BERLIN ENDGAME 1945

For Robert, my agent; and for Kate, Marcus, Emily, Gemma, and everyone else at Osprey who have all walked this long road with me.

OSPREY PUBLISHING
Bloomsbury Publishing Plc
Kemp House, Chawley Park, Cumnor Hill, Oxford OX2 9PH, UK
Bloomsbury Publishing Ireland Limited,
29 Earlsfort Terrace, Dublin 2, D02 AY28, Ireland
1385 Broadway, 5th Floor, New York, NY 10018, USA
E-mail: info@ospreypublishing.com
www.ospreypublishing.com

OSPREY is a trademark of Osprey Publishing Ltd

First published in Great Britain in 2026

© Prit Buttar, 2026

Prit Buttar has asserted his right under the Copyright, Designs and Patents Act, 1988, to be identified as Author of this work.

All rights reserved. No part of this publication may be: i) reproduced or transmitted in any form, electronic or mechanical, including photocopying, recording or by means of any information storage or retrieval system without prior permission in writing from the publishers; or ii) used or reproduced in any way for the training, development or operation of artificial intelligence (AI) technologies, including generative AI technologies. The rights holders expressly reserve this publication from the text and data mining exception as per Article 4(3) of the Digital Single Market Directive (EU) 2019/790

A catalogue record for this book is available from the British Library

ISBN: HB 9781472869661; eBook 9781472869685; ePDF 9781472869630; XML 9781472869647

26 27 28 29 30   10 9 8 7 6 5 4 3 2 1

Plate section image credits are given in full in the List of Illustrations (pp. 7–8).
Maps by Prit Buttar
Index by Fionbar Lyons

Typeset by Lumina Datamatics Ltd
Printed and bound in Great Britain by Clays Ltd, Elcograf S.p.A.

Editor's note
For ease of comparison, please refer to the following conversion table:
1 mile = 1.6km
1 yd = 0.9m
1 ft = 0.3m
1 in. = 2.54cm/25.4mm
1 lb = 0.45kg

Osprey Publishing supports the Woodland Trust, the UK's leading woodland conservation charity.

To find out more about our authors and books visit www.ospreypublishing.com. Here you will find extracts, author interviews, details of forthcoming events and the option to sign up for our newsletter.

For product safety related questions contact productsafety@bloomsbury.com

CONTENTS

List of Illustrations   7

List of Maps   9

Dramatis Personae   10

Introduction: The Road to Berlin   17

Chapter 1: The City on the Spree   25

Chapter 2: 'Call Me Meier'   57

Chapter 3: Preparing for the Last Stand:
The German Defences   81

Chapter 4: The Red Army: Plans For Vengeance   117

Chapter 5: The Storm Bursts: 16 April   147

Chapter 6: Breakthrough: 17–18 April   177

Chapter 7: To the Gates of Berlin: 19–20 April   207

Chapter 8: *Der Krieg ist verloren*: 21–22 April   239

Chapter 9: Into the City: 23–25 April   269

Chapter 10: Disintegration: 26–28 April   307

Chapter 11: The Bitterest of Ends: Berlin, 29 April–2 May   341

Chapter 12: The Roads to the West: 29 April–8 May   365

Chapter 13: Conclusion: An Uneasy Silence   393

Notes   413

Bibliography   429

Index   436

LIST OF ILLUSTRATIONS

'That's how Berlin is going to look!': the soldiers of the Red Army were eager to exact revenge for the destruction of Stalingrad by the Germans in 1942–1943. (RIA Novosti Archive, image #602161 / Zelma, Wikimedia Commons, CC BY-SA 3.0, https://creativecommons.org/licenses/by-sa/3.0)
Members of *Volkssturm* heading for the front on the River Oder in March 1945. These civilians, previously regarded as too young, too old, or too infirm for military service, were deployed in the final defence of Germany with very limited equipment and almost no training. (Photo by Mondadori via Getty Images)
A Soviet fighter-bomber squadron over Berlin, 28 April 1945. While the Red Army infantry and tank units were supported by air strikes, it was notoriously difficult to carry out attacks on precise targets and indiscriminate devastation was inflicted across the city. (Photo by Mark Redkin/FotoSoyuz/Getty Images)
Members of the Hitler Youth defending Berlin with a machine gun in April 1945. After being under the influence of Nazi indoctrination for almost all their lives, many of these teenagers were fanatically committed to defending Germany at all costs. (Photo by Arthur Grimm/ullstein bild via Getty Images)
Soviet artillery positioned to fire at the at the German defences on the Seelow Heights. For the Red Army, its artillery was the 'god of war', and there was widespread expectation that, if used effectively, it could smash the enemy defences and make an advance relatively simple. (Photo by Fine Art Images/Heritage Images/Getty Images)
As the Red Army approached in April 1945, tens of thousands of civilians discovered too late that few arrangements for their evacuation had been made; many people made desperate attempts on foot, under enemy fire, with no provision for medical aid or supplies. (Photo by: Sovfoto/Universal Images Group via Getty Images)
A soldier instructing a woman in the use of a *Panzerfaust*. These weapons were widely feared by Soviet tank crews – although their range was limited,

they were capable of burning through the armour of almost any tank they encountered. (Photo by ullstein bild/ullstein bild via Getty Images)

Members of the *Volkssturm* being instructed in the use of a *Panzerfaust* amongst the rubble of Berlin. The officer wears the insignia of a *Volkssturm* battalion commander; the *Volkssturm* used a mixture of Wehrmacht and SS insignia, which may have contributed to many of them being mis-identified by Soviet soldiers as SS and executed when they surrendered. (Photo by ullstein bild/ullstein bild via Getty Images)

Troops from the Soviet Thirty-Third Army entered Berlin from the north during the morning of 23 April. The following days saw bitter fighting amidst the rubble of the city. (Photo by Serge Plantureux/Corbis via Getty Images)

In many cases, the Soviet troops were in no mood to take prisoners. Zakhar Yevseyevich Krasilchikov recounted: 'We threw grenades through the windows of houses and basements from which they were firing at us, then cleared the buildings of Germans who were fighting to the last bullet.' (Photo by ullstein bild/ullstein bild via Getty Images)

Although the building had been in ruins since the fire of 1933, the Red Army placed great importance on capturing the Reichstag. (Photo by MOROZOV/RIA NOVOSTI/AFP via Getty Images)

Fires were ignited by the huge number of high explosives dropped on the city. These fires were whipped up by the strong wind and spread across Berlin – it was often days before the flames went out, having reduced almost everything in their path to ash. (Photo by ADN-Bildarchiv/ullstein bild via Getty Images)

In his final hours, Hitler dictated his personal testament to his secretary, Traudl Junge, photographed here on her wedding day. Junge remained in the Führerbunker until Hitler's death on 30 April 1945; her 2002 memoir details the last days of the Nazi regime. (Photo by Imagno/Getty Images)

After the battle, weary columns of German prisoners were gathered and began to march out of Berlin. Some Soviet soldiers gathered to jeer at them, but most were either busy celebrating, or simply glad that the fighting was over. (Photo by Mondadori via Getty Images)

The Reichstag became a magnet for Soviet soldiers. Along with hundreds of others, Yakov Fadeyev left his mark on the building: 'On the seventh column from the entrance, I and others wrote on the walls. I wrote: "I, Fadeyev, reached Berlin."' (Photo by ullstein bild/ullstein bild via Getty Images)

An aerial photo showing a devastated Berlin in 1945. Bombing, artillery fire, and intense combat in the streets left over 90 per cent of the city in ruins by the end of the war. (Photo by: Photo12/Universal Images Group via Getty Images)

LIST OF MAPS

The Opposing Forces, April 1945	103
Berlin Defence Sectors	115
1st Belarusian Front Sector, 16 April	160
1st Ukrainian Front Sector, 16 April	172
1st Belarusian Front Sector, 17 April	180
1st Ukrainian Front Sector, 17 April	187
1st Belarusian Front Sector, 18 April	196
Konev's Exploitation	204
1st Belarusian Front Sector, 19 April	216
The Approaches to Berlin, 20 April 1945	229
2nd Belarusian Front Sector, 20 April	234
LXXIX Rifle Corps' Advance Through Pankow and Schönholtz	258
Fighting to the South of Berlin, 24–25 April	283
Friedrichshain, 24 April	286
Central Berlin	288
Operations South of Berlin, 26 April–2 May	338
Between Berlin and the Elbe	381

DRAMATIS PERSONAE

Germany

Altner, Helmut – private, young recruit
Ansat, John – Generalleutnant, commander *Festung Swinemünde Korps*
Averdieck, Fritz – panzergrenadier, 20th Panzergrenadier Division
Axmann, Artur – head of Hitler Youth
Bärenfänger, Erich – Generalmajor, then Brigadeführer – commander Berlin Defence Zones A and B
Biehler, Ernst – Oberst, *Kampfkommandant* Frankfurt-an-der-Oder
Bormann, Martin – personal secretary to Hitler
Böttcher, Friedrich – Oberst, operations officer 18th Panzergrenadier Division
Bräuer, Bruno – General, commander 9th Fallschirmjäger Division
Burgdorf, Wilhelm – General, senior adjutant to Hitler and head of the army's personnel department
Burmeister, Arnold – Generalleutnant, commander 25th Panzergrenadier Division
Busse, Theodor – General, commander Ninth Army
Diers, Georg – Unterscharführer, Tiger tank commander in Berlin
Dönitz, Karl – Grand Admiral, commander of the *Kriegsmarine* and German head of state from 30 April 1945
Dufving, Theodor von – Oberst, chief of staff XLI Panzer Corps
Edelsheim, Maximilian von – Generalleutnant, commander XLVIII Panzer Corps
Eismann, Hans-Georg – Oberst, operations officer Army Group Vistula
Engel, Gerhard – Generalleutnant, commander *Ulrich von Hutten* Infantry Division
Fegelein, Gretl (née Braun) – sister to Eva Braun, wife of Hermann Fegelein
Fegelein, Hermann – Gruppenführer, adjutant to Himmler
Friedeburg, Hans-Georg von – Admiral, ceasefire negotiator

Dramatis Personae

Fritsche, Hans – diplomat in propaganda ministry
Gareis, Martin – Generalleutnant, commander XLVI Panzer Corps (General from 1 April)
Goebbels, Joseph – propaganda minister, *Gauleiter* of Berlin, Plenipotentiary for Total War
Göring, Hermann – head of the Luftwaffe, Hitler's appointed heir
Gräser, Fritz-Hubert – General, commander Fourth Panzer Army
Greim, Robert Ritter von – Generalfeldmarschall, last head of the Luftwaffe
Guderian, Heinz – Generaloberst, chief of general staff at *OKH*
Hachtel, Erich – Leutnant, company commander 5th Jäger Division
Harmel, Heinz – Brigadeführer, commander *SS-Frundsberg* Panzer Division
Harzer, Walter – Oberführer, commander *SS-Polizei* Panzergrenadier Division
Heinrici, Gotthard – Generaloberst, commander Army Group Vistula
Henseler, Hans – Untersturmführer, sapper officer in *SS-Nordland*
Herrmann, Harry – Oberstleutnant, commander 9th Fallschirmjäger Division
Himmler, Heinrich – Reichsführer-SS, head of the SS
Högl, Peter – Obersturmbannführer, deputy commander of Hitler's personal SS bodyguards
Holste, Rudolf – Generalleutnant, commander XLI Panzer Corps
Hölz, Johannes – Oberst, chief of staff Ninth Army
Huber, Johann – officer cadet, 7th Panzer Division
Jacobi, Alfred – Generalleutnant, *Festungskommandant* Stettin
Jeckeln, Friedrich – Obergruppenführer, commander V SS Mountain Corps
Jodl, Alfred – Generaloberst, Chief of Operations Staff at *OKW*
Jolasse, Erwin – Generalmajor, commander 344th Volksgrenadier Division
Jüttner, Hans – Obergruppenführer, head of the *Ersatzheer*
Käther, Ernst – Oberst, temporarily Generalleutnant, *Kampfkommandant* Berlin
Kausch, Paul-Albert – Obersturmbannführer, commander 11th SS-Panzer Regiment
Keitel, Wilhelm – Generalfeldmarschall, head of *OKW*
Keller, Kurt – panzergrenadier, *Müncheberg* Panzer Division
Kempin, Hans – Standartenführer, commander of *SS-30. Januar* Grenadier Division
Kercher, Fritz – Leutnant, tank company commander in 25th Panzergrenadier Division
Klein, Gerhard – Oberst, commander *Friedrich Ludwig Jahn* Infantry Division
Kleinheisterkamp, Matthias – Obergruppenführer, commander XI SS-Panzer Corps
Köhler, Karl-Erik – General, commander XX Corps

Kordes, Gerhard – infantryman, 9th Fallschirmjäger Division
Krebs, Hans – General, chief of general staff at *OKH*
Krukenberg, Gustav – Brigadeführer, commander *SS-Charlemagne*, then commander *SS-Nordland*
Liebknecht, Karl – co-founder of Spartacist movement
Lindner, Rudi – officer-cadet in 712th Infantry Division
Loringhoven, Berndt Freytag von – Major, adjutant to chief of staff of *OKH*
Luck, Hans von – Oberst, panzer regiment commander 21st Panzer Division
Luxembourg, Rosa – co-founder of Spartacist movement
Manteuffel, Hasso von – General, commander Third Panzer Army
Marcks, Werner – Generalleutnant, commander 21st Panzer Division
Menze, Erika – teenager trapped in Halbe pocket
Mohnke, Wilhelm – Brigadeführer, commander central Berlin defence zone
Mummert, Werner – Generalmajor, commander *Müncheberg* Panzer Division, later commander Berlin Defence Zones A and B
Naumann, Werner – propaganda minister after Hitler's death
Papen, Franz von – chancellor of Germany, 1932, then vice-chancellor with Hitler
Pipkorn, Rüdiger – Oberst and acting Standartenführer, commander 35th *SS-und-Polizei- Grenadier* Division
Rattenhuber, Johann – Gruppenführer, commander of Hitler's personal SS bodyguards
Rauch, Josef – Generalleutnant, commander 18th Panzergrenadier Division
Refior, Hans – Oberst, chief of staff to *Kampfkommandant* Berlin
Reichhelm, Günther – Oberst, chief of staff Twelfth Army
Reitsch, Hanna – German test pilot
Remer, Otto-Ernst – Generalmajor, commander *Führer-Begleit* Panzergrenadier Division
Reymann, Helmuth – Generalleutnant, *Kampfkommandant* Berlin
Schack, Friedrich-August – General, commander XXXII Corps
Scholze, Georg – Generalmajor, commander 20th Panzergrenadier Division
Schöneck, Friedhelm – infantryman, *Berlin* Infantry Division
Schörner, Ferdinand, Generalfeldmarschall – commander Army Group Centre
Schünemann, Hans-Wolfgang – Oberst, commander 303rd *Döberitz* Infantry Division
Seydlitz-Kurzbach, Walther von – General, former commander LI Corps, member of *Bund Deutsche Offiziere* and *Nationalkomitee Freies Deutschland*
Siefert, Ernst – Oberst, commander Berlin Defence Zone Z
Sixt, Friedrich – Generalleutnant, commander CI Corps

Speer, Albert – armaments minister
Steiner, Felix – Obergruppenführer, commander III SS-Panzer Corps and eponymous *Armeegruppe*
Streng, Ernst – Scharführer, tank commander *SS-Schwere-Panzer-Abteilung 502*
Sydow, Otto – Generalleutnant, commander *Flak-Division Berlin*
Tams, Karl-Hermann – Leutnant, junior officer 20th Panzergrenadier Division
Thoma, Helmut – Major, operations officer *Müncheberg* Panzer Division
Tippelskirch, Kurt von – General, commander Twenty-First Army, then acting commander Army Group Vistula
Trotha, Ivo-Thilo von – Generalleutnant, chief of staff Army Group Vistula
Voigtsberger, Heinrich – Generalmajor, commander *Berlin* Infantry Division
Wäger, Kurt – General, commander V Corps
Weidling, Helmuth – General, commander LVI Panzer Corps
Wenck, Walther – General, commander Twelfth Army
Witzleben, Henning von – Oberst, commander 3rd Marine Division
Ziegler, Joachim – Brigadeführer, commander *SS-Nordland* Panzergrenadier Division
Zobel, Horst – Hauptmann, panzer battalion commander in *Müncheberg* Panzer Division

SOVIET UNION

Abyzov, Vladimir Ivanovich – rifleman, 39th Guards Rifle Division
Antipenko, Nikolai Aleksandrovich – Lieutenant General, head of logistics department, 1st Belarusian Front
Babadzhanian, Aranesp Khachaturovich – Colonel, commander XI Guards Tank Corps
Badigin, Mikhail Petrovich – anti-tank gunner
Batov, Pavel Ivanovich – Colonel General, commander Sixty-Fifth Army
Belov, Yevtikhii Yemelianovich – Lieutenant General, commander X Guards Tank Corps
Belov, Pavel Alekseyevich – Colonel General, commander Sixty-First Army
Berzarin, Nikolai Erastovich – General, commander Fifth Shock Army
Blanter, Matvei Isaakovich – composer accompanying Eighth Guards Army
Bogdanov, Semen Ilyich – Colonel General, commander Second Guards Tank Army
Bokov, Fedor Yefimovich – Lieutenant General, head of political section Fifth Shock Army

Chuikov, Vasily Ivanovich – Colonel General, commander Eighth Guards Army
Dremov, Ivan Fedorovich – Major General, commander VIII Guards Mechanised Corps
Erastov, Konstantin Maksimovich – Lieutenant General, commander XLVI Rifle Corps
Esipenko, Khariton Fyodorovich – Colonel, chief of staff XXIX Guards Rifle Corps
Fadeyev, Yakov Ivanovich – young Red Army soldier
Fedyuninsky, Ivan Ivanovich – Colonel General, commander Second Shock Army
Firsov, Pavel Andreyevich – Lieutenant General, commander XXVI Guards Rifle Corps
Galitsky, Ivan Pavlovich – Colonel General, head of engineers, 1st Ukrainian Front
Gerko, Nikofor Ignatyevich – Major General, deputy commander of tank forces, 1st Belarusian Front
Getman, Andrei Lavrentyevich – Lieutenant General, deputy commander First Guards Tank Army
Glazunov, Vasily Asanavovich – Lieutenant General, commander IV Guard Rifle Corps
Goloborodko, Grigory Stepanovich – Senior Lieutenant, company commander 58th Guards Rifle Division
Golovach, Vladimir Nikitovich – tank crewman
Gordov, Vasily Nikolayevich – Colonel General, commander Third Guards Army
Grishin, Ivan Tikhonovich – Colonel General, commander Forty-Ninth Army
Gusakovsky, Iosif Irakliyevich – Colonel, commander 44th Guards Tank Brigade
Ivanov, Aleksei Petrovich – sapper
Katukov, Mikhail Yefimovich – Colonel General, commander First Guards Tank Army
Kazakov, Vladimir Ivanovich – Colonel General, head of artillery 1st Belarusian Front
Khetagurov, Georgy Ivanovich – Major General, commander 82nd Guards Rifle Division
Konev, Ivan Stepanovich – Marshal, commander 1st Ukrainian Front
Konstantinov, Mikhail Petrovich – Lieutenant General, commander VII Guards Cavalry Corps

Dramatis Personae

Koretsky, Vasily Ignatyevich – Major General, commander VI Guards Mechanised Corps
Kostylev, Vladimir Ivanovich – Major General, chief of operations 1st Ukrainian Front, later commander Second Polish Army
Kuznetsov, Vasily Ivanovich – Colonel General, commander Third Shock Army
Lelyushenko, Dmitry Danilovich – General, commander Fourth Guards Tank Army
Luchinsky, Aleksandr Aleksandrovich – Lieutenant General, commander Twenty-Eighth Army
Malinin, Mikhail Sergeyevich – Colonel General, chief of staff 1st Belarusian Front
Maslov, Ivan Vladimirovich – junior officer, Third Guards Tank Army
Morgunov, Nikolai Viktorovich – Colonel, commander 45th Guards Tank Brigade
Myasnikov, Vladimir Vladimirovich – flamethrower operator
Neustroyev, Stepan Andreyevich – Captain, battalion commander in LXXIX Rifle Corps
Osinovsky, Dmitry Filippovich – junior artillery officer
Perevertkin, Semen Nikoforovich – Major General, commander LXXIX Rifle Corps
Perkhorovich, Frantz Iosifovich – Major General, commander Forty-Seventh Army
Petrov, Ivan Yefimovich – General, chief of staff 1st Ukrainian Front
Polyakov, Uri Nikolayevich – assault gun crewman
Poplavski, Stanislav Gilyarovich – General, commander First Polish Army
Popov, Vasily Stepanovich – Colonel General, commander Seventieth Army
Pukhov, Nikolai Pavlovich – Colonel General, commander Thirteenth Army
Rokossovsky, Konstantin Konstantinovich – Marshal, commander 2nd Belarusian Front
Rudenko, Sergei Ignatyevich – Colonel General, commander Sixteenth Air Army
Rybalko, Pavel Semenovich – General, commander Third Guards Tank Army
Shalin, Mikhail Alekseyevich – Lieutenant General, chief of staff First Guards Tank Army
Shemenkov, Afanasy Dmitriyevich – Major General, commander XXIX Guards Rifle Corps
Shtemenko, Sergei Matveyevich – Colonel General, head of Operations Staff in *Stavka*
Skorobogatkin, Konstantin Fedorovich – Major General, commander 193rd Rifle Division

Sokolovsky, Vasily Danilovich – General, deputy commander 1st Belarusian Front

Sukhorukov, Ivan Fedorovich – Colonel, commander 242nd Guards Rifle Regiment

Sukhov, Ivan Prokofiyevich – Lieutenant General, commander IX Mechanised Corps

Telegin, Konstantin Fedorovich – Lieutenant General, head of political section, 1st Belarusian Front

Tsvang, Semen Ruvimovich – Soviet rifleman

Vasilevsky, Aleksandr Mikhailovich – Marshal, chief of the Soviet General Staff

Vesterman, Arkady Grigoryevich – junior tank officer

Vishnevsky, Vsevolod Vitalyevich – Soviet writer accompanying Eighth Guards Army

Zaitsev, Vasily Ivanovich – Colonel, commander LXI Guards Tank Brigade

Zhadov, Aleksei Semenovich – Colonel General, commander Fifth Guards Army

Zhukov, Georgy Konstantinovich – Marshal, commander 1st Belarusian Front

OTHERS

Gavin, James – General, commander 82nd Airborne Division (US)

Moore, James – Major General, chief of staff Ninth Army (US)

Spaatz, Carl – General, commander of Allied Strategic Air Forces (US)

Vassiltchikov, Marie Illarionovna ('Missie') – Russian exile in Berlin

INTRODUCTION: THE ROAD TO BERLIN

As the long, hard winter of 1944–45 came to an end, much of the world was preparing for the end of the war in Europe. On the side of the Allied Powers, there was relief that the long, bloody conflict would soon be over. Huge resources, both human and industrial, had been spent in grinding the Axis Powers to the brink of final collapse, and for the fighting men there was a deep yearning for a chance to go home and to put behind them the fatigue and dirt, the horror and fear, that had been such a major part of their lives for many years. Across the front line, the mood was varied. For some, there was still blind belief in the Führer to conjure a miraculous victory; for others, all that remained was to fight on to the bitter end, even though defeat seemed certain. Many – perhaps most – were even more exhausted than the soldiers and civilians of the nations arrayed against Germany, and simply wanted their ordeal to come to an end. Such was the fractured state of Nazi Germany that many people were able to hold more than one – and in some cases all – of these views at the same time.

In many respects, it seemed fitting that in a war of huge battles and manoeuvres on a massive scale, a conflict that had reached the capital cities of so many nations, the final battle would be for control of Berlin. It was from this city that Hitler's regime had planned and executed its wars on its neighbours, and it was here that the last resources of the once-invincible Wehrmacht would make their last stand. There would be little concern for the safety and well-being of the civilian population; indeed, Hitler and his entourage expected and required ordinary men and women to join the ranks of the last formations of the German Army to defend the capital against the enemy hordes. And there was no question that those hordes were coming. The great Soviet offensive of January and February had carried the front line from the Vistula River to, and in places across, the Oder River, and the leading Red Army units were just 43 miles from the eastern outskirts of Berlin. Once reinforcements and supplies had brought its formations back to strength, the Soviet war machine would attack once more. And despite its battered, exhausted state, the Wehrmacht would mount a determined defence of the capital of Germany.

At what stage did such an apocalyptic end to the war become inevitable? In many respects, Hitler made his intentions regarding the Soviet Union clear as early as 1925 when the future Führer of the Thousand-Year Reich wrote his autobiographical manifesto, *Mein Kampf*. He made no secret of his contempt for the people of the Soviet Union and his intention to secure a land empire at their expense:

> We National Socialists consciously draw a line through the foreign policy trend of our pre-War period [i.e. before 1914]. We take up at the halting place of six hundred years ago. We terminate the endless German drive to the south and west of Europe, and direct our gaze towards the lands in the east. We finally terminate the colonial and trade policy of the pre-War period, and proceed to the territorial policy of the future.
>
> But if we talk about the new soil and territory in Europe today, we can think primarily only of Russia and its vassal border states.[1]

When Nazi Germany agreed a non-aggression treaty with the Soviet Union in the late summer of 1939 – the infamous Molotov–Ribbentrop Pact, named after the foreign ministers of the two states – it seemed that, superficially at least, Hitler was not pursuing a war of conquest against the Soviet Union, but from the outset the pact was little more than an attempt by both sides to buy time. Even as Joachim von Ribbentrop was negotiating the final details of the pact, Hitler met Carl Burckhardt, a Swiss German diplomat who was the League of Nations High Commissioner in Danzig, in the Berghof overlooking Berchtesgaden:

> Everything I undertake is directed against Russia; if the west is too stupid and blind to understand this, I will be forced to come to terms with the Russians, to strike at the west, and then after subduing it to turn against the Soviet Union with my massed forces.[2]

Within days, as the world absorbed the implications of the non-aggression treaty, Stalin made a similar comment to those around him:

> Of course, it's all a game to see who can fool whom. I know what Hitler's up to. He thinks he's outsmarted me but actually it's I who have tricked him.[3]

Both sides continued to plan for war against each other, but Operation *Barbarossa* – the invasion of the Soviet Union in June 1941 – seems to have taken Stalin by

Introduction: The Road to Berlin

surprise. He can have had no doubt that an attack was coming, but his plans to strengthen the defences of the Soviet Union needed more time and he refused to accept any reports that suggested that this time was not going to be available. Intelligence reports provided by the British and by Soviet agents were dismissed as attempts to mislead the Soviet government, and Stalin resolutely refused to accept any of the intelligence reports from his own agencies – more time was needed, therefore anything that suggested otherwise was dismissed. Like Hitler, Stalin was so convinced of his personal infallibility that anything that suggested he might be wrong was at best inaccurate, at worst deliberate treason.

It is arguable that from the outset, the Wehrmacht had no real chance of defeating the Red Army. German war plans were based upon incomplete and inadequate intelligence about Soviet resources, and the expectation was that the Soviet units – which had performed badly in the advance into Poland in the last two weeks of September 1939 and in the Winter War against Finland in 1939–40 – would rapidly disintegrate. Knowledge of roads and railways in the Soviet Union was largely based on Soviet maps and limited aerial reconnaissance of the regions close to the frontier, and from the outset, everything depended upon a quick victory. In order to provide sufficient motorised support, trucks had been requisitioned from every occupied country as well as from Germany itself, creating huge logistic problems in terms of replacement parts, tyres etc., and in any case most of the civilian trucks were not robust enough to survive on the primitive roads of the Soviet interior. The scale of German mobilisation was such that previously exempt groups of workers were called up in the expectation that they would soon be released back to their civilian jobs, and the failure to complete a quick victory left Germany with workforce shortages that persisted to a greater or lesser extent throughout the rest of the war.

Despite this, the Wehrmacht seemed to be close to achieving an astonishing triumph as the invasion progressed. On every front, huge numbers of prisoners were taken and the scale of territory that was overrun was immense. Nevertheless, resistance grew and German strength slowly declined through a mixture of logistic difficulties and rising casualties. Perhaps by a narrow margin, the Red Army succeeded in surviving the tremendous onslaught of the German forces. As the days grew shorter and the weather deteriorated, it was clear that the swift defeat of the Soviet Union and the seizure of Leningrad in the north and Moscow in the centre would not take place. Thereafter, the balance of power tilted slowly against Germany.

Once the tide of war began to flow towards the west, all German thoughts of creating a new land empire from territory acquired from the Soviet Union were replaced by growing fear of what would happen if the Red Army should reach

German territory. The rhetoric of Joseph Goebbels, the Reich's propaganda minister, emphasised the zero-sum nature of the war against the Soviet Union: there was room in the world for either Bolshevism or National Socialism, and the triumph of one required the destruction of the other. From the days of *Mein Kampf*, Hitler and his followers had deliberately made little distinction between Jews and Bolsheviks, frequently referring to the Soviet system as 'Jewish Bolshevism', and other nuances began to grow stronger in official proclamations. The Red Army was portrayed as an Asiatic force bent upon the destruction of European civilisation, and Germany was the bulwark against this existential threat. The enemy had to be kept away from German territory at all costs.

There was, of course, a further reason to fear the arrival of the Red Army. Although many Germans, both military and civilians, would later deny any knowledge of the atrocities committed by German forces in the occupied territories of Europe, the reality was that awareness of these crimes was widespread. Many senior German officers worked closely with the US Army Historical Division after the war, writing accounts of their battles against the Red Army, and they and other officers produced growing numbers of memoirs as the years passed. Few if any of these accounts make any mention of the widespread slaughter of Jews and Slavs across the Soviet Union, or of the brutal mistreatment of prisoners of war in the east. Where mention of such crimes was unavoidable, the authors always blamed the atrocities on the SS or other agencies, insisting that the Wehrmacht itself was almost completely innocent. Even the SS attempted to whitewash its reputation. Oberstgruppenführer Paul Hausser, one of the most senior and most capable SS commanders, became a leading activist in the *Hilfsgemeinschaft auf Gegenseitigkeit der Angehörigen der Ehemaligen Waffen-SS* ('Mutual Aid Association of Former Waffen-SS Members', usually abbreviated to *HIAG*), a group that campaigned energetically to portray the military formations of the SS as elite soldiers rather than the perpetrators of war crimes. One of Hausser's books, *Soldaten wie Andere Auch* ('Soldiers Like Any Other'), even used this theme in its title.[4] But the reality was that every branch of the German military machine was involved in war crimes. Front-line units sometimes took part in so-called anti-partisan sweeps, in which thousands of innocent civilians were indiscriminately killed; some units 'loaned' sub-formations for operations against Jews and other victims of the occupation; higher commands routinely provided logistic support for the *Einsatzgruppen* of the SS, which were responsible for the hundreds of thousands of deaths that occurred in the first months of the German invasion; and all parts of the military were involved in the scorched earth policy during the long retreat that left so many Soviet cities, towns, and villages reduced to ruins.

Introduction: The Road to Berlin

Throughout the war, German soldiers returned to their home cities from time to time. Some were granted short periods of leave, while others spent time in Germany recovering from their wounds. During such visits, they shared the information that they had about what was happening in the east. This may have been imprecise in many cases, but there can be no doubt that most Germans had at least an inkling of the terrible atrocities that were being committed. Many might have viewed these – at least during the years of victory – as justified and a distasteful but necessary precursor to final victory, but as the war progressed, there was growing anxiety in German towns and cities. If the Red Army were to arrive on German soil, there was no doubt that it would wreak a terrible revenge. Any uncertainties about this disappeared after the events of October 1944 when the Red Army briefly advanced into East Prussia before being repulsed. When German troops recaptured the village of Nemmersdorf, they reported finding dozens of slaughtered civilians, many of whom had been tortured before being killed. Reassessments of the events in and around Nemmersdorf suggest that Goebbels deliberately embellished and exaggerated the scale of the atrocities, but nevertheless many civilians had been raped and murdered, and the German propaganda machine was quick to take advantage of the gruesome results.

Stories of the Nemmersdorf massacre were broadcast widely by the German authorities and were used to stiffen the resolve of German soldiers to defend their families from the menace from the east. But despite Goebbels' invitation to Red Cross officials from Sweden and Switzerland to visit East Prussia to confirm the stories of rape and massacre, attempts to win support internationally made little or no impact. The Soviet advances that took its leading units into East Prussia had also uncovered the death camp at Majdanek, and the horrific images appearing from there overshadowed any German claims of Soviet atrocities. Most people outside Germany – and indeed, many within Germany too – saw any crimes committed by the Red Army as little more than vengeance for the greater crimes committed by the Germans.

Fear of the Red Army and a lingering belief that somehow Hitler would defy the odds were large parts of the motivation that kept the Germans fighting, but there was huge war-weariness in all circles by early 1945. German losses on all fronts in the preceding few months had greatly exceeded all losses in earlier years combined, and although Albert Speer, the armaments minister, was able to keep production of weapons and munitions going through a mixture of desperate and ingenious measures, it was almost impossible to replace what had been destroyed by the Western Allies in northern France and by the Red Army first in its advance across the western parts of the Soviet Union and then the devastating and swift surge from the Vistula to the Oder and Neisse Rivers. Perhaps even more significant than the loss of equipment were the casualties suffered by the combat units. Like all armies with a strong tradition of officers leading from close to the front line, the losses of experienced junior officers and senior NCOs had been high and it was impossible to find replacements of a similar calibre. Everything – experienced troops and leaders, tanks and guns, ammunition and fuel – was in short supply. Nevertheless, almost nobody was in favour of simply capitulating to the Soviet forces assembling for the last battle. It is impossible to know how many soldiers and civilians were resigned to the unavoidable defeat of Germany, as the widespread repression that followed the failed July Plot of 1944 to kill Hitler meant that anyone who voiced such opinions faced arrest, imprisonment, and even summary execution. But amongst those who recognised the inevitable catastrophe that lay ahead, many still felt that resisting the Red Army was worthwhile. It increased the chances of the Western Allies advancing further into Germany, thus avoiding the horror of occupation by the vengeful Soviet forces.

However, many in the upper circles of the German military knew that any such hopes were largely forlorn. After suffering heavy losses in their ultimately successful breakout from the Normandy beaches, the Western Allies had little appetite for the casualties that they anticipated if they were to press on to Berlin. Germany had been divided into occupation zones at the Yalta Conference in February 1945 and the Americans in particular could see little merit in spilling the blood of their soldiers to seize towns and cities that would then be handed over to the Soviet authorities. In Britain, Churchill repeatedly expressed concerns in private about the future influence of the Soviet Union over Europe, but his doubts had largely been sidelined by Roosevelt and Stalin at Yalta. The only possible circumstances in which American and British troops might be sent to take control of Berlin were in the event of a sudden, complete collapse of Nazi rule and the disintegration of the Wehrmacht. In such circumstances, airborne forces would land in and around Berlin while ground forces then moved up to establish contact. Under the codename *Eclipse*, three US formations – 17th, 82nd, and 101st Airborne Divisions – and a British parachute brigade were to capture the main airfields at Tempelhof, Rahnsdorf, Gatow, and Oranienburg, while Montgomery's 21st Army Group would cross the lower Rhine and march rapidly to Berlin.[5]

Eclipse would only be possible if Hitler was dead and the German leadership was in disarray. In any other circumstances, wrote General Omar Bradley, commander of 12th Army Group, a battle for control of the German capital could cost at least 100,000 casualties. Moreover, the use of massed airborne forces had proved to be problematic. Heavy casualties were suffered during Operation *Market Garden* in September 1944 in the failed attempt to seize the

Introduction: The Road to Berlin

Rhine bridge at Arnhem, and even modest resistance by the Germans in their capital city could cost the lightly armed airborne forces dearly. Bradley was aware of the plans for Berlin to lie within the Soviet zone of occupation, and could see little benefit in his forces suffering heavy losses for territory that was to be handed back to the Soviet Union; destruction of the remaining German forces in the west was given greater priority. Eisenhower agreed, and ordered the armies of the Western Allies to halt on the Elbe in the centre, and to concentrate their efforts in a drive into Bavaria and on to Austria. Only in the north, where parts of the east bank of the Elbe were to be in the British occupation zone, would there be any major crossing of the river.

On the Soviet side, there was clear elation that the end of a war that had cost the Soviet Union such terrible casualties was close, but there were also numerous tensions. Since the end of the summer campaigns of 1944, Stalin had been moving to assert greater personal authority over the military. The massively centralised system that existed before the war had proved to be too unwieldy and slow to deal with the German onslaught and – in fits and starts – Stalin had been forced to permit greater freedom of action and initiative amongst his senior commanders. As the middle years of the war passed, a small body of experienced and capable officers emerged to win his confidence and he rewarded this by giving them increasing responsibilities for prosecuting the war. But as the end of the conflict approached, it seems that he began to take steps to reassert his personal primacy. In the years that followed the end of the war, Soviet historiography would concentrate on portraying the Great Patriotic War against Fascism as a unique victory, made possible by the united determination of all components of the Soviet Union under the leadership of the Communist Party. In turn, the Communist Party was portrayed as having been inspired and led by the infallible figure of Stalin. Soviet setbacks in the war were to be blamed upon subordinates or were simply ignored and largely forgotten – in particular, the infallibility of both the Communist Party and Stalin was to be unquestioned. And other figures who had played leading roles in defeating Nazi Germany were to have their status greatly reduced.

In an operation that commenced in mid-January 1945, three Red Army Fronts – 1st Ukrainian Front in the south, 1st Belarusian Front in the centre, and 2nd Belarusian Front in the north – advanced rapidly across Poland and the eastern territories of Germany. Much like Hitler, Stalin enjoyed pitting his subordinates against each other, and he must have been pleased at the manner in which the commanders of 1st Ukrainian Front and 1st Belarusian Front – Marshals Ivan Stepanovich Konev and Georgy Konstantinovich Zhukov respectively – attempted to outshine each other. Zhukov had been given the prized central sector of the great offensive, astride the main route to Berlin, but although Konev's armies were turned away to the southwest to ensure the rapid conquest of Silesia, he nonetheless ensured that by the end of the operation, he had substantial forces on the Neisse from where they could thrust into central Germany. Even at this stage, he could see that just a small diversion to the northwest would put his armies close to Berlin. Zhukov's armies on the central Oder were clearly much closer to the German capital, but, if at all possible, Konev intended to seize some of the glory of the final victory over the Nazi enemy.

Despite the agreement secured in Yalta for the partition of Germany after the war, Stalin remained deeply suspicious to the very end of the war that the Western Allies would find some opportunity to betray him and would attempt to make a separate peace with Hitler. Accordingly, he now ordered his subordinates to make their preparations for the final assault on the German capital. With Berlin in his hands, he would be able to ensure adherence to the agreements reached with the Americans and the British. Moreover, he could establish his personal credentials as the man who had masterfully oversaw the defeat of Fascist Germany.

CHAPTER 1

THE CITY ON THE SPREE

The Spree River is a somewhat unusual waterway, in that it is actually longer – running for 250 miles – than the Havel River, of which it is a tributary. It arises in the Lusatian Mountains on the modern border between Germany and Czechia, and then flows north and northwest until it joins the Havel. Over the last few miles of its course, it passes across a relatively flat, sandy region; it was on this marshy ground, and particularly on an island in the river, that the city of Berlin arose. Its growth from a small, insignificant settlement to the capital of Germany both shaped and was influenced by the character of its inhabitants, who would be forced to endure the horrors of urban warfare as the Third Reich drew to a close in 1945.

The foundation of Berlin as a town is generally accepted as taking place in 1237, but there had been inhabitants on the banks of the Spree in this region for hundreds of years. Merchants established a settlement on the island in the middle of the stream, now known as *Museumsinsel* or Museum Island, and the name 'Berlin' began to appear in documents and on maps from about 1250. The population remained modest for many years; inhabitants numbered about 8,000 in 1400, and 200 years later had risen to just 12,000. The Thirty Years War had a devastating effect on the region, with up to a third of the town being destroyed and half the population being killed or fleeing, but by the middle of the 17th century Berlin was thriving, with 20,000 inhabitants. Waves of new residents arrived in the city over the last part of that century, including large numbers of Jews and Huguenots. Further refugees fleeing violence to the east and southeast boosted the population and when Elector Friedrich III of Prussia declared himself King in Prussia in 1701, he made Berlin his capital. When he died in 1713, the city numbered 55,000 residents.

Friedrich was the first of many rulers of Germany to have great ambitions for the city, but first and foremost, he was an authoritarian autocrat. He set out to ensure complete control over Berlin, increasing the already significant size of the military garrison. His son, Friedrich II, carried his father's plans forward with the intention of creating what he described as a 'new Athens'; he wrote to Voltaire and other great personalities of the era, inviting them to come to Berlin for prolonged visits. At the same time, he continued the tradition of ensuring firm control: when the city's population passed 100,000 in his time, about a fifth consisted of soldiers. But despite the strict attitude of its rulers – in 1806, Graf Friedrich Wilhelm von der Schulenberg, one of the garrison commanders, declared that it was the primary duty of Berliners to show docility to royal authority – Berlin was never happy with such attempts to restrict its freedom.[1] When Europe was shaken by a wave of unrest in 1848, there were protests in the city. Demonstrators gathered outside the palace, demanding the withdrawal of the royal garrison and the creation of a citizens' militia, which would be answerable to city officials rather than royal appointees.

When the crowds showed no signs of dispersing, King Friedrich Wilhelm IV issued orders for the city garrison to clear the palace square, but specified that little or no force was to be used. The officers commanding the garrison had other ideas. Several charged into the protesters on horseback, laying about them with their sabres, and a few shots were fired. The tense situation exploded, with the protesters erecting barricades across the city, and there were bloody clashes with the garrison, leaving nearly 300 dead. Rather than engage in a pitched battle for Berlin against its citizens, Friedrich Wilhelm ordered his men back to their barracks. A mass funeral was held for the victims of the violence and several political prisoners were released. Constituent assemblies were created in Berlin and other German cities, but their power was strictly limited. In any case, there was little unity amongst those opposed to authoritarian rule by the Hohenzollern crown, and by the end of 1848 Berlin was once more tightly under the control of the authorities and their troops. However, there was a lasting legacy of the brief uprising: the rulers of Berlin came to view the people of the city as prone to disobedience, and the civilian population acquired a taste for being assertive.

As the capital of Prussia, Berlin grew substantially and was embellished by its rulers with fine buildings and palaces. In the first half of the 19th century, the city was the fourth largest in Europe and it continued to prosper during the Industrial Revolution. For the government at least, it was the natural choice as capital of the newly unified Germany in 1871, but from the outset this was greeted by many with a mixture of dismay and scepticism. Prussia originally referred to what later became known as East Prussia, a region further to the east, with its well-established capital of Königsberg. Founded at roughly the same time as Berlin, Königsberg was successively the capital of the Teutonic Knights, the Duchy of Prussia, and finally the province of East Prussia. It was the birthplace of many famous thinkers and musicians, including the philosopher Immanuel Kant; its Albertina University, founded in 1544, was one of the great centres of learning in all of Europe. Other German cities such as Munich and Hamburg could also claim to be more significant and important to German culture, commerce, and industry than Berlin, and many viewed the city with disdain; in 1907, when a French traveller told a friend in Hamburg that he planned to visit Berlin for two months, the response was astonishment: 'What could you possibly find to do for two whole months in Berlin?'[2]

When Germany came into being, Europe – and indeed the world – was dominated by the capitals of the European Powers. Paris and especially London were viewed as great metropolitan powerhouses, with long histories of dominance over their respective countries. By contrast, Berlin became the capital of a nation that was far more decentralised. Each region had its distinctive culture, dialect, and traditions, and in many respects Berlin struggled to establish its credibility both at home and abroad. But most were caught up in the energy of the time. The brash, assertive new state at the heart of Europe was a hub of industrial and military activity, and many of those who flocked to Berlin were eager to embrace a new age with all its excitement and energy. The result was a curious mix of old and new. Alongside the rather prudish and puritan memories of the past, there were widespread signs of change, and each wave of change left its older residents increasingly bewildered and those outside the capital increasingly contemptuous. Even Kaiser Wilhelm I had doubts about the selection of Berlin as Germany's capital; perhaps recalling how Berliners had risen up in rebellion in 1848, he would have preferred Potsdam, which had long been a favourite for the Hohenzollerns. But Otto von Bismarck, his chancellor and the architect of German unification, was adamant. Many of the reasons for his preference were precisely the reasons why so many others would have preferred an alternative. The smaller states of Germany felt threatened by the capital of Prussia – the most powerful of the pre-unification states – now becoming the capital of all of Germany. For Bismarck, this was a means of cementing the primary place of Prussia and its values in the new Germany. By contrast, the Catholics of Bavaria – and the residents of ancient cities in the west that could trace their origins to the Roman era – saw the austere, Protestant Prussia as overbearing, puritanical, and uncultured, and Berlin was a brash, vulgar, and irreverent upstart. There seems to have been no awareness amongst the Catholic Bavarians that the Lutheran and Calvinist Prussians, whom they instinctively disliked, were just as suspicious of Berlin as they were.

It was almost inevitable that the capital of the new nation would celebrate the birth of Germany with a huge military parade, and about 40,000 men marched and rode through the city in blazing summer sunshine in June 1871. The route that they followed was bedecked with pennants and banners, including dozens of French regimental flags captured in the recently ended Franco-Prussian War. Despite their reputation for being 'difficult', Berliners showed little unhappiness about paying a surcharge on their tax to pay for the celebrations. But in its early years the German capital wasn't a pleasant place in which to live, despite all its attempts to embrace modernity. August Bebel, who was one of the founders of the Social Democratic Party, recalled how infrastructure had not kept pace with the rapidly growing population:

> Wastewater from the houses collected in the gutters running alongside the kerbs and emitted a truly fearsome smell. There were no public toilets in the streets or squares. Visitors, especially women, often became desperate when nature called. In the public buildings the sanitary facilities were unbelievably primitive.[3]

Matters improved rapidly with the construction of a modern sewage system that commenced in 1879; this was followed by creation of the subway or *U-Bahn* between 1896 and 1902. Large numbers of tenement blocks were built to house the booming population, with further waves of immigrants arriving from most regions of Germany but especially from the east – from East Prussia, Silesia, and nearby rural areas. As early as 1860, there had been tentative plans for the orderly growth of Berlin, with wide avenues and street grids, but the pace of growth resulted in wild land speculation and many of the well-intentioned plans were ignored. There was a proliferation of what became known as *Mietskasernen* ('rental barracks'), five floors high, covering entire city blocks with small central courtyards. Cooking and sanitary facilities were communal, and waves of infectious diseases frequently originated in and spread rapidly through these blocks. Compared to its rival capitals, Berlin was heavily overcrowded, with seven times as many people living in each building lot as was the case in London, and a third more than in Paris. Despite this, rents rose rapidly, forcing many people to move several times in search of cheaper accommodation. Many of these *Mietskasernen* would become battlefields in April 1945.

Amongst the newcomers in Berlin were large numbers of Jews. In 1860, Berlin was home to fewer than 19,000 Jews; by 1880, nearly 54,000 Jews were residents. But to a large extent, this was proportionate to the expanding population of the city, and the Jewish community never exceeded 5 per cent of the total. They brought with them memories of persecution in lands to the east, particularly territories controlled by Russia. By contrast, Berlin seemed a safe haven and a place of great opportunity for them to put their knowledge, education, and skills to good use. But whilst Germany was unquestionably a better environment for Jews than the Russian Empire, antisemitism was widespread throughout Europe at the time and Berlin was no exception. With so much of Germany's financial sector dominated by Jewish families, there was resentment in many non-Jewish circles. The views that one writer expressed were shared by many: 'The Jewish element – no longer restrained, as of old, within particular limits, and today so insolently dominant in Berlin – exercises a continually increasing influence.'[4]

Many Jewish financiers – one of the most notable was Henry Bethel Strousberg, who became famous as the richest man in Germany – became hugely wealthy and lived in magnificent residences, as did others who benefited from the boom that followed German unification. By contrast, many of the 'traditional' families who had dominated Prussian society for centuries found themselves struggling. In an earlier era when the population of Prussia was largely rural, the *Junker* families with their rural estates controlled the character and attitude of their state, and their prestigious names continued to carry a certain cachet; but the newly enriched urban entrepreneurs now had far greater spending power and visible wealth. A curious mismatch developed between the two groups – the traditional Prussians continued to hold considerable status in Germany, but their wealth and spending power was at best modest, while the urban elite that arose from the entrepreneurs who flocked to Berlin hankered after the social status of the *Junker* families and found that their wealth was an incomplete substitute.

With such a mix of people from widely differing regions and cultural and social backgrounds, the city became a place where there was no single prevailing ethos. Traditional Prussians lived close to Bohemian hedonists; Jews rubbed shoulders with Catholics; and ordinary workers from all backgrounds rapidly realised that despite their differences, they shared a life of squalor, poverty, and hard work. In many respects, this fed into the culture that was already present in Berlin of a city that was unruly and independently minded. This was a marked contrast with the authoritarian and heavy-handed nature of government, both at a local and national level.

In keeping with many other cities of Europe, the eastern sections became the locations of most of the industrial areas with dense, overcrowded housing for their workers, while western sections – particularly in the southwest, in Charlottenburg, Steglitz, and Zehlendorf – were the preferred areas of the growing middle classes. Opera and theatrical houses were built, museums were established, and there were attempts to create new monuments to mark the arrival of Berlin and Germany on the world scene. One of the most notable was the *Siegessäule* ('Victory Column') that was erected at one end of Unter den Linden, the main avenue through the heart of old Berlin. It was decorated with friezes commemorating the wars of unification and surrounded by cannon captured in the defeat of France; at its summit stood a gilded Goddess of Victory, a winged figure holding a staff in one hand and a victory wreath in the other. With what was becoming an increasingly common attitude, many Berliners treated the monument with amusement and irreverence. The Goddess of Victory looked alone and poorly proportioned to many, and her unsmiling expression contributed to many referring to her as the 'only lady in town without a lover'.[5]

The rapid growth of Berlin and widespread speculation almost inevitably resulted in a financial crash after just a few years. For many, the Jewish financiers who were at the heart of the German business community were to blame. By the beginning of the new century, this downturn had passed and Berlin was widely regarded as an outstanding example of a modern, well-organised city. The amused disdain shown by visitors in the first few years of the German state, making unfavourable comparisons with Paris and London, were replaced by comments that Berlin was transformed from the dirty, unhygienic sprawl of building sites of the early 1870s. As early as 1891, when he stayed in the German capital with his family for five months, Mark Twain was deeply impressed. In a letter to the *Chicago Daily Tribune* after his return home, he wrote:

> [A striking feature] is the spaciousness, the roominess of the city. There is no other city, in any country, where streets are so generally wide ... Unter den Linden is three streets in one; the Potsdamerstrasse is bordered on both sides by sidewalks which are themselves wider than some of the historic thoroughfares of the old European capitals; there seem to be no lanes or alleys ... here and there, where several important streets empty into a common centre, that centre's circumference is of a magnitude calculated to bring that word spaciousness into your mind again. The park in the middle of the city [Tiergarten] is so huge that it calls up that expression once more.[6]

Clearly, Twain didn't visit any of the *Mietkasernen*.

The new German state had little prospect of any rapprochement with France – at the end of the Franco-Prussian War, Germany annexed the provinces of Alsace and Lorraine and demanded huge financial reparations – and the British were wary of a new power in the heart of Europe that threatened to overturn 'traditional' British foreign policy of preventing any one nation from dominating the continent. At first, Germany found a receptive audience in the court of the tsar; the Austro-Hungarian Empire, which had been defeated by the Prussians during the wars of unification, was perhaps a more lukewarm friend. And hostility to the new Germany and particularly its rulers was not restricted to other countries. In 1878, Max Hödel, a plumber from Leipzig, fired at Kaiser Wilhelm I with a revolver; he was promptly arrested and tried for treason. He was executed later that year. Shortly after Hödel's failed attack, there was a second attempt, this time by Karl Nobiling, who had grown up in the Prussian province of Posen (now the Polish Poznań). After firing at the Kaiser with a shotgun and slightly wounding him, Nobiling drew a pistol and shot himself in the head, dying shortly after. Wilhelm was both alarmed and baffled by these attacks. 'I don't understand why I'm always being shot at,' he complained irritably to Bismarck.[7] For the chancellor, the attacks were proof that political liberalisation had gone too far. Hödel had been a member of the Social Democratic Party or *SPD* in the past, and although there was no conclusive evidence of any such link on the part of Nobiling, the attacks were used to vilify the Social Democrats and their allies, but Berliners demonstrated their unruliness once again in the Reichstag elections of 1878, increasing the vote of the Social Democrats.

If Bismarck and other traditionally minded Prussians hoped that they could suppress what they saw as the subversive left with increasingly restrictive legislation, they were to be disappointed. In the months that followed, the Berlin police reported that the *SPD* had effectively become an underground organisation that continued to enjoy widespread support. In later elections, the *SPD* ran their candidates as independents and bypassed the bans on printing pro-Social Democrat newspapers by publishing them abroad and then bringing them into Germany. Attempts to ban the display of red pro-*SPD* emblems ended in farce. The wearing of red flowers resulted in numerous arrests and the courts ruled that whilst people were entitled to wear whatever colour of flower they wished, the wearing of red flowers by all people in an assembly was illegal. Female *SPD* supporters responded by wearing red petticoats and lifting their outer skirts to display them to the police, aware that the societal rules on decency would greatly constrain the ability of the police to take any action against them.[8] Frustrated by the manner in which the brash, vibrant city refused to comply with his vision of Prussian austerity, order, and deference, during the 1880s the German chancellor began to speculate about moving the centre of government out of Berlin. However, Bismarck's dominance was coming to an end. In 1888, the 90-year-old Kaiser Wilhelm I died. His successor, Friedrich, was already terminally ill with throat cancer and died later the same year, to be succeeded by Wilhelm II. From the outset, the new Kaiser had a far cooler relationship with Bismarck, openly opposing his constant attempts to suppress trade unions, the *SPD*, and other real and imagined opponents. This ultimately resulted in the chancellor being forced to resign in March 1890.

The new Kaiser enthusiastically embraced the mood to develop Berlin into as important and as dominant a city as places like London, Paris, and New York, and there was a huge surge in development that continued up to the start of the First World War. Many Berliners welcomed this and rejoiced in what they and others saw as the creation of a thoroughly modern city, but the traditionalists were less impressed. In many respects, the waves of immigrants moving to the city, largely from the eastern provinces of Germany, found it more congenial than its existing residents, many of whom remembered a quieter, perhaps more dignified city. Such views were not restricted to parts of the Berlin population. The regional wariness about Berlin continued, with other parts of Germany recoiling from the sprawling, industrialised metropolis with its noise, pollution, and scandalous nightlife. Even Wilhelm, who wanted to create a glittering capital that could outshine other European cities, had mixed feelings about Berlin; he had been brought up to believe in absolute authoritarian power and disliked the unruliness of the city's inhabitants, and he was disdainful of what he saw as attitudes that were too civilian, too feminine. Nevertheless, he spent much of his reign embellishing Berlin with new buildings, many of which were decorated with neo-Gothic ornamentation that clashed terribly with earlier constructions. A new avenue was created in the Tiergarten, named the Siegesallee ('Victory Avenue'). Marble statues of Hohenzollern figures of the past were placed along the new avenue; on the orders of Wilhelm, many of the statues had their faces modelled on those of his friends and associates. Far from impressing Berlin, Germany, and the entire world, the avenue was widely mocked as the epitome of the pretentions of Wilhelmine Germany. It wasn't long before Berliners gave it their own, unofficial name of Puppenallee ('Dolls' Avenue').

Berlin continued to have a substantial military presence throughout the years between German unification and the First World War. The old barracks of the Prussian Army had been enlarged over the years, particularly after the 1848 protests, and Wilhelm wasn't the only person in Berlin to show a remarkable level of deference to men in uniform. In typical Berlin fashion, this resulted in an episode that highlighted the absurdity of this attitude in a hilarious manner. Wilhelm Voigt was a shoemaker who was originally from East Prussia, and had a history of criminal behaviour; he was first imprisoned for two weeks aged just 14 for theft, and over the years that followed he was sentenced to a total of 25 years' imprisonment for various crimes – theft, forgery, and attempted burglary. In 1906, at the age of 57, he was living in Berlin with his sister, but was ordered to leave the city by the police as his past criminal record made him an undesirable person. Like many of Berlin's poorer residents, most of his clothes were purchased second-hand from market stalls and he had acquired most of the components of the uniform of an army Hauptmann (captain in British and US forces). He donned the uniform and, inspired by the manner in which his clothing resulted in everyone he encountered treating him respectfully, marched up to four soldiers and their sergeant who were about to return to their barracks. After dismissing the sergeant, he ordered the others to accompany him, adding a further six soldiers from a nearby rifle range, and the small group boarded a train to the suburb of Köpenick. Here, he took control of the city hall and ordered the local police to prevent unrest and to occupy the post office so that they could block any telephone calls to central Berlin for an hour.

Voigt then had the mayor and treasurer of Köpenick placed under arrest for financial irregularities. He demanded that they hand over all the funds that they held and took away a little over 4,000 Marks (slightly more than four times the average annual income); with punctilious courtesy and correctness, he signed a receipt in the name of the director of one of the many jails in which he had served time. Two soldiers were dispatched in a carriage with the arrested officials to the royal guard house at Neue Wache while Voigt slipped away to the railway station. Ten days later, he was arrested after a former cellmate gave his name to the police, telling the authorities that Voigt had mentioned some such plan in the past.

The incident caused great amusement both in Germany and elsewhere. Kaiser Wilhelm clearly saw the absurdity of the story, but was also delighted at the obvious respect shown to an officer of his army. Foreign journalists saw the story as confirmation for the widespread stereotypical views about German militarism. Writing in the *Illustrated London News*, a journalist commented that the Kaiser had spent many years instilling reverence for his military, and the level to which he had succeeded was shown by the attitude of the mayor and treasurer who accepted being placed under arrest without any warrant or police authority being invoked.[9] Voigt was found guilty of forgery, impersonating an officer, and wrongful imprisonment, and was given a four-year jail sentence, but most of the population saw him as an amusing rogue and Wilhelm decided to pardon him after just two years' imprisonment. For Berliners from all walks of life, but particularly those in the industrial areas of the east, Voigt became a celebrity.

The heartlands of Germany's industrial revolution were to the west, along the Ruhr valley, and in the southeast, particularly in Upper Silesia. Like industrial areas in other countries, the development of these regions was driven by the ready availability of coal and minerals from local resources, and industrialisation was already extensive when Germany was unified. Despite having no local coal or mineral mines, Berlin rapidly developed as a manufacturing centre and by the mid-1890s accounted for about 7 per cent of German industrial production, at a time when its population formed less than 3.5 per cent of the total. The number of people employed in such industries increased greatly over the next few years, but as was the case in many other cities struggling with rapid industrial growth, working and living conditions were poor. Trade unions had little or no legal status and were often ignored by employers; as a result, their only recourse was industrial action, and throughout the decade before the First World War there were numerous strikes. Such actions weren't limited to matters of employment, pay, etc.; on occasion, there were protests and strikes about the electoral system that was explicitly designed to minimise the voice of ordinary people. The tendency of Berlin's workers to organise for protest, and the willingness of the police to use force in response, would continue beyond the First World War and was part of the political violence that led to Hitler's accession of power.

The coming of the First World War was greeted with a wave of popular patriotism in many of Europe's capitals, and Berlin was no exception. A large crowd gathered outside the Royal Palace, singing patriotic songs and shouting demands for the Kaiser to appear. Wilhelm addressed the gathering from a balcony, expressing his thanks for their support and proclaiming that he saw just a united *Volk*, no longer riven by political parties. In the days that followed, the *SPD*, which had at first been hostile to a major war, joined most other parties in creating a united pro-war front. All partisan disputes were formally put to one side in what became known as the *Burgfrieden*, the traditional name for the arrangement in a city or fortress under siege in which all factions stood together to defend their home. For some in Berlin, it was an opportunity to address the wider dislike of the city across Germany. Adolf Wermuth, the mayor of Berlin, declared that as the capital of the Reich, Berlin would lead in terms of willingness and sacrifice.[10] But when the anticipated rapid victory over France, Russia, and Britain failed to appear, the mood changed quickly. A combination of mobilisation and loss of overseas markets resulted in a huge slump in employment and therefore family income across Germany, and attempts to alleviate this by increasing unemployment benefits, augmented by local efforts in Berlin to create communal soup kitchens and to provide aid for rent, only partially compensated the urban population.

The attempts to improve the image of Berlin within Germany were unsuccessful. Large numbers of men – over 92,000 in some estimates – returned to the city from the army because they were deemed to be skilled industrial workers who would be needed in Berlin's factories if the war was to continue for longer than anticipated. Other factors also reduced the contribution made by the Reich capital to the front line. For example, factory workers tended to be less physically fit and of smaller stature than rural workers, and were therefore more likely to be deemed medically unsuitable. The development of new branches of government to regulate and organise production of weapons and munitions resulted in increasing centralisation of power within Berlin. Residents in the countryside and in other German cities began to refer to the capital in disparaging tones as the *Kriegslieblingskind* ('favoured war child').

Food shortages that arose from a combination of the British naval blockade, the cessation of trade across much of Europe, and particularly the bad harvest of 1917, left their scars on the population of the entire country, but as is always the case, poorer people suffered the greatest shortages. The working-class areas of Berlin were full of resentment for the alleged comfortable life of the largely rural population of Bavaria and suspected farmers of hoarding food, but those in other parts of the country felt that the higher rations allocated to the factory workers of Berlin were unfair. Although the government – increasingly dominated by the military – took measures to increase armaments production, this resulted largely in a boom of contracts for private concerns, and certain parts of society continued to be almost completely sheltered from hardship and shortages. Much of Berlin's nightlife continued, to the dismay of soldiers who returned to the capital either on leave or while convalescing from wounds. Amongst the soldiers who visited the city in 1916 was the 27-year-old private Adolf Hitler, who concluded that Berlin was full of people evading front-line duty or agitating for peace. A few years later, looking back on his visit – and a second trip a year later – Hitler modified his opinion, feeling that these distasteful impressions were due to the excessive influence of the city's Jews.[11]

As the war dragged on, some doggedly insisted that the nation had to persevere to see the matter to a successful conclusion, but others were horrified at the cost, both at home and in the front line. The failure of the *SPD* to fight for the rights of the working classes resulted in growing support for other left-wing groups in industrial areas of Berlin. In early 1916, Rosa Luxembourg and Karl Liebknecht founded the Spartacist movement and led an anti-war protest on 1 May through the heart of the capital, resulting in the arrest and imprisonment of the two leaders. At the same time, those who were determined to fight on to secure victory regardless of the price being paid also began to organise into political groupings. Inevitably, both the left-wing anti-war groups and the right-wing militarists were centred on Berlin. The political scene in the city therefore became increasingly polarised as hardships steadily worsened, and in mid-1917 the more centrist parties attempted to regain the initiative. Although they succeeded in passing a motion in the Reichstag calling for a compromise peace without reparations, the military government simply ignored it. In early 1918, there was increasing industrial unrest in Berlin and other regions; this resulted in draconian measures, with armed soldiers patrolling the streets of working-class areas of the capital and the arrest and imprisonment of trade union leaders. But the failure of the 1918 offensives in the west resulted in recognition in all factions in Berlin that the war could not be won.

After desperate attempts at belated reform, the Kaiser abdicated. Any hope of continuing the monarchy in some form was swept away by the growing flood of protests. The new government began to take shape in lengthy discussions in the city of Weimar, a location chosen because so many regions of Germany continued to distrust Berlin. In the meantime, in a nation exhausted by war and starvation, political views polarised still further. Many from the labouring classes were inspired by the events taking place in Russia and saw a great opportunity for German workers to seize power; others, the traditionalists and militarists who had prospered under the old regime and had always regarded Berlin and its irreverent inhabitants with disdain, were filled with horror at the demise of the Kaiser and were desperate to prevent any further slide towards revolution. And everywhere, those who were driven into increasingly hard-line left- and right-wing positions regarded the traditional political parties as unrepresentative of their views. Amidst this turbulence, it was no surprise that as the centre of government and the home of so many ordinary labourers, it was Berlin that became the cockpit of violence.

Mutinous sailors from Kiel formed the *Volksmarinedivision* ('People's Naval Division') and marched to Berlin in support of the Spartacists, resulting in clashes with regular troops. Large numbers of soldiers remained under arms despite the end of the war, many of them enrolled into the ranks of the *Freikorps*, units of 'volunteers' that were sometimes built around the old divisions and regiments of the Kaiser's army and on other occasions were little more than armed gangs loyal to their leader. Despite no overall structure of command and control, the various *Freikorps* units were united in one aspect: they were quite ready to use whatever force was required to crush left-wing protesters who threatened to replicate the Bolshevik seizure of power. There was outright warfare between left- and right-wing groups with hundreds of deaths, and in January 1919, after a failed attempt by the Spartacists to seize power, Liebknecht and Luxembourg were captured and taken to the Eden Hotel where they were brutally interrogated. Both were battered senseless. Luxembourg was taken to a car where she was shot in the head and dumped in the Landwehr Canal; her body remained undiscovered for several months. Liebknecht was also taken away in a car but as it was passing through the Tiergarten, he was pushed out and then shot.

Despite all the violence and deaths of the past few weeks, these political killings resulted in widespread shock. The official story – that Luxembourg had been seized by a mob and dragged away into the night, and that Liebknecht was shot while trying to escape – was greeted with general disbelief. Many were horrified that a government with prominent *SPD* figures might have participated in such murders; this created a permanent rift that effectively poisoned any attempts at cooperation by the parties of the left and centre-left. Other parts of the political spectrum took a different view. A precedent had been established for extrajudicial killings of political opponents, and this trend would steadily worsen in the years that followed. Many months after the deaths of Luxembourg and Liebknecht, attempts were made to prosecute the soldiers involved, but although two – Otto Runge, who had struck the prisoners until they were unconscious, and Kurt Vogel, who threw Luxembourg's corpse into the canal – were sentenced to prison terms, they were swiftly released. In later years, the Nazi regime even paid them compensation.

But the violence in Berlin was compartmentalised, with many areas almost unaffected. Harry Graf Kessler, an Anglo-German aristocrat who had variously been a publisher, a theatrical organiser, and a soldier, described his experiences in the city:

> In the evening [of 17 January] I went to a cabaret ... The sound of a shot cracked through the performance of a fiery Spanish dancer. Nobody took any notice. It underlined the slight impression that the revolution has made on metropolitan life. I only began to appreciate the Babylonian, unfathomably deep, primordial and titanic quality of Berlin when I saw how this historic, colossal event has caused no more than local ripples on the even more colossally eddying movement of Berlin existence. An elephant stabbed with a penknife shakes itself and strides on as if nothing has happened.[12]

Fighting continued across Germany until early May, with up to 5,000 people losing their lives. In Berlin, unrest flared up from time to time; despite the crushing of the Spartacists, many left-wing groups remained determined to bring about radical changes, including the introduction of legal safeguards for councils representing workers and soldiers in emulation of similar arrangements in Russia after the fall of the tsar. On 3 March, strikes spread across the German capital, and the military responded with force, attacking and occupying the offices of the newspaper *Rote Fahne* ('Red Flag'). Some workers – many of the organisers of the strike claimed that these were agents provocateurs and attempted to distance themselves from the rising wave of violence – responded by attacking police stations and seizing weapons.

Supported by artillery and aircraft, the *Freikorps* struck at resistance wherever they encountered it, particularly in and around Alexanderplatz.

Fighting continued until the middle of March, despite attempts by the mayor of the Berlin district of Lichtenberg to negotiate a ceasefire. The army claimed that it had suffered the loss of 75 men; casualties amongst their opponents were far greater, ranging from a low estimate of 1,200 to an upper estimate of 3,000. Many more were rounded up and arrested, and several of them were wounded and died of neglect in the days that followed.[13] But although there was far more violence than in the attempted Spartacist uprising that ended with the deaths of Liebknecht and Luxembourg, it remained limited to distinct areas of Berlin, like Lichtenberg. Just a few city blocks away, restaurants and theatres continued to function normally, and most wealthy Berliners continued life almost as normal. In some respects, it was characteristic of the increasing polarisation of Berlin and indeed of Germany as a whole. Working-class districts licked their wounds and remained openly hostile to the government, while the inhabitants of the more comfortable suburbs in the west and southwest of Berlin were relieved that the socialists were being put firmly in their place. Fully aware of how the Russian aristocracy and bourgeoisie had suffered during the Bolshevik seizure of power, they were quite content to turn a blind eye to the brutal manner in which the army and *Freikorps* had acted. Few, if any, perceived the peril of men becoming accustomed to the violent repression of those of different political opinions.

Both Berlin and Germany were badly in need of a period of calm. The months since the end of fighting on the Western Front had seen almost constant turmoil, and the entire nation desperately needed time for the chaos created by the fall of the Kaiser to dissipate, and for new institutions and procedures to be established and to gain credibility. With impeccable timing, the victorious enemies of Germany took a step that was effectively guaranteed to do quite the opposite. On 7 May, a draft Treaty of Versailles was presented to the German delegation. Germany was to accept all responsibility for the recent war and was to commit to paying as-yet unknown reparations. The German Army would be limited to just 100,000 men; the Rhineland would be occupied by France and Britain for 15 years and would thereafter be a demilitarised zone. When the Germans submitted counterproposals, these were rejected out of hand. Germany was given a deadline to accept the terms or to face invasion.

Aware of the country's desperate need for peace almost at any price, Friedrich Ebert, the president of the new republic, faced rebellion in his government but managed to put together a cabinet that was prepared to sign the treaty, albeit at the last moment and under protest. But already, a myth was beginning to take shape in Germany, particularly amongst the military. Oberst Max Bauer, a close personal friend and protégé of General Erich Ludendorff, published a short book in early 1919. In this, he declared that the defeat of Germany was 'exclusively due to the failure of the homeland', a view that was shared by many in the army – they believed that they had been retreating intact towards Germany's frontiers and had not been defeated on the battlefield.[14] Such a view was at best a very narrow and partial interpretation of events, but it allowed senior officers – particularly Ludendorff and Hindenburg, who had effectively been in charge of a military dictatorship in Germany in the closing phases of the war – to absolve themselves of any responsibility for what had happened.

Fearing plots to overthrow his government, Ebert ordered the disbandment of army units and of the *Freikorps* in keeping with the terms of the treaty, leading to a fierce argument with General Walther von Lüttwitz, the commander of all army units in and around Berlin. At the centre of the dispute was *Marinebrigade Ehrhardt*, a *Freikorps* unit made up largely of former sailors; its commander, Korvettenkapitän Hermann Ehrhardt, had led his men, numbering up to 6,000 at the peak of their strength, in the ruthless repression of socialist groups in Wilhelmshaven and then in Bavaria, where the unit gained a reputation for brutality. Ehrhardt often acted without any orders or even contrary to his instructions, but although some senior navy figures called for its disbandment, *Marinebrigade Ehrhardt* was moved to the barracks at Döberitz, a short distance to the west of Berlin. In early 1920, Ebert ordered its disbandment, but Lüttwitz refused on the grounds that the unit was essential for the safety of Berlin. When Ebert insisted and also added a list of other units to be disbanded, Lüttwitz ordered Ehrhardt to march on the capital.

To date, the civilian government had cooperated, with varying degrees of willingness, with the army and with right-wing groups to prevent groups like the Spartacists seizing power. Now, there was the real prospect of strife with the very forces that had been used to suppress left-wing groups in Berlin and elsewhere. When Gustav Noske – the *SPD* defence minister – demanded that regular army units intervene, the new commander of the German Army, General Hans von Seeckt, refused on the grounds that he could not order German soldiers to open fire on men they regarded as their former comrades. Ehrhardt's brigade marched into Berlin unopposed before dawn on 13 March 1920, where it was greeted by Ludendorff and Wolfgang Kapp, a founder of the *Vaterlandpartei* ('Fatherland Party'). The government fled and Kapp was declared the new chancellor.

Ebert and his government responded quickly. Even as they travelled from one location to another, eventually reaching Stuttgart, Ebert's cabinet issued calls for a general strike to oppose the coup attempt. It was a remarkable moment: politicians who had in recent weeks and months been condemning workers for taking industrial action to promote political causes were now urging their former opponents to take action against Kapp and Lüttwitz. The workers of Berlin and other cities were aware that regardless of their distrust and dislike of Ebert and others who had been involved in suppressing left-wing groups in 1919, their hatred of the hard right as represented by the coup plotters was even greater. Immediately, strikes broke out across all of Germany. Until now, strikes had paralysed parts of Berlin, but on this occasion the disruption was at a different level. All transport was shut down and electricity supplies disrupted. Civil servants and shop assistants – even, according to some reports, many prostitutes – joined the strike. So complete was the shutdown of the capital that it took Kapp and his accomplices two days to type and print a proclamation of their new government.

Elsewhere in Germany, there were attempts by supporters of the coup to assist Kapp and his followers. The Iron Division was a *Freikorps* unit that had been involved in attempts to establish a pro-German regime in Latvia and had just returned by sea, and its current commander, Hauptmann Rudolf Berthold, ordered his men to board trains for Berlin. Rail workers immediately went on strike. The soldiers then commandeered a train on 14 March, using it to move to the outskirts of Hamburg, but they found that the commander of a regular army battalion had already been arrested by local government representatives, and that the leaderless soldiers had declared themselves as supporters of the socialist party officials. These officials now ordered Berthold and his men to a nearby school where they were to bed down. The following morning, the soldiers found that the school was surrounded by large numbers of civilians, many of them armed. After a tense stand-off, a brief gun battle took place, resulting in deaths on both sides, but Berthold's men were both outnumbered and short of ammunition and had no choice but to surrender. Despite assurances that they would be treated well, the soldiers were attacked by groups of civilians. Berthold took shelter in a nearby bar but was pulled out into the street, and when he drew his pistol to defend himself, it was seized and used to kill him.[15]

There was little or no military resistance to Kapp and Lüttwitz, with many senior figures declaring themselves supporters of the coup. Others were clearly sympathetic, but took an official position of neutrality and waited to see how matters would unfold. Adolf Hitler had been in contact with the coup plotters before the seizure of Berlin and attempted to fly to the capital to join Kapp and Lüttwitz. His plane landed near Berlin where it was surrounded by striking workers; hastily disguising himself, Hitler managed to complete his journey by car. But despite his support and the quiet acquiescence of the police and military, the coup was rapidly unravelling. Communications in Berlin were completely silenced by the strikers, forcing Kapp and Lüttwitz to issue orders via couriers. Threats of dire punishment – including execution – for taking part in strikes had no effect, and Kapp had to face the reality of failure. He and his fellow conspirators were desperate to save face and were aided by many in the centre and centre-right of German politics, who saw little benefit in alienating large sections of the military. Kapp agreed to resign, handing power to Lüttwitz, who was also forced to step down. The coup was effectively over after just four days.

To date, the resistance in Berlin had been by way of the highly effective general strike, but violence was almost inevitable. Ehrhardt and his brigade had been assured by Seeckt that they would be permitted to leave Berlin without hindrance; when they marched out of the city centre, they were surrounded by a heckling crowd. Some of the soldiers attacked a young boy who was mocking them and then opened fire on the crowd; 12 people were killed and 30 were wounded. Elsewhere in Berlin, there were confrontations between small *Freikorps* units and civilians, ranging from scuffles to exchanges of fire, leaving several hundred more killed or wounded. Kapp and Lüttwitz were both permitted to leave Berlin without hindrance; Kapp eventually fled to Sweden in April, and Lüttwitz travelled to Hungary. Legal proceedings against some of the conspirators finally took place a year later, and Kapp returned to Germany to protest that he and his followers were innocent. He was found to have a tumour behind his eye and died before he could be brought to trial. Lüttwitz remained in Hungary until he was granted amnesty in 1924. He returned to Germany and died in Breslau in 1942. Ehrhardt, whose brigade had seized Berlin, went into hiding after his unit was finally disbanded in May 1920, but continued to conspire with some of his former soldiers. They carried out several assassinations in the hope of triggering unrest sufficient to lead to the military seizing power, and Ehrhardt was forced to flee to Hungary in 1922. When he returned to Germany late that year, he was promptly arrested, though he soon escaped custody. Hoping for a role as the leader of the radical right, he opposed Hitler's rise to power. Although he later joined the SS, he was one of those intended for execution when Hitler purged the Nazi Party in 1934. He fled to Switzerland, later returning to live quietly in Germany until his death in 1971.

In many ways, the coup attempts by the Spartacists and by Kapp and Lüttwitz set the tone for events across all of Germany. The years that followed would see an increasingly bitter struggle between right and left for control, with both sides pursuing their objectives without any thought of compromise. Berlin was as polarised as any other part of the country, but two further factors added to governmental difficulties. The enormous debt incurred during the years of war, compounded by the crippling reparations imposed by the Allied Powers at Versailles, doomed the German economy to chaotic inflation. With the international value of the German currency plummeting, prices soared. In mid-1922, it seemed as if things were stabilising, with the US dollar worth about 320 German marks, compared with 90 marks in 1921, but suddenly a new wave of hyperinflation began. By late 1923, a dollar was worth a staggering 4,210 *billion* marks. It took severe financial measures, including the introduction of a new Reichsmark, to restore stability, but hundreds of thousands of Germans were left destitute and this fed into the political unrest in the country, particularly in large cities. The echoes of this period continue even into the modern era, with successive German governments regarding the control of inflation as paramount.

The second factor that added to the turmoil in Berlin was the expansion of the city. In 1920, the city boundaries were increased to incorporate several surrounding areas that had technically been separate towns. The result was the creation of a metropolis of nearly four million people, the third largest city in Europe. The divisions between those on the left of politics and the centre-left, created by the use of force by the *SPD* government to suppress the Spartacists, remained unresolved, resulting in a series of unstable coalitions in local government. City finances were in as big a mess as national finances, and as is always the case in periods of economic turmoil, the impact varied according to the status of individuals. Wealthy Berliners, particularly those who had foreign currency reserves and assets, were able to manage with little difficulty, and members of powerful trade unions – that were able to demand ever-higher wages – were at least buffered from the worst effects of the financial problems. Those who were dependent upon fixed incomes, such as pensioners, and those who had invested heavily in war bonds, suffered the worst. Many took ruthless advantage of the situation to purchase property and businesses with comparatively small amounts of foreign currency and there was widespread resentment at the visibly ostentatious and luxurious lifestyles of the rich, particularly foreigners, in the German capital. Alfred Polgar, a freelance journalist from Vienna who had moved to Berlin, wrote contemptuously about visitors from America who dined in a hotel close to where he lived:

> A small flag with the stars and stripes stands in a vase amongst the flowers. A plate is overflowing with the whitest sliced bread bursting with wheat. A glass cover protects glistening real butter, of golden yellow. There are strange boxes and cans, round or square, containing only God knows what delicacies. Delicate aromas of spices and spirits rise from bowls and bottles. The locals at neighbouring tables look with awe at this culinary display. Here dine the victors, the Americans! Hail to them! It is due to their intervention in the war that we owe this peace with its Fourteen Points [the list of requirements stipulated by President Woodrow Wilson as the price of peace], these bundles of dollars, this democracy, this sense of being eaten out of our houses and homes. We love America![16]

Inevitably, rapidly worsening poverty brought a wave of crime, ranging from petty theft to major fraud, from prostitution to drug and alcohol misuse. Whilst the scale of vice in Berlin was worse than in other capital cities, it was exceptional in its openness. This made the city an attractive destination for many foreigners, but most rapidly tired of the frenetic, gaudy nature of Berlin's excesses and left for quieter and less feverish cities. But it would be wrong to describe the Berlin of the Weimar Republic as no more than a seedy den of vice. It was also a centre of academic and cultural experimentation and triumph. Great scientists like Albert Einstein were based there, as were writers like Vladimir Nabokov, Berthold Brecht, and Franz Kafka. The city also embraced the new medium of cinema, with pioneers like Fritz Lang leading the way, but life for ordinary Berliners was hard, living in a city that faced worsening unemployment and food shortages. Some right-wing newspapers were quick to blame the Jewish community for making matters worse, directing their ire particularly at the latest wave of Jews who had arrived recently from territories to the east. This led to attacks on the Jewish community, with a particularly violent episode sweeping through the Scheunenviertel – home to many Jewish families and businesses – on 7 November 1923. Whilst some saw this as a regrettable venting of the frustration of ordinary people, others correctly interpreted the violence as a harbinger of a dark future.

It was against this backdrop that Joseph Goebbels, who studied history and literature at university before pursuing a career as a private tutor, journalist, and bank clerk, became a member of the Nazi Party in 1924. Despite at one time expressing doubts about Hitler's opposition to socialism, he rapidly became a close adherent of the Nazi Party leader and became *Gauleiter* (regional leader) of the Party in Berlin in 1926.[17] But by the mid-1920s, opportunities for the advancement of the Nazi Party seemed diminished. The economic and political turmoil that had repeatedly shaken the city was greatly reduced and, partly through substantial loans from American banks, life in Berlin was beginning to improve. The population grew steadily, as did industry and commerce, and the political infighting of recent years was replaced by a general mood of support for the new republic, at least in principle. At a time when most of the rest of Germany remained sceptical about republicanism, this further increased the gap between Berlin and other towns and cities; the enthusiastic embracing of American culture, particularly in popular music, and the activities of left-wing writers and artists, led many conservative Germans to regard their capital as a distasteful combination of the worst aspects of Chicago and Moscow.

The foreign influences in Berlin – particularly American jazz and the continued activities of the political left – were anathema to Goebbels and the Nazis. Almost from the moment that he took office as *Gauleiter* in Berlin,

Goebbels organised a series of provocative marches through working-class areas, leading to increasingly violent clashes. In March 1929, several hundred Nazi supporters – members of the *Sturmabteilungen* ('Assault units' or *SA*) – attacked and beat about 30 Communists at a railway station in southwest Berlin before proceeding to the city centre where they assaulted several Jews. A new weekly publication of the Nazis, entitled *Der Angriff* ('The Attack'), railed against the corruption of German culture by Jews, and the notoriety gained by the local party through its attacks slowly attracted followers. In May 1927, the city administration responded to the worsening violence by banning the Nazi Party in Berlin for nearly a year, and in the national elections of May 1928, the Nazis secured only 1.5 per cent of the vote in the capital. Nevertheless, attacks – both physical and via *Der Angriff* – on opponents of the Nazis continued to escalate. Partly because of a bribery scandal that involved two wealthy Jewish businessmen and the city mayor, the Nazis enjoyed a modest degree of success in the local elections in November 1929; their share of the vote remained barely at 3 per cent, but they managed to secure a seat in the city assembly. Almost immediately after, the world faced further economic and financial turmoil as a result of the Wall Street Crash. A new centre-right government imposed austerity measures, and political violence worsened across all Germany.

In Berlin, there occurred an incident that in almost any other era would have had little or no political effect. Horst Wessel was a 22-year-old living in the eastern Berlin district of Friedrichshain; he had been a member of several increasingly radical right-wing groups before joining the Nazi Party and the *SA* while studying law. He soon abandoned his studies to devote himself full-time to the Nazis and became one of Goebbels' rising stars, recruiting new members and organising violent attacks on Communists and their sympathisers. However, a childhood injury had left him with a weakened, deformed arm, limiting his personal involvement in the fighting. At this stage, he was living with a woman described variously as a prostitute or ex-prostitute, and he may have functioned as her pimp. When he had a dispute with the landlady of the apartment over unpaid rent, the landlady turned to friends of her dead husband who were prominent Communists for help. At the time, Wessel was a well-known target for the Communists and one of their number shot Wessel in mid-January 1930. Wessel died several weeks later from septicaemia.

The death of a violent young man who was probably a pimp would have barely been noticed, particularly at a time when street clashes between right and left resulted in almost daily injuries, but Goebbels made the most of the moment. Wessel was promoted into a kind of Nazi saint who had sacrificed himself for the Party and for his vision of a future Germany. Nazi newspapers wrote extensively about Wessel, and in the years that followed there were several occasions when Nazis who were killed in street violence were described as having joined Wessel's ethereal combat group. A song written by Wessel, the *Horst Wessel Lied*, became the Nazi Party anthem.[18]

The political polarisation of Germany worsened. In 1930, the Communists secured 27 per cent of the vote while the Nazis won nearly 15 per cent. Goebbels immediately organised demonstrations in central Berlin, leading to clashes with the police, though there were ominous signs that many police officers were sympathetic to the Nazis and refused to take firm or timely action. Communist groups also indulged in violent attacks, on both the Nazis and the police, and many newspapers, not just those directly linked to the Nazi Party, began to portray the Nazis as the only means of stopping left-wing violence. But the Communists weren't the only source of difficulties for Goebbels and his followers. The *SA* was increasingly unruly and inclined to follow a different path, something that would ultimately lead to Hitler's purge of the *SA* and parts of the Nazi Party during the Night of the Long Knives at the end of June 1934.

Despite the violence, the reputation of Berlin's nightlife continued to attract visitors. In many respects, the energy with which the city threw itself into hedonistic celebrations every night seemed like a reaction to the grim reality of daytime street battles. Harold Nicolson, a British diplomat, compared the German capital to other great European cities:

> Those who in London or in Paris would already have drooped in sleep are busy in Berlin, inquisitive, acquisitive, searching, even at 4am, for some new experience or idea … London is an old lady in black lace and diamonds who guards her secrets with dignity and to whom one would not tell those secrets of which one is ashamed. Paris is a woman in the prime of life to whom one would only tell those secrets that one desires to be repeated. But Berlin is a girl in a pullover, not much powder on her face, Hölderin [a German poet of the Romantic movement] in her pocket, thighs like those of Atalanta, an undigested education, a heart that is almost too ready to sympathise, and a breadth of view that charms one's repressions from their poison, and shames one's correctitude.[19]

The endless nocturnal search for pleasure was also an escape from the grinding reality of unemployment and financial hardship that continued to dominate life for so many, both in Berlin and elsewhere. Struggling to make ends meet, the government imposed a pay cut on transport workers in the capital; both the Nazis and the Communists called their followers out on strike, and groups of strikers from both parties even marched together through the city, threatening and attacking strike-breakers. When the continuing wrangling in the Reichstag triggered another round of elections, the Nazis lost support as middle-class voters turned against them for openly cooperating with the Communists and the latter became the largest party in Berlin. With a mixture of relief and triumph, many proclaimed that the Nazis were a spent force and would now fade into obscurity.

Such a point of view may have seemed credible in Berlin, where support for the Nazis had consistently been in a minority, but violence continued on the streets. On many occasions, the police attempted to prevent attacks by one side on the other, but this was more often to protect pro-Nazi groups than their opponents. Equally fierce battles were being fought behind closed doors as Hitler and other politicians held discussions about the future government of Germany. Men like the chancellor, General Kurt von Schleicher, believed that they could manipulate and control Hitler, and put pressure on President Paul von Hindenburg to agree to Hitler becoming chancellor. The elderly president showed open contempt for the future Führer, telling former chancellor Franz von Papen that the highest post that Hitler could aspire to was as a postmaster, but he was eventually persuaded by those who believed that they could use Hitler and the Nazis to crush the Communists, and would then be able to discard them. Schleicher was forced to resign in January 1933 and many expected Papen to become chancellor once more, but instead, he agreed to become vice-chancellor to Hitler.

The Nazi accession to power in 1933 was greeted with jubilation by Hitler's supporters throughout Germany and a triumphal torchlit procession through the capital was joined by thousands of ordinary Berliners. But the large numbers of supporters of the *SPD* and the Communists were at best sceptical and many were openly hostile. When a march led by the *SA* deliberately moved through a pro-Communist part of Berlin, shots were fired and a marcher was killed, triggering a major crackdown on the Communists by the police. In his role as interior minister of the regional Prussian government, Hermann Göring announced that all members of the *SA* and SS were deputised as auxiliary police to help keep law and order. A few days later, the Reichstag was burned down. Whether this was a secret act by the Nazis or was genuinely carried out by the Dutch Communist Marinus van der Lubbe, what is certain is that it was not an act planned by Berlin's Communists as a prelude to a general uprising, as the Nazis claimed. Nonetheless, the government used the incident as justification for wide-ranging repression and suspension of civil liberties. Prominent political opponents were rapidly detained and the persecution of Berlin's 160,000 Jews, which had commenced as soon as Hitler was in place, escalated – after all, in the eyes of the Nazis, Jews and Bolsheviks were effectively the same, so the Jews must have been involved in any Communist plot. Others were also targeted. During a single week in the summer of 1933, the *SA* rounded up over 500 members of left-wing groups and took them to improvised prisons where they were brutally tortured, and 91 died in the weeks that followed.

Belatedly realising that they had no control over the monster that they had unleashed, Papen and others made increasingly denunciatory statements about the Nazis. The army was also uneasy, given how the *SA* repeatedly demanded that it should be the core of a new National Socialist military. Hitler's response was to order the Night of the Long Knives in the summer of 1934. Ernst Röhm, the head of the *SA*, was the highest profile victim, but the killings spread beyond the ranks of the Nazis. Many prominent right-wing politicians were also killed, including Schleicher and several close associates of Papen. At that stage, Papen was too prominent and Hitler too unsure of his own position for the former chancellor to be arrested and shot, but the message was clear: dissent would not be tolerated. There was consternation both in Germany and abroad, but most people within the country had come to regard the *SA* as synonymous with political violence, and concluded that whilst the measures taken against it had been brutal, they were needed to restore order. Some foreigners like the British writer Christopher Isherwood noted that most Berliners seemed complacent and docile; after more than a decade of polarised politics and the resulting violence, after the economic devastation first of the period of hyperinflation and then of the worldwide depression that followed the Wall Street Crash, most were desperate for a period of calm. Provided that they weren't personally threatened with arrest or worse, they were quite willing to turn a blind eye to the extrajudicial excesses of the Nazis.

The wild, uninhibited nightlife of Berlin was anathema to many senior Nazis and it was inevitable that the new regime would take action to turn the capital into a more 'decent' and 'respectable' city. Some of the more notorious venues where drug-taking and homosexuality were rife were swiftly closed down, and there were numerous arrests of homosexuals for 'social deviancy'. There were also steps taken against the numerous newspapers in the capital. At first, only two – the Communist *Rote Fahne* and the pro-*SPD Vorwärts* – were banned, but others came under severe pressure to dismiss left-wing and Jewish members of staff. Goebbels, newly appointed *Reichsminister für Volksaufklärung und Propaganda* ('Reich Minister for Public Enlightenment and Propaganda'), forced all newspapers to print articles condemning those that the Nazis saw as enemies of Germany, particularly the Jews. Gradually, the centrist and left-wing newspapers declined and faded. Many newspapers on the right showed little inclination to oppose the Nazis, enthusiastically embracing the new regime and loudly trumpeting its messages to the masses. Attempts to impose Nazi values on other aspects of Berlin life were less successful. American jazz had established firm roots in Berlin and the association of this form of music with black and Jewish American culture made it particularly distasteful to the Nazis; every opportunity was taken to expel foreign jazz musicians and to ban Jewish performers. Fritz Stege, a musician and composer who was an enthusiastic supporter of the Nazis, became head of the *Arbeitsgemeinschaft Deutscher Musikkritiker* ('Association of German Music Critics') in 1933 and proudly proclaimed the banning of 'Negro jazz' from Berlin's radio station, but jazz enthusiasts in Berlin merely tuned into foreign radio stations. Finally recognising that the elimination of jazz was impossible, the regime attempted to introduce an acceptable version, holding a nationwide competition for bands that could play something that sounded like jazz but incorporated marching themes in keeping with the rising militaristic culture. The winners of the competition faded rapidly from memory, and although both the music and the venues for jazz in Berlin were shadows of their Weimar incarnations, they continued to attract audiences. As Stege glumly noted in 1937, 'It is true: jazz is still with us, in spite of prohibitions and decrees.'[20]

The numerous aspects of Berlin that had both scandalised and amazed visitors over the preceding years steadily dropped away after Hitler's rise to power. Some artists, writers, and intellectuals embraced the new regime's vision; others attempted to find ground for coexistence. Many simply left Germany for other countries. At first, most of Berlin's 160,000 Jews tried to keep their heads down, hoping that the Nazi grip on power would be short-lived, and many of their fellow Berliners saw the city's Jews as authentic Berliners and the Nazis as newcomers. Goebbels demanded a boycott of Jewish businesses almost as soon as he became propaganda minister, but despite attempts by *SA* men to enforce such boycotts – they daubed Jewish shops with graffiti and attempted to intimidate Berliners who entered – most people in the capital simply carried on as normal. Other steps against the Jews were more effective. When they came to power, the Nazis were appalled to discover that three quarters of Berlin's lawyers were Jewish or at least had Jewish heritage. Jewish judges were soon dismissed and law schools forbidden from accepting Jewish students. The medical profession was also purged of Jews, who were restricted to working at a Jewish hospital (which could only be used by Jewish patients). Where they could, the city authorities forced the closure of Jewish shops and businesses, but although this resulted in many Jews deciding to seek new lives abroad, their numbers were offset by new arrivals from the east. For a time in 1936, anti-Jewish measures became less prominent – Hitler wanted to avoid foreign criticism during the Olympic Games – but were then reinforced with vigour.

Matters came to a head late in 1938. On 7 November, the 17-year-old Herschel Grynszpan, a Polish-German Jew, went to the German embassy in Paris. He asked to see an official in connection with the deportation of his family from Germany to Poland. When he met Ernst vom Rath, the third secretary in the embassy, he produced a handgun and shot him five times. The diplomat survived for two days before succumbing to his wounds.

The Nazis had been waiting for an excuse for further attacks on the Jews. Many of the Party *Gauleiters* were keen to seize Jewish property to replenish depleted local Party funds, while others simply wanted an excuse to conduct a pogrom. As soon as news broke of Rath's shooting, the regime acted swiftly. Jewish children were banned from state elementary schools, all Jewish cultural activities were suspended, and the rights of Jews were further restricted – the range of measures and the speed with which they were implemented hint at premeditation and preparation. Jewish businesses had been required to paint their names in large white letters on the front of their properties, making identification easy for any attack. But worse was to follow. Hitler and other figures were celebrating the anniversary of the failed Beer Hall Putsch of 1923 on 9 November when the first reports arrived that Rath had died. Goebbels gave a speech that evening, declaring that the Führer had ordered that whilst the Nazi Party was not to be seen organising or promoting attacks on the Jews of Germany, the authorities shouldn't stand in the way of any 'spontaneous' actions. Reinhard Heydrich, head of the *Sicherheitspolizei* ('Security Police'), issued instructions both to the police and to the SA for attacks on Jews – again, the speed with which these instructions were issued, and the level of organisation with which they were implemented, suggests that such measures had been prepared long in advance.

The result was what became known as *Kristallnacht*. Thousands of Jewish businesses, homes, and synagogues were attacked across Germany and Austria. There were assaults on Jews resulting in dozens of deaths and rapes, and tens of thousands of Jews were arrested and taken to concentration camps. The following day, Peter Fröhlich – a 15-year-old secular Jew – cycled through the city along his usual route to his workplace, where he received a message from his father advising him to return home immediately:

> I ... pedalled through a city that seemed to have been visited by an army of vandals ... The route ... happened to be through Tauentzienstrasse, lined on three or four long blocks with large specialty shops. Their facades had been efficiently reduced to rubble, their huge display windows shattered, their mannequins and merchandise scattered on the sidewalk ...

> My father ... and Emil Busse [a Gentile family friend] ... had sauntered through the heart of the city to inspect the damage, just two Berliners on a stroll. The scene that most appalled them was the assault on a small hotel on the Spree, one of the few hostelries still owned by a Jew. The mob had gone through the place methodically floor by floor, breaking all the windows, bursting into the rooms to demolish the furniture, slicing open blankets and pillowcases, and throwing heaps of feathers into the street below ...
>
> I walked over to my cousin's house. The family was there, in misery. Tante Hede tight-lipped, Onkel Samuel weeping. This was not the way my parents or I would respond, but after I saw what had happened to their store, it struck me that they had good cause to lament.
>
> It was pure chaos. If there was ever a commercial establishment that might tempt hoodlums to do some enjoyable trashing, it was *Fröhlich* on Olivaerplatz. Its waist-high glass counters holding stockings, gloves, and ladies' underwear had proved irresistible; they had been smashed and their contents savagely torn to pieces. But the wall cabinets had given the wrathful German people ... even more entertaining targets. One of the cabinets, well over five feet tall, with an array of shallow glass-fronted drawers, had held innumerable fine shadings of thread; the other, quite as high and as minutely subdivided, had contained buttons ... Both had been ripped from the wall and emptied pell-mell, their contents mingling with glass fragments strewn all over the floor.[21]

Many Germans were horrified by the violence and some – including a small number of police officers – actively took steps to protect their Jewish neighbours; a solitary police officer defied the *SA* mob that descended on the large synagogue in Oranienburgerstrasse in Berlin and prevented its destruction. One Berliner looked on in horror and commented that 'they must have emptied the insane asylums and penitentiaries to find people who'd do things like that!'[22] He was wrong. These were the same violent thugs who had fought pitched battles in the streets of the capital against Communists and *SPD* supporters, and who now turned their fury on the Jews. Indeed, some of them had previously fought on the side of the Communists – men for whom violence was an end in itself.

The majority of Germans stood by and watched in silence, many fearing that they would become victims of the violence if they attempted to intervene. The rioters often forced bystanders to take part in the attacks on property or Jews, and the years of dehumanising the Jews of Germany bore fruit, with many Germans joining the attacks voluntarily, even with enthusiasm. In Berlin, there was further evidence of preparatory action: the police chief had ordered that gas and telephone lines to Jewish properties should be cut off before the attacks began. As daylight broke, Goebbels announced exultantly that the pogrom had achieved all the desired and expected outcomes, but others in the Nazi regime were less enthusiastic. Some, like Göring, were concerned about the material cost of replacing so much broken glass; others, like Himmler, feared that the *SA* – which was meant to have been neutered after the Night of the Long Knives – would once more bring about widespread disturbances. Most blamed Goebbels for triggering the attacks, but he responded by levying a fine on the Jews for the violence, effectively forcing them to pay for the damage that had been done to their properties. Further restrictions followed, with Jewish businessmen forced to sell their companies to non-Jewish owners at heavily discounted prices. Those who could leave Berlin accelerated their plans, and by the outbreak of the Second World War, about half the Jewish population of the city had left.

Grynszpan, the assassin who had triggered *Kristallnacht*, was arrested by the French and held in prison awaiting trial. He briefly escaped in 1940 before being captured by the invading Germans and taken to Sachsenhausen concentration camp. Goebbels intended to hold a trial that would highlight the murder of Rath as part of a widespread Jewish conspiracy, but when he learned that Grynszpan might use the proceedings to allege that he had been seduced into a homosexual relationship by Rath, he abandoned his plans. At some unknown date before the end of the war, Grynszpan died in the camp.

The attitude of the population of Berlin to the Nazis – ambivalent at best – had been a source of concern and irritation for Hitler and the upper leadership from the moment they seized power, and the outbreak of war in 1939 did little to change things. All across Germany, large patriotic crowds had gathered in 1914 to greet the commencement of the war. In 1939, the mood was different. There was an air of resignation and apathy, with little appetite for the extra editions of newspapers that appeared in Berlin and elsewhere. At first, the only significant impacts seemed to be the nightly blackout and rationing, though this was carefully moderated; Goebbels was keen to avoid the shortages and resultant discontent that had contributed to the collapse of Germany's home front in the First World War. The biggest change for most Berliners was that the blackout resulted in an increase in fatal road accidents and a crime wave, ranging from burglaries to murders.

With so many men mobilised into the armed forces, women took up the jobs that became vacant and female conductors on Berlin's trams were an early sign of changed circumstances. Even as German victories in the first 12 months of the war accumulated – the rapid defeats of first Poland, then Norway and Denmark – there was little enthusiasm in Berlin for what was being done to create Hitler's vision of a new Europe. When 218th Infantry Division, which had been raised in the capital, carried out a victory march through Berlin on 6 July after the defeat of France, there was considerable celebration with thousands turning out to watch the troops coming home, many with rare luxuries 'appropriated' in France and elsewhere, but the enthusiasm was more for the loot they brought home and indeed the fact that they had returned safely; perhaps the war might really be over quickly, without significant hardship for the country and for Berlin. George Kennan, a US diplomat in the city, noted that few Berliners expressed their views about the war and seemed far more preoccupied with their parochial difficulties:

> I rode miles, that afternoon, on the enclosed upper deck of a bus, where practically everyone's conversation was audible. I heard no one as much as mention the event; the talk was all of food cards and the price of stockings. Indeed, what struck one most about wartime Berlin was the undemonstrative but unmistakeable inner detachment of the people from the pretentious purposes of the regime ... The war dominated the prints; but it was, so far as concerned the Berliners ... the regime's war, not theirs.[23]

Just as earlier rulers had considered moving the capital to another city, some senior Nazi figures suggested that it would be better to designate somewhere like Munich – where there was much stronger support for the Nazis – as the capital of the Reich, but Hitler had recognised from the outset the importance of Berlin and was determined to make it conform with his views of how the city's residents should behave and think. He also intended to change the appearance of the city.

From an early stage, Hitler had grand plans for the capital of the Reich. Over the years preceding the war and several times after the conflict began, he talked about his vision of rebuilding much of the city centre to create what he described as *Welthauptstadt Germania* ('World Capital City Germania'). On one occasion, he outlined his vision to his close associates, one of whom later recalled an after-dinner conversation with the Führer:

> Just as Bismarck had to impress upon the Bavarians and Prussians his concept of a German Idea [i.e. the unification of Germany], so too must the Germanic peoples of continental Europe be steered deliberately towards the Germanic concept. He even sees value in renaming Berlin, the capital of the Reich, as 'Germania'.[24]

Albert Speer, Hitler's preferred architect – who would later be appointed armaments minister – heard the first hint of Hitler's plans in the spring of 1936, but didn't discover the full scale of what was intended for Berlin until the summer months. There was to be a great central avenue through the city, which the Führer stipulated had to be 130 metres wide; Julius Lippert, the mayor of Berlin, repeatedly offered plans that showed the avenue only 100 metres wide, and ultimately this resulted in his dismissal. Railway lines would be redirected and two major stations – the Anhalt and Potsdam termini – would be moved to new locations to make space for the grandiose vision. The huge avenue, named the *Prachtallee* ('Avenue of Splendour') would run from north to south for three miles, with a great east–west axis crossing its northern end. This great avenue was to be clear of traffic, with a special highway built in a tunnel for vehicles. At the junction of the two axes would be a great open plaza of about 350,000 square metres, nearly 600 metres on each side; around this would stand several great buildings, including a palace for the Führer. The military high command would have a new home on this square, and the Reichstag was to be reconstructed too.

One of the most ambitious parts of the grandiose scheme was the planned *Grosse Halle* ('Great Hall'), which was to stand on the north side of the great plaza. This immense building would have required a minor change in the course of the Spree; on a square base measuring 1,034 feet on each side and rising 243 feet above the ground would be a huge dome rising a further 322 feet. Hitler planned for the hall to be an open building for great rallies with up to 150,000 people attending, but Speer considered this simplistic and wanted a different internal arrangement, not least because he could see the shortcomings of Hitler's vision – the lectern from which the Führer intended to address the gathered thousands would be dwarfed by the vast space, reducing him to 'an optical nothingness'.[25]

At the southern end of the *Prachtallee*, which was to be lined with neo-classical buildings to house all the departments of the German government, would be a second gigantic construction, a victory arch inscribed with the names of all the soldiers who had died to create Hitler's world-dominating empire. This would be about 330 feet tall, and as Hitler described his visions to Speer, he showed him drawings he had made:

[Hitler said] 'I made these drawings ten years ago. I've always saved them, because I never doubted that someday I would build these two edifices. And this is how we will carry it out now.' ...
What is startling is less the grandiosity of the project than the obsessiveness with which he had been planning triumphant monumental buildings when there was not a shred of hope that they could ever be built.[26]

The unprecedented size and mass of these proposed buildings was such that there were doubts about the ability of the relatively soft ground of Berlin to support them. To investigate this further, Speer had a 'test structure' built near the planned site of the triumphal arch. The *Schwerbelastungskörper* ('heavy load-bearing body') was a concrete cylinder, 50 feet high and nearly 70 feet in diameter, with a mass of 12,650 tons. Completed in 1941, the structure sank seven inches over the following three years; Speer had calculated that the maximum permissible amount of subsidence was a third of this, and the planned mega-structures would therefore have required extensive work on additional foundations.

Even before the *Schwerbelastungskörper* was built, clearance of buildings had begun at the northern end of the planned *Prachtallee*. Many of the buildings that were demolished were residential, the *Mietskaserne* that housed so many of Berlin's workers, and this created difficulties for the civil administration. Berlin was already short of housing, and although Hitler's scheme also included the construction of tens of thousands of new apartments, they only existed in his mind at this stage, and the demolition of existing housing seemed to many to be premature. Work stopped in September 1939 when Germany invaded Poland and then restarted after the Wehrmacht's swift victory, only to be suspended again in 1940 during the campaign in the west. After the fall of France, Hitler visited Paris with Speer and stressed the importance of resuming construction in Berlin so that it would outshine the French capital; just a year later, the commencement of the war with the Soviet Union brought all further building to an end.

Writing after the war, Speer was critical of the planned rebuilding of central Berlin, though he made few if any objections at the time and happily accepted a generous salary for overseeing the project:

> Hitler's city plan had one major fault: it had not been thought through to the end. He had become so set on the notion of a Berlin Champs Elysées two and a half times the length of the original in Paris that he entirely lost sight of the structure of existing Berlin, a city of four million people. For a city planner such an avenue could only have a meaning and function as the core of a general reorganisation of the city. For Hitler, however, it was a display piece and an end in itself. Moreover, it did not solve the Berlin railroad problem. The huge wedge of tracks that divided the city into two parts would merely be shifted a few miles to the south.[27]

Speer's alternative suggestion, supported by several figures including Georg Leibbrand, the Minister for Reich Traffic, was to expand the existing *Ringbahn*, a circle route around the inner city, and to construct two large stations at the northern and southern points of the ring. Existing land used for railway yards would see the construction of housing for up to 400,000 people, and the great east–west avenue would be extended until it reached the *Autobahn* ring around the Greater Berlin area. In many respects, it was a more comprehensive plan, but the additional building requirements would have added greatly to the cost. Moreover, Speer didn't address a fundamental problem: if his new project was to include new homes for 400,000 people and would involve the demolition of existing tenements to create space for new buildings, where were these people expected to live until construction was completed?

Ultimately, few of the planned new buildings emerged, though several residential areas were cleared in preparation, thus exacerbating existing housing shortages. Part of the complex that was to house the air ministry was built; it is now the home of the German Ministry of Finance. The massive *Schwerbelastungskörper* also survives as a mute monument to the grandiose dreams of the past. The abandoned Nazi plans would have brought great changes, but the enemies of the Reich were about to inflict changes of their own on Berlin.

Chapter 2

'Call Me Meier'

Ultimately, Hitler's dreams of demolishing large parts of central Berlin and replacing them with the edifices of his new city came to nothing, but destruction on a far greater scale commenced in 1940 and would continue until the end of the war. By 1945, despite the hopes of many in Germany, there was no prospect of the Western Allies arriving in Berlin before the Red Army, but although the forces advancing across the Rhine from the west stopped broadly along the line of the Elbe River, the Americans and British contributed fully to the terrible destruction of the German capital.

British bombers struck the German capital on many occasions, the first such raid taking place on 25 August 1940; this raid did minimal damage, but played a part in Hitler's decision to direct the Luftwaffe to switch its priority during the Battle of Britain and to attack British cities instead of concentrating on degrading the RAF.[1] In a speech to Luftwaffe officers in September 1939, Hermann Göring had boasted that 'No enemy bomber can reach the Ruhr. If one reaches the Ruhr, my name is not Göring. You may call me Meier.'[2] In some accounts of this speech, he was quoted as saying all of Germany was inviolable, not just the Ruhr. 'Meier' was a common surname in Germany; some claimed it was a reference to a popular stand-up comedian in Berlin night-clubs of the 1930s. As air raids on German cities in the Ruhr and elsewhere became a regular occurrence, air raid sirens were mockingly referred to by civilians as 'Meier's trumpets' and many Berliners frequently referred to Göring as 'Meier' in private conversations. On one occasion, Göring is reputed to have taken cover in a *U-Bahn* station during an air raid in Berlin; when the civilians huddled in the semi-darkness glared at him reproachfully, he beamed back at them and proclaimed, '*Guten Abend, meine Damen und Herren. Nennen Sie mich Meier.*' ('Good evening, ladies and gentlemen. Call me Meier.')

That first attack on Berlin in August 1940 did little physical damage, but caused widespread consternation amongst Berliners who rushed into the air raid shelters, listening with a mixture of fear and disbelief to the sound of anti-aircraft guns and the unmistakeable drone of the bombers passing overhead. A second raid at the end of August killed ten Berliners and wounded a further 29, but as William Shirer, an American journalist, noted, the general consternation wasn't about the casualties: 'The populace of Berlin is more affected by the fact that the British planes have been able to penetrate to the centre of Berlin without trouble than they are by the first casualties. For the first time, the war has been brought home to them.'[3]

Attacks on German cities continued on a modest scale over the following months after the initial attacks, but Berlin lay at the extreme range of RAF bombers and there were too few aircraft available to inflict major damage. The limitations of night bombing meant that these raids rarely struck important targets, but there was widespread satisfaction that at a time when London and other British cities were suffering considerable damage, Berliners were also being inconvenienced. Air Chief Marshal Charles Portal, head of the RAF's Air Staff, commented that the losses suffered on the raids were justified by forcing four million Germans from their beds and into air raid shelters.[4] Whilst the raids were causing many to suffer from loss of sleep, the British might have been disappointed to learn that on many occasions, Berliners recorded that their main fear was being hit by shrapnel from the anti-aircraft guns that defended them. The German defences were capable of inflicting serious losses on attacking bombers and a raid in November 1941 by 160 RAF bombers resulted in the loss of 21 with little damage being done to Berlin. The consequence of this raid was that Air Marshal Richard Pierse, head of Bomber Command, was dismissed. His replacement was a man who would have a profound effect on the conduct of the air war against Germany.

Air Marshal Arthur Harris had been Portal's deputy since the summer of 1940 and his appointment was part of the response of the RAF to increasingly severe criticism of its bombing policies. In addition to the disastrous raid on Berlin of November 1941, there had been widespread shock both within the service and in government circles at the Butt Report of August 1941, which examined the efficacy of air raids on Germany and occupied Europe. The report concluded that of those aircraft that had actually been recorded as reaching their targets (as opposed to being shot down or having to turn back before they could drop their bombs), only a third managed to get within five miles of their actual objective, and in the case of the Ruhr industrial region, poor visibility (due to cloud, smoke, and fog) reduced this to just one in ten planes bombing the true target.[5] Portal and others protested that there were methodological errors in the report but there was widespread concern about the failure of air raids to have any meaningful impact, and the effect of the bombing of cities by any side was criticised as a means of crippling the enemy's war effort. In February 1942, one MP declared in the House of Commons:

> The total casualties [in the UK] in air raids – in killed – since the beginning of the war are only two thirds of those we lost as prisoners of war at Singapore ... The loss of production in the worst month of the Blitz was about equal to that due to the Easter holidays.[6]

There was now a fierce debate between those who doubted that strategic bombing was capable of delivering meaningful results and those who attempted to dismiss the Butt Report. Lord Cherwell, a close confidant and scientific adviser to Churchill, wrote a document that became known as the 'Dehousing Paper' in March 1942, describing how the inaccuracy of the air raids on German cities could be put to one side. Instead of attempting – frequently without any success – to target specific installations, the bomber force should be deployed for area attacks on cities. The paper attempted to extrapolate from evidence of the effect of German raids on British cities:

> Careful analysis of the effects of raids on Birmingham, Hull and elsewhere have shown that on average, one ton of bombs dropped on a built-up area demolishes 20–40 dwellings and turns 100–200 people out of house and home.
>
> We know from our experience that we can count on nearly 14 operational sorties per bomber produced. The average lift of the bombers we are going to produce over the next 15 months will be about three tons. It follows that each of these bombers will in its lifetime drop about 40 tons of bombs. If these are dropped on built-up areas they will make 4,000–8,000 people homeless.
>
> In 1938, over 22 million Germans lived in 58 towns of over 100,000 inhabitants which, with modern equipment, should be easy to find and hit. Our forecast output of heavy bombers (including Wellingtons) between now and the middle of 1943 is about 10,000. If even half the total load of 10,000 bombers were dropped on the built-up areas of these 58 German towns the great majority of their inhabitants (about one third of the German population) would be turned out of house and home.[7]

The report added that this took no account of the anticipated arrival of thousands of American bombers. But there were serious problems with the report. Extrapolating from the estimated effect of one ton of bombs to the effect of many times a greater weight of explosives ignored the fact that in large air raids, the bombing patterns of aircraft were likely to overlap and cause damage to the same areas, thus reducing the overall impact of any one plane's contribution. If attempts were made to compensate by spreading the bombing over a larger area, this increased the chances of bombs falling harmlessly in open ground or into lakes and rivers. There were other criticisms of Cherwell's paper. Some pointed out that many of the navigational aids required were still many months away from delivery in large quantities. In any case, the estimate of damage done by a single ton of bombs, from which the entire case was extrapolated, was demonstrated to be a considerable exaggeration.

Nevertheless, the concept of area bombing of German towns and cities was adopted by the RAF, and 'Bomber' Harris, the new head of Bomber Command, would be its greatest proponent. Even before he was appointed, he regarded strategic bombing as the best way to win the war; in 1940, he told Portal that given the manner in which the Nazi regime had unleashed the Luftwaffe on cities across Europe, it was inevitable that they would have to face similar attacks on German population centres.[8] But at first, he had to hold his plans in check. The pressing priority was to attack bases from which U-boats were threatening British supply lines across the Atlantic and during 1942, there were only nine occasions when air raid sirens sounded in Berlin.[9] In January 1943, on the tenth anniversary of Hitler's accession to power, RAF Mosquitos raided Berlin in a daylight attack timed to arrive at precisely the moment that Göring and Goebbels would be making important speeches. On 2 March, there was a heavier attack. It left about 700 Berliners dead and a further 65,000 with damaged or destroyed homes. A further attack by Mosquitos took place on 20 April, Hitler's birthday.

The slowly rising number of attacks on Berlin had a growing impact on the well-being of Berliners. It became customary for city residents to wish each other *Bolona* when they parted at the end of the day – an abbreviation of *bombenlose Nacht* ('bombless night'), so that they could sleep undisturbed. Nevertheless, the practicalities of day-to-day life were of greater importance to most. The Nazis had announced that everyone should have one evening a week when they made a vegetable stew rather than eating meat, and wealthier Berliners noted with dismay that this had even spread to the city's best hotels and restaurants by the end of 1940. Amongst its many responsibilities, the *Sicherheitsdienst* ('Security Office' or *SD*, effectively the intelligence service of the SS) monitored public opinion closely and reported in the spring of 1941 that there were grumblings about beer shortages, and there was concern and exasperation in higher Nazi circles to the reaction of Berliners to the news of an unexpected development in May 1941. Rudolf Hess, a grim Bavarian and fanatical supporter of Hitler, was *Stellvertreter des Führers* ('deputy Führer') but was effectively third in line behind

Hitler and Göring. He took it upon himself to fly solo to Britain in an attempt to negotiate a peace settlement.

Marie Illarionovna Vassiltchikov, known to her friends as 'Missie', was a Russian princess who had fled her homeland in 1919 as a small child. In 1940, the 23-year-old moved to Berlin with her older sister Tatiana and managed to secure a job first with the *Drahtlose Dienst* ('Wireless Service' or *DD*) and then as a secretary and translator working for the *Auswärtiges Amt*, the information office of the German foreign ministry. Her diary, kept in secret throughout the war, recorded various aspects of life in Berlin, and she commented that when she dined with a German diplomat and a couple from the Italian embassy, the conversation was dominated by Hess' flight, which everyone found 'comical'. A few days later, she noted wryly the jokes that were circulating amongst Berliners, who continued to hold onto the irreverent sense of humour that had irritated almost every ruler of the city and defied the official line that Hess was delusional, offering their own versions of events:

> [Here are some] examples:
> 'Augsburg [from where Hess departed], city of the German ascension'
> 'The BBC [reports that] "on Sunday night no further German cabinet ministers flew in"'
> '*OKW* [*Oberkommando der Wehrmacht*, 'Military High Command'] bulletin: Göring and Goebbels are still firmly in German hands'
> 'The Thousand Year Reich has now become a Hundred-Year Reich. One zero is gone'
> In a broad Berlin accent, 'That our government is mad, is something that we have known for a long time; but that they admit it, *that* is something new'
> 'Churchill asks Hess: "Are you the madman?" "No, only his deputy"'[10]

If there had been general indifference in Berlin to the war itself, the mood changed in the summer of 1941 with the invasion of the Soviet Union; given the earlier preoccupations of Berliners, it was inevitably the impact of increasing rationing that caused the most consternation. The availability of meat was greatly reduced and beer shortages – and watering down of beer – became widespread. Missie Vassiltchikov had already described the very limited menu at her workplace canteen with disdain at the end of the previous year:

> [The menu] is short and not very imaginative:
> Monday: Red cabbage with meat sauce
> Tuesday: Meatless day. Codfish in mustard sauce

Wednesday: Stonefish patties (this tastes exactly as it sounds)

Thursday: Assorted vegetable dish (red cabbage, white cabbage, potatoes, red cabbage, white cabbage ...)

Friday: Mussels in wine sauce (this is a 'special dish' which vanishes within minutes, so that one has to fall back on potato dumplings in sauce)

Saturday: One of the above

Sunday: Another of the above

Dessert all through the week: vanilla pudding with raspberry sauce.[11]

Even potatoes were in short supply, and Goebbels began to fear that civilian morale might start to crack. He countered this with increased propaganda, decrying British air attacks as attempts to exterminate German civilians and ordering the publication of accounts – many of which were fictional – about the phlegmatic determination of ordinary Berliners to carry on, come what may. He also stepped up the regime's attempts to dehumanise the 70,000 Jews who remained in the city. The wearing of a yellow Star of David became compulsory in September 1941, and Goebbels and Heinrich Himmler, head of the SS, waited with impatience for the rapid defeat of the Soviet Union; this would permit the transfer of large numbers of Jews to the new territories conquered in the east, where they would be worked to death. In the meantime, Jews were forbidden from using 'Aryan' air raid shelters and had to seek cover in designated Jewish shelters. The official policy regarding Germany's Jews remained the same as before: the Jews were to be transported to the east for resettlement. In practice, the intention was to move them to ghettos across Poland, which would have been emptied of their population by the transfer of their residents into the Soviet Union. To create space in Ukraine, Belarus, and the Baltic States for this transfer, the SS – with considerable assistance from the Wehrmacht – instigated what would become known as the 'Holocaust by bullets', the slaughter of hundreds of thousands of Jews in mass shootings. Despite the rising wave of propaganda against the Jews, there was concern in higher Nazi circles about the possible reaction of the civilian population if the measures being used in the east were employed against German Jews, particularly those from Berlin. It was therefore important to preserve the illusion of resettlement in some undefined location to the east.

Even though the plans for working the Jews to death in the occupied lands had to be shelved, the Jews of Berlin began to be moved east. Whilst most Germans kept any opinions on the gradual disappearance of Jews to themselves, some enthusiastically welcomed the transfers, while others did what they could to help Jewish friends, hiding them from the authorities or assisting them in leaving for possibly safer parts of Europe. Despite the attempts of the regime to prevent it, there was a steady trickle of reports from the east – often from soldiers returning home for convalescence or on leave – about mass killings. The most common feeling amongst civilians in Berlin and elsewhere seems to have been one of helplessness. By late 1942, even skilled Jewish factory workers who had been exempted from transfers to Poland were being rounded up; they were to be replaced by non-Jewish workers from Poland. Despite Goebbels' boasts that Berlin was *Judenfrei* ('free of Jews') by the summer of 1943, deportations continued until the end of the war; the last train, carrying 117 Jews, left the capital on 27 March 1945.

As 1943 progressed, Harris continued to promote the cause of area bombing. In some respects, he had little choice. The aircraft available to RAF Bomber Command and the technology of the day meant that more precise air attacks were simply impossible. In response to criticisms of the huge numbers of civilians killed in the devastating attacks on Hamburg, he responded:

> The aim of the combined bomber offensive … should be unambiguously and publicly stated. That aim is the destruction of German cities, the killing of German workers and the disruption of civilised community life throughout Germany.
>
> It should be emphasised that the destruction of houses, public utilities, transport and lives, the creation of a refugee problem on an unprecedented scale, and the breakdown of morale both at home and at the battle fronts by fear of extended and intensified bombing, are accepted and intended aims of our bombing policy. They are not by-products of attempts to hit factories.[12]

Although the RAF struck cities in the western parts of Germany with increasing force throughout 1943, serious attacks on Berlin and cities to the east of the Elbe had to wait until November when RAF Lancasters were available in sufficient numbers. At first, these raids had little impact; Missie Vassiltchikov, now living in Potsdam just outside Berlin, commented in late 1943 that there were raids on most nights, but they usually took place when she was having a bath and seemed relatively ineffective.

However, once large numbers of Lancasters were deployed, the RAF returned to the German capital over several consecutive nights, and by the end of 1943 it was estimated that up to 25 per cent of housing in Berlin was damaged or destroyed. Speer, now the armaments minister, later described one such raid on 22 November. Both the raid and its aftermath were described in several accounts:

> I was having a conference in my private office … when the air-raid alarm sounded. It was about 7.30pm. A large fleet of bombers was reported heading towards

Berlin. When the bombers reached Potsdam, I called off the meeting to drive to a nearby flak tower, intending to watch the attack from its platform, as was my wont. But I scarcely reached the top of the tower when I had to take shelter inside it; in spite of the tower's stout concrete walls, heavy hits nearby were shaking it. Injured anti-aircraft gunners crowded down the stairs behind me; the air pressure from the exploding bombs had hurled them into the walls. For 20 minutes explosion followed explosion. From above I looked down into the well of the tower, where a closely packed crowd stood in the thickening haze formed by cement dust falling from the walls. When the rain of bombs ceased, I ventured out on the platform again. My nearby ministry was one gigantic conflagration. I drove there at once. A few secretaries, looking like Amazons in their steel helmets, were trying to save files even while isolated time bombs went off in the vicinity. In place of my private office, I found nothing but a huge bomb crater ...

From the flak tower the air raids on Berlin were an unforgettable sight, and I had constantly to remind myself of the cruel reality in order not to be completely entranced by the scene: the illumination of the parachute flares, which the Berliners called 'Christmas trees', followed by flashes of explosions which were caught by the clouds of smoke, the innumerable probing searchlights, the excitement when a plane was caught and tried to escape the cone of light, the brief flaming torch when it was hit. No doubt about it, this apocalypse provided a magnificent spectacle.[13]

At first, many Berliners assumed that this raid would be brief and ineffective, as it was raining heavily. Despite the dense cloud, the bombers struck the city centre with devastating effect. Missie Vassiltchikov was sheltering in a basement during the raid:

The all-clear came only half an hour after the last planes had departed, but long before that we were called out of the house by an unknown naval officer. The wind, he told us, thus far non-existent, had suddenly risen and the fires, therefore, were spreading. We all went out into our little square and, sure enough, the sky on three sides was blood-red. This, the officer explained, was only the beginning; the greatest danger would come in a few hours' time, when the fire storm really got going. Maria [von Gersdorff] had given each of us a wet towel with which to smother our faces before leaving the house – a wise precaution, for our square was already filled with smoke and one could hardly breathe.

We went back into the house ... the electricity, gas and water no longer worked and we had to grope our way around with electric torches and candles. Luckily we had had time to fill every available bath tub, wash basin, kitchen sink and pail. By now the wind had increased alarmingly, roaring like a gale at sea. When we looked out of the window we could see a steady shower of sparks raining down on our and the neighbouring houses and all the time the air was getting thicker and hotter, while the smoke billowed in through the gaping window frames ...

Towards 2am I decided to sleep for a while ... Every now and then a crashing building or delayed time bomb would tear one awake and I would sit up with a pounding heart. By now the fire storm had reached its peak and the roar outside was like a train going through a tunnel.[14]

As the war progressed, fewer foreign journalists lingered on in Berlin. Theo Findahl was a Norwegian who had written an article for an Oslo newspaper in April 1940 warning Norwegians that an attack on their country was imminent, but had been ignored. He was caught up in the air raid of 22 November 1943, and was making one of his regular telephone calls to Oslo when the sirens sounded. After checking his apartment's lights were extinguished and the windows were open – to reduce the risk of pressure waves shattering the windowpanes – he walked to the nearby *U-Bahn* station at Grosser Stern where he joined a group of friends. Sirens had gone off almost every night for over a week without any raids, but this time the people in the shelter emerged an hour later to a transformed landscape:

From the square it seemed as if the entire city was ablaze. All of the Hansaviertel [the city district to the northwest of the Tiergarten] was burning. I had to get home to see if anything could be saved! The water main in Altonaerstrasse had burst and the street was like an inland lake. Impossible to get through to Hansaplatz along this road. The Tiergarten was like a jungle, branches and stems slapped at your face if you tried to push forward past the fallen tree trunks. Händelallee – a sea of flames. I went on and turned into Klopstockstrasse. The road was as hot as a bakery oven – at a few points people were trying to save what they could, here and there belongings had been stacked in the street, but most had given up and just let everything burn. Hopeless, I reached Number 33 – a hot wind raced along the street, the house was a single fireball. From the large house opposite, which had perhaps the best cellar in the city, a group of dazed women emerged, an adolescent girl screamed hysterically, but most were quite quiet as if half-stunned. Suddenly there flashed before my eyes the memory of the pale, moaning Frenchwoman who dragged herself along the wall of her house in Bergues three years ago after the Germans had reduced the town to ashes and rubble. The best thing to do was to go back to the Tiergarten where the air wasn't so acrid with soot and smoke – get away from this place quickly, which had been our home for three years.[15]

Konrad Warner was another foreign correspondent in Berlin, from Switzerland. He hurried to join his neighbours in a cellar:

Shortly after I joined them, the burning stairwell collapsed above us. The way up was blocked.

The cellar filled with smoke. We had to get out of this hellish hole. People pressed past each other without a glance ... Others sat exhausted and listless on their chairs and cots. Some had soaked blankets, scarves and handkerchiefs in the water basins to protect against fire and as a shield against flying sparks.

We crawled through a break in the wall into the air raid shelter of the next house in order to reach the next road, along which we could get to a *U-Bahn* station. These were the catacombs of the 20th Century. We dragged ourselves through various shelters and crawled through new openings until we reached the last house on the next street, from where we had to continue on the surface. The elderly managed to get through these small tunnels only with difficulty, children and babies were passed through and suitcases pushed across. All the houses above us were ablaze and we couldn't have moved along the streets.[16]

Attacks continued into 1944, causing widespread devastation; the raids killed nearly 4,000 and injured over twice as many, and left nearly half a million people homeless.[17] However, the RAF lost over 500 aircraft, an unsustainable loss rate. Despite the claims of Harris and other proponents of area bombing, the 'Battle of Berlin' was widely seen to be a failure. German night-fighters were deployed in strength to defend the German capital, and three flak towers had been built in Berlin itself in a triangular arrangement around the city. Construction of these commenced almost immediately after the first RAF attack in 1940. Each consisted of a *Gefechtsturm* ('combat tower'), a square concrete blockhouse about 230 feet on each side, rising about 130 feet above the ground, and armed with eight 128mm guns arranged in pairs in corner emplacements. There were also numerous smaller 37mm and 20mm guns, though these lacked the range to engage most of the attacking bombers. In addition, each location – one in the Tiergarten, one in Friedrichshain, and one in Humboldthain – had a *Leitturm* ('lead tower' or 'command tower') that had a few guns but was primarily tasked with fire control. Each tower complex had a retractable radar and walls up to 11.5 feet thick and could provide shelter for thousands of civilians; a further four towers were planned for Berlin, but were not built. The heavy guns could reach nearly nine miles with their shells and were effectively invulnerable to the hail of bombs falling on the city.

The flak towers were impressive constructions and would play a major role in the fighting in Berlin when Soviet troops attacked the city in 1945. But together with other facilities such as air raid shelters, they represented only about 15 per cent of the planned total. Much of the work had been delayed due to misplaced confidence in German fighter defences and the difficulties posed for the British and Americans in attacking a major city so far to the east, and by the time it became clear that Germany's enemies had long-range aircraft capable of such missions and were prepared to risk the losses suffered in such raids, there were many competing demands on Germany's construction resources. The majority of Berliners were forced to use improvised shelters, either in their basements or in *U-Bahn* stations.

The US Army Air Forces (USAAF) had also planned for strategic bombing as a means of bringing the war to a rapid conclusion, but its emphasis was on daylight attacks aimed at specific industrial areas. Despite growing evidence to the contrary, USAAF doctrine continued to embrace the pre-war theory that close formations of heavily armed bombers would be able to fend off fighter attacks and would thus be able to reach their targets.[18] But when raids took place, unescorted bombers proved to be too vulnerable to German fighter attacks. In particular, two raids intended to disrupt German military production by hitting ball-bearing factories in Schweinfurt in September and October 1943 resulted in unacceptable losses; out of 291 B-17s sent to attack the German city in October, 60 were shot down, 17 returned but were too badly damaged to be repaired, and 121 others suffered damage. About 22 per cent of the crews committed were lost.

Many within the US military thought that it would be impossible to build single-engined fighters with the range to act as escorts for bombing missions, but by the last quarter of 1943 there was growing belief that several aircraft – in particular, the P-47 Thunderbolt and the P-51 Mustang – would be suitable for such roles if they were fitted with additional external fuel tanks. Of these, the P-51 proved to be the best solution and it was decided that until sufficient numbers were available to escort such raids, it would be unwise to continue with attempts to penetrate into the German heartland. The Germans were aware that US fighters provided effective escort capabilities and had deliberately withdrawn many of their fighter squadrons to Germany in the expectation that by the time US bombers had flown that far, their fighter escorts would have been forced to turn back; the P-51 effectively neutralised this redeployment.

In July 1943, a massive Anglo-American attack on Hamburg – codenamed *Gomorrah* – killed about 37,000 residents, wounded a further 180,000, and left over half the city in ruins. Aware that it would not be long before the Western Allies had the capability of delivering similar attacks to other cities, the Germans took measures to reduce the likely death toll. In August, Goebbels – who, as *Gauleiter* of Berlin, was also the *Reichsverteidigungskommissar* ('Reich defence commissar') for the city – issued a proclamation to the civilian population. Those with family contacts outside Berlin were urged to leave. They were told that appropriate documents giving permission to travel would be issued. Women and children and the elderly were given priority, and by the end of 1943 between 800,000 and 1.2 million Berliners had left. But despite this, there were concerns that too few children had been evacuated. Many of those evacuated returned to their homes, and the families of others had refused to allow them to leave. The *SD* wrote a report of 10 February 1944 that looked at the issue of evacuation and the attempts made to encourage people to take advantage of the opportunities being offered:

> The parents of children in 28th and 29th Elementary Schools were shown a film about a *KLV* ['*Kinderlandverschickung*', or 'child relocation to the countryside'] camp. The young people present were enthusiastic, but their mothers were more reserved. When the narrator explained that it was possible that boys or girls would have to sleep on straw for a few days but at least would not be woken by air raid alarms and wouldn't have to make their way to bunkers, there was the first interjection: 'But it's good in the bunker!' When it was pointed out that Berlin was a war zone in which children had no place, some mothers shouted, 'But neither do we!' The narrator then explained that the mothers should be grateful that their children were safe, and someone interjected, 'But the children don't want to [leave]!' ... Parents responded with loud laughter to the statement that children under ten were to be placed in family homes because they were not considered suitable for camp life. When the narrator, who had so far dealt with the heckling with considerable skill, was unable to give precise information when asked where the children aged under ten would be sent, the majority of parents left the meeting.[19]

In addition to evacuating civilians, particularly those that Goebbels described in his diary as 'superfluous mouths', some of Berlin's factories were moved to locations less likely to be bombed. In part, this was due to Speer's instructions to avoid the creation of gigantic manufacturing complexes – although these benefited from efficiencies due to all parts of the construction and assembly processes being on one large site, they were attractive targets for bombers, and dispersing them over several locations was judged to be a safer option.

Remarkably, theatres in Berlin continued to function – albeit with increasing difficulty – until they were formally closed in August 1944. The state opera theatre had been destroyed in one of the early heavy raids and Hitler ordered its immediate reconstruction, but by the time that Goebbels ordered the closure of theatres, audiences had plummeted. Few were willing to risk spending an evening away from air raid shelters. Instead, they gathered in the shelters with their fellow Berliners and waited to see if they would survive the night – many of the city's underground stations were not deep enough to survive direct hits, which made the heavily fortified shelters increasingly popular. Ursula von Kardorff was a journalist living in Berlin and in her diary she described a typical evening spent in the public shelter of the *Zoobunker*, as the flak tower in the Tiergarten was generally known:

> It's spooky. As the flak begins to fire, a herd of human animals runs in the dark towards the entrance, which is small and far too narrow. Flashlights are switched on and everyone starts shouting, 'Lights out!' Then the people push and shove and thrust their way in and one is surprised that despite this it all goes fairly well. The bunker walls, made of massive blocks of stone, look like the stage set of the prison scene from *Fidelio*. An illuminated elevator rises and falls silently, apparently for those who are sick ... Snappy policemen and officials drive the unwilling crowd slowly up the stairs to distribute them across the different floors. Everyone stops again at every landing. A woman begins to scream. She thinks she would sooner die up there in the open: 'I have a husband and a son at the front,' she shouts, weeping, 'I'm not going up!' Finally, she is taken away. There are spiral stairs in the towers. This is where lovers sit – a travesty of some form of fancy dress party. When the batteries above open fire, the building shakes, and everyone ducks together as if a scythe is passing over them. Everything is in disarray: frightened wealthy people, tired women, ragged foreigners who drag their belongings behind them in huge sacks, and soldiers with rather embarrassed expressions. If panic should break out here, then God have mercy on us, I think to myself.[20]

A few of the foreigners noted by Kardorff would have been forced labourers. Most such workers were employed in factories and other industrial concerns, but some were used as domestic servants. In the central part of Berlin, though, most foreigners were those who were employed in rather better circumstances. Given the manner in which the Nazi regime recorded racial characteristics so carefully, it is no surprise that air raid reports listed the dead and wounded not only in terms of sex and whether the victims were adults or children or were in the military, but also whether they were foreign workers or prisoners of war. For example, a report about a raid in October 1944 punctiliously recorded that the dead included 100 men, 51 women, eight children, 13 soldiers, five police officers, 36 foreign men, six foreign women, and one prisoner of war.[21]

In early 1944, the P-51 began to appear in sufficient numbers for major US attacks to be resumed against targets anywhere within bomber range, and, in combination with RAF bombers, operations were mounted in the second half of February in what became known as 'Big Week'. This was part of an operation codenamed *Pointblank*, a deliberate attempt to force the Luftwaffe into battle on unfavourable terms so that it could be degraded prior to the planned invasion of Europe, and in many respects the roles of fighters and bombers employed in the attacks were swapped. Instead of the prime purpose being the bombing of German cities, the intention was to mount attacks that the Germans couldn't ignore and would have to try to intercept. The intention was, put simply, to kill Luftwaffe pilots and destroy German aircraft.

Losses during *Pointblank* were substantial on both sides, but in percentage terms the bomber forces suffered less than they had in the past. The P-51s enjoyed considerable advantages over their German opponents. The large two-engined Messerschmitt Me-110s proved to be too unmanoeuvrable to be able to engage in combat against the excellent P-51s, and even single-engined German fighters like the BF-109 and FW-190 couldn't fight the US aircraft on even terms; they had been re-armed with heavier guns during the winter of 1943–44 in order to be able to do substantial damage to the heavy bombers and this reduced their performance against the P-51s, which remained tuned for air-to-air combat against enemy fighters. After *Pointblank*, with planning for the Normandy Landings now taking priority, bomber forces switched their objectives to prepare the way for the invasion of northern France, but intermittent attacks on the German capital continued in 1944 and heavy attacks returned in early 1945. By this stage of the war, the combination of large numbers of escorting fighters and the Luftwaffe's decline ensured that bomber losses were far lower than in the past. Indeed, such was the state of the German military that ammunition was in short supply for all kinds of weapons, ranging from small arms to the large-calibre anti-aircraft guns that were deployed around Berlin and other cities.

Plans for a massive raid or series of raids on Berlin had been drawn up as early as the summer of 1944 as revenge for the use of V-1s by Germany against London, but other priorities had intervened. Improved air defences across southeast England greatly reduced the danger posed by the German flying bombs, removing the need for some form of retribution against Berlin, and the plan, codenamed *Thunderclap*, was shelved until a time when its implementation might trigger the complete collapse of Germany. In January 1945 it was thought that such a moment might have arrived. The Ardennes offensive was over, with heavy losses inflicted on the German units involved, and the Red Army had torn apart the German defences along the Vistula and was rapidly approaching the Oder River. Still insisting on the ability of area bombing to bring about the complete collapse of civilian morale, the RAF was keen to take advantage of the reports of widespread gloom and panic in German circles as the Soviet forces drove forward towards Berlin. In addition to the impact on enemy morale, there were expectations that *Thunderclap* would also greatly hinder the transfer of German forces from the west to the east, thus aiding the Red Army. Moreover, German night-fighter capability had almost completely collapsed, allowing RAF Bomber Command to operate over Germany with little danger other than from anti-aircraft fire. On 25 January, the British Joint Intelligence Committee made its recommendations:

> [*Thunderclap* will] create great confusion, interfere with the orderly movement of troops to the front, and hamper the German military and administrative machine ...
>
> [There is also] political value in demonstrating to the Russians, in the best way open to us, a desire on the part of the British and Americans to assist them in the present battle.[22]

Thunderclap would, by its very nature, be somewhat contrary to the existing policy of giving priority to the bombing of targets such as oil and armaments production facilities, and many within the air forces were reluctant to divert resources from these previously agreed objectives. However, there was growing political pressure for raids such as *Thunderclap*. Churchill had become involved in the discussions and demanded that Portal draw up plans for a series of major strikes against cities in the eastern parts of Germany. Many of these – places like Chemnitz, Leipzig, and Dresden – had experienced little bombing to date, and were now crowded with refugees fleeing the Soviet advance. Attacks on these, Churchill and others insisted, would cause severe disruption to German plans for ongoing resistance. Additional impetus for the execution of *Thunderclap* came with intelligence reports that the German Sixth SS-Panzer Army had been withdrawn from the west, where it had played a major role in the Ardennes offensive, and was heading east. It was assumed that it would attempt to intervene against the Soviet advance towards Berlin. In fact, it was destined to be sent to Hungary, but this was not known to the Western Allies at the time, and they hoped that a major raid on Berlin would at least disrupt its transfer to the east and might inflict significant casualties too.

The efficacy of strategic bombing raids on civilian morale was an issue that was raised repeatedly during the war, both by the Allied Powers and by the Germans. Bombing enthusiasts on both sides believed that inflicting major damage on urban areas would destroy the will of the enemy to continue the war, often in the face of evidence from their own cities that whilst such raids caused considerable damage and loss of life, their impact on morale was far more nuanced. Unquestionably, German civilians were shocked and dismayed by the damage to their neighbourhoods; but their ability to turn this into measures that might bring down the German government was almost non-existent. The degradation of German morale was not limited to the devastating use of explosives and incendiaries; on many occasions, leaflets were dropped on cities too. One such leaflet fell on Berlin on 22 March 1944:

> The fateful question:
> Where is the Luftwaffe?
> That is the question that your soldiers on the Eastern Front and in Italy have asked again and again.
> 'The Luftwaffe is defending the homeland,' they were told.
> Now, in bright daylight, American bombers fly *en masse* over Berlin. Today they were over the Reich capital for the fifth time. Of course, you too are now asking:
> 'Where is the Luftwaffe?'
> Ask Göring! Ask Hitler![23]

There is nothing to suggest that these taunting leaflets had any significant impact on the population, but whilst area bombing failed to trigger mass unrest against the regime, it undoubtedly damaged confidence in the ability of Germany's rulers to defend its citizens. Göring was increasingly the target of private derision and contempt, and the *SD* reports mentioned a small but growing number of incidents in which civilians angrily remonstrated with Nazi Party officials, complaining that the widespread destruction in Berlin (and other cities) was effectively their fault. On 23 August 1943, Missie Vassiltchikov and a friend, Loremarie Schönburg, had made a journey to the outskirts to try to find a farmer who would sell them fresh fruit. The following day, they returned to the city centre, where Missie was staying with the family of Oberst Rudolf-Christopher Freiherr von Gersdorff, one of the anti-Hitler conspirators in the army:

> Martha, the Gersdorffs' cook, fell into my arms sobbing. She had been scared silly, but the house was all right. Not so Loremarie, who has a gaping hole in the ceiling

over her bed. She is greatly impressed and announces that she is evidently predestined for bigger and better things ... All the top floors of the houses on and around the Kurfürstendamm ... had burned down. After the raid Goebbels toured some of the worst-hit districts, but when he asked for 30 volunteers to fight the fire he got, we are told, a cool reception.[24]

As detailed planning for the implementation of *Thunderclap* was carried out in the closing days of January 1945, Lieutenant General James Doolittle, commander of Eighth Air Force, expressed doubts about the impact of what was being proposed. He wrote to General Carl Spaatz, the commander of Strategic Air Forces in Europe, that it was impossible for large numbers of bombers to reach Berlin without the population having plenty of time to take shelter:

The chances of terrorising into submission, by merely an increased concentration of bombing, a people who have been subjected to intense bombing for four years is extremely remote ...

We will, in what may be one of our last and best-remembered operations regardless of its effectiveness, violate the basic American principle of precision bombing of targets of strictly military significance for which our tactics were designed and our crews trained and indoctrinated.[25]

Spaatz's response was evasive. Weather conditions did not always permit the bombing of oil production facilities, he wrote, and in such conditions a large area target like Berlin was a permissible diversion of resources. Accordingly, *Thunderclap* was approved for 2 February.

Whilst the weather might have prevented attacks on the usual priority targets, it also intervened in the planned raid on Berlin, forcing a postponement of 24 hours. Interestingly, the final instructions issued by Spaatz to his air forces played down the original intention to use *Thunderclap* as a means of bringing about the final collapse of German morale. Instead, the value of the raid in adding to the widespread disruption of movement and military production in Germany was emphasised. This may have been an attempt to deflect any future criticism if the hoped-for collapse of morale did not take place. Film crews were to accompany the bombers, with the intention of producing newsreels that would demonstrate the willingness and ability of the Western Allies to support the Soviet forces advancing from the east.

Berlin was defended by about 300 heavy anti-aircraft guns. Although they were alerted to the air raid as the bombers crossed the coast and headed inland, the shortage of ammunition prevented them from having as much impact as they might have done, but many bomber crews later reported that they were forced into violent manoeuvres to avoid being hit. Perhaps 50 or more aircraft suffered damage from the bursting shells and 23 were downed; no German fighters managed to penetrate the fighter shield around the bomber force. Several planes failed to reach Berlin for a variety of reasons, but 932 B-17s dropped a total of nearly 2,300 tons of bombs, of which only about 250 tons were incendiaries.

The railway network around Berlin suffered considerable damage. The Anhalter railway station was wrecked, with moderate damage to the Schlesischer railway station and the Tempelhof railway martialling yards. But other areas were also heavily hit. The districts of Friedrichstadt, Luisenstadt, and Friedrichshain suffered considerable damage. Many important buildings in Berlin were reduced to ruins; most of the buildings lining Wilhemstrasse, Friedrichstrasse, Unter den Linden, and the surrounding areas were smashed, and the Reich Chancellery and the Gestapo headquarters were badly damaged. Although the great bulk of munitions dropped on the city were high explosives, the explosions ignited fires that were whipped up by the strong wind and spread steadily eastwards. It was four days before the flames went out, having reduced almost everything in their path to ash. For some in Berlin, there was a small degree of solace in the news that the People's Court had been badly hit. It was here that the conspirators in the July 1944 Plot had been tried and humiliated before being taken away for slow and painful executions. The brutal Roland Freisler, who had presided over the prosecutions and had a long history of aiding Nazi policies, including involvement in the infamous Wannsee Conference of January 1942 where the decision to implement mass gassing of Jews was taken, was amongst those who were killed in the air attack.

Analysis of photographs taken after the raid resulted in a report produced by the USAAF that claimed that *Thunderclap* was 'undoubtedly one of the outstanding operations conducted by this air force'. The bombers of the first wave were able to aim visually, and the report assessed that 80 per cent of the bombs fell within 4,400 feet of their target – it is an indication of the imprecision of bombing in the 1940s that this as regarded as a great success. The second wave was less accurate, as much of Berlin was obscured by smoke and increasing cloud cover, and a third of their bombs fell at least three miles from their targets; the rest were spread over larger areas than those dropped by the first wave, contributing greatly to the devastation of civilian areas. The report concluded that overall, only 4 per cent of bombs fell within 1,000 feet of the aiming point, and less than a third fell within a mile.[26]

German propaganda classed all bombing attacks, whether by day or night, as 'terror raids' and reported the USAAF raid of 3 February in the same light. German news media reported 20,000 dead, a number that was taken up by newspapers in other countries, but this was a major exaggeration. The true figure was about 2,900 dead, with 120,000 left homeless.[27] The number of wounded is described as ranging between 2,000 and 20,000.[28] There was significant disruption to industrial output from factories particularly in the southern sectors of Berlin, but this time the impact on rail movements was modest. By this stage of the war, the Germans were adept at rapidly restoring damaged railway lines, and even the damage to industrial infrastructure was limited. Speer's policy of dispersing production to multiple locations and moving industrial plant into caves and underground sites meant that much of German industry continued to function despite the raids. The impact upon civilian morale is almost impossible to assess, but it fell far short of triggering a final collapse of the German will to resist. After *Thunderclap*, when General Henry Arnold, head of the USAAF, urged Spaatz to achieve decisive successes with air power, Spaatz replied: 'Your comment on the decisiveness of results achieved by airpower leads me to believe you might be following the chimera of the one air operation that will end the war.'[29]

Clearly, Spaatz had turned his back on the idea of precipitating the collapse of the enemy through one devastating blow. But on 13–15 February, British and American bombers struck the city of Dresden with huge force. From the outset, the intention of the RAF was to create a firestorm and in this the plan was highly effective, and the loss of life in a city overcrowded with refugees fleeing the Red Army's penetration into Upper Silesia and East Prussia was terrible. At least 25,000 people perished, and the lack of accurate data about the numbers of refugees in the city makes it impossible to know the true death toll.

Even as the bombers were destroying Dresden, attention turned once more to the use of air power to strike at German lines of communication. Under the codename *Clarion*, plans had been drawn up in 1944 for widespread attacks on road and rail infrastructure, and it was inevitable that such raids would result in widespread damage to civilian areas, as had been the case with *Thunderclap*. But support for *Clarion* was far from universal, with several senior figures beginning to doubt the impact of mass attacks on railways, especially given that these attacks were usually so imprecise that huge civilian casualties were almost inevitable. The proponents of *Clarion* countered by raising once more the possibility that such casualties would help erode the will of the German nation to continue the war, but increasing numbers of senior officers were sceptical. Colonel Thetus Odom, a staff officer in the USAAF, wrote:

> There is absolutely no basis for the hope that such an operation would cause disorder among the civilian population of Germany by the feeling of fear …

> The operation constitutes open war against civilians, who would react badly ... and [would] place our forces in a defensive position before the world.[30]

Odom also raised the fear that Germans might be so angered by the endless death toll amongst German civilians that they would seek revenge upon US prisoners of war, but the objections that he and others raised were overruled. Perhaps mindful of some of the outcry that followed the Dresden bombing, Spaatz attempted to shape the narrative:

> It is important that public relations and communiqué officers be advised to state clearly in communiqués and all press releases the military nature of all targets attacked. Special care should be taken against giving any impression that this operation is aimed at the civilian population or intended to terrorise them. In addition to the above, care must be taken to ensure that all crews are thoroughly briefed that attacks will be limited to military objectives.[31]

A later copy of this memorandum added that such measures were extremely important for the safety of any crews who were shot down and captured.

The aircraft that took part in *Clarion*, which was executed on 22 and 23 February, generally attacked from lower altitudes than in earlier raids. Railway facilities in small towns were targeted in addition to those in large cities, and the bombing patterns were far more compact than in earlier raids, resulting in fewer civilian losses. Considerable quantities of locomotives and rolling stock were destroyed, reducing the overall capacity of the Reich's railways for the rest of the war, but the hoped-for disruption – through a mixture of destruction of railway lines and the creation of a climate of fear amongst railway workers – proved to be modest.

Berlin was not specifically targeted in *Clarion*, but on 26 February the German capital was struck once more. The bombers of Eighth Air Force intended to strike at several railway stations, but the city was covered in thick cloud, decreasing bombing accuracy. This attack – and a night raid by RAF Mosquitos that followed immediately after – left a further 80,000 Berliners without homes. Attacks continued the following month, with Harris in particular continuing his implacable drive to destroy German cities with no regard for civilian casualties, but the mood was changing. Earlier, Churchill had been an ardent supporter of Harris and had demanded area bombing of German cities, but now he took a different position. Thoughts were turning to how wartime leaders might be perceived after the conflict, something with which Churchill was increasingly preoccupied, and towards the end of March he wrote a note to Portal:

The moment has come when the question of bombing German cities simply for the sake of increasing the terror, though under other pretexts, should be reviewed. Otherwise, we shall come into control of an utterly ruined land. The destruction of Dresden remains a serious query against the conduct of Allied bombing. I am of the opinion that military objectives must henceforward be more strictly studied in our own interests rather than that of the enemy ... I feel the need for more precise concentration upon military objectives such as oil and communications behind the immediate battle zone, rather than on mere acts of terror and wanton destruction, however impressive.[32]

This was, at best, a deeply disingenuous note, given Churchill's enthusiasm for such attacks in the past and his urging for strikes against cities like Dresden and Chemnitz that had escaped heavy bombing in earlier years, however much he attempted to dress up his criticism on the grounds that German infrastructure needed to be preserved to make the tasks of future occupation forces easier. Harris responded furiously. He accepted that attacks on cities were repugnant, but justified them on strategic grounds, adding that any measures that reduced potential casualties amongst friendly forces were entirely acceptable. Under considerable pressure, Churchill reworded his note in a milder form.

Despite the growing unease in both British and American circles about area bombing, such attacks continued on Berlin. On 15 March, when weather forecasts suggested favourable conditions that would normally have resulted in the targeting of oil facilities, Spaatz intervened with new orders. Bombers were to strike at Zossen, immediately to the south of Berlin, where the German *Oberkommando des Heeres* ('Army High Command' or *OKH*, responsible for the Eastern Front) was based, and also at the northern suburb of Oranienburg. This second target was officially an attempt to disrupt the railway yards, but the true target was a series of laboratories in Oranienburg. The intelligence services of the Western Allies had identified these as the centre of Germany's atomic weapons programme, and the agreements reached in the Yalta Conference in February would place the area under Soviet control at the end of the war. The destruction of these laboratories would therefore serve two purposes: it would damage or even destroy the German atomic weapons programme; and it would prevent such material from falling into the hands of the Soviet Union.

Accordingly, a force of about 600 bombers struck Oranienburg on 15 March. Despite the favourable weather forecast, there was patchy cloud. Nevertheless, given the compact target area, there was widespread destruction, though some bombers strayed from their designated targets; several bombs fell on the concentration camp at Sachsenhausen, a short distance to the north. A similar bomber force struck Zossen, where several members of the German general staff were killed or wounded, but the dispersed nature of the *OKH* facilities lessened the impact of the raid.

US bombers carried out incendiary attacks on rail targets in Berlin on 18 March. A teenage girl later recalled how she and her friends took shelter during the raid:

> The room was full of chattering and laughter. But there is a background of nerve-racking tension. There, an impact close by! The anti-aircraft guns begin to fire. The vibrations get stronger and stronger. The chatter dies down and the laughter stops completely. Suddenly, a deafening bang! The light flickers and the room sways. We flinch in fear. The old woman across from me begins to pray quietly. A child buries his face in his mother's lap, sobbing. His whimpers hang in the air like an embodiment of our fear. Blow after blow! Everyone feels the approach of death. Perhaps three more minutes, two more, maybe just one! The young woman next to me stares into space with dull eyes. Like all of us, she's had enough of life.
>
> There, smoke is coming out of the little crack in the wall! It's a barely noticeable puff, but the heavy cellar air is contaminated with smoke in just a few minutes. A woman screams. 'We're done for!' she cries, grabs her belongings, and rushes to the door that leads to the back rooms. Many others join her. When the room becomes pitch black, even the last who are left can't take it any more. The earth roars with bomb impacts. It's as if all manner of energies have been unleashed. Then comes news that the exit is blocked. But immediately afterwards, a man shouts, 'Everything above us is on fire, we have to get out!' Children scream, women cry, fearful confusion sweeps over everyone. What's going to become of us? Smoke penetrates into this room at the back too. The air is humid, the hot smoke stings our eyes as we stand crushed together. Death has his hand stretched over us.
>
> 'The emergency exits are blocked,' says the air raid warden. 'We'll have to wait until it's cleared.'
>
> 'We have to wait? So we're stuck here!' groans a young woman, whose child clings to her with fear. An old man suffers an angina attack. And we wait – we wait for death!
>
> There, a breath of fresh air! An exit has been cleared! Who can describe the joy that one feels at avoiding death. And everyone pushes their way out. 'We have to hurry!' shout the wardens, 'There's a danger of collapse!' Nobody knows if the attack is over, as the alarm system has been destroyed. We climb out. Everything above and around us is ablaze.[33]

Ten days later, the US bombers were back. On this occasion, they dropped over a thousand tons of bombs on the Berlin suburb of Spandau. These were the last mass attacks, though bombing continued right up to the arrival of Soviet troops. In total, the USAAF dropped about 23,000 tons of explosives on the German capital during the war; the RAF added a further 41,000 tons.[34] By the end of March 1945, there had been no fewer than 314 air raids on Berlin. Of these, 85 – 27 per cent of the total – had occurred in the preceding 12 months.[35] The result was widespread devastation. At least half of all civilian housing in the city had been damaged, with up to a third rendered uninhabitable. A third of the urban area had been reduced to a sea of rubble, but despite German propaganda claims that the attacks had cost the lives of up to 50,000 people, the true figure is more likely to have been about 20,000.[36] The widespread *U-Bahn* system of Berlin, the use of cellars, and the construction of official air raid shelters capable of housing up to 65,000 people had reduced casualties considerably, particularly as attacking bombers had to fly a long distance over German territory and there was therefore ample time for civilians to be alerted and to take cover. In addition, over a million civilians had been evacuated from Berlin to areas where they might be safer from air attack. Unfortunately, such locations included cities like Dresden.

More people had been killed in the attacks on Dresden in mid-February than all the raids on Berlin combined, and the loss of life in Japanese cities was even greater. The firebombing of Tokyo on the night of 9–10 March 1945 resulted in devastating fires that killed between 87,700 and 124,700 people; most of the victims were the elderly, women, or children.[37] It is worth noting that at the time, the devastation of Tokyo was regarded as a great victory both by the military personnel involved and US politicians; there was little of the unease that existed about inflicting civilian casualties in German cities.[38] General Henry Arnold, head of the USAAF, sent a congratulatory message to Major General Curtis LeMay, commander of Twentieth Air Force, adding that 'this mission shows your crews have the guts for anything.'[39] Henry Stimson, Roosevelt's Secretary of War, expressed concerns in private and commented on the general indifference to the deaths in Japan compared with the deaths in Germany, but kept these opinions largely to himself.[40]

CHAPTER 3

PREPARING FOR THE LAST STAND: THE GERMAN DEFENCES

In January 1945, the Red Army had launched its long-anticipated assault on the German armies defending East Prussia and Poland. Even in the best possible circumstances, the Wehrmacht was now too weak to be able to deal with attacks on so many axes – in addition to continuing their drive across Hungary, Soviet forces erupted from three bridgeheads over the Vistula River south of Warsaw and also pushed into East Prussia from the north and east. Moreover, despite the German propaganda about the Ardennes offensive of late 1944, the operation had failed with heavy losses, and a renewed assault on the Reich from the west was merely a matter of time. But Hitler's micro-management of military affairs ensured that whatever small chances the Germans had of local successes on the Eastern Front were lost. Permission to pull back to a shorter line – a proposal codenamed *Schlittenfahrt* ('Sleighride') – was refused and the already inadequate reserves held behind the front line were further reduced by Hitler insisting on moving formations to Hungary. By the end of January, the Red Army had surged across Poland into Silesia, the last relatively intact region of vital industrial production in the Reich, and had crossed the old German–Polish frontier. On 31 January, riflemen of the Soviet Fifth Shock Army reached and crossed the frozen Oder River, seizing the small town of Kienitz, directly to the east of Berlin. After an advance of over 270 miles, they were just 45 miles from the centre of the German capital. Predictably, there was consternation in Berlin, not least because the shattered German units that had been swept away by the Red Army were in no shape or position to erect strong defences between the Oder and the capital. It seemed as if the long-anticipated defeat of Germany was at hand and might take place in the following few days. The Red Army's spectacular surge across

Poland and into the eastern parts of Germany carried its leading units to the Oder River in less than three weeks. After capturing the town of Landsberg an der Warthe, Colonel Khariton Fyodorovich Esipenko, the chief of staff of Fifth Shock Army's XXIX Guards Rifle Corps, led a small group towards the Oder, which flows just 28 miles further west. His mixed battlegroup reached the river early on 31 January:

> At 0800 on 31 January, Majors Platonov and Cherednik led their battalions across the Oder on foot across thin ice and captured a small bridgehead in the Kienitz area. The rifle units immediately began to prepare defences. Tanks and most of the self-propelled artillery couldn't cross to the west bank; the ice was too weak. Instead, they took up positions on the right bank in readiness to provide fire support for the advanced detachments ... At this point, the main forces of Fifth Shock Army were still 30–40km from the bridgehead.
>
> The rapid advances of Soviet troops to the Oder were so surprising to the Fascist command that they didn't even have enough time to suspend railway movements. Without firing a single shot, our soldiers captured a military train that arrived from Berlin at the station in Kienitz, complete with six anti-aircraft guns and 13 officers and 63 cadets from the anti-aircraft artillery school. The appearance of Soviet troops also threw the German civilian population into confusion. After all, Berlin Radio had just broadcast a message that 'the valiant troops of the Führer, successfully conducting an organised battle, are pulling back to previously prepared positions on the Bzura River'. And here, just 68km from Berlin, there were Soviet tanks and artillery, and Russian voices could be heard ...
>
> The station chief turned to Colonel Esipenko: 'Will you permit me to dispatch the train to Berlin?'
>
> With exaggerated politeness and a serious demeanour, Khariton Fyodorovich replied, 'I'm sorry, Station Manager, but it's impossible. Passenger traffic to Berlin will be interrupted for a short time – well, at least until the end of the war. Please take your passengers to the basements and bomb shelters.'[1]

This last detail is an invention; although there was a railway station in Kienitz, it was on a small branch line and only local trains ran through it. Nonetheless, the anecdote exemplifies the confusion created by the swift Soviet advance. At that moment, there were few – if any – organised formations between Esipenko and Berlin. German reconnaissance aircraft appeared overhead as the day drew on and the first air attacks took place before dusk, followed by ground attacks the following morning. Although Soviet accounts described these attacks as powerful and supported by armour, they are unlikely to have been more than reconnaissance probes.

Despite the disarray of the Wehrmacht, the Red Army faced considerable difficulties in exploiting this spectacular advance. Some 100 miles to the east, the German garrison of the 'fortress' of Poznań continued to hold out, tying down substantial Soviet forces and blocking the movement of supplies and reinforcements. This logistic disruption was perhaps the more important consideration; without fuel, ammunition, food, and replacements for destroyed or damaged equipment and casualties, the spearheads that had reached or were closing up with the Oder would be unable to achieve anything further. A swift attack towards Berlin would be highly risky.

When the conflict between the Soviet Union and Germany broke out in the summer of 1941, the Wehrmacht entered the fighting with a strong doctrine of delegated decision-making, built around a highly trained staff officer system. Over many decades, accepting that it would be impossible for even the most capable senior commander to keep abreast of all events on a fast-changing battlefield, the German military had devised and then steadily developed a system in which local commanders were entrusted to show initiative and improvisation in the face of unexpected developments. Their orders would have made clear the overall objectives of their superiors, and they were sufficiently trained to deliver those objectives even if they had to deviate from their precise orders to do so. By contrast, the years of Stalin's purges in the late 1930s had stripped the Red Army of any sense of showing initiative – to do anything other than slavishly following orders invited suspicion, scrutiny, arrest, and even execution. This difference contributed greatly to the rapidity of the German advance and the disastrous performance of the Red Army in 1941, but in the years that followed, both sides changed significantly. Stalin slowly relaxed his restrictions on his senior commanders, permitting them greater freedom to react rapidly to developments on the battlefield. The ability of lower-level commanders in the Red Army to show such initiative was, however, very limited – the years of rigid diktat had left their mark, and Soviet reports throughout the war repeatedly highlighted the lack of initiative of corps and division commanders, who persevered stubbornly in attacks on positions that had already repulsed their earlier assaults rather than attempting to find ways of outflanking or bypassing them. Even by 1945, there was ongoing frustration at this tendency, but although the overall improvement of command arrangements in the Red Army had been fairly modest, it nonetheless resulted in a far more effective approach to operations than had been the case in earlier years.

During those years, the Wehrmacht evolved in the reverse direction. Hitler imposed increasingly rigid top-down control, eroding and almost eliminating the freedom to improvise and make decisions on the ground without first seeking permission. The result was almost always disastrous. The rapidity of developments on the battlefield was such that even contacting corps or army headquarters prior to issuing orders to subordinates would add unacceptable delays; but Hitler insisted that such clearance had to come from even higher in the chain of command. Faced with a rapidly deteriorating battlefield, division commanders had to pass requests to corps commanders, who in turn forwarded them to their army commanders. They too were effectively powerless and had to seek clearance from their army group commanders, who would then contact *OKH*. Generaloberst Heinz Guderian, chief of staff at *OKH*, then had to present the proposals to Hitler at the daily conferences, argue the case with the Führer, and then pass any decision back down the same command chain by which time the situation on the battlefield would have changed beyond recognition. To make matters worse, when Hitler was asked to approve courses of action that he didn't wish to follow, he would prevaricate and put off a decision for a day or more. On almost every occasion, the result was catastrophic. But far from accepting responsibility for the outcome, Hitler's response was that the lower-level commanders had failed to adhere to their instructions, and he simply increased the rigidity of the command system. It was against this background that the final battles of the Reich were fought.

The blows that tore apart the German front line in mid-January resulted in yawning gaps opening up, and there were major changes to the command structure. In particular, a new German command was created to fill the largest gap: Army Group Vistula. At first, it inherited Second Army from its northern neighbour and Ninth Army from its southern neighbour, but both were badly degraded by the heavy losses they had suffered. In addition, new units would have to be sent to the area to restore some semblance of continuity. The announcement of the commander of the new army group was greeted by many in the German military hierarchy with a mixture of surprise and dismay. Guderian had proposed Generalfeldmarschall Maximilian von Weichs for the role; Weichs had just completed a difficult withdrawal through Greece and Yugoslavia by Army Group F with considerable skill. But the withdrawal – which Weichs had justified on the perfectly rational grounds that his entire army group risked destruction if it remained in situ – merely fed into Hitler's conviction that traditional senior Wehrmacht officers lacked the required determination to stand firm against the Red Army. Hitler's trust in the senior figures in the Wehrmacht had never been strong and deteriorated with each setback suffered by Germany. After the July Plot of 1944, the Führer's trust almost completely collapsed. As a result, he dismissed Guderian's suggestions that the highly competent Weichs should take command of the new army group, preferring instead a candidate that he believed would show the required level of fanatical determination.

Prior to commanding Army Group F, Weichs' life had followed the course of a typical son of German military aristocracy. After the invasion of the Soviet Union, he had a brief spell in charge of Second Army, and then oversaw the advance to Stalingrad as commander of Army Group B. By this stage, he had already attracted a degree of mistrust from Hitler. Firstly, he was one of the Prussian aristocracy that the Führer disliked strongly, and secondly, he repeatedly urged Hitler to authorise a withdrawal from Stalingrad as it became clear that Sixth Army lacked the strength to complete the capture of the city. His concerns were confirmed when the Red Army launched Operation *Uranus* and encircled Stalingrad, but Hitler transferred much of the army group to the new Army Group Don, commanded by Manstein. When Army Group B was formally disbanded in July 1943, he had a spell of home leave before being sent to the Balkans. He was therefore a man with extensive experience of command at every level, both as a field commander and as a staff officer. The man that Hitler chose instead of him had little meaningful command experience and no training whatever.

Heinrich Himmler was born in 1900, the same year that Weichs became an officer cadet. He was drafted into the army during the First World War but had not completed training before the conflict came to an end. He showed great interest in martial matters while studying at Munich University after the war, but was unable to join the 100,000-strong *Reichswehr* permitted by the Treaty of Versailles. Instead, he was attracted to Ernst Röhm, the founder of the *SA*, and joined his *Bund Reichkriegsflagge* ('Imperial War Flag Society'), where he was immersed in an environment of antisemitism and willingness to use violence for political ends. After joining the Nazi Party in 1923 and the SS in 1925, he became *Reichsführer-SS* four years later, at a time when the organisation was growing in both the size and the roles that it undertook. In his teenage years, Himmler had shown little inclination for antisemitism, but by this stage of his life his views had changed radically. When he recruited senior figures for the SS, he was careful to select men who fitted his vision of what the new service should be: he preferred technocrats, ideally not associated with what he saw as the failed institutions of the past like the Prussian aristocracy. Those who displayed strong commitment to antisemitism and were prepared to push the boundaries of what had previously been regarded as acceptable caught his eye and were promoted rapidly. He displayed a distinctly two-faced attitude to those he had chosen for greatness. On the one hand, he demanded what he described as 'decency' and strict adherence to morality, but on the other hand, he went to great lengths to shield his protégés from the consequences of their often openly criminal behaviour. By the beginning of the Second World War, he held numerous roles in the Nazi machine. In addition to overseeing all aspects of the SS – including the rapidly growing Waffen-SS – he was head of police and security services via his role as Germany's interior minister. Whilst his lack of specific training for his political roles was little different from other appointees, his place at the head of the Waffen-SS was another matter. Repeatedly, he selected senior officers on the basis of their commitment to Nazi ideology rather than their military experience or training.

It wasn't until 1944 that he received any personal experience of military affairs, when he became *Befehlshaber Oberrhein* ('Commander Upper Rhine') in the west. However, this was little more than a title, with him being involved in almost no military decision-making. Even in such a position, he left a poor impression on the professional soldiers around him, both in the army and the Waffen-SS. Oberstgruppenführer Paul Hausser was one of the most senior figures in the armed wing of the SS and unlike Himmler had extensive command experience from the First World War and the Weimar years. He was stunned when it was announced that Himmler had been selected by Hitler to command the new Army Group Vistula, and he later wrote:

> Himmler had no authority as a military leader … he was also unaware that he lacked military experience and knowledge … it was a tragedy – no, a crime – to entrust this army group to Himmler in this most desperate situation.[2]

To place a man with no military training or experience in such a senior role was, to put it mildly, a contentious and risky step. If Himmler had been a man who ensured that he was surrounded by people who could give him sound advice and had possessed the required capacity for hard work and rapid learning, at least some of this risk could have been mitigated. But Himmler possessed neither of these traits. He was one of those who believed that fanatical determination would more than compensate for material deficiencies in the field and dismissed the objections of professional soldiers to his orders as indications of their failed and limited thinking. Moreover, he had a lifetime problem with vague intestinal complaints, which had led to him adopting a regime of regular rest and carefully calculated meals; as a consequence, it was impossible for him to spend much more than five hours per day in a working role. As interior minister, head of the SS, and (following the July Plot) commander of the *Ersatzheer* ('Replacement Army'), this would have made it almost impossible for him to deal with his responsibilities fully. The additional requirements of commanding a new army group that was being formed whilst fighting for its life and trying to hold back the Red Army's thrust towards Berlin demanded a level of energy and work rate that was completely beyond him.

Preparing for the Last Stand: The German Defences

Oberst Hans-Georg Eismann was appointed as the operations officer of Army Group Vistula and travelled to take up his new post, passing the debris of refugees streaming westwards accompanied by the shattered remnants of army formations as he made his way first to Schneidemühl, from where he was directed to Deutsch-Krone. Finally, he found Himmler aboard his luxurious personal train, *Steiermark*, and met the new army group commander. Himmler was not a physically impressive figure, of average height and build with soft features and a receding chin, and the outline that he gave Eismann of the overall military situation lacked coherence and detail, other than confirming that the German front line had a huge gap that Army Group Vistula had to close. Eismann wrote about the meeting:

> I then asked, 'What will we use to close this breach and then hold the new front line?' The entire campaign in the east had been fought with no reserves, or at least no strategic reserves and usually without tactical reserves either … Up to this point, Himmler had been speaking while sweeping his pointer energetically around the map. The core of his rather rambling briefing, however, had been that he would bring the Russians to a halt with Army Group Vistula and would then crush them and throw them back. This was quite a declaration. Any great field commander should of course strive for the highest objectives with self-belief … But a degree of sound judgement regarding the relevant military circumstances must accompany this. Here, I had the involuntary impression that I was talking about colours with a blind man …
>
> It was clear to me that the great breach created by the penetration would persist and that the army group's mission would be impossible unless the high command provided fresh formations as quickly as possible. Therefore I asked Himmler what additional forces would be provided, and when they would arrive.
>
> Instead of an answer, I now received a rather loud and rude lecture from my new commander about my typical 'general staff attitude' that climaxed with an accusation that staff officers only had misgivings, were too academically trained, couldn't improvise, had defeatist attitudes, and so on. He, Himmler, would end any such misgivings by attacking with ruthless determination. That was the only way that such difficult problems could be overcome.[3]

The dispiriting journey to Himmler's headquarters and the clear lack of grasp of the new commander were sufficient to leave any officer with a profound sense of pessimism, but worse was to follow. The German military machine operated with each commander from division level upwards being assigned a chief of staff who had been through the rigorous selection and training programme that made the German general staff such an effective organisation. In addition to overseeing the detailed staff work of his headquarters, the chief of staff would often complement his commander by taking control of the headquarters, permitting the commander to visit front-line units and to concentrate on decision-making. There was also a strong tradition of chiefs of staff being able to challenge the decisions of the commander, both face-to-face and by raising the matter with the chief of staff at the next level of command. Given Himmler's singular unfitness for the role of commander of an army group, it was essential that he had a competent and efficient chief of staff. Eismann was now stunned to learn that the man who would take up the post was Gruppenführer Heinz Lammerding, a personal favourite of Himmler who had commanded the panzer division *SS-Das Reich* through much of 1944. Like many other senior SS figures, he had no formal military training and was widely regarded in both the army and the Waffen-SS as being completely unfit to command a field division.[4] The involvement of his division in atrocities in France during 1944 – including the Oradour-sur-Glane massacre of 654 civilians – merely proved to Himmler that he had a suitable level of fanaticism for the task of defeating the Red Army.

Eismann was left to carry out the tasks of both operations officer and chief of staff until Lammerding arrived. During these days, he had to work in a surreal environment aboard the *Steiermark*. Carriages were divided into offices that ran all of the various parts of Himmler's empire, relying on a connection to the civilian telephone system, a single teleprinter, and just one radio set. Eismann found himself trying to organise the army group from what amounted to half a railway carriage and sharing a desk with several other people. A few days after being appointed, Lammerding finally reached Himmler's headquarters, and Eismann was distinctly unimpressed:

> With him, there was always the impression of insecurity. That was compounded by the fact that he was a cautious man who was inclined to compromise. In his new post, he avoided taking personal responsibility ... At first he didn't involve himself in the business of commanding the army group and took a laissez-faire attitude. He was reluctant to express his views on the operational situation to Himmler.[5]

Even in the surreal world inhabited by the Nazi leadership in 1945, the appointment of Himmler was an extraordinary development. Such a decision was probably influenced by several factors. Prior to the July Plot, Hitler accepted the necessity of relying on the traditionally minded officers of the German military, even in the case of individuals who were openly critical and disdainful of the Nazis. With the exception of a brief period of time around the Stalingrad debacle, Hitler was unable to accept personal responsibility for any of the setbacks suffered by Germany, and the succession of major defeats, followed by the failed assassination attempt, left him openly questioning the wisdom of relying on men whom he regarded as having let him down so badly. Another possible explanation for the bizarre appointment of Himmler is that despite the impending final defeat of Germany, senior Nazi figures continued their personal struggles for advantage over each other. Throughout his time in power, Hitler had encouraged what he regarded as a Darwinist form of competition, and such behaviour was now deeply imbedded throughout the regime. Martin Bormann, who as Hitler's personal secretary wielded great influence as access to the Führer required his cooperation, was keen to use any opportunity to expand his personal power and may have encouraged Hitler to appoint Himmler in the knowledge that he was almost certain to fail as an army group commander. As a result, Hitler might see fit to reduce Himmler's status and strip him of some of his powers, providing opportunities for Bormann and others to increase their personal fiefdoms. The catastrophic consequences of this failure for Germany were ignored in the pursuit of personal gain.

Strong-minded, authoritarian leaders rarely allow those in their inner circle to be openly critical, but by the end of 1944, Hitler's earlier lack of tolerance of disagreement had reached new levels. Most of those around him – civilians like Bormann and Goebbels, military figures like Generaloberst Alfred Jodl (chief of the operations staff at *OKW*) and Generalfeldmarschall Wilhelm Keitel (head of *OKW*), had rarely shown any inclination to express reservations about the Führer's plans, and even those who had disagreed openly in the past were now far more cautious. During the Battle of Moscow at the end of 1941, Guderian, commanding a panzer group outside the Soviet capital, had been involved in several increasingly angry exchanges with Hitler, culminating in his dismissal. Now, as chief of the general staff at *OKH*, he was a different figure. In his memoirs, he later described how he was careful to raise objections in a reasoned manner, trying to avoid confrontations that would merely drive Hitler into a more rigid mindset. But there were many areas where he showed no readiness at all to argue against the Führer's decisions. In particular, the manner in which he acquiesced and even actively cooperated with the repression of suspected anti-Hitler conspirators shows just how much he had changed from the argumentative, independently minded officer of earlier years. Nevertheless, the appointment of a dilettante like Himmler to such a critical role as commander of Army Group Vistula would test his patience to and ultimately beyond the limits of endurance.

The headquarters of Army Group Vistula lacked everything that mattered – maps, communications equipment, and the multitude of staff officers and personnel required to coordinate field units and their supply and support formations. Despite this, Himmler insisted on taking Second and Ninth Armies under his command on 18 January, when secure communications with both armies were almost non-existent. His lack of grasp of military realities reduced Eismann to despair:

> [Himmler] was simply not capable of a strategic evaluation of the big picture. He just stared as if spellbound at the huge breach that he had to close. He looked at the Russian advance towards Poznań as a unique opportunity to attack the flank of the Russian armies from a line running from Schneidemühl to Bydgoszcz and thus to destroy them. He constantly used words like 'aggressively' and 'thrust into the flank'. It never seemed to occur to him that the Russians might be planning a flank attack against the hard-pressed Second Army. One look at the map that was always spread before him should have made that obvious.
>
> For him, 'attack' seemed the only option ...
>
> Himmler wanted to direct the battle himself. He issued orders indiscriminately to individual battalions until it was possible for us to put a halt to this. I particularly remember that he seemed to not know how to measure distances on a map and constantly confused the scales of the standard general staff maps; he sent a battalion out from Schneidemühl completely on its own with the simple mission of attacking the enemy and then holding him until the flank attack could take place ... The battalion commander, an elderly reservist, was completely nonplussed. He didn't dare raise objections against the army group commander. The battalion would end up in open countryside 30km south of Schneidemühl without any communications or contact on its flanks because Himmler had no comprehension that a 10cm distance on the map represented 30km on the ground. No more was ever heard of that battalion.[6]

In addition to the two armies that Himmler inherited from the army groups to north and south, new units would be needed to repair the breach in the front line. Several headquarters were already en route to the area, and these would take control of a mixture of broken formations, improvised battlegroups, and large numbers of *Volkssturm* – German males previously regarded as too young, too old, or too infirm for military service, and now deployed in improvised battalions with very limited equipment and almost no training. From north to south, three SS corps headquarters were deployed – XVI SS Corps, X SS Corps, and V SS-Mountain Corps. Three corps, if properly constituted, would comprise a full army and would be able to restore the German front line; in practice, they possessed just one Latvian SS division between them, together with a few assault guns and several battalions of *Volkssturm*. Himmler was enthusiastic about the three corps commanders, all of whom had shown the requisite commitment to Hitler and Nazism by ruthlessly conducting campaigns of mass murder in the east, but officers like Eismann saw no prospect of being able to hold back the Red Army with such pitiful resources, let alone mount annihilating counterattacks of the kind demanded by the army group commander. The Soviet advance bypassed the isolated city of Poznań and rapidly penetrated the fortifications that had been constructed along the old German–Polish frontier; if these defences had been manned by adequate forces with mobile reinforcements available for counterattacks, there would have been considerable scope for fighting a prolonged delaying action, but the weak units available were rapidly driven away by the Red Army. But despite these setbacks, Himmler returned to his headquarters on 26 January after a trip to Berlin, clearly excited by what he had been told. A new army was to be created near Stettin, to the east of the lower Oder, from where it would strike into the northern flank of the Soviet armies that were approaching the river. Originally, it was envisaged that a second thrust would be made from the south, but Hitler insisted on diverting the units designated for this to Hungary and all that remained was the northern part of the operation.

Although Zhukov's 1st Belarusian Front had made a spectacular advance from the Vistula, this left its flanks exposed to just the sort of attack that Himmler was now describing. On 26 January, the same day that Himmler enthusiastically told Eismann and Lammerding about the planned counteroffensive, Zhukov and Stalin discussed the situation; the latter warned Zhukov that it would be best to wait until 2nd Belarusian Front, on the northern flank, was able to move up alongside. It was in this context that reports began to arrive of the new German concentration to the east of the lower Oder. The German counteroffensive – ultimately codenamed *Sonnenwende* ('Solstice') – would be conducted by a newly formed army. Originally, this was designated Eleventh Army, and was formed using staff from a group on the upper Rhine, together with the headquarters personnel of Third Panzer Army, which had been fighting in East Prussia; with all its formations either destroyed or transferred to other armies, it was now redundant. But Himmler insisted on naming the new formation Eleventh SS-Panzer Army, and this created a degree of confusion in Soviet circles. The Red Army was aware of German units concentrating close to the northern flank of their drive towards the Oder, and with intelligence arriving from different sources, it seemed as if a profusion of units, new and old, were being sent to the area. Dealing with this threat was therefore a priority.

All of the Soviet units that had driven across Poland and the eastern parts of Germany were significantly degraded by their long advance, having suffered substantial losses from both German action and breakdowns of tanks and other vehicles. Supplies of all kinds and significant reinforcements would have to be brought forward, and this was greatly hindered by the persistent resistance of the German garrison in Poznań. Whilst a delay in striking towards Berlin would give the Germans time to move reinforcements to defend the Reich's capital, Stalin and Zhukov agreed that this was unavoidable.

One of the formations in Zhukov's 1st Belarusian Front was Eighth Guards Army. Originally designated Sixty-Second Army, it had fought the Germans to a standstill in the ruins of Stalingrad and, as had been the case in the desperate days of 1942, it remained under the command of Vasily Ivanovich Chuikov, now holding the rank of colonel general. The stocky Chuikov, with a head of thick, dark hair, was well known to his soldiers; he made a point of visiting the front-line units regularly. His memoirs are engagingly written, but like all memoirs they should be treated with a degree of caution; some of the anecdotes that he describes may well have happened, but he was not above embellishing them to make them more interesting or dramatic. Nor did he hesitate to adapt his account to fit with the prevailing political dogma. In the years after the war, Stalin deliberately attempted to downplay the role of Zhukov in the war. Chuikov's memoirs were amongst the first to be authorised after the war, and he was careful to ensure that they complied with Stalin's vision of recent history. At dawn on 2 February, his units reached the Oder River to the south of the city of Küstrin and – in the face of repeated German air attacks – attempted to establish bridgeheads across the river. Venturing out onto the thin ice, the soldiers of Eighth Guards Army could take only light weapons with them and the foothold that they secured was tenuous, as Colonel Aranesp Khachaturovich Babadzhanian, commander of XI Guards Tank Corps, later described:

> Even after crossing the Oder, units of Eighth Guards Army needed to spend a lot of effort and time – about two weeks – to expand their bridgehead on the west bank to a size that would allow 1st Belarusian Front to concentrate the required number of troops there to begin a powerful attack on Berlin. And even after our troops secured bridgeheads on the west bank of the Oder, the enemy continued to hold a fortified bridgehead centred on the city of Küstrin. A significant number of enemy troops, although surrounded, continued to hold important locations like Schneidemühl, Poznań, and Breslau, tying down our forces … The lines of communication of our troops were now stretched over 500km and more, the railways were not functioning, the railway bridges over the Vistula had not yet been restored, supplies were exhausted, and military equipment and weapons needed repair and replacement. A direct attack on Berlin was out of the question.[7]

Perhaps in awareness of Stalin's wishes to reduce Zhukov's reputation after the war, Chuikov took a different position, suggesting that Zhukov, Babadzhanian, and others were wrong to call for a pause, though acknowledging that continuing immediately towards Berlin was not without risk:

> As for the risk, in war you often have to take chances. But in this case the risk was justified. Our troops had already covered over 500km in the Vistula–Oder Operation and only a further 60–80km remained from the Oder to Berlin …
>
> If we objectively assess the strength of the grouping of Nazi forces in Pomerania, we can see that any threat to our strike forces on the Berlin axis could well have been contained by the troops of 2nd Belarusian Front.[8]

In a separate article written after the war, he recognised the logistic difficulties faced by the Red Army at the time:

> If *Stavka* and the Front headquarters had organised supplies properly and had managed to deliver the required amount of ammunition, fuel and food to the Oder on time, if aviation assets had time to relocate to the Oder airfields, and the bridging units could ensure the crossing of troops over the Oder, then our four armies – Fifth Shock, Eighth Guards, and First and Second Tank – could have developed a further attack on Berlin in February, advanced another 80–100km, and completed the gigantic operation by capturing the German capital.[9]

This was little more than wishful thinking. It was physically impossible for supplies to be organised in the manner that Chuikov acknowledged was necessary; in the absence of such supplies, a further advance was simply impossible. He also failed to recognise the difficult terrain that lay between the Oder and the German capital. Attempting to push forward through this area without adequate supplies of ammunition and without at least attempting to replenish the depleted ranks of the Red Army was more than merely risky. In any event, dealing with the build-up of German forces around Stettin was deemed to be more important.

Sonnenwende, Himmler's great counterattack from the north, failed to make significant headway and was abandoned on 18 February after both sides had suffered significant losses; with the element of surprise lost, there was little or no prospect of a decisive victory being achieved by the German forces and such was the desperate situation faced by the Reich that the armoured assets that had been concentrated in Eleventh SS-Panzer Army were badly needed to intervene elsewhere. Even as the decision to call off *Sonnenwende* was being made, Zhukov and Marshal Konstantin Konstantinovich Rokossovsky launched a powerful drive into Pomerania, rapidly thrusting north to the Baltic coast and destroying the few units that had been deployed under the aegis of the three SS corps that Himmler had deployed in their path. Second Army, originally the northern flank of Army Group Vistula, was now isolated around the Bay of Danzig to the east, and Ninth Army had been driven back to the Oder River. After most of the panzer formations used in *Sonnenwende* had departed, the remnants were once more renamed, becoming Third Panzer Army once again, tasked with defending the German front line from the Baltic coast to Ninth Army's positions to the east of Berlin.

With his army group in utter disarray, Himmler took to his bed, claiming that he was suffering from influenza. In reports to Hitler, he was deeply critical of Generaloberst Walter Weiss, commander of Second Army; Weiss had repeatedly warned Himmler of the risk of his army being cut off in and around Danzig and had reported that prolonged defence was impossible with so few reserves available to deal with Soviet attacks. Unable to send Weiss any reinforcements, Himmler had responded with platitudes and demands for evergreater fanaticism. In Himmler's absence, Lammerding – probably leaning heavily on Eismann – was left to try to extract the debris of the other shattered front-line units from the disaster that had unfolded across Pomerania.

As was frequently the case after military setbacks, there was a change of personnel. Generalleutnant Eberhard Kinzel had been commanding 337th Volksgrenadier Division on the Eastern Front during the retreat along the lower Vistula valley towards Danzig; he was a man with at best a chequered military record, having held many significant staff posts but few field commands prior to the recent fighting. His most notable tour of duty had been immediately before and during Operation *Barbarossa*, the invasion of the Soviet Union in 1941, when he had been head of *Fremde Heere Ost* ('Foreign Armies East' or *FHO*), the intelligence arm of the German general staff with special responsibility for gathering information on actual and potential enemies to the east of the Reich. In this role, he was responsible for the intelligence assessments of the Red Army on the basis of which the German invasion was planned; he had taken up the post with no formal intelligence training or experience, and his reports vastly underestimated the strength of the Soviet Union's military, in terms of its field forces and its reserves. Kinzel would later claim that his initial assessments had been accurate, but Hitler had insisted that they exaggerated the strength of the Red Army and demanded that new documents be drawn up; the truth of the matter will never be known.

After being dismissed from *FHO* in early 1942, Kinzel served as chief of staff first at corps level and then with Army Group North outside Leningrad before being assigned to 337th Volksgrenadier Division. He now suddenly appeared at the headquarters of Army Group Vistula, having been ordered there by *OKH* but with little idea of what his role would be. At first, the rather vague instructions from Guderian suggested that he serve as an additional chief of staff alongside Lammerding to help manage matters while Himmler was apparently incapacitated by illness. There was no precedent for an army group effectively having two chiefs of staff; nor were there any guidelines on how they were to divide the work, but Lammerding rapidly imposed his own solution. If he had been out of his depth as a division commander, he was in even greater difficulties as chief of staff of Army Group Vistula, and he now took advantage of Kinzel's arrival and left almost all decision-making to the new man.

There were other changes too. Generaloberst Erhard Raus, the commander of Third Panzer Army, had watched helplessly as his formations were smashed and driven back first in East Prussia and then in Pomerania, and he was summoned to Berlin. After he had given a detailed and inevitably pessimistic report of the recent fighting and the prospects for the future, he was told that he was being removed from command. For what remained of the war, Third Panzer Army would be commanded by General Hasso von Manteuffel. In some respects, he was the epitome of the traditional German officer that Hitler openly detested by this stage of the conflict: the son of a distinguished military family, he served in a Prussian cavalry regiment in the First World War and commanded panzer divisions in North Africa and on the Eastern Front in the Second World War, and his most recent post had been to lead Fifth Panzer Army in the Ardennes offensive. Weiss, the commander of the isolated Second Army, was also dismissed, probably because of the reports that Himmler had submitted.

But regardless of Himmler's attempts to pass blame onto his subordinates, Hitler had to face the reality that Himmler was utterly unfit to command any field formation, let alone an army group. Guderian learned that the *Reichsführer-SS* was still languishing in hospital and decided to visit him. Despite Himmler's fall from grace, he remained a powerful person in the Nazi regime and Guderian had to tread carefully:

> I drove there immediately and met Himmler, who seemed fairly well, and I reflected that a slight cold would not have led me to leave my troops in such a tense situation.
>
> I made it clear to the SS supremo that he combined a number of the highest Reich positions in his person: the posts of *Reichsführer-SS*, Chief of the German Police, Reich Minister of the Interior, Commander-in-Chief of the Reserve Army and finally Commander-in-Chief of Army Group Vistula. Each of these posts required the full attention of a man, especially in serious times of war, and although I had confidence in him to do all sorts of things, the burden of his duties

exceeded the strength of a single person. By now he must have realized that it wasn't so easy to lead troops at the front.

I therefore suggested that he relinquish his command of the army group and resume his other offices.

Himmler was no longer as confident as he used to be. He wavered: 'I can't tell the Führer that. He won't allow me to do this.'

I saw my chance: 'Then allow me to tell him.' Now Himmler had to agree. That same evening I suggested to Hitler that he relieve Himmler of his command and asked him to appoint Generaloberst [Gotthard] Heinrici, previously commander of First Panzer Army in the Carpathians, as commander-in-chief of Army Group Vistula in his place. Muttering grumpily, Hitler agreed. On March 20, Heinrici was appointed.[10]

The contrast between the outgoing army group commander and his replacement could not have been starker. With a lifetime in the army and extensive command experience on the Eastern Front, Heinrici was a highly respected officer with an established record for successful defensive actions. In almost every respect, he was a product of his era. The descendant of Dutch settlers who had moved to East Prussia in the 17th century, he served in the First World War with the combination of military professionalism and blindness to politics that characterised so many German officers. The brash glitter of the Wilhelmine era left many with distaste for political affairs, and this helped men like Heinrici embrace the *Dolchstoss* legend – the belief that the German Army was betrayed by a 'stab in the back' when politicians brought down the government – that played such a major part in stoking resentment in German military circles during the Weimar years. With little knowledge of, or interest in, the civilian political landscape of Germany during the war, Heinrici and others could not understand or accept that suffering on the home front had escalated to unsustainable levels. He also shared the casual antisemitism of other Germans of his background and accepted without question the view that German Jews held too much wealth and prominence. In 1939, after listening to a speech by Alfred Rosenberg, the Nazi Party's racial specialist, Heinrici wrote to his mother:

> The Jewish question will only be solved when there are no more Jews in Germany and they [the Nazis] are determined to carry this out too. It would be best of all if there were no more Jews across Europe.[11]

Yet despite accepting Nazi policies against Jews, he married a half-Jewish woman, ultimately having to go through the process of securing the *Deutschblütigkeitserklärung* ('German blood certificate') for her that declared her an honorary Aryan. In the opening phases of *Barbarossa*, he was a corps commander and seems to have accepted with little question the need for harsh measures to prevent and later repress partisan movements – he only objected to mass executions when they took place close to his headquarters and insisted that they should be conducted out of his sight – but his letters to his wife gradually showed a growing awareness that the conflict had degenerated into an utterly brutal war that could not be won. However, his memories of what he saw as the betrayal of the German Army in the First World War left him with no inclination to join those plotting against Hitler. Like many other senior figures, he believed that another *Dolchstoss* had to be avoided at all costs, even if that cost were to include the near-complete destruction of Germany, its cities, and its people. A stocky man of modest height, Heinrici was popular with his men for his forthright and sometimes abrasive manner of speech when he visited them and was widely known – in most cases affectionately – as the *Giftzwerg* ('poison dwarf'). His career had not been spectacular; he was not a man for eye-catching or dramatic operations, but his breadth of experience was almost unmatched, as was his reputation for determined defence. These defensive skills would be tested to the limit in the coming battles to prevent the Red Army from reaching Berlin.

Having been relieved of command of Army Group Vistula, Himmler enjoyed a remarkable return to health. When Heinrici arrived at the headquarters of the army group on 22 March, he was greeted by Lammerding, who informed him that Himmler was busy in a very important meeting and couldn't be disturbed. After waiting for perhaps 15 minutes, Heinrici lost patience and sent his aide-de-camp to find Lammerding, insisting that the handover of command should begin immediately.

The long-suffering Eismann was present at the meeting that followed:

> Sitting in the midst of mountains of situation maps and other papers, Himmler held forth to Generaloberst Heinrici about his military career for, I believe, three hours. Here, for the last time, the pure layman held the spotlight. The most inconsequential things were presented in great detail. After three hours nobody knew what this actually related to. It was shocking, and had that effect on the new [army group] commander. To this man, especially, such a totally theatrical military swansong, untroubled by any factual knowledge, in a military situation that was more than serious, was deeply astonishing, indeed, downright insulting.[12]

As the rambling discourse dragged on, the telephone on Himmler's desk suddenly started ringing. After listening for a moment, Himmler passed the handset to Heinrici, telling him, 'You are the new commander, and this call concerns you.'[13] Heinrici found himself talking to General Theodor Busse, commander of

Ninth Army; as is described below, the new army group commander found himself dealing with a crisis almost as he was taking command. But Himmler wasn't finished. After Heinrici had given brief instructions to Busse, the *Reichsführer-SS* attempted to resume his monologue, but Heinrici interrupted with his characteristic bluntness and asked Himmler for his opinion about the future of Germany. Taking Heinrici to the far end of the room where the two men couldn't be overheard, Himmler informed him in a quiet tone that he was taking steps via a neutral country to commence negotiations with the Western Powers.

For Heinrici, it was staggering news. What Himmler had outlined amounted to treason – it was inconceivable that any such steps were being undertaken with Hitler's permission. Before Heinrici could learn more, Himmler left both the room and shortly after the headquarters aboard the *Steiermark*. The truth was that via an intermediary, Himmler had made contact with Count Folke Bernadotte, head of the Swedish Red Cross, and was exploring the possibility of handing over concentration camp prisoners as a prelude to arranging a ceasefire in the west, but in the paranoid environment that prevailed in German circles after the July Plot, Heinrici was left wondering whether Himmler had been attempting to draw him into an indiscretion.

The matter about which Busse had telephoned the headquarters of Army Group Vistula related to fighting near the city of Küstrin, immediately to the east of the Oder. Here, the Red Army had secured bridgeheads across the river to the north and south of the city and were gradually compressing the German toehold on the east bank. Busse now reported that the two Soviet bridgeheads on the west bank had made convergent attacks and were attempting to cut off the city entirely; prior to this, a narrow corridor had been held open, albeit constantly swept by Soviet artillery fire. In his brief conversation with Busse, Heinrici had authorised an immediate counterattack by the only armoured forces available, 25th Panzergrenadier Division and the *Müncheberg* panzer division, but by nightfall the German units were reporting that they had made little progress. The following morning, they began to be forced back.

From the moment he arrived aboard the *Steiermark* to take command of Army Group Vistula, Himmler made no personal visits to his subordinate armies. By contrast, Heinrici set off immediately. First he travelled to the headquarters of Third Panzer Army, where Manteuffel informed him that his troops were thinly spread, doing little more than monitoring the front rather than holding it in strength. He then visited Busse, who updated him on the bitter fighting around Küstrin. There seemed little hope of establishing a permanent, safe corridor to the city, and the best option was for the armoured forces in the west to launch an attack at the same time that the garrison attempted to break out towards the west.

Heinrici agreed with this assessment, but when he spoke to Guderian, he learned that Hitler had different plans. Abandoning Küstrin was forbidden; instead, an attack was to be made from the city of Frankfurt-an-der-Oder, 16 miles to the south of Küstrin, where the Germans held another small bridgehead on the east bank. A powerful force was to be concentrated here to strike towards the north, thus cutting off and destroying the Soviet Eighth Guards Army, which had closed up to and had crossed the Oder south of Küstrin. Heinrici now travelled to Berlin and persuaded Hitler that such an operation had no prospect of success. Moreover, he managed to ensure that 25th Panzergrenadier Division would remain in place rather than being sent to Frankfurt to take part in this attack. Instead, there would be a single attack on the west bank to try once more to establish firm contact with the Küstrin garrison.

In the meantime, Hitler ordered that the Luftwaffe and Kriegsmarine make strenuous attempts to destroy the bridges that the Red Army was establishing over the Oder. The only strike aircraft available were from *Kampfgeschwader 200*, effectively a special operations unit of the Luftwaffe that tested and developed new bombs, flew captured aircraft, and undertook particularly difficult missions. Oberst Werner Baumbach, the unit commander, had just a single squadron of Stukas available to attack the Oder crossings, and after the first attempt to hit the bridges, he reported to Eismann that the attacks were futile. Even if his planes could damage a bridge, it was easy for the Soviet engineers to repair them quickly, and the intense fire of anti-aircraft guns around the bridges would wear down his squadron at a disproportionate rate. Just as importantly, the aviation fuel resources available to the entire sector were so low that Baumbach suggested it would be better to use the limited fuel for fighter aircraft rather than the ineffective bombing missions. The attempt by naval engineers to destroy the bridges, using radio-controlled boats, proved to be just as ineffective.

Meanwhile, Busse's Ninth Army gathered its strength and attacked towards Küstrin again on 27 March. At first, the armour made encouraging progress, but the following day the advance came to an abrupt halt. It had been easy for the Soviet defenders to anticipate the likely axis of attack and they had positioned their anti-tank defences with skill. After suffering the losses of several tanks, the German forces faced a powerful counterattack that drove them back to their start line. In the best possible circumstances, an attack along a predicted route would have been a difficult task, but the reality was that XXXIX Panzer Corps, which oversaw the operation, was greatly outnumbered by the units of Eighth Guards Army that opposed it.

Regardless of the realities of the situation, Hitler responded to this latest setback with another of his increasingly frequent and bitter outbursts. When Guderian and others presented the details of the unsuccessful operation to the Führer, he placed the blame on Busse, complaining that the army commander had failed to provide adequate ammunition for proper artillery preparation – in the First World War, he lectured them, barrages had consumed at least ten times as many shells. Guderian responded that all of Ninth Army was struggling with crippling shortages of artillery ammunition, which led to a further outburst: Guderian should have ensured that sufficient ammunition was available. By this stage, Guderian too was growing angry. He had been struggling with poorly controlled hypertension and angina as well as a huge workload, compounded by Hitler's intransigence and interference and injuries amongst his staff – his two deputies, Generals Walther Wenck and Hans Krebs, had been injured recently, the former in a car crash and the latter less severely in the US bombing raid that struck Zossen on 15 March. Moreover, the operations staff of *OKH* was barely functional after several key figures had been placed under arrest on Hitler's orders following the abandonment of Warsaw in January contrary to the Führer's express instructions. When Hitler raged that the soldiers in the attack had failed him, Guderian responded in vain that the heavy casualties they had suffered suggested no lack of effort on their part.

When he returned to the headquarters of *OKH* in Zossen, Guderian prepared a detailed written briefing about the ammunition shortages and the casualties suffered by XXXIX Panzer Corps. Unwilling to face Hitler again, he dispatched the ailing Krebs to the evening conference. Krebs returned after midnight and informed Guderian that Hitler demanded the presence of Guderian and Busse the following day, and Guderian described the meeting:

> At 1400 on 28 March, the usual group gathered in the confined bunker in the Reich Chancellery, including General Busse. Hitler appeared. Busse was asked to present his report. After a few sentences, Hitler interrupted the general and accused him of the same omissions that I thought I had refuted the day before. After two or three sentences I was overcome with anger. I broke into Hitler's condemnations: 'Permit me to interrupt. Yesterday I explained to you in detail, both verbally and in writing, that General Busse was not to blame for the failure of the attack at Küstrin. Ninth Army used the ammunition that was assigned to it for the attack. The troops did their duty. This is proved by their unusually high losses. I therefore request that you do not blame General Busse.'
>
> Hitler then said, 'I ask all those present to leave the room except the Generalfeldmarschall [Keitel] and the Generaloberst [Guderian].' After the large audience had gone into the anteroom, Hitler spoke briefly. 'Generaloberst Guderian, your health requires an immediate six-week leave of absence.'
>
> I raised my right hand. 'I take my leave.' I walked to the door. When I had my hand on the door handle, Hitler called me back and asked, 'Please stay here until the end of the conference.' I returned to my seat in silence. The conference

participants were called back into the room and discussions continued as if nothing had happened. However, Hitler refrained from any further attacks against Busse. I was briefly asked for my opinion two or three times, and then – after endless hours – this too was over. The participants left the bunker. Keitel, Jodl, Burgdorf [Hitler's senior adjutant] and I were asked to stay.

[Hitler said,] 'Please ensure your health is restored. In six weeks the situation will be very critical. Then I will need you urgently. Where do you want to go?'

Keitel advised me to go to Bad Liebenstein. It was very nice there. I replied that the Americans had already reached there. 'Well, then to Bad Sachsa am Harz,' said the caring Generalfeldmarschall. I thanked him for his kindness and remarked that I would choose my own location and would select somewhere that could not be occupied by the enemy within the next 48 hours.

I raised my right hand again, then, accompanied by Keitel, I left the Führerbunker forever. On the way to my car, Keitel assured me that it was very right that I didn't say anything further to Hitler. What else could I have said in this situation? Any reply would have been too much.[14]

Guderian surrendered to American forces on 10 May. There were requests from the Soviet Union for him to be handed over to face war crimes charges relating to his time on the Eastern Front in 1941, but the Western Allies declined; together with other senior German officers, he joined the US Army Historical Division and helped it in writing accounts of the Second World War. These invariably attempted to show the Wehrmacht in the best possible light, fighting a highly skilled war and losing only because of Hitler's interference and overwhelming enemy numbers. Much of the post-war 'whitewashing' of the Wehrmacht – the attempt to exonerate it of any war crimes and to place all blame for such events on parts of the SS and rear area organisations – originated with the group working for the US Army. Despite his denials, there can be little question that Guderian was aware of atrocities and did nothing to prevent them – the numbers of Jews and others killed in the area behind his panzer divisions in 1941 were no different from killings elsewhere. Indeed, he participated in a propaganda film in late 1944 denying the Holocaust, even though the Soviet liberation of several concentration camps had already laid bare the atrocities that had been committed. Moreover, as chief of the general staff from mid-1944, in addition to enforcing the Nazification of the army after the failed July Plot, he oversaw the suppression of the Warsaw Uprising, doing nothing to restrain the mass slaughter of innocent civilians by German units. His claims after the war that Germany had been fighting for its very existence and had been the bulwark of Europe against the evils of Bolshevism may have had some resonance in the Cold War era, but now seem to be little more than post-facto rationalisation. He died in 1954.

Guderian had expected that Wenck would be his successor as chief of the general staff. There was no doubt that Wenck was a highly gifted and energetic staff officer, but he was still in hospital following his car crash. Instead, Krebs was given the role. He had learned Russian in the years between the wars and served as military attaché in Moscow in 1933–34 and again in 1940. Thereafter, he held a number of senior staff posts. Most of his contemporaries regarded him as a faithful follower of Hitler; whilst this may have been a factor in his replacing Guderian, the reality was that there were no obvious alternatives for the post in what remained of the Wehrmacht.

In the west, the US Army had already seized a bridge over the Rhine at Remagen on 7 March, but had established only a small bridgehead across the river. That changed on 22 and 23 March when the US Third Army and Montgomery's 21st Army Group swept across the Rhine, securing major bridgeheads. Badly worn down by fighting in the Reichswald to the west of the river, the German First Parachute Army could do little to oppose the overwhelming forces deployed against it and began to retreat towards the northeast, leaving a growing gap to the German Fifteenth Army around the Ruhr. In the days that followed, the German forces in the west fought against the Western Powers with varying degrees of determination; some, particularly SS units and those with large numbers of heavily indoctrinated teenage recruits, put up resistance that was every bit as fanatical as Hitler might have desired, but others simply laid down their weapons at the first opportunity. On 1 April, British and American forces that had bypassed the Ruhr to the north and south met at Lippstadt after an advance of about 70 miles, encircling nearly half a million German soldiers in the industrial heartland. Regardless of the willingness or otherwise of German units to put up strong resistance, there was now almost nothing between the advancing armies of the Western Powers and Berlin. In the week that followed, US forces surged forward to the Elbe, and there seemed to be a very real prospect of the German capital being captured by the Western Powers rather than the feared Red Army. Heinrici and others were aware that Germany's enemies intended to partition the country after the war, and that it was unlikely that the British and Americans would be willing to risk heavy losses by attempting to take Berlin – which would lie deep within the Soviet zone of occupation – but there remained a hope that if the Oder front could be held for long enough, the mood might change and the terror of Soviet conquest might be avoided.

The ability of the armies defending the Oder to stop the Red Army for long was questionable. At army and corps level, the names of formations were reminiscent of earlier days of victory – Third Panzer Army in the north, originally named Third Panzer Group, was one of the two major armoured forces that

Preparing for the Last Stand: The German Defences

advanced rapidly into the Soviet Union in 1941 as the main striking force of the German Army Group Centre and – briefly – threatened Moscow as winter closed in. Thereafter, it declined steadily in strength, losing most of its armoured units. Now, it had been forced back over the lower Oder with heavy losses, and on 12 March its last toehold across the river at Altdamm came under heavy attack. Briefly, during its transformation into Eleventh SS-Panzer Army, it had substantial panzer forces under its control, but many of these had been sent south to take part in the attempts to restore the corridor to Küstrin. With what remained, Manteuffel could do nothing to hold the position around Altdamm and on 19 March Hitler grudgingly gave permission for its abandonment. The last German troops pulled back across the Oder on 21 March; they left behind over 50,000 dead or missing, excessive casualties for a position of little major consequence, especially at a time when the decisive battle for Berlin was imminent.

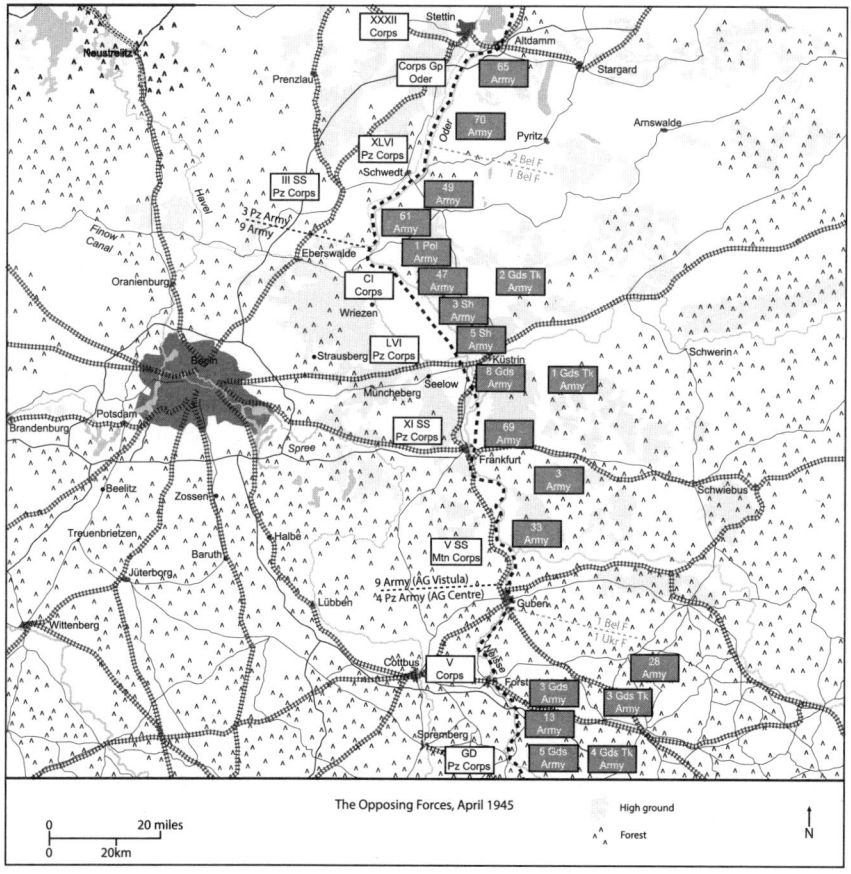

The Opposing Forces, April 1945

Manteuffel still had several corps headquarters under his command, but many were badly weakened by the recent fighting in Pomerania. The so-called 3rd Marine Division had been created in early April from the wreckage of 163rd Infantry Division, effectively destroyed in Pomerania, using naval personnel to replenish its ranks; it held a position between the lagoon of the Stettiner Haff and the coast. It was technically part of the *Festung Swinemünde Korps* ('Fortress Swinemünde Corps'); in addition to the redeployed sailors, the corps had 402nd Division, which had existed in several forms since 1940. Its latest incarnation was as a training division, using whatever units could be scraped together. The corps commander, Generalleutnant John Ansat, had commanded an infantry division in the central sector of the Eastern Front in 1941–42 and knew the reality of what lay ahead; he had little confidence that his weak units would be able to put up prolonged resistance.

Immediately to the south was XXXII Corps under General Friedrich-August Schack with another improvised division, *Divisionsgruppe Voigt* (in reality no more than three or four weak battalions), 549th Volksgrenadier Division, 281st Infantry Division, and the garrison of the city of Stettin. Schack's southern neighbour was *Korps Oder*, with a mixture of army and SS personnel forming its headquarters. It oversaw numerous units of very limited fighting power. Several anti-aircraft battalions had been grouped together as *Flak-Regiment 21*, armed with a variety of weapons that could be used against both aircraft and ground targets. *Divisionsgruppe Müller* was the most powerful unit in the corps, with two SS battlegroups, an armoured anti-tank battalion, and an armoured reconnaissance battalion. By contrast, 610th Security Division consisted of three weak SS police regiments with no artillery. Another so-called division – *Infanterie-Division Klossek* – had a single battalion of regular troops, two battalions of *Volkssturm*, and a mixture of training units, without any heavy weapons.

Defending the Oder around the town of Schwedt were the formations of XLVI Panzer Corps and III SS-Panzer Corps. The former was led by the highly experienced Generalleutnant Martin Gareis, and on paper at least was a formidable formation. In addition to numerous corps-level units, including two assault gun brigades and a heavy tank battalion armed with Tiger tanks, Gareis had several divisions. One was 547th Volksgrenadier Division, which included many of the surviving elements of 23rd *SS-Panzergrenadier-Division Nederland*. Although it was originally raised from Dutch volunteers, the units that were still in existence in March 1945 were mainly made up of Germans, including large numbers of redeployed naval personnel. Gareis also had 1st Marine Division, another unit of sailors, and 11th *SS-Panzergrenadier-Division Nordland*. Raised in 1943 around Danish and Norwegian volunteers, the division had been heavily involved in fighting on the Eastern Front for most of its existence and had a good reputation in combat.

The commander of III SS-Panzer Corps was Obergruppenführer Felix Steiner, who would be heavily involved in the final attempts by Hitler to save Berlin. After serving throughout the First World War, he joined one of the *Freikorps* formations in the turbulent years that followed and then the Reichswehr, leaving the army in 1933 to join the ranks of the Nazi Party. He was involved in the tentative plans to turn the *SA* into a new National Socialist army, and after Hitler's purge of the *SA* he became a member of the SS, steadily rising through its ranks. In late 1943, he took command of the newly formed III SS-Panzer Corps, and made rigorous changes to training regimes. In order to avoid costly trench warfare, he developed a doctrine of small assault groups of infantry, stressing the importance of initiative and physical fitness and strength. He commanded the short-lived Eleventh SS-Panzer Army before resuming command of his old corps, which now consisted of three divisions. One, *SS-Nederland*, was little more than three weak battalions, with many of its units still subordinated to 547th Volksgrenadier Division. One of his other divisions was rather stronger – 27th *SS-Grenadier-Division Langemarck*, originally made up of Flemish Belgian volunteers, had two grenadier regiments and an armoured anti-tank battalion. Steiner's last unit was 18th Panzergrenadier Division, which was in the process of being rebuilt after losing most of its personnel in fighting in East Prussia.

In addition, Manteuffel had two divisions that he held as reserves at army level. Both were made up of foreign volunteers who were serving with the SS. The first was 28th *SS-Grenadier-Division Wallonien*, another formation formed using Belgian volunteers, this time from the Walloon community. Despite its name, the division was far from division strength, with just two grenadier battalions. The other reserve formation was 33rd *SS-Grenadier Division Charlemagne*, with French volunteers. It too was in reality little more than a regiment of two grenadier battalions and a support battalion.

The army that would bear the brunt of the fighting when the Red Army attacked Berlin was Busse's Ninth Army. Busse had served as a senior staff officer for much of the war, notably as Manstein's chief of staff, first in Eleventh Army and then in Army Group South. Manstein clearly thought highly of him and he was undoubtedly a highly competent staff officer. But on many occasions, he insisted on subordinates simply obeying the instructions that he had received from above, and in particular showed little inclination to modify or ameliorate orders from Hitler that were clearly unsuited to the reality of the battlefield. It was perhaps because of this that he retained the trust of the Führer, taking command of Ninth Army as it was being badly mauled by the Soviet advance in Poland in January 1945.

Busse's most northern formation was CI Corps, originally formed as an eponymous corps commanded by General Wilhelm Berlin, who handed over command to Generalleutnant Friedrich Sixt on the eve of the Soviet attack. The strongest infantry unit in the corps was 5th Jäger Division, which Sixt had led in the past. The other two infantry units were far weaker. The first was 606th Infantry Division, with three weak regiments made up of hastily mobilised rear area units and lacking any heavy weapons; the other was *Infanterie-Division Berlin*, with just three battalions. The strongest unit in Sixt's corps was 25th Panzergrenadier Division, despite its losses in the failed battles to hold Küstrin, but although it was part of CI Corps, it could only be sent into action with Hitler's permission.

Facing the Red Army near Küstrin was General Helmuth Weidling's LVI Panzer Corps; it had been effectively destroyed in Pomerania and had been re-established using personnel from other disbanded corps headquarters. Weidling had commanded an infantry division on the Eastern Front in 1942–43 before taking command of LVI Panzer Corps. During this time, Weidling issued orders for tens of thousands of Soviet civilians to be rounded up in his area of operations and incarcerated in primitive compounds where typhus and other diseases were rife – indeed, there were suggestions that they were deliberately infected with typhus in the expectation that the disease would spread to Red Army troops who were advancing towards the area. As he prepared to face the Red Army in 1945, he had three divisions under his command. The first was 9th Fallschirmjäger Division; the second was 20th Panzergrenadier Division; and the third was *Panzer-Division Müncheberg*.

To Weidling's south was XI SS-Panzer Corps, commanded by Obergruppenführer Matthias Kleinheisterkamp. He had three infantry divisions – 303rd *Infanterie-Division Döberitz*, 169th Infantry Division, and 712th Infantry Division. All were far from full strength. He also had the new *Panzergrenadier-Division Kurmark*, created in early 1945 around replacement and training units of the *Grossdeutschland* panzergrenadier division. The final unit in Ninth Army's defensive line was Obergruppenführer Friedrich Jeckeln's V SS-Mountain Corps. It had the weak 286th Infantry Division and 391st Security Division, 32nd *SS-Freiwilligen-Grenadier Division 30. Januar*, created in great haste at the end of January around the personnel of training units strengthened by just a handful of experienced front-line soldiers. A further unit, *Division Rägener*, consisted of just three *Volkssturm* battalions, a police battalion, and the personnel of a training unit.

Beyond the southern flank of Ninth Army was Fourth Panzer Army, commanded by General Fritz-Hubert Gräser and part of Schörner's Army Group

Centre. When Konev's Front erupted out of the Sandomierz bridgehead across the Vistula in January 1945, Fourth Panzer Army was effectively destroyed in just a few days, and its latest incarnation included the usual mixture of the remnants of former units and new, improvised formations. Gräser had three corps – from north to south, V Corps, *Panzerkorps Grossdeutschland*, and LVI Panzer Corps. It would be General Kurt Wäger's V Corps, with 342nd, 72nd, and 275th Infantry Divisions, that would face the main weight of the coming offensive. In reality, none of these amounted to even a single regiment, but they were expected to hold the same frontage as a full-strength infantry division.

Ever since the terrible winter battles outside Moscow in late 1941, German officers had repeatedly complained about the poor quality of replacement drafts. Training regimes that might have been appropriate in earlier years no longer sufficed, particularly for men who were thrown into the inferno of the Eastern Front. Recruits arrived in the front line with a reasonable level of basic training, but often with little or no familiarity with heavy weapons such as mortars, anti-tank guns, and even machine-guns. Most German armies rapidly established 'schools' behind the front line where they attempted to remedy these deficiencies, but as the war progressed recruits were sent to the front after shorter and shorter spells of initial preparation. By the closing stages of the war, this had reached previously unimaginable levels. In late March 1945, Helmut Altner, a young Berliner aged just 17, received his conscription papers and was ordered to report to an army depot in the city. His memoir reflects the ability of many Germans at the time to hold contradictory points of view at the same time: on the one hand, his descriptions of the devastation of his home city as a result of air raids and the increasingly wretched state of the population are vivid; but on the other hand, he remained convinced that Germany was about to turn the tables on its enemies and final victory could still be achieved. In his diary, he noted the scenes as his transport took him to the barracks in Spandau, in the west of Berlin:

> We rapidly approach the centre of Spandau and here, for the first time, we see the powerful extent of the damage. The empty window frames of a burnt-out factory across the way stare accusingly at the world, fallen beams glowing gently and occasionally flaring up with the breeze, while the owners of a still burning house watch from across the street speechlessly as the fruits of years of hard toil go sky high. Dark figures slink through the destroyed quarter, looking about them furtively like hyenas on the prowl …
>
> The further we penetrate this destroyed, burning quarter, the more depressed we get by the atmosphere. Women are crying quietly, stopping people to ask anxiously about certain streets and if many have been killed. They are answered in

low voices. One no longer recognises in these faces the heroism mentioned so often by Goebbels in the first years of the war. On the contrary, one sees only a dull, undisguised despair.[15]

Altner and his fellow teenage recruits – with a few older men who had been deemed either too old or too disabled for military service in the past – spent barely a week in Spandau. They were issued ill-assorted items of uniform, documentation, and given a few sessions of drill; they were also required to witness executions of men who had been found guilty of desertion or cowardice. Then, without having fired a shot (or in many cases even held a weapon), they were sent east by train. In Seelow, they switched to a train on a local line, and while they awaited their departure they saw a train that had just arrived from Frankfurt-an-der-Oder. Women on the train had bundles of potatoes and other food items that they had scavenged or bartered and were attempting to take back to Berlin, and the recruits witnessed railway police supported by SS personnel – probably men from the *Allgemeine-SS* ('General Service SS') rather than the front-line *Waffen-SS* ('Armed SS') – forcing the women to hand over their packages of food. Silently, a group of experienced soldiers who were aboard the same train as Altner dismounted and formed a cordon between the civilians and the SS, even pointing their weapons at the SS personnel. They then escorted the women back aboard their train and ensured they departed without further intervention.[16]

Other men heading for Army Group Vistula were rather better prepared. The 21-year-old Leutnant Karl-Hermann Tams had already been wounded twice on the Eastern Front and had just completed a company commanders' course when he was sent east at the end of March. His return to 20th Panzergrenadier Division raised mixed feelings: on the one hand, he was back with old comrades; on the other hand, they all feared what lay ahead. He was assigned to the division's field replacement battalion and oversaw the training of the newest arrivals:

> One could hardly believe it, but these men had been assigned to us because of the lack of ships for them to man, there being no alternative for them. They were all experienced in naval warfare, many of them having had their ships sunk under them, and I should stress that these sailors generally made an outstanding impression on us. They were a very likeable lot, as were our own soldiers, who were all up to Ivan's cunning tricks and knew how to turn them to our own advantage. In a short time, however, all of them were killed in action. I still maintain that our regiment in Seelow was undermined by the faulty assessment of these men's ability to convert into infantry. That applies above all to the employment of two *Volkssturm* companies in our sector. Their losses were devastating.[17]

Preparing for the Last Stand: The German Defences

After taking command of Army Group Vistula, Heinrici wasted no time, visiting his subordinates and studying reconnaissance information about the Soviet units facing him. He rapidly determined that the Red Army was concentrating significant forces immediately to the north of Küstrin; there seemed little likelihood of any attacks being made between this area and the coast. This was unsurprising – the flat terrain, with widespread areas of soft ground, was unsuitable for conducting a major offensive. Similarly, the area south of Frankfurt-an-der-Oder looked an unlikely area for an attack due to the dense woodland to the west of the Oder. Most of the coming assault was correctly viewed as likely to strike in the Frankfurt–Küstrin sector; this represented the most direct line of advance to Berlin, and it was important to strengthen the defences in this region. By doing so, Heinrici and his army commanders were left with no additional infantry resources in reserve. Once the units in the front line were worn down, there would be no prospect of replenishing them or building a new line of resistance. In an attempt to make their inadequate resources stretch further, the Germans deployed *Volkssturm* in areas where they assessed there was little chance of a Soviet attack; these units were desperately weak, but major risks had to be taken merely to create a continuous front line.

In the midst of his preparations, Heinrici was invited to lunch with Göring. In the 1930s, Göring had acquired a large estate to the northeast of Berlin and had extensively rebuilt the hunting lodge, turning it into a rural retreat that he later stocked with art treasures looted from occupied Europe. Named Carinhall in honour of Göring's first wife, it was the venue of many grand feasts and parties during the Nazi era and it was just a few miles from Heinrici's headquarters. Although Göring was no longer the dominant figure within the regime that he had been in earlier years, it was impossible for Heinrici to ignore the invitation and he had to make time for the lunch appointment. He almost certainly had an inkling of the reason for the invitation. Unlike the armed forces of other nations, the German parachute formations were part of the Luftwaffe rather than the army, and one of the divisions that had been assigned to Heinrici was 9th Fallschirmjäger Division. Heinrici had been assured that these men were veteran soldiers with valuable combat experience of battlefields like Monte Cassino in Italy and elsewhere, but Heinrici knew that even if the division contained a small core of such veterans, most of its personnel were likely to be far less experienced – either new recruits, or men who had been reassigned from other parts of the Luftwaffe and had little training or aptitude for ground warfare. He had expressed his doubts about the resilience of the division, and the following day Göring had telephoned Heinrici to complain about the criticism. Göring announced that he would not assign a second *Fallschirmjäger* division to Army Group Vistula. Instead, he would send it to Schörner's Army Group Centre further to the south; it was another example of how the whims of senior figures in the Nazi regime could take precedence over purely military considerations. At the lunch, Göring criticised Heinrici further, telling him that he had decided to tour the nearby defensive positions and had concluded that the men were too indisciplined, relaxing in their dugouts and playing cards rather than improving their entrenchments. Heinrici chose not to argue and left as soon as he could. The lavishly decorated 'hunting lodge' with its beautifully manicured gardens and estate, heavily guarded by Göring's personal bodyguard of Luftwaffe personnel, was a jarring contrast to the devastated state of nearby Berlin or the muddy squalor in which most of the soldiers of Army Group Vistula prepared to face the Red Army.[18]

Despite all of these handicaps, Heinrici and his subordinates had grounds for cautious confidence. If the Red Army attacked along the shortest axis towards Berlin, the terrain would work in favour of the defenders. The Oder itself had been artificially widened by the retreating Germans, with floodgates being opened to make both banks swampy; this forced the Red Army into constructing ever longer bridges that spanned both the river and the muddy banks. It also reduced the area on the west of the Oder, within the Soviet bridgeheads, where assault forces could assemble. The west bank of the river forms a generally flat area up to five miles from the shore, known as the Oderbruch, before rising steeply to a ridge: the Seelow Heights, from where there is a commanding view of the line of approach of an army attacking from the east. There were few routes from the Oderbruch to the top of the ridge that could be used by tanks, and this gave Heinrici and his forces a good chance of concentrating their firepower where it would be most needed.

During their long retreat across the western Soviet Union and Poland, the Germans had come to adopt a defensive plan that consisted of three defensive zones. The first would be on the western edge of the Oderbruch, consisting of three distinct defensive lines; the first two were handicapped by the high water table, preventing proper trenches from being dug, and shortages of concrete and other supplies further hindered the construction of a comprehensive defensive line. Nevertheless, there were abundant quantities of mines and these were deployed in large numbers. Ideally, the second and third lines would have been as strong as the first, but in many cases the positions consisted of little more than shallow foxholes. However, this worked both ways: whilst the defences might be modest, they were also difficult to detect and it seems that Soviet reconnaissance failed to spot them.

The second defensive zone was known as the *Hardenbergstellung* ('Hardenberg Position') and ran along the edge of the Seelow Heights. It consisted of two lines of trenches and foxholes, with much of the field artillery deployed in the second line. It was normal practice to construct multiple firing positions for guns so that they could be moved quickly, and to confuse Soviet reconnaissance about which were actually intended for use during the coming battle, but the shortage of fuel and trucks meant that many of the guns were effectively static. Nevertheless, if the Soviet forces were to penetrate through the first zone and then the first line of the *Hardenbergstellung*, the artillery positions would provide retreating German units with an area where they could rally and resume the battle.

The final line of defence was the *Wotanstellung* ('Wotan Position'), a further six to eight miles to the west. This consisted of three defensive lines; ideally, this was where armoured forces would be held in readiness for counterattacks, but there were few such units available. Busse later described the terrain on which his army would fight:

> Despite the difficulties arising from the lack of cover and the limitations in the construction of positions there was an advantage with this terrain in which ditches and swamps precluded the use of armour. Attacks could only succeed using great masses of infantry, strong artillery with plentiful ammunition, and strong air forces. For the defence it was essential to destroy the attackers without the loss of too much ground ... A counterattack with armoured forces would only be successful on the heights west of the Oderbruch. This would have to be done by hook or by crook before the enemy could establish himself, for the heights formed the critical point for the Russian armoured forces. Their retention or loss, dependent upon the situation and strengths, would decide the result of the coming battle.[19]

It was essential to stockpile as much ammunition as possible for the coming fighting, but supplies were desperately limited. German factories were still producing large quantities of weapons and munitions, but the widespread disruption of rail transport as a result of strategic bombing and shortages of coal for locomotives made distribution of factory production very difficult. At best, Busse's gunners would have sufficient shells for two days of combat.

Between 5 and 7 April, Heinrici attended several conferences in Hitler's bunker. Whilst the Luftwaffe was a shadow of its former self, it was still able to conduct valuable reconnaissance missions and reports indicated that huge columns of Soviet vehicles and troops were assembling along the Oder line. There could be no doubt that an offensive was imminent. What was particularly worrying was the growing strength of the Red Army along the lower Oder, opposite Third Panzer Army – all calculations to date had been based on an assumption that the coming battle would be fought almost exclusively in Ninth Army's sector, but there was now evidence of additional attacks to the north. Heinrici had been forced to release several panzer divisions for use elsewhere – Hitler had decreed that they were needed for a counteroffensive in Hungary, where the last oilfields available to Germany were being overrun. When Heinrici asked for this decision to be reversed, Hitler replied that the threat facing Army Group Centre, in Saxony and Czechoslovakia, was far greater: Generalfeldmarschall Ferdinand Schörner, the commander of the army group, feared a major Soviet offensive of even greater power than that facing Heinrici, directed towards Prague. Heinrici pointed out that without reinforcements, his units would be unable to defend Berlin against the coming offensive, but Hitler had no answer other than to demand ever greater degrees of fanatical determination by the troops in the front line.

As was often the case, other senior figures at the conference now made offers of help in an attempt to appease Hitler. Göring declared that he could release 100,000 men from the Luftwaffe as there were insufficient aircraft and fuel for all his units. Himmler also offered to provide reinforcements, claiming that the SS had reserves of 25,000 men. Admiral Karl Dönitz, head of the navy, also promised to release men no longer needed to man large warships. Heinrici knew better than to challenge the reality of these numbers, and instead expressed reservations about the value of men with little or no field training or experience. Krebs, the new chief of the general staff at *OKH*, suggested that they could be deployed in key positions in the *Hardenbergstellung* – this would spare them the ordeal of being caught in any preliminary Soviet bombardment. Hitler declared his agreement. In the event, only about 30,000 Luftwaffe personnel appeared, with few weapons and no training. The few naval personnel who were provided could do little more than occupy secondary positions in Third Panzer Army's sector, and almost none of the SS reserves that Himmler had described ever materialised.

Although he was unable to reverse Hitler's decision to transfer the priceless panzer divisions to the south, Heinrici's concerns about the efficacy of the soldiers he was being offered gave him an opportunity to ask Hitler for other concessions. During 1942, 1943, and 1944, German commanders on the Eastern Front had devised a means of mitigating the effect of the increasingly heavy Red Army bombardments that preceded Soviet offensives. When it was judged that the attack was imminent, troops were ordered to abandon their forward positions and fall back to the second defensive line, which was intended as the main line of resistance. The Soviet shells would then strike empty positions and even if a proportion of the barrage was directed against the second line, it would nonetheless have less effect than if the full weight of shelling had fallen on the defenders. Hitler had steadily increased the rigidity of his supervision of the military, insisting that any withdrawals could only be carried out with his specific permission, and this threatened to make the use of the last-minute withdrawal impossible. Heinrici had executed precisely such a manoeuvre – in contravention of Hitler's standing orders – a few weeks before in Czechoslovakia with great success, and he now raised the issue with Hitler, informing the Führer of his intention to use these tactics in defence of Berlin. He described the preparatory steps he had already ordered to create a second line of defences prior to the conference with Hitler:

> This second line of battle was set up … although there were some difficulties because the troops never understood the reason for this and raised objections. They declared: 'We have been building for four weeks and have made dugouts and want to defend ourselves. Now, when the battle is about to begin, we are supposed to leave these good fortifications and move away.' It never occurred to them that nothing would be left of these good fortifications if they were to fight, and nothing would be left of them [the soldiers] either. I have always used the comparison that, if I'm in a steel mill, I don't put my head under the trip hammer that comes down and smashes it, but that I pull it back and withdraw in time. This tactic was, in this case, also approved by Hitler, to the surprise of all listeners.[20]

The unhappiness of the soldiers constructing the positions is interesting. Veterans of the Eastern Front would have had no doubts about the wisdom of the plan and, despite the back-breaking work involved, would have been willing to construct a second line in order to avoid having to endure the brutal Soviet artillery preparation; rather, it is likely that the incomprehension and complaints came from the numerous replacement drafts, *Volkssturm*, and redeployed sailors and Luftwaffe personnel. This in turn indicates that a significant proportion of the German defenders had little hard experience of warfare against the Red Army.

There was a further meeting in Berlin on 8 April, where the latest intelligence information about the Red Army's dispositions was assessed. Once again, with limited reconnaissance resources and aircraft, the Luftwaffe seems to have had little difficulty in conducting far-ranging flights over territory occupied by the Red Army. Accounts written after the war by Soviet aviators frequently comment on the ease with which they dealt with the few remaining German planes that appeared, but the reports presented to the Führer's conference on 8 April suggest that Soviet air superiority did not translate into complete control of the airspace. Several major redeployments of Red Army units had been detected, and it was clear that three Fronts – 2nd Belarusian Front in the north, 1st Belarusian Front in the critical sector closest to Berlin, and 1st Ukrainian Front to the south – were concentrating their resources. Schörner, the commander of Army Group Centre, was present at the conference and his view – that he would have to bear the brunt of the offensive by 1st Ukrainian Front – seems to have been generally accepted. At the very least, there was no awareness that 1st Ukrainian Front intended to make its main effort northwest towards Berlin rather than west and southwest towards Prague. Given the nature of the theatre in which the coming battles would be fought, it was impossible for the Red Army to hide its concentrations, and the Germans also had considerable experience of calculating precisely when the preparations would be complete and the offensive would begin. The conference was told that the likely start date of the assault would be in one week, on 15 April. Such an assessment was crucial if Heinrici's planned withdrawal to his second line, in order to avoid the brutal punishment of the Soviet artillery preparation, was to be successful.

Berlin itself was divided into nine defence zones, designated by the letters A to H, with Z for the central area. As is described later, the command arrangements for the city were unnecessarily complex, with overlapping agencies competing for resources and often issuing contradictory instructions. Obstacles were prepared by different bodies with little or no regard to arrangements being made by other groups; the army, which would ultimately fight in the German capital, was barely consulted. Civilians were dragooned into work parties to dig trenches and bunkers; damaged tramcars were filled with rubble and used as roadblocks; and the city's widespread *S-Bahn* system, which in many places ran on rails raised above the streets, was also put to use for defence. Just how effective these defences would be was questionable.

Meanwhile, Altner and his fellow recruits were belatedly receiving a modicum of training. They had been deployed in the third defensive zone and spent several hours of most days undergoing weapons training, both firing guns and familiarising themselves with them. A week after they had left Spandau, they felt competent in the use of machine-guns and had undergone basic training in the use of *Panzerfausts*, but there was no opportunity for even the most rudimentary training in fieldcraft or tactics. On 12 April, the recruits discussed the latest news reports: Roosevelt, the American president, was dead. Was this the moment that the alliance arrayed against Germany would break apart? In some parts of Germany, the news of the US president's death was greeted with jubilation. Goebbels had unearthed two astrological charts prepared in earlier years, one in 1918 and one in 1933. He highlighted that these documents had predicted early German victories

Preparing for the Last Stand: The German Defences

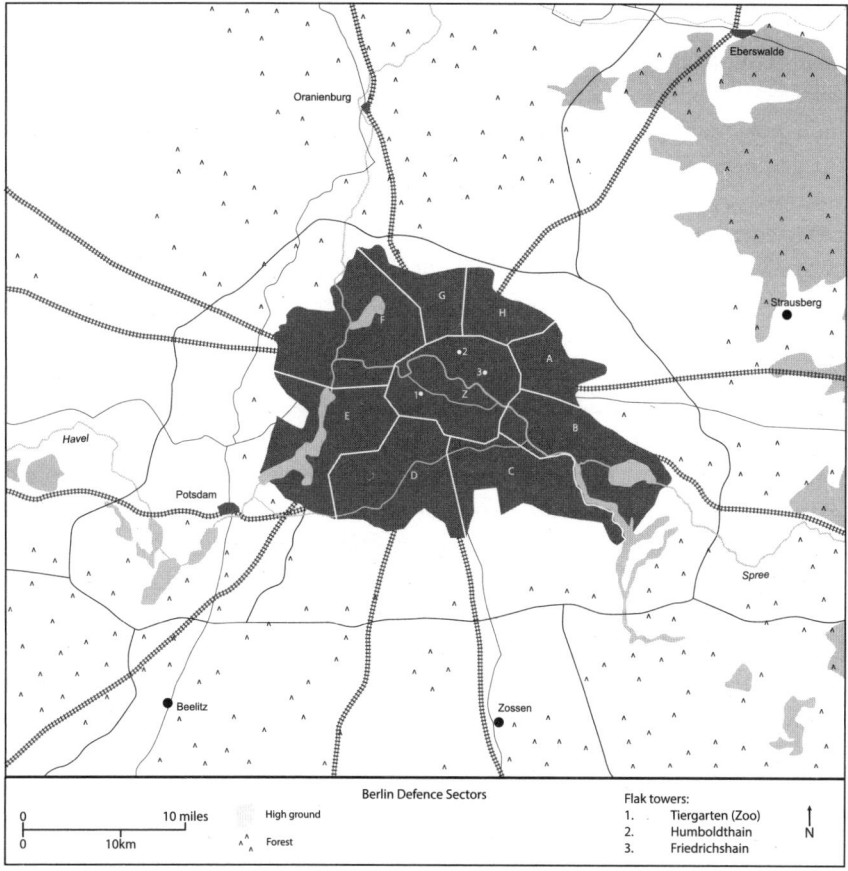

in a war commencing in the late 1930s, followed by widespread setbacks and a stunning victory in April 1945. Excitedly, he drew parallels between Roosevelt's death and previous moments of history. In 1762, Czarina Elizabeth had died at a moment when Frederick II's Prussia seemed to be facing certain defeat, and this had heralded both the withdrawal of Russia from the alliance against Prussia and a resurgence in the fortunes of Frederick. For Goebbels, this was no coincidence. History was surely about to repeat itself, and as had been the case in 1762, the unwieldy alliance against Germany would collapse.

Other rumours added to the general sense that there might be new developments in Germany's favour. In the trenches of Army Group Vistula, there was talk of imminent reinforcements – these were the tens of thousands of soldiers promised by Göring and Himmler – and there were suggestions that the Red Army was overstretched and would collapse rapidly. Once the reinforcements arrived, said the rumours, a new offensive would commence, timed for Hitler's birthday – the Führer had promised at least 500 new tanks and a thousand artillery pieces. A few of Altner's fellow recruits openly questioned such beliefs, but if others also had doubts, they kept them to themselves.[21]

Early on 12 April, reports reached Heinrici's headquarters that the front line was under shellfire. Clarification rapidly followed: the bombardment, though heavy, was restricted to just a few locations. This was no surprise. A standard part of Soviet operations was to launch preliminary attacks under the guise of 'reconnaissance in force'. This served several purposes. Firstly, there was the possibility that the Germans would respond to these attacks and thus reveal the firing positions of their artillery and other heavy weapons. Secondly, German reserves might be drawn into the front line and thus rendered unavailable when the real offensive started. And thirdly, the Red Army hoped to secure better starting positions for the offensive. In this case, most of the activity was around the bridgehead over the Oder to the north of Küstrin. The probing attack was precisely directed, with its main weight falling on the seam between two improvised German divisions – 606th Division, which had been created from the remnants of 344th Infantry Division and had recently been transferred from the lower Rhine in the Netherlands, and *Infanterie-Division Berlin*. Both divisions were forced back. The following day, the Red Army widened its attack to encompass the divisions to the north and south. The northern assault was made across the Oder against 5th Jäger Division; despite the use of a smokescreen to try to give the attacking troops some cover as they crossed the river, the Germans inflicted heavy losses with a mixture of machine-gun and artillery fire and the attack failed. But elsewhere, the defences were driven back once again. The only consolation for Heinrici and Busse was that the aggressive probing attacks were still contained largely within the first defensive zone on the Oderbruch. The vital Seelow Heights remained firmly in German hands. But the bridgehead to the north of Küstrin was significantly enlarged and observers on the heights could see more Soviet troops crossing the river from the east. Everything suggested that the predictions about the date of the attack looked reasonably accurate: the real test of Busse's defences was about to begin. Late on 15 April, Heinrici ordered his troops to commence their last-moment withdrawal from their foremost positions.

Chapter 4

THE RED ARMY: PLANS FOR VENGEANCE

Amongst the German units destroyed in Stalingrad in early 1943 was 297th Infantry Division. As the last exhausted, emaciated soldiers of the division surrendered to the Red Army in February, a Soviet officer stood on a pile of rubble and watched them trudge past. He gestured at the ruins of Stalingrad, the gaunt windowless buildings and the mounds of debris, and shouted at the prisoners: 'That's how Berlin is going to look!'[1] Now, a little over two years later, the fulfilment of that promise was imminent. Revenge for the devastation inflicted upon Stalingrad and so many other cities and towns across the Soviet Union would be delivered by arguably three of the best senior commanders in the Red Army.

Konstantin Konstantinovich Rokossovsky was born in 1896, the son of a family with connections to the Polish aristocracy. His birthname was Konstany Ksaweriewicz, and his place of birth is variously described as being Warsaw or Velikiye Luki. Orphaned as a child, he joined the cavalry as a teenager and Russified his name to make it easier for his fellow soldiers to pronounce. He proved to be a skilled soldier, surviving two wounds, and was an early adherent of the Red Army, leading cavalry formations during the Russian Civil War. In the years that followed, he became a close associate of other men who would be prominent in the Red Army, particularly Zhukov and Semen Konstantinovich Timoshenko, and enthusiastically embraced the concepts articulated by Marshal Mikhail Nikolayevich Tukhashevsky about the use of armoured and mechanised forces to conduct 'deep battle' operations. This may have contributed to his arrest in 1937, when Stalin's purges of Soviet society reached the ranks of the Red Army – Tukhashevsky was arrested in May and tortured into signing a confession that he had been plotting against Stalin, and similar arrests and mistreatment of known associates followed. Many signed confessions and implicated others purely in attempts at self-preservation, hoping that such denunciations might result in leniency, and it is possible that some arrested officers may have named Rokossovsky. In any case, his Polish ancestry and his enthusiasm for tanks (as opposed to cavalry, still favoured by several of Stalin's closest associates) were sufficient to bring him under suspicion.

Despite severe mistreatment – including having several teeth knocked out of his mouth – Rokossovsky refused to sign confessions to having links with Polish and Japanese intelligence officers. During his captivity, he refused to assign blame to Stalin for his arrest; he told fellow prisoners that the purges and persecutions were entirely the work of the *Narodny Komissariat Vnutrennikh Del* ('People's Commissariat of Internal Affairs' or '*NKVD*', the forerunner of the *KGB*). He remained in captivity until March 1940 when he was released without having been charged or convicted. He was sent to the Black Sea coast to recuperate from his ordeal; he studiously refused to discuss or write about his prison experiences in the years that followed.

The failures of the Red Army in the years immediately before the German invasion of 1941 – first during the occupation of eastern Poland in the autumn of 1939, then during the Winter War with Finland – had led to major restructuring of the armed forces and there was an urgent need for experienced and talented officers. Timoshenko, now in charge of the military reforms, appointed Rokossovsky as commander of V Cavalry Corps. The German invasion of the Soviet Union found him commanding a mechanised corps, and within weeks he was appointed to lead Fourth Army, but almost immediately he was ordered to take command of a mixture of units in the Battle of Smolensk. During the heavy fighting for the city, he mounted repeated counterattacks and helped thousands of Soviet soldiers escape encirclement; the fierce battles and the consequent delay on the German advance were major factors in preventing the Wehrmacht from achieving its intention to destroy the Red Army and to capture Leningrad, Moscow, and other key locations before the onset of winter.

After playing a leading role in the defence of Moscow in the winter of 1941–42, Rokossovsky was hospitalised after being wounded and returned to service in the summer as a Front commander, first in the central sector and then in the crucial battles around Stalingrad, where his Don Front formed the northern pincer of the forces that encircled the German Sixth Army. He then oversaw the crushing of the trapped German forces. He commanded the defence of the northern side of the Kursk salient during the summer of 1943 and his Front was renamed 1st Belarusian Front later that year. The following year, this Front played a major role in *Bagration*, the devastating Soviet offensive that tore apart the German Army Group Centre and overran Belarus, and Rokossovsky then advanced to the eastern suburbs of Warsaw. This placed his armies on the most direct axis leading west towards Berlin, and Rokossovsky spent much of the autumn fending off German counterattacks and making preparations for the next phase of operations, which would take the Soviet troops across Poland. As Rokossovsky's staff officers began the laborious business of drawing up detailed plans and orders, he visited Sixty-Ninth Army on 12 November, deployed in a bridgehead over the Vistula near Warsaw:

> I returned to the Front command post in the evening. We had just assembled in the mess when the duty officer reported that *Stavka* wanted me on the telephone. Stalin was on the other end, and he told me that I was being appointed commander of 2nd Belarusian Front. This was so unexpected that I blurted without thinking, 'What have I done to be transferred from the main to a secondary sector?'[2]

Rokossovsky's new command was immediately to the north, facing East Prussia and northern Poland. Stalin placated him by saying that this would not be a secondary sector; the next offensive would require close cooperation between 1st Ukrainian Front in the south and 1st and 2nd Belarusian Fronts in the north, and all would play key roles in the operation. Rokossovsky moved to his new command and led his forces in the January offensive in an advance that skirted the southern part of East Prussia before angling north to reach the Baltic coast. Thereafter, his armies played a leading role in the conquest of Pomerania, and by the end of the winter were gathering along the lower Oder, ready to strike into north Germany to isolate Berlin from the north.

Rokossovsky's replacement as commander of 1st Belarusian Front was Zhukov, perhaps the most famous Soviet commander of the war. In the early stages of the war, Stalin appointed senior figures to oversee the cooperation of two or more fronts in major operations, and at first turned to his inner circle of old comrades from the days of the Russian Civil War – Timoshenko, and Marshals Semen Mikhailovich Budenny and Kliment Yefremovich Voroshilov – but in many respects the skills that had brought them to prominence in the 1920s were now out of date, and their operational performance was usually poor. Instead, as the conflict progressed, Stalin called upon two other figures to play leading roles in such coordinating tasks. One was Aleksandr Mikhailovich Vasilevsky, who in 1945 was chief of the general staff. Amongst those on all sides who survived the war to write their memoirs, Vasilevsky is almost unique in that his personal account makes little attempt to glorify his own contribution. Instead, the self-effacing Vasilevsky went to great lengths to give credit to other officers, even interpreting unfair personal criticism from Stalin as no more than the stress of high command. Stalin rapidly recognised his lack of personal political ambition and showed a great deal of trust in him; the planning and execution of the encirclement of the German Sixth Army at Stalingrad can be attributed largely to Vasilevsky, but it is typical of the man that his name rarely features in many accounts of the decisive campaign. When the Red Army launched Operation *Bagration* to destroy the German Army Group Centre in Belarus in the summer of 1944, Vasilevsky coordinated the efforts of 3rd Belarusian and 1st Baltic Fronts on the northern side of the operation with great success and then took control of all Fronts that were advancing into the Baltic region. In February 1945, Colonel General Ivan Danilovich Cherniakhovsky, commander of 3rd Belarusian Front, was killed in an explosion in East Prussia, caused either by a landmine or random artillery fire, and Vasilevsky took control of the Front for the rest of the war.

The other man to whom Stalin repeatedly turned throughout the war to coordinate the actions of several Fronts was Zhukov, who first came to prominence in 1939 when he led the Red Army to a crushing victory over Japanese forces at Khalkin Gol in the far east. Even at that stage of his career, he had established a fearsome reputation for stubbornness and ruthless determination, showing little hesitation in dismissing or arresting any officers that he regarded as failing to carry out his orders. During the fighting against the Japanese, Petr Grigoryevich Grigorenko was a staff officer in the headquarters to which Zhukov was answerable, and he later recalled that Zhukov submitted large numbers of reports of severe punishments:

> At this time, there were already 17 men condemned to death. It wasn't just lawyers who were shocked by the details of the cases. In every case, there was either a report from the chief of staff, in which he wrote 'So-and-so received such-and-such an order and did not follow it' and a resolution on the report of 'Tribunal. Judge. To be shot' or a note from Zhukov: 'So-and-so received such-and-such an order from me personally and did not carry it out. Judgement: to be shot.' A verdict, nothing more. No interrogation protocols, no investigations, no examination. Nothing at all. Just a single piece of paper and a sentence.[3]

In the context of Stalin's purges of the armed forces, such brutal and often arbitrary imposition of the harshest discipline was entirely acceptable, and Zhukov seemed just the sort of officer that Stalin wanted in the upper ranks of the army. Shortly after the war with Germany began, Zhukov was sent to some of the most difficult theatres and further enhanced his standing with the Soviet leader, though the extent to which he was justified in claiming credit is questionable. When he arrived in Leningrad as the Wehrmacht approached the city, the German forces had already been ordered not to proceed into the urban area and instead to establish a siege perimeter from which Leningrad could be bombarded while its occupants starved to death. Characteristically, Zhukov imposed harsh discipline on the defending forces, summarily dismissing those whom he deemed to have failed to show the required standard of leadership, and returned to oversee the defence of Moscow with his reputation embellished. It is open to question just how effective his interventions in Leningrad were; at best, they stiffened the resolve of some of the defenders, but most of those trying to protect Leningrad needed little motivation to continue the struggle.

Zhukov also received considerable credit for the conduct of the fighting around Moscow in which the German forces were thrown back in disarray, and on this occasion, the credit was more justified. However, the Soviet victory outside Moscow owed a great deal to factors beyond Zhukov's control. The German forces arrayed against the city represented most of the panzer formations that were on the Eastern Front backed by a formidable array of infantry divisions, but all of these formations were far from full strength. The Wehrmacht was operating at the end of grossly over-extended lines of communication and simply supplying front-line units was a huge challenge. Partly due to the poor road network, partly due to fuel shortages, and partly due to the sheer quantities of supplies needed, operations in the Soviet Union were highly dependent upon railway lines, and the Soviet railways were of a different gauge to those to the west. Work on re-pinning lines so that trains could run without interruption was slow, and although Zhukov marshalled his armies with great effect to defeat the German pincers that were closing on Moscow, it is unlikely that the Wehrmacht had the strength to capture the city. Just as the Germans were determined to fight for their capital in 1945, regardless of how hopeless the overall situation seemed, the Red Army would have been equally committed to making a stand in Moscow, and the German infantry units in particular lacked the numbers needed to fight their way through such a large urban area.

The undoubted success of the Red Army in beating back the German spearheads was followed by a series of costly offensives, resulting in heavy losses for little significant gain. In his memoirs, Zhukov attempted to assign responsibility for this to Stalin. He described a conference held on 5 January 1942:

After [Marshal Boris Mikhailovich] Shaposhnikov [at that time, chief of the general staff] had given information about the situation on all parts of the front and a presentation of the draft plans, Stalin said, 'The Germans are dismayed after the defeat near Moscow; they are poorly prepared for winter. Now is the most opportune moment to launch a general offensive. The enemy expects us to delay our offensive until spring so that, having gathered our strength, we will then resume active operations. He wants to buy time to get his breath back.'

As I recall, nobody present objected to this, and Stalin developed his idea further. 'Our task,' he reasoned, pacing as usual around the office, 'is to deny the Germans any respite, to drive them west without pause, to force them to use up their reserves before spring …'

Having outlined the plans, Stalin invited those present to speak.

'In the western sector [i.e. to the west of Moscow],' I reported, 'where the most favourable conditions have been created and the enemy hasn't yet managed to restore the combat effectiveness of his units, we must continue the offensive. But for a successful outcome, it is necessary to replenish and strengthen our troops with fresh drafts, military equipment, and reserves, primarily with tank units. If we do not receive this reinforcement, the offensive cannot be successful.

'As for the [proposed] offensive of our troops near Leningrad and in the southwest sector, our troops there face substantial enemy defences. Without the presence of powerful artillery formations, they won't be able to break through these defences; they will become exhausted and will suffer large, unjustified losses. I am in favour of strengthening the western sector and conducting a more powerful offensive there.'

'We currently don't yet have the material capabilities sufficient to ensure a simultaneous offensive on all fronts,' [Nikolai Alekseyevich] Voznesensky [a senior member of Stalin's government] added in support of me.

'I spoke with Timoshenko,' replied Stalin. 'He is in favour of action in the southwest sector. We need to grind down the Germans faster so that they cannot attack in the spring. Who else wishes to speak?' There was no answer …

As we left the conference room, Shaposhnikov said, 'You argued in vain. The issue was decided in advance by the supreme commander.'

'Then why did he ask our opinion?'

'I don't know, my dear fellow, I don't know,' replied Boris Mikhailovich, sighing deeply.[4]

Whilst it is possible that Zhukov raised doubts about the wisdom of such widespread attacks, he showed no hesitation in imposing his customary harsh discipline on his subordinates in executing the planned attacks, even though they were clearly resulting in precisely the heavy, unjustified losses he had anticipated. He then followed this with a series of bloody and futile assaults on the German-held salient around Rzhev, resulting in huge loss of life for no significant gain.[5] Later, this entire series of operations would be largely forgotten in Soviet accounts, and any mention was restricted to claims that the attacks tied down or degraded German resources. Nonetheless, Zhukov managed to emerge from these ferocious battles with his reputation remarkably intact and then played a prominent role in the Battle of Kursk in 1943 before overseeing operations in Ukraine and Belarus in 1944.

During Operation *Bagration* in the summer of 1944, Zhukov had oversight of the two southern Fronts involved in the assault, while Vasilevsky oversaw the northern half of the immense operation. Zhukov often seemed as concerned about how his part in the battle would be perceived by Stalin as he was in the elimination of the opposing German forces. The units in Vasilevsky's northern sector were rapidly approaching the city of Vilnius and Zhukov was anxious to be able to claim a comparable victory. As his Sixty-Fifth Army approached the city of Baranovichi, Colonel General Pavel Ivanovich Batov faced angry criticism from Zhukov who accused him of not proceeding with the required speed:

> Never in my long service did I ever encounter such humiliating behaviour. [Major General Nikolai Antonovich] Radetsky's [political commissar, Sixty-Fifth Army] face was frozen. When I finally got a chance to speak and reported that our troops were making good progress, and that the city could be taken at any moment, the marshal started raging again.
>
> 'The army commander's report corresponds with the facts,' said Radetsky. But he was ignored. When Radetsky repeated himself, the marshal turned on him too. This undignified scene ended with Zhukov ordering Radetsky to go to Baranovichi and not to return until the city was in our hands. He then kicked aside his chair and left the room, slamming the door behind him.
>
> There was an oppressive silence. 'Don't worry about it,' Radetsky assured me. 'We don't serve Zhukov, we serve the Soviet armed forces. Let's have our evening meal. It's all nonsense. But I'd like to know what got the marshal so agitated.' I didn't really care, but Radetsky continued. 'I think I can see what's going on. Vasilevsky's already outside Vilnius. Zhukov's wrestling with him for attention, to be the first to report a major success to *Stavka*. But I'll have to go. Orders are orders!'
>
> So I was left alone. I didn't have to worry about my troops. The battle was proceeding as planned. Still, I couldn't find any solace. We army commanders were unaccustomed to being treated like this by our superiors. Late that night [7–8 July] Radetsky contacted me. 'Everything's going as planned.'

'Where are you calling from?'

'I'm in Baranovichi. I've driven around the whole city with Alekseev. I'm in [Major General Kuzma Yevdokimovich] Grebennik's command post [15th Rifle Division] in the cemetery. Our troops are about 1.5km further west, advancing successfully.'

A senior officer was hunched over a briefcase in front of the hut where Zhukov was sleeping. I had the marshal awakened and informed him that Baranovichi had been taken.

'Are there any reports from Vilnius?' he asked. 'No? Then I'll sleep a little more.'[6]

Perhaps Zhukov had good reason to be anxious about retaining Stalin's favour. As 1944 drew to an end and Stalin looked increasingly at how he wanted the Soviet war effort to be portrayed in the years to come, he informed Zhukov that he would not be employed in the final assaults across Poland and on to Berlin in the same overseeing role that he had performed in the past. Instead, this function would be carried out by *Stavka* under the close supervision of Stalin. But – arguably in an attempt to soften the blow for Zhukov – Stalin gave him command of 1st Belarusian Front, which was now deployed immediately north of Konev's 1st Ukrainian Front and faced Warsaw. In the coming battles, this Front would be on the main axis that led to Berlin.

Nevertheless, it was unquestionably a demotion for Zhukov, and although it was the first clearly visible example of Stalin's intention to reduce Zhukov's status, the Soviet leader had been seeking means of denigrating Zhukov for several years. As early as 1942, he asked Viktor Semenovich Abakumov (a senior NKVD officer who would become head of *SMERSH*, the Soviet counter-intelligence service, when it was formally created in 1943) to find incriminating evidence; despite several arrests and brutal interrogations of men associated with Zhukov, Abakumov failed to uncover anything of use. After *Bagration*, Stalin tried again, this time tasking Nikolai Aleksandrovich Bulganin, a senior member of the Politburo and deputy defence minister, to take up the investigation. The only 'evidence' that Bulganin could find was two artillery manuals that Zhukov had authorised without approval from *Stavka*.[7]

There are many biographies of Zhukov, and like his personal memoirs they concentrate on his military achievements. There has been little attempt to describe him as a human being, and even the accounts written by his contemporaries are open to question. After the war, Stalin's desire to give himself the leading role in Soviet historiography at the expense of all others resulted in many other senior figures making unflattering comments about Zhukov.

The Red Army: Plans for Vengeance

In many respects, this was hardly difficult, given the reputation for stubborn, brutal imposition of orders that Zhukov had established. All of his operations were characterised by heavy casualties and he showed little regard for the lives of ordinary soldiers. But despite the glaring failures of the attacks on the Rzhev salient, he also had a fearsome reputation for success. Junior officers and ordinary soldiers knew that if they were serving in one of the units under his command, they could expect heavy fighting, but they were also confident that he would deliver victory.

The final figure who would play a leading part in the coming battle for Berlin was the commander of 1st Ukrainian Front, to the south of Zhukov's 1st Belarusian Front. Like several other senior figures, Ivan Stepanovich Konev served in the First World War in the Russian Army before joining the Red Army, but his early path was as a commissar, responsible for the political education of soldiers and ensuring that officers followed Communist Party doctrine. He then became a division commander and was involved in the Battle of Khalkin Gol; some accounts suggest that his performance was poor, resulting in criticism from Zhukov in official reports.[8] Despite this, he started the war with Germany first as an army commander and then as a Front commander. Although he was caught up in the disasters that befell the Red Army in the opening months of the conflict, he appears to have caught Stalin's eye and escaped blame; like many others, the early successes of his troops in the counteroffensive outside Moscow in 1941 were praised and recognised, while the subsequent failures to turn an advantageous position into a decisive victory were overlooked. He then served as a Front commander during the fighting around the Rzhev salient, once more escaping criticism for the huge losses suffered by his troops for minimal gain.

Having played no part in the Battle of Stalingrad, Konev next had a chance to impress at Kursk. Here, his Steppe Front was used in the counteroffensive that followed the German failure to amputate the salient and he led his units – soon renamed 2nd Ukrainian Front – across central Ukraine. In early 1944, his Front formed the southern part of the offensive that encircled a substantial group of German forces in the Battle of Cherkassy; as the surrounded Germans attempted to break out and link up with relief columns being sent to their aid, Konev showed an adroit political touch, seeking to claim all credit for the operation at the expense of General Nikolai Fedorovich Vatutin, whose 1st Ukrainian Front had formed the northern part of the encirclement operation. In the summer of 1944, Konev took command of 1st Ukrainian Front and although he played no part in *Bagration*, he launched a powerful assault to complement the main offensive, thrusting west via Lviv to reach and cross the Vistula, creating the large bridgehead around the city of Sandomierz. From here, his Front burst into

Poland in January 1945 before overrunning Silesia and ending the operation along the line of the Oder and Neisse Rivers.

In the eyes of many, Zhukov and Konev were rivals for the attention and approval of Stalin. Both had reputations for accepting heavy casualties to achieve victories, but there were additional nuances. Colonel General Aleksandr Petrovich Pokrovsky, who had served as Konev's chief of staff on several occasions, later wrote:

> There were many similarities in the leadership styles of Zhukov and Konev. But amongst all the Front commanders with whom I served, Konev was the more engaging and energetic personality. It is true that something else should also be remembered. He was hot-tempered, but easy-going. He could become very angry and enraged and would start to shout, but he calmed down quickly. In general, in my memory, I must say that of all the Front commanders with whom I dealt, Konev was – how can I put it? He was the most soldierly, he had the most humanity in his character, and was the kindest. I accompanied him on many trips to his armies. One day we walked with him along the trenches of the front line for a whole day, and listened to him talking to the soldiers. His conversation wasn't condescending; he simply talked to the soldiers in a natural way. This was his essential soldier's nature. He spoke to his men in this completely natural way because it was the only way that he could, with complete understanding of the life and soul of soldiers, without any trace of anything pompous or calculated.[9]

Whilst all such accounts should be treated with caution, it is worth noting that there are few, if any, such descriptions of Zhukov chatting with the ordinary rank and file. Konev seems to have been identified by Stalin at a relatively early stage of the war as a useful counterweight to Zhukov, and this may account for the manner in which his earlier failures were passed over with few lasting consequences.

The forces deployed by the Red Army for the coming offensive were impressive; given the weakness of the Wehrmacht, they represented an overwhelming advantage. In the north, Rokossovsky's 2nd Belarusian Front had Second Shock Army and Forty-Ninth, Sixty-Fifth, and Seventieth Armies, supported by three tank corps, a mechanised corps, a cavalry corps, and an air army. To his south was Zhukov's 1st Belarusian Front. It had Third and Fifth Shock Armies, Eighth Guards Army, Third, Thirty-Third, Forty-Seventh, Sixty-First, and Sixty-Ninth Armies, First and Second Guards Tank Armies, First Polish Army, two tank corps, two cavalry corps, and an air army. Finally, 1st Ukrainian Front to the south fielded Third and Fifth Guards Armies, Thirteenth,

Twenty-Eighth, and Fifty-Second Armies, Second Polish Army, Third and Fourth Guards Tank Armies, two tank corps, a mechanised corps, a cavalry corps, and an air army. In numerical terms, these forces were perhaps smaller than the troops that had been deployed the previous summer for *Bagration*, but they still greatly outnumbered the Germans: Zhukov's 1st Belarusian Front had 768,000 men, nearly 1,800 tanks, 1,300 assault guns, nearly 17,000 guns and mortars, 1,500 rocket launchers, and over 3,800 aircraft. To his south, Konev's 1st Ukrainian Front fielded over 511,000 men, nearly 1,400 tanks, nearly 700 assault guns, 11,700 guns and mortars, 900 rocket launchers, and 2,100 aircraft.[10]

Details for the coming operation were drawn up at the beginning of April. In a conference in Moscow, Stalin, Zhukov, Konev, and other senior figures met to consider how to proceed. Here, Konev later wrote, he and Zhukov were informed that the Western Allies were actively planning to seize Berlin before the Red Army could arrive. The reality was that the only concrete plans for such an operation had been drawn up to cover the possibility of an unexpectedly rapid collapse of German resistance; whether the misinterpretation of this by Stalin and his associates was accidental or deliberate is open to question. Regardless, Konev and Zhukov were ordered by Stalin to draw up their proposals for the operation. They presented their plans the following day, and Konev later described his thoughts:

> According to the original plans, Berlin was intended to be captured by 1st Belarusian Front. However, the right wing of 1st Ukrainian Front, on which the main strike group was concentrated, would pass close to the south of Berlin. Who could anticipate how the operation would unfold, what surprises we might encounter in different sectors, and what new decisions and adjustments to earlier plans would have to be made as matters progressed?
>
> In any case, I had already assumed a likely course of events that, with the successful advance of the units on the right wing of our front, we might find ourselves in an advantageous position to manoeuvre and strike at Berlin from the south. I considered it premature to express these considerations, although I had the impression that without explicitly saying it, Stalin allowed for such an option in the future. This impression grew when, approving the composition of the groupings and the direction of the attacks, Stalin began to draw the demarcation line between 1st Belarusian and 1st Ukrainian Fronts on the map with a pencil. In the original plans, this line extended through Lübben and onwards somewhat south of Berlin. Drawing the line with his pencil, Stalin abruptly stopped it in the city of Lübben, about 60km southeast of Berlin. He stopped it there and didn't take it any further. He didn't say anything at the time, but I think Zhukov also saw the meaning behind this. The demarcation line was cut off approximately

where we were supposed to reach on the third day of the operation. Obviously depending on the situation, it was tacitly assumed that the Front commands would then have further possibilities for initiative.

In any case, for me the end of the demarcation line at Lübben meant that the speed of the breakthrough, and the rapid manoeuvre and development of actions on the right wing of our Front could subsequently create a situation in which it would be advantageous for us to attack Berlin from the south.

Was there an unspoken call for competition between the Fronts by ending the demarcation line at Lübben? I admit this possibility. In any event, I can't rule it out. This becomes all the more likely if we think back to that time and recall how we viewed Berlin and the passionate desire of everyone, from ordinary soldier to general, to see this city with their own eyes, to take possession of it with the power of their weapons.

Of course, that was my passionate wish too. I'm not afraid to admit it now. It would be odd to portray oneself in the last months of the war as a person devoid of passions – on the contrary, we were filled with them at the time.[11]

General Ivan Yefimovich Petrov, Konev's chief of staff, recalled matters slightly differently, as his biographer related:

Participants at the meeting recall how Stalin stood over the map for some time, thinking, and then took a pencil and crossed out that part of the dividing line between the sphere of action of 1st Belarusian and 1st Ukrainian Fronts, which had cut off 1st Ukrainian Front from Berlin, and retained only part of this line as far as Lübben ... and said:

'Whoever breaks through first, can take Berlin.'[12]

There is a clear difference here: Petrov's account suggests that Stalin was persuaded to change the original demarcation and was explicit in permitting the two Front commanders to compete for the glory of capturing Berlin, whereas Konev describes the demarcation as always being a little ambiguous. Colonel General Sergei Matveyevich Shtemenko, head of the operations directorate of *Stavka*, largely corroborated Petrov's account when he later wrote that Konev had raised objections to the demarcation lines between his armies and those of Zhukov on 31 March, and that when the full conference took place the following day, Stalin responded to this:

The chief of the general staff [Vasilevsky] considered it necessary to draw the supreme commander's attention once again to the demarcation line between the

The Red Army: Plans for Vengeance

two Fronts. It was emphasised that this line virtually excluded the armies of 1st Ukrainian Front from direct participation in the fighting for Berlin, and that this might make it difficult to carry out the operation as scheduled. Marshal Konev spoke in the same vein, arguing in favour of aiming part of the forces of 1st Ukrainian Front, particularly the tank armies, at the southwest suburbs of Berlin.

Stalin decided on a compromise. He did not completely abandon his own idea, nor did he entirely reject Marshal Konev's considerations, supported by the general staff. On the map showing the plan of the operation he silently crossed out the section of the demarcation line that cut off 1st Ukrainian Front from Berlin.[13]

In his memoirs, Zhukov went to some lengths to portray the demarcation, and the subsequent movements of Konev's forces, as entirely originating with Stalin, but Konev had persuaded Stalin to modify plans in his favour in the past – all Front commanders would have had private conversations with Stalin, either in person or via telephone, and it is possible that the discrepancies in the accounts of decision-making in 1945 reflect the suspicions of senior officers about Konev's record of manoeuvring for personal advantage.

The overall intention of the Berlin Operation was to defeat and destroy the concentration of German forces defending Berlin, to capture the city, and to reach the line of the Elbe to establish contact with the Western Allies. Each Front was assigned missions to achieve this objective. Rokossovsky's armies were to cross the lower Oder and isolate Berlin from the north, protecting the northern flank of 1st Belarusian Front from any German counterattacks, and then to secure the northeast coastline of Germany as far to the west as possible. At this stage of the war, the future western boundary of the Soviet occupation zone had been agreed with Churchill and Roosevelt, but Stalin contemplated a rapid collapse of German positions, permitting Rokossovsky to advance to the German border with Denmark and perhaps even to overrun Denmark before German forces there could surrender to the Western Allies. In the centre, Zhukov's 1st Belarusian Front was to attack directly towards Berlin and then to press on to the Elbe, reaching the river no later than 15 days after the commencement of the operation. Finally, in the south, 1st Belarusian Front was to isolate Berlin from German forces further to the south and to destroy Wehrmacht formations in the area around the city of Cottbus, and then to reach the Elbe in 12 days to establish contact with US forces – though the possibility of turning north to reach Berlin remained a possibility.

Each Front commander assigned the units under his command to specific missions. Rokossovsky intended to commit three of his armies to the main attack towards the west. As his units were still forming up after completing their advance in eastern Pomerania and towards Danzig, he scheduled his start date as four days after the Fronts to the south had commenced operations. Closest to the coast, Second Shock Army was to complete the clearance of the Oder estuary and would then seize the German islands in the Baltic Sea; although it was designated a shock army and therefore – at least in theory – possessed additional resources to aid a breakthrough, it was badly understrength after being involved in heavy fighting in and around Danzig. The main thrust by 2nd Belarusian Front was to be led by the other three armies in the general direction of Neustrelitz, with the tank and cavalry units being held in reserve to exploit initial successes.

For Zhukov, the first task was to secure the Oderbruch and the access routes up onto the ridge of the Seelow Heights. As was almost always the case with his operations, Zhukov chose to attack with combined arms armies – from north to south, Forty-Seventh Army, Third and Fifth Shock Armies, Eighth Guards Army, and Third Army. Most of these would commence their attacks from positions already secured on the west bank and the two tank armies would be committed once the first wave of attacks had cleared the Germans from the Oderbruch and had penetrated into – and ideally through – the second defensive positions along the Seelow Heights. On his northern flank, Zhukov intended Sixty-First and First Polish Armies to advance and secure his right wing, while Sixty-Ninth and Thirty-Third Armies performed the same task on the southern flank.

The Germans had concluded that the forces being assembled by Konev to the south would be used to attack directly west and southwest and would not necessarily be involved in the coming battle for Berlin. Contrary to their expectations, 1st Ukrainian Front intended only Second Polish Army and elements of Fifty-Second Army to advance towards Dresden. The real weight of the Front, with Thirteenth Army in the north, Fifth Guards Army in the centre, and Third Guards Army in the south, was directed at Spremberg and Cottbus, with the two tank armies waiting to exploit deep into Germany once the front line had been breached.

The commanders of the Soviet armies that would make the assault were seasoned veterans. General Pavel Semenovich Rybalko had a frustrating start to the Second World War; he was a senior lecturer in a tank school and wasn't given a field command until late 1942, when he was assigned to the new Third Tank Army. He led it with distinction in the battles around Stalingrad, but his units were badly mauled in the German counteroffensive that restored the front line before the spring of 1943. Renamed Third Guards Tank Army, the formation was rebuilt and took part in the Battle of Kursk before being heavily involved in the Soviet advance across central and western Ukraine. During the surge across

The Red Army: Plans for Vengeance

Poland in early 1945, he showed his ability to improvise and redeploy his units quickly as the battles unfolded, and Third Guards Tank Army was now the northern exploitation force of 1st Ukrainian Front.

General Dmitry Danilovich Lelyushenko, commander of Fourth Guards Tank Army, was to advance on Rybalko's southern flank. In an era in which delegation of command to subordinate commanders was increasingly seen as an effective way of handling large formations, Lelyushenko was a man who preferred to visit the front line and make decisions personally. On the one hand, this sometimes led to delays and a degree of inflexibility; but on the other hand, his willingness to visit units in the thick of the action earned the approval of his subordinates. He took part in the Battle of Moscow, playing a leading role in fending off the southern pincer of the German attacks on the Soviet capital. During the battles around Stalingrad, he was rebuked by Stalin for frequently being absent from his headquarters – Stalin would often telephone his army commanders for personal updates. In 1944, Lelyushenko took command of Fourth Tank Army and took part in the operations that drove the Germans from Ukrainian soil; during these battles, his units lost up to 90 per cent of their vehicles, and required a lengthy spell of replenishment to recover their strength. In early 1945, the army was upgraded to 'Guards' status, and fought in the advance across Poland, reaching the upper Oder and Neisse.

Similarly, Zhukov's two tank armies were under experienced command. The northerly force was Second Guards Tank Army, commanded by Colonel General Semen Ilyich Bogdanov, who had held the post since September 1943. In July 1944 he was shot in the shoulder by a German sniper; the wound left him with permanently restricted movement and required five months of hospitalisation, but when he returned to his command immediately before the Soviet advance across Poland in January 1945, he showed that he had lost none of his energy and determination. To his south was First Guards Tank Army, commanded by Colonel General Mikhail Yefimovich Katukov. He had been in this post since early 1943, leading his army with skill and distinction in advances from the Battle of Kursk into the heart of Ukraine. But whilst his tanks had led the drive across northern Poland in January and February, he had severe reservations about repeating that performance in the coming battle. Zhukov held conferences with his army commanders and their staff officers in early April, and Katukov later wrote:

> During a map exercise after the initial discussions using maps and a model of Berlin, it became quite obvious to us that the terrain was conducive to defensive operations. Swampy rivers and rivulets, canals, and lakes formed advantageous terrain where you couldn't pin down the enemy, and the leading elements would

suffer heavy attrition. There were additional difficulties for our tank units. The west bank of the Oder [the Oderbruch] is a swampy floodplain. And beyond this floodplain lie the Seelow Heights. They loomed over us like sheer cliffs. Also, there was a railway running from north to south on the eastern edge of the Seelow Heights, in a deep cutting. This created a further serious obstacle …

Looking at the approaches of the German capital on the model and the map, we immediately realised that it would not be possible to repeat the deep breakthrough of the Vistula–Oder Operation in this terrain: these were no conditions for armoured manoeuvres. We would have to wage a stubborn struggle, advancing step by step, gnawing through the Nazis' defences in bloody fighting.

However, we had no doubt that regardless of this we would sweep away all the enemy's fortifications covering the approaches to the capital. And this confidence was based on the victories that Soviet troops had won in past battles.[14]

Eighth Guards Army, which was roughly in the centre of Zhukov's attacks, was originally Sixty-Second Army, earning its Guards status as a result of its heroic defence of Stalingrad. Its commander, both then and outside Berlin, was Chuikov, who has already been described in connection with the initial Soviet attempts to cross the lower Oder. His army had been involved in heavy fighting to defeat the isolated German forces in Poznań and had suffered considerable losses. The weeks that followed were spent in trying to bring units back to combat strength with replacement drafts, but like Katukov, Chuikov could see that the coming operation would not be an easy one:

The tasks that the Front command assigned to us were extremely difficult. It is true that we had considerable resources for strengthening our armies. For example, for Eighth Guards Army in its 7km frontage for the assault, we had 77 artillery and ten tank and assault gun regiments, amounting to 266 guns and mortars and up to 40 tanks per kilometre of front line. However, these assets couldn't strike both German defensive positions at the same time. After overrunning the first line, it would be necessary to move forward thousands of guns and hundreds of observation posts, and then establish communications and cooperation with the advancing units. All of this would take time.

We had strong aviation assets, but they were assigned to strike the same positions that the artillery was targeting. Without intelligence data, the pilots couldn't know about the carefully camouflaged enemy defences in forested areas …

The dominant heights of the ridge at Seelow that remained in enemy hands made it possible for him to observe the entire valley where our troops were concentrated. It was very difficult for us to conceal our movements.[15]

The Red Army: Plans for Vengeance

It was clear to Soviet commanders that the coming battle would be a different matter from the dramatic sweep across Poland in January and February, and inevitably there were disagreements. Babadzhanian, commander of First Guards Tank Army's XI Guards Tank Corps, had been at the tip of the spear in the Vistula–Oder Operation. He was present at a conference of senior officers of Zhukov's Front on 5 April where Bogdanov, commander of Second Guards Tank Army, expressed uneasiness at the corridor of advance allocated to his formations; rather than risking his tanks being drawn into the built-up areas around Berlin, he wanted to bypass the city further to the north. Zhukov reprimanded him, reminding him that the swift capture of Berlin was the primary objective.[16] He had already pointed out the location of key buildings such as the ruins of the Reichstag and the old Hohenzollern palaces, making a point of asking his army commanders if they wanted to capture them before Konev's troops – in Zhukov's mind at least, there was no doubt that he was in direct competition with his rival.

Throughout the war, the losses suffered by Soviet units were shockingly high. Whereas experiences in the First World War had left the public, the political leadership, and the military of the Western Powers with great reluctance to countenance the casualties that had been suffered in 1914–18, the attitude within the Soviet Union was very different. The battles that raged along the Eastern Front prior to the collapse of Imperial Russia in 1917 were every bit as bloody as the more familiar battles of Flanders, and moreover were accompanied by great advances and retreats, but in a nation with far lower levels of literacy and with its population spread over such a vast area, Russia did not react to these losses in the same manner as nations in the west. Moreover, the deaths of the war were then followed by further carnage as the Russian Civil War raged, and this in turn was succeeded by terrible death rates from famines, both natural and man-made. Far from engendering an abhorrence of such deaths, these experiences seemed to habituate Soviet society – civilian, political, and military – to the near-inevitability of deaths on a huge scale. A few Soviet commanders genuinely attempted to minimise battlefield losses, and many more claimed to have done so when they wrote their memoirs, but throughout the war the Soviet units suffered casualties at rates that would have been regarded as horrific by the armies of the Western Powers.

As is usually the case in war, these casualties were disproportionately high amongst the newest recruits. Men who survived their first few episodes of combat learned the difficult skills of reducing their personal risk and it was on this core of veterans – diminishing steadily as the war progressed – that the Red Army's final victory was built. As casualties climbed ever higher, basic training of recruits was often truncated and men were dispatched to the front with levels of training that would have been unthinkably minimal in other armies. To compound problems, the Red Army had a practice – inherited from the old Imperial Russian Army and passed on in turn to the modern Russian Army – of expecting and requiring front-line units to convert recruits straight out of basic training into fully trained soldiers. Such a policy might have been possible in peacetime, but in the midst of almost continuous combat it was often impossible to implement meaningfully. Nor did the Red Army have a tradition of professional NCOs, experienced men who could oversee such training. Most NCOs were either veterans who had earned promotion or, more commonly, raw recruits who had shown promise and had caught the eye of their training cadres.

In addition to the modestly trained replacement drafts arriving from the Soviet hinterland, reinforcements came in the form of men from recently reconquered areas of the Soviet Union. Instead of waiting for governmental authorities to re-establish normal procedures, advancing armies simply press-ganged local people and, after screening them to exclude those who might have collaborated with the occupiers, sent some to training establishments and put the rest through the most rudimentary induction before incorporating them into their ranks. Yakov Ivanovich Fadeyev was aged 17 when the Red Army recaptured Odessa, where he had lived under Romanian occupation. He was delighted when the local schools reopened, but just two weeks after resuming his studies he was drafted into the army. In many respects, he was fortunate, in that he was sent to a proper training base to the northeast of Moscow:

> There, in a reserve regiment, we were thoroughly starved, as if it was being made clear to us that we would either die here through hunger or heroically at the front. From there we were sent to the border of the USSR, to Rava-Ruska near Lviv. We were ordered to a forest … and the village of Turinka. Those who had some kind of education were selected for further studies, and the rest spent about a month in a training battalion. I don't know what I did to merit it, but I was awarded the rank of senior sergeant. During this time we were taught to shoot with rifles and machine-guns. And then, when 70th Tank Brigade received new tanks, we were sent to Colonel General [Pavel Semenovich] Rybalko's Third Tank Army [later renamed Third Guards Tank Army].
>
> By that time [autumn 1944] our troops had already crossed the Vistula and we crossed the river across a bridge. Our offensive operations had already stopped and we were on the defensive. We began to dig trenches and to build dugouts. I was appointed to the post of deputy commander of a tank rider platoon. But in November 1944 I fell ill with typhoid fever and I was sent to a hospital in Lviv for treatment.

> I was discharged only on 9 March [1945], but I didn't return to my unit. I went to a reserve regiment and then to the 1st Assault Battalion, commanded by Major Mitin, of 236th Rifle Regiment, 106th Rifle Division, Third Guards Army. I was in 2nd Company, commanded by Lieutenant Lomayev, a Siberian of short stature.
>
> I was appointed commander of the 1st Assault Platoon. The major introduced me to the soldiers, telling them that I was an experienced veteran, but I just blinked in amazement – why was he lying to them? After all, not only had I not smelled the smoke of battle, I still barely knew how to fire a gun! Only later did it dawn on me that in this way the battalion commander wanted to establish my authority among the soldiers from the very outset. Since I had no idea what an assault platoon was, I asked the battalion commander what we were meant to be assaulting. Major Mitin replied that we had to storm the Fascist lair – Berlin, which was 110km away. In the meantime, we were to prepare for the decisive battle; we carried out repeated reconnaissance probes, searching for 'tongues' [Red Army slang for prisoners seized for interrogation].[17]

Generally, the armies awarded 'Guards' status received the best and most numerous reinforcements. Fadeyev's account suggests that in many cases, even those deemed to be high-quality replacements were barely capable of performing in combat. The recruits sent to units like tank formations, that required a greater degree of training, were little better. Arkady Grigoryevich Vesterman's experience as an officer cadet was of brutal instructors who imposed draconian discipline:

> We were out in the field in short cadet overcoats lined with 'fish fur' [Red Army slang for the thin woollen lining of cheap winter garments] and we were put through tactical lessons, walking on foot 'like tanks'. We were constantly hungry as our cadet rations and everything else were shamelessly stolen by everyone, from quartermasters to command staff. The commanders we came across were merciless bastards who, in order to avoid being sent to the front themselves, drove us hard and went out of their way to demonstrate their zeal and severity in front of higher authorities. Our company commander was a real beast, named Tseptsov, and I had no luck at all with my platoon commander who fiercely hated Jews. When an order was received to release 50 recruits from the battalion to be sent as replenishments to an infantry unit, the company and platoon commanders immediately added all the Jews of the company to that list. Of the 50 finally selected for the infantry, exactly half of us turned out to be Jewish recruits. We were waiting to leave when suddenly some commission headed by a colonel appeared and checked who was being sent to the trenches 'to die the death of the

brave'. They reached me and asked my commanders: 'How are his studies? How is his discipline?' I had studied well – I had graduated from school with honours, giving me the right to be sent to a Guards unit. The commission ordered several other cadets and me to return to the battalion, and the rest were sent to the front line. And of them, apart from one individual, none survived. All of them ended up in a rifle regiment and died when they were surrounded, and the only surviving cadet later wrote a letter to us to inform us of the terrible fate of our comrades.

Amongst the cadets there were many former front-line soldiers who had been sent for further training after being treated for wounds and based on the stories these veterans told us, we all believed that soon after arriving at the front we would go up in flames in our tanks in the very first battles. I became friends with one of them, Sergeant Yakov Sher, who arrived at the school from the front. Sher and I later ended up in the same brigade, and he died before my eyes, his head torn clean off. And my other comrade, Kim Shevchenko, burned in a tank at the very end of the war.

As for combat training: we received only the basics of the knowledge required to be a tank commander. There was only one session of live firing; we fired three rounds each. The tank training area was located next to the school and each of the cadets was given ten to twelve driving lessons, including training in overcoming ditches, bridges, and overpasses, and several hours of night driving with the driver's hatch closed. In June 1943, after graduating from the college, we were sent to Nizhny Tagil [in the Ural Mountains], to a tank factory. We were taken to the workshops, to the production line, and told: 'Here are your tanks, being assembled. The T-34s will be ready in two days.'[18]

The quality of soldiers sent to non-Guards armies was even poorer. This meant that the ability of those units to conduct complex manoeuvres was almost non-existent. As a result, fearing the wrath of superiors like Zhukov with their fearsome reputations, junior commanders simply threw their men forward in human waves, adding greatly to the already terrible casualty rate suffered by the Red Army. In their memoirs, many senior Soviet commanders described how they organised special training exercises to prepare their men for operations, including the construction of German positions so that soldiers could plan and rehearse how they intended to attack, but interviews with survivors after the war suggest that in most cases, such training was of little value. Men were led through the simulated German defences at walking pace, then at a higher tempo, with only rudimentary measures taken to replicate the noise and chaos of real combat. There was no attempt to create situations in which junior commanders would have to improvise or come up with alternative plans in the face of setbacks.

But despite the murderous casualties suffered in the war and the poor quality of replacement drafts, there was a paradox: the Red Army actually improved its performance as the war continued. This was due to several factors. Firstly, the starting point was a low one; in almost every respect, the Red Army of 1941 was in poor shape. Its equipment was often outdated and poorly maintained; its force structure was unwieldy; the assumptions underlying its operational doctrine were largely wrong; training was poor; and its leadership was rigid and too fearful of being seen to have deviated from orders. By 1945, a great deal had changed. The equipment of the army was far superior in almost every respect, and the concentration on a small number of tank designs, for example, resulted in greatly improved availability of replacement parts. The structure of divisions, brigades, corps, and armies had been repeatedly altered to improve functionality, and although many officers were still inclined to enforce orders regardless of the reality on the ground, there were sufficient numbers of experienced commanders at every level to ensure that in many cases, innovation and flexibility were increasingly common features on the battlefield. Training of individual recruits remained poor, but everything else had changed, at least to some extent.

In almost every major battle on the Eastern Front, there were incidents of Soviet riflemen being simply terrified by the noise of their own artillery bombardment to the point where they were unwilling to leave their trenches and advance close behind the barrage. As a result, the initial benefit of driving the Germans to take shelter was lost and the defenders were often manning their positions when the riflemen finally moved forward. All of these consequences of poor training were inevitable in a huge army that had suffered such heavy losses in preceding years and moreover had no tradition of high-quality training. Looking just at what the Soviet Union classified as 'irrecoverable losses' – men killed, missing, taken prisoner, or too badly injured to return to service – the annual totals are almost unimaginable. Between the onset of hostilities on 22 June 1941 and the end of 1941, these losses came to over 3.1 million. A further 3.3 million were lost in 1942, 2.3 million in 1943, and 1.8 million in 1944; the fall in the annual death rate reflects both the improving performance of the Red Army and the fact that as it was now largely on the offensive, it was losing fewer men as prisoners. Between the beginning of 1945 and the moment when the Soviet armies were drawn up along the Oder and were preparing for their assault on Berlin, another 550,000 men had been lost, making a total of nearly 11 million irrecoverable losses to date. Even if the majority of these were the relatively inexperienced new drafts in their first few battles, hundreds of thousands of irreplaceable veterans were also gone.[19]

Making good at least some of the losses of the advance from the Vistula to the Oder was an essential step before pressing on to Berlin, but a prolonged pause was also needed to allow supplies to be brought forward. Despite the speed of their retreat, the Wehrmacht units that were driven back across Poland carried out a ruthless scorched earth policy, destroying bridges and railways to hinder the Soviet advance. The railways were particularly important at a time when this was the primary means of moving the huge quantities of supplies needed for the Red Army. Railway bridges had to be constructed over the Vistula and then maintained in difficult conditions – the winter ice was breaking up, often damaging or sweeping away pontoon bridges, forcing the logistics teams to take unusual measures. Lieutenant General Nikolai Aleksandrovich Antipenko was head of logistics for Zhukov's 1st Belarusian Front:

> Saving the bridges required a major operation. The railway troops and special teams of the logistic services acted with unprecedented determination. At that time, 13th Bridging Column was in the area of the rail bridge at Dęblin [south of Warsaw]; its commander, Colonel Moskalev, showed rare resourcefulness in creating ice corridors to direct broken ice floes under the bridge spans. In other words, he used the still-solid ice to protect the piers, fighting ice with ice.
>
> This clever innovation proved to be quite effective. To break up the approaching floes, we turned to the aviators and sappers for help. Planes carried out constant bombing of large ice floes even at some distance. Heavy bridge trusses, swept from their places in 1st Ukrainian Front's zone somewhere further upstream, threatened our bridges but as a result of aerial bombs and the sappers' demolition charges were often broken into fragments that passed unhindered under the bridge spans ...
>
> The railway bridge in Warsaw was saved using another original solution. It was attached by cables to the banks from different points and about 100 platforms loaded with cobblestones from the streets were placed on top of the bridge to increase the stability of the supports ... At the most critical moment, the pressure of ice on this bridge was so great that it became curved and concave. When trains crossed, the whole structure looked like it would break ...
>
> Soldiers and officers of 20th Bridging Battalion ... climbed on the ice floes near the bridge, pushing them with poles under the spans. Sometimes, blocks of ice piled up as high as the bridge deck and it was difficult to keep one's footing on this moving, rumbling, living mass of ice – some of the bridge workers fell into the water, but grabbing ropes that were thrown to them, they promptly climbed back onto the ice floes and once more entered the fray.

Things were worse for our right-hand neighbour, 2nd Belarusian Front. The only railway bridge in its section of the Vistula, near Toruń, couldn't withstand the onslaught of ice and was demolished. For almost half a month, we had to allot railway capacity for trains going to 2nd Belarusian Front via the Warsaw bridge until the Toruń bridge was restored.[20]

One of the consequences of the problems with railway lines and particularly the Vistula bridges was a logjam of trains on the lines immediately to the east. Up to 25 trains carrying supplies arrived every day and with so few able to proceed further, railway sidings became increasingly clogged. To complicate matters further, the lines that continued to the west were of the narrower European gauge rather than the wide gauge used in the Soviet Union. Some lines were re-pinned to the Soviet gauge, but many trains had to transfer their loads to captured rolling stock on the west bank. There were further delays to the west where it was necessary to stockpile huge quantities of ammunition, fuel, and other materiel as close to the assault troops as possible. A large-capacity bridge over the Oder was essential:

> Since the construction area was within range of enemy artillery and mortars and was also the target of repeated air attacks, construction had to be done at night using elements of bridge structures manufactured during the day in the surrounding forests. Despite this, the road and bridge units suffered heavy losses. During the day, the bridge was often damaged by enemy aircraft in one or other of their attacks; piledrivers with diesel hammers mounted on pontoons often sank after being struck by bomb fragments. And yet, the bridge was built in just seven days. During this week, the bridge builders lost 163 men killed, 38 drowned, and 186 wounded. The construction of the bridge was at a heavy price, but it made possible the transfer of military equipment to the bridgehead, first to hold it, then to expand it.
>
> Enemy aircraft did their best to disrupt the Küstrin bridges across the Oder. On the night of 18 April, when work was completed on a railway bridge across the Oder and Warta, the enemy launched a serious air raid on them and destroyed both bridges. Under constant bombardment and constantly suffering casualties the men of 29th Railway Brigade and Moskalev's bridging column selflessly set about restoring both crossings, completing the task in just one week.[21]

Although Soviet aviation greatly outnumbered the Luftwaffe and the latter was crippled by fuel shortages, the ability of German aircraft to continue attacking the crossings and to conduct reconnaissance missions is striking. A clue to this can be found in the recollections of Anatoly Nikolayevich Gordeyev, a fighter pilot. Although he described the problems associated with escorting Soviet bombers on their raids, he suggests that the level of command and control of air assets fell far short of what was commonplace in the Luftwaffe and the air forces of the Western Allies:

> Our task was to provide 'cover for the attacking aircraft' – and that was all we were told, nothing about where they were flying or what and where their targets were. This was a major oversight by our headquarters, and led to losses and all manner of confusion. Sometimes you would find yourself in air-to-air combat, you drove off the enemy, and you then had to catch up with the bombers – but you didn't know where they had gone. Cooperation was poorly developed even by the time of the Berlin Operation – we accompanied a group of Pe-2 bombers on their first combat mission of the offensive, but we had no idea where they were going.[22]

Other aspects of the use of air power were also relatively primitive. Unlike the Germans or the Western Allies, Soviet aviation generally operated on the basis of attacking targets that were specified in advance of the mission; the routine use of aircraft to provide assistance to ground units that encountered unexpected resistance, a feature of Luftwaffe operations since the beginning of the war, developed only slowly. Zhukov's 1st Belarusian Front included Sixteenth Air Army, commanded by Colonel General Sergei Ignatyevich Rudenko, and in an account of the fighting he made no secret of the poor level of cooperation between ground and air units in earlier campaigns as he described the preparations made for 1945:

> The main task assigned to the ground attack aircraft was to support the operation of our tanks and mechanised forces. After analysis of the accumulated experience of cooperation between aviation and mobile forces, especially in the Belarusian Operation [*Bagration*], we realised that we had significant shortcomings in this matter. The main issue was that the interaction of aviation with tank and mechanised units was organised and coordinated only at the level of the commanders and headquarters of armies, corps, and in a few cases divisions. Consequently, if new tasks arose or aviation had to be redirected to other targets, the order had to pass through several command bodies, which took a significant amount of time. For this reason, our aviation was often late in delivering air strikes, which would have to be avoided during the Vistula–Oder Operation. To ensure a high rate of offensive action while breaking through the enemy's strong, deeply

echeloned defences, it was necessary for the commanders of forward detachments and even of small units to be able to establish contact with air units operating above the battlefield, to indicate to them the most important targets requiring action, and to exchange information with air units for immediate assistance.

Admittedly, the 'old timers' of our army – 2nd Guards and 299th Assault Aviation Divisions ... had little experience of such cooperation during the Belarusian Operation. Moreover, there was a prevailing opinion that the commander of a tank battalion, company, or forward detachment, being in a tank on the move, would not see or hear enough and therefore there could be no question of his communication and interaction with aviation.

To analyse this matter, we prepared a joint conference of aviators and tank crews. This turned out to be a very interesting and useful discussion, an exchange of combat experience, and a business-like conversation between tank crews and pilots about joint military operations on the battlefield took place. Many experienced ground and air veterans were involved.

I particularly recall the speech of one tank commander ... who said something like this: 'Those who have already spoken, mainly from amongst representatives of higher headquarters, have argued that it is impossible to see or hear aircraft from the ground while moving forward. I have driven in a tank from the Volga to the Vistula and I can't agree with this opinion. We tankers always see planes coming towards us or to either side. The fact is that a tank only has its hatch closed when entering a breakthrough or during an attack. The rest of the time, especially when moving in the operational depths of the attack, hatches are not closed; tankers can observe aircraft, maintain contact with them, and thus receive help from them.'

Other experienced tank crews, as well as pilots, said much the same thing. After the conference, we conducted an experimental exercise on radio communication between tanks on the move and aircraft in the air. The first experience was disappointing, mainly for technical reasons. The specialists had much work to do, tuning and configuring radio equipment on tanks and aircraft. After this, in a second exercise, the results were excellent. Everyone was satisfied that it was possible to maintain reliable communication from a tank on the move with aircraft flying overhead. And if communication was established, cooperation became possible.

Subsequently, several tactical exercises were conducted between aviation units and small units of tank crews. At the same time, issues of mutual identification of tanks and aircraft were worked out, and methods of target designation were made consistent, allowing new missions and retargeting of air groups that were operating in support of tank forces.[23]

It is worth noting that this still fell far short of the practice adopted by other armed forces, which had dedicated, specially trained air liaison officers accompanying ground units. Nevertheless, Zhukov's drive from the Vistula to the Oder saw a modest but marked improvement in coordination between air and ground forces. Rudenko spent the weeks of preparation for the advance on Berlin to ensure that this was improved further: in addition to bringing all units up to full strength and incorporating additional squadrons, he and his staff officers worked hard to ensure that all new aircrew personnel were aware of the improved communications that had been implemented in the advance from the Vistula. To develop cooperation further, pilots spent time in the trenches where ground units were preparing, to give them a 'feel' for the conditions in which infantry and tank crews would be operating.

Despite the logistic difficulties, compounded by the disruptive raids of the Luftwaffe, Antipenko succeeded in stockpiling huge quantities of supplies. He estimated that one 'load' of supplies for all of 1st Belarusian Front amounted to 43,000 tons. For the artillery, this meant nearly 360 tons of ammunition for every kilometre of front line. But even these huge stockpiles were dwarfed by the overall requirements of the assembled forces. Antipenko worried that the first day of the operation would consume half of the stocks he had assembled. He warned Colonel General Mikhail Sergeyevich Malinin, Zhukov's chief of staff, of the potential shortages, but there was little that could be done if the offensive was to commence on time. Malinin's only reassurance to Antipenko was that at the commencement of the advance from the Vistula in January, Zhukov had shortened the initial bombardment when the first attacking probes seemed to be making good progress; perhaps a similar approach might be possible here, leaving the gunners with plenty of shells for later in the operation.

In keeping with usual practice, the Soviet forces that had assembled for what was expected to be the last showdown with the Wehrmacht carried out aggressive reconnaissance probes in the two days before the offensive began. After the war, senior officers usually wrote about the great value of reconnaissance in force in identifying the true disposition of German defences, forcing German artillery to open fire and thus reveal its location, and securing favourable start lines for the main offensive. The soldiers who were involved in these probes rarely shared this view. Although the memoirs of army commanders describe battalions being trained specially for reconnaissance in force, the soldiers themselves later recalled that on the few occasions that any such training took place, it was rudimentary at best, and in most cases companies and battalions in the front line were simply ordered to conduct the reconnaissance in force with little or no preparation. There was usually a degree of artillery bombardment prior to the probes, but this was limited by the overall shortage of ammunition and the German defences were rarely suppressed to any significant degree. Consequently, heavy casualties in the battalions tasked with reconnaissance in force were inevitable.

The combination of the aggressive reconnaissance probes and Heinrici's planned abandonment of the foremost defences meant that some Soviet units moved forward on the very eve of the attack into ground that had until recently been in German hands. This was not always without incident. Mikhail Petrovich Badigin was the commander of an anti-tank gun:

> As soon as it got dark [on the eve of the attack], we began to move closer to the front-line infantry, which in our sector had advanced 2–3km. The guns of 3rd Battery were advancing on our left. They were unlucky – they found themselves in a German anti-tank minefield. From external appearances, the field looked perfectly ordinary without hillocks or bald patches of earth – the typical signs of hasty minelaying. During the preceding day, our sappers had searched this entire low-lying area and cleared hundreds of mines. And yet, the sappers apparently overlooked this area, or perhaps the Germans managed to restore part of the minefield. And here was the tragic consequence: 3rd Battery hit the mines. A big explosion shook the air. The lead vehicle jerked strangely and was blown onto its side, the second vehicle was left with its front wheels in the air. The column came to a halt. The shell-shocked men were quickly evacuated and given medical aid.
>
> Our battery apparently made it through the minefield only by a miracle. To avoid setting off any more vehicle-triggered mines, we carried heavy boxes of shells on our shoulders all night from the road to our new firing position. The vehicles stayed behind.[24]

Accounts written during the Soviet era inevitably place great value on the work of political officers. In addition to ensuring conformity with Communist Party doctrine, these individuals had an additional important task at this stage of the war. Throughout the conflict, many Soviet soldiers had dealt with the high likelihood of being killed or wounded by adopting a fatalistic attitude: they persuaded themselves that they had no hope of surviving the conflict and having thus accepted their inevitable death, they concluded that it made little difference whether they perished today, tomorrow, or next week. But by 1945, weariness of the slaughter and brutal fighting was a growing problem, and with an end to the war apparently within reach, it was only human for soldiers to wonder whether they might actually live to see peace. In such circumstances, they might be less willing to risk their lives. The political officers therefore had to keep motivation high, and there was a concerted campaign to highlight the crimes committed by the Germans during the time that they had occupied the western parts of the Soviet Union. Revenge was used as a motivator, and although post-war accounts claimed that soldiers were constantly lectured on the need to maintain 'fraternal' relationships with ordinary working-class Germans, the reality was somewhat different and most soldiers knew that if they were to loot, rape, or kill as they advanced, no action would be taken against them. Nonetheless, some political officers attempted to make stirring speeches to motivate the rank and file. From a modern perspective, the value of such political speeches seems questionable, but this was a conflict between two sides made up of soldiers who had grown up in tightly controlled environments, constantly fed a particular political orthodoxy. An indication of the efficacy of the speeches is that many young soldiers felt motivated to apply for Communist Party membership on the eve of the offensive.

Finally, all was ready. Zhukov had moved as many troops as he could into their bridgeheads; to the south, where there were fewer bridgeheads, Konev had massed many of his men in preparation for assault crossings. Colonel General Ivan Pavlovich Galitsky, head of 1st Ukrainian Front's engineers, described the final preparations:

> Two days before the offensive, sappers removed our minefields in front of our foremost lines. The engineering and pontoon bridge units deployed, positioning themselves at their concentration points, ready to construct crossings, landing stages, ferries, floating bridges, and low-water bridges [partially submerged, to make them more difficult to spot from the air]. We ensured they had established contact with all formations for whom they were to provide crossings.
>
> On the night of 15–16 April, groups tasked with clearing passages in enemy minefields gathered in the trenches with the assault infantry's foremost battalions.
>
> With the permission of the Front commander, my staff and I ... went to Colonel General [Vasily Nikolayevich] Gordov's Third Guards Army to supervise the preparation of bridge crossings for the tank armies of Generals Rybalko and Lelyushenko, and to monitor the progress of the crossing ... we arrived there at midnight. We stopped in the dugout of Major General [Aleksandr Nikiforovich] Gusev [commander of Third Army's engineers], where we spent the night.
>
> Before dawn, together with Gusev, we went to the army command post. The commanders of 6th Pontoon Bridge Brigade, Colonel Berzin, and 16th Assault Engineer Brigade, Colonel Kordyukov, were already there. Part of the battalions of these formations was assigned to support Third Guards Army, and Berzin planned to build a 60-ton pontoon bridge to allow Rybalko's tank army to cross as it advanced; Kordyukov would build two nine-ton bridges from the light column for Third Guards Army.

The Red Army: Plans for Vengeance

In the room, lit by electric bulbs from a car's headlamps, there were two tables that had been knocked together by the sappers. On one of them was a telephone and a large-scale map. This showed all the crossings that had been established in Third Guards Army's zone over the river. The locations, capacity, start times for new crossings, the responsible officers, and the commandants of the crossings were all indicated.

The time for artillery preparation was approaching. Every now and then we glanced at the clock. Time passed extremely slowly. But finally the hands showed 0615 and immediately there was a deafening salvo of thousands of guns and mortars. The roar intensified and grew, shaking everything around us. There were about 270 guns and mortars for every kilometre of the front. Huge, crushing power! We tried to speak to each other, but the words were drowned by the incessant roar. We had to explain ourselves as if we were deaf and dumb, using gestures and facial expressions.[25]

The preparations were over and the battle had commenced. In their positions, the German and Soviet soldiers waited for the bombardment to end, knowing that many of them would be dead before the day was out. The commanders on both sides had done all they could. And to the rear of the German lines, the people of Berlin waited with fear for the outcome of a battle that would decide their fates.

Chapter 5

THE STORM BURSTS: 16 APRIL

Before dawn on 16 April, the massed guns of 1st Ukrainian Front and 1st Belarusian Front opened fire on the German defences. For the Red Army, its artillery was the 'god of war', and there was widespread expectation that, if used effectively, it could smash the enemy defences and make an advance relatively simple. Despite repeated failures to achieve such an outcome, this belief persisted even in 1945.

Like all armies in the First World War, the Russian Army had been caught by surprise by the huge consumption of ammunition by its artillery formations. Ever since the invention of artillery, soldiers had learned the benefit of digging trenches and other earthworks to avoid being pulverised by bombardments, and artillery had evolved to try to overcome this. Solid shot was replaced by explosive ammunition, and the weight of fire – in terms of both the size of individual shells and the number of guns deployed – increased steadily, particularly through the First World War. When initial barrages repeatedly failed to deliver the desired results, the conclusion was usually the same: more guns, more ammunition, longer bombardments would have to be used in future.

But such analysis often failed to identify a recurring issue. Regardless of the weight of shelling, bombardments were often too haphazard. Even if an entire area was heavily shelled, positions that had been carefully constructed could survive anything other than a direct hit by a heavy shell, and the troops that would man these fortifications were often safe in deep bunkers, ready to take up defensive positions when the ground attack began. Defensive artillery was also used to devastating effect, catching attacking troops as they advanced across open ground. The use of rolling barrages – effectively a curtain of shelling that steadily progressed through the depths of the defensive positions while attacking troops advanced as close as possible behind the bombardment – could be countered by ordering defensive artillery to fire either on pre-identified forming-up areas for attacking troops, on the strips of no-man's land that they (and any reinforcements for the attacking wave) would have to cross, or immediately behind the rolling barrage, to catch attackers as they tried to move forward as close to the curtain as possible. Of course, such defensive measures required the artillery assets of the defenders to survive the initial bombardment, and this further emphasised the importance of proper targeting. That, in turn, relied on high-quality reconnaissance.

Unlike the German armed forces and those of the Western Powers, Soviet forces did not have any aircraft that had been specifically designed for aerial reconnaissance. Most of the planes used were converted bombers, and although the quality of photography improved steadily through the war – not least through the provision of cameras from the West as part of the huge quantities of aid dispatched to the Soviet Union – the quality of reconnaissance prior to attacks remained variable. Partly, this was because the Germans had become adept at building multiple firing positions and moving their guns and other assets from one to the other, making it difficult to predict which would be occupied at any particular time. Improved camouflage of such positions made them harder to detect, and dummy positions were constructed – if time and resources permitted – to add to the difficulties of Soviet reconnaissance. In their memoirs, Red Army commanders wrote about the thousands of highly detailed photographs that were taken before the commencement of the assault in April 1945, but this was merely the first step: analysis of these photographs and proper targeting of identified positions was critical. In January 1945, Konev's 1st Ukrainian Front made its attack out of the large bridgehead over the Vistula near Sandomierz after a devastating bombardment that was both heavy and precisely targeted, and for perhaps the first time in the conflict, the 'god of war' delivered what had been expected. Now, in April, as they prepared to fight for the capital of the Reich, both sides waited to see how accurate the initial bombardment would be.

Writing after the war, Heinrici described the Soviet preparatory bombardment as possibly the heaviest of the war; however, the weight of shelling prior to almost any Red Army attack was often described in such terms. Nonetheless, the guns hammered at the German lines while aircraft flew forward to strike at targets further to the rear and, visually at least, it was an impressive commencement to the operation. Colonel General Vladimir Ivanovich Kazakov, Zhukov's artillery chief, wrote:

> At 0500 Moscow time (locally, it was 0300) on 16 April, a powerful salvo fired by a huge mass of guns and mortars heralded the start of the artillery preparation.

The Storm Bursts: 16 April

The spectacle was truly astounding: tens of thousands of flashes appeared across a wide front from the firing positions, followed by the flashes of explosions in the enemy positions. The salvoes of *Katyusha* rockets made a particularly strong impression. Even experienced artillerymen were transfixed by this spectacle, all the more menacing because it took place at night rather than in daylight.[1]

The salvo rocket launchers known to the Red Army as the *Katyusha* and to the Germans as the *Stalinorgel* ('Stalin Organ') had been in use throughout the war, but their efficacy was questionable. The visual and auditory impact was great, and a battery of four launchers could fire a salvo that delivered over four tons of explosives, but the range was less than that of conventional artillery and it was also far less accurate. Reloading the launchers took a considerable amount of time, meaning that *Katyushas* could really be used in just a single salvo. It was normal Red Army practice to deploy them for a massive area bombardment, often immediately before the ground attack commenced, but this was a questionable practice – at that stage, any defending troops would still be safe in their bunkers, and the Germans rapidly realised that however unnerving the shrieking rockets were, their use at the end of a bombardment provided the defenders with ample warning of the advance of ground troops. By 1945, Soviet artillery officers were mixing their tactics, often adding a further conventional bombardment of front-line positions shortly after the *Katyusha* salvoes to catch any Germans who might have emerged from their shelters in anticipation of a ground attack; some accounts of this attack describe the use of *Katyushas* at a very early stage of the bombardment rather than as a finale.

The bombardment was shorter than Antipenko, Zhukov's logistics chief, had feared; he could hope that at least there would be sufficient ammunition for further bombardments if required. For the Germans on the receiving end, even this shortened artillery preparation was a brutal experience. Tams, the company commander in 20th Panzergrenadier Division, was on the Seelow Heights:

> It seemed as if the dawn was suddenly upon us, then vanished again. The whole Oder valley bed shook. In the bridgehead [the Soviet positions on the west bank of the Oder] it was as light as day. The hurricane of fire reached out to the Seelow Heights. It seemed as if the earth was reaching up into the sky like a dense wall. Everything around us started dancing, rattling about. Whatever was not securely fastened down fell from the shelves and cupboards. Pictures fell off the walls and crashed to the floor. Glass splinters jumped out of window frames. We were soon covered in sand, dirt, and glass splinters. None of us had experienced anything like it before, and would not have believed it possible. There was no escape.

The greatest concentration of artillery fire in history was directed immediately in front of us. We had the impression that every square yard of earth would be ploughed up. After two or three hours, the fire was suddenly lifted. Cautiously we risked a peep over the Heights down into the Oderbruch, and what we saw made the blood run cold. As far as we could see in the grey light of dawn came a single wave of heavy tanks. As the first row came closer we saw behind them another, and then hordes of running infantry.[2]

Tams' description of the bombardment continuing for 'two or three hours' is incorrect. Further south, Konev's 1st Ukrainian Front conducted a longer bombardment, but after the first 30 minutes, Zhukov's artillery had largely shifted its fire to deeper locations. Moreover, aerial attacks added to the explosions and smoke, and these two factors may have contributed to Tams feeling as if his position, at least, was still being bombarded even when the shelling of the front line had stopped. Altner and his comrades were in the third defensive belt and experienced the artillery bombardment from further to the rear:

We are woken in the middle of the night by the sudden shaking and shuddering of the earth beneath us ... I quickly pull on my boots, take my greatcoat and pack under my arm, and stumble out into the night. The earth is quaking and the night is full of lightning and roaring. Heavy shells are passing over us and we can see each other's tired faces whenever an explosion bursts and a flash of light hangs briefly in the night ...

The thundering of guns has turned into a single roar and the air is full of howls, whistles and a quivering and buzzing. Heavy bangs come from behind us between the lesser explosions, sounding like railway wagons shunting into each other. A vast red wall of fire rises up into the sky in front of us, clouds of smoke rising with it. The shapes of bombers appear like giant birds in the black clouds. Fountains of dirt and iron erupt. We duck deeper in our trenches ...

We are in a vast cauldron. In front of us, around us and behind us is an enveloping hell as the Russians drum on our trenches. The explosions go on and on. Our ears have long since been deafened. Hardly anyone speaks. Only when a fountain of dirt and steel erupts close by does an angry word escape that one can read from their lips.

Burning barns and villages stand out in the distance like torches in the night, and refugees are coming back dragging their belongings in prams and handcarts, or on their backs. A woman in a dressing gown that flaps in the wind stumbles past with her hair loosened, her eyes a complete blank. She has a coffee mill in her hand which she keeps turning endlessly. Her mouth moves but makes no sound.[3]

The Storm Bursts: 16 April

In keeping with Heinrici's orders to abandon the foremost positions at the last moment, some of the soldiers of 9th Fallschirmjäger Division were still in the process of pulling back when the bombardment began, resulting in many men being killed, including Oberst Arthur Menke, commander of one of the division's regiments. From the moment that the division was assigned to him, Heinrici had questioned the credentials of the paratroopers as an elite, veteran formation; now, the resilience of the division was sorely tested from the outset. Of its three regiments, one was made up of veterans, most of them fully trained parachutists; another had been involved in combat in Hungary and France and had at least some experienced soldiers, and the third was typical of German units of the closing stages of the war, made up largely of rear area units hastily repurposed as infantry. The other elements of the division – its artillery, anti-tank battalion, combat engineers – existed more on paper than in reality and in many cases were deployed elsewhere.

In addition to modifications of traditional fire plans, Zhukov's units had organised a further innovation in an attempt to confuse the Germans. Hundreds of powerful searchlights, usually used as part of air defences, had been brought to the front line. Most were manned by the volunteer crews that had used them in Soviet cities, and front-line soldiers were surprised to find large numbers of women in their trenches. After just 25 minutes, as the artillery barrage moved on to targets further to the rear of the German front line and the assault troops set off, the searchlights were switched on, directed at the German positions. It seems that the intention of this was twofold. Firstly, it would illuminate the battlefield during the pre-dawn attack. Secondly, it was expected that the powerful lights would dazzle the defenders. Some senior officers involved in the offensive regarded this innovation as a great success – Kazakov, Zhukov's artillery commander, later wrote that the innovation illuminated the ground over which the attacking troops were to advance – but the men in the front line had mixed views. Aleksei Petrovich Ivanov was a 'tank rider', assigned to go into battle on the back of an assault gun. He later remembered how his men were given their final preparations for the attack:

> All of us were gathered together and the platoon commander distributed bottles of alcohol, one between five men. We poured 100g each and early in the morning the artillery preparation began. The *Katyushas* fired first, then artillery of all calibres joined in. Thick clouds of smoke and dust were everywhere, and when the attack began the searchlights were switched on. The widespread clouds, which covered everything, became like yellow smoke in the light. We couldn't turn back because the searchlights were so blinding, and all we could make out were silhouettes, we couldn't see anything else.[4]

Chuikov, who was joined in his bunker by Zhukov during the initial bombardment, was equally unimpressed:

> In my army's zone, the light of artillery fire was so bright that it was difficult to get any impression from the command post of the first moment when the searchlights were switched on. As we didn't sense it, the Front commander and I even wondered why the searchlights hadn't been activated. We were surprised when they told us that they were actually operating.
>
> I must say that while we admired the power and effect of the searchlights during training, none of us could predict accurately what it would look like in a combat situation. It is difficult for me to judge how things were in other sectors of the front but in the zone of my Eighth Guards Army, I saw how the powerful beams of light from the searchlights fell on a swirling curtain of smoke, dust and flames raised above the enemy positions. No searchlights could penetrate this barrier and it was difficult for us to observe the battlefield directly. As luck would have it, the wind was also blowing against us. Consequently, Hill 81.5, where my command post was located, was soon shrouded in impenetrable smoke. We couldn't see anything at all and had to rely on the radio telephone and messengers to communicate with and control our troops.[5]

As they laboured forward over the heavily cratered landscape, many of the Soviet soldiers realised that far from aiding them, the searchlights were merely providing any German gunners who were still active with a brightly lit background against which the advancing troops were clearly silhouetted. Several company and battalion commanders sent back urgent requests for the lights to be switched off; Zhukov and Kazakov refused and overruled the requests. With no prior experience of operating with such bright lights turning the clouds of smoke and dust into a glowing fog, many infantry units chose to remain in their trenches until dawn.

Even with all the careful planning, the scale of the operation meant that there was considerable confusion. Vladimir Vladimirovich Myasnikov, whose unit was armed with flamethrowers, had clearly received no advance warning that the offensive was commencing and the artillery bombardment took him and his comrades by surprise. Then the battalion chief of staff arrived in the trench:

> He ordered the flamethrowers to be brought up and prepared to move forward. Everywhere it seemed as if there was a thick fog, it was like walking in milk, we couldn't see anything. We pulled the flamethrowers out of the trench and were checking them when trucks arrived. We were loaded aboard and off we went. Somewhere up ahead our troops were held up and we were to help them gain a

The Storm Bursts: 16 April

foothold. We were given the command: 'Deploy the flamethrowers in such-and-such a position'. We quickly dismounted, dug in, and waited for the order to attack. But there was no attack. Instead, we were ordered once again, 'Mount up'.[6]

Despite the hope of logistics officers like Antipenko that the truncated bombardment might result in stocks of ammunition being saved, many gunners had been issued barely enough even for the initial barrage. Dmitry Filippovich Osinovsky had missed the bombardment – suffering from severe toothache, he had been sent to the rear to find medical help. After a fruitless search, he returned to his battery:

> During this offensive, our brigade had just a couple of shells [per gun] left and there were no more supplies, so the guns were mainly just left in the woods. But as the artillery division's intelligence officer, I was sent to the headquarters of the rifle corps to provide artillery support for the infantry. Although our brigade didn't fire a further shot, I was dispatched to the front 'on a dashing horse', which in reality was a damaged truck, with a radio operator and driver.[7]

All along the front line, Soviet troops were moving forward. Chuikov later wrote that there was little by way of defensive fire at first from the German lines, something that he attributed to the efficacy of the initial artillery preparation, but much of the apparent silence from the German gunners was due to Heinrici's plan to pull back from the foremost positions:

> For the first two kilometres, our rifle units and tanks advanced successfully, albeit slowly, behind the barrage of fire. And then, as the ground was blocked by streams and canals, the tanks and assault guns began to lag behind the infantry. Cooperation between artillery, infantry and armour was disrupted. The precisely timed artillery barrage had to be stopped and the guns switched to supporting the infantry and tanks with sequential concentration of fire. The surviving enemy guns and mortars came to life at dawn and began to fire on the routes along which our troops and equipment were moving forward. In some regiments and battalions, this resulted in chaos. All of this affected the pace of the assault.
>
> The enemy showed particularly stubborn resistance along the *Hauptgraben* ['Main Canal'], which runs through the valley, skirting the foot of the Seelow Heights. The spring waters made it deep, impassable for our tanks and assault guns. And the few bridges over it were shelled by artillery and mortars from behind the Seelow Heights, and were covered by direct fire from dug-in, well-camouflaged tanks and assault guns.

Here, our advance slowed even more. While the sappers tried to establish crossings, the troops came to a standstill. It was impossible for vehicles and tanks to manoeuvre; the roads were clogged, and it was impossible to move directly across the swampy floodplain and the mine-strewn fields.[8]

Ivanov and his sappers were accompanying assault guns that supported Chuikov's Eighth Guards Army in its attack:

> We reached the Seelow Heights around noon, because they were only 6km from our front line. As it was spring and this was a low-lying floodplain and a rather swampy area, there were few roads and numerous canals and ditches. By the time we moved forward, all the craters left by our artillery barrage were already filled with water.
>
> And let me describe what the Seelow Heights were like in our area. Imagine being on a plain, and then in front of you is a steep slope, covered with forest, a slope of about 70 degrees. I can tell you with certainty that these heights were completely insurmountable for any vehicles, and the only possible passages were along the few roads that crossed the heights. In our sector, even ordinary artillery couldn't fire on them, because the barrels would have to be raised too steeply, so the only fire was from mortars.[9]

At the outset of the war, Soviet tank units often consisted of a mixture of light, medium, and heavy tanks. This proved to be an unwieldy arrangement. Travelling at different speeds, the tanks struggled to move as a coherent whole, and the heavy tanks – ranging from the strange multi-turreted vehicles like the T-35 to the more conventional KV series – often damaged roads and bridges, making movement of reinforcements and supplies much more difficult. As the war progressed, the heavy tanks – now mainly the far more effective vehicles of the IS series – were grouped in separate heavy tank regiments, intended for use as breakthrough units. The Seelow Heights were almost impossible for any motor vehicle to ascend, and these heavy tanks, weighing more than 40 tons, now came to an almost complete halt. The German defenders had anticipated this, and Tams' panzergrenadier division was quick to take advantage. In addition to its anti-tank weapons, the division was supported by numerous groups of lethal 88mm dual-purpose guns, manned by Luftwaffe anti-aircraft crews:

> With their barrels fully depressed the anti-aircraft guns dug in on the ridge along the chain of hills directed their murderous fire on the Soviets. Tank after tank

went up in flames, the infantry sitting on them being swept off. The survivors charged on with piercing cries. The Luftwaffe gun crews were firing into the packs of Red soldiers and the attack began to collapse in front of our eyes. Several T-34s had broken through and were now being knocked out by our troops as they tried to roll up the slope of *Reichstrasse 1* [the main east-west highway running over the heights to Berlin] into Seelow. As it became full light, the enemy was beaten back with heavy losses for the Soviets.[10]

For the men of 20th Panzergrenadier Division, it felt like a moment of vindication. They had been forced back in the previous two days by powerful 'reconnaissance in force' attacks, and in a fit of temper, Hitler had ordered all soldiers of the division to remove their medals and other decorations.[11] If they had tried to hold their positions as the Führer demanded, many of their guns would have been destroyed by the Soviet bombardment and their defensive fire against advancing Soviet tanks would have been far less effective.

Arkady Vesterman, whose experiences as a recruit were described above, was waiting in his T-34, hoping and expecting that the heavyweight IS tanks would be able to create a breakthrough. When his battalion was ordered forward at midday, they passed a field full of burning IS-2s; Vesterman counted 21 wrecks.[12] Most Soviet soldiers regarded these behemoths as almost invulnerable, and the sight of so many of them destroyed had a sobering effect. Uri Nikolayevich Polyakov was a crewman in an assault gun and when his battalion advanced late on 16 April, he too stared at the wrecks in amazement:

> That was where I first saw our IS-2 tanks that had been destroyed. I thought nothing at all could harm them. I had seen a damaged IS before, its gun had been knocked off and there were God knows how many dents on the turret and hull, but there were no penetrations of its armour. But here on the Seelow Heights, the Müncheberg road twisted its way up the slope. We passed one bend and stared – there were two burned-out ISs standing there. We were surprised – what had happened? We drove by and I turned and looked, and both of them had huge holes in their frontal armour. It seemed impossible because this armour was 180mm thick [maximum thickness was actually 120mm]. We drove another 100m and there we saw stationary German anti-aircraft guns in concrete firing wells, apparently from the air defence belt. It seemed the tanks were crawling around the bend and the Germans hit them at point-blank range. No armour could withstand that.[13]

Heinrici's decision not to contest the Oderbruch and to rely instead on the barrier of the Seelow Heights proved to be correct. Ivanov and his sappers had gathered at the bottom of the slope:

> In general, the battle seemed to have died down at about midday when we reached the foot of the heights. The Germans weren't firing, and nor were we. A lieutenant colonel, the deputy regiment commander and the former head of the regiment's reconnaissance company, told me: 'Come with me to scout out the front line.'
>
> Running from crater to crater, we reached our front trench. There along the high ground there were birch trees and some kind of a ditch, not particularly deep. When the infantry approached the heights, they had dug in along this ditch, as it was the only shelter around. We jumped into it, and what a nightmare confronted us. The entire ditch was filled with our wounded soldiers, some without arms or legs. They saw us and began to beg, 'Help us, guys!' But we had a completely different task – to scout out a route for tanks, and besides, how could we help such a mass of wounded men? It was horrific. As we moved along the trench, the lieutenant colonel told the wounded that we needed to carry out our reconnaissance. We moved on. In one place I saw a German helmet. I kicked it, and the German wearing it stood up. Can you imagine? He was 40 or 50 years old, and unkempt. Usually the Germans were very neat, but this one's face was literally covered with stubble. He immediately dropped his rifle and raised his hands. I searched him promptly in case he had a grenade or something else but I didn't find anything ... I knew a few words of German and somehow explained to him with gestures, 'Run that way, to our rear area.' The German turned, raised his hands, and ran off. It was clear to me that he was running and waiting for me to shoot him in his back ... And when we looked around, there were about 200 Germans raising their hands and coming up to us to surrender. If they had seen me shooting that first German before their eyes, they would have fired on us and definitely wouldn't have surrendered.[14]

Such a large-scale surrender was probably unusual, given that most of the German positions on the Oderbruch at the foot of the Seelow Heights had already been abandoned. But the old soldier described by Ivanov was one of the last wave of people mobilised by Germany for its final defence, and these drafts had little or no experience of warfare. It is hardly surprising that many chose to surrender and save their own lives at the first opportunity.

From a point about three miles north of Seelow, the ridge of the Seelow Heights runs south, angling slightly to the east, until it reaches Mallnow, about seven miles from its origin. Here, it angles sharply to the northeast, forming a narrow spur that extends as far as the village of Reitwein. This spur was the only part of the high ground that was already under the control of the Red Army at the beginning of the offensive; Chuikov's command post was located here, and he and his fellow senior officers peered in vain through the smoke and dust to assess progress. When the initial reports arrived, the news was neither unexpected nor positive: the assault waves were struggling to make any progress. All three of Chuikov's rifle corps had been involved in the initial assault and as they laboured forward over the cratered floodplain of the Oderbruch, German artillery began to fire with increasing weight and effect. Despite every attempt at reconnaissance, both on the ground and in the air, the Red Army had failed to identify all of the German artillery positions on the high ground.

After overrunning most of the Oderbruch, Chuikov ordered his artillery units to move forward so that they could make a second bombardment, this time of the German lines along the Seelow Heights. After a renewed burst of shelling, the infantry and armour were ordered forward once again. There were just three good roads that Soviet tanks could use to ascend the ridge, and the most accessible was *Reichsstrasse 1,* running in an almost straight line from the Oder at Küstrin to Seelow. The Germans had of course covered this with their best anti-tank formations, including a group of Panther and Tiger tanks from the *Müncheberg* panzer division. The battalion of 20 tanks moved into pre-reconnoitred positions close to the *Hauptgraben* at the foot of the slope and waited for the Soviet armour. It was here that many of the advancing IS tanks were destroyed; although the Soviet heavy tanks had powerful 122mm guns, capable of destroying either a Panther or a Tiger, they suffered from a slow rate of fire. From their camouflaged positions, the Germans also had the advantage of firing the first shots, and at short range they could hardly miss. They rapidly destroyed or crippled the first wave of tanks attempting to ascend the slope.

A little to the north, the German lines proved less robust. When Soviet riflemen advanced towards the southern edge of the village of Werbig at the foot of the Seelow Heights, the inexperienced and poorly trained German defenders in some areas simply abandoned their trenches and fled. The small garrison in Werbig succeeded in holding the village, but the Soviet 47th Guards Rifle Division – part of Eighth Guards Army's IV Guards Rifle Corps – managed to ascend the slope and secure a foothold on the heights. A desperate German counterattack dislodged most of the Soviet troops, briefly stabilising the situation.

Frustrated by the slow progress, Zhukov decided to send his two tank armies into action. He later wrote that he had considered this as a possibility during the planning of the operation. On numerous occasions during the war, tank forces that had been intended to be inserted through breaches created by the combined arms armies were obliged to lend their weight to the initial assaults in order to help create the breaches, but this ran the risk that the tank formations would be weakened by these initial battles, thus limiting their efficacy in exploiting into the depths of the German lines. Zhukov later wrote that after consulting his army commanders, he ordered the two tank armies to join the assault in the early afternoon. Chuikov's account suggests that contrary to Zhukov's account, there had been no prior discussion about such an early deployment of the tank armies, and Katukov took a similar view. He was discussing matters with Lieutenant General Mikhail Alekseyevich Shalin, his chief of staff:

> Our conversation was interrupted by a radio call. The familiar voice of the Front commander sounded from the phone. An unexpected order followed: without waiting for a complete breakthrough of the enemy defences, First Guards Tank Army was to go into battle, tasked with completing the breakthrough of the enemy's tactical defence zone in conjunction with Eighth Guards Army.
>
> Although the prospect of throwing vehicles at unsuppressed enemy firing points was not encouraging, I could see that in the current situation the Front commander had no other choice; during nine hours of constant attacks, Chuikov's infantry had been able to wedge itself into the enemy's defensive lines in only a few areas.[15]

Regardless of whether this was a change of plan or not, Katukov acted quickly. He sent all three of his corps – XI Tank Corps on the northern flank, XI Guards Tank Corps in the centre, and VIII Guards Mechanised Corps on the southern flank – into action. But despite the additional weight of troops, the attackers made little progress. With only three roads ascending the Seelow Heights, and these now partly choked with the wrecked vehicles destroyed in earlier attacks, it was almost impossible for Katukov's tanks to do more than strengthen the positions held by Chuikov's infantry.

As the day progressed, Hauptmann Horst Zobel, commander of the *Muncheberg* panzer battalion that was helping defend the Seelow Heights against the Soviet attack, became aware that he was in danger of being outflanked. Despite the steadily rising number of destroyed and disabled Red Army tanks at the bottom of the slope, one group of attackers was beginning to climb towards the ridge. Babadzhanian's XI Guards Tank Corps had been led across Poland and eastern Germany by 44th Guards Tank Brigade, commanded by the resourceful Colonel Iosif Irakliyevich Gusakovsky; during the advance through the German defences to the west of Poznań, he had shown a level of independence of mind that was unusual in the Red Army, willingly taking risks and operating almost unsupported in order to keep up the tempo of the attack. Now, his brigade was involved in the first attempt to force *Reichstrasse 1*; the attack rapidly broke down despite the other two brigades of Babadzhanian's tank corps joining the attack. Lieutenant General Andrei Lavrentyevich Getman, second-in-command of First Guards Tank Army, described how the fighting unfolded, and although his account is full of the flourishes typical of Soviet historiography, it gives a good picture of the battle:

> Meanwhile, having become convinced of the futility of the attempts to break through to Seelow with a frontal attack, the commander of the leading unit, Colonel Gusakovsky, decided to try to bypass this strongpoint from the south. After advancing towards the southwest, 44th Guards Tank Brigade reached the farm at Ludwigslust at 2000.
>
> Here, the famed tank platoon of Lieutenant Kravchenko, already awarded Hero of the Soviet Union, distinguished itself once more. Deployed as reconnaissance, it was the first to approach Ludwigslust. Despite heavy enemy fire, the brave tankers immediately rushed into the farm. Then, from the other side of the farm, enemy tanks and infantry moved towards them. But the platoon had already taken up an advantageous position. Hidden from enemy sight, our tankers nonetheless had a good view of the single road through the farm. Lieutenant Kravchenko was in a good position for an ambush.
>
> The Nazis apparently expected to encounter Soviet reconnaissance troops and, taking advantage of their superior forces, to destroy them. But as soon as they ventured into the ambush, Kravchenko's platoon opened fire on them. The lead Tiger was hit by the first shot from Junior Lieutenant Osminkin's tank. Immediately after this, a Panther and two more Tigers caught fire. The others quickly turned back. The enemy infantry also fled, suffering significant losses.[16]

This farm was a little to the east of Friedersdorf, at the lip of the Seelow Heights. What Getman doesn't mention is that the first attempt to force the road leading through Ludwigslust towards Friedersdorf failed when Zobel's tanks shot up several Soviet tanks, striking their thinner side armour, but this initial setback proved to be the key to Gusakovsky's success: Kravchenko's platoon was then able to move up the slope using the wrecked tanks from the first attack for cover. Zobel had lost four of his tanks during the day, but had accounted for far more Red Army tanks – his men claimed up to 50 'kills', but many of these would have been disabled rather than destroyed.

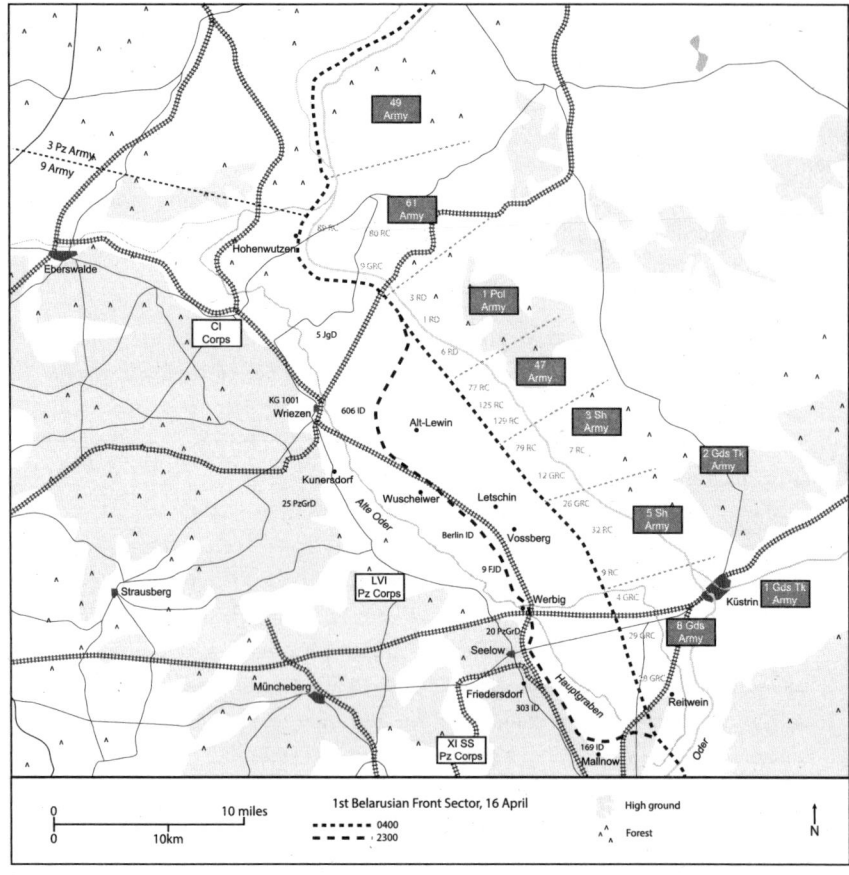

Elsewhere in Zhukov's sector of the front line, there was variable progress. His most northern formations were Sixty-First Army and First Polish Army. The units of Sixty-First Army occupied a bend in the river that projects towards the west, and there were options for attacks towards either the northwest or the southwest. The commander of the army was Colonel General Pavel Alekseyevich Belov, who had achieved fame in the aftermath of the Battle of Moscow in the winter of 1941–42. At the head of I Guards Cavalry Corps, he had broken into the rear of the German lines and, supported by several thousand paratroopers, his men had roamed almost unchecked across a large area in the German rear area, ultimately forcing the diversion of several German divisions. After an eventful few weeks, Belov and his men managed to break out to reach safety, and even senior Germans praised him for his resourcefulness. Faced with

The Storm Bursts: 16 April

the Oder, he concluded that an attack towards the northwest and the town of Schwedt would be difficult as the west bank was another floodplain, too soft for tanks to manoeuvre off-road. Consequently, he made only a limited attack here with two reinforced rifle companies. His main effort was towards the southwest, attacking towards Hohenwutzen. Here, his LXXXIX Corps threw two battalions across the river either side of the main road bridge, triggering energetic German counterattacks. The northern bridgehead was rapidly eliminated and the southern bridgehead was screened off.

On Belov's southern flank, First Polish Army was able to deploy some units in the northern edge of a bridgehead held by Forty-Seventh Army to the south. As these troops attacked towards the west and northwest, other Polish units undertook the difficult task of crossing the Oder under fire. Unlike Belov's troops, the Poles had considerable success despite fierce resistance, establishing bridgeheads over the Oder and linking up with their compatriots who were advancing from Forty-Seventh Army's bridgehead. Further south, Major General Frantz Iosifovich Perkhorovich's Forty-Seventh Army had concentrated a considerable force in his small bridgehead and attacked towards the southwest with five rifle divisions supported by a heavy tank regiment and four assault gun regiments. Despite this formidable array, his army struggled to make much progress. The line of advance was crossed by several water obstacles and there were limited crossing points suitable for armoured vehicles. In the path of the Soviet troops was 606th Infantry Division, created from the remnants of 541st Volksgrenadier Division, which had been fighting in East Prussia where it was largely destroyed. The new division had been in existence for less than a week and had three weak regiments, each in reality no more than a single battalion, supported by a battalion of sappers and an anti-tank company. Nonetheless, it fought doggedly through the day, preventing the Soviet units from breaking out. As darkness fell, the division reported that its men were exhausted and almost completely out of ammunition. They would be unable to continue holding back the Soviet assault if it continued the following day.

In an attempt to stabilise the southern flank of 606th Infantry Division, the Germans mounted several counterattacks with a mixed battlegroup of two SS battalions, the anti-aircraft battalion of 25th Panzergrenadier Division, and the weak battalions of an improvised regiment of Luftwaffe officer cadets. Constantly harassed from the air, the Germans were driven from the village of Alt-Lewin and pulled back towards Kunersdorf. This threatened to break open the German defences in the area and a further counterattack was essential to restore the situation. One of the units ordered to concentrate a little to the north of the Soviet advance was a unit with the unlikely name of *Kampfgruppe 1001 Nachts*

('1001 Nights Battlegroup'), originally formed around three companies of men who had been guarding V-2 rocket sites. They had been reinforced with three companies of Hetzer tank destroyers, a motorcycle company, and a few assault guns and armoured cars from 27th *SS-Langemark*, giving it a total strength of about 500 men and 43 armoured vehicles. At the end of March, it fought its first battle in an unsuccessful attack to try to reduce the Soviet Forty-Seventh Army's bridgehead, and its men now probed forward cautiously from Wriezen to try to ascertain the size of the penetration to the south of the town. They reported the presence of up to 20 Soviet tanks and deployed a thin screen to cover the Soviet troops but lacked the strength to do more.

There were few reserves available for the Germans to conduct the sort of powerful counterattack that was such a hallmark of German tactical and operational doctrine. The only significant reserve in the area was 25th Panzergrenadier Division and late in the afternoon Hitler authorised its release to CI Corps. The division had patiently endured a day of almost constant air attacks and now began to move forward into position. At the end of the day, a battalion from 119th Panzergrenadier Regiment took up covering positions a little to the south of Wriezen. The panzergrenadiers had no contact with any units to north or south; they could only hope that other German formations were covering the gaps.

To make matters worse for the Wehrmacht, Third Shock Army, on Forty-Seventh Army's southern flank, was also attacking. The fighting here concentrated on the small village of Letschin, which had been heavily fortified by elements of the *Infanterie-Division Berlin*. Combat continued into the night both in the village and along the railway embankment to the west, as Friedhelm Schöneck, one of the soldiers in the *Berlin* division, later described:

> By late afternoon our position on the railway embankment was untenable. The ammunition was almost exhausted. The losses in dead and wounded were terrible. We were lying there, a forgotten outpost. There was no question of a command structure, everyone was fighting for himself alone without any set task or orders ...
>
> Going through Seitzing, which we left burning behind us, we reached the road to Wuschewier, but it was no longer a road, only a cratered landscape over which we staggered. The village was just a single heap of rubble. Shattered vehicles were scattered about as if in a scrapyard, with ammunition boxes and equipment around. In between, dead and yet more dead ...
>
> [Later, as pursuing Soviet troops caught up,] machine-gun salvoes whipped across the street, and hand grenades exploded in doorways and cellar shafts: cries, shouts and groans ...

> The whole night through we fought against an enemy who would allow us no rest. Time and again we were showered with splinters from a hail of mortar fire. Where exactly the enemy was located was impossible to establish in this confusion. Gradually the fighting drew towards the southwest corner of the village. It was increasingly obvious that the Russians had already surrounded us and that we, a colourful, thrown-together band of various units, were fighting our war in a lost outpost.[17]

Schöneck and his comrades were almost the last surviving elements of the *Berlin* division. Already weakened by fending off the Soviet reconnaissance probes of the previous two days, all of its units were short of ammunition and most were rapidly overwhelmed or put to flight. Advancing Soviet troops surprised the division headquarters; several senior officers were captured, and the rest dispersed. Generalmajor Heinrich Voigtsberger, the division commander, was amongst those who escaped. He eventually surrendered to British forces advancing from the west in May.

Fifth Shock Army, to the south of Third Shock Army, attacked the lines of 9th Fallschirmjäger Division, some of which had been caught in the forward line by the Soviet artillery preparation. Gerhard Kordes, an 18-year-old recruit, was fortunate to be in the trenches along the base of the ridge line of the Seelow Heights rather than attempting to withdraw from the Oderbruch at the last moment, and watched with horror and amazement as shells rained down on the floodplain before him. When the shelling stopped and Zhukov's searchlights lit up the battlefield, Kordes could see men running towards him; he gripped his rifle in anticipation, but realised that they were Germans who leapt into his trench before clambering out and continuing towards the west, shouting, 'The Russians are coming!' By now, it was beginning to grow light and Kordes stared at what must have seemed like a tidal wave of Soviet armour accompanied by infantry. Suddenly, the artillery batteries deployed in support of 9th Fallschirmjäger Division opened fire and the masses of Soviet riflemen seemed to melt away before Kordes' eyes. The tanks ground forward to the foot of the slope and came to an abrupt halt; Kordes continued to watch as several were hit by anti-tank guns and set ablaze.

As had been the case with Buikov's assault, the Soviet attack foundered as it grew fully light and the surviving tanks and riflemen pulled back a short distance. As they glanced around, the young *Fallschirmjäger* recruits were relieved to see that they had suffered few losses. Shortly after, they received orders to pull back to a new position part-way up the slope of the ridge.[18]

Despite Heinrici's misgivings, the Luftwaffe soldiers fought with great determination, and in many sectors mounted repeated, costly counterattacks against the Soviet units. In an echo of earlier wars, Lieutenant General Fedor Yefimovich Bokov, the head of Fifth Shock Army's political section, ordered the battle flags of all regiments to be carried through the trenches on the night before the assault. Bokov described how the assault developed immediately to the south of Letschin:

> It was striking that at first our rifle, tank, and assault gun units suffered almost no losses. But it became progressively harder to move forward. Due to thick smoke, the accuracy of aimed fire was significantly reduced. Although the density of artillery was very high, the shelling was concentrated in specific areas, meaning that some enemy batteries and machine-gun positions in hardened shelters were unsuppressed. The enemy recovered quickly from their initial shock and began to resist stubbornly.
>
> Lieutenant General [Pavel Andreyevich] Firsov's XXVI Guards Rifle Corps was on the right flank of the army. Overcoming enemy resistance and successfully repelling counterattacks, the corps' soldiers had already reached the second defensive line by midday and by evening were in possession of all three positions of the enemy's forward defensive line. During this day of fighting, they advanced 6–8km ...
>
> The soldiers ... bypassed the enemy strongpoints at the sugar factory in Vossberg and then, attacking at several points, dealt a crushing blow to the German 652nd Regiment ... Each room [in the factory] had to be stormed successively.[19]

A regiment from one of Firsov's divisions was in the forefront of the battle for Letschin, eventually seizing the ruins but only at a high cost. A little to the south, the other formations of General Nikolai Erastovich Berzarin's Fifth Shock Army also suffered considerable casualties as they fought their way forward through the thinning ranks of 9th Fallschirmjäger Division and elements of *Panzer-Division Müncheberg*. Fifth Shock Army faced additional difficulties due to the slowness of Chuikov's advance and had to guard against German attacks from that direction, but managed to fight forward to Werbig. Here, the southern flank of the German defenders who had been shaken in the earlier attack from the south were now fighting more effectively, and Soviet losses soared as Berzarin's troops found themselves facing strengthened strongpoints protected by minefields. An armoured train, with several 88mm guns, repeatedly engaged Soviet tanks and drove them back; some German accounts later described seeing 'thousands' of dead Soviet riflemen along the railway embankment. Nevertheless, after repeatedly bombarding the German positions with heavy artillery, the Red Army units ground down their opponents. Kurt Keller, a panzergrenadier in the *Müncheberg* panzer division, was caught in the midst of the fighting:

> The Russians shelled us with their artillery and other tanks for a further one and a half hours, so that we had to crouch down in shell holes between the goods station and the regimental command post as best we could. We tried jumping from one shell hole to another back to the regimental command post to find better cover and then to break through via the farmsteads to Werbig. However, this didn't work out as we were taking heavy casualties from the Russian submachine-gun and mortar fire, as well as machine-gun fire. Some time between 1100 and 1130 our last regimental commander, a major from Bruchköbel, surrendered with the remains of the regiment.
>
> After the surrender the Russians shot all the wounded who were unable to march any more, as well as some soldiers that were not wounded, standing them up against the wall. I myself stood up against a wall three times until an older Russian took me away, saying to me, 'You are not SS,' and placing me in a group of prisoners being led away.[20]

By this stage of the war, such treatment of wounded men was commonplace on both sides. Keller was fortunate to escape execution, and shortly after managed to slip away and make his way back to German lines.

By the end of the day, the Soviet Second Guards Tank Army was moving forward through the depleted lines of the first wave of attacking infantry to take up the battle and hopefully to advance at a faster rate. As darkness fell, senior Soviet officers began to take stock. Berzarin, Bokov, and other senior figures of Fifth Shock Army were pleased that their units had advanced further than those of Chuikov's Eighth Army to the south, but as they reviewed the performance of their troops, they knew they had fallen short of the day's objectives:

> Due to poor tactical management of some commanders, individual rifle units manoeuvred poorly on the battlefield. Instead of bypassing enemy strongpoints with their main forces, leaving their elimination to the second echelon, officers sometimes threw their regiments into protracted frontal assaults, delaying the overall advance.
>
> When preparing for the offensive, our reconnaissance was unable to establish the enemy's fire system accurately, and consequently during our artillery preparation, it wasn't possible to suppress his weapons completely. In addition, at

the very beginning of the battle, not all units used guns for direct fire support effectively. Due to shortcomings in engineering support in some formation, tanks and artillery lagged behind the infantry, delaying the entry of the second echelon into the battle.[21]

With few exceptions, almost exactly the same issues had been identified ever since the disappointing end to the Battle of Moscow. Training manuals had been altered, but years of fearing to show any initiative could not be overcome easily. Chuikov, too, reflected on his lack of success:

> Why, despite our significant superiority in forces, were we obliged to content ourselves with such modest progress on the first day of the operation? Apparently, the enemy took into account their experiences of past battles and changed the principles of his defensive deployments. Previously, he had positioned his main forces on the first defensive line; the second and third positions, although prepared in depth, were not always occupied by troops of second and third echelons. Also, as a rule, reserves – tank or motorised divisions – did not occupy defensive lines, but were located close by to the rear, ready for counterattacks against any units that broke through. Having studied this plan, we crushed the enemy on his main defensive line. At the same time, aviation and long-range artillery attacked his reserves, disrupting them and preventing the enemy from organising counterattacks. After defeating the enemy troops in the main defensive line, we brought our mobile reserves into battle, usually tank corps and tank armies, which crushed the enemy reserves and advanced into the operational space. This was the case in Ukraine, and again near Kovel and in the Vistula–Oder Operation, when tank armies under the command of Bogdanov and Katukov were introduced into a clean breakthrough made by the combined arms armies in the enemy's main defensive line. These powerful tank formations drove deep into the enemy rear and expanded the breakthrough towards the flanks for hundreds of kilometres.
>
> Now, the enemy organised his defences in a new way. He manned not only the first, but also the second and third zones, placing large numbers of infantry, tanks, and artillery there. In addition, the enemy had strong reserves in the depths of his defences. After breaking through the first defensive line along the banks of the Alte Oder and the Haupt Canal, our troops encountered the enemy's organised second line of defence, already manned by his troops.
>
> We must also bear in mind the fact that the Nazis turned the entire space from the Oder to Berlin into essentially a continuous fortified area, where in addition to powerful field positions, numerous buildings, forests, and water barriers were adapted for defence.

> We did not pay sufficient attention to the uniqueness of the area, which is replete with natural barriers – canals, streams, and lakes. The lack of roads hampered our ability to manoeuvre and made it impossible to introduce large formations into the attacks. On top of that, there were many villages where every house had to be stormed.
>
> The first day of the offensive showed that the enemy would fight stubbornly for every defensive line. Large numbers of special teams of SS troops were deployed; they were ordered, according to prisoners, to shoot anyone who tried to retreat or showed lack of resolve. We had to storm every trench and every dugout, not to mention residential areas.[22]

By the end of the first day, Eighth Guards Army had barely reached the Seelow Heights, and had advanced over ground that had been clearly visible to the Red Army for several weeks. Failure to take proper account of the defensive possibilities open to the Germans in this area is astonishing and difficult to understand; nor are Chuikov's comments consistent with earlier statements about the comprehensive reconnaissance that had been carried out. It is possible that a degree of complacency had crept into Soviet thinking. After the catastrophic losses suffered by the Germans in their retreat across Poland, and the clearly imminent end of the war, perhaps Chuikov and others anticipated a relatively straightforward advance. But just as Soviet troops had fought with great determination to defend Moscow in 1941, it was surely inevitable that regardless of the likelihood of final defeat, German soldiers would make a major effort to defend their capital against the Red Army.

Further to the south, Konev's 1st Ukrainian Front opened its offensive at the same time. In earlier operations, different Fronts had staggered their start days, for several reasons. Firstly, it was sometimes not possible for reasons of logistics and command and control for huge forces to attack on the same day; secondly, by attacking on consecutive days, there was an increased chance that any German reserves would already have been committed by the time that other Fronts joined the attack. On this occasion, though, Konev's gunners hammered the German lines facing them at the same time as Zhukov's artillery. The Front commander was in the command post of Thirteenth Army with Colonel General Nikolai Pavlovich Pukhov, in preparation for the assault across the Neisse River. Pukhov later described the moment when a chance shot nearly had a major impact on the coming battle:

> Just before the assault on the German defences on the Neisse, Marshal Konev arrived at my observation post. About 15 minutes before the start of the artillery

preparation, he and I entered the dugout located on the bank of the river in the forest. We sat down at the stereoscopic viewers for the last time, and suddenly an enemy bullet glanced off the Marshal's stereoscope. Ivan Stepanovich pretended that he didn't even notice it. I couldn't help but envy his *sang-froid*.

The morning was calm and silent. There was mist over the river. Soon, the silence was shattered by the powerful roar of thousands of shells and mortar bombs. The banks of the Neisse are sandy and from the very first explosions a terrible cloud of dust rose up. When our infantry went forward to attack, there was a solid yellow veil over the west bank of the river. But then a strong gust of wind dispersed it and among the dense trees on the far bank I saw Soviet soldiers and officers running forward rapidly.[23]

Konev later wrote that he hadn't even noticed the sniper's bullet and only became aware of it when he read Pukhov's memoir. After about 90 minutes of shelling of the west bank, Konev's guns moved their barrage further to the west and a smokescreen was laid by Soviet aircraft across the Neisse, adding to the mist and dust:

The entire forest [on the west bank] was covered in a triple layer of smoke – from shell explosions, from the smoke screen, and from fires. This concealed our progress but also created difficulties. It is generally not easy to fight in a forest, even more so in one that is burning. But as events subsequently showed, the artillery preparation was carried out effectively and we were able to break through the main German defensive line on the west bank of the Neisse and, having overcome it, to advance deeper.

The leading battalions began to cross the Neisse at 0655, after the initial artillery bombardment and under cover of the smokescreen. The crossing of the first echelon of the main forces was completed quickly – within one hour. Immediately after the seizure of a bridgehead on the west bank of the Neisse, bridges began to be built throughout the entire breakthrough sector. The leading battalions crossed on boats, dragging components of assault bridges behind them. As soon as the end of such an assault bridge was secured on the opposite bank, infantrymen ran across.

Light pontoon bridges were built in about 50 minutes. Bridges with a capacity of 30 tons took about two hours, and bridges capable of handling 60-ton loads about four to five hours. This latter type could handle tanks of all types. Some of the field artillery was dragged across the river using ropes at the same time that the leading battalions were crossing.

Some 10–15 minutes after the first soldiers reached the west bank of the Neisse, the first 85mm guns were taken across to provide direct fire support against German tanks. This immediately created a sense of security in the first small bridgeheads. In addition to the bridges, crossings were carried out using ferries, which transferred the first groups of tanks to the other shore for direct support of the infantry.[24]

Pukhov's Thirteenth Army was in the centre of Konev's assault, with Third Guards Army operating to the north near Forst and Fifth Guards Army to the south near Muskau. All three armies established secure bridgeheads in the first attack. The defences here consisted of 342nd Infantry Division around Forst and 545th Volksgrenadier Division (part of *Panzerkorps Grossdeutschland*) covering the rest of the sector; the former had suffered almost complete destruction in the battles in Poland in January and February and consisted of no more than a weak battlegroup; and, like all *Volksgrenadier* divisions, its southern neighbour was also a weak formation, with its personnel having had little or no opportunity for these men to establish the rapport and camaraderie that was needed for them to survive combat as a coherent whole. Moreover, neither 342nd Infantry Division's battlegroup nor 545th Volksgrenadier Division had much by way of artillery. They could do little to interfere with the Soviet crossings and by the end of the day, the southern edge of Forst was in the hands of Third Guards Army.

Colonel General Aleksei Semenovich Zhadov's Fifth Guards Army also made rapid progress, as he later described:

> From the reports of my signalmen, I knew things were proceeding well in all my divisions, but I couldn't resist asking the telephonist to put me in touch with one of the division commanders. The first who could be contacted was Major General Vladimir Vasilevich Rusakov, commander of 58th Guards Rifle Division. Before I could ask him the inevitable question of how things were going, his excited voice was already speaking: 'In our sector, Comrade Army Commander, everything is going according to plan, the men are working miracles.' He then added that when one of the links of the assault bridge broke free at the beginning of the attack and floated away ... [four privates] stood up to their chests in the icy water, carrying planks on their shoulders to restore the missing link and thus allowing the infantry battalion to cross. At another site ... [four other soldiers] did the same.
>
> During the second phase of the artillery preparation, all artillery, mortar, and tank units accompanying the assault troops crossed after the rifle battalions. The first echelon of the army's main force had completed its crossing within one hour. The advancing units captured sections of the first trench line and swiftly expanded their bridgeheads. Three hours after the start of the crossing, engineers had built seven bridges along the army's main axis: two nine-ton bridges, four 30-ton

bridges, and a sixty-ton bridge, and after five hours there were already ten bridges functioning. The sappers spent many hours in the icy water building them.

During this time, tanks operating in close support and the remaining forward artillery units crossed to the west bank. The troops were preparing for a concerted attack. At 0840, under cover of artillery fire and with aviation support, the units that had crossed launched an attack on the enemy's main defence line. The Hitlerite troops defended fiercely. Enemy aircraft in groups of up to 12 planes raided our battle formations.

By 1100 the army's troops had broken through the first two lines of the main defensive sector on the primary axis of advance, covering 3–4km and capturing several important strongpoints. The Nazis fought back fiercely. Strong counterattacks followed in quick succession against the right flank and centre of XXXII Guards Rifle Corps and the left flank of XXXIV Guards Rifle Corps. Here, the enemy counterattacked with part of his reserves ... in order to stop our troops and to ensure the second defensive line, codenamed *Matilda*, continued to hold ...

By the end of the first day, XXXII Guards Rifle Corps had broken the main defensive line and was approaching the second, having advanced 10km.[25]

Muskau was captured in the early evening. Unlike in Zhukov's sector, Konev had not needed to throw his tank armies into the battle to overcome the German defensive line; he was anxious to use them for a rapid, deep exploitation, not least because this would allow him maximum leeway in the ambiguity of Stalin's demarcation between the two Soviet Fronts. Lelyushenko's Fourth Guards Tank Army was ready to move through the lines of Fifth Guards Army, and Lelyushenko had established his command post close to Zhadov's headquarters. As soon as the heavy-capacity bridges were operating, the tanks began to cross, with X Guards Tank Corps leading the way. After clashing with small groups of German tanks, the Soviet armour motored forward throughout the following night, maximising the dislocation of the German defences. It seems that the rapid deployment of Lelyushenko's army was hindered more by the almost inevitable confusion of so many units operating close together than by German action. Colonel Vasily Ivanovich Zaitsev's LXI Guards Tank Brigade, part of X Guards Tank Corps, crossed the Neisse close behind Fifth Guards Army:

> The area between the Neisse and Spree Rivers is wooded. The forests were set ablaze by the artillery barrage, which complicated our forward movement. Resourceful paratroopers, who were being used as tank riders, donned their gas masks to avoid

smoke inhalation. Several men were wounded and when they were sent to the rear in their gas masks, panic broke out there as many people concluded that the enemy was using poison gas and the rear area soldiers didn't have masks. The matter came to the attention of the corps commander who contacted me via the radio to ask what was happening and why the men were wearing gas masks. After I explained the reason for the commotion, Lieutenant General [Yevtikhii Yemelianovich] Belov swiftly put an end to the panic amongst the rear area units.[26]

Further north, Rybalko's Third Guards Tank Army was also crossing the Neisse and concentrating on the west bank in preparation for a rapid advance. Despite the description by senior commanders of the operation unfolding smoothly, there were some unnerving moments. Lieutenant Ivan Vladimirovich Maslov was a tank company commander in Third Guards Tank Army:

> About 60 tanks of our brigade crossed the Neisse ... Right in front of Rybalko, the army commander, a few metres from the bridge, my tank hit a mine. Rybalko stood at the crossing with a group of brigade commanders about 100m from the explosion. I got out of my tank, unhurt but badly concussed. A captain ran up to me and ordered, 'Come with me immediately to the commander!'
>
> Staggering slightly, I approached Rybalko and saluted. He asked, 'Who's your company commander?'
>
> 'I am, Senior Lieutenant Maslov!'
>
> 'Well come on, Maslov, change to another tank. I'll need my company commanders in Berlin,' replied Rybalko. I got into tank 217.[27]

Despite the intensity of the fighting around the Seelow Heights and the ominously effective crossing of the Neisse by Konev's 1st Ukrainian Front, the senior German leadership continued to believe that the main Soviet effort in this area would not be against Berlin. Instead, Hitler informed Schörner that evening that he expected the Soviet units to angle towards the southwest, striking towards Dresden. The Führer was at one time described by Nazi propaganda as *Grösster Feldherr Aller Zeiten* – 'greatest general of all time', often abbreviated by soldiers to *Gröfaz* and used as a derogatory term as the war progressed; despite his alleged prowess and intuition, it didn't seem to occur to Hitler that 1st Ukrainian Front had ample forces to attack towards both Dresden and Berlin at the same time, particularly given the weakness of the German Fourth Panzer Army in its path.

But if 1st Ukrainian Front was making good progress, having carried out the difficult task of securing crossings over the Neisse, the same was clearly not the

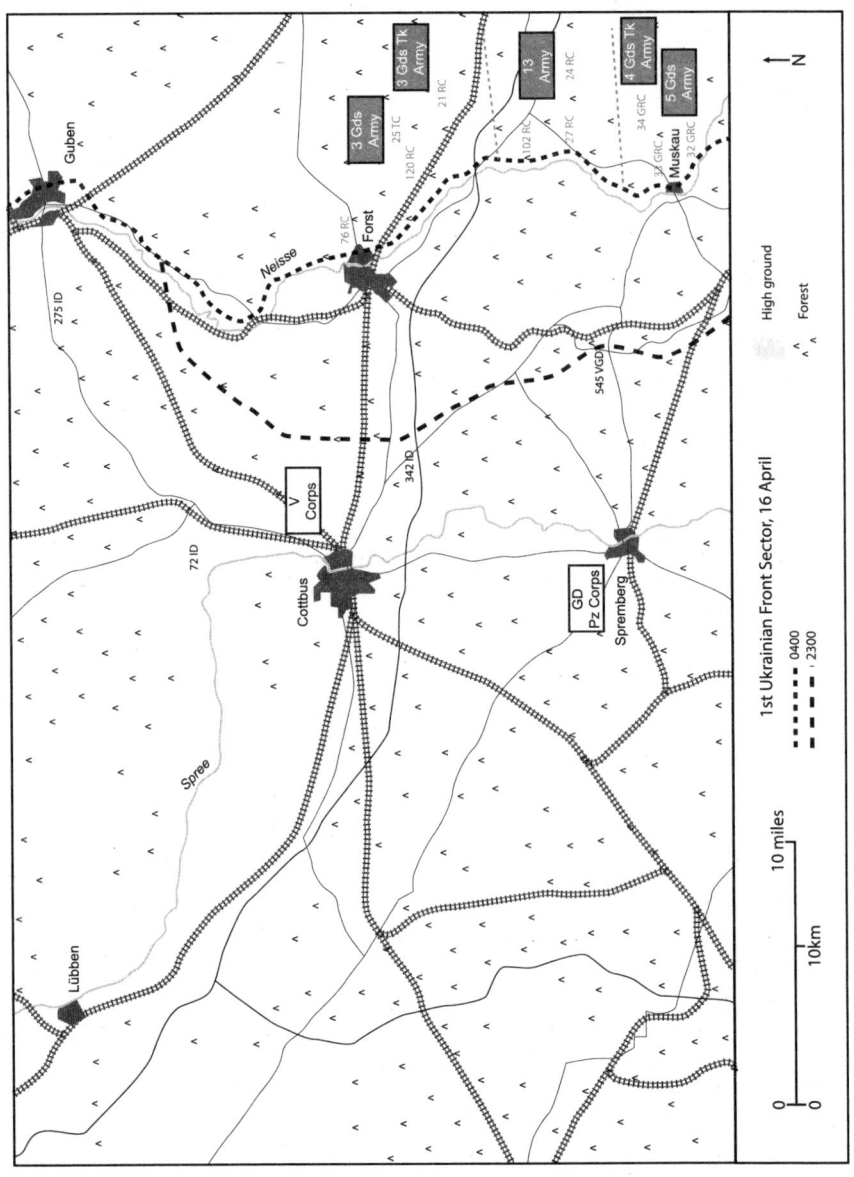

The Storm Bursts: 16 April

case with 1st Belarusian Front. During the late afternoon of 16 April, Zhukov contacted Stalin:

> I called *Stavka* and reported that we had broken through the first and second positions of the enemy's defences and the Front's troops had advanced up to 6km, but then encountered serious resistance along the line of the Seelow Heights where, apparently, the enemy's defences had mostly survived [the initial bombardment]. To strengthen the impact of the combined arms armies, I had brought both tank armies into the battle. I believed that by the end of the following day we would break through the enemy's defences.
>
> Stalin listened attentively and said, 'It seems that you underestimated the enemy on the Berlin axis. I thought that you would already be approaching Berlin, but you're still on the Seelow Heights. Things have started more successfully for Konev. Shouldn't we change the boundaries between the Fronts and turn Konev's and Rokossovsky's main forces towards Berlin? The enemy's defences in front of Konev turned out to be weak,' he continued. 'Konev crossed the Neisse without difficulty and is moving forward without much resistance. Support the attack of your tank armies with bombers. Call me in the evening to tell me how things are progressing.'
>
> That evening, I again spoke to the supreme commander about the difficulties encountered on the approaches to the Seelow Heights and said that it would not be possible to clear this line before the following day. This time, Stalin didn't speak as calmly as he had earlier in the day. 'Your commitment of First Guards Tank Army in Eighth Guards Army's sector instead of where *Stavka* had planned was in vain,' he said sharply, and added, 'Do you have confidence that you will take the Seelow defences tomorrow?'
>
> Trying to remain calm, I replied, 'Tomorrow, 17 April, by the end of the day the defences at the Seelow Heights will have been penetrated. I believe that the more the enemy commits his troops against our forces here, the easier and faster it will be to take Berlin, since it's easier to defeat enemy troops in open country than in a fortified city.'
>
> 'We are considering ordering Konev to turn the tank armies of Rybalko and Lelyushenko towards Berlin from the south and ordering Rokossovsky to accelerate his crossing [of the Oder] and to strike at Berlin from the north,' said Stalin.
>
> I answered, 'Konev's tank armies are quite capable of advancing quickly and they should be turned towards Berlin, but Rokossovsky will not be able to launch an offensive [towards Berlin] earlier than 23 April, since he will face delays in crossing the Oder.'

'Goodbye,' said Stalin rather dryly and hung up.

My mood was not good. But I knew Stalin; even when there were small setbacks, he got irritated very easily.[28]

However Zhukov chose to interpret Stalin's displeasure, the day had been a chastening setback. The assault by 1st Belarusian Front had failed to achieve the level of success expected, and there was now a clear race to Berlin between Zhukov, whose forces were suffering heavy losses for minimal gains, and Konev, who had overcome the barrier of the Neisse and was poised to commit his armour in a rapid advance. Confirmation came in the form of new orders from *Stavka*: Zhukov's chief of staff informed him that Konev had been told to send Third Guards Tank Army to Berlin via Zossen while Fourth Guards Tank Army advanced on Potsdam, and Rokossovsky was to accelerate his plans to cross the Oder and to use some of his exploitation forces to sweep around Berlin from the north. In other words, *Stavka* was directing the Fronts on either side of Zhukov effectively to take over many of the tasks previously assigned to 1st Belarusian Front. Within two days, Rokossovsky's orders were altered once more, instructing him to revert to his original objective of advancing west to secure the coast and to link up with the forces of the Western Allies near Hamburg. In his memoirs, Zhukov gave a frank assessment:

> When preparing the operation, we somewhat underestimated the complexity of the terrain in the Seelow Heights area, where the enemy had the opportunity to organise a very strong defence. Located 10–12km from our start line and dug deep into the ground, especially on the reverse slope of the heights, the enemy could protect his forces and equipment from our artillery bombardment and aerial attacks. It is true that we had very limited time to prepare the Berlin Operation, but this cannot serve as an excuse.
>
> Firstly, I must take the blame for the overall flaw in the planning. I think that, if not publicly, then in my internal reflections, responsibility for the lack of readiness to take the Seelow Heights at the level of armies should lie with the corresponding army commanders and the Front artillery commander, Kazakov, who should have taken into account the difficulties of destroying the enemy defences in this area when planning the artillery bombardment.
>
> Now, a long time later, thinking about the plan for the Berlin Operation, I conclude that whilst the defeat of the enemy's Berlin group and the capture of Berlin itself were conducted correctly, this [initial phase of the operation] could have been carried out somewhat differently.[29]

This version of events is dishonest, according to other veterans of the operation. Writing his memoirs after Zhukov's account was published, Babadzhanian was quick to point this out:

> The Seelow Heights dominate the Oderbruch and form a very serious obstacle on the route to Berlin. The troops of Eighth Guards Army – infantry, artillery, and the tanks assigned to it – all clustered at the foot of the heights, unable to move further.
>
> I remember that in the meeting on 5 April, some of our generals persistently argued to the Front commander that the enemy's main line of defence was not the first, but the second line, which passed through the Seelow Heights, and that artillery and aviation attacks should be concentrated not on the first line, but on the second. However, their opinion was not taken into account.[30]

In other words: Zhukov ignored the concerns of his subordinates. His personal reflections were meaningless to the thousands of dead and wounded men, most of whom were still lying on the approaches to the Seelow Heights. It is noteworthy that Kazakov, the artillery commander of 1st Belarusian Front, makes no mention whatever of the lack of efficacy of the bombardment in his memoirs. Regardless of the time pressure under which Zhukov and his subordinates were working, the soldiers paid with their blood for this failure to assess the German defences accurately.

Chapter 6

BREAKTHROUGH: 17–18 APRIL

17 April

Many miles to the west of the Seelow Heights, the more astute residents of Berlin were aware that trouble was approaching. They had endured increasingly heavy air attacks for several years; now, there were clear signs that they faced a new ordeal. In the Pankow district in the northeast of the city, Sigmund Mehring, who had been an artilleryman in the First World War, heard the distant rumble on 16 April and had no doubt that it was a massive artillery bombardment. In other parts of Berlin, the gunfire wasn't audible, but word spread rapidly. Shortly after, the radio announced that a major Soviet offensive had commenced.

As the day drew to a close, there were other signs. The first refugees fleeing from the east arrived in Berlin, and some of the city's inhabitants received news by telephone from friends and relatives in the towns closer to the Oder. But many Berliners showed their practical nature during the warm afternoon, queuing for hours to buy bread and other items – if the Red Army were to arrive, they reasoned, it would be prudent to have as much food stockpiled as possible. Cinemas continued to function normally, and one of the very few measures that were taken in view of the seemingly inevitable battle for the city was the implementation of a plan to evacuate the Berlin Philharmonic Orchestra. Acting without any authorisation, Albert Speer – Hitler's armaments minister, who later wrote at length about his personal attempts to undermine the Führer's orders to destroy everything in Germany rather than let it fall into enemy hands – told Gerhart von Westerman, the artistic director of the orchestra, that there would be just one more performance on the evening of 16 April before the musicians departed for Bayreuth. To the surprise of Westerman and Speer, most of the musicians refused to leave. They had too many personal ties to the city and intended to take their chances with the rest of the population. In view of this, Westerman too decided to stay.[1]

On both sides of the front line, there was enormous activity through the night. The Red Army laboured to bring forward reinforcements and supplies of all kinds in preparation for a new attack; aware of the progress being made by Konev, Zhukov was determined to overcome the stubborn German defences along the Seelow Heights regardless of the cost in blood. Meanwhile, Konev was preparing to exploit his successes. In particular, his two tank armies were ready to be unleashed. Unlike Zhukov's tank formations, Third and Fourth Guards Tank Armies had suffered almost no losses. Fuel tanks were topped up, track pins were checked, minor maintenance was carried out on the engines. Some of Lelyushenko's armour had been active during the night, taking full advantage of the dislocated German defences to push forward a short distance. Immediately to the rear of the tanks, bridging units were formed up on the roads running back to the Neisse crossings; Konev had ensured that the engineers attached to his tank armies were not used in the initial river crossing, as he knew that several more water barriers lay ahead. He intended his tanks to be able to advance with as few hold-ups as possible.

Petrov, Konev's capable chief of staff, spent a sleepless night. A wealth of intelligence information was streaming back through the various field headquarters – prisoner interrogations, captured documents, data on German units identified in the fighting – and all of this had to be considered in case it might have an impact on the plans for 17 April. Amongst the documents that were captured was one signed by Generalmajor Otto-Ernst Remer, commander of the *Führer-Begleit* panzergrenadier division. Remer had enjoyed a rapid rise of rank since the summer of 1944, when he was a major in command of a guard battalion of the *Grossdeutschland* division in Berlin. On 20 July he was ordered by Stauffenberg, who had just returned from East Prussia where he believed his briefcase bomb had killed Hitler, to place Goebbels under arrest. Goebbels insisted that Remer speak to Hitler on the telephone; by chance Remer had met the Führer a short while before, and he recognised the voice on the other end of the line. He then used his troops to arrest many of the conspirators. His reward was immediate: a double promotion to Oberst, followed by further promotion in early 1945. The document captured by the advancing Soviet troops on 16 April stated that heavy Soviet armoured attacks were expected the following day, and Remer's division – with the subordinated *Panzer-Ausbildungsverband Böhmen* ('Armour Training Unit Bohemia') – was to stop the attacks on the Matilda Line.[2] By the time that Lelyushenko read the document, his leading X Guards Tank Corps, advancing during the night, had already dislocated this German position.

BREAKTHROUGH: 17–18 APRIL

At the same time, the new directive from *Stavka* had arrived: the tank armies were to drive northwest, aiming to reach Zehlendorf, in the southwest part of Berlin. In order to avoid any lengthy delay caused by redeployment, Konev and Petrov agreed to permit Rybalko and Lelyushenko to advance west, as originally planned, so that they could secure crossings over the Spree and reach better terrain for armoured operations. Then, at the end of 17 April, Rybalko was to turn his Third Guards Tank Army to the north and northwest, crossing the Spree and reaching Berlin by the end of 20 April. Alongside him, Lelyushenko was to reach Potsdam at about the same time.[3] It wasn't the first time that Rybalko had been ordered to change direction at short notice. In the fighting in eastern Ukraine in early 1943, he had executed such a manoeuvre with speed and skill, at a time when most Soviet motorised units were still being handled clumsily; then, during the rapid advance from the Vistula across Poland and Silesia in January and February of 1945, he had again altered direction on more than one occasion as Konev's priorities changed. The new orders were passed on swiftly. At this level at least, the Red Army was a far more efficient and effective force than it had been in the past.

Both tank army commanders were eager to carry out their orders. Their subordinate units had suffered considerable losses since breaking out of the Sandomierz bridgehead on the Vistula in January, but had been brought back to almost full strength – on the eve of the offensive, Rybalko's Third Guards Tank Army had 668 tanks and assault guns available, compared with an establishment strength of 704.[4] Lelyushenko's army was in a similar state, with adequate fuel stockpiled for at least three complete resupplies. Ammunition stocks were slightly lower, averaging two full reloads, but even one of these armies would have been sufficient to crush the German forces in their path. Rybalko's intelligence officers had briefed him that, at best, Fourth Panzer Army's units in the zone through which his tanks would be advancing amounted to no more than about 13,000 soldiers, supported by 155 artillery pieces and perhaps 30 tanks.[5] Even if the Germans were able to dispatch reserves to shore up their lines, there was almost no prospect of stopping the torrent of Soviet armour that was moving across the Neisse and advancing towards the Spree.

On the German side of the front line, Heinrici and Busse in the north had cause to be satisfied with the performance of their troops on the first day of battle, but they were also aware of the price of their resistance. Heinrici reported to *OKH* that XI SS-Panzer Corps had suffered 'not inconsiderable' losses of armour and infantry, and that nearly half the ammunition stockpiled over recent weeks had been consumed; he anticipated that casualties would rise significantly the following day. Busse, too, reported that he doubted the ability of his men to continue resisting. He was pleased that the Luftwaffe had flown a number of missions in support of his troops, but was also aware that the parlous fuel situation meant that even if the planes involved weren't shot down by their Soviet opponents, they would be unable to continue mounting raids for more than another day or two.[6] To the south of Busse's Ninth Army, however, the situation looked grim. Gräser's Fourth Panzer Army was in a poor state. Any plans for counterattacks on 17 April using the *Führer-Begleit* panzergrenadier division were already in disarray following the night attacks by Soviet armour. Whilst it lacked the commanding presence of the Seelow Heights, the terrain was not unfavourable for defensive fighting, with numerous waterways and forests, but Gräser lacked the manpower for a sustained battle.

Zhukov's armies commenced the new day with a further artillery bombardment. This time, firing commenced at first light and continued for 30 minutes. Partly because of the improved light and partly because so many hitherto-undetected

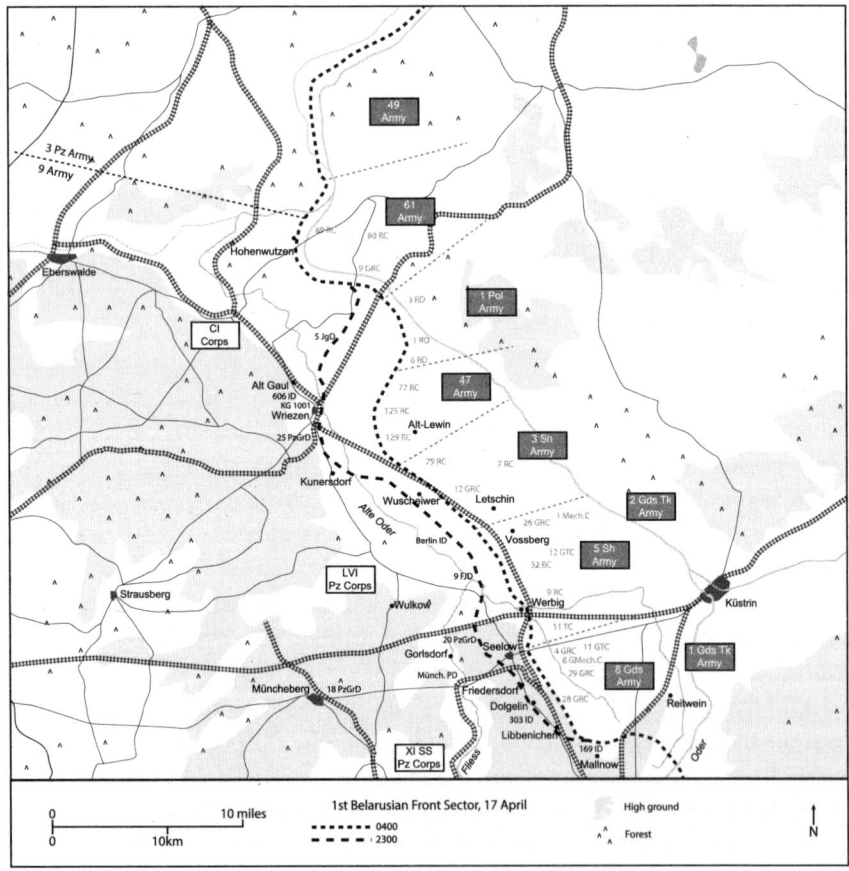

German positions had been identified in the first day of fighting, Chuikov hoped that this fresh barrage was far more effective than had been the case on 16 April. He had regrouped his units, ordering IV Guards Rifle Corps on his northern flank to concentrate a little to the south and to strike towards Gorlsdorf, with support from XI Tank Corps. Its southern neighbour, XXIX Guards Rifle Corps, was to storm the German defences at Ludwigslust and Friedersdorf, and XXVIII Guards Rifle Corps was to capture Dolgelin; all three corps were to clear the line of the Fliess River, a little over three miles to the west of the ridge line of the Seelow Heights.

However, when they moved forward, the Soviet riflemen found that the German defences were still intact. Ivanov, the sapper who had seen the maimed soldiers at the foot of the high ground the previous day and had taken part in the capture of a group of Germans, was now with a company of SU-76 assault guns. These light vehicles were effective in combat, even though their crew often referred to them disparagingly as 'four-man coffins' due to their vulnerability if they were engaged by German armour, and as they moved forward, Ivanov saw for himself just how easily they could be knocked out:

> The night passed quietly. I spent it in a dugout, with either the regiment or battalion commander, I can't remember which. Early in the morning I returned to the regiment headquarters and listened as our commander assigned tasks to the officers: 'Comrade, we have been ordered to take this position at any cost! If the lead vehicle is hit, then the next one must move up and take its place, and so on, until the very last is knocked out!' However powerful our assault guns were, this was actually just sending our guys to their deaths.
>
> The first vehicle moved forward. Bang! Right, the second moved past it. Bang! The same outcome. The third assault gun managed to move up, followed by the fourth and all the others, although we didn't have many vehicles left, maybe only six or eight in total. But still, they made a hole and the T-34s poured through the narrow corridor like locusts.[7]

It actually took until the afternoon to force the German positions. The weak remnants of 303rd *Döberitz* Infantry Division fought hard, despite their losses of the first day of fighting. The division commander, Oberst Hans-Wolfgang Schünemann, had been badly wounded on 16 April, and, with support from a handful of tanks from the *Müncheberg* panzer division, his men inflicted heavy losses on the attackers throughout the morning of 17 April. But during the afternoon – after further artillery bombardment and with Soviet aviators repeatedly attacking – Eighth Guards Army captured the lip of the Seelow Heights from Friedersdorf to Libbenichen; however, the Soviet troops were still some distance short of the Fliess River, and the Germans had deliberately allowed the waterway to flood the neighbouring meadows, making this relatively small river into a substantial barrier. The two days of fighting had cost *Müncheberg* 14 of its 21 Panther tanks and five of its ten Tigers.[8]

It would have been customary for the Wehrmacht to mount an energetic counterattack at this stage of the battle, aiming to catch the exhausted Soviet attackers off-balance before they could dig in. It had been Busse's intention to mount such an operation with 18th and 25th Panzergrenadier Divisions operating in close cooperation, but 18th Panzergrenadier Division had been ordered to concentrate near Müncheberg the preceding night and was earmarked for strengthening the sagging defences around Seelow; 25th Panzergrenadier Division was already in the front line in Wriezen to the north. During the afternoon, Busse had a telephone conversation with Heinrici. The only armoured reserves still available consisted of two SS formations – and 14th *Nordland* and 23rd *Nederland* Panzergrenadier Divisions – and they were ordered to move up to support Busse's exhausted units, particularly LVI Panzer Corps on the vital axis of *Reichstrasse 1*.

Writing after the war, Heinrici recalled that he wanted to concentrate *SS-Nordland* and *SS-Nederland* close to Müncheberg before the Soviet offensive began, where they would be ideally positioned to counterattack along *Reichstrasse 1*. But Eismann, his operations officer, had advised against this, as there was at the time insufficient fuel to move both divisions into position. Moreover, if they were then required elsewhere, precious fuel would have been wasted sending them to Müncheberg. Had the divisions been where Heinrici had wanted them, they would have been able to get into battle a day sooner than later proved to be the case.[9] Other reinforcements were of far less value. Several hundred teenagers of the Hitler Youth had been ordered to the front line by the Nazi Party; these youngsters had no military training and despite the fanatical devotion of many to Hitler, they were of no use and were actually a hindrance. Busse had them sent to sapper units that were strengthening fortifications in the third defensive zone.

To the north of the critical battle for the Seelow Heights, Soviet attacks continued throughout 17 April. Zhukov's most northern formation, Sixty-First Army, made another assault across the Oder. On this occasion, the crossing was led by the men of 8th Independent Penal Battalion, a unit made up of soldiers of all ranks who had fallen foul of the authorities. Men could be sent to the penal battalion for a large number of reasons, including having been captured by the Germans and subsequently escaping but being unable to give a 'satisfactory' reason why they had been captured in the first place. If they performed adequately in the penal battalions, they might be restored to their former ranks and returned to their units, but the use of these units in costly attacks made survival unlikely.

This attack was no exception: out of an original force of 120 men, only 20 survived the day, with the German 5th Jäger Division mounting energetic counterattacks against the small bridgehead. But even if this German division was still holding its lines, it was in danger of being outflanked to the south, where 606th Infantry Division had reached the limits of its ability to resist by the end of 16 April. More units of First Polish Army were fed into the attack, crushing the remaining pockets of German resistance, and 5th Jäger Division was forced to deploy some of its subunits southwards to try to shore up the line; at the same time, it attempted to incorporate the remnants of 606th Infantry Division into its ranks. Leutnant Erich Hachtel was in command of one such group:

> My regimental commander tasked me with making contact with the headquarters of 606th Infantry Division. I took a couple of men with me … and we raced south with our tracked motorcycle combination through our own lines towards the manor farmhouse at Alt Gaul, where according to the latest information 606th Infantry Division's command post should be. We were well aware that we could come across the Russians at any moment and be shot at … We reached the manor at about midday. Defensive positions had been set up around it, occupied by infantry. We drove up to the manor and I went down the steps to a big cellar that was the division's command post. I entered this room, in which several officers were sitting around a big table, at one end of which was a colonel, who was the commander of this division. I was looked at in astonishment when I reported my mission to the colonel. All appeared to be fixed in the belief that they were surrounded and only waiting for the Russians to arrive, for the colonel asked me in a friendly tone, '*Kamerad*, how did you get through to us?' I explained the current situation to these gentlemen and suggested they join me.[10]

Despite the near-collapse of 606th Infantry Division, the rapid deployment of 25th Panzergrenadier Division meant that the German line was still just about intact. The Soviet Forty-Seventh Army made several powerful attacks during 17 April and bitter fighting engulfed Wriezen, where the German defences around the edge of the town were captured in heavy fighting. Under constant artillery fire, the panzergrenadiers counterattacked late in the day, recovering some of their positions; further south, a mixture of infantry from various units, supported by a group of *Hetzer* tank destroyers, blocked every attempt by the Soviet Forty-Seventh Army to break through, but by the end of the day were forced back to the ridge running south from Wriezen.

The advance of Third Shock Army was also held up by determined resistance. It took all of 17 April for the Soviet troops to fight their way to the base of the long ridge at Kunersdorf and Metzdorf, and tank support was held up while engineers struggled forward with bridging equipment to deal with a canal that crossed the line of advance. Trying to make up for lost time, Colonel General Vasily Ivanovich Kuznetsov, the army commander, ordered attacks to continue all through the following night, but these achieved little more than further casualties. To make matters worse, Neu Trebbin, two miles to the east of the ridge, remained in German hands, hindering attempts to reinforce the depleted Soviet units that had succeeded in bypassing the village. Schöneck and a few other survivors of the *Berlin* infantry division spent much of the night of 16–17 April isolated in Wuschewier before deciding to try to escape towards the west:

> It was 0400 on 17 April when we assembled for the breakout at the western exit of the village behind the last houses. Grenade detonations ripped through the early morning air. We fired madly in the diffuse darkness to where we supposed Ivan was. His reply came by return of post. Heavy machine-gun fire forced us back into the village.
>
> While a group returned fire from the village, some of us crept up to the Russian machine-gun position from behind. Hand grenades exploded simultaneously on the left and right. The machine-guns fell silent. We stormed ahead across the fields towards Grube.[11]

In Grube, the survivors caught their breath. They could see flares being fired by the beleaguered garrison of Neu Trebbin, barely a mile away, and set up makeshift positions and while they waited for daylight, Schöneck and several others were overcome by exhaustion. He awoke suddenly to find himself facing a soldier he hadn't seen before; after a moment, the stranger disappeared while Schöneck took cover from an exploding shell. One of his comrades described a similar incident, and they attributed it to the presence of *Seydlitz-Truppen* – the catch-all phrase used by the Germans for soldiers who had been captured by the Red Army and had agreed to fight against Germany. Shortly after, under heavy shellfire, the rag-tag group of men from the *Berlin* division, mixed with stragglers from SS and improvised Luftwaffe battlegroups, managed to reach Neu Trebbin, adding their numbers to the garrison.

Fifth Shock Army, a little to the south, also renewed its attacks, commencing with a further heavy artillery preparation. What remained of 9th Fallschirmjäger Division was unable to prevent the Soviet 266th Rifle Division from reaching Neu Hardenberg, at the foot of the ridge. As was the case elsewhere, the terrain proved as much of a hindrance to the Soviet forces as German resistance; in this case, the Alte Oder, a former main channel of the Oder River, crossed the line of

Breakthrough: 17–18 April

advance. The units of Second Guards Tank Army were meant to move up in support of Fifth Shock Army's riflemen but there were few crossings that could sustain the weight of the tanks, resulting in long delays. On the southern flank of Fifth Shock Army, the Soviet IX Rifle Corps threw two divisions at the German troops in Gusow. Here, a mixture of men from 9th Fallschirmjäger Division and 20th Panzergrenadier Division found themselves under heavy pressure as Soviet aircraft joined the attack. After a bitter struggle, the village was captured in the early afternoon, and the attacking riflemen established contact with Soviet tanks to the south of Gusow that were cooperating with Chuikov's Eighth Guards Army. Supported by these tanks, IX Rifle Corps turned around and pushed northwest along the road running to Platkow. After suffering further losses, the remnants of 9th Fallschirmjäger Division pulled back to the west into a forested area where the survivors were able to regroup; they then took up positions along the ridge around Wulkow.

It was a considerable success for Berzarin's Fifth Shock Army and importantly it seemed to open a route for Second Guards Tank Army to break through the German lines. The undulating landscape to the west of Wulkow was unfavourable for tanks, and was sharply delineated to the northwest by the Stobberow River, a relatively modest waterway that ran through a deep gorge. However, beyond the Stobberow, there was a good road that ran southwest along high ground. If the Soviet units could reach this, they might be able to advance more swiftly. To make matters worse, 20th Panzergrenadier Division had fallen back towards the southwest, creating a gap in the line, and the sudden Soviet advance through Gusow threatened to unhinge the German defences. Tams and his panzergrenadier company had already endured further artillery bombardment and air attacks, before their northern flank came under unexpected pressure. Tams rushed over to investigate and discovered that his men had no contact with any friendly units to their north – there was meant to be a company of *Volkssturm* holding positions as far as the southern flank of 9th Fallschirmjäger Division, but it had disappeared. A platoon of SS soldiers, survivors of the Küstrin garrison, had also been in the area on 16 April but had vanished by the following day. When several T-34s appeared driving along the road from Gusow, Tams had no choice but to fall back on Seelow:

> I had not expected to be attacked from the north so soon. I still remember a long white wall about 2m high leading past the knacker's yard, which gave us cover from fire from the north.
>
> The Russians must have seen us, for the wall received a broadside from the barrels of several tank guns and disintegrated swiftly in smoke as soon as I had passed ...

Our battalion command post was in the cellar of a storehouse and reached via the loading ramp through a large sliding door. I reached the top of the steps out of breath and called down: 'Everyone outside, the Russians are here!' The faces that I saw were apathetic, virtually defeated. The command post as such had already been evacuated, and the soldiers remaining there were seeking shelter and cover from the bombardment. One of the soldiers told me that our commander, Oberst Stammerjohn, was dead …

The soldiers came back to life when Feldwebel Stein aimed a shot at a Soviet officer as they were leaving the storehouse through the sliding door. Two T-34s were standing in the yard with their engines running and their gun barrels aimed in our direction. The man on the tank with a red band on his hat fell, apparently hit. The shock caused by the Russian presence spread among the men emerging from the building along the ramp. The ensuing unequal exchange of fire caused panic among us, so that my original intention to lead the men back to the centre of town to redeploy them was forcibly abandoned. Meanwhile a third tank entered the yard, and there being no anti-tank weapon ready to hand, the men disappeared.[12]

Gathering what men he could, Tams withdrew to the local railway line immediately to the south of Seelow and followed the embankment to the west; near Friedersdorf, he encountered more survivors of his company. He now had 13 men under his command, barely a tenth of the number with which he had started 16 April. Aware of the risk of the Soviet forces exploiting their success to the full, Generalleutnant Josef Rauch, commander of 18th Panzergrenadier Division, deployed two of his panzergrenadier battalions around Wulkow to shore up the exhausted *Fallschirmjäger* survivors.

If Zhukov's armies were merely grinding forward despite suffering – and inflicting – heavy losses, the situation was very different in Konev's sector. Zaitsev's tank brigade had spent much of the night driving cautiously through the darkness and moved forward swiftly at first light. It was only when the brigade advanced towards the Spree River that it suffered its first loss when the leading tank fell into a well-camouflaged anti-tank ditch. One of Zaitsev's battalion commanders was hit by a sniper round and there were exchanges of fire with German infantry armed with *Panzerfausts*, but by the end of the day Zaitsev was on the banks of the Spree a little to the north of Spremberg, waiting for bridging equipment to catch up with him.[13] Zhadov's Fifth Guards Army was meant to be moving up to the Spree alongside Zaitsev's tanks but ran into the German *Führer-Begleit* panzergrenadier division. Fending off constant counterattacks, particularly on their southern flank, Zhadov's troops fought their way forward towards the river.

Breakthrough: 17–18 April

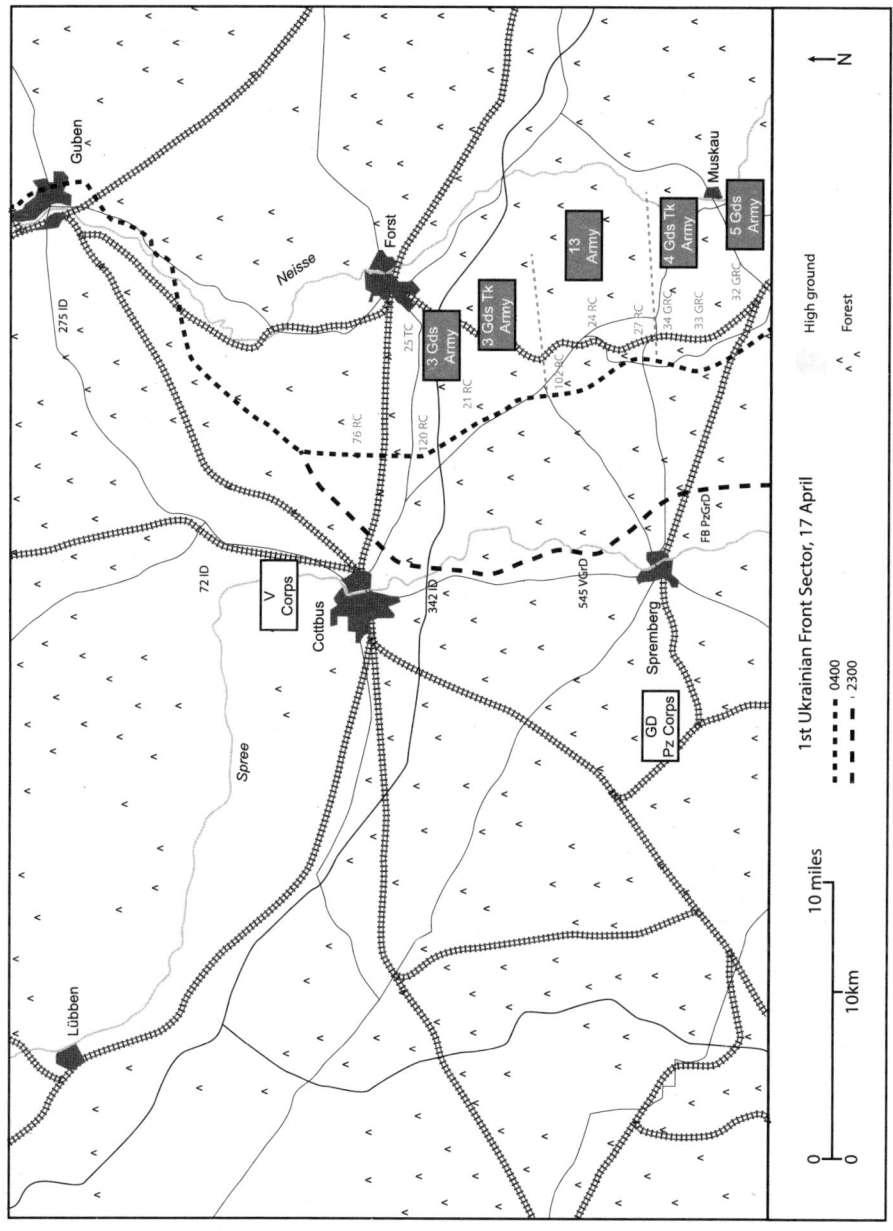

As they moved forward, Rybalko's tank formations also found themselves involved in fierce clashes that were often over almost as soon as they began. In one such exchange of fire, 54th Guards Tank Brigade reported that it had been engaged by German armour, including Tiger tanks, that it tentatively identified as belonging to 21st Panzer Division. It was commonplace for soldiers on all sides to identify enemy tanks as being the most potent that they might face, as this made their own losses more explicable, and Tigers were often misreported as being present; regardless of the tank types involved, the Soviet tank brigade reported that it had driven off the German counterattack, leaving 15 wrecks burning on the battlefield, for the loss of 12 of its own vehicles.[14]

At the headquarters of Fourth Panzer Army, there was a growing sense of helplessness. There were few assets available at corps level to use as reinforcements or for counterattacks. Ideally, Gräser would have preferred to hold units like the *Brandenburg* panzergrenadier division in reserve, but the weakness of the front line had required its deployment in the main defensive line immediately to the south of Konev's assault. His limited assets were fully committed and were fighting hard, but once the Red Army reached and crossed the line of the Spree between Cottbus and Spremberg, there would be nothing that could be done to stop their onward advance. Nor could he expect any help from higher commands. Schörner, the commander of Army Group Centre, wanted to hold back whatever reserves he had in anticipation of a Soviet attack towards Prague.

By contrast to Gräser, Konev was in good spirits. The shoulders of his breakthrough, at Cottbus and Spremberg, were causing him some concern, but it seemed only a matter of time before he could clear them. On the evening of 17 April, he spoke to Stalin:

> When I was finishing my report, Stalin suddenly interrupted me, saying: 'But things are not going well for Zhukov. He's still trying to break through the defensive lines.' After saying this, Stalin fell silent. I was also silent and waited to see what he would say next. Suddenly, he asked, 'Is it not possible, after transferring Zhukov's mobile troops, to send them towards Berlin through the gap that has formed in your Front's sector?'
>
> I gave him my opinion. 'Comrade Stalin, this will take a lot of time and cause great confusion. There is no need to transfer tank units from 1st Belarusian Front to our breakthrough. Events are developing favourably for us, and we have enough forces and are able to direct both of our tank armies towards Berlin.'[15]

In view of the unreliability of Konev's memoirs on other occasions, this account should be treated with caution, but given the lack of progress by 1st Belarusian

BREAKTHROUGH: 17–18 APRIL

Front, it seems credible that Stalin was thinking of transferring at least part of Zhukov's two tank armies to the south. However, extracting the tank units from the fighting on the Seelow Heights would have been a difficult, time-consuming undertaking even before moving the units south. Moreover, all of their supplies and support services would also have to redeploy, and there was then the additional complexity of introducing them into an area already congested by Konev's armies. By the time that all this had taken place, new maps had been distributed, commanders had been oriented to the terrain and circumstances, orders had been drawn up, etc., the battle would probably have been over. It is certainly arguable that the original plan to commit two tank armies to the assault on the Seelow Heights was an error, and that they might have been better deployed either in Konev's sector or further north in Rokossovsky's sector; but moving them once the operation commenced would have been almost impossible.

Between the two Soviet Fronts was the German city of Frankfurt-an-der-Oder. Like many such cities, Hitler had declared it a fortress in the last week of January – it was to be held to the last man, and could only be abandoned with the Führer's specific position. Given its location, such a declaration was inevitable and work had commenced towards the end of 1944 to build fortifications. The Dammvorstadt – the part of the city on the east bank, now the Polish town of Słubice – was evacuated on 4 February and most civilians in other areas were ordered to leave the following day. The *Festungskommandant* ('Fortress Commandant') was originally Generalleutnant Hermann Meyer-Rabingen, but he was then transferred to the command of 404th Division and replaced by his deputy, Oberst Ernst Biehler. Even before the Soviet offensive commenced, Heinrici had attempted to have the fortress status of the city cancelled – he could see little prospect of holding it and preferred to defend a shorter line to the east. When Heinrici summoned Biehler to Berlin to try to persuade Hitler of the futility of defending Frankfurt, the Führer's response was to dismiss Biehler from his post, only to reverse the decision in the face of Heinrici's protests. On 16 April, the city came under fire as part of the overall preparatory bombardment and Biehler implemented plans drawn up many days in advance. He abandoned the Dammvorstadt, but it is worth noting that Hitler didn't give permission for such a withdrawal – with the proviso that it could only be carried out in an extreme emergency – until the following day. Despite Heinrici's requests, the city remained a fortress, and Hitler added that he fully expected it to hold out even if it found itself encircled.

As darkness fell on 17 April, the first reconnaissance platoons of 1st Ukrainian Front's Third Guards Army were already across the Spree. The formations of Konev's two tank armies had either reached the river or were approaching it, and would begin crossing during the night. The advance of 1st Ukrainian Front had been rapid, but there were significant groups of German troops behind the Red Army's front line, and fierce clashes continued for several days as these groups ran into Soviet formations. Nevertheless, Konev had good reason for satisfaction. Only Fifth Guards Army was running behind schedule, but it was tying down one of the few mobile formations available to the Wehrmacht. Once the intact tank armies crossed the river, Konev was confident that there would be rapid progress; in fact, his Front had effectively achieved operational freedom. Only the physical obstacle of the Spree was delaying his advance.

By contrast, the mood in Zhukov's headquarters continued to be one of angry frustration. Significant advances had been made, but the stubborn defences along the ridge of the Seelow Heights had not been cleared completely. Casualties had been expected, but they were far higher than Zhukov and his army commanders had anticipated, and this raised concerns for the future. To date, all of the fighting had been in the first German defensive belt, and there were two further belts to be cleared before the Red Army reached Berlin. Zhukov knew that breaking this first belt would be the toughest task prior to reaching the German capital, but nonetheless he anticipated heavy fighting in the second and third belts, and everyone expected the Wehrmacht to make one last defensive effort in Berlin itself. There was now the real possibility that 1st Belarusian Front's armies would be too weak to make a major impression on Berlin, and that the capture of the city would be left to Zhukov's rival, Konev.

In his evening report to Zhukov, Chuikov confirmed that his men had finally secured a large section of the Seelow Heights, but at a terrible cost, not only to themselves but to the tank army operating in support of Eighth Guards Army. At best, the operation was a full day behind its expected schedule. But there was a small degree of consolation for Zhukov. Like the other army commanders, Chuikov was quick to stress the serious damage being inflicted on the German units that were fighting with such determination, and it was questionable how long they could continue to expend ammunition, equipment, and manpower in such a manner. Accordingly, Zhukov issued fresh instructions to Chuikov. Whilst every effort was to be made to advance beyond the ridge line that had cost so much blood, the emphasis for Eighth Guards Army on 18 April was to maximise the attrition of the German units in its path. This would further reduce the ability of the Germans to sustain a prolonged defence, and might result in weaknesses elsewhere in the front line, allowing other armies of 1st Belarusian Front to make faster progress.[16]

In many respects, this was not a welcome development for Chuikov. He and many of his men had fought together since the desperate days in Stalingrad in 1942, and had long cherished the dream of achieving the ultimate revenge on the Germans

BREAKTHROUGH: 17–18 APRIL

for the damage done to the city on the Volga – they wanted to be the Red Army formation that led the way into Berlin. But Chuikov had to face reality, with the consolation that in any event, the outskirts of Berlin were just 34 miles to the west. Even if Eighth Guards Army continued to take heavy losses, it was surely certain to play a part in the final defeat of the hated enemy. While Chuikov and Katukov continued to smash their way forward along *Reichstrasse 1*, the other armies of 1st Belarusian Front were urged to accelerate their advance, particularly Bogdanov's Second Guards Tank Army. If it could break out of the hilly region immediately west of the ridge line that had held up Zhukov's troops, it might be able to advance swiftly towards Berlin.

Babadzhanian, whose tank corps had suffered serious losses in helping Chuikov force his way up the Seelow Heights, was reorganising his units late on 17 April in preparation for the following day when a visitor surprised him:

Major General [Nikofor Ignatyevich] Gerko [deputy commander of tank forces, 1st Belarusian Front] arrived at my command post and informed me that I was to return to Seelow with him, to a meeting with [Lieutenant General Konstantin Fedorovich] Telegin, of the Front Military Council.

'Now?'

'Right now.'

I was perplexed. In the midst of dealing with the enemy's frenzied counterattacks, should I abandon my troops and go to some sort of meeting? Gerko simply shrugged in response: 'Orders are orders.'

Travelling along a road that had been ploughed up by bombs and shells, we reached the ruins of Seelow late at night. After the attacks that had been thrown at this town, it would have been astonishing if anything had remained intact. We could barely drive through the streets, as they were choked with the rubble of destroyed houses and the pavements were littered with masonry. We finally reached the miraculously intact house where the meeting was being held.

The flickering light from a lamp illuminated the faces of those gathered. In the middle, of those seated at the table, I recognised Telegin; his face was stern, and he looked very unhappy.

Based on the comments of those present, Gerko and I realised that this was an 'analysis' of the delay of the offensive at the Seelow Heights … I noted to myself that among the commanders standing in front of the members of the Military Council, the majority were tankers. It seemed as if the tankers were to be blamed for the fact that they were not given sufficient space to manoeuvre.

It was after midnight that we finally got the opportunity to return to our units, which were fighting a determined enemy.[17]

It isn't clear whether the Military Council was acting on behalf of Zhukov, trying to shield him from criticism, or had been ordered by Stalin to investigate the failure of 1st Belarusian Front to advance rapidly. Regardless, it was an unwelcome distraction for officers struggling to conduct the battle.

Despite the tribulations of Babadzhanian and others, the balance was tilting steadily in favour of the Red Army. German losses had been severe and many units had effectively been worn away in the two days of fighting. Just as Telegin and others sought to allocate blame for the slow advance of the Red Army, some figures in the German chain of command were also quick to find scapegoats. When an exhausted regiment of 303rd Infantry Division fell back from its positions to the south of Seelow, rumours reached the headquarters of XI SS Corps that it had been given permission for its retreat by the commander of the neighbouring regiment, Oberstleutnant Helmut Weber. Kleinheisterkamp, the commander of XI SS Corps, was at the headquarters of 303rd Infantry Division when Weber made his evening report:

> I was able to refute [the rumour] immediately with the help of my liaison officer. The corps commander ... wanted to court-martial me. Filthy dirty as I was, I sought to justify myself before him, and the chief of staff only managed to hold me back with difficulty. The consequence was that the unknown neighbouring regiment was stripped of all its awards and decorations, and the regimental commander shot himself. I do not know what he had been accused of.[18]

There was little love lost between the regular army and the SS. With some justification, officers like Weber regarded many senior SS figures as owing their status more to patronage within the SS than to any military aptitude, and there was often considerable friction when regular army units were placed under SS command.

In the rear of the German troops engaged in combat, the recruits in the third defensive belt had a mixed day. On the one hand, they were spared the danger of artillery fire; but on the other hand, they came under air attack. Helmut Altner and his comrades recognised a group of aircraft as German Messerschmitts, and were horrified when the planes plunged down towards them, opening fire with their machine-guns. Shortly after, they learned that the planes had been captured by the Red Army and pressed into service. In addition to strafing attacks, the planes dropped bundles of leaflets calling on the Germans to surrender.[19]

At his command post just outside Strausberg, Heinrici knew that despite the severe check that his army group had inflicted on Zhukov's 1st Belarusian Front, it would be impossible to continue the battle at the same intensity in the days to come. A brief discussion with his staff confirmed his fears: there was no possibility of releasing troops from other sectors to send to Ninth Army and Fourth Panzer Army as reinforcements. The only area where there was no heavy fighting was in the north, where Third Panzer Army held the line to the Baltic coast, and here there were clear signs of an imminent assault by Rokossovsky's 2nd Belarusian Front. Reports from the corps and division commanders suggested that there would be sufficient ammunition left for one more major day of fighting before Ninth Army was forced back, but the front line was looking increasingly fragile. The Germans had correctly identified the entry of units of First and Second Guards Tank Armies into the battle and Heinrici reported to *OKH* that although counterattacks had been launched, the Red Army had secured deep penetrations of the defensive line. He concluded that he intended to use *SS-Nordland* to stop Soviet units from advancing west from Seelow while *SS-Nederland* would counterattack towards the south against the formations of 1st Ukrainian Front.

Busse at the headquarters of Ninth Army also submitted a report. The armoured reconnaissance battalion of 25th Panzergrenadier Division had been completely destroyed during the day's fighting around Neu Trebbin and other units were hard-pressed. In the middle of trying to deal with the growing pressure on his units, Busse received an unexpected request from General Bruno Bräuer, commander of 9th Fallschirmjäger Division, which he passed on to Heinrici. Army Group Vistula's operations officers' diary recorded:

> General Bräuer, the division commander ... reported that his units were in complete disarray and that after hard fighting were no longer as steadfast as they had been before. He then made the absurd request that his division be pulled out [of the front line] for 24 hours. I [Heinrici] have relieved him of command and replaced him with Oberstleutnant [Harry] Herrmann. He is a particularly good leader. In addition, I have sent the division reinforcements in the form of a march battalion [i.e. a replacement draft] and set up a special catch line to the rear [of the division, to catch any stragglers].[20]

Unlike many of the officers assigned to Luftwaffe ground units, Bräuer was an experienced paratrooper, having served in the army since 1936. He played a major role in the conquest of Crete and its subsequent occupation. His dismissal from command of 9th Fallschirmjäger Division brought his military career to an end and he was captured by British soldiers two days after the end of hostilities. The Greek authorities then successfully applied for his extradition to face charges of war crimes committed during his time in Crete and in 1947 he was convicted of the deportation of several hundred Jews from the island to death camps in Poland. He was executed shortly after. His replacement, Harry Herrmann, stayed with the remnants of 9th Fallschirmjäger Division for the rest of the war and subsequently was held by the Soviet Union until 1955. After his release, he joined the West German Bundeswehr with the rank of Oberst, serving until 1967.[21]

For Busse, in addition to the rapidly accelerating degradation of his units, there was the added fear that even if by a miracle his men were able to continue holding back the weight of 1st Belarusian Front, the rapid collapse of Fourth Panzer Army to the south left Ninth Army's southern flank completely exposed. Busse later wrote:

> By the evening of 17 April there was already a threat to our own southern flank, which in a short time had reached the point of requiring a withdrawal. Fully supported by the army group, Ninth Army tried to contact *OKH* with the urgent request that because of the situation of Ninth Army and in order to continue firm contact on the boundary with Third Panzer Army, it was necessary to pull back before the entire front collapsed. The only response received by Ninth Army was a sharp order from Hitler to hold its front line and to re-establish its position at critical points with counterattacks.[22]

In many respects, Busse felt that his army had done all that could be expected of it. Despite being attacked by hugely superior Soviet forces, it had clung to the Seelow Heights in intense fighting for two days, inflicting huge casualties on the Red Army. But the price of this defiant defence was unsustainable. The infantry and armoured units in the front line were melting away and the artillery operating in support was almost out of ammunition. Busse's mindset is difficult to determine with any certainty; he wrote about the battle after the war, but his account was of course coloured by hindsight. At the time, he appears to have been able to hold almost contradictory views at the same time. On the one hand, he had spent most of the war rigidly passing on and enforcing orders from above, even when his professional training must have told him that they were incorrect; but on the other hand, he had confided in Heinrici that he had little hope of being able to stop the Red Army from reaching Berlin. Instead, he would delay the Soviet advance as much as he could, in the hope that the Western Allies would reach the German capital first, thus sparing the population from the wrath of the Soviet troops. Heinrici had made him aware of intelligence reports that showed the intentions of the Allied Powers to divide Germany into zones of occupation, with Berlin lying within the Soviet zone; in such circumstances, Heinrici told him, it was highly unlikely that the British or Americans would risk heavy casualties storming the German capital when they would have to hand it back to the Soviet Union. Busse's response was that he would do all he could to hinder the Soviet advance, in the hope that a severe setback for the Red Army might encourage the Western Powers to advance towards Berlin anyway. But as his exhausted army ended the second day of battle, there was no sign of any such advance. The Americans had a small bridgehead over the Elbe at Magdeburg, just 73 miles from the centre of Berlin, but showed no intention of exploiting it.[23]

18 APRIL

Chuikov urged his subordinates to complete the penetration of what was still the first belt of German defences. In places, Soviet infantry and armour had reached the second belt, but until the first belt was completely cleared, it would be impossible to concentrate sufficient forces to advance decisively towards Berlin. The storming of the ridge of the Seelow Heights had been a bloody, exhausting business, but Eighth Guards Army and Fifth Shock Army to its north now found themselves struggling through equally difficult terrain – the hills and woodland of an area known as the Märkische Schweiz, with few good roads and numerous small streams and rivers running through steep-sided folds in the land. It was ideal terrain for defensive warfare; only the heavy losses suffered by the Germans in the preceding days gave any hope that the advance might be accelerated. Nevertheless, Zhukov continued to demand faster progress, bombarding his army commanders with repeated exhortations. In his memoirs, Chuikov reproduced one of the signals he received:

The Front commander orders:
    1. Increase the speed of the offensive immediately. If we permit a slow advance in the Berlin Operation, the troops will be exhausted and will use up all their material reserves without taking Berlin.
    2. All [army] commanders must position themselves in the command posts of the corps commanders leading the attack on the main axis. I categorically prohibit [army commanders] staying to the rear of the troops.
    3. All artillery, including heavy artillery, is to be assigned to the first echelon and must be kept no further than 2–3km behind the echelon that is engaged in combat. Concentrate artillery operations in those areas where the breakthrough is to be created.
    Keep in mind that all the way to Berlin, the enemy will resist and will cling to every house and copse, and therefore tankers, assault guns, and infantry should not wait until the artillery has killed all the Nazis and has gifted them the privilege of moving through open space.
    4. Hammer the enemy mercilessly and move forward day and night towards Berlin, so that it will soon be in our hands.[24]

Such instructions were either unnecessary or meaningless. Every soldier, from ordinary riflemen to army commanders, was already trying their utmost to advance as quickly as possible. Having secured at least a segment of the ridge of the Seelow Heights, Chuikov was anxious to push beyond the Fliess River as quickly as he could so that Katukov's tanks could be unleashed, and threw the relatively fresh 82nd Guards Rifle Division, which had been waiting in reserve, into a morning attack to storm the high ground to the west of the river, just south of Gorlsdorf. The first objective was a wooded hill to the north of *Reichstrasse 1*, and this was cleared by early afternoon. It took the rest of the day to clear the small village of Worin, just to the north, but the defenders were completely exhausted and the Soviet riflemen also pushed down *Reichstrasse 1* to Jahnsfelde.[25]

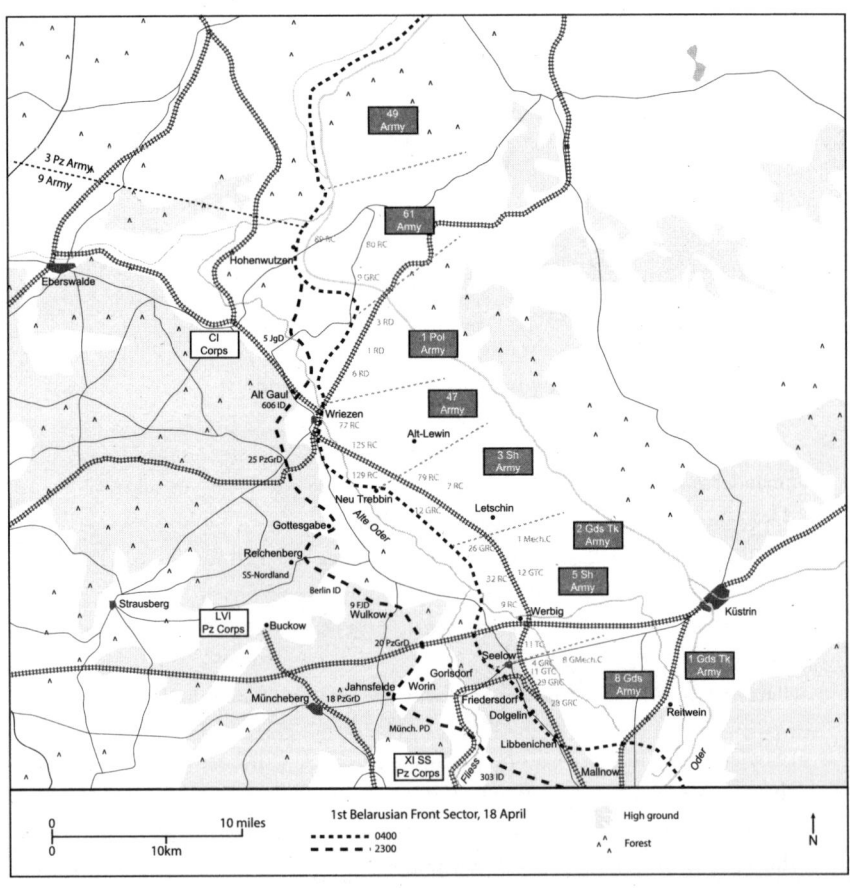

Altner and his fellow raw recruits were put into the front line to the southeast of Müncheberg in a reserve position. There were rumours of all kinds circulating: many German cities had already fallen and the Red Army was driving forward towards Berlin unchecked; both flanks of Ninth Army had been turned and encirclement was imminent; and General Walther von Seydlitz-Kurzbach, who had surrendered in Stalingrad and after whom the German soldiers fighting alongside the Red Army were named, was said to be in Seelow. There was even talk of his tank being destroyed by a determined German civilian armed with a *Panzerfaust*. Suddenly, the recruits came under heavy artillery fire:

> We find ourselves lying in an inferno of fire and horror. Fire strikes from the heavens and licks the earth, howling around us. I lie there half dead with fear, scratching the earth with my fingernails, ripping at the turf. If only one could sink into the bowels of the earth! All around us fire and dark smoke as the earth is ploughed up metre by metre. More keep coming – Stalin Organs [the German name for *Katyusha* rockets] – God have mercy on us![26]

After a brief barrage that must have seemed like an eternity to the inexperienced recruits, the Red Army attacked – a mixture of regular riflemen and the dreaded *Seydlitz-Truppen*. Supported by a few tanks and regular troops, Altner and his comrades found themselves in a counterattack, driving the Soviet attack back in disarray:

> We reach the first row of trenches and stop, not wanting to go any further. Reinforcements occupy the trenches. There is the occasional shot. The company commander appears and collects us together. We go back.
>
> Dead lie between the craters, many of them in field grey uniforms, nearly all German, some with swastikas on their chests, some with the black-white-red armband [worn by the *Seydlitz-Truppen*], their medals shining faintly. Now they lie close to each other, peaceful in death.
>
> We are tired and despondent, burnt out. We have a big emptiness inside us. We have lost all hope.[27]

Several Soviet attempts to crush the German defences foundered almost as soon as they began. Major General Afanasy Dmitriyevich Shemenkov, commander of XXIX Guards Rifle Corps, had been ordered to attack with support from Babadzhanian's tanks at 0800, but when Babadzhanian reached his command post, Shemenkov told him that he had postponed the start time by an hour to complete his preparations. At 0800, Chuikov and Katukov appeared in Shemenkov's command post, as Babadzhanian described:

> 'Are the troops ready to begin the breakthrough?' asked Chuikov. Shemenkov began to explain why he had postponed the start time of the assault. 'How could you "postpone" it?' demanded Chuikov.
> I don't know what happened next at the command post of the rifle corps, because Katukov said to me in a low voice, 'There's nothing for you to do here. Hurry up and join your men – the order must be executed on time!'[28]

Just before the Berlin Operation commenced, Shemenkov had been awarded Hero of the Soviet Union with the Order of Lenin and the Gold Star medal for his leadership the previous August in the capture of the city of Magnuszew, creating one of the bridgeheads from which the Red Army would attack in January 1945. Perhaps because of this recent award, he seems to have survived this episode with little more than Chuikov venting his frustration and wrath on his subordinate.

Tams and his panzergrenadiers had withdrawn to a series of trenches behind two 88mm anti-tank guns. The gunners told the infantrymen that they had very limited ammunition, just five shells per gun, and intended to use them to maximum effect at first light on 18 April before destroying their guns and falling back. During the preceding night, they fought off an attempt by a group of T-34s to bypass them, and the exhausted Tams fell into a deep sleep. Shortly after dawn, he and his men saw figures approaching from the east and opened fire, realising too late that the men they had spotted were the gunners, pulling back from their abandoned and disabled guns. But Soviet infantry were close behind, and a furious battle developed:

> The Russian artillery laid a barrage on the railway embankment behind us, as their infantry broke into our trenches. The picture that now plays in front of my eyes still haunts me in my sleep. Although I had been a soldier for three and a half years, of which 17 months had been in action with a front-line unit, I had never experienced anything like this, nor believed it possible. Men were fighting with clubs and knives just as in the Middle Ages.
> 'I can't take any more of this!' I felt like shouting. When I stood up over the trench, a second of panic gripped me and I ran back to the wall of fire on the railway embankment. Subconsciously, I noticed that someone was following me. It must have been only seconds before we were about 50m from the railway embankment and crawling up to it. Two terrifying explosions immediately behind

us forced us against the embankment. Gefreiter Schröder asked me if I had been hit. Yes, a shot through the right lower leg and a hit in the left foot. For a moment I was unable to get up. Schröder ... quickly pulled me over the railway line into cover on the far side.[29]

It was the end of Tams' war; he was evacuated to the rear, and then decided to return to his home city of Hamburg as the war was clearly close to its end. When his parents saw him, his father's first question was whether he was a deserter. His anxiety eased only when Tams assured him that he had been wounded and was unable to fight.

The incident of 'friendly fire', with Tams' panzergrenadiers shooting at – and presumably hitting – several of the retreating anti-tank gunners, was an inevitable consequence of the confusion of war. It wasn't restricted to any side. Semen Ruvimovich Tsvang, a rifleman in one of the tank armies, described an episode as he and his comrades marched towards the German capital:

Many men died due to poor communication and lack of cooperation between various units. [There was a lot of] confusion. No one really knew where a particular brigade or regiment was, or how many kilometres they had managed to advance. As we moved towards Berlin, an entire rifle battalion was killed before my eyes by a massive volley of its own supporting *Katyushas*. It was horrific to look at the field strewn with the corpses of more than 200 young guys with cropped haircuts. [It looked] like the set of a science fiction film.[30]

Fritz Averdieck, a Feldwebel signaller in 20th Panzergrenadier Division, was facing the northern flank of Chuikov's attempts to break through the German lines. The left flank of his company's position was threatened by Soviet tanks at dawn on 18 April and the Germans pulled back to Worin, roughly midway between Seelow and Müncheberg. The village soon came under attack, forcing a further withdrawal; they were to take up positions close to Müncheberg, but after just a short distance they learned that Jahnsfelde was already in Soviet hands and they were effectively cut off. Matters were made worse by contamination of the fuel for Averdieck's half-track, which constantly threatened to stop working:

The only possibility was to break through to our lines along a route unknown to the enemy. Our regiment commander, a Leutnant, organised those on foot, and our APC [armoured personnel carrier] was taken in tow by a Tiger. At dusk we took up positions along the edge of the woods. Firing behind us indicated that Ivan had followed us into the woods from Worin. As soon as it was dark enough, we broke out of the woods and encountered no resistance. We passed through the burning village of Jahnsfelde without incident and reached the main road to Müncheberg and then, a little later, our own lines, which we occupied immediately.[31]

Despite Chuikov's constant urging, the battle was being decided a little further north, around Wriezen. The stubborn defence of Neu Trebbin came to an end shortly after dawn on 18 April and Schöneck and the rest of the survivors of the garrison managed to reach the small village of Gottesgabe. Command and control were rapidly breaking down; as they staggered back to the west, Schöneck and a few of his exhausted comrades came across an abandoned supply dump and collapsed, too tired to continue. To north and south, Soviet troops took possession of the ridge line and began to move west.

The divisions of First Polish Army made repeated attacks on 5th Jäger Division to the north of Wriezen and succeeded in reaching – but not crossing – the Alte Oder. There was bitter fighting first to the east of Wriezen, and then in the town itself, as the Soviet Forty-Seventh Army threw its divisions at the German defences. Shortly after dusk, the Germans abandoned the ruins and pulled back to the west. The battalions of 35th Panzergrenadier Regiment, part of 25th Panzergrenadier Division, had fought all day to hold the town and were reduced to fewer than 100 men each. To the south of Wriezen too, the Germans were driven back to the high ground to the west with Third Shock Army in close pursuit. There were too few defenders left to prevent Kuznetsov's riflemen from pressing into the villages of Möglin and Batzlow, where bitter fighting continued through the following night. Generalleutnant Arnold Burmeister, commander of 25th Panzergrenadier Division, ordered what remained of his units to try to set up a defensive line facing southeast, but he had little idea of the exact location of 18th Panzergrenadier Division to his south. Many – perhaps most – German units were still fighting hard, but the losses of the three days of battle, combined with the almost complete lack of reserves, meant that holes were now appearing in the front line.

For Busse and Heinrici, much had rested on the planned counterattacks by *SS-Nordland* and *SS-Nederland*. The movement of these divisions proved to be a difficult undertaking. Fuel was in desperately short supply, and much of it was contaminated – a tanker had been partially sunk during an air attack near Stettin, and the recovered fuel constantly blocked the carburettors of tanks and half-tracks. Panzergrenadiers were forced to march on foot, and the clearing skies permitted Soviet aviators to range freely over the area, attacking columns at will.

Obersturmbannführer Paul-Albert Kausch's 11th SS-Panzer Regiment, part of *SS-Nordland*, moved forward to support the exhausted 9th Fallschirmjäger

Division; knowing that his men were effectively finished as a fighting force, Herrmann, who had just taken command of the paratroopers, asked Kausch to deploy his tanks in defensive positions. Kausch refused, preferring to take up an ambush position on a ridge running north from Buckow. Almost immediately after it had deployed, the SS regiment came under attack on its northern flank by the leading units of Second Guards Tank Army near Reichenberg. The SS tank crews claimed to have destroyed at least 50 Soviet tanks by nightfall; regardless of the true number of 'kills', they had effectively brought Bogdanov's tank army to a standstill. But as other elements of *SS-Nordland* took up positions in the dense woodland to the south of the panzer regiment, there was confused fighting with units from both sides having little idea of the location of friendly or hostile forces. There was no coherent front line, merely groups of vehicles and men probing through the dense woodland and stumbling into enemies and friends almost at random.

SS-Nederland, which had been allocated to XI SS Corps, was able to concentrate barely a single battlegroup by the end of the day. The division started the battle badly understrength – at the end of March, it had reported that it had just 1,355 combatants as a result of its heavy losses in the failed *Sonnenwende* counteroffensive. Parts of the division were left close to their starting positions in Third Panzer Army's sector, and scattered companies and platoons were commandeered by LVI Panzer Corps as they moved south. The effective disintegration of the division was unavoidable given the fuel shortages and transport difficulties, but there may have been a deliberate decision to avoid being drawn into the hopeless battles against the Red Army. The division had served in Steiner's III SS-Panzer Corps. In the week before Zhukov and Chuikov launched their attacks towards Berlin, Steiner had summoned several officers of III SS-Panzer Corps to his headquarters in Third Panzer Army's sector, where he told them that he believed it was important to reduce the strength of the forces being deployed in the west along the Elbe. By doing so, he hoped, the Western Allies might be tempted to cross the river and occupy large parts of Germany before the arrival of the Red Army.[32] A Leutnant in one of the divisions later recalled:

> The man who spoke was a man who was weary, infinitely weary, not in body, but in his soul. He said that the apparatus of the state no longer functioned. We had to see how we could help ourselves. I was terrified. Yes, it had gotten to that. The state was no longer in order. It no longer functioned for us! Nothing could have made our situation clearer to me in that hour of hopelessness than those words of the weary general who stood before us ... The conviction of the infallibility of the

organisation of the German state had been so strong in me that the thought that it was no longer in order pressed down on me with immense weight. What would happen to us now? Was there any way for us young soldiers to personally come through this great collapse?[33]

Steiner was highly regarded both in the SS and by his army contemporaries. When III SS-Panzer Corps was in Estonia in 1944, he had conducted an exemplary defence of the Sinimäed Hills; but when Hitler ordered him to withdraw to Tallinn to establish a 'bridgehead' around the city, he ensured that by evacuating all of his rear area formations to the south, such a bridgehead could not be held, and thus saved his men from becoming trapped in a pointless pocket on the northeast corner of the Baltic Sea. Now, like many, he could see the inevitable end of the war approaching, but unlike a large proportion of senior officers, he was determined to take steps to protect his men, just as he had done in Estonia. He had already had private conversations with Himmler, urging the *Reichsführer-SS* to open discussions with the Western Allies to secure a ceasefire in the west while Germany continued to fight against the Soviet Union. When *SS-Nordland* and *SS-Nederland* were sent to Busse's aid, Steiner spoke to the division commanders, urging them to avoid their units being sucked into urban warfare in Berlin. If at all possible, they were to withdraw to the west around the outskirts if the Red Army proved to be unstoppable.

Once the Soviet drive on Berlin commenced, Steiner dragged his feet when ordered to dispatch troops to the south, and Heinrici suspected that he was hoping to retreat to the west at the earliest opportunity so that his men could surrender to the Western Allies. If this was the case, Heinrici had good reason to be angered, as this reduced still further his options for attempting to retain control of the battle, but Steiner's attitude is understandable. Although he was a member of the SS, he clearly saw the defeat of Germany as unavoidable. Many of his units had fought against the Red Army since III SS-Panzer Corps was first deployed between Leningrad and the Estonian border in early 1944, and he would have known that as members of the hated SS, their chances of surviving Soviet captivity were slim. Moreover, many of the soldiers in III SS-Panzer Corps were from occupied countries in the north and west – Norway, Denmark, the Netherlands, and Belgium. It was natural that they might wish to try to avoid capture by the Red Army and would seek to make their way home, or at least surrender to the Western Allies.

In Konev's sector, Third and Fourth Guards Tank Armies were beginning to cross the Spree. Lelyushenko's VI Guards Mechanised Corps was tied down on his southern flank, fighting in support of Zhadov's Fifth Guards

Army, but his other two main formations – X Tank Corps and V Guards Mechanised Corps – were past the last German defensive line and driving into 'operational space'. Lelyushenko had received new orders a few hours before dawn:

> In pursuance of orders from *Stavka* to Fourth Guards Tank Army, we were to capture the area of Beelitz–Treuenbrietzen–Luckenwalde [to the southwest of Berlin] by the end of 20 April, and during the night to 21 April we were to capture Potsdam and the southwest part of Berlin. The neighbour to our right, Third Guards Tank Army, was tasked with crossing the Spree before dawn on 18 April and then rapidly to develop an offensive in the general direction of Vetschau–Baruth–Teltow and the southern outskirts of Berlin, and then to break into Berlin from the south during the night of 20–21 April.
>
> This directive set us a new task – an attack on Berlin, in contrast to the previous plan, which aimed to attack in the general direction of Dessau [between Magdeburg and Leipzig]. This new development didn't come as a surprise to us. At army headquarters, we had considered this even before the operation began. Therefore, without any lengthy loss of time, new missions were assigned: X Guards Tank Corps was to develop an attack in the direction of Luckau–Dahme–Luckenwalde, cross the Teltow Canal, and then capture southwest Berlin by the end of 21 April; VI Guards Mechanised Corps, after capturing the city of Spremberg, was to advance on Nauen [to the west of Berlin] and establish contact with the troops of 1st Belarusian Front [i.e. completing the encirclement of Berlin]; and VI Guards Mechanised Corps would advance towards Jüterborg, and by the end of 21 April capture Beelitz–Treuenbrietzen, securing the left flank of the army from possible enemy attacks from the west and creating an external front of encirclement of the enemy's Berlin group.[34]

Just a few years before, such rapid implementation of new plans, however much they might have been anticipated, would have been beyond the abilities of Soviet commanders and their staff. It is a measure of how far and fast the Red Army had evolved in the brutal environment of war, transforming from a lumbering, inflexible force into a highly effective weapon. Casualties remained at levels that no western nation would have contemplated, but unlike in earlier years, those losses could be offset by considerable tactical and operational successes. The bulk of X Guards Tank Corps and V Guards Mechanised Corps advanced rapidly on 18 April between Cottbus and Spremberg, reaching Drebkau and Neupetershain by the end of the day; their leading reconnaissance elements were even further forward, about 42 miles from the start line of the offensive.

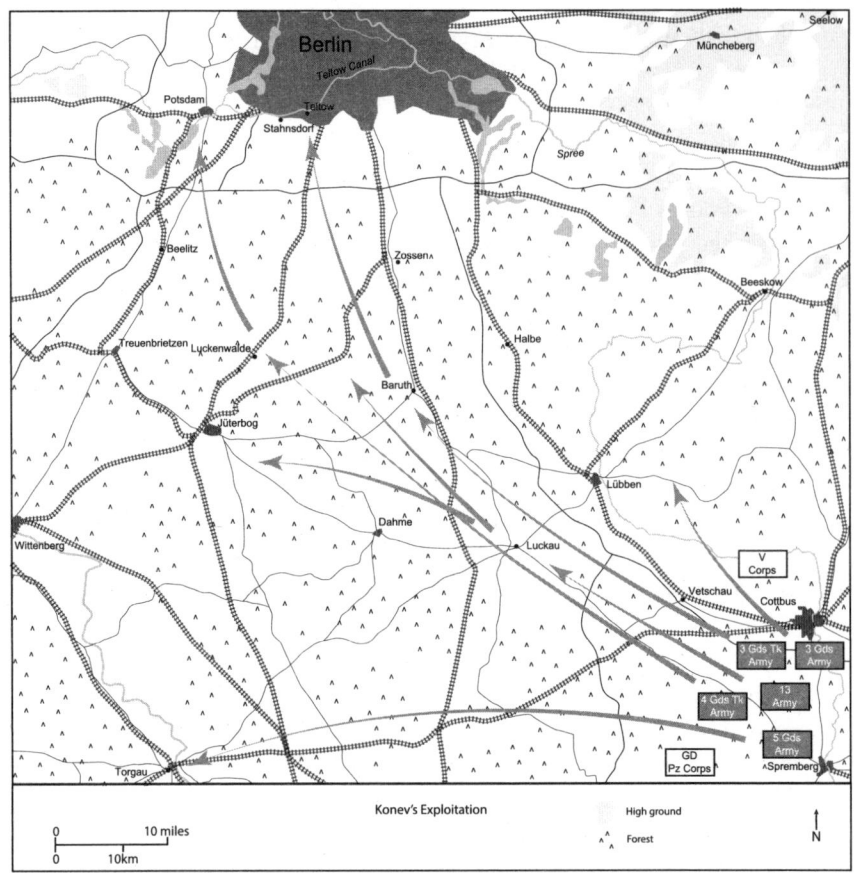

Rybalko's Third Guards Tank Army had a more difficult time. It took until midday on 18 April for the main body of armour to complete its crossing of the Spree. Bridging equipment had been held up in traffic congestion and the first attempts to cross at a ford ended with a tank being abandoned after the ford proved to be deeper than expected. Shortly after, several usable fords were located and the tanks began to cross, but most of Rybalko's armour didn't cross the Spree until the following night; it was a major frustration for the army commander, as reconnaissance units were reporting that the only opposition in his path consisted of a few companies of *Volkssturm*.[35] All afternoon, Rybalko – and Konev, who had moved his command post to the Spree – urged the units that had crossed to try to make up for lost time. By nightfall on 18 April, the leading elements were about 18 miles beyond the Spree. The combined arms armies had also closed up with the river and were beginning to cross, even though isolated, fierce clashes continued in the forests between the Spree and the Neisse.

As had been the case in Ninth Army's sector, the Germans had intended to fight their main defensive battle in the second line of trenches and fortifications, but Gräser's Fourth Panzer Army had already suffered heavy losses before the fighting reached this line; unlike Busse's troops, who had largely been able to pull back on the eve of the Soviet offensive, most of Fourth Panzer Army's forward units were badly mauled as Konev's units surged across the Neisse towards the Spree. They were further hampered by Hitler's insistence that the Neisse should be defended for as long as possible – this effectively denied the field commanders any flexibility in how they conducted their battle. By the morning of 18 April, the German front line had disintegrated. What remained of 545th Volksgrenadier Division had fallen back to Spremberg while its northern neighbour, 342nd Infantry Division, retreated into Cottbus. Further south was the *Brandenburg* panzergrenadier division, released from reserve and facing the Soviet Thirteenth Army. In January, *Brandenburg* had been hastily moved from East Prussia to try to stem the torrent of Soviet forces streaming west from the Vistula and had been in almost continuous combat since; although it had received some replacement drafts, these were either poorly trained recruits or improvised battalions of men who had previously been classified as unfit for front-line service. Fighting in a densely forested area, the division managed to hold up, but not stop, the Soviet attacks on the first day of the offensive; by 18 April, what remained of the division was fighting isolated battles, each group having little knowledge about what was going on to north or south. The counterattack by the *Führer-Begleit* panzergrenadier division delayed the Red Army's advance but failed to restore the situation and by the end of 18 April, Remer's division had been forced away to the south and was defending the town of Schleife.[36]

Three days of fighting had shattered the defences of Fourth Panzer Army. Konev's armour was operating almost unhindered; even if Busse continued to hold off Zhukov's forces in the dense forests and hills of the Seelow Heights, the Red Army looked likely to reach Berlin either by the direct route from the east or from the southeast. There was little that Gräser could have done, given the inflexibility of his orders and the lack of any meaningful reserves, but Hitler raged that the collapse of the front line along the Neisse was due to betrayal. Some of those around him sought refuge in fantasy. Gerda Bormann, wife of Martin Bormann, Hitler's secretary, wrote to her husband that the situation reminded her of the epic Germanic work *Edda*, specifically the *Götterdämmerung* ('Twilight of the Gods'):

> The Giants and the Dwarfs, the wolf Fenris and the snake Mitgard, all the powers of evil ... are storming over the bridge of the Gods ... the citadel of the Gods is tottering and all seems lost. But suddenly a new citadel rises, more beautiful than the one before, and Baldur lives again.[37]

For the thousands of soldiers fighting and dying in the front line, any such talk would have been incomprehensible. Similarly, the inhabitants of Berlin were about to learn the true horror of warfare. They had endured much from bombing raids, but their ordeal was about to worsen a hundredfold.

Chapter 7

TO THE GATES OF BERLIN: 19–20 APRIL

19 April

During the night of 18–19 April, Heinrici received numerous messages from his subordinate formations. In the north, Manteuffel reported that the Soviet units facing Third Panzer Army across the lower Oder looked as if they had almost completed their preparations for an offensive. He doubted the ability of his army to hold back the attack for long, particularly as he had no reserves available for counterattacks. Many of the soldiers of 7th Panzer Division, which had been fighting in the small German-held pocket immediately to the north of Danzig, had been evacuated by sea and brought to the west to be re-equipped, but at present they had little significant combat strength. A few tanks had been made available to the division, but fuel and ammunition shortages rendered them of little value.

In Berlin, the growing threat posed by the Soviet tank armies from 1st Ukrainian Front received little attention. Many in the upper echelons of the regime continued to believe that these units were intending to drive towards Dresden in order to link up with the US forces advancing from the west, rather than angling to the northwest towards the German capital. There was far more concern about the growing signs of collapse of Busse's Ninth Army. In addition to fighting a desperate battle with diminishing resources, Busse had to deal with constant telephone calls from Goebbels. In addition to his role as propaganda minister, Goebbels was also the *Gauleiter* of Berlin and therefore in control of the city's *Volkssturm*, and *Generalbevollmächtigten für Total Kriegeinsatz*

('Plenipotentiary for Total War'). He therefore regarded the battle to defend Berlin as being part of his overall sphere of interest and bombarded Busse with requests for information. On 19 April, he spoke to Oberst Johannes Hölz, Busse's chief of staff, and offered another four battalions of soldiers – some were *Volkssturm* and others had been designated as part of Berlin's garrison in anticipation of the fighting reaching the city. This raised a vital matter: was the decisive battle for Berlin to be fought in the city itself, or on the approaches?

When it became increasingly likely towards the end of 1944 that enemy forces might reach Berlin, Hitler appointed Generalleutnant Bruno Ritter von Hauenschild, commander of the military district that encompassed the city, as head of the Berlin Defence Area, but he became seriously unwell with influenza in February, necessitating hospitalisation. His replacement was Generalleutnant Helmuth Reymann, who had served with distinction as commander of 11th Infantry Division in the northern sector of the Eastern Front. He arrived in Berlin to discover that although numerous obstacles and barricades were in place on the main roads into the city, there were almost no defenders available other than *Volkssturm* and the improvised battalions of rear area units. He also had to contend with the tangled, competitive spheres of influence that prevailed in so many parts of Nazi Germany.

Given the limited resources available, Reymann and his staff had concluded that their task was simply to ensure that there were sufficient fortifications in place for use by retreating German field formations – the troops that they had could not be expected to defend such a large urban area and could do no more than support whatever German divisions pulled back to Berlin. When Reymann and his chief of staff, Oberst Hans Refior, attempted to coordinate such plans with Goebbels and other competing authorities, they were met with indifference at best, and deliberate obstruction at worst. Until 16 April, many senior civilian figures in Berlin seemed to persist in the belief that the Red Army could be held at arm's length indefinitely and therefore saw little reason for the inevitable disruption that would result from preparations for fighting within Berlin itself. Now, with the Red Army attacking Müncheberg, only 29 miles to the east of central Berlin, most of these figures simply packed up their families and fled for towns and cities closer to the west with the intention of ensuring that they were not in an area that would come under Soviet occupation. Others responded to the growing crisis with even greater determination to cling to whatever little authority they had.[1]

Goebbels regarded the organisation of Berlin's defence as his remit, and in addition there were several senior SS figures whose areas of authority overlapped with Reymann's. The *Gauleiter* of Berlin insisted on a daily meeting with Reymann, but this was rarely an opportunity for sensible collaboration; instead, Reymann and his chief of staff were subjected to instructions that often conflicted with their own preparations. Struggling with constant interference, Reymann organised his defences into three distinct belts, with eight different sectors. The outermost line was along the perimeter of the Greater Berlin area; the middle belt largely followed a raised *S-Bahn* railway line through the suburban districts; and the final defensive belt was around the central part of Berlin with the Landwehr Canal to the south, the Spree to the east and north, and the Tiergarten to the west. This inner zone would benefit from the firepower of the three flak towers if the Red Army penetrated into the city centre. Construction of defences was difficult because of shortages of raw materials, and the promised labour force rarely approached the numbers required. Often, this was due to the disruption of transport by American and British air raids; on other occasions, it merely reflected the widespread practice of officials promising more than they could deliver as they attempted to compete for the approval of Hitler and other senior figures. Other important preparations, particularly the possible evacuation of civilians, were never discussed properly, let alone implemented. Reymann wanted to have clear plans for a mass evacuation, and was unimpressed by Goebbels' attempts to dismiss his requests with bland assurances that measures were in place. When he investigated, the garrison commander discovered that these measures merely consisted of two designated routes marked on a map. There was no provision for medical aid or supplies for the hundreds of thousands of civilians who would have to attempt to walk out of the city along these routes. When Reymann requested that at least the estimated 120,000 children in Berlin should be evacuated as it would be impossible to ensure adequate food supplies if fighting reached the city, Goebbels replied that there would be sufficient milk for the duration of the fighting, and if necessary the Nazi Party would organise the transfer of herds of cows into Berlin to provide milk. Questions from Reymann and Refior about where Goebbels expected to find fodder for such herds of cattle went unanswered.[2]

Never a man for half measures, Goebbels energetically threw himself into sending as many reinforcements as he could to the German units fighting to the east of Berlin. The promised transfer of several battalions of *Volkssturm* to Busse's Ninth Army was merely a part of the units that Goebbels intended to send against the threat from 1st Belarusian Front, and Reymann protested in dismay that even before this weakening of his garrison, he didn't have sufficient men to defend Berlin. By transferring any troops to the battles raging in the east, any possibility of sustained defence was effectively brought to an end; nor would there be any contingency to deal with an unexpected threat, for example from the southeast or from the west. On this occasion, the SS figures involved in Berlin's defence sided with him, perhaps because Goebbels' plans would weaken their personal commands and therefore their importance in the eyes of the Nazi hierarchy. After a futile conversation with Goebbels, Reymann spoke to General Wilhelm Burgdorf, Hitler's senior adjutant, asking him to raise the matter with Hitler for a final decision at the Führer conference later that day. Having some insight into what these conferences entailed, Reymann must have known that he was unlikely to receive a satisfactory response.

As the war progressed and the ability of Germany to dictate the course of events steadily declined, the daily conference with the Führer assumed an ever more surreal aspect. The people who attended it changed as the years went by; Göring, who had been present at most conferences in the early years, was still nominally Hitler's heir, but his status within the Nazi system had declined as the ability of the Luftwaffe to wage war – and in particular to defend German cities from attack – deteriorated. Increasingly, Göring attempted to avoid the conferences or to leave them early before the latest air raids were discussed. Keitel, head of *OKW*, and Jodl, head of the Operations Department of *OKW*, were almost always present with their aides. Despite constantly siding with the Führer in any disputes, Jodl retained a degree of respect amongst other officers. Major Bernd Freytag von Loringhoven was adjutant to the chief of staff of *OKH* and worked with Guderian and then Krebs, and he later wrote:

> Jodl was ... always calm and considered. The words he uttered were deliberate and carefully chosen. [He] was far too intelligent to fall under Hitler's spell. In the last years of the war his viewpoint on military operations seldom coincided with those of the Führer, whom he never feared to contradict. That would put Hitler in a very bad mood and he would not shake hands [with Jodl] for several days. During the final months, Jodl expressed himself freely in front of Hitler, as few others would have dared to do ... [But] I believed him to be, like Keitel, wholly dedicated to Hitler, by virtue of his long service with *OKW*.[3]

This summary is perhaps overly generous to Jodl. However much he may have disagreed in discussions with Hitler, he rarely showed the independence of thought described by Loringhoven and had not hesitated to implement Hitler's instructions, however damaging they might be. But however generous men like Loringhoven were towards Jodl, there was little respect for Keitel from anyone. Many thought of him as honest and congenial, but almost everyone agreed that as Generalfeldmarschall and head of *OKW*, he was significantly over-promoted and functioning beyond his level of competence. He was clearly overawed by

Hitler and took every opportunity to try to appease the Führer, siding with him unquestioningly whenever disputes arose; other officers often referred to him in private as *Lakeitel* ('lackey'). Generalfeldmarschall Ewald von Kleist, who commanded panzer armies and army groups on the Eastern Front for much of the war, referred to Keitel as a 'stupid follower of Hitler' and Göring was equally disdainful, describing him as having the mind of a sergeant in the body of a field marshal.[4] He had at least a degree of insight, writing in his personal notes that he was deeply unhappy with being in his post and that he attempted on at least three occasions to persuade Hitler to allow him to resign.[5] But his strict sense of duty left him inextricably tied to his head of state, unable to break free as the years passed.

Burgdorf was head of the army's personnel office when General Rudolf Schmundt, Hitler's senior adjutant, died of injuries sustained in the failed attempt to assassinate the Führer in July 1944. Given his well-known, uncompromising belief in both Hitler and National Socialism, Burgdorf was a natural replacement. Loringhoven's opinion of him was mirrored by most of the traditional officers of the army:

> Burgdorf subscribed body and soul to Hitler and the Party. Uncultivated, coarse, and vulgar, he embodied perfectly the Nazi clique. His … mediocre career in the armed forces had nurtured his resentment against the generals and members of the [general] staff.
>
> Burgdorf battled energetically against traditionalism and elitism, seeking at any price to impose the Nazi ideal of *Volksoffizier* ['people's officer'] within the officer corps, and was nicknamed *Vomag* or *Volksoffizier mit Arbeitergesicht* ['people's officer with a worker's head'].[6]

Like Göring, Himmler was suffering from declining prominence. He remained head of the SS and the entire police and security apparatus of the Reich, but his personal performance during his brief spell as commander of Army Group Vistula had greatly damaged his prestige. He was often represented at conferences by Gruppenführer Hermann Fegelein, one of the most detested individuals in a regime that featured such a large number of abhorrent men. In his memoirs, Speer described him as 'the most disgusting man in Hitler's circle'.[7] An ardent horseman, he was instrumental in forming a cavalry unit in the SS; this was deployed in Poland in late 1939 where it took part in mass executions of members of Polish society who were thought to be potential leaders of anti-German resistance. He assiduously sought Himmler's favour, becoming one of an inner circle of SS officers to whom Himmler extended personal patronage and protection, and this proved to be very useful. When Fegelein was charged with several offences, ranging from unauthorised acquisition of money and luxury goods to having unlawful sex with a Polish woman and attempting to procure an abortion for her, Himmler intervened to quash any investigations. Fegelein's cavalry unit had grown to the size of a regiment by 1941 and was deployed in so-called anti-partisan operations; in reality, it was responsible for the massacre of thousands of Soviet civilians in occupied areas, often with little justification other than Fegelein's desire to present Himmler with an impressive 'body count'.[8] After being wounded in 1943, Fegelein was summoned back to Berlin by Himmler and given the role of being his liaison officer in Hitler's headquarters. During these months, he assiduously courted and then married Gretl Braun, sister of Hitler's mistress Eva Braun; this appears to have been purely a careerist move and had no effect on his numerous affairs. Loringhoven's opinion of Fegelein was brutally scathing:

> The multiple functions of the *Reichsführer* [Himmler] enabled this arrogant, corrupt dandy to interfere in everything, from interior policy to police matters and military affairs. During situation briefings he would interrupt people, including Hitler himself, in a manner verging on insolence.[9]

Eismann, who had endured the misfortune of being Himmler's operations officer during the brief reign of the *Reichsführer-SS* at the headquarters of Army Group Vistula, had an equally low opinion of Fegelein:

> He was ... the most lying and evil intriguer whom I ever experienced during this war. He had his filthy fingers into everything. His unashamed arrogant conduct toward older, experienced men was unparalleled. Even toward Himmler, with whom he was familiar, he employed a tone in private which was, at the very least, remarkable.[10]

Given such characterisations, it is unsurprising that throughout Himmler's time as commander of Army Group Vistula, Fegelein was actively undermining the *Reichsführer-SS* in private conversations with Hitler.

In addition to these military and SS figures, the daily conference with Hitler was attended by numerous Party officials. The person who had gained the most from the declining status of both Göring and Himmler was Martin Bormann, Hitler's personal secretary and head of the chancellery staff. By having almost complete control on who could see Hitler, he exerted great influence; known as the *Braune Eminenz* ('Brown Eminence'), a mocking reference to the powerful

Cardinal Richelieu of 16th-century France and his brown Nazi Party uniform, he became a frequent attender of the daily conferences as the war drew to a close. He, Burgdorf, and Fegelein spent many evenings together in drinking sessions, and like many within the Party he was openly hostile towards the conservative aristocrats who made up such a large proportion of the army's senior officers, seeing the traditional *Junker* class as an obstacle to the Party's control of German society. But whilst Bormann was widely regarded both by the military and by other Party officials as a coarse, overbearing bully, Joseph Goebbels, also increasingly present at the daily briefings, was a far more urbane figure. Well-spoken and intelligent, he was acquiring a growing reputation for remaining calm and composed as catastrophe loomed. However, this was offset by constant frustration on the part of army officers when it came to the handling of the *Volkssturm*; with no military experience or training, Goebbels constantly interfered in mobilisation, training, and deployment.

The daily conference usually started in mid-afternoon. The situations on the Western and Eastern Fronts would be presented by Jodl and Krebs respectively, with Hitler demanding huge amounts of detail about troop deployments and movements. Usually, Hitler was the only person to be seated; everyone else gathered around the conference table, waiting their turn with a mixture of anxiety and anticipation, as Hitler studied the maps prepared laboriously by men like Loringhoven:

> The maps, minutely designed, with tiny flags illustrating the positions of army corps, divisions, and other formations, conveyed a pleasing illusion of the actual capacities of the German fighting forces. Looking at them, one might think that the continuous lines corresponded to divisions with fully operational troops. Those who understood the harsh realities of the front knew that these scrupulously designed maps were no more than a sham. During the last year of the war, the majority of divisions had been wiped out and were mere empty shells. Countless thousands of men were missing. Nonetheless, the same was expected of them as of divisions still capable of fighting. Data was available as to the real condition of the troops, but Hitler never took any notice. The Führer stuck obstinately to his analyses, captivated by the magic of the lines and marks on the maps.[11]

After the situation briefings, discussions moved to other matters, mainly how the diminishing resources of the Reich were to be used. The division of responsibility of the theatres of war – with *OKH* responsible for the Eastern Front while *OKW* dealt with all other regions – led to further competition and chaos; although Jodl and Krebs (and before him, Guderian) often tried to take into account the needs of theatres other than their own, it was inevitable that they often regarded their own areas of responsibility as being the most important. Hitler would then be the sole arbiter of where any precious resources were allocated, something that further increased the importance of access to the Führer, via Bormann. Throughout the conference, which might last several hours, Hitler would often embark on a rambling digression, either speculating pointlessly about new weapons that he still dreamed would be produced in the future, or attempting to impress the professional soldiers around him by displaying detailed – and largely irrelevant – knowledge about specific weapons. On occasions, the setbacks on the various front lines would trigger outbursts of anger from Hitler. Throughout the war, he had been minded to see defeats as being due to the incompetence of field commanders rather than any reflection on the overall strategy that he imposed, or the operational and even tactical interference upon which he insisted. After the failed July Plot, all setbacks were interpreted as signs of outright treachery and betrayal. Sometimes, Jodl would speak up in defence of army officers, and Guderian had done so on many occasions before he was dismissed; Krebs was too cautious to risk attracting the Führer's wrath by any such objections, which were in any case almost pointless.

The Führer conference of 19 April was in many ways typical of those that had preceded it, dragging on for several wearying hours and diverting officers from their important tasks in managing their commands. Late in the day, Burgdorf telephoned Reymann about the plan by Goebbels to send *Volkssturm* battalions to the east as reinforcements for Busse's Ninth Army. The issue had been discussed, he informed Reymann, and Hitler had sided with Goebbels.[12] Burgdorf added that Heinrici had supported the transfer of the *Volkssturm*; it was only later that day that in a telephone conversation with Heinrici, Reymann learned that the commander of Army Group Vistula had done so in an attempt to ensure that the final battle of the Third Reich was fought outside the urban area, and the civilian population was thus spared the horror of being in a battlefield.

There were other developments too, but Reymann was not informed about these. To the north of Berlin, Steiner's III SS-Panzer Corps had effectively been stripped of its main assets when *SS-Nordland* and *SS-Nederland* were transferred south. Now, there were discussions about assigning 4th *SS-Polizei* Panzergrenadier Division to the corps; this unit, which had been badly degraded in fighting around Danzig, was being evacuated to the west by sea. Even before it embarked on ships for the west, the division was little more than a single battlegroup, consisting of just five infantry battalions, a combat engineer battalion, and three French SS companies. After leaving their vehicles in the small pocket still controlled by German forces in the eastern Baltic, these men were effectively dismounted infantry with few heavy weapons and no artillery support.

Nonetheless, Hitler behaved as if it was a full-strength panzergrenadier division. Hitler speculated about using III SS-Panzer Corps, now restyled *Armeegruppe Steiner*, in a powerful counterattack from the north against the Soviet forces in the coming days. It was pure fantasy. Having lost his two SS panzergrenadier divisions, Steiner was currently left with just a few companies of combat engineers, an anti-aircraft company, and an armoured reconnaissance battalion.[13]

Throughout the day, the battle on the approaches to Berlin continued. It was on the main axis to Berlin that Heinrici faced his severest problems. Ninth Army's most northern formation, CI Corps, was being driven back only slowly, but the losses suffered were nevertheless so great that it was likely the Soviet advance would accelerate in the coming days. Weidling's LVI Panzer Corps was also being levered out of its positions and although 18th Panzergrenadier Division had been ordered to counterattack, the reality was that it ran into Second Guards Tank Army and was almost immediately forced into a defensive posture. Weidling had been angered late on 18 April to learn that *Reichsjugendführer* ('Reich Youth Leader') Artur Axmann, head of the Hitler Youth, had organised a battalion of teenagers armed with *Panzerfausts* and had brought them to the rear area of LVI Panzer Corps. Weidling refused to deploy the untrained youths and extracted a promise from Axmann that they would be withdrawn, but Axmann's order for their withdrawal was either not received or was ignored; after being under the influence of Nazi indoctrination for almost all their lives, the teenagers of the Hitler Youth were fanatically committed to defending Germany at all costs. In March, Axmann himself had issued a proclamation to the Hitler Youth:

> There is only victory or annihilation. Know no bounds in your love of your people; equally know no bounds in your hatred of the enemy. It is your duty to watch when others tire, to stand when others weaken. Your greatest honour is your unshakeable fidelity to Adolf Hitler![14]

The resultant tragedy was entirely predictable. The youths remained in the battlefield, attempting to ambush Soviet armour wherever they encountered it. The Red Army showed little mercy and took few prisoners when they encountered the tank hunters. Some German veterans later described with approval how the teenagers fought with almost complete disregard for their lives; others were horrified at what was increasingly obvious: it was a pointless slaughter that achieved little to hold back the Soviet forces.

Having pulled back hastily to Rüdersdorf, immediately to the east of Berlin, Fritz Averdieck and the rest of his panzergrenadier regiment had an opportunity to catch their breath. They had started the battle far from full strength, but when they assembled on the morning of 19 April, they had just 90 men left; this was doubled by combing through the rear area elements, but the regiment – which should have consisted of two battalions, each with three companies and a heavy weapons company – still fielded less than two full-strength companies. Under intermittent air attack, the 'regiment' set off towards the north, where it was to take up a blocking position between two lakes; by the time it reached its destination, 30 men from the rear area formations had slipped away. To the surprise of the panzergrenadiers, a Soviet IS-2 suddenly erupted out of the woodland, shot up a German Panther tank, and charged through their positions, only coming to a halt when it encountered a roadblock. As it attempted to manoeuvre past the obstacle, it was hit by *Panzerfausts* and then knocked out by a second Panther. As darkness fell, the men dug in, but during the night there were further Soviet attacks and most of the remaining rear area personnel disappeared into the darkness.[15]

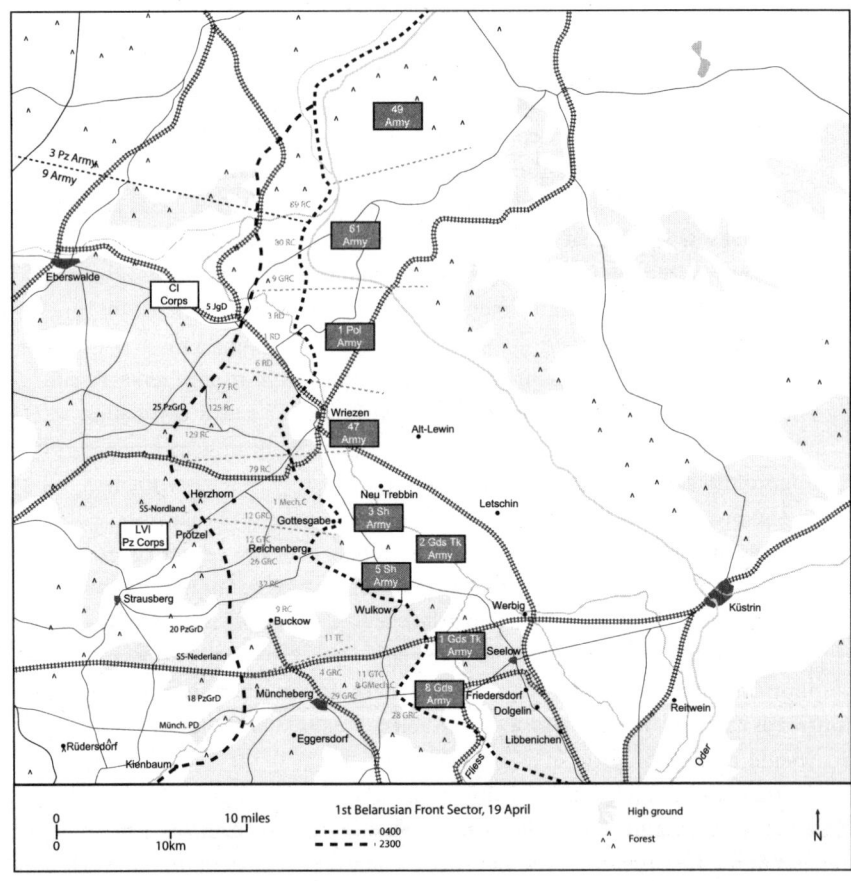

To the south, XI SS-Panzer Corps was no longer able to hold a continuous front line, with isolated companies of units like the *Kurmark* panzergrenadier division fighting against overwhelming odds. Kleinheisterkamp's corps had responsibility for the front line as far as Frankfurt-an-der-Oder and reported that although his southern units remained broadly in position, the Soviet penetration around Seelow had created a gap to LVI Panzer Corps in the north. To make matters worse, Heinrici was aware of the rapidly accelerating collapse of Fourth Panzer Army to the south of his army group; the leading Soviet units were already behind his southern flank.

Given the clear competition between Zhukov and Konev that Stalin had repeatedly encouraged, Zhukov must have been almost incandescent with frustration as his armies continued to gnaw their way through the German defences at huge cost, while Konev's formations raced west and began to turn towards Berlin. He issued fresh orders before dawn on 19 April for a renewed major effort that was to commence at midday. The military councils were to ensure that they sent political officers to all formations in order to ensure compliance, and the order ended on an uncompromising note: 'All officers who have shown themselves incapable of carrying out assignments and have displayed lack of resolution will be replaced by able and courageous officers.'[16]

It was a typical reaction of Zhukov to failure. In some respects, his attitude to such setbacks was not dissimilar to that of Hitler – he showed little or no willingness to accept that his orders might have been at fault, only grudgingly accepting responsibility in his memoirs long after the event. Inevitably, his subordinates had learned that the only sure way of shielding themselves from the consequences of failure was to throw their men into assaults regardless of casualties. By this stage of the war, there were few, if any, officers left in the combat elements of the Red Army who were genuinely short of resolution; nor were there plentiful numbers of more 'able and courageous' officers available to replace them.

Inevitably, it was Chuikov's battered Eighth Guards Army that was to lead the attack, with Fifth Shock Army on its northern flank; they would be supported by First and Second Guards Tank Armies respectively. Chuikov felt that the timetable was impossible to deliver. He particularly resented the section of the orders that subordinated the tank armies to the commanders of the combined arms armies, without any clarification of whether the tank armies remained under direct control of Zhukov's headquarters. Nevertheless, he and his staff issued instructions and made their preparations to storm Müncheberg. If they could capture the town, they would be halfway from their start line to Berlin; perhaps more importantly, they could be hopeful that they would have destroyed the bulk of the remaining German forces in their path.

On the battlefield, there were further episodes of friendly fire. Aleksei Ivanov, the assault gun officer who had struggled up the slope of the Seelow Heights in the initial attack, was now with the leading troops of Eighth Guards Army:

> We were assigned to a rifle battalion to take a factory. The regiment commander ordered me to collect three assault guns from the workshops and move to firing positions, and to make sure they had supplies of shells and fuel. I sat on the deck of the first vehicle and took them to where we had been ordered. I found the officer and reported, 'Comrade Lieutenant Colonel, three combat vehicles are here at your disposal.'
>
> I asked him about shells and fuel, and he answered, 'We have plenty of everything, you can relax.' I turned around and had trotted 50–70m, no more, when I heard the hiss of a flying shell. An experienced front-line solder can always distinguish the whistle of a shell that's going to fall somewhere nearby. It's only when a shell – like a bullet – is flying straight towards you that you don't hear it.
>
> I threw myself to the ground and there was an explosion. I got up and everything seemed fine, but then the lieutenant colonel's orderly ran up. 'They killed everyone!' It turned out that they had gathered for a meeting: the infantry regiment commander, the battalion commanders, and the deputy regimental commander. And the shell fell right in the middle and killed everyone in an instant. And this was just 20km from Berlin! Moreover, the worst thing was that this shell wasn't German, but one of ours.[17]

On the German side of the line, reinforcements arrived in the rear of the positions around Müncheberg: five battalions of *Volkssturm* from Berlin and three battalions of Latvian SS. The only lingering hope for Heinrici was that *SS-Nederland* might be able to mount a counterattack that would restore contact between LVI Panzer Corps and XI SS-Panzer Corps, but the leading elements of the division clashed with Soviet armour immediately to the east of Müncheberg and were driven back by Colonel Nikolai Viktorovich Morgunov's Soviet 45th Guards Tank Brigade. However, the result of this first clash was that the Soviet attack towards Müncheberg from the east suffered a check. The Soviet tank brigade had already sustained heavy losses – all three of its battalion commanders were either dead or wounded, and some of its tank companies were reduced to barely half their establishment strength. By midday, the attack by XI Guards Tank Corps had almost come to a halt. Babadzhanian, the corps commander, ordered his depleted units to bypass Müncheberg to the south.

Meanwhile, Chuikov's artillery had begun to bombard Müncheberg and shortly after midday – a little later than Zhukov had stipulated – Eighth Guards

Army joined the assault on the town. XXIX Guards Rifle Corps was in the lead, with its 82nd Guards Rifle Division attempting to thrust down *Reichstrasse 1*. The Germans had of course prepared extensive defences on this route and the attack was rapidly halted, whereupon Colonel Ivan Fedorovich Sukhorukov, a regiment commander in the division, diverted his men into the forest north of the road. The Soviet riflemen infiltrated through the woodland around the flank of the German defences and penetrated into Müncheberg, and heavy close-quarter combat broke out. Despite being wounded, Sukhorukov stayed with his men, urging them on in the best possible interpretation of Zhukov's orders.

The commander of 82nd Rifle Division was Major General Georgy Ivanovich Khetagurov. He described the fighting for Müncheberg:

> By 1800, 246th and 244th Guards Rifle Regiments were approaching Müncheberg from the northeast. I had sent [Sukhorukov's] 242nd Guards Rifle Regiment through the forests to march west, to bypass the city. The bulk of our artillery began methodically shelling the eastern approaches. Here, the enemy had deployed artillery and mortar batteries, had dug trenches and prepared machine-gun positions. From my command post, on high, forested ground, all this was clearly visible.
>
> I had continuous radio communication with Sukhorukov, and when he reported that having moved through the forest, his regiment had bypassed Müncheberg and had turned back towards the east, I gave the command to Pavlenko and Plyakin [the other two regiment commanders]: 'Start the attack!'
>
> The two regiments immediately opened fire, attracting the attention of the Nazis. Meanwhile, Sukhorukov's regiment, using its own vehicles and half-tracks as well as captured ones, burst into the city from the Berlin direction almost unhindered.
>
> The enemy resisted desperately in the trap, but our well-trained assault groups took block after block. By 2000 the division had completely captured this most important Nazi stronghold on the approaches to Berlin ...
>
> When the last pockets of enemy resistance in the city were suppressed, I reported this to Chuikov, and at first he seemed doubtful: 'Have you really managed to clear it all?'
>
> '[Major General Aleksei Mikhailovich] Pronin [a senior member of Eighth Guards Army's military council] just left us, he saw everything and will confirm my report,' I answered.[18]

Chuikov then informed Khetagurov that he was to take command of XXIX Guards Rifle Corps for the rest of the operation; for the first time since the offensive had begun, the commander of Eighth Guards Army sounded cheerful, with good reason. Babadzhanian's XI Guards Tank Corps, operating in conjunction with XXIX Guards Rifle Corps, had succeeded in moving past the southern edge of Müncheberg during the afternoon and reached Eggersdorf, cutting the road to the south of Müncheberg, at sunset. Fighting continued into the night; by dawn, the leading Soviet units had reached Kienbaum, to the southwest of Müncheberg. Here, their onward route was blocked by the Löcknitz River, a modest stream but with sufficiently steep banks to make crossing difficult for tanks. The retreating Germans had destroyed the bridge in the village, but riflemen accompanying the tanks waded across and secured a foothold on the west bank.[19]

Both Chuikov and Khetagurov portrayed the capture of Müncheberg as a relatively straightforward battle, but the accounts of the tank armies give a very different picture, with tough fighting both on the approaches to the city and in the urban area, with repeated German counterattacks and several parts of the city changing hands many times before the Germans were finally driven off. Like many others, Katukov was critical of the planning of the Berlin Operation:

> Thus, during the first four days of the operation, First and Second Guards Tank Armies actually performed the task of direct infantry support. Now that all the details of the breakthrough at the Seelow Heights are known, it is obvious that the Front command made a number of significant miscalculations. Firstly, it did not take into account the strength of the enemy's second line of defences, which ran along the Seelow Heights. During the offensive, it became clear the enemy concentrated his main efforts on defending the ridge of the Seelow Heights. In addition, the Nazi high command transferred significant parts of the forces and resources from other parts of the front line to this sector.
>
> As a result, the rapid offensive didn't work out as planned. The troops of the Front slowly 'gnawed through' the enemy's defensive positions one after another.
>
> There was a further difficulty for our offensive in the fact that the left flank of the units that had advanced closer to Berlin remained open. During this time, there was a strong Nazi grouping at Frankfurt-an-der-Oder. Shalin [Katukov's chief of staff] received alarming messages from our intelligence officers: the Germans near Frankfurt numbered up to 100,000 men. This was a substantial force for a counterattack into our flank.
>
> We expected that the troops of 1st Ukrainian Front would deal with the enemy's Frankfurt group, advancing to the left of our 1st Belarusian Front. But it transpired that they hadn't yet done so and [Major General Ivan Fedorovich] Dremov's VIII Guards Mechanised Corps had to disperse its forces … [and]

continuously repelled flank counterattacks. The Nazis were determined and persistent and we had to transfer other units to the fighting on our left flank that we could have used effectively to develop the attack on Berlin.[20]

Katukov's assessment of the threat from Frankfurt-an-der-Oder is an exaggeration. Biehler, the fortress commander, had very modest forces at his disposal, largely consisting of *Festungs-Division* ('Fortress Division') *Frankfurt-an-der-Oder*. Although it had nine infantry battalions, two machine-gun battalions, four artillery battalions, a combat engineer battalion, and a tank-hunter battalion, none of these were at full strength and they were made up largely of *Volkssturm* and hastily redeployed rear area and training units. The division also had very limited mobility – certainly not enough to mount counterattacks of the kind that Katukov described. Throughout the fighting for the Seelow Heights and Müncheberg, the garrison was effectively immobile and unable to intervene in the fighting on either flank. When Katukov and Chuikov were storming Müncheberg, the only significant event in Frankfurt was the demolition of the bridge over the Oder.

However, his criticism of Zhukov for not realising the strength of the German positions along the ridge of the Seelow Heights is both correct and, remarkably, not the first time that Zhukov was criticised for such failings. During 1942, Zhukov oversaw several attempts to break into and to destroy the German-held salient around Rzhev, to the west of Moscow. In this heavily forested country, crisscrossed by steep-sided gullies, Zhukov conducted operations with little or no regard for the near-impossibility of mounting major operations in such difficult terrain. He repeatedly failed to recognise the ease with which the Germans could create and hold defensive positions, and raged at the failure of his army commanders to move forward reinforcements, ammunition, and artillery, when even a rudimentary glance at the maps of the area would have shown that there were few roads that could be used. To make matters worse, the Rzhev salient was close to the region where he had grown up as a child, and he must have been aware of the nature of the terrain. In the attempts to relieve Leningrad, he had also demanded recurrent attacks over difficult terrain, but at least in that case there was the justification that if the siege of the city was to be lifted, there were few avenues for a relief effort to be mounted. On the Oder front in 1945, the dominating ridge line should have been an obvious hindrance to any attempt to advance on Berlin by the most direct route, and his armies paid a huge price for his failure to assess this properly. But Zhukov is – probably – not the only person at fault. Although several other senior figures later wrote that they had serious reservations about attacking such a position, these accounts may be less than entirely accurate. Detailed notes from the original meetings are not available; nor are there any written documents from the planning phase in which commanders raise doubts.

Not far from Müncheberg, Helmut Altner and his comrades had buried the 23 men of their company who had been killed the previous day and whose bodies could be found – another seven were missing, believed to have been torn to pieces by the salvoes of *Katyusha* rockets that had struck their trenches. Shortly after dawn on 19 April, their positions were shelled once more and Soviet troops then attacked. Reinforcements arrived permitting a counterattack. In a brief lull, the recruits received some remarkable news:

> The battalion commander comes forward and addresses us: 'Hold on another 24 hours, comrades,' he says in a moving voice. 'Hitler has issued an order: "Hold on another 24 hours and the great change in the war will come! Reinforcements are rolling forward! *Wunderwaffen* are coming. Guns and tanks are being unloaded in their thousands. Hold on another 24 hours, comrades! Peace with the British. Peace with the Americans. The guns are silent on the Western Front. The Western Army is marching to the support of you brave Eastern Front warriors. Thousands of British and Americans are volunteering to join our ranks to drive out the Bolsheviks. Hundreds of British and American aircraft stand ready to take part in the battle for Europe. Hold on another 24 hours, my comrades. Churchill is in Berlin negotiating with me."'[21]

For a moment, morale was boosted and the exhausted youths rallied once more. But as the day progressed, repeated Soviet attacks levered them out of their trenches to the south of Müncheberg. As darkness fell, the survivors of a regiment that had been holding positions a little further forward joined Altner and his comrades – the major commanding the regiment had just 78 men left. During the night, he and two other men crept forward into the lines of the Red Army and returned with a prisoner and attempted to interrogate him. Shortly after, Altner saw the prisoner being led away into the darkness, and a single pistol shot rang out.

To the north of Müncheberg, the German 5th Jäger Division was forced to pull back towards the northwest, unable to make contact with any units to its south; all that remained was a series of isolated groups, some no more than a handful of men, fighting uncoordinated battles in the hilly, forested terrain. Both sides were struggling to make sense of the situation. A young Leutnant from 5th Jäger Division was in command of what was effectively the division's rearguard, and at the end of 19 April his men had an encounter that was typical of the confusion:

> I had given my sentry orders to stop the tank company led by Leutnant Kercher, as I wanted to speak to him about something. Shortly afterwards the sentry reported that tanks were coming along the road. Expecting this to be Leutnant Kercher and his tank company, we did nothing. The tanks rattled at full speed past our sentry, whom fortunately they did not recognise. The sentry returned breathlessly to our dimly lighted room to say that he had been lucky yet again for that had not been Leutnant Kercher's company, but Russian T-34s. After half an hour these tanks came back through our location. It would seem that they had lost their way, thinking they were on the road to Berlin![22]

Fritz Kercher was the commander of a company of tank destroyers from 25th Panzergrenadier Division, which was now dispersed over a wide area. The remnants of two battalions of its panzergrenadiers continued to cling to positions around a mill near Wriezen, far behind the advancing Soviet units. Schöneck, who had escaped from Neu Trebbin with a handful of other stragglers, reached Batzlow, where they were added to a defensive line made up of *Volkssturm*, redeployed sailors, and Hitler Youth. Fighting flared around the village that night as XII Guards Rifle Corps, part of Kuznetsov's Third Shock Army, made repeated assaults, finally driving the Germans out. Schöneck continued his slow retreat, eventually reaching Prädikow, just to the east of Prötzel, where he encountered a battery from his *Berlin* division's artillery regiment; he and his comrades were promptly incorporated into its ranks as gunners.

It was in this sector that the first elements of *SS-Nordland* were deployed early on 19 April. They were able to take up concealed positions near Herzhorn, where a large column of Soviet tanks from Second Guards Tank Army appeared as the day progressed. Heavy fighting erupted with numerous Soviet tanks being hit and set ablaze, but the attackers rapidly recovered and, supported by artillery and aircraft, struck back at *SS-Nordland*. By the end of 19 April, the SS division had been forced to withdraw to Strausberg without being able to mount the sort of decisive counterattack that senior commanders had hoped for.[23] One of the most effective units of *SS-Nordland* was *SS-Schwere-Panzer-Abteilung 503*, with fewer than a dozen King Tiger tanks; these were in constant action on the two roads that ran to Strausberg from the east, fighting alongside both SS troops and isolated bands from 9th Fallschirmjäger Division. The tank crews would claim that they had shot up large numbers of Soviet tanks – Hauptscharführer Karl Körner, commanding one tank, reported that he destroyed seven tanks at first light near Grunow, while Obersturmführer Bruno Müller claimed a further 23 nearby, and the total for the day came to 70 – but regardless of the true number of 'kills', the Soviet troops edged closer to Strausberg.[24]

Despite *SS-Nordland*'s determined battle against Second Guards Tank Army, both Busse and Heinrici had their doubts about the division's reliability. Rumours of Steiner's comments to his officers before *SS-Nordland* and *SS-Nederland* were detached from III SS-Panzer Corps may have reached Heinrici, but the withdrawal of *SS-Nordland* to Strausberg was the result of unrelenting Soviet pressure rather than any attempt to escape to the west in order to avoid becoming prisoners of war in the east. The southern elements of the division, linking up with the survivors of 9th Fallschirmjäger Division, fought close-range battles with Soviet tanks and infantry in the forests to the north of Müncheberg. Like the teenagers of the Hitler Youth, many of the panzergrenadiers from *SS-Nordland* made good use of their *Panzerfausts*, which were widely feared by Soviet tank crews – although their range was limited, these weapons were capable of burning through the armour of almost any tank they encountered, and fighting in built-up areas or forests provided plenty of cover for small teams of tank hunters. Vladimir Nikitovich Golovach, a Soviet tank crewman, later described fighting against German troops using these weapons:

> *Panzerfaust* rounds caused a lot of damage to our tanks, but they also resulted in heavy losses for their users. After all, it was only possible to fire an aimed shot from such a weapon at a range of 50m and with clear line of sight. We became especially good at spotting *Faustniki* at night: when they fired, a stream of sparks flew from their tailpipes, and our machine-gunners responded immediately. Sometimes we captured them alive instead of shooting at them, including many teenagers and old people.[25]

There were several moments of remarkable acts of bravery during the withdrawal of *SS-Nordland*. A Panther tank from the division had broken down in Prötzel and was still stranded in the village when Soviet tanks approached. The SS crewmen waited until the T-34s were at almost point-blank range before opening fire; they then used their last round to render the Panther unusable before withdrawing on foot. When they reached German lines, they claimed to have destroyed at least 20 T-34s; the true number is unknown, but Second Guards Tank Army lost several dozen tanks in the day's fighting at various locations. Despite such incidents, Heinrici's doubts about the SS division would resurface in the coming days.

For the moment, though, the army group commander's main concerns were about the practicalities of continuing the battle. He felt that his troops had done as much as they possibly could, and with his front line now reduced to isolated

'That's how Berlin is going to look!': the soldiers of the Red Army were eager to exact revenge for the destruction of Stalingrad by the Germans in 1942–1943. (RIA Novosti Archive)

Members of *Volkssturm* heading for the front on the River Oder in March 1945. These civilians, previously regarded as too young, too old, or too infirm for military service, were deployed in the final defence of Germany with very limited equipment and almost no training. (Getty Images)

A Soviet fighter-bomber squadron over Berlin, 28 April 1945. While the Red Army infantry and tank units were supported by air strikes, it was notoriously difficult to carry out attacks on precise targets and indiscriminate devastation was inflicted across the city. (Getty Images)

Members of the Hitler Youth defending Berlin with a machine gun in April 1945. After being under the influence of Nazi indoctrination for almost all their lives, many of these teenagers were fanatically committed to defending Germany at all costs. (Getty Images)

Soviet artillery positioned to fire at the at the German defences on the Seelow Heights. For the Red Army, its artillery was the 'god of war', and there was widespread expectation that, if used effectively, it could smash the enemy defences and make an advance relatively simple. (Getty Images)

As the Red Army approached in April 1945, tens of thousands of civilians discovered too late that few arrangements for their evacuation had been made; many people made desperate attempts on foot, under enemy fire, with no provision for medical aid or supplies. (Getty Images)

A soldier instructing a woman in the use of a *Panzerfaust*. These weapons were widely feared by Soviet tank crews – although their range was limited, they were capable of burning through the armour of almost any tank they encountered. (Getty Images)

Members of the *Volkssturm* being instructed in the use of a *Panzerfaust* amongst the rubble of Berlin. The officer wears the insignia of a *Volkssturm* battalion commander; the *Volkssturm* used a mixture of Wehrmacht and SS insignia, which may have contributed to many of them being mis-identified by Soviet soldiers as SS and executed when they surrendered. (Getty Images)

Troops from the Soviet Thirty-Third Army entered Berlin from the north during the morning of 23 April. The following days saw bitter fighting amidst the rubble of the city. (Getty Images)

In many cases, the Soviet troops were in no mood to take prisoners. Zakhar Yevseyevich Krasilchikov recounted: 'We threw grenades through the windows of houses and basements from which they were firing at us, then cleared the buildings of Germans who were fighting to the last bullet.' (Getty Images)

Although the building had been in ruins since the fire of 1933, the Red Army placed great importance on capturing the Reichstag. (Getty Images)

Fires were ignited by the huge number of high explosives dropped on the city. These fires were whipped up by the strong wind and spread across Berlin – it was often days before the flames went out, having reduced almost everything in their path to ash. (Getty Images)

In his final hours, Hitler dictated his personal testament to his secretary, Traudl Junge, photographed here on her wedding day. Junge remained in the Führerbunker until Hitler's death on 30 April 1945; her 2002 memoir details the last days of the Nazi regime. (Getty Images)

After the battle, weary columns of German prisoners were gathered and began to march out of Berlin. Some Soviet soldiers gathered to jeer at them, but most were either busy celebrating, or simply glad that the fighting was over. (Getty Images)

The Reichstag became a magnet for Soviet soldiers. Along with hundreds of others, Yakov Fadeyev left his mark on the building: 'On the seventh column from the entrance, I and others wrote on the walls. I wrote: "I, Fadeyev, reached Berlin."' (Getty Images)

An aerial photo showing a devastated Berlin in 1945. Bombing, artillery fire, and intense combat in the streets left over 90 per cent of the city in ruins by the end of the war. (Getty Images)

groups with little or no contact with each other, he contacted *OKH* during 19 April. He later wrote:

> The commander of Army Group Vistula requested Hitler's permission to withdraw Ninth Army from the Oder and bring it back to the planned positions on the Hohenzollern and Finow Canals on both sides of Berlin ... His request was rejected with harsh words, and he was told that this was the point of crisis in the battle, which had to be endured and turned into victory by the counterattack of *SS-Nederland* and *SS-Nordland*. The [army group commander] made it unambiguously clear that these divisions would not be able to penetrate the enemy's lines. They were immediately forced onto the defensive and ultimately served to delay the enemy's advance towards Berlin.[26]

Further south, the armies of Konev's 1st Ukrainian Front continued their rapid progress. On the northern flank of the advance was the city of Cottbus. In February 1945, USAAF bombers intending to strike the synthetic oil production facilities in Ruhland, about 30 miles to the southwest, were unable to locate their target due to adverse weather and bombed Cottbus instead, leaving about 1,000 civilians dead and many more injured. The ruins that they left were now the scene of fierce fighting. At dawn on 19 April, Gordov's Third Guards Army was just four miles to the southeast of the city centre. The leading formation, XXI Rifle Corps, was driving back the remnants of the German 342nd Infantry Division; in an attempt to prevent his front line from collapsing, Gräser had brought much of 275th Infantry Division, originally deployed further north, to the area as reinforcements. In earlier years, the Germans would rightly have calculated that a Wehrmacht infantry division was capable of holding its lines against a Red Army rifle corps, but by 1945 the balance in such a battle lay firmly with the Soviet forces, particularly as in this case, they were reinforced by additional tank units. By the end of the day, the Germans had been driven back into Cottbus, where the battle became less one-sided; as armies have repeatedly discovered, relatively weak forces are far harder to dislodge in an urban environment – particularly where extensive ruins and rubble provide plentiful cover – than in open countryside.

On the southern side of the torrent of Soviet forces pouring west was Spremberg. By 19 April, the Soviet Fifth Guards Army's formations were approaching the city from the south, east, and north, squeezing its defenders into a small eastward-projecting salient around Spremberg. In addition to the units of the *Führer-Begleit* panzergrenadier division that had managed to reach the area, there was also a large part of 10th *SS-Panzer-Division Frundsberg* dispatched to the area as reinforcements, the remnants of 344th Infantry Division, and one or two battalions of *Volkssturm*. Konev could derive considerable satisfaction from the overall speed of his advance, but the determined resistance of the German forces on his flanks in Cottbus and Spremberg were causes for concern. He travelled to the command post of Thirteenth Army in the centre of this Front to discuss the matter with Pukhov and the two men agreed that Thirteenth Army's XXVII Rifle Corps should attack towards the southwest while Fifth Guards Army attempted to cross the Spree south of Spremberg with the intention of linking up with Pukhov's new thrust, thus surrounding the Germans in the city.[27] But Fifth Guards Army was still struggling to subdue the German units around Weisswasser, further to the east; it took all of 19 April for the Red Army to concentrate sufficient forces to reach the Spree and the southern outskirts of Spremberg.

Meanwhile, the two tank armies of 1st Ukrainian Front continued their headlong advance, much as they had done in January and February across Poland. Lelyushenko fretted about the absence of XI Guards Mechanised Corps, still tied down in helping protect the southern flank of the breakthrough, but was confident that it would rejoin the rest of his army in time for the final attack on Berlin. To his north, Rybalko had another successful day. His VI Guards Tank Corps reached Vetschau, and the leading elements continued almost unopposed into the night. By the end of the day, reconnaissance units were in Lübben, just 26 miles southeast of Zossen. The motorised units continued to clash with small groups of *Volkssturm*, losing tanks and other vehicles to ambushes with *Panzerfausts*, but the advance continued unchecked.

Eismann was still the operations officer of Army Group Vistula. That evening, he drew up an analysis of the current situation. Busse's Ninth Army was strung out over a frontage of about 90 miles, with substantial gaps in the line. The first defensive belt along the ridge of the Seelow Heights had fallen after heavy fighting and the second defensive belt – known in many German accounts as the *Hardenbergstellung* – had been breached with the fall of Müncheberg. This left the third belt, the *Wotanstellung*. Eismann calculated that this line, including the lakes that it incorporated, amounted to about 66 miles. A full withdrawal to the *Wotanstellung* would reduce the front line by a substantial amount, giving the depleted units of Ninth Army a better chance of creating a continuous front line. However, some Soviet units – particularly to the southwest of Wriezen – were already at least part-way through the *Wotanstellung*. Eismann calculated that with the southern flank of Ninth Army still sitting on the Oder at Frankfurt, it would take up to two days for a complete withdrawal to this shorter line, during which it could be expected that the Red Army would continue its relentless attacks. It was therefore essential, he concluded, that any order to withdraw had to be given immediately. Moreover, troops would have to be transferred north from the units pulling back from Frankfurt. A major breach had opened up in the German lines between CI Corps, which was being pushed back towards the northwest, and LVI Panzer Corps, which was pulling back towards the southwest. There was a further gap opening up on the south of LVI Panzer Corps, with XI SS-Panzer Corps and V SS-Mountain Corps continuing the line as far as Frankfurt. General Stanislav Gilyarovich Poplavski's First Polish Army was moving into the gap to the north of Weidling's LVI Panzer Corps, forcing it and CI Corps further apart. Eismann warned that a transfer of troops from the two southern corps to help repair these gaps required the pooling of all the transport resources of Ninth Army, and concluded his report with an ominous sentence: 'If there is a [Soviet] breakthrough on 19 April, extraction and reconsolidation will not be possible.'[28] This breakthrough had effectively already occurred.

Heinrici had already been refused permission for a formal withdrawal, and could do nothing to help his subordinates. In the north, Manteuffel reported that an assault by 2nd Belarusian Front across the Oder was imminent; he lacked the strength to do more than fight a delaying action. Ninth Army was effectively fighting as three separate groups, and even within each corps area many units had lost touch with each other or with higher headquarters. Without reinforcements, total collapse seemed just a matter of time. Eismann made several anxious calls to investigate the status of *SS-Polizei*, urging that, if necessary, weapons would have to be appropriated from every possible source in order to bring the division up to combat-ready status as quickly as possible. Additional troops were also beginning to appear – more elements of 549th Volksgrenadier Division had been evacuated from East Prussia by sea and were to be sent to Third Panzer Army, in the hope that this would permit Manteuffel to release troops for Ninth Army. For the moment, other than the *Volkssturm* already dispatched by Goebbels, the only reinforcements for Busse consisted of a battalion of Latvian SS. These men had also been brought west by sea; their parent unit, 15th *SS-Waffen-Grenadier* Division, had been badly mauled in Pomerania, and like all the units being brought back by sea, the men had few heavy weapons and nothing by way of support services.

The four days of fighting had cost Ninth Army over 12,000 men killed and many more wounded or missing. Busse's intention had always been to delay the advance of the Red Army for as long as possible in the hope that the Western Allies might reach Berlin first, but this was now clearly not going to happen. In any event, Busse had no intention of fighting a protracted urban battle and wanted to withdraw his army towards the west – the end of the war was close, and he intended his men to surrender to the Western Allies if at all possible. The best that he could now hope to achieve was for LVI Panzer Corps to re-establish contact with the two SS corps to its south, and for this group then to conduct a fighting withdrawal past the southern edge of Berlin. To the north, CI Corps would fall back towards *Armeegruppe Steiner*.

At last, Zhukov could see a possibility that his armies would reach Berlin before 1st Ukrainian Front. In an attempt to accelerate his advance, he made further alterations to the deployment of his forces. Bogdanov, commander of Second Guards Tank Army, was dismayed when he received orders that effectively broke up his command. His IX Tank Corps was to support Forty-Seventh Army, with the combined force pushing forward past the northern edge of Berlin and then driving south towards Potsdam in order to link up with the spearheads of 1st Ukrainian Front. The other two formations, I Mechanised Corps and XII Guards Tank Corps, were to support Third and Fifth Shock Armies respectively in their attacks towards the northeast suburbs of Berlin. Once these missions were accomplished, Zhukov assured Bogdanov, the tank army would concentrate once more and would be assigned the task of capturing the northern parts of the city. The price of driving through the German defences on the Seelow Heights had been terrible. Soviet accounts written after the war generally give a figure of about 33,000 dead, but the true number is thought to be at least twice as high. In addition, Zhukov's Front had lost nearly 750 tanks and assault guns, roughly a quarter of the number with which it started the battle.[29]

20 APRIL

In many respects, the battle for Berlin had been decided by dawn. Much hard fighting lay ahead, but there was no longer any possibility of the Wehrmacht being able to hold the Red Army at arm's length from the German capital, even for a brief period. There was no longer any clear front line – merely fragmented units attempting to pull back to the west with little or no contact with their neighbours, and often already bypassed by Soviet spearheads. It was a day that had always been marked with celebrations in Hitler's inner circle and – at least in earlier years – across Germany: it was Hitler's birthday. The Führer was 56 years old. For the preceding 34 nights, RAF Mosquito bombers had attacked Berlin, and there was a further raid on the night preceding 20 April. There would be a final British attack the following night.

The Soviet Eighth Guards Army attacked to the south of Müncheberg, driving the Germans back between *Reichstrasse 1* and Fürstenwalde. Chuikov recorded that German resistance was less than in preceding days, but progress remained slow, which he blamed on dense woodland that favoured defensive fighting, but a glance at contemporary maps suggests that he was now operating in somewhat more open ground. The continued slowness of his offensive more likely reflects the losses his units had suffered, and the difficulties of moving supplies forward. Attempts to release First Guards Tank Army for a faster thrust proved fruitless. Katukov complained to Zhukov that his tank army was hamstrung by the absence of his VIII Guards Mechanised Corps, guarding the increasingly long southern flank of the assault; Zhukov ordered a cavalry corps, currently held in reserve, to relieve Dremov's mechanised corps so that it could be made available for the thrust towards Berlin. Despite all of these problems, the combined bulk of the two Soviet armies reached Jänickendorf, still a little to the east of the advanced units that had reached Kienbaum the day before, with a further area of tangled woodland lying in front of them before the *Autobahn* ring around Berlin.

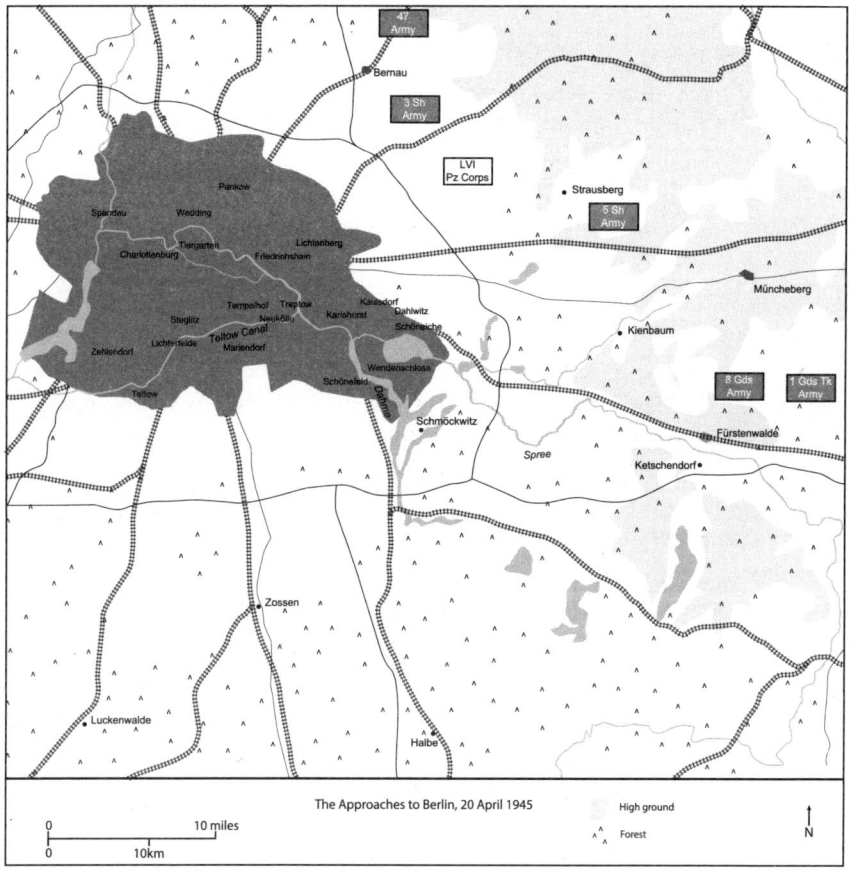

The Approaches to Berlin, 20 April 1945

Altner was in a small village in the path of Eighth Guards Army. His unit was ordered to pull back just as an artillery bombardment began, and the recruits scrambled through the burning buildings with shells falling around them. When they reached a farmhouse where their battalion headquarters was supposed to be stationed, they found it was empty and abandoned. Only a young Leutnant was present and after a brief rest the small group continued their withdrawal, first south past the western edge of Fürstenwalde and then towards the west. As they passed Ketschendorf, immediately south of Fürstenwalde, some of them may have noticed a compound protected by barbed wire. It was a satellite camp of the Sachsenhausen concentration camp, where up to a thousand prisoners had been held at a time, used by the SS as slave labour in various construction projects and subjected to brutal treatment and arbitrary beatings and executions. By the time that Altner and his comrades hurried past, the work camp was deserted, but Ketschendorf would soon be home to another such institution. Shortly after the fighting had passed, the *NKVD* established a camp in nearby workers' housing where German civilians were interned. These included large numbers of teenagers suspected of being involved in the *Werwolf* resistance movement that the Nazis had intended to create. Conditions were little better than those in the camp run by the SS, and it is estimated that out of about 10,000 who were imprisoned in the *NKVD* camp, up to half died during its two years of existence.

Babadzhanian was quick to exploit the small bridgehead secured over the Löcknitz at Kienbaum and after sappers had located a ford, the tanks of 44th Guards Tank Brigade began to make their way across the river. There was almost nothing in their path, and accompanied by tank riders, the T-34s rolled west. During the evening, they reached Rüdersdorf, where they finally encountered German defenders. An energetic counterattack from the west brought them to a halt, and they dug in to await the arrival of further rifle and artillery units.

To the north of Chuikov's riflemen and Katukov's tanks, the two shock armies advanced far faster, making the most of the capture of Müncheberg and the growing dislocation of the German lines. While Berzarin's Fifth Shock Army cleared the Germans from Strausberg and other towns and villages, Kuznetsov's Third Shock Army advanced against far weaker resistance. The two tank corps that had been detached from Bogdanov's tank army finally achieved something approaching the rapidity of advance that had been expected of them, and by evening had reached the area around and to the south of Bernau. They were now just 11 miles to the northeast of central Berlin. The Soviet units to the north of Fifth Shock Army – Forty-Seventh Army and First Polish Army – were also able to exploit the growing gaps in the German lines following the capture of Wriezen and rapidly approached the town of Eberswalde, where air raid sirens were activated to warn the population of the approach of Soviet tanks. In the early afternoon, there was a further dramatic development. Third Shock Army's LXXIX Rifle Corps was its leading formation and its longest-range guns, probably from an independent artillery unit that had been assigned to the corps, were now in range of Berlin and fired a salvo of shells at the German capital. Shortly after, guns of an artillery brigade of Forty-Seventh Army also opened fire on Berlin. For the Red Army, it was a most satisfying way to mark Hitler's birthday; for civilians in Berlin, it was a confirmation that their ordeal was about to get far worse.

Like Fürstenwalde, Eberswalde was the location of a satellite work camp, this time attached to the Ravensbrück concentration camp; prisoners worked in nearby factories manufacturing components for the German V-weapons programme. They had been evacuated before the Red Army approached, but throughout the region tens of thousands of civilians discovered too late that few provisions for their evacuation had been made. A few energetic local Party officials made attempts to secure transport and to mark evacuation routes, but – much to the chagrin of senior figures like Goebbels – the majority of Nazi Party figures took the first opportunity available to flee, taking their families with them and trying to reach western areas where they might avoid being captured by the Red Army. One of those who fled the area was Göring, whose country estate Carinhall, the scene of many lavish dinners during the war, was about 13 miles to the northwest. A column of 24 trucks left for Bavaria that morning, laden with paintings, furniture, and other expensive items. It should be noted that motorised transport was almost never available for the evacuation of ordinary German civilians. Göring ordered the main building to be wired for demolition and left the same day, walking purposefully away from the house. As he passed the point where the fuses for the explosive charges would be triggered, he glanced at the tangle of wires and said quietly to one of his personal guards, 'When you're Crown Prince, you have to do these things sometimes.' He then made his way to Berlin to take part in Hitler's birthday celebrations, while Carinhall was rapidly reduced to rubble.[30]

Soviet soldiers had already established a grim reputation as they advanced through German-held territory. Even before the Red Army had cleared the Wehrmacht from the occupied parts of the Soviet Union, there had been incidents of rape and looting, but this worsened greatly when German territory was reached. Official Soviet historiography attempted to claim that such incidents were very rare, but German accounts demonstrated the falseness of this. In the years after the fall of the Soviet Union, some veterans shed their previous inhibitions about the conduct of the Red Army as it crossed Poland and the eastern parts of Germany. Many continued to deny personal involvement, but others were quite frank about what happened, describing it as the completely predictable consequences of the atrocities committed by Germans in the Soviet Union. Whilst revenge was a major factor, other elements were also at work. Many of the soldiers of the Red Army had been away from their homes for several years with little or no opportunity for sexual encounters with women, and the combination of surviving violent combat and the imminent end of the war added further to the widespread rapes. As far as looting was concerned, there was widespread incomprehension that a nation as wealthy as Germany could have chosen to go to war against the Soviet Union. Soldiers seized items almost regardless of their utility. There were several occasions when soldiers – including officers – had toilets torn out of German houses and shipped home, even though there was no sanitation system in their villages to which they could connect the toilets. Jewellery of all kinds was regarded as a great prize, not least because it was easily portable, and many soldiers grabbed watches in large quantities. Some had little or no idea that a stopped watch could be restarted simply by winding it, and in the closing weeks of the war – and for some time after – Soviet soldiers wearing several watches at the same time became a common sight. Indiscipline through the use of alcohol was also widespread, adding to the violence against civilians. Osinovsky, the artilleryman quoted earlier, described some of the disorder as he and his comrades marched towards Berlin:

> There was an episode when our advanced units captured a populated area and moved on. The radio that I carried with me no longer had the range required and we remained in the captured village. There were just old people, women, and children there. We drank coffee with them and had a pleasant chat. But then the second echelon of the Front arrived and these soldiers caused a lot of destruction. The [elderly] men were shot immediately, the women and children were locked in a barn and systematically robbed. The newly arrived soldiers shouted insults at me, saying that I had been hanging around with Fascists. That was the kind of offensive that we were conducting.
>
> The second echelon often didn't actually fight, but robbed and killed with impunity.
>
> During this period, something else occurred. Near Berlin there were many copses – in other words, the forests there aren't dense. At night, the rifle unit to which I was attached received an order to go to the aid of a battalion that was surrounded. The Germans no longer had a continuous front line, but just separate groups that fought 'according to the situation'. And one regiment of the Red Army got completely drunk and wandered into an area where there were Germans

all around, who fired on them. The poor fellows radioed for help and our infantry was given the command to go and rescue these Red Army soldiers.

We set off in darkness and at dawn we came across our Red Army soldiers without any contact with the Germans. They were all so drunk! I saw their commander, a major, who in slurred speech told us how they got lost and ended up encircled by the Germans.[31]

Many accounts – both Soviet and German – described how the troops of the first echelon usually moved through German towns and villages rapidly; they might have taken some jewellery and watches, but they were usually too busy pursuing the retreating Wehrmacht to indulge in widespread violence and looting. On many occasions, these Soviet soldiers warned civilians about the indiscipline of the second echelon, which often included disproportionate numbers of poorly trained troops, many of them incorporated into the ranks of the Red Army as it came across prison camps in Poland and eastern Germany. It is easy to imagine how men who had been held prisoner by the Germans and had suffered terribly at the hands of their captors were eager to take revenge when the opportunity arose.

For several days, the sounds of explosions and gunfire had been growing louder in Berlin as the battle approached the city. On Hitler's birthday, the noise was even greater, and many Berliners were already becoming accustomed to the rumble of gunfire. A female journalist kept an anonymous diary of her experiences in the German capital during and immediately after the last weeks of the Third Reich's existence, and her account starts on this day:

> What was yesterday a distant rumble has now become a constant roar. We breathe the din: our ears are deadened to all but the heaviest guns ...
>
> A little before 3pm the newspaper wagon drove up to the kiosk ... It's not a real paper any more, just a kind of newssheet printed on two sides and damp on both. The first thing I read is the Wehrmacht report. New place names: Müncheberg, Seelow, Buchholz – they sound awfully close ... I barely glanced at the news from the Western Front. What does it matter to us now? Our fate is rolling in from the east and it will transform the climate, like another ice age ...
>
> No one knows anything for sure. There's no *Völkischer Beobachter* [a virulently strident Nazi newspaper] on the stairs any more. No Frau Weiers coming up to read me the headlines about rape over breakfast. 'Old woman of 70 defiled. Nun violated 24 times.' (I wonder who was counting?) ... Are [these headlines] supposed to spur the men of Berlin to protect and defend us women? Ridiculous. Their only effect is to send thousands more helpless women and children running

out of town, jamming the roads heading west, where they're likely to starve or die under fire from enemy planes. Whenever she read the paper, Frau Weiers' eyes would get big and glaze over. Something in her actually enjoyed that brand of horror.[32]

That night, there was a further air raid – the last time that RAF planes would bomb the city. The diarist spent much of the night in the local air raid shelter.

Hitler's birthday also saw the entry of Rokossovsky's 2nd Belarusian Front into the fighting. Preparations for an imminent attack against Third Panzer Army had been continuing in the preceding days, and a heavy artillery bombardment of the German positions along the lower Oder was followed by the creation of a smokescreen to protect the troops making the assault. The river divides into two streams, the East and West Oders, and in most places the Red Army had already

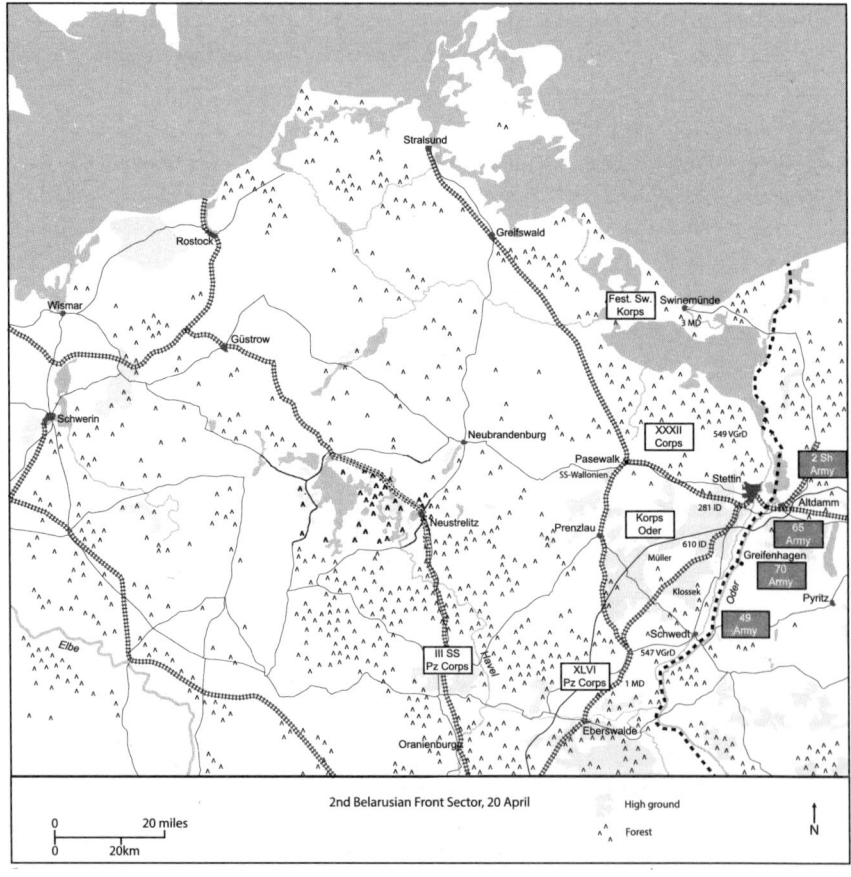

crossed the former. The first to attack were elements of Colonel General Pavel Ivanovich Batov's Sixty-Fifth Army, and the army commander peered anxiously through his binoculars as Lieutenant General Konstantin Maksimovich Erastov's XLVI Rifle Corps set off across the Oder. By the afternoon, Batov was able to report to Rokossovsky that the first wave of troops from five rifle divisions had crossed and was fighting on the west bank. By the afternoon, Batov had two ferries operating on his section of the river, permitting the transfer of guns, mortars, and the light SU-76 assault guns to the west. Impressed by the progress of Sixty-Fifth Army, Rokossovsky promised Batov reinforcements in the shape of I Guards Tank Corps; he also sent orders to Second Shock Army, waiting a little to the north, to make use of the crossings that Batov had secured.

To the south of Sixty-Fifth Army was Seventieth Army, commanded by Colonel General Vasily Stepanovich Popov. The attack here started a little later, and the stubborn resistance of German troops opposite Greifenhagen held up the attacks for much of the day. The defenders, yet another improvised unit known as *Gruppe Wellmann*, were finally driven back after inflicting heavy losses on the Soviet troops, and construction of a 50-ton pontoon bridge commenced. The third Soviet army to be involved in the offensive was Forty-Ninth Army, on the southern flank of Rokossovsky's Front, and when he reached Colonel General Ivan Tikhonovich Grishin's command post, Rokossovsky was disappointed to find that there had been almost no progress:

> We had placed great hopes in Forty-Ninth Army. Its task was to cooperate with the right-flank troops of First Belarusian Front … and deliver a cleaving blow against the enemy, throwing units of his Third Panzer Army to the north and northwest, where they were to be engaged by Seventieth Army. In view of the importance of the task, Forty-Ninth Army had received more reinforcements than the others. And now Grishin was marking time.
>
> We analysed the causes of the setback. The main one was a mistake of the army's reconnaissance. In this sector, the flooded island between the two channels [of the Oder] was crossed by several canals, one of which the scouts had mistaken for the main stream of the West Oder. As a consequence, all artillery fire had been converged on the bank of this canal, held by minor enemy forces. When our infantry crossed the canal and reached the West Oder they were met by fierce enemy fire and were unable to force a crossing.[33]

Everywhere, the German defences on the Eastern Front were disintegrating. Konev's armies were rolling forward, brushing aside the small groups of *Volkssturm* that tried from time to time to stop them. At *OKH*, Krebs – obediently complying with Hitler's opinion – had expected the tank armies to turn southwest towards Dresden and the Elbe, so that they could link up with the American forces that had reached the river; instead, news came of the turn of Lelyushenko's and Rybalko's formations towards the northwest and Berlin. Spremberg, at the southern edge of Konev's breakthrough, was subjected to another brutal bombardment at dawn, and in mid-morning Zhadov's Fifth Guards Army attacked the town. By late afternoon, the ruins of Spremberg were in Soviet hands and the attacking riflemen had pushed on a few kilometres to the west beyond the town. The various Soviet groups converging on Spremberg linked up with each other, creating multiple small encirclements to the west.

The German *Führer-Begleit* panzergrenadier division had received uncompromising orders to hold its positions at all costs. Remer might have impressed Hitler with his loyalty during the coup attempt of 20 July, but his rapid promotion and appointment to command of the division took no account of his relative lack of experience. Throughout 19 April, there were heated arguments between Remer and other officers – some of them his direct subordinates within the division, others commanding various groups of stragglers – about the situation. Remer was minded to continue holding Spremberg and the area to the east, but other more experienced officers repeatedly urged him to withdraw to the west while there was still time. Finally, during the second half of 19 April, *Führer-Begleit* withdrew to an area immediately west of Spremberg, and even at this stage it had to take up all-round defensive positions as the locations of Soviet units were not fully known. For 20 April, Remer was ordered to hold his current positions in anticipation of a counterattack by two SS panzer divisions, and the division spent the day under constant air attack and being assailed on all sides by Soviet units. As darkness fell, Remer realised that the counterattack either had failed or had never even commenced. There was a further conference of the senior officers in what was now clearly an encirclement; they agreed to wait until dawn before deciding in what direction they should move.[34]

The speed of the advance of Konev's armoured forces brought its own problems. Rybalko was concerned that his northern flank was relatively unprotected, forcing him to leave small groups of tanks at key road junctions as cover. This measure brought a rebuke from Konev in a signal sent to Third Guards Tank Army during 20 April:

> Comrade Rybalko, you are moving like a snail. One brigade is fighting, the rest of the army is stationary. I order you to cross the Baruth–Luckenwalde line through the swamps along multiple routes, deployed in full battle order. Report when this has been accomplished.[35]

With fighting continuing all along the front into the night, there was little or no opportunity for the Germans to reorganise the meagre forces that remained available. For Busse, even Eismann's proposal of adopting a shortened front line was too much; in a conversation with Eismann during the evening, he informed the operations officer that he regarded it as impossible for his remaining troops to defend even 48 miles of front line. He added that with Fourth Panzer Army's front line effectively breached, it made no sense for troops to remain in Cottbus – it would be better if they withdrew to the northwest and were attached to Ninth Army.[36] The reality was that Ninth Army no longer existed as a coherent organisation. There had been no contact with the headquarters of Weidling's LVI Panzer Corps since mid-evening, with gaps in the front line on either flank of the corps.

Heinrici spent most of the evening with CI Corps. He spoke to Eismann shortly after Busse's telephone call, reporting that the units of the corps were effectively at the end of their strength. He emphasised that 25th Panzergrenadier Division was in no state to make any attacks on the Soviet forces. Eismann then spoke to Krebs at *OKH*. Despite the reports from both Army Group Vistula and Ninth Army, Krebs simply passed on the instructions dictated by the Führer. In order to restore contact between CI Corps and LVI Panzer Corps, 25th Panzergrenadier Division was to be extracted from its current positions and deployed on the southern flank of CI Corps. Krebs assured Eismann that this would be made possible by the transfer of 3rd Marine Division from Third Panzer Army. Eismann replied that it was increasingly difficult for Busse's headquarters to retain contact with CI Corps, and it might be better if this formation was assigned to Third Panzer Army, but Krebs was unwilling to agree to this. There was a tendency for formations to withdraw towards the 'centre of mass' of their parent formations, and he was concerned that if CI Corps was attached to Third Panzer Army, it would be more likely to retreat towards the northwest, thus creating an even larger gap in the German lines, but eventually Eismann was able to persuade Krebs to approve the transfer. The discussion concluded with further information about the timing of the transfer of 3rd Marine Division. Eismann concluded the day glumly with the observation that 'Whether or not relief of 5th Jäger Division [by the marine division] is possible will be revealed tomorrow.'[37]

Heinrici returned to his headquarters that night and immediately contacted Krebs to demand permission for Ninth Army to pull back. In response to every argument that Heinrici raised, Krebs replied simply that the Führer insisted that Ninth Army hold its positions. Moreover, it was to concentrate forces on its southern flank to attack towards the south in order to help relieve the pressure on

Schörner's Army Group Centre. Finally, Heinrici gave Krebs an ultimatum. He told the chief of the general staff that he had not been given sufficient freedom to deploy his formations as he had wished. Adding that he had an established reputation for stubborn defence, he said that a withdrawal was essential not out of any sense of unfounded pessimism, but simply because Ninth Army faced imminent destruction. The instructions for a counterattack were impossible to implement – if Heinrici was not given permission to withdraw, he asked for permission to resign and to fight as an ordinary infantryman. After a pause, Krebs asked if he really wanted this message to be delivered in full to Hitler. Heinrici replied that he insisted on it. Shortly after, Krebs called him back. Hitler's orders remained unchanged, and Heinrici had been refused permission to resign his command.[38]

The surreal atmosphere of Hitler's bunker continued its increasing separation from reality. For several days, there had been discussions about moving various senior commands out of Berlin, and it was widely assumed that Hitler would escape to his mountain headquarters near Berchtesgaden in Bavaria to continue the war. It seems that Goebbels played a major role in changing Hitler's mind. He argued that if Hitler had to face death, then it was better that this should be in Berlin, rather than what he disparagingly described as a 'summer house' far from the capital. With even the most fanciful talk of a miraculous military victory becoming increasingly absurd, many figures like Goebbels turned their thoughts to the legacy that they would leave behind, and the propaganda minister stressed the symbolic importance of Hitler remaining in his capital to the very end. Much of the Nazi era was dominated by a dark obsession with death as the only alternative to complete victory, and in such an atmosphere the thought of some sort of inspiring, heroic last stand that would be remembered by future generations assumed an importance out of all proportion to reality. Hitler now declared that he would remain in Berlin. When he informed those gathered around him in the bunker of his decision, most urged him to change his mind and to leave, but as was often the case, the Führer was adamant. He told his entourage that he couldn't call on the troops defending Berlin to continue fighting if he personally fled to a safer location and that fate would decide his personal outcome, but he gave others permission to leave if they wished.[39] Amongst the first to leave was Göring, citing urgent matters that awaited him in Bavaria. Hitler stared at him silently. It was an ignominious end to a relationship that stretched back to the early days of the Party.

Chapter 8

DER KRIEG IST VERLOREN: 21–22 APRIL

21 April

With the entry of 2nd Belarusian Front into the offensive on 20 April, the battlefront extended from the estuary of the Oder to the approaches to Dresden. In the north, Rokossovsky pushed his armies forward as fast as possible. Batov's Sixty-Fifth Army had started the offensive far from full strength; the army commander later wrote that only one of his three rifle corps had received replacement drafts and most of his divisions were at less than half their establishment strength. The German units facing Batov were in even poorer shape, thus accounting for the initial Soviet successes on 21 April, but fighting was tougher the following day. Although he had repeatedly refused permission for a full evacuation of the German forces trapped in Courland, Hitler had grudgingly agreed to the transfer of individual formations to the west, and amongst these was 281st Security Division. The security divisions were originally raised to act behind the front line on the Eastern Front, responsible for tasks ranging from protecting lines of communication, through anti-partisan operations, to supporting the *Einsatzgruppen* in their mass killings of Jews, but as the war continued most of these divisions found themselves in the front line. Although their personnel were often older men and the divisions lacked much of the artillery and other heavy weaponry of regular infantry divisions, Hitler repeatedly treated them as if they were capable of functioning in an identical manner. Towards the end of 1944, 281st Security Division was evacuated by sea from Courland to northern Germany where it was redesignated 281st Infantry

Division and assigned reinforcements of artillery and anti-tank units, and by the time that Rokossovsky's armies surged across the Oder it had already been involved in heavy fighting in Pomerania. It was now ordered to take part in a counterattack to drive back Batov's Sixty-Fifth Army, alongside elements of the 'fortress garrison' of Stettin. At first, the German attack made some progress, but was soon halted and then driven back. Heinrici later commented on a bitter lesson learned repeatedly on the Eastern Front:

> The experience gained in Russia several times proved to be true in this case too: once the Russians had gained ground on the enemy's riverside, it was almost impossible to drive them off from there again. They quickly and skilfully entrenched themselves into the slopes running down towards the river and could neither really be reached by artillery nor by mortars. Their way back was blocked by the water and the commissars standing on the other side of the river, who without any qualms shot fleeing solders. Thus the Russians were clinging to the earth and holding out, for only holding on could offer them a slight chance to save their lives.[1]

Batov's southern flank was causing him problems due to the limited progress of his neighbouring army. The units of the German Third Panzer Army mounted repeated counterattacks, but fuel shortages and communications difficulties made it almost impossible to coordinate them effectively. Nevertheless, there were worrying moments, with the Soviet riflemen using dozens of captured *Panzerfausts* to fight off the German attacks. The Soviet 37th Guards Rifle Division had some difficult moments, as Batov later described:

> I remember how towards the end of the morning, when the violent counterattacks on the left wing had subsided, [Major General Kuzma Yevdokimovich] Grebennik [commander of 37th Guards Rifle Division] told me: 'If the enemy had advanced in a more organised manner and struck with better concentrated force, we would already be back in the water.' I recalled our own bitter experiences of the first year of the war, when our tank formations had wasted their resources trying to plug holes in our defences. Now it was the Germans who did this, or rather were forced to so do. They were unable to form a concentrated shock wedge and their improvised attacks did little to help them, although they were repeated frequently and carried out with bitter determination.[2]

Slowly, Batov's troops edged forward, but elsewhere there was less progress. Both Seventieth and Forty-Ninth Armies made little headway, and during the afternoon Rokossovsky switched his Front-level assets that he had assigned to these armies to Batov instead. The emphasis of 2nd Belarusian Front thus shifted to its northern flank. Heinrici and Manteuffel assessed the fighting and concluded that, given its weak resources, Third Panzer Army had done all that was possible. Between Stettin and the Baltic Sea, the front line remained relatively quiet and it was possible to extract much of 549th Volksgrenadier Division so that it could be sent as reinforcements to face the Soviet Sixty-Fifth Army. In addition, Manteuffel ordered his only reserve, *SS-Wallonien*, to deploy south of Stettin. It was hoped that these two divisions would be able to make a fresh attempt to destroy the bridgehead secured by Batov's troops, but there was little prospect of any such attack being possible before the following day.

Just before dawn on 21 April, Zhukov issued a new proclamation to his Front:

> The decisive hour of the battle has arrived. Before you lies Berlin, the capital of the German Fascist state, and beyond Berlin a link-up with the troops of our allies and complete victory over the enemy. Despite being doomed to destruction, the remnants of German units continue to resist. The German command is scraping together the last remnants of *Volkssturm* reserves, sparing neither the elderly nor 15-year-old children, and is trying to hold back our offensive to delay its death just for a few hours.
>
> Comrade officers, NCOs, and soldiers of the Red Army! Your units have covered themselves with eternal glory. There was nothing that could stop you either in the ruins of Stalingrad, or in the Ukrainian steppes, or the forests and swamps of Belarus. You were not stopped by the strong fortifications that you have now overcome on the approaches to Berlin.
>
> Before you, Soviet heroes, is Berlin. You must take Berlin, and take it as quickly as possible, so as not to give the enemy time to come to his senses. Let us unleash the full power of our military on the enemy, bring forth all our will to win, all our skill. Let us not disgrace our honour as soldiers, the honour of our battle flags.
>
> To storm Berlin – to complete the final victory, comrades! With daring and courage, close cooperation of all branches of the military, good mutual support, sweep away all obstacles and move forward, only forward, to the centre of the city, to its southern and western outskirts – towards the allied troops moving from the west. Forward to victory![3]

There was, of course, another reason for Zhukov to urge all possible speed: he firmly intended that it should be his armies, not those of Konev, that received the accolade of conquerors of Berlin.

Given the heavy losses suffered in the slow, brutal grind across the Seelow Heights, it was inevitable that new orders had to be issued. As had been the case since the beginning of the offensive, Eighth Guards Army and First Guards Tank Army were to function as a combined group, driving along *Reichstrasse 1* towards Berlin. When they reached the outskirts of the German capital, they were to turn south, crossing first the Spree and then the Dahme. Once they had passed these waterways, they would turn west once more, driving through the southern part of Berlin, until they reached the Havel. Here, they would link up with Second Guards Tank Army, which by this stage was expected to be re-unified as a single group. Third Shock Army was to penetrate into Berlin from the northeast, while Fifth Shock Army on its southern flank conquered the eastern suburbs. Three armies – Sixty-Ninth and Thirty-Third Army, together with Third Army, which until now had been in reserve – were tasked with completing the destruction of the German Ninth Army.[4] Again, there was a specific reason for directing Eighth Guards Army and First Guards Tank Army to capture southern Berlin. This would block off any attempt by Konev's armies to reach the German capital.

On the northern flank of Zhukov's Front, Soviet troops were rapidly exploiting the gap that had appeared in the German lines following the near disintegration of Ninth Army. Generalleutnant Friedrich Sixt, who took over CI Corps on the eve of the Soviet attack, now had a command that existed largely on paper. With little contact with many of his subordinate formations, he attempted to pull back towards the west, but powerful Soviet units had already bypassed his southern flank and he was forced to retreat towards the northwest, thus widening the breach that already existed. The scattered German battlegroups further south continued to inflict losses on the advancing Soviet units, but could do little to hold them back.

After several days of bitter fighting, the Soviet Eighth Guards Army, with the accompanying tanks of First Guards Tank Army, reached the Berlin ring road on 21 April. Chuikov regarded the orders for his forces to turn south with concern; he worried about possible German counterattacks from Berlin into what might be an exposed western flank of his army, and ordered his IV Guards Rifle Corps to continue pushing directly towards Berlin while the rest of the army angled towards the southwest. As 21 April progressed, the fighting reached the suburbs of the German capital with clashes in Köpenick. Babadzhanian, whose tanks were in the forefront of the advance, fretted about the dangers of urban warfare – his armour would surely be better deployed in open ground away from the threat of ambushes at close range by Germans using *Panzerfausts* – but balanced this with the desire to be part of the final battle against the enemy.

As they penetrated into the urban area, Soviet troops came across increasing signs of the brutal measures taken by the German military police to maintain discipline. Several accounts describe the corpses of executed German soldiers hanging from lampposts with placards around their neck stating that they had betrayed Germany. Many buildings were emblazoned with painted slogans, declaring that Berlin would always be German; Babadzhanian wryly noted that in some cases, advancing Soviet troops had added a footnote: 'Yes, but without Fascists'.[5]

During the afternoon of 21 April, Babadzhanian's tankers had an unexpected encounter, as Katukov later described:

> Babadzhanian called me: 'I have some Japanese people here, Comrade Commander.'
>
> 'What sort of Japanese people?' I didn't understand. 'Where did they come from?'
>
> 'They say they are diplomats. From the Japanese embassy in Berlin.'
>
> 'Send them to me.'
>
> An hour later, a whole diplomatic mission appeared at my checkpoint. The diplomats continually bowed and smiled. It seemed that they were not at all confident of a warm welcome from us. While they were crossing the front line, they had endured some anxious moments. One of the diplomats, quite a tall man, spoke passable Russian. He said that, unwilling to endure the horrors of battle, the employees of the Japanese embassy had decided to seek help and protection from the Soviet command. 'We want to return to our homeland.'
>
> Although I had no great desire to help representatives of a country which at that time was an ally of our enemy, I still had to provide the refugees with transport and send them to the Front headquarters in order to avoid diplomatic repercussions.[6]

Helmut Altner spent the day struggling back towards the west along the *Autobahn* running from Frankfurt-an-der-Oder to Berlin. The road was a tangle of wrecked and abandoned vehicles with military police attempting in vain to restore order. Bridges along the road had already been demolished and small groups of *Volkssturm* were digging trenches on either side. Altner 'liberated' a bicycle from a staff sergeant who was busy directing traffic, and accompanied by his comrade Fritz Stroschn he reached a village where the remnants of the company had gathered. Here, they learned that Soviet troops had taken control of Fürstenwalde and had then pushed on to the west and had reached Erkner, on the eastern edge of Berlin. Routes to the southwest seemed clear and the company set off for

Storkow, only to learn that Soviet tanks were in the village. They spent a dispirited night in a farm near Storkow, wondering how they were going to escape from the Soviet forces that seemed to be on all sides.[7]

Other fragments of Ninth Army were also being driven away towards the southwest. With Soviet forces bypassing both flanks, encirclement and complete destruction seemed inevitable and Heinrici continued to submit requests for as much of Busse's army as possible to be ordered to withdraw west towards Potsdam. Already, it was too late for all units to escape encirclement, but there remained at least a possibility that much of the southern fragment of Ninth Army could be saved. But as was often the way when a crisis demanded immediate action, Hitler chose to place great faith in reports that he believed were more favourable. Army Group Centre, to the south of Heinrici's formations, was commanded by Schörner, a long-time favourite of Hitler, who had a grim reputation for rigid enforcement of orders and summary execution of those who disobeyed. He was also skilled at playing on Hitler's beliefs and had submitted wildly optimistic reports that his forces were counterattacking successfully into the southern flank of the advance by 1st Ukrainian Front. Citing these developments, Hitler ordered Heinrici and Busse to make an attack of their own towards the south towards Cottbus. From there, it would be possible to re-establish firm contact with Army Group Centre and thus isolate Konev's two tank armies that were rapidly approaching Berlin. It was an absurd order, given the shattered state of Ninth Army; and in any case, Schörner's reports were exaggerated.

On the Oder River, the garrison of Frankfurt remained in place. Heinrici had repeatedly requested its withdrawal and had been rebuffed on every occasion, but he now finally persuaded Hitler that the 'fortress' had no further value. Finally, during the afternoon of 21 April, Hitler grudgingly agreed. Orders were passed swiftly to the garrison, but constant air attacks made preparations difficult and it would not be possible to commence a withdrawal to the west until the following day. They weren't the only units that were struggling to move in a timely manner. Eismann's doubts that 3rd Marine Division would arrive in time to release 5th Jäger Division proved to be entirely justified; harassed by Soviet aircraft and hamstrung by fuel shortages, the sailors of the division made their way south largely on foot and by the end of 21 April, Oberst Henning von Witzleben, the division commander, could report only that his leading elements had reached Zehdenick, about 26 miles north of Berlin's outskirts, and it would take at least another four days for the division to assemble.

In the centre of the fragmented Ninth Army, Weidling's LVI Panzer Corps struggled back towards the eastern edge of Berlin, with no contact with higher commands; late on 21 April, Army Group Vistula reported that the last report it had received from Weidling, via Ninth Army, was over 24 hours old. In turn, Busse was struggling to keep in regular contact with Heinrici's headquarters. In one radio conversation, Busse rejected Heinrici's instructions that Ninth Army should attempt to extend its line north of Berlin on the grounds that he lacked both the troops and the required fuel. Staff officers struggled to produce reports using information that was fragmentary at best, and almost always out of date by the time it was received. But with Ninth Army effectively disintegrating, there was a clear threat that despite its southern flank holding firm, Third Panzer Army faced the possibility of being driven away towards the northwest. To deal with this, Hitler once more demonstrated his tendency to treat units on his situation maps as if they were at full strength. He had already speculated about deploying the grandiosely named *Armeegruppe Steiner* in an attack in this area, and now issued orders for Steiner to drive back the Soviet units that were attempting to cross the Finow and Hohenzollern Canals near Oranienburg and to link up with LVI Panzer Corps. In addition to the units already under Steiner's command, he was assigned two improvised Luftwaffe divisions that had been promised by Göring, made up of redeployed airmen and ground personnel. The orders demonstrate the level of fantasy that now prevailed:

> It is the essential mission of *Armeegruppe Steiner* to establish and maintain contact under all circumstances with LVI Panzer Corps that are near Werneuchen. It will do this by attacking from the north with 4th *SS-Polizei* Division and elements of 5th Jäger Division and 25th Panzergrenadier Division. These elements – which need to be as strong as possible – will be freed up by 3rd Marine Division.
>
> It is expressly forbidden for any unit to fall back to the west. Officers who do not unconditionally follow this order are to be arrested and shot on the spot. I make you, yourself, responsible with your own head for carrying out this order.
>
> The fate of the capital of the German Reich depends on the success of your mission.[8]

Faced with clearly impossible orders, Steiner contacted Heinrici and requested the return of *SS-Nordland* and *SS-Nederland* to his command. Both of these formations had suffered further losses and would have contributed little to the striking power of *Armeegruppe Steiner*, leaving Heinrici with further suspicions that Steiner was merely trying to move as many of his foreign SS as possible to positions from where they could escape to the west. In any event, it was impossible to release these divisions from their current commitments and the request was denied.

Meanwhile, Soviet armour came ever closer to Berlin. The tank units that Zhukov had dispatched to sweep around the northern side of the city reached

Buch, on the outskirts, and encountered few organised defenders, as a young lieutenant in the leading reconnaissance unit described:

> On the approaches to Buch, the German resistance was absolutely insignificant. Discarded functional vehicles and other equipment showed that the enemy had run away in a hurry, and the corpses of its soldiers and its smashed artillery in firing positions convinced us that our fighters and bombers had not done a bad job here.
>
> My patrol vehicle went freely to the eastern outskirts of [Buch]. The entire reconnaissance detail followed the vehicle. We ran into individual Hitlerite soldiers shuffling along. After raising their hands, they cried out, '*Hitler kaput!*'
>
> We made our way into the town. The news that Soviet tanks had appeared on the streets flew through the neighbourhood. Russians, Ukrainians, Frenchmen, and Poles who had been forcibly taken there by the Fascists started to make their way out of the cellars, shelters, and dugouts. At first they approached our vehicles with the red stars on the turrets cautiously, and later with growing boldness.[9]

Learning from local people that the German defenders had pulled back a short distance and had set up three barricades, the reconnaissance commander pressed on. The first two obstacles proved to be easy to bypass, but sniper and *Panzerfaust* fire at the third obstacle brought the advance to a brief halt. Rapidly deploying from the line of march, the Soviet tankers made short work of the defenders and by early evening had reached Karow, a little to the west. Here they found another German slave labour camp and set up all-round defence for the night.

In the southern sector, Konev enjoyed another successful day. His two tank armies were now far in advance of the combined arms armies behind them – by the end of 21 April, the gap had increased to 21 miles and in many cases had reached the *Autobahn* ring around Berlin. In other circumstances, such a wide gap might have invited a powerful German counterattack, but even if sufficient troops had been available for such an operation, Germany no longer had the means of supplying the essential fuel and ammunition. But the lengthening supply lines were causing difficulties for the Soviet units. The leading tanks were short of fuel and were forced to pause a short distance from Zossen, where *OKH* had its headquarters in two underground bunkers. Here, they had encountered a small group of German armoured vehicles that formed part of the guard force at *OKH*. While the Soviet tanks exchanged fire with this makeshift force, Krebs held a last conference with his staff. Shortly after midday, there was a telephone call from Hitler's bunker: Krebs was given permission to transfer his headquarters to an army base just north of Potsdam. Most of the non-essential personnel of *OKH* were put aboard a convoy of vehicles that left for Bavaria; as they made their way through the streets, they were perilously close to the leading Soviet armoured columns and, to add to their troubles, they came under sudden air attack. But the aircraft were from the Luftwaffe, mounting one of their last sorties of the war, and the pilots had mis-identified the vehicles.[10]

Having refuelled, the Soviet tanks probed into Zossen and came across the bunkers from which *OKH* had conducted the war in the east. It seems that few of the senior Soviet commanders were aware of where *OKH* had been based, and the tank column was met by the civilian caretaker. To the astonishment of the tank crews, he invited their officers to accompany him on a tour and then led them through the bunkers with their still-functioning communication equipment. The large telephone exchange, linking *OKH* with German units in every corner of Europe, was still intact; a departing German officer had left a message written in his best Russian, advising any Soviet soldiers that this was valuable and useful equipment that should not be damaged. At one point, a telephone in the conference room began to ring. It was a German staff officer asking for an urgent update; the soldier who had answered the phone replied in Russian: 'Ivan is here. Go to hell.'[11]

Not far away, Lelyushenko's men, like other Soviet units, came across a work camp, this time with unexpectedly prominent prisoners:

> Our 65th Guards Tank Brigade, under the command of Colonel Fomichev, was the spearhead of Fourth Guards Tank Army and after defeating the enemy garrison in Babelsberg [immediately to the east of Potsdam] liberated about seven thousand prisoners of various nationalities from concentration camps. Among them was French Prime Minister Eduart Herriot [actually, he was a former prime minister and had been mayor of Lyon until he was arrested for refusing to cooperate with the German occupation authorities] and his wife. He had been imprisoned first in a camp near Paris and when the Nazis were forced to leave the French capital, he was transported to Babelsberg. Herriot was liberated by 2nd Machine-Gun Company under the command of Lieutenant Vitold Stanislavovich Yezersky. He was informed about the presence of a senior French political figure in the camp by Tamara Prusachenko, a Stalingrader who was in the same camp. The machine-gun company stormed the camp, killing any guards who resisted ...
>
> The tankers fed Herriot and his wife lunch, gave them a car, and then sent them under escort to Front headquarters for rest and onward departure for their homeland. Chatting with his guards, Herriot thanked them heartily, writing

down the address of his liberator, and promised to write to him on his return to France. He kept his word.[12]

The most northern of Konev's combined arms armies, Gordov's Third Guards Army, continued to fight in and around Cottbus, where the thinning ranks of the garrison continued to resist. With his divisions being bled white in the fighting, Gordov requested permission to screen off the city, but Konev refused:

> We could not limit ourselves to surrounding the Cottbus concentration. This was too sensitively located close to our rear area services. Until the city was taken, we had to bypass it on small country roads, causing great difficulty in organising the supply of fuel and ammunition, especially for the tank armies. On this day [21 April], I visited Gordov and carried out, as they say, 'educational work'. My intention was to strengthen the determination of the command of Third Guards Army to overcome the Cottbus grouping as soon as possible.
> A general attack on the urban area was planned for the next day, and this included helping Gordov with large forces of both aviation and artillery.[13]

There was a further concern. Even if Cottbus was captured rather than encircled, Gordov's army was certain to be involved in what was rapidly developing into the encirclement of the German Ninth Army, with 1st Ukrainian Front approaching from the south and 1st Belarusian Front bearing down from the north. The distance between Gordov's western flank and the tank armies approaching Berlin was growing steadily, and Gordov expressed concern that the Germans might attempt to escape through this gap. Konev had Lieutenant General Aleksandr Aleksandrovich Luchinsky's Twenty-Eighth Army in reserve, recently transferred from the Königsberg theatre. Although its divisions were badly depleted by the losses suffered during the battle for the capital of East Prussia, it was now ordered to proceed with all possible speed into the gap between Gordov's troops and Third Guards Tank Army. Meanwhile, Rybalko's tanks were now probing into Königs Wusterhausen, at the southeast edge of Berlin. By the end of the day, they were separated from the riflemen of Chuikov's Eighth Guards Army to the north by a series of lakes and waterways, but both Soviet forces were unaware of the presence of the other. Astonishingly, there seems to have been no direct liaison between Konev's and Zhukov's headquarters; both relied on information from *Stavka* about the location of the other. To an extent, this was a consequence of the top-down command structure of the Red Army, but the rivalry between Konev and Zhukov also contributed to their unwillingness to cooperate closely. This lack of communication would have serious consequences in the days that followed.

The southern side of Konev's breakthrough, around Spremberg, also saw a day of hard fighting. With his Fourth Panzer Army scattered to the winds, Gräser sent an order to the *Führer-Begleit* division during the morning, instructing it to try to break out to the west. Hastily, the division organised itself into two battlegroups, but Zhadov's Fifth Guards Army attacked even while preparations were underway. The intention had been to hold the current position until midday to allow other units to reach the area, but Soviet pressure was too intense and Remer ordered the breakout to begin immediately. The first objective was Kausche, about seven miles to the west of Spremberg, and under constant artillery and mortar fire, the two battlegroups struggled along forest roads to the village, leaving in their wake a string of abandoned trucks and tanks, their fuel tanks empty. The village fell to the Germans after a fierce battle and the small number of armoured vehicles that remained mobile pushed on to Neupetershain, a further two miles to the west. They found the town firmly in Soviet hands and the remnants of *Führer-Begleit*, together with soldiers from other units, gathered in the forests a little to the northeast.

Here, Remer held a brief conference with Brigadeführer Heinz Harmel, commander of *SS-Frundsberg*, and Generalmajor Erwin Jolasse, commander of 344th Volksgrenadier Division. They agreed that the only option was for the remaining armoured vehicles to lead a breakout attempt by *Führer-Begleit* towards the west; the rest of the troops would attempt to form a rearguard and would then follow if possible. Under sporadic artillery fire throughout the night, the exhausted soldiers prepared for what many feared would be their last battle.[14]

In Berlin, Reymann – the *Kampfkommandant* of the garrison – found himself inundated with requests to leave the city throughout 21 April. He had already argued in vain for a timely evacuation of non-essential civilians, but Goebbels had brusquely dismissed his requests, saying that the SS and local police authorities would conduct an evacuation when Goebbels alone ordered it. Goebbels then announced that no able-bodied men were permitted to leave Berlin – all were to make themselves available for service in the *Volkssturm*, and dozens of Party officials now besieged Reymann's headquarters to try to secure permits that would allow them and their families to flee to the west. Reymann had no interest in detaining them – he had decided that the *Volkssturm* were of little practical military value, and correctly assessed that whatever modest fighting ability they had would be eroded if they included large numbers of men who were anxious to escape at the earliest opportunity. He therefore instructed his staff to issue the relevant documents; by the end of the day, over 2,000 Party officials were in the process of leaving the city. Oberst Hans von Refior, Reymann's chief of staff, wryly commented on the 'rats leaving the sinking ship'.[15] The flight of so many Party officials who found themselves in the path of the advancing Red Army had started as soon as Soviet troops approached the frontiers of the Reich, much to the irritation of Goebbels and others; for the officers of the army, who had endured constant criticism from Party members about their constant retreats and had then endured the suspicion and disdain of senior figures after the failure of the July Plot, it was final proof, if any were needed, of the hypocrisy and self-serving character of those who had strutted and preened themselves in earlier years.

Reymann's willingness to allow so many Party officials to leave Berlin had serious consequences. He had made no secret of his doubts about the ability of his forces to do any more than prepare defences for the regular troops that retreated into Berlin, and even at this late hour, there were figures in the Nazi hierarchy who were eager to take advantage of any passing opportunity to indulge in the pseudo-Darwinist internal struggles that were a recurring theme of the past few years. Burgdorf, who in addition to acting as Hitler's adjutant was head of the army's personnel department, had already briefed against Reymann, and, declaring that permitting so many Party officials to leave Berlin amounted to defeatism, he now informed Hitler that the *Kampfkommandant* was not showing the required level of 'fanatical' determination. Goebbels had also taken a dislike to Reymann, particularly when he learned that he had used Goebbels' offer of *Volkssturm* battalions for the fighting to the east as an opportunity to move large numbers of *Volkssturm* out of Berlin. He too advised Hitler that Reymann was not the right man to take command of Berlin's defenders in the coming battle.

During the late afternoon, Reymann was dismissed from his post and ordered to go to Potsdam where he was to take command of another newly improvised division. There were intense discussions about who should replace him as *Kampfkommandant*; during the evening, Oberst Ernst Käther – promptly given a double promotion to Generalleutnant – was declared the new commander of Berlin. He had commanded an infantry regiment on the Eastern Front earlier in the war, but his main credential for his new post was that he was a senior *Nazionalsozialistischer Führungsoffizer* ('National Socialist Leadership Officer' or *NSFO*), responsible for ensuring that the rank and file were sufficiently indoctrinated in Party policy.

Heinrici continued to argue for greater freedom of action, even though his ability to influence the course of events was diminishing by the hour. The encirclement of what remained of Ninth Army seemed imminent and could only be avoided by an immediate withdrawal to the edge of Berlin itself, but Krebs insisted that Hitler's orders had to be followed, and that the Führer explicitly took full responsibility for these orders. In vain, Heinrici protested that this was irrelevant, and that he had to act in the best interests of the men under his command. He had already offered his resignation the day before and he now repeated his request; the response was the same as before. He sent a signal to Busse advising him to try to disengage from battle with the Soviet forces facing Ninth Army, regardless of Hitler's instructions, but Busse was not a man inclined to such acts of disobedience. His command had changed markedly in the preceding week, with CI Corps now detached from his northern flank and assigned to Third Panzer Army and LVI Panzer Corps falling back towards Berlin. To the south, he had gained control of the isolated V Corps from Fourth Panzer Army, and he limited his response to Heinrici's orders to drawing up plans for V Corps and V SS-Mountain Corps to pull back in two stages to the Spree and the Oder–Spree Canal.[16] However, no practical steps were taken to facilitate implementation of these orders.

Accompanied by Jodl, Heinrici travelled to Steiner's headquarters to see what was being done to implement Hitler's instructions for an attack from the north. Steiner cut across their enquiries, asking them, 'Has either of you actually seen my units?' Jodl then requested details of the attack that was meant to take place early on 22 April, and Heinrici added the last sentence of Hitler's orders, stressing that the fate of the capital of the Reich depended on the success of the operation. He then added, 'You have to attack, Steiner – for the sake of your Führer.' Knowing that there wasn't the slightest possibility of his troops being able to carry out the attack, Steiner snapped back, 'But he's *your* Führer too!'[17] He pointedly gave no assurances to his visitors that the attack would take place.

There was growing disquiet about the inability to contact LVI Panzer Corps. Late on 21 April, confused reports reached both Berlin and Busse's headquarters that Weidling was retreating towards the west and had already moved his headquarters to Döberitz. There was no truth in these reports, but Hitler's response was immediate: Weidling was withdrawing without permission in direct contravention of the Führer's instructions and was to be arrested and shot immediately. To his discredit, Busse issued the same order. The reality was that Weidling's corps was fighting its own private war against the Red Army with little or no contact with any other forces. But the isolation and confusion that had led to the order for Weidling's arrest and execution also made it impossible for this order to be carried out – the breakdown in communications worked in both directions.

The confusion about Weidling's location and intentions arose for multiple reasons. Firstly, contact with many units, including with Weidling's headquarters, had been badly disrupted. Secondly, some rear area elements of LVI Panzer Corps had actually been ordered to Döberitz by the corps chief of staff, and when higher commands learned of this, they misinterpreted it as evidence that the entire corps was heading west. Thirdly, additional confusion was caused by the activity of the *Seydlitz-Truppen*. Although some such troops were used in combat, their main use seems to have been to disrupt German command and communications, and several Wehrmacht units reported episodes involving the appearance of individuals or small groups of officers who issued verbal orders and then disappeared. One such group directed much of 20th Panzergrenadier Division to move to Döberitz, resulting in the division breaking up into disconnected battlegroups.[18]

Berlin was now under increasing artillery fire from the east. Despite the almost complete collapse of Hitler's Thousand-Year Reich, some continued to have faith in the Führer. The anonymous female diarist living in Berlin spent much of the morning sheltering in a cellar:

> After the earlier wave of shells 'Siegismund' turned up, an elderly gentleman from the neighbourhood. His nickname comes from *Sieg* ['victory']; he keeps talking about the victory at hand, the certain victory, *Sieg* this and *Sieg* that, which is presumably why he was kicked out of his own basement. Siegismund genuinely believes that salvation is at hand, and 'that man' (as we now call A.H.) knows exactly what he's doing. Whenever he talks the people sitting nearby exchange silent, meaningful glances. No one challenges Siegismund. Who wants to argue with a madman? Besides, madmen can be dangerous.[19]

She was wise to keep silent. Throughout all parts of Germany where the Party still maintained control, civilians who spoke openly that they no longer believed in victory were often arrested and hanged in public.

22 April

The following day, Rokossovsky's armies continued their drive into northern Germany, but despite Manteuffel's misgivings about the ability of his troops to keep fighting, Batov's Sixty-Fifth Army found that German resistance was increasing. Several villages in the path of the Soviet forces had been heavily fortified and clearing these proved to be a costly and time-consuming task. The most important achievement of the day in 2nd Belarusian Front's sector was the establishment of more bridges, allowing relatively free movement of reinforcements and supplies across the Oder. The Luftwaffe was in no position to intervene and units from Rokossovsky's other two armies were able to use these crossings without any German interference. Despite only modest advances, Rokossovsky was satisfied with the day's efforts; his units were in position to pick up the pace in coming days. On the other side of the front line, Manteuffel could only await further assaults. What little capacity his Third Panzer Army possessed for counterattacks had been directed to the south to try to restore the situation closer to Berlin. His units were fighting hard, but once they were overcome, the front line would collapse rapidly.

The city of Stettin on the northern flank of Rokossovsky's Front, with its garrison, increasingly acted as a drag on the Soviet advance. A few German warships in the port opened fire on the river crossings on which the advance was dependent until Soviet bombers attacked the town. There were further counterattacks, mainly by the Flemish soldiers of *SS-Langemarck*, backed by 281st Infantry Division in Stettin. Other German units also counterattacked; Batov later claimed that his army was faced by over 30,000 German elite troops, but this is an exaggeration in terms of both quantity and quality. Other Soviet commanders like Major General Konstantin Fedorovich Skorobogatkin, commander of 193rd Rifle Division, had a rather more sanguine opinion of the Germans being thrown at them:

> I particularly recall one counterattack, in which the enemy deployed several thousand men: poorly trained, mainly very young or older men, victims of the Fascists' total war mentality, who were in the main fighting their first battle. Counterthrusts with such forces could of course bring no success for the German leadership, merely heavy and pointless casualties.[20]

As the day progressed, more elements of Colonel General Ivan Ivanovich Fedyuninsky's Second Shock Army crossed into Batov's bridgehead and took up positions facing Stettin, eliminating any danger to the bridgehead from the north. Other German attacks from the south slowly petered out, leaving the swampy meadows strewn with dead.

The gap between Third Panzer Army and Ninth Army in the south was growing wider. What remained of CI Corps, cut off from the rest of Busse's army and now subordinated to Third Panzer Army, had been forced away towards the northwest, and its last units were driven out of Bernau, a little to the northeast of Berlin, during 22 April. From here, there was little to stop the Soviet forces either rolling up Third Panzer Army from the south while Rokossovsky's armies pinned the Germans in their defensive positions, or advancing freely to the west and enveloping Berlin. Neither Busse nor Heinrici had any idea of the location of the headquarters of Weidling's LVI Panzer Corps or any of its armoured formations; in particular, they had expected *SS-Nordland* to be defending this area, but the division had effectively disappeared. To date, only two battalions of 3rd Marine Division had completed their deployment south from Stettin, and together with a mixture of *Volkssturm*, fragments of retreating units, and the formations of *Armeegruppe Steiner*, they took up defensive positions along the line of the Havel River to the northwest of Berlin. Throughout 22 April, the Soviet units on the eastern side of the river grew in strength, and the first major attack came during the afternoon. A small German bridgehead across the Havel in Oranienburg was abandoned, but the line along the river either side of the town remained intact.

However, a little further south, Soviet reconnaissance units discovered that the Havel was barely defended and demonstrated once again their prowess at improvising river crossings. Using a mixture of small boats and timber they had swiftly felled in the forested area around Hennigsdorf, they rapidly established a bridgehead across the river. On the northern side of Oranienburg, too, the Red Army made some progress. Here, Second Polish Army attacked the remnants of 5th Jäger Division and 25th Panzergrenadier Division, slowly pushing them back.

Unaware that he had been sentenced to death, Weidling continued to try to coordinate his divisions in the fighting immediately to the east of Berlin. On the morning of 22 April, he discussed the situation with his division commanders. There was still no contact with higher commands, and it was therefore impossible to know the overall situation. In these circumstances, what was the best course of action? There was near unanimity: using what remained of its diminishing strength, LVI Panzer Corps should concentrate its forces to make an attack towards the south, where it was believed that the rest of Ninth Army was still fighting. Once contact had been restored with Busse's headquarters, it would be possible to make further plans.

There was only one dissenting voice. Brigadeführer Joachim Ziegler, commander of *SS-Nordland*, argued that if an attack was to be made, it should be to the northwest, towards *Armeegruppe Steiner*. The reasons for his preference are not clear, and there are several possibilities; indeed, it is likely that most or all of these played a part in his thinking. Firstly, his division had originally been part of Steiner's III SS-Panzer Corps, and it was perhaps understandable that he wished to return to Steiner's command. This was reinforced by the longstanding friction between commanders in the Waffen-SS and their regular army contemporaries. Secondly, *SS-Nordland* was made up largely of men from the Scandinavian countries, and with the end of the war clearly just a matter of days or weeks away, Ziegler may have wanted to try to get his men to the north of Berlin, from where there was at least the possibility that they would be able to fall back to a region closer to their homes. In any case, Weidling refused. If possible, the corps would fight its way south towards Ninth Army.

There is a different account of Ziegler's wishes at this time. Untersturmführer Hans Henseler, a junior officer in the division's combat engineer battalion, later described how he was one of several officers summoned by Ziegler to a meeting. The division commander then told his subordinates that *SS-Nordland* was to concentrate its forces before heading west around the outskirts of Berlin; Ziegler intended to surrender to the Western Allies or at least to reach *Armeegruppe Steiner*. In order to carry out this unauthorised withdrawal, it was essential to secure crossings over the Havel and the combat engineers were tasked with moving west immediately either to ensure that the bridges were safe, or to gather boats for a crossing.[21] The plan was rapidly overtaken by events, but Ziegler wasn't the only senior officer to make his own arrangements in the face of the imminent collapse of Germany. The newly promoted Generalmajor Georg Scholze, commander of 20th Panzergrenadier Division, became aware that some parts of his division had already moved west, in some cases due to the interference of *Seydlitz-Truppen*. He now ordered the rest of his division to try to follow, without any authorisation from higher commands. Like Ziegler, he found that his orders were impossible to carry out in the confusion of battle.

Far from withdrawing towards *Armeegruppe Steiner*, *SS-Nordland* was now attempting to hold back the combined weight of Eighth Guards Army and First Guards Tank Army in and around Mahlsdorf, just to the east of Berlin. As the day progressed, the division finally began to disintegrate. Its units were bloodily levered out of their positions, and it became impossible for Ziegler to communicate with all of his subordinate officers. Many elements of the division began to fall back into Berlin itself, and by the end of the day most of its remaining strength was gathered in Karlshorst. They had not received anything approaching adequate supplies for several days, and were close to the end of their strength.

Not far away, the *Berlin* infantry division also retreated into the city. Made up in haste around the remnants of 309th Infantry Division with rear area units and *Volkssturm*, it had fought as hard as any regular formation during the bitter battles on the Seelow Heights, but it had no more fighting capability left – most of the division's modest complement of heavy weapons had been lost, and there was little or no ammunition for what remained. Voigtsberger, the division commander, gathered what remained of the division around him late on 21 April. He told them that further fighting was senseless, and that their priority should be to get home safely. Many took his advice and attempted to slip away into Berlin to seek out their families; they would have to evade the constant patrols of military police and self-appointed SS vigilantes who summarily executed any soldiers found behind the front line without written orders. Others remained in the ranks, including Voigtsberger, who attached himself to Weidling's headquarters.[22]

Still believing that *Armeegruppe Steiner* represented a substantial force and that Ninth Army was a functioning, coordinated formation, Hitler issued orders through Krebs for the two forces to attack towards each other with the intention of destroying the Soviet armour that had reached the northern fringe of the city. Even if they had been aware of these German intentions, Zhukov's troops were increasingly confident that the strength of the enemy had been broken. Released from Front reserves, Lieutenant General Mikhail Petrovich Konstantinov's VII Guards Cavalry Corps crossed the Havel via the bridgehead seized the previous day at Hennigsdorf and began scouting around the northwest edge of the urban area. Belatedly, the Germans dispatched a battlegroup to the Havel to try to plug this gap, but it disappeared in the general confusion.

Zhukov's two shock armies were now preparing for the storming of Berlin. The heavy losses they had suffered and their long supply lines forced a slower tempo, and even though they continued to outnumber the forces deployed against them, urban fighting conditions greatly favoured the defenders. The leading division of Third Shock Army's LXXIX Rifle Corps battled into Pankow in northeast Berlin and its battle for the suburb highlights both the depleted state of the Soviet units and the modest opposition that they encountered:

> By this time, there were just 35–40 men in the battalion's companies, of which 25–30 men were riflemen, while the companies themselves comprised two platoons ...
>
> The battalion commander decided to attack along a broad front in small groups, infiltrating into the depth of the enemy defence through gardens, cleared areas, and vegetable patches, bypassing buildings that were defended by the enemy wherever possible ...
>
> The battalion's artillery and mortars commenced a powerful bombardment of the suburb's buildings at 0850 against identified firing points. Deployed in a single line, the battalion attacked at 0900, breaking into the first buildings in groups of three to four men. There were few Germans in these buildings because they had retreated during the artillery bombardment and occupied buildings in the centre of the suburb, a small distance from the outskirts.
>
> After seizing the first buildings, groups of riflemen began to advance through the gardens to the next buildings accompanied by 45mm guns, constantly trying to spot the enemy and firing on some buildings on the orders of the rifle companies' officers. Following a few shots from the guns and taking advantage of the enemy's disarray, the soldiers broke into the buildings and overcame the Germans positioned there and continued the attack without pause ...

By 1000 the battalion had reached the Panke River and taken 20 prisoners, and the battalion commander concentrated his men here. He had lost 15 men in the fighting, mainly stragglers. The regimental commander reinforced the battalion with a battery of 76mm guns and six more 45mm guns, ordering it to continue its advance.

After crossing the Panke, the battalion first attacked along its bank, clearing the Germans from the buildings along Schlossallee north of the river, and then turned south. After recrossing the Panke, the soldiers attacked westward bypassing the residential area of Pankow from the north, through the Schlosspark. This was defended by *Volkssturm* in foxholes and trenches … At 1100, after seizing the park, the battalion approached the junction of Kaiserin-Augustastrasse and Grabbeallee. After a brief reconnaissance, the battalion commander decided to seize some buildings near the junction that had been turned into a strongpoint by the Germans and blocked the road to Schönholtz. He intended to outflank it with two companies to the north and south …

At 1200 the battalion commander called in a ten-minute artillery bombardment against the buildings and under its cover both companies began their outflanking manoeuvres. Linking up 200m west of the strongpoint, the companies turned back to the east … After a 30-minute battle the Germans' strongpoint was overcome by this blow from its rear, with the loss of 80 Germans killed and 30 captured. The battalion continued its attack towards the west, taking Schönholtz by 1400. It lost 14 men killed and wounded in the fighting.[23]

Whilst these may seem modest losses, the battalion had commenced the day with barely 100 combatants. Many Soviet rifle formations had started the operation far from their establishment strength and the heavy fighting to the east of Berlin had reduced their ranks still further.

By the end of 22 April, Chuikov's Eighth Guards Army had seized much of southeast Berlin:

Advancing through the eastern suburbs of Berlin, the army's soldiers captured Dahlwitz, Schöneiche, Fichtenau, Rahnsdorf, Friedrichshagen, and Wendenschloss. There was particularly strong resistance to IV Guards Rifle Corps in Kaulsdorf and Karlshorst. Indeed, the offensive in this direction came to a halt …

The tank crews of First Guards Tank Army faced a difficult task. Moving through deserted squares and streets in urban battles, where the enemy defends from buildings, lofts and basements, tankers can't see the enemy and can't penetrate into these places. At the same time, tanks are good targets for soldiers armed with Molotov cocktails and *Panzerfaust* launchers. This doesn't mean that

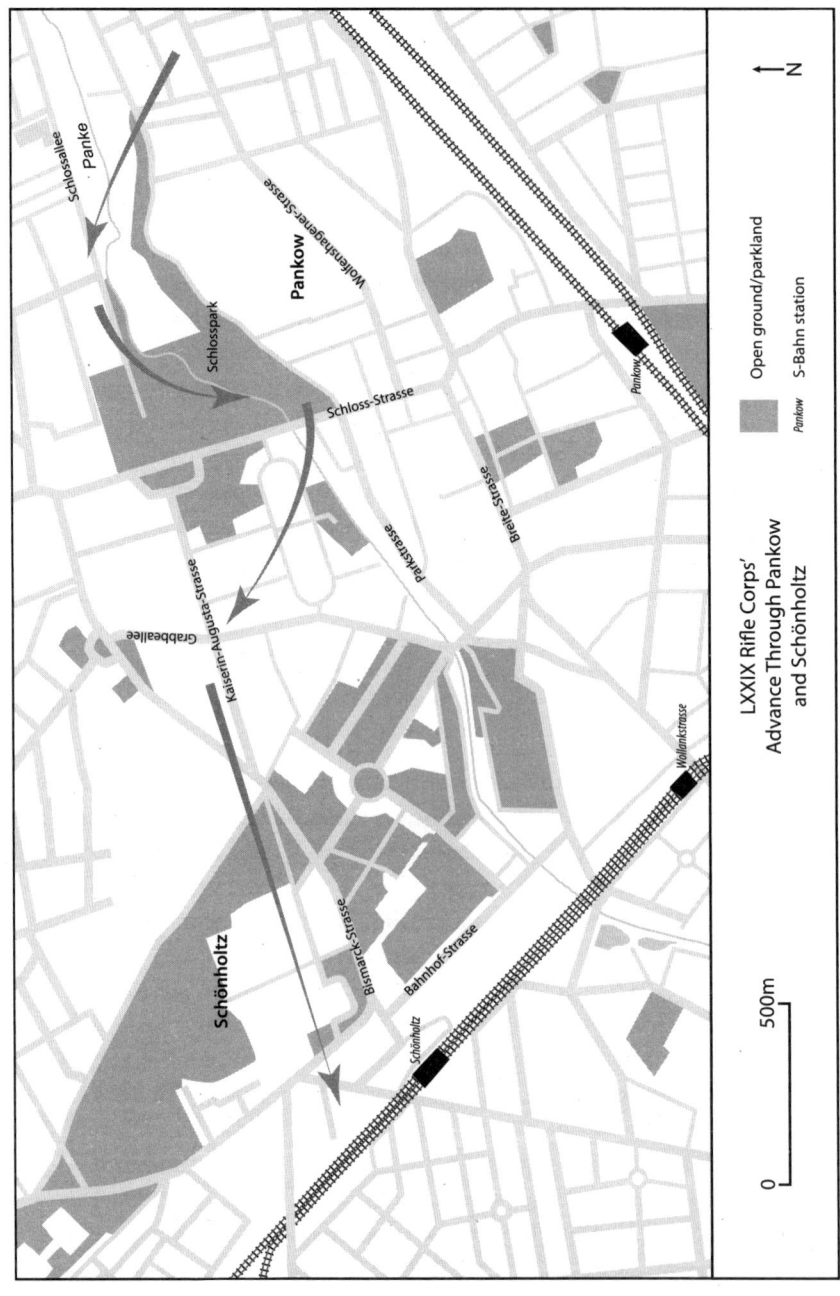

LXXIX Rifle Corps' Advance Through Pankow and Schönholtz

tanks and tankers aren't needed and aren't suitable for urban fighting – far from it. They are essential, but not as an independent force, rather for joint actions with units of other branches of the military in special assault groups.

Only in cooperation with rifle units, artillerymen, sappers, and other specialists, will tank crews be aware of where danger lies. The assault group infantry will inform them. They will indicate in which building, on which floor, loft or basement the enemy is holed up, and who must be destroyed through joint efforts. In this close interaction, tanks most often are used as tracked artillery, and the tankers as artillerymen protected by armour.

Without pausing the offensive through the suburbs of Berlin, we reorganised our battle formations on the fly into assault groups and detachments.[24]

The heavy resistance in Karlshorst and Kaulsdorf was from the various units of *SS-Nordland*. The division's rear area units had been sent back into Berlin, where Sturmbannführer Rudolf Ternedde hastily organised their personnel into ad hoc infantry companies. A battalion of the division's 24th *SS-Panzergrenadier-Regiment Danmark* was cut off to the northeast, with some of its personnel succeeding in fighting their way west where they were able to link up with Steiner's troops. The rest of the division fought against the growing strength of the Soviet troops attempting to break into Karlshorst and succeeded for the moment in holding its positions, but at a heavy cost.

Far to the south, the Soviet units on the northern flank of Konev's breakthrough finally overcame the stubborn German defenders of Cottbus. Over half the city, already damaged by US bombers, had been reduced to ruins and of its pre-war civilian population of 55,000, only about 3,000 remained. Most of the defending force – made up of soldiers of 275th and 342nd Infantry Divisions, supported by a few SS tank crews and several battalions of *Volkssturm* – perished in the battle, with the Red Army taking fewer than 2,000 prisoners. Generalleutnant Ralf Sodan, who had commanded an infantry division earlier in the war and had been in command of the defence of Cottbus, took his own life rather than surrender.

On the other flank of 1st Ukrainian Front's penetration, the breakout by the encircled German troops began at first light. A junior staff officer in *Führer-Begleit* later described the moment:

> I stood at the edge of a small wood and peered across to Neu-Petershain, where the Russians were just bringing two anti-tank guns into position … 500m separated us from the town, whose farmsteads stood out ever more sharply against the brightening sky. General Remer ordered an 88mm flak gun to go into position and open fire on the anti-tank gun position.

No one knew exactly what was supposed to happen now. There was no communication with higher command. There was a great deal of confusion. The gun had just reached the edge of the forest when there were several flashes in quick succession over at the edge of the town. Instinctively I took cover. The first shot was too short, the second struck the tractor, which immediately burst into flames, and the third knocked out the gun itself. The driver of the tractor, who was killed immediately, was tossed into the ditch by the blast of the exploding shell, while a member of the gun crew lay writhing in pain on the asphalt with a shattered leg and frightful burns. Everyone else suffered more or less serious wounds.

I wanted to cross the 70m to recover the seriously wounded; but I didn't get far, for suddenly there were bullets whizzing around me. The Russians were spraying the edge of the forest and the burning tractor with machine-gun fire. The seriously wounded man was suddenly still. He must have been fatally hit. At the same time, hellish mortar fire began falling on the entire wood. I dashed back into the forest, where our armoured troop carriers and tanks were sitting ...

We couldn't retreat, for the village at our back, where we had forced a breakthrough yesterday [Kausche] ... had been re-occupied by the Russians during the night. And we lacked the necessary ammunition, but especially the fuel, to make a frontal attack against Neu-Petershain, which was likewise heavily defended by anti-tank weapons. We therefore had only one possibility of getting out of this witch's cauldron. We would have to try to break out over the large meadow to the south.[25]

This became known to the survivors of the division as the *Todeswiese* ('meadow of death'). The entire open space was clearly visible to Soviet troops in Kausche and Neupetershain, and as the remaining vehicles of *Führer-Begleit* began to drive across the meadow, accompanied by hundreds of men on foot, firing grew ever more intense. Some of the division's half-tracks were carrying groups of civilian refugees, and casualties were heavy. When they reached the line of trees at the southern edge of the meadow, the Germans were dismayed to find that another open area lay before them, once more swept by Soviet fire. Few of the armoured vehicles survived the first meadow, and almost all were destroyed before they could reach the southern edge of the second meadow. Only about 400 men of the division, including Remer, succeeded in this breakout, but small groups of survivors continued to trickle back over the following days.

Harmel, the commander of *SS-Frundsberg*, fought a determined rearguard action before infiltrating through the encirclement to safety. Schörner, the commander of Army Group Centre, had ordered Harmel to hold his positions and not to retreat; instead, he was to mount an energetic counterattack into the southern flank of Konev's breakthrough. When he learned that the SS officer had ignored his instructions, Schörner ordered his dismissal. Harmel ended the war commanding an improvised SS battlegroup in Austria, where he surrendered to the British.[26] Remer fought in the defence of Dresden before escaping in civilian clothing towards the west, where he surrendered to American troops.[27]

The two tank armies of 1st Ukrainian Front continued to lead the advance. Lelyushenko's units overran several towns to the southwest of Berlin while one of his tank corps turned towards the city itself. A little further north, Rybalko's Third Guards Tank Army advanced through Stahnsdorf and reached the Teltow Canal; here, the Soviet troops found that the defenders had organised a series of strongpoints manned by the usual variety of *Volkssturm* and improvised battlegroups. Although they were relatively weak, the tankers were unwilling to risk a battle at close quarters against men armed with the deadly *Panzerfausts* and Rybalko ordered his men to regroup in preparation for a major assault the following day.

As the day drew to a close, the Soviet units around Berlin were in position to complete two encirclements. To the east of the German capital, Rybalko's right flank was only seven miles from Chuikov's leading elements; a link-up here would leave Busse's Ninth Army surrounded to the southeast of Berlin, in and around Halbe. To the west of Berlin, the leading units of the two Soviet Fronts were separated by about 24 miles. Fresh orders arrived for both Fronts that evening. The original demarcation line between Zhukov and Konev was further modified, now running from Lübben to Mariendorf in southern Berlin and then on to the Anhalter railway station just to the south of the Brandenburg Gate. For Konev, this was recognition of the speed with which his armies had swept towards the German capital; Zhukov, who had hoped to be the conqueror of the capital of the Reich, made little mention of this further snub in his memoirs, but his orders to Chuikov's Eighth Guards Army – to push on as fast as possible to reach Steglitz, immediately to the southwest of central Berlin – were a further deliberate attempt to forestall the advance of his rival and to prevent Konev's armies from being the first to get to the city centre.

During the afternoon of 22 April, senior figures gathered in Hitler's bunker for the daily conference. Hitler listened to the reports of Soviet advances in silence, looking increasingly grim as the briefing concluded with the forecast that Berlin would be completely surrounded within 48 hours. The scene has been immortalised in the film *Der Untergang* ('Downfall'), made in 2004, and the actor Bruno Ganz achieved lasting fame when his portrayal of Hitler during this conference became the basis of countless memes on social media. After listening to the briefing from Krebs, Hitler indicated the symbols on his map that marked the position of *Armeegruppe Steiner* and dismissed concerns about the northern pincer of the imminent encirclement, telling those present that Steiner would soon deal with this threat. Throughout the morning, Hitler had repeatedly asked for information about the progress of the attack by Steiner that he had ordered in unequivocal terms, but had received no clear answer. Now, Krebs and the others could no longer avoid the subject. Hesitantly, Krebs informed Hitler that Steiner's units had not moved, and no attack was coming.

Until now, Hitler had remained relatively calm, but he now lost his temper in a furious outburst. Loringhoven, who was present, described the scene:

> Hitler suddenly jumped up from his chair and furiously threw the coloured pencils he always carried with him during situation discussions across the table. Then he began to scream. His voice, which had been weak and flat for weeks, once again regained some of its former strength. Struggling for words, he denounced the world and the cowardice, baseness, and disloyalty around him. He reviled the generals, condemned their constant resistance against which he had had to fight; for years he had been surrounded by traitors and failures. While all stared straight ahead in embarrassment, Hitler, gesticulating, cleared a space for himself and stumbled unsteadily up and down the narrow room. Several times he tried to regain his composure, only to erupt again immediately. Utterly beside himself, he pounded his fist into his palm while tears ran down his face. Under these circumstances, he repeated again and again, he could no longer lead; any orders he gave were a waste of his breath; he didn't know how to go on.[28]

As his rage subsided, Hitler stared at the map on the table and muttered: '*Der Krieg ist verloren*' ('The war is lost'). It was a statement greeted in stunned silence. None of those present can have been in any doubt that the war had indeed been lost a considerable time earlier, but to hear it from Hitler seemed a shocking revelation. Hitler went on to tell them that he intended to remain in Berlin, and would take his own life at the very end. Despite having made similar statements themselves in private conversations in the past few days and weeks about the futility of continuing the war, his entourage urged him not to lose hope. Hitler shrugged in response, telling them, 'Do whatever you want. I'm not giving any more orders.'[29] He told Jodl and Keitel that they should leave and dictated a public announcement that would tell Berliners of his intention to remain in the city to the bitter end.

Whilst imprisoned and awaiting trial after the war, Keitel wrote an account of this conference that barely makes any mention of Hitler's fury at Steiner. Instead, he concentrated on the Führer's decision to stay in Berlin:

I had the conference chamber cleared, and found myself alone with Hitler, as Jodl had just been summoned to the telephone. As so often in my life, Hitler cut me short after my very first few words and broke in to say: 'I know already what you're going to tell me: "The decision has got to be taken now!" I have already taken a decision: I will never leave Berlin again; I will defend the city with my dying breath. Either I direct the battle for the Reich capital – if Wenck can keep the Americans off my back and throw them back over the Elbe – or I will go down with my troops in Berlin, fighting for the symbol of the Reich!'

I told him bluntly that that was madness, and that in the present situation I was obliged to demand that he fly that very night to Berchtesgaden to ensure the continuity of command over the Reich and the Wehrmacht, something that could not be guaranteed in Berlin where communications might be severed at any moment.

The Führer explained: 'There is nothing to stop you flying to Berchtesgaden at once. In fact I order you to do so. But I myself am going to stay in Berlin. I have already announced that to the German people and the Reich capital on the radio an hour ago. I am not in the position to retract.'

At that moment, Jodl came in. In his presence, I explained that I had no intention whatsoever of flying to Berchtesgaden without him, Hitler; that was quite out of the question. It was not just a matter of the defence or loss of Berlin, but the command of all the armed forces on every front, which could not be guaranteed from the Reich Chancellery if the situation in the capital worsened any more. Jodl fervently agreed, and explained that if their signals communications with the south were to break down altogether – and the big cable had already been cut in the Thuringian Forest – then there would be no further possibility of directing the operations of the Army Groups of Schörner [Centre], Rendulic [South], the Balkans, Italy, or West; radio communication alone would not suffice ...

The Führer called in Bormann, and he repeated to the three of us the order to fly to Berchtesgaden that night, where I was to take command, with Göring as his personal representative. All three of us announced that we refused to do so. I said: 'In seven years I have never refused to execute an order from you, but this is one order I shall never carry out. You cannot and should not leave the Wehrmacht in the lurch, still less at a time like this.' He replied: 'I am stopping here, and that is that. I have deliberately announced this without your knowledge so as to commit myself. If there has got to be any negotiating with the enemy – as there has now – then Göring is better at that than I am. Either I fight and win the battle of Berlin – or I am killed in Berlin. That is my final and irrevocable decision.'[30]

Later, Bormann asked Goebbels to persuade Hitler to escape to Bavaria while it was still possible. But when he spoke to Hitler in private, Goebbels informed the Führer that he too would stay in Berlin to the very end and would also end his life rather than attempt to escape. He summoned his wife and six children to the bunker, making clear that they would never leave.

Many of those who had been in the conference room during the afternoon met again during the early evening, and there was a small glimmer of light for those who were still desperate for Hitler to continue leading the war. A little earlier, he had spoken to Jodl in private. The intention of the Allied Powers to partition Germany was well known to the inner circle, but many had doubted that the British and American armies advancing from the west would stop at the Elbe. Indeed, some privately hoped that they would press on to Berlin, thus giving more Germans a chance to surrender to them rather than to the vengeful Soviet forces. But with the US armies clearly coming to a stop along the Elbe, Jodl suggested to Hitler that this might provide Germany with one last opportunity for victory. General Walther Wenck had been a rising star in the Wehrmacht since the dark days of Stalingrad, where his imaginative flair had played a major role in restoring order to the shattered German front line. More recently, he had served as Guderian's deputy when Guderian was chief of the general staff at *OKH*; Guderian had expected that Wenck would eventually replace him and in early 1945 had battled hard to have Wenck appointed to oversee the counteroffensive that Army Group Vistula – at that time under the control of Himmler – was about to launch to the east of the Oder. While driving between Berlin and the front line, Wenck had been involved in a serious car crash and had been hospitalised, but on 10 April he was given a new post. The German forces being organised along the Elbe were renamed Twelfth Army, and Wenck was placed in command.

Like all German forces that were being created in haste in the dying weeks of the war, Twelfth Army existed more on paper than in reality, but Wenck was able to mount an energetic defence in Magdeburg. Now, with the US forces making little serious attempt to advance any further – there was some limited fighting around Magdeburg, during which a small bridgehead was established on the east bank – Jodl suggested that Twelfth Army should be ordered to attack towards the east, against the Soviet forces closing in on the capital from the southeast. At the same time, Steiner was to be urged once more to attack from the north, and Busse's Ninth Army would break out of its imminent encirclement to link up with Wenck's men advancing from the west. Like a drowning man, Hitler feverishly grabbed at this new slender hope.

That night, Keitel travelled to Twelfth Army's headquarters, located in woodland a little to the east of the city of Magdeburg. When he met Wenck, he bluntly stated, 'We must rescue the Führer!' Whilst being held in Nuremberg after the war, Keitel recalled:

> In a *tête-à-tête* with General Wenck I outlined the situation that had developed the previous afternoon in the Reich Chancellery, and made it clear to him that my last hope of fetching the Führer out of Berlin rested solely on the success of his [Wenck's] breaking through to the capital and linking up with Ninth Army. I was thinking in terms of nothing less than abducting the Führer – if necessary by force – from the Reich Chancellery if we were to be unable to bring him to his senses, something which I hardly dared to hope after his calamitous performance during the previous afternoon. Everything depended, I told him, on the success of our operation, whatever the cost.
>
> Wenck called in his chief of staff; with a map, I sketched in the situation around Berlin as best I knew it from the previous day; then I left the men alone and set about my supper in the hall of the forester's house while Wenck dictated the new order to his army I had asked him for, to take back to the Führer. About an hour later, I drove off again with the army order in my pocket, having offered to hand Wenck's order to General [Karl-Erik] Köhler [commander of XX Corps] on the way back, and to brief him personally and visit his division commanders during the night as well. I wanted to bring my own personal influence to bear on all these troop commanders and bring home to them both the rough significance of the task lying ahead of them and the assurance that if things went wrong, it would augur ill for Germany. Wenck was – and stayed – the only one to learn my innermost thoughts and of my intention to abduct the Führer from Berlin before the capital's fate was sealed.[31]

Even after allowing for the widely held view that Keitel was overpromoted and out of his depth, it is difficult to see what he hoped to achieve. A link-up by Ninth and Twelfth Armies would be a difficult undertaking, and to expect them to have sufficient strength left to reach the bunker under the Reich Chancellery was absurd. If such a miracle was achieved and Hitler was persuaded to leave Berlin, or was forcibly abducted – what did Keitel imagine would happen next? The Ruhr and Upper Silesia were in enemy hands, depriving the Reich of any meaningful industrial capacity, and with much of Germany occupied by the Allied Powers, it would be almost impossible to raise more troops. It seems that like many around Hitler, Keitel – and Jodl, who had first suggested that Wenck should simply turn his back on the US armies opposing him and march to the relief of Berlin – could not contemplate a future without Hitler.

Hitler continued to believe that his generals had betrayed him, despite reassurances from Jodl and Keitel that Twelfth Army was marching to his aid.

Not trusting the military chain of command to carry out his instructions, he insisted on an uncoded radio broadcast:

> The Führer has issued orders from Berlin that units fighting the Americans are to be transferred east rapidly to defend Berlin. Sixteen divisions are already on the move and can be expected to arrive in Berlin any hour.[32]

The intention was twofold. Firstly, it would make clear to the world that if Wenck failed to march to Berlin, he was directly disobeying the Führer. Secondly, it gave an impression that US forces were no longer attacking German units, adding to the Nazi Party view that ultimately, the alliance fielded against Germany would fall apart and the Western Powers would align themselves alongside Germany against the Bolshevik threat from the east.

Wenck's later recollection of his discussion with Keitel gives a slightly different picture. He wrote that he expressed doubts about the success of the proposed operation and in any case would need two days to concentrate his men. Rather than conduct an operation to the south of Berlin, he wanted to aim for a point to the west of the city, close to where the Soviet encirclement pincers would meet, as this offered a better chance of reaching the outskirts of Berlin and linking up with elements of the city's defenders who might attempt to break out to the west. In particular, he wished to avoid getting his troops sucked into the urban area. His proposal was rejected. After Keitel had left with Wenck's assurances that an attack would be made as soon as possible, Wenck summoned the rest of his staff and addressed them:

> We will advance as close as possible to Berlin, but without abandoning our positions on the Elbe and with one flank on the river we will keep open an escape route to the west. It would be nonsensical simply to thrust towards Berlin and then to be encircled by the Russians. We will try to unite with Ninth Army and then give as many soldiers and civilians as possible the chance to escape to the west.[33]

The forces available to Wenck were modest. In theory, he had command of several corps, each with several divisions, but in reality these divisions largely existed only on paper. Few numbered more than a single regiment in strength, and none had the normal complement of artillery and other heavy weapons. Nevertheless, even if Jodl and Keitel still clutched at fantasies of continued resistance, Wenck was now explicitly working towards the least bad ultimate outcome. He saw his task simply as saving as many Germans as possible from the wrath of the Red Army. But whilst his combat assets might have been limited, Wenck enjoyed a substantial advantage over other German commanders. Purely by chance, the zone controlled by his Twelfth Army had accumulated large quantities of supplies as rail, road, and barge transports stopped there, unable to complete their journeys to their intended destinations. With no orders from above on how he should distribute these supplies, Wenck ordered his staff to make the most of their good fortune and to ensure that the units that would be involved in this new operation would at least have sufficient fuel, ammunition, and food.[34]

News of Hitler's outburst at the afternoon conference rapidly spread through the senior figures of the regime. Himmler had already left Berlin and was in Hohenlychen, to the north of the German capital. He had anticipated an end to Hitler's rule and had made preparations to advance his own cause in such circumstances. During the evening of 22 April, Fegelein telephoned him from the Chancellery bunker and gave him a brief but inaccurate outline of what had happened. Crucially, by emphasising that the Führer had declared that he would give no further orders, he left Himmler with the impression that Hitler had resigned. He immediately took steps to make contact with the Western Allies; he intended to try to persuade them that he and his SS would be invaluable for their occupation plans, and would ask for weapons and supplies so that the SS divisions could continue the fight against the Red Army. 'Everyone in Berlin has lost their minds,' he told his staff disparagingly, with no insight whatever that his personal viewpoint was also not based on any sense of reality.[35]

At about midnight, Heinrici spoke to Wenck by telephone, having been informed of the new plans. The two men agreed that the priority was to save Ninth Army, and Heinrici then spoke to Busse. To a large extent, he exaggerated the forces that were preparing to march to Ninth Army's rescue, probably in an attempt to raise Busse's morale, and the commander of Ninth Army was ordered to make preparations for an attack towards the relief column. These instructions specified the troops that could be freed by withdrawing from the most eastern positions held by Ninth Army, but took little account that the units concerned were reduced to mere fragments. Busse would later claim that these orders permitted him a degree of freedom, allowing him to move forces west for a breakout, but in reality he was merely following instructions from above. He remained almost inflexible in his sense of duty and his intention to obey all orders, regardless of the consequences for his men.

A strange situation therefore existed by the end of 22 April. In Berlin, Krebs, Keitel, and Jodl were drawing up orders on the assumption that the combined forces of Steiner, Busse, and Wenck were going to make one last attempt to save

Berlin from the Red Army. At the same time, Wenck, Busse, and Heinrici were preparing to avoid any entanglement in the city and were focussed purely on getting as many troops out to the west as possible, and Steiner continued to avoid committing his troops to any attack. But the public announcement by Hitler that Wenck was marching to Berlin resulted in some Berliners beginning to feel hopeful for the first time in weeks. Wenck was coming to their aid. If the Red Army could be held at arm's length just a short while longer, the worst might be avoided.

CHAPTER 9

INTO THE CITY: 23–25 APRIL

23 APRIL

To the north of Berlin, Rokossovsky's armies continued their slow advance across northern Germany, and Fedyuninsky's Second Shock Army began preparations for a formal attack on Stettin. The city was already badly damaged by air raids carried out by the Western Powers – British raids in August 1944 had inflicted particularly heavy damage, destroying over 90 per cent of the Old Town and most of the port facilities.[1] The garrison of the 'fortress' had already been partly depleted to reinforce other sectors and there was little or no prospect of prolonged defence; rather than permit the remaining troops to be encircled, Manteuffel gave orders that they were to abandon the city at the last possible moment and escape towards the west.

On the southern flank of Third Panzer Army, *Armeegruppe Steiner* received orders from *OKH* to take up positions around Oranienburg, from where it was to launch an attack towards Berlin. These instructions were issued without any attempt to inform Manteuffel, and were already out of date; Soviet troops were fighting in Oranienburg against 1st Marine Division, making such a redeployment impossible. In response to Steiner's continuing objections on the grounds that his forces were too weak to mount a major attack, *OKH* ordered Manteuffel to release 25th Panzergrenadier Division and 7th Panzer Division and send them south. Manteuffel raised the matter with Heinrici, pointing out that even if he retained these divisions, he desperately needed to shorten his line to prevent it collapsing. In any event, the forces demanded by *OKH* would make little difference to the strength of *Armeegruppe Steiner*. After being involved in heavy fighting against Rokossovsky's armies, 25th Panzergrenadier Division was reduced to little more than a battlegroup and like almost all German mechanised units at this stage of the war it lacked the fuel for a major redeployment. The state of 7th Panzer Division was even worse. It was a panzer division in name only, consisting of little more than the equivalent of a weak tank battalion with little fuel, and an infantry regiment with only light weaponry.

In eastern Berlin, Chuikov's Eighth Guards Army had reached the Spree late on 22 April and plans were made for an assault crossing at dawn on 23 April, to be preceded by a heavy artillery bombardment of the west bank. But the leading units took it upon themselves to press forward during the night:

> Units of XXVIII and XXIX Guards Rifle Corps reached the Spree. Here, the soldiers found many rowing boats and motorboats as well as several large barges. Without waiting for orders or instructions, the unit commanders ordered their men aboard these boats and crossed first the Spree, then the Dahme under cover of darkness. Units of 88th Guards Rifle Division commanded by Major General [Boris Nikiforovich] Pankov crossed first ...
>
> We owed this success to the initiative of Captain Afanasy Ivanovich Semakin, the commander of 2nd Battalion, 269th Regiment, of 88th Guards Rifle Division. A long-serving officer and participant in many battles, he showed the best qualities of a commander here on the outskirts of Berlin: courage, energy, and creativity in solving combat problems. The battalion advanced from the Berlin ring road through woodland. On the way, he encountered an intermediate enemy defensive line. His battalion had no guns or mortars. Semakin didn't wait for guns or other reinforcements to be brought up – the enemy could retreat or force a battle in circumstances that were most favourable to him. It was necessary to overcome him immediately, on the move, with a surprise attack ... In a short battle, the battalion captured more than 100 enemy soldiers and destroyed three half-tracks.
>
> As it later turned out, this was the only obstacle on the route to the Spree crossings. After moving forward a few hundred metres, the battalion reached the riverbank. The Soviet soldiers cleared it of a few enemy groups and, following their commander – some swimming, others using improvised means – crossed the river.[2]

By the end of the day, Eighth Guards Army was across the Spree at numerous points. It could have been a formidable defensive line, had sufficient troops been available and had appropriate preparations been made; but Heinrici and Reymann had ensured that as many *Volkssturm* as possible were moved out to the east of Berlin before the fighting began. Late on 22 April, Goebbels – belatedly realising that the army commanders were deliberately moving *Volkssturm* battalions out of the city to avoid battles in the urban areas – had insisted that he took personal command of the defence of Berlin, excluding the city from Army Group Vistula's influence.

Chuikov described how several *Volkssturm* surrendered without putting up much resistance, but at the same time emphasised the unpredictable and often savage nature of urban warfare; even at this late stage of the war, there were plenty of Germans, particularly amongst the teenage ranks of the Hitler Youth, who remained fanatically devoted to Hitler and were prepared to lay down their lives. Babadzhanian's tank crews had a difficult time:

> Danger lurked for Soviet soldiers at every turn during these street battles. Enemy soldiers, surrounded in one house, moved through underground passages, of which there were many in the old part of the city, to another house. The enemy also used the widespread sewer system for this purpose. They shot at us from behind, and from around every corner. Leaflets in Russian were scattered everywhere, trying to intimidate us: 'There are 600,000 houses in Berlin, and each house is a fortress that will be your grave.'[3]

Vladimir Myasnikov, whose flamethrower detachment had not been warned of the start of the offensive when in position on the Oder, was now with the troops pressing into the urban area:

> We were attached to 144th Rifle Division, which was part of Fifth Shock Army. When it reached the Spree, the division came across a bridge, but couldn't capture it for some time. The bridge had two decks. The first level was a pedestrian bridge, and to its right there was a road, with a second higher level with railway and metro. On the right of the bridge was a wall, about a metre high, and to the left were pillars that supported the upper deck. As they retreated, the Germans blew up the road and railway at two points, but the pedestrian walkway remained intact.
>
> The regiment tried to cross this bridge on the move, but achieved nothing. Then the command decided to send in flamethrowers at night. I should add that in Berlin the fighting continued day and night with us operating in assault groups, so my platoon was divided into two groups of 15 men, one commanded by me, the other by the platoon commander. One group operated during the day and the other at night.
>
> At 0100 [on 23 April], the company commander told me to capture the bridge and to knock out the houses on the embankment. I led my group of 15 forward onto the bridge under constant fire from the Germans. It was absolute hell. The Germans fired at us with machine-guns, rifles, mortars, and *Panzerfausts*. The only protection was from the square pillars, about half a metre wide. We took

cover behind these pillars, and it was important to stand still when the fire hit the pillars – sparks and fragments of concrete flew through the air and you stood, not rushing forward. When the Germans shifted their fire – then you could run to another pillar. Thus, we reached the middle of the bridge where there were two towers containing a mechanism for raising the bridge.

By the time we reached the middle, it was getting light. On the German side, either side of the bridge, there were two buildings from which they were firing, and as soon as it grew light the Germans intensified their fire. I decided to move the flamethrower towards the right house to set it ablaze and suppress the defensive fire. Two soldiers crawled across towards the house with the flamethrower. I was lying behind some rubble and trying to coordinate the attack. They crawled 100m towards the house into position to fire, but nothing happened. I saw the soldiers discard the flamethrower and run to the other side of the bridge, lying down by the pillars. A large piece of shrapnel had damaged the ignition mechanism and the flamethrower wouldn't light.

It was now morning and the Germans increased their fire to try to knock us out. But the regiment gave us support. On our side of the bridge was a large building where our guns were positioned, and they fired on the house to the left of the bridge. The house caught fire and without waiting we rushed over to it. I knew that with just my 15 men I couldn't drive the Germans out of the house, so we entered its basement and then, moving from one basement to the next, we reached the end of the block onto the street running parallel to the river. We crawled out of the basement about 300m from the bridge and fired on the house to our right with two flamethrowers. The house caught fire … and we made our way back to the embankment, setting fire to all the houses on our route. We fired into the basement of another house and immediately a German appeared with a white flag, saying there were about 60 Germans – soldiers and civilians – in the house and they would surrender if we spared their lives. I ordered a flamethrower into position and told the Germans to come out without weapons.

To exploit our success, I sent a messenger for the other half of our platoon. When they arrived, we numbered 30 men. The company commander saw our success and sent another platoon over.[4]

In many cases, the Soviet troops were in no mood to take prisoners. Zakhar Yevseyevich Krasilchikov was a soldier in a heavy machine-gun company of a reconnaissance battalion:

We were entering Köpenick, an industrial district, where there was a railway junction. The company took part in these battles on foot, with the DShK

['Degtyarev-Shpagina-Krupnokalibery'] on wheels, a pair of backpack flamethrowers and a dozen submachine-gunners attached to each machine-gun platoon. I commanded the combined assault group and if I'm honest, I really enjoyed our battles in Berlin.

We threw grenades through the windows of houses and basements from which they were firing at us, then cleared the buildings of Germans who were fighting to the last bullet with machine-gun fire and flamethrowers, and we were surprised at how many 'Krauts' we killed. We worked very efficiently. But in close street-fighting, the gun crews were not under cover and any fire from a *Panzerfaust* or a sniper meant the death of the gun crew ...

There were also so-called 'non-combat losses'. The railway station was captured, but there was a tank of alcohol on the tracks. The men fired several bursts at it with machine-guns and alcohol began to flow from the holes and men filled their helmets, but that wasn't enough for one man who climbed onto the tank, opened the hatch, and fell inside with a large hat in his hands. He suffocated from the alcohol fumes and drowned.[5]

Goebbels had declared that the *Panzerfaust* would be the decisive weapon in urban warfare; he had boasted that it was simple enough for a child to use effectively. Its main limitation was its short range, but this was of little consequence in streetfighting. As they retreated into Berlin, soldiers from the reconnaissance battalion of *SS-Nordland* watched Hitler Youth using the weapons against Soviet tanks:

Over there in the foxholes crouched three small figures, clutching their *Panzerfausts* firmly, listening to the growing thunder of tank engines with their hearts thumping. Humans against machines! Now the whole ground trembled under the enormous weight of the giants. We stared at them, rigid with tension. They were less than 50m away. Those three were nerveless. The tanks were separated from each other by very small distances, only 10–15m, as they rolled forward. They had seen our infantry retreating and hardly thought that death awaited them in the abandoned positions. Soon they were close to the foxholes ...

The tanks had driven into a perfect position for the three comrades lying in wait. The small gaps between them ensured their destruction. When the first tank was within 10m, three heads and *Panzerfausts* came up in a flash, three swift bangs, fire shot out from the *Panzerfausts* and three tanks were hit. Two burned immediately. One of them exploded. The third turned on the spot, its tracks damaged. The three heads dipped down quickly and emerged with three new *Panzerfausts*. Before it could withdraw from the short range of fire, the last tank received a fatal blow.[6]

The veterans of *SS-Nordland* were both impressed and horrified by the fanatic devotion of the Hitler Youth to the Führer, but even seasoned soldiers were growing tired of the fighting. One group of soldiers from 1st Flak Division began to retreat as Soviet troops bore down on them and showed little willingness to listen to their commander until he pulled a pistol and shot one of them. But when the next firefight began, one of the soldiers shot the officer in the head, and he and his comrades slipped away into the ruins.[7] The anonymous female diarist described the appearance of a new face in her bunker:

> We have a new resident, the husband of the woman who was bombed out of her home in Adlersdorf and who moved in here with her mother. He showed up very quietly, still in uniform; an hour later he was wearing civilian clothes. How could he get away with it? No one's even noticed, or else they don't care. Anyway no one's saying anything. A hard-boiled soldier from the front, he still looks pretty strong. We're happy to have him.
>
> Deserting suddenly seems like a perfectly understandable thing to do – a good idea, in fact.[8]

When they overran an airfield in Schönefeld, the soldiers of Eighth Guards Army were surprised to be met by a group of Red Army tanks – the leading elements of Rybalko's Third Guards Tank Army, advancing from the south. Chuikov promptly reported this to 1st Belarusian Front headquarters, and was startled by the response: he was ordered to send staff officers to the airfield to confirm that this was actually true, and to identify the units from 1st Ukrainian Front and discover the orders they had been given.[9] Clearly, the appearance of units of Konev's Front so close to Berlin came as an unpleasant surprise to Zhukov.

On the southern flank of Fifth Shock Army, a little to the north of where Chuikov's Eighth Guards Army had established tenuous contact with the units of 1st Ukrainian Front advancing from the south, the solders of IX Rifle Corps – backed by a tank corps – found themselves on the Spree, opposed by two battalions from *SS-Panzergrenadier-Regiment Danmark*. The bridge across the river was still partially intact with a small German bridgehead held by *Volkssturm* on the east bank; this was swiftly eliminated, but every attempt to cross the bridge was defeated by the Danes with heavy losses for the attackers. A brigade of combat engineers arrived during the afternoon with assault boats and the Soviet troops crossed the river close to either flank of the SS lines, with the northern crossing penetrating into the Treptower Park. The Germans launched powerful counterattacks to try to eliminate this bridgehead; there were heavy casualties on both sides, but the foothold across the Spree remained in Soviet hands.

Weidling's LVI Panzer Corps moved its headquarters into Rudow in southeast Berlin before dawn on 23 April. Here, Weidling was finally able to make contact with Ninth Army after being out of touch for over a day, and Voigtsberger – the commander of the disbanded *Berlin* division – was sent to Busse's headquarters. He returned an hour later and told a startled Weidling that there were orders from both Hitler and Busse for the arrest and execution of Weidling and Oberst Friedrich Böttcher, operations officer of 18th Panzergrenadier Division, for retreating without permission. A furious Weidling immediately handed over control of his corps to Oberst Theodor von Dufving, his chief of staff, and headed for the Reich Chancellery; he ordered Dufving to try to establish firm contact with Ninth Army to the southeast, with the intention of avoiding LVI Panzer Corps being drawn into urban fighting.

To the south of Berlin, Konev's troops prepared to storm the German defensive line along the Teltow Canal:

> The Germans prepared a strong defence – they dug trenches, set up reinforced concrete pillboxes, and dug in tanks and assault guns. Overlooking the canal was an almost continuous wall of houses – stone buildings with walls a metre or more thick. Reinforced buildings of industrial concerns stretched along the shore, their blind rear sides facing the canal and resembling a medieval fortress wall descending to the water ... A few bridges across the canal were prepared for demolition and some had already been destroyed. The canal itself was a serious obstacle: it was 40–50m wide, and 2–3m deep ...
>
> In the 12km sector where Rybalko's tankers waited, the enemy rounded up everything available – 15,000 men ... And the enemy had more than 250 guns and mortars, 130 tanks and half-tracks, and over 500 machine-guns. And an unlimited number of *Panzerfausts*. Moreover, for the Fascist soldiers and officers defending the Teltow Canal, this was the last line at which they could hold us. Behind them was [central] Berlin. And besides Berlin and their desperate determination to fight to the end and to die rather than let us into the city (and judging by the ferocity of the battles, most of the last defenders of the German capital had such determination), they also had behind them the SS tribunals, swiftly meting out justice to those who tried to slip away.[10]

Konev exaggerates the number of defenders and perhaps the determination of many of them to fight, but the canal was nonetheless a difficult obstacle. His artillerymen had laboured through the preceding night to move guns and ammunition into place, and the leading units of Rybalko's Third Guards Tank Army were relieved to be reinforced by a rifle division from Twenty-Eighth Army;

an assault across the canal without adequate infantry support would have been disastrous. With little time for formal reconnaissance, Konev ordered his artillery to concentrate on the buildings immediately facing the canal, but it would take most of 23 April for preparations to be completed. The assault could not begin until the following day.

The main developments to the south of Berlin were on either side of the city. To the east, two brigades of Third Guards Tank Army moved forward and made contact with the leading units of Zhukov's 1st Belarusian Front, thus completing a tentative encirclement of the German Ninth Army. Further west, Lelyushenko was pleased to have his VI Guards Mechanised Corps – delayed by the ongoing fighting around Spremberg – returned to him and immediately put it in the forefront of his advance. The corps stormed into Fresdorf to the south of Potsdam where it battled against the *Friedrich Ludwig Jahn* infantry division, which had been created around the remnants of 251st Infantry Division using men who had previously been part of the *Reichsarbeitsdienst* ('Reich Labour Administration' or *RAD*), *Volkssturm,* and Hitler Youth. The division was part of *Armeegruppe Reymann*, the conglomeration of ad hoc units now commanded by the former *Kampfkommandant* of Berlin, and lacked any artillery or heavy weapons; it was swiftly driven out of Fresdorf and its commander, Oberst Gerhard Klein, was captured. Lelyushenko described how he visited the headquarters of VI Guards Mechanised Corps and met Klein and other prisoners:

> The captured colonel was brought to us, and we learned that the division had been formed in early April and included youngsters aged only 15–16. I lost my temper and demanded, 'Why are you driving innocent teenage boys to slaughter on the eve of an inevitable catastrophe?' His lips moved convulsively, one eyelid twitched, and his legs trembled. This Nazi warrior looked pitiful and disgusting.[11]

It should be pointed out that young Soviet teenagers fought against the Germans in the ranks of the partisans and, had the Wehrmacht penetrated into Leningrad and Moscow, would undoubtedly have taken up arms to defend their cities. By the end of 23 April, Fourth Guards Tank Army had completed the envelopment of southern Berlin and its leading elements were now only 15 miles from IX Guards Tank Corps, part of Bodganov's Second Guards Tank Army, which was approaching from the north.

Like the two tank armies, the combined arms armies of 1st Ukrainian Front spent 23 April carrying out a mixture of advances and regroupings. Gordov's Third Guards Army was now covering the southern flank of the German Ninth Army. The garrison of Frankfurt-an-der-Oder pulled out of the city late on 22 April and

INTO THE CITY: 23–25 APRIL

troops from the Soviet Thirty-Third Army entered the city from the north during the morning of 23 April. Over 90 per cent of the city was reduced to ruins, and numerous fires were burning. Other fires broke out over the following days. In the years that followed, Communist officials in East Germany and the Soviet Union would blame this arson on retreating SS troops, but the timings suggest that whilst some of the destruction might have been deliberately carried out before the garrison withdrew, much took place after the Soviet forces arrived. Polish forced labourers returning to Poland may also have been responsible for some of the arson.

On the western flank of Third Guards Army, Twenty-Eighth Army was deploying rapidly; some of its leading elements moved up to support Third Guards Tank Army in preparation for the crossing of the Teltow Canal, while other units completed the southern encirclement of Busse's Ninth Army. Largely undetected by the Red Army, Busse's men were beginning the redeployment ordered by Heinrici and moving west. They were protected by the woodland of the Spreewald, which made aerial observation difficult, and the numerous waterways of the region hampered any Soviet attempts to pursue them. A little to the south, Pukhov's Thirteenth Army regrouped after the capture of Cottbus and moved west towards the Elbe. Konev later wrote – as did Fedyuninsky – that steps were taken in case the Germans attempted to march to the relief of Berlin from the west, but although they would have been aware of Hitler's order to Wenck's Twelfth Army, not least because it had been broadcast by German radio stations, it is likely that at this stage they had little clear idea of whether such an attack was going to take place, or its likely strength. Zhadov's Fifth Guards Army reached the Elbe during the morning of 23 April along a stretch close to the town of Riese, midway between Dresden and Leipzig. For the moment, the far bank was unoccupied by either German or US troops.

Despite his successes, Konev was worried by developments on his southern flank. Here, Schörner's Army Group Centre had launched a counterattack towards Spremberg and by the end of 23 April had penetrated about 18 miles into the seam between Fifty-Second Army and Second Polish Army. The attack had taken the Soviet units by surprise and rapidly broke through the front line, resulting in chaotic fighting in the rear areas for a period of time, but Konev was able to dispatch sufficient reinforcements to stabilise the situation. In any event, Schörner's thrust was going nowhere. If the intention had been to reach the remnants of the German units encircled near Spremberg, it was too late to make any difference, and once the Soviet units recovered their balance – and the German units had exhausted their limited fuel and ammunition – the moment of crisis passed rapidly. The Germans were soon forced to pull back to their start line.[12]

In his bunker beneath the Reich Chancellery, Hitler seemed to have recovered from his near collapse of the previous day. He was now confident that Steiner would finally attack towards Berlin while Wenck and Busse carried out their attacks from the southwest and southeast respectively, but others in the bunker tried to take advantage of the situation for their own ends. The almost universally detested Fegelein could see that the end was near and repeatedly suggested to Hitler that it would be better to place *Armeegruppe Steiner* under more reliable command, i.e. Fegelein himself. Hitler gave him no heed.

During the day, the Führer again ordered Jodl and Keitel to leave Berlin while escape was still possible, so that they could continue to oversee Wehrmacht operations in northern Germany. Originally, the intention had been for senior figures to head south to Bavaria, but the headquarters staff of *OKW* were to move to Krampnitz, just to the north of Potsdam. With a link-up between the Red Army and the forces of the Western Powers now imminent, the division of the remaining territory controlled by the Reich was inevitable and Hitler placed the northern part under the control of Admiral Dönitz, with Generalfeldmarschall Albert Kesselring in command of the southern part. In Berlin itself, he made a further appointment, telling Brigadeführer Wilhelm Mohnke that he was to take command of the forces defending the 'citadel', Hitler's description of Berlin's government quarter. Mohnke saw service on several fronts during the war and was implicated in the massacres of British prisoners in 1940 and Canadian soldiers in Normandy in 1944. He was also commander of the division *Leibstandarte-SS-Adolf-Hitler* or *LSSAH* during the Ardennes offensive of late 1944; one of his subordinate units, *Kampfgruppe Peiper*, was involved in yet another war crime when US prisoners were gunned down at Malmedy. He was wounded – his third wound of the war – in Hungary, and was still recovering from his injuries when he received this new appointment. The units available to him were modest, amounting to barely two weak regiments.

After several delays in the rubble-strewn streets of Berlin, Weidling finally reached the Reich Chancellery at about 1800 on 23 April and met Krebs and Burgdorf. The exasperated corps commander explained that far from retreating to the west of Berlin, his men had been involved in bitter fighting against the Red Army and were still trying to re-establish a common front with the rest of Ninth Army. By this time, it had become clear to the senior officers in the bunker that defence of Berlin would be impossible – Reymann's preparations had been largely to create positions that retreating Wehrmacht forces might use, and he had then managed to move most of the *Volkssturm* battalions out of Berlin. Now, with the news that LVI Panzer Corps was actually fighting in the eastern part of the city, it seemed that sufficient forces for some sort of defence had miraculously appeared. Krebs ordered Weidling to pull back his formations into Berlin, where they would hold the city while the relief effort by Twelfth Army and Ninth Army was carried out.

Weidling was accompanied by his operations officer, Major Siegfried Knapp, and he now spoke to Dufving by telephone to make him aware of the new orders. Dufving replied that Busse had sent orders by teleprinter to LVI Corps, informing Dufving that Weidling was dismissed from his post and was to be replaced by Burmeister, commander of 25th Panzergrenadier Division. Weidling's temper was already stretched to the limit; he and his men had conducted a difficult fighting withdrawal under immense pressure, and yet he was being blamed for a retreat that he had not carried out. He demanded permission to leave and hand over to his successor, but instead was told that Hitler wished to speak to him.

Weidling would later describe his shock when he met the Führer; Hitler had a rigid expression and his left leg twitched back and forth constantly. The despondency that had shocked Keitel and Jodl the day before was gone. Instead, Hitler was enthused by the new plan for the relief of Berlin and he now told Weidling that he was to move his corps into Berlin, where he would become the new *Kampfkommandant*, directly under Hitler's command. Weidling protested that it would be better to declare Berlin an open city, but Krebs sided with Hitler. Käther, the rapidly promoted general who had been put in command after Reymann's dismissal, found himself demoted just as rapidly back to Oberst.

Next, Weidling contacted Dufving and brought him up to date. When he was told that the corps was to pull back into Berlin, the chief of staff protested bitterly. The units of LVI Panzer Corps were already attempting to implement Weidling's earlier orders to try to move south towards the rest of Ninth Army and this new set of instructions would cause chaos, particularly as all formations were heavily engaged in fighting. He warned Weidling that trying to implement a withdrawal into Berlin might cost the corps up to 60 per cent of its combat effectiveness. Weidling replied that there was no doubt of what would happen to him personally if the order wasn't carried out. Later that night, after he had returned to his headquarters, Weidling told Dufving: 'The end of the war is near anyway and if I have to die, I want to do it honourably.'[13]

It is a measure of how badly communications had broken down, with the consequent disruption of the normal chain of command, that Heinrici at the headquarters of Army Group Vistula was one of the last to learn about Weidling's reappearance and appointment as *Kampfkommandant* of Berlin. Busse had informed him that the first elements of LVI Panzer Corps had made contact with his northwest flank near Schmöckwitz to the southeast of Berlin, but it was only shortly before midnight that Käther telephoned Heinrici and brought him fully up to date. For the man who had intended to avoid a battle in Berlin at all costs, it was a bitter blow. He protested that the units that had reached Schmöckwitz were vital to protect the flank of Busse's Ninth Army and then attempted to contact Krebs. It wasn't until after 0100 that he made contact, complaining that it was unacceptable for *OKH* – on Hitler's orders – to order LVI Panzer Corps back into Berlin without informing either Ninth Army or Army Group Vistula. Krebs blamed communications difficulties; Heinrici concluded the call by saying that the withdrawal from Schmöckwitz left Ninth Army with no line of retreat. Soviet units had established tenuous contact between the army and Berlin, and he now regarded the firm encirclement of Busse's forces as inevitable.

Weidling wasn't the only visitor to the bunker on 23 April. Speer, the armaments minister, chose to fly back into Berlin to say goodbye to his Führer. He later wrote that Hitler asked him if he should heed the advice of Jodl and Keitel and leave Berlin, but Speer advised him to stay in the capital.

> He said nothing more of an imminent turning point or that there was still hope. Rather apathetically, wearily and as if it were already a matter of course, he began speaking of his death: 'I too have resolved to stay here. I only wanted to hear your view once more.' Without excitement, he continued: 'I shall not fight personally. There is always the danger that I would only be wounded and fall into the hands of the Russians alive. I don't want my enemies to disgrace my body either. I've given orders that I be cremated. Fraülein Braun wants to depart this life with me, and I'll shoot Blondi [his dog] beforehand. Believe me, Speer, it is easy for me to end my life. A brief moment and I'm freed of everything, liberated from this painful existence.'[14]

Speer stayed in the bunker when Krebs began the daily briefing. As the *OKH* chief of staff outlined the situation on a large map – with communications breaking down, only a general description was possible – Hitler seemed to become more optimistic, and Speer watched with bafflement as the two men discussed divisions and other units that had in reality ceased to exist several days before.

Meanwhile, the repercussions of Hitler's behaviour on 22 April continued. Messages arrived from Göring, who was in Bavaria, to several figures. Speer caught sight of a telegram to Joachim von Ribbentrop, the Reich foreign minister:

> I have asked the Führer to provide me with instructions by 2200 on 23 April. If by this time it is apparent that the Führer has been deprived of his freedom of action to conduct the affairs of the Reich, his decree of 29 June 1941 becomes effective, according to which I am heir to all his offices as his deputy. If by midnight 23 April 1945 you receive no word either from the Führer directly or from me, you are to come to me at once by air.[15]

Immediately, Bormann seized on this as evidence of Göring's intention to conduct a *coup d'état*. He roused Hitler to a further outburst of rage, and Göring was stripped of all his titles and privileges – but perhaps as a small act of recognition of all the years that Göring had served the Nazi cause, he was permitted to resign on grounds of ill health, and in return would escape any further punishment.

Like other soldiers in the disintegrating German units that had pulled back from the Seelow Heights, Altner and his comrades had spent a desperate couple of days attempting to head west. At one point they were fortunate enough to board a train, but were soon forced to disembark when they learned that the track had been cut by advancing Soviet troops. They reached the airfield at Tempelhof early on 23 April and marched on past an air raid shelter where they rested a short time. The civilians in the shelter stared at the newcomers:

> Astonishment shows in their eyes. They look at us as if we were ghosts ... The eyes of several of them show anger, even hatred. Hatred of us because we are continuing the fight. Hatred of us for having not yet cast aside the fetters of duty. They shyly draw aside to make room for us and the comrades collapse on the benches or roll on the stone floor. I lie on the bench with my pack under my head. My legs are stiff and my skull aches as if to burst. We soon go out again, leaving the people behind sleeping, waiting and hoping.[16]

In places, the hostility towards those still fighting against the inevitable resulted in acts of violence. Despite constant repression during the Nazi era, there were still many Communists in the industrial suburbs of east and north Berlin. Many mocked the retreating German soldiers, but some took up arms and sniped at them regardless of whether they were SS, Wehrmacht, or *Volkssturm*. But a greater threat came from those still zealously enforcing Hitler's orders. Altner and the others continued their march:

> SS patrols in cars are driving along the streets, stopping a man here and picking one up there, their engines humming. *Volkssturm*, here mainly in SS uniform, close the anti-tank barriers behind them, while Hitler Youth go about proudly carrying *Panzerfausts*.
>
> There is a big square to our right lined with the facades of burnt-out buildings. Two SA men are standing beneath a lamppost from which a handcuffed civilian is hanging with a red electricity cable around his neck that has cut deep into his flesh. His face is blue and his eyes hang deep in their sockets. Around his neck is hung a white cardboard placard, on which is written in shaky writing: 'I, Otto

Meyer, was too cowardly to fight for my wife and child. That is why I am hanging here. I am a swine.' I feel I am going to be sick. I want to look away but cannot take my eyes off this gruesome sight. The SA men are laughing and smiling as the dead man swings slowly in the wind. A passing civilian tells us in a low voice why the soldier has been hanged. Like us he had come back tired and burnt out from the fighting and encirclement before Berlin. He was young. His wife begged him to stay. He gave in and was then betrayed by a neighbour.[17]

Eventually, Altner reached the barracks in the western part of Berlin from where he had been sent to the Seelow Heights. Of the 150 who had departed with him, only 58 remained.

While Altner was trudging west, the encirclement of Ninth Army was firmly established behind him as a mechanised brigade from Rybalko's Third Guards Tank Army established firm contact with Chuikov's Eighth Guards Army near Schönefeld. Elsewhere, Zhukov's orders for Chuikov to drive on into southern Berlin and thus to block any advance by Konev's forces into the city centre were frustrated by elements of *SS-Nordland* that put up tough resistance in and around Neukölln. However, units of Eighth Guards Army continued to overrun the southeast parts of Berlin and elements reached the Teltow Canal to the south, not far from where Rybalko's forces were preparing to cross. Having taken command of the defences of Berlin, Weidling had issued orders for all bridges over the canal to be destroyed as soon as any remaining German soldiers to the south had withdrawn, but the confusion caused by chaotic command arrangements – with local Party officials believing they had complete authority – and the breakdown of communications meant that his instructions were often not obeyed. Untersturmführer Hans Henseler, part of a battalion of combat engineers, was at one such crossing and had to insist that the bridge was destroyed; when the demolition charge was finally triggered, it merely blew a small hole in the centre of the roadway. While the local Party official hurried away, ostensibly to find more explosives, Henseler and his men took up defensive positions. Around them, men of the *Volkssturm* had also been deployed, but their numbers diminished steadily as they slipped away into the city. Leaving the bridge, Henseler continued into Berlin, trying to make contact with the rest of his battalion, and encountered a major and a group of armed men who bluntly ordered them to turn around and face the Soviet troops, refusing to accept Henseler's word that he was under orders to find the rest of his unit. It was only when Henseler's men emerged from the buildings around him, their weapons pointed at the major and those accompanying him, that the small group of sappers was permitted to continue.[18]

24 APRIL

Rybalko's assault across the Teltow Canal began before dawn on 24 April, shortly after Henseler and his men left the area. Artillery battered the buildings of Lichterfelde and Zehlendorf and when the assault began, it encountered determined resistance from what remained of 20th Panzergrenadier Division, reinforced by local units. The panzergrenadier division was a shadow of its former strength, and matters had been made worse towards the end of the previous day when Scholze, its commander, shot himself in despair at the imminent fall of the capital and the disintegration of his division. Nonetheless, his troops fought hard and it took most of the day for the Soviet units to establish a firm foothold north of the canal. A little to the east, there was better progress, and Rybalko ordered future attacks to be concentrated here.

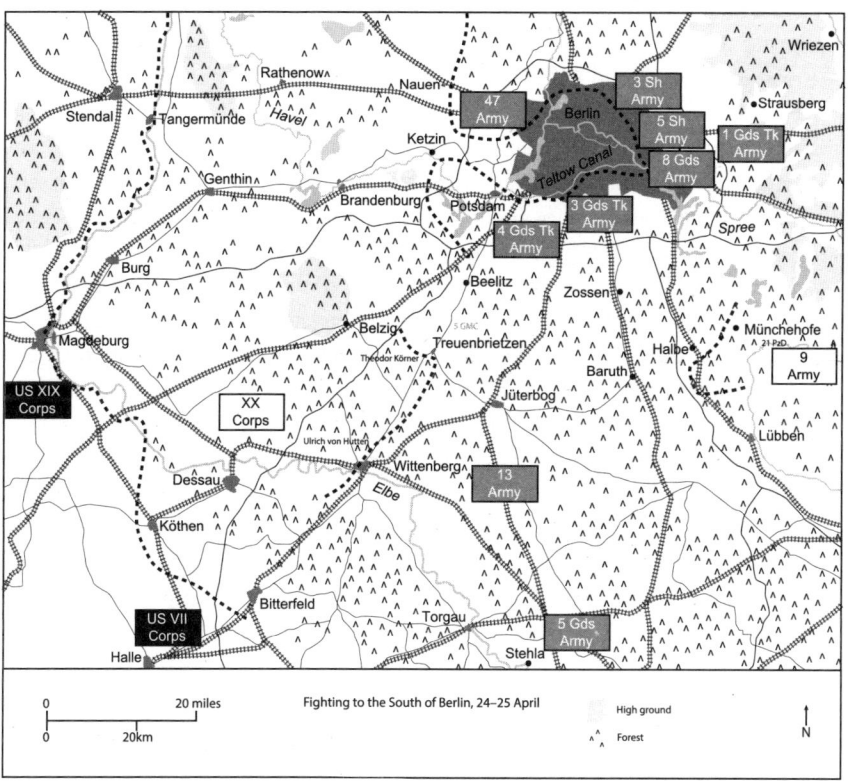

Fighting to the South of Berlin, 24–25 April

Fritz Altner, a signaller from 20th Panzergrenadier Division, was in central Berlin. He heard a report that the division's rear area units were in Döberitz, to the west of the city, and managed to get a written order to go there. On their way west, they found their half-track – they had been separated from it for several days – and drove west. Near Ketzin, to the west of Potsdam, they encountered several assault guns from their division and joined them in an attack to clear Ketzin of Soviet troops, and after being warned that further Soviet units were to their west, they turned towards the northwest. In the village of Wutzetz, they found more elements of 20th Panzergrenadier Division, and for the first time there were a few officers present who were able to start reorganising them into an improvised battlegroup. By adding the division's rear area personnel, they were able to gather two infantry battalions, two artillery batteries, an armoured company of eight assault guns, and a few anti-aircraft guns and mortars. Altner noted grimly that whilst the remaining combat elements of the division were still disciplined and prepared to fight, the rear area troops took every opportunity to disappear. But worse was to come – over the following two days, even some of the officers, including the brigade commander, abandoned the brigade.[19]

Further west, Lelyushenko was now close to linking up with Soviet units pressing down from the north, completing the encirclement of Berlin. By the end of the day, the gap between the pincers was no more than three miles. Around the eastern and northeastern parts of the German capital, Zhukov's two shock armies were battering their way into Berlin. Here, they encountered a formidable obstacle: the flak tower at Friedrichshain. Its powerful 128mm guns had been providing long-range fire support for the defenders throughout the previous day, but the battle intensified on 23 April. An attempt to outflank the tower failed with the loss of several Soviet tanks and a second assault succeeded in reaching the trenches close to the tower before being driven back by intense fire. By the end of the day, the gunners of the tower reported with satisfaction that they had fired over 1,200 128mm rounds and a similar number of smaller calibre rounds during the day.[20] In the urban landscape, the numerical superiority of the Red Army was of little benefit and – as Goebbels had anticipated – the *Panzerfaust* became one of the most potent weapons available. Suffering heavy losses, Third Shock Army's VII Rifle Corps was brought to a halt in the city blocks around the park in the northern part of Friedrichshain, in bitter fighting amidst the rubble of a bombed-out large cement factory. The neighbouring Fifth Shock Army did little better with its XXVI Guards Rifle Corps and XXXII Rifle Corps, backed by two tank brigades, running into a *Volkssturm* battalion to the west of the *S-Bahn* station on Frankfurter Allee. The withering fire from the Friedrichshain Flak Tower drove the tanks back and the *Volkssturm* – who were, after all, fighting for

Into the City: 23–25 April

their homes – held their positions with dogged courage, even when XXVI Guards Rifle Corps outflanked them to the north by penetrating through the cluster of buildings that had been Berlin's main slaughterhouse. Frustrated by this resistance, Berzarin ordered his artillery to level the entire area in a brutal bombardment. The terrified inhabitants of Friedrichshain cowered in cellars and *U-Bahn* stations, but as had been the case in other urban battlefields, turning city blocks into rubble hindered attackers as much as defenders, with the streets filled with debris and plentiful cover for German soldiers to use in close-range clashes. The slaughterhouse area reaped a new harvest of corpses and by the end of the day, the exhausted soldiers of XXXII Rifle Corps managed to reach and capture Baltenplatz. After the war, the square would be renamed Bersarinplatz in honour of the general whose artillery reduced the entire area to rubble. For both Third and Fifth Shock Armies, Alexanderplatz – regarded by many Berliners as the heart of the city – remained just out of reach.

German reinforcements also arrived in this area, including the surviving Panther tanks of the *Müncheberg* panzer division, regular SS troops, and groups of Hitler Youth and *Volkssturm*. Amongst them were some of the survivors of 15th *SS-Waffen-Grenadier* Division, one of two Latvian divisions raised by the SS. They had originally been deployed as part of Army Group Vistula but, distrustful of the foreign 'volunteers' serving in the SS, Heinrici had ordered many of these units out of the front line. Although they were meant to remain in the area to the rear of the front line, the commander of the greatly reduced division, Standartenführer Vilis Janums, decided that the war was effectively over and further loss of life was to be avoided at all costs. Without authorisation, he broke his unit into several groups with orders to march west on foot past Berlin and then to head west in the hope of surrendering to the Western Powers. Perhaps two thirds reached the lines of the US Army; the rest were rounded up and deployed in Berlin. Alongside them was another foreign contingent. When Germany invaded the Soviet Union in 1941, a Spanish division was raised and sent to the east, where it became part of Army Group North and fought during the battles around Leningrad as 250th Infantry Division, often known as *División Azul* ('Blue Division') on account of the blue shoulder flashes worn by its personnel. Although the Germans repeatedly complained about indiscipline and lack of fighting ability of the Blue Division, its performance was no worse than that of regular German units, but it was disbanded in late 1943 and its personnel were ordered to return to Spain. Many of them chose to remain and were reorganised into the Blue Legion, and some of these now found themselves in this last battle to defend the capital of the Reich.

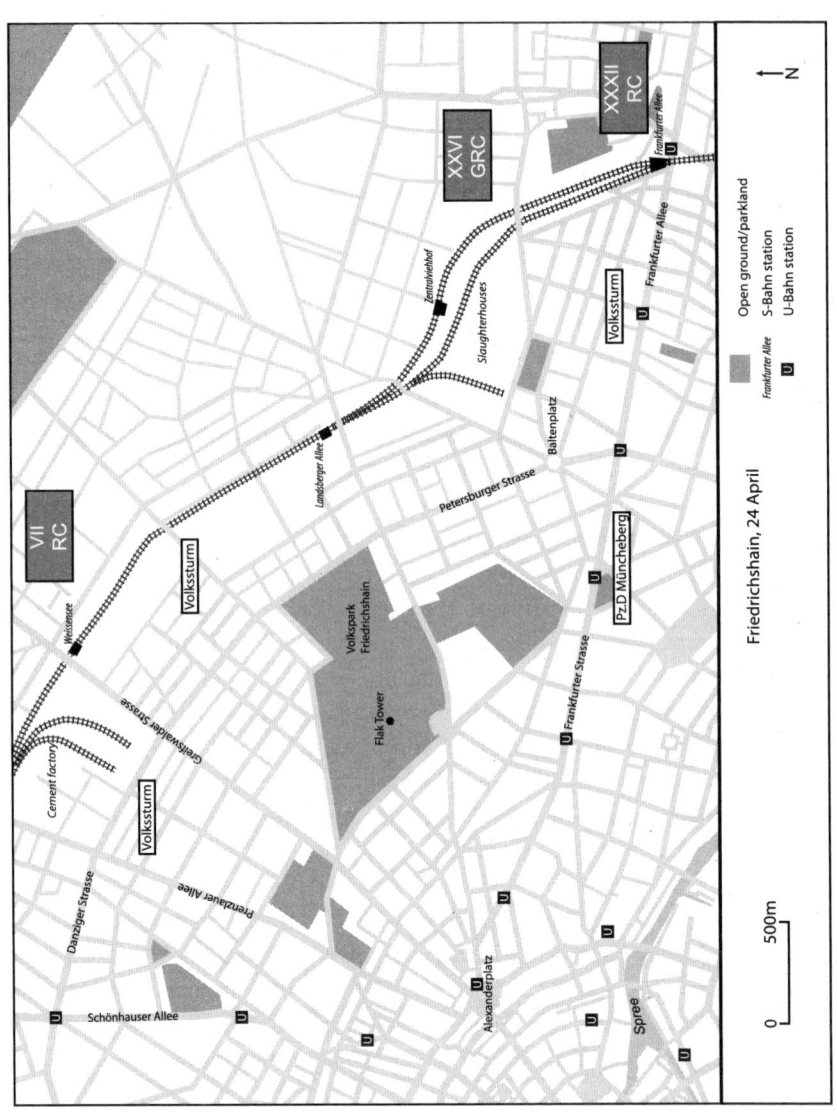

The stubborn defence of the Spree by *SS-Panzergrenadier-Regiment Danmark* came to an end on 24 April with Soviet units seizing most of the west bank of the Spree in southeast Berlin. The surviving Danish soldiers pulled back to form a strongpoint behind the substantial walls of a school on Köpenickerstrasse where they held up the Soviet advance for most of the day before being driven back by a combination of heavy mortar fire and the appearance of the Soviet 50th Guards Heavy Tank Regiment with its IS-2 tanks. During the evening, the Soviet units – now largely mixed together, with elements of different divisions overlapping with each other in the urban area – continued towards the west, reaching Oranienplatz. The survivors of the German defensive force pulled back further to Leipzigerstrasse, on the southern edge of central Berlin. Zhukov would have received reports of this costly advance with a sense of relief: as he had hoped, his units were now almost far enough to the west to block off a thrust into the city centre by his rival Konev.

To the west of Berlin, Wenck began preparations for his attempt to reach Busse's Ninth Army. To his irritation, leaflets were dropped throughout the area by aircraft acting on Hitler's orders:

Soldiers of *Armee Wenck*!
   An order of the greatest importance has summoned you from your assembly areas against our western enemies and set you on a march towards the east. Your mission is clear:
   Berlin remains German!
   The barbarian assault of Bolshevism, bent on destroying the *Volk*, must be smashed before and on the walls of the Reich capital.
   The Führer stands in the forefront of the defence of Berlin.
   He has informed your brave commander that, trusting in your quick and decisive intervention, he anticipates with confidence the decisive battle for Berlin.
   Soldiers of *Armee Wenck*!
   Not just your Führer, all of Berlin waits with hope for you.
   In the outer parts of the Reich capital there is already bitter fighting. The Bolsheviks are trying with all their strength first to seize Berlin, then to wipe out the Reich capital and thus to hold the trump card for the great forthcoming power struggle in San Francisco [where Hitler expected the Allies to hold their postwar conference]. As you know, they are resisted by the Wehrmacht, police, Volkssturm, *OT* [*Organization Todt*, one of the Reich's labour organisations] and the working men and women of Berlin with all their energy; the conquest of Berlin by the Bolsheviks could never be reversed. Where Bolshevism takes hold, all life comes to an end. The first terrible reports from the suburbs already show

BERLIN

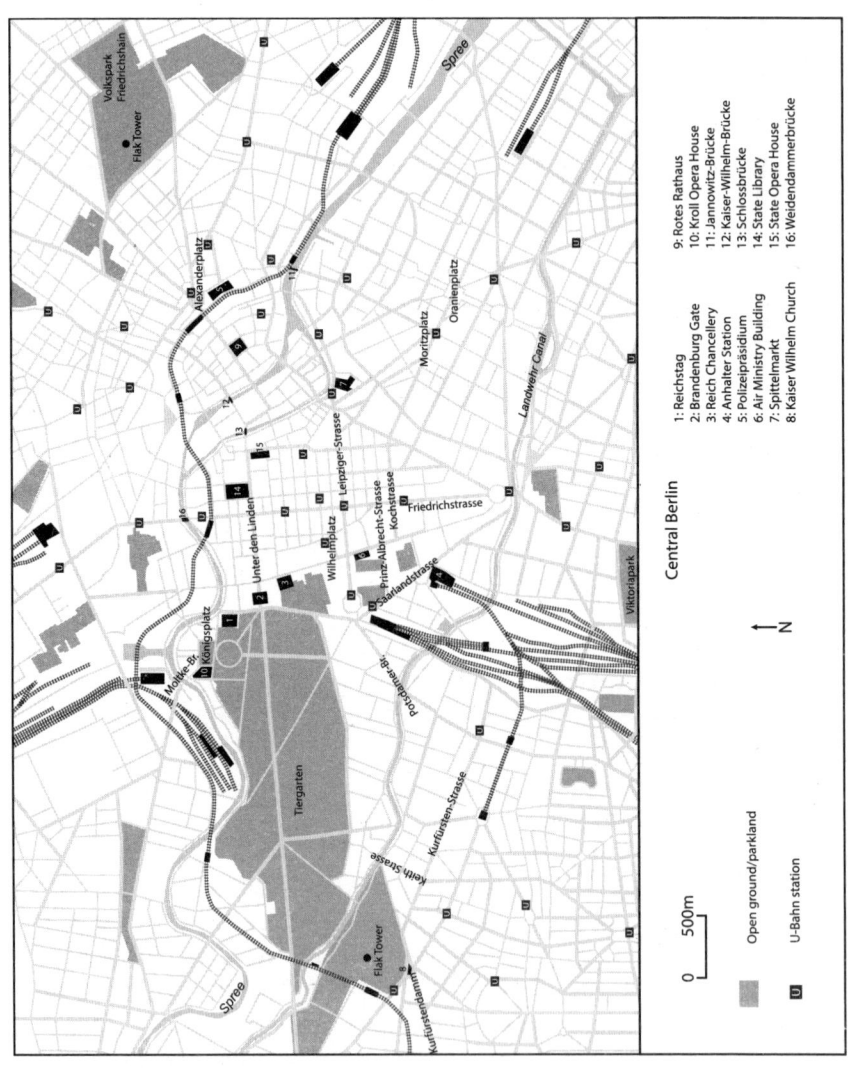

that as ordered, the Soviet soldiery is committing the same atrocities in the city as in the eastern regions.[21]

Wenck had no intention of having his army drawn into the fighting in Berlin; the leaflet therefore gave an impression that he wished to avoid, and furthermore might raise hopes amongst civilians of something that was not going to happen. He ordered his men to destroy any leaflets that they found, but he could do nothing about the radio broadcasts that were spreading similar rumours. In Berlin, the anonymous female diarist sheltered in the cellar once more during the evening – although air raids had stopped, the area was now under sporadic artillery fire:

> A new rumour floats around the basement, which the wife of the liquor distiller heard from a reliable, very secret source and announces with a heaving bosom: the Yanks and Tommies have quarrelled with Ivan and are thinking of joining with us to chase Ivan out of the country. Scornful laughter and heated discussion.[22]

Oberst Günther Reichhelm, Wenck's chief of staff, later described how he and Wenck had concluded that it was feasible for Twelfth Army to fight either against the Western Allies or against the Red Army, but attempting both at the same time would result in disaster. Although neither man seems to have known about the future division of Germany, they had correctly deduced that the halting of US forces along the Elbe and the cessation of further air attacks suggested that it was safe for them to turn east in strength. All they could do was leave minimal forces facing west and hope that the current near-ceasefire would continue.

Amongst the formations in Twelfth Army was Köhler's XX Corps, made up of a series of improvised divisions – in reality, little more than groups of infantry with little by way of heavy weaponry. Two of these, the *Theodor Körner* and *Ulrich von Hutten* infantry divisions, were on the Elbe facing the US Army and were ordered to move east to try to establish a corridor to Ninth Army; they were supported by a handful of assault guns. Only one division – the *Scharnhorst* infantry division – would be left facing the Elbe, with another unit, the *Ferdinand von Schill* infantry division, joining the push to the east with a further assault gun brigade. None of these divisions had more than 9,000 men and contained a mixture of the remnants of earlier units, training formations, rear area personnel, labour battalions, and new recruits. But such was the urgency of the situation that they moved with alacrity, reaching their start lines by dawn on 24 April. The speed of the redeployment was aided considerably by two factors. Firstly, the excellent German *Autobahn* network in the area provided several good march routes; and secondly, air attacks by the USAAF had effectively ceased. Moving out at first light, *Ulrich von Hutten* immediately encountered soldiers of Pukhov's Thirteenth Army near Wittenberg. Contrary to what Konev implied in his account, the Soviet soldiers were clearly not expecting an attack from the west and were rapidly driven off. The attack had left *Ulrich von Hutten* temporarily out of fuel, but the situation was remedied speedily by a surprising discovery. A local civilian informed the soldiers that the Nazi Party *Kreisleiter* for Wittenberg had a personal stockpile of fuel, and this was rapidly located; about 40,000 litres of gasoline was swiftly distributed to the division's units.[23] A little to the north, *Theodor Körner* advanced to Treuenbrietzen with little difficulty, but then came under attack from 10th Guards Mechanised Brigade, part of Lelyushenko's V Guards Mechanised Corps. The fighting intensified through the day with neither side able to claim victory.

As news of Wenck's attack spread, hope soared amongst German soldiers and civilians. This was at least partly due to the lack of action by the Western Allies to take any steps to intervene – their complete air superiority would have permitted them to interdict any troop movements, and attacks across the Elbe would have prevented Wenck from pulling out his divisions for use in the east. Many Germans chose to interpret this inaction as evidence that the alliance against Germany was finally falling apart; the reality was that US commanders were under strict orders to avoid further loss of lives, as almost all the territory that was to be under the control of the Western Powers was already in their hands. Alarmed by the attacks from the west, Konev urged Lelyushenko to concentrate V Guards Mechanised Corps in the path of the German attack and promised as much air support as he could muster.

To the east, Busse's Ninth Army struggled to redeploy. All supplies were running out and morale and discipline were also at low levels. Much of 21st Panzer Division was in the encirclement and it succeeded in withdrawing more or less intact through Münchehofe, but the division's artillery regiment took matters into its own hands, as the division's armoured reconnaissance battalion's commander later described:

> The artillery staff … commandeered my fuel and fled to the northwest. Through lack of fuel my own unit was reduced to 70 per cent effectiveness, so future attempts to make a motorised breakout on our own would prove futile.
>
> Resistance was only coming from the panzer divisions, the SS, and in the beginning the units from the city. There was no longer any operational direction higher than division. Units with unpopular officers were running away. Death sentences were no longer being carried out. From the orders given, the High

Command was clearly demanding the constant sacrifice of our army, which was why our operational tasks made no sense. Everyone, from the leaders of reconnaissance units to senior staff officers, was in the dark about what was going on.

The question arose whether to flee with one's troops on one's own responsibility, or stay with the parent division – a question of conscience. I sent my adjutant, Leutnant Kielhorn, home to his mother in Berlin by the last remaining route, as he was an only child. One hour later the ring was closed.

The results were simply indescribable chaos: hassle, no sleep, no supplies, contaminated drinking water, unbelievable casualties, the encirclement constantly closing in, ferocious enemy air attacks, and massive artillery bombardment. During this phase there was a visible sinking of morale in my own unit. The chief of staff, Major Renner, had already fled. Unit leaders took control. The generals were no longer exercising their authority.[24]

Meanwhile, another group of foreign SS were about to become embroiled in the fighting for Berlin. A French Legion had been raised for service with the SS in 1943, growing into a brigade in 1944 before being expanded still further in February 1945 into 33rd *SS-Waffen-Grenadier Division Charlemagne*. The division was involved in fighting against Rokossovsky's 2nd Belarusian Front around Neustrelitz, and its commander, Brigadeführer Gustav Krukenberg, was summoned to Berlin. Accompanied by several hundred French SS, he drove to the capital along chaotic roads choked with refugees and other units – these included elements of *SS-Nordland*, attempting to follow earlier orders to head west, and even Soviet units that Krukenberg carefully avoided. Some of the soldiers they passed mocked the French SS, telling them they were heading the wrong way. Many civilians cheered the small column of trucks, mistaking them for the vanguard of Wenck's army. There seemed to be little by way of defensive forces, and leaving his men near the Olympic Stadium, Krukenberg drove on to the Reich Chancellery. He arrived shortly before midnight and, to his astonishment, was able to enter the building and the underground bunker unchallenged.

The bunker was now far less crowded than had been the case just a few days before, with so many Nazi officials having taken advantage of Hitler's collapse of 22 April to leave the city. But there was rubbish everywhere and sanitary facilities were no longer working properly; empty alcohol bottles littered some of the rooms and corridors as some of the remaining inhabitants made use of the stockpiles in the bunker before the inevitable end. Krukenberg was greeted by Fegelein, and shortly after Krebs appeared. He told Krukenberg that negotiations were underway with the US forces to allow them into Berlin – an entirely false statement – and all that was required was for Berlin to hold out against the Red Army for a further week. Krukenberg's role in this would be command of *SS-Nordland*; Ziegler was being removed from his post.²⁵ Despite a creditable past record, Ziegler had fallen out of favour, perhaps because of his earlier insistence that his division be permitted to rejoin *Armeegruppe Steiner*. For the moment, he remained in the Berlin area with rear area units of *SS-Nordland*. He would have a part to play in the final stages of the battle.

That evening, *OKW* issued a summary that stressed the difficulties being experienced by Ninth Army in reorganising its forces for a breakout towards the west. To some extent, this was based on guesswork, as Busse's headquarters was able to give superior commands only the most general outline of the locations of its various formations. But one item in the *OKW* report was absolutely correct: the isolated units of Ninth Army were running low on fuel and ammunition, particularly armour-piercing rounds. There had been some attempts by the Luftwaffe to fly supplies into the area, but few if any planes reached their destination, falling victim to Soviet anti-aircraft fire or being intercepted by Soviet fighters.

25 APRIL

The slow disintegration of Army Group Vistula's last significant formation, Third Panzer Army, continued its inexorable path. The counterattacks that had held up the Red Army for the preceding two days were at an end, with the Germans completely out of ammunition and fuel, and Sixty-Fifth Army continued to move west, as Batov described:

> At 1100 on 25 April, after powerful artillery preparation, our rifle divisions commenced an attack that proceeded quickly from the outset. At about 1300 our troops took the strongpoints of Schmellenthin and Pommellen [in reality, two small villages about seven miles southwest of central Stettin]. We then prevented counterattacks from coming within 300m of our positions. The police units and naval infantry regiments deployed by the German command in the forefront of their CI Corps were completely destroyed by our artillery and airmen. At 1250 [I Guards] tank corps was inserted into the breakthrough. Heavy artillery continued to fire on our troops from the Stettin defensive area, but we continued to advance inexorably towards the northwest.
>
> Units of 17th Tank Brigade and 1st Mechanised Infantry Brigade [from I Guards Tank Corps] bypassed Barnimskunow where the enemy had four tanks and two artillery batteries, then the Hohenholz Forest where there were eight to

ten tanks and around two infantry regiments, and advanced quickly towards Krackow–Gladkow.

Borisov's guardsmen [from 44th Guards Rifle Division] captured the strongpoint of Barnimskunow in cooperation with 413th Rifle Division. Teremov [108th Rifle Division] took Hohenhof. Grebennik [37th Guards Rifle Division] destroyed the German troops in Hohenholz Forest while Makarov's 69th Rifle Division overran the forces screening them and marched on Krackow.

During the evening of 25 April our tanks reached the Randow River and tried to seize a crossing near Krackow, north of Löcknitz. The bridges were blown up. Our rifle units, which reached the river that night, began to cross it on the move.[26]

The advance of Sixty-Fifth Army – nine miles west of the Oder – put its leading units to the southwest of Stettin and Manteuffel acted quickly. He ordered the troops that remained in the city to leave and escape to the west before they were cut off. During the evening and night, they completed their preparations and set off at about midnight, hoping that the roads were still open.

Despite the weakness of his units, Steiner finally made an attack across the Finow Canal. Elements of 7th Panzer Division had reached his lines together with a few other disparate groups of men and tanks, but it took one more intervention from Jodl to persuade Steiner to start moving. It was only when Jodl warned him that his command might be broken up and its units handed back to Third Panzer Army that Steiner ordered an attack. It was at best a half-hearted attempt and rapidly petered out, but a group from *SS-Polizei* Division, led by Oberführer Walter Harzer, the division commander, moved to seize the bridge over the Havel River in Spandau, on the west flank of *Armeegruppe Steiner*. He had orders to hold it for as long as possible, so that there remained a corridor to the west through which troops might be able to escape. The move came just in time. The Soviet Forty-Seventh Army attempted to penetrate into Spandau, but this first attack was poorly coordinated and Harzer's troops were able to drive the attackers back with little difficulty.

To the west of Berlin, the leading tanks of the Soviet 35th Guards Mechanised Brigade were leading Lelyushenko's Fourth Guards Tank Army towards the northwest. Just before dawn on 25 April, a machine-gun platoon led by Lieutenant Tsygankov moved through the ruined streets of Ketzin, to the northwest of Potsdam, and made contact with soldiers from 328th Rifle Division and tanks from 65th Guards Tank Brigade, units of 1st Belarusian Front. The pincers around Berlin had closed and the city was cut off. Throughout the morning, more Soviet units arrived to strengthen the ring. With most of the German defenders of Berlin deployed to the east and south of the city centre, the western and northern parts of Berlin were relatively unprotected and the Soviet units began to move through the suburbs, encountering little resistance. In the working-class district of Wedding, a former Communist stronghold, many people greeted the Soviet units with cheers and applause. There were isolated pockets of resistance, for example around the prison in Plötzensee and the *S-Bahn* station in Wedding, but these were rapidly crushed with heavy artillery fire. But as had been the case before, the flak towers continued to frustrate the advance. As XII Guards Rifle Corps moved through Wedding, its eastern flank came under heavy fire from the guns of the Humboldthain Flak Tower, protected by a deep railway cutting. The Soviet troops cautiously bypassed it. The dominating position of the flak towers and the power of their guns enabled them to intervene in fighting at some considerable distance; the Zoo tower, to the west of the city centre, was able to fire on Soviet units four miles to the east.[27]

Further to the east, the defence of the city was stronger. Here, Weidling had the formations of both his LVI Panzer Corps and the better elements of the city garrison at his disposal. To the east of the Humboldthain Flak Tower, the city had suffered heavy damage from air raids earlier in the war and the sea of rubble proved to be an excellent defensive position for tank hunters operating with *Panzerfausts*. The remnants of the paratroopers who had fought on the Seelow Heights were deployed here, but coordination between the various defensive units remained poor – communications were limited and often non-existent, and in any case no commanders had an adequate picture of the battle to be able to do more than make local decisions. Nonetheless, the progress of Third and Fifth Shock Armies into the city in this area was slow, with German troops organising themselves into small combat groups around energetic, experienced officers and NCOs. Operating as combined battalions was almost impossible and would have invited the Red Army to use the full destructive power of its artillery, but small teams of men unconsciously emulated the tactics used by Polish fighters during the Warsaw Uprising of 1944, unaware that in that earlier battle, the Germans had condemned such measures as criminal partisan activity.

After being appointed commander of *SS-Nordland*, Krukenberg had returned to the Olympic Stadium where he had left his French SS soldiers, and then made his way to the headquarters of his new command. For the moment, it was located in Neukölln, in the southern part of Berlin, and he was unimpressed by what he found:

> The entire division was scattered all over the place. Many of the men had simply moved off. The division seemed to have lost its unity … No information was available on the situation in the area … I looked out of the window and in the distance I saw Russian tanks.[28]

Into the City: 23–25 April

The change of command threatened to degenerate into chaos, exacerbated by the high levels of stress under which the soldiers were operating. Krukenberg had ordered his French SS to stand guard outside the headquarters and shortly after Ziegler had departed, a group of half-tracks appeared, carrying wounded men from the division. The French soldiers ordered them to halt, but – perhaps fearing that the men from *SS-Charlemagne* were pro-Russian 'Seydlitz troops' – the driver of the leading half-track ignored them and attempted to drive on. The Frenchmen opened fire, triggering a burst of machine-gun fire in response. Several of the French SS were wounded.[29]

After receiving what little information was available, Krukenberg drove to Weidling's headquarters and told him that *SS-Nordland* amounted to no more than 1,500 men and six assault guns. The division's surviving artillery was in the Tiergarten, with the rear area units somewhere to the west near Spandau. Weidling ordered him to pull any remaining elements of the division out of Neukölln and to move to the east of the city, where they were to be subordinated to Oberst Ernst Siefert, commander of Zone Z. To his dismay, he found that none of the defensive positions that he was supposed to hold actually existed; it added to his growing realisation that the defence of Berlin was utterly disorganised, with overlapping commands and no overall plan.

Chuikov had spent the preceding night preparing for a major assault by his Eighth Guards Army. His divisions were badly depleted, but he still had plentiful artillery to support them:

> I went to my observation post in the morning, in a large five-floor building near the airfield in Johannisthal [between the Spree and a waterway connecting the Teltow and Landwehr Canals]. From the corner room, Berlin was visible through a jagged hole in the wall ... An endless sea of roofs, with gaps here and there – the scars left by bombing. In the distance were factory chimneys and church spires. Parks and squares, already bedecked with young foliage, seemed like pockets of green flames from a distance. The morning fog, mixed with dust from the night's artillery fire, spread through the streets. In places it alternated with black clouds of thick smoke. And somewhere in the centre, yellow bursts of explosions rose into the sky – heavy bombers had already begun working on the main objectives of the coming attack.
>
> Suddenly, the floor beneath my feet trembled and shuddered. Thousands of guns heralded the start of the assault. Looking through the gap in the wall, I could see the outline of the city's defences along the Teltow, Havel, and Tegel Canals, and along the railway lines encircling the city centre. Every house here seemed to be a fortress. And where the walls of the old town rose, there lay the strongest

Nazi defences. The Landwehr Canal and the tight curve of the Spree with its high concrete banks protected the government buildings, including the Reich Chancellery and the Reichstag.

From my observation post I could see the weight of fire that fell on the enemy positions. The walls of houses, loopholed with firing points, collapsed, rubble and barricades blocking the streets flew into the air. Thousands of Germans were dying senselessly, given weapons by Hitler and forced to go to their deaths under our destructive fire.[30]

Chuikov described how his men had reorganised for urban warfare, with small teams of riflemen combining with sappers, mortar units, gun teams, and tanks. Despite having fought in other cities as they advanced west, it seems that many units had to learn the realities of street-fighting once more; at first, columns of tanks had attempted to advance with little support and were then unable to deal with attacks by infantry armed with *Panzerfausts*. Just as the German commanders often had little opportunity to coordinate their various units, the attackers too found that local initiative and resourcefulness were often more important than careful control from above. Suffering and inflicting casualties throughout the day, Eighth Guards Army's divisions managed to penetrate perhaps two miles into southern Berlin, and by the end of the day held a line running from the Spree near the Treptower Park to Mariendorf in the west. There was particularly heavy fighting at the airfield at Tempelhof, where the defenders were reinforced by immobilised tanks that had been dug in up to their turrets. By the end of the day, the Soviet gunners were able to stop the airfield from operating by sweeping its runways with gunfire, but had not succeeded in driving the Germans out of their positions.

Although Chuikov gives the impression of a well-coordinated offensive, the reality around much of Berlin was that the Soviet divisions and corps often didn't cooperate effectively with their neighbours. Zhukov continued to urge his men forward, determined to capture Berlin before Konev's forces from the south could seize the key prestigious positions in the city centre, and this pressure for haste added to the steadily rising casualties on both sides, with Soviet commanders frequently using brutal artillery fire to smash any obstacles in their path. The lack of proper coordination occurred at every level. Rifle companies sometimes found themselves running into the path of attack of neighbouring units; regiments and divisions rarely had a clear understanding of the demarcation lines on their flanks; and although Zhukov issued instructions for boundaries between his armies, these were often ignored by the soldiers on the ground. And as already described, coordination and cooperation at the highest levels were deliberately poor. In particular, Zhukov wanted Eighth Guards Army and First Guards Tank Army to envelop central Berlin from the south in order to block any advance by Konev's armies and he continued to issue orders without any attempt to coordinate with his rival.

Perhaps the worst example of the chaotic consequences of such disregard for neighbouring units occurred when Zhukov ordered his air assets, the bomber squadrons of Sixteenth and Eighteenth Air Armies, to conduct a two-day assault on the German defences. This was codenamed *Privetstviye* ('Salute') and was carried out by about 500 planes. As the British and US aircrews had discovered, precise bombing was almost impossible, and the proximity of Soviet and German ground units worsened matters considerably. Konev described the results:

> During street-fighting in a city, it is generally very difficult to target precise air strikes on the exact objects that are to be attacked. Everything is reduced to ruins, shrouded in flames, smoke, and dust. From above, it is generally difficult to make out where everything is.
>
> From Rybalko's reports, I learned that there were isolated cases when he suffered losses from our air strikes. It was not easy to distinguish which Front's aircraft were hitting their own side in the turmoil of street battles.
>
> And if as a result of certain errors, our own men were hit in the front line, this was always perceived as a severe and dramatic event. This was especially so during the battles for Berlin, and such reports arrived constantly through the entire day of 25 April, both to me and to Zhukov.
>
> The commanders of both Fronts turned to *Stavka* for clarification on the further interaction of the troops fighting in Berlin and to eliminate unnecessary disputes. As a result, a directive from *Stavka* established a new demarcation line running through Mittenwalde, Mariendorf, Tempelhof, and Potsdam Station. All of these locations, as described in the orders, were included in 1st Ukrainian Front's sector.
>
> It was evening before the demarcation line was established, and most of Rybalko's tanks and Batitsky's corps were far beyond the line, in a region that was now under 1st Belarusian Front's control. They had to be pulled back across the line … Everyone knew how psychologically difficult it was for Rybalko to pull his tankers back. After all, they were the first through the breakthrough, the first to turn towards Berlin, to capture Zossen, to cross the Teltow Canal, and to break into the city centre from the outskirts of Berlin in the most brutal and bloody battles, only to receive an order in the midst of the last battle to hand over their sector to their neighbour. Is such a matter easy to accept?

Of course, orders are orders, and must be carried out unconditionally. Everything was accomplished, but it was not easy.[31]

Rybalko's units suffered substantial casualties from Zhukov's air strike; about 100 men were killed, and 16 tanks and six artillery pieces were destroyed. Angrily, Rybalko demanded an investigation into this 'outrageous' incident. If such an enquiry was ever conducted, the outcome was not made public.[32]

Zhukov's memoir contains no mention of the losses suffered by Rybalko's tank units from the air attacks:

> Each army that stormed Berlin had advance routes determined in advance. Units and subunits were given specific objectives – areas, streets, squares. Behind the seeming chaos of urban battles there was a harmonious, carefully thought-out system. The main objectives in the city were taken under devastating fire ...
>
> The goal of street-fighting in Berlin was to deprive the enemy of the opportunity to gather his forces into a concentrated force, to split the garrison into separate pockets and to destroy them rapidly. The necessary preconditions for this solution had been created by the beginning of the operation. First, our troops on the approaches to the city had worn down a significant part of the enemy's manpower and equipment. Secondly, by encircling Berlin quickly, we had deprived the Germans of the opportunity to manoeuvre their reserves. Thirdly, the German reserves that had gathered in Berlin were quickly routed. All of this allowed us, despite numerous obstacles, to reduce street-fighting to a minimum and made it easier for our troops to destroy the enemy's defences inside the city.
>
> Every infantry and tank attack was supported by massive artillery and air strikes, which were carried out on all sections of the front. About 11,000 guns of different calibres opened fire simultaneously at certain moments. From 21 April to 2 May, 1.8 million artillery shells were fired at Berlin. In total, more than 36,000 tons of munitions were hurled at the enemy defences in the city.[33]

This account is misleading on several points. Firstly, boundaries between armies and Fronts had been drawn up, but Zhukov deliberately ignored the boundary dictated by *Stavka* between his 1st Belarusian Front and Konev's 1st Ukrainian Front. Secondly, although boundaries and axes of advance were set for individual armies, the ability of army, corps, and division commanders to keep their forces within their narrow boundaries – especially as armies converged on the centre of Berlin and their frontages became narrower – was frequently compromised, with units often moving laterally to try to bypass German strongpoints. Thirdly, there

Into the City: 23–25 April

is an obvious inconsistency in claiming that street-fighting was kept to a minimum whilst saying that every attack was supported by massive artillery and air power. This may have reduced the amount of ground combat, but at the price of indiscriminate devastation. But by the end of 25 April, Zhukov could relax a little. The change in boundaries dictated by *Stavka* ensured that it would be his armies that took the central part of Berlin.

Konev had his hands full dealing with multiple problems. There remained a threat from the south, where Schörner's attack towards Spremberg had been halted, but difficulties persisted for Second Polish Army. To the west, Wenck's troops were clearly becoming active in their move towards the east. There was heavy fighting along the southern outskirts of Berlin in the north; and to the east, Konev knew that the encircled forces of the German Ninth Army remained intact. Correctly assuming that they would attempt to escape to the west, he took precautions. One of the formations in his Front was 1st Guards Breakthrough Artillery Division, consisting of three mortar brigades, two howitzer brigades, and a field gun brigade. One of its mortar brigades had been sent to Third Guards Tank Army to support its planned attack across the Teltow Canal, but the rest was ordered to deploy in the anticipated path of a breakout by Busse's Ninth Army, supporting two rifle corps. Throughout the war, defending forces on the Eastern Front – particularly on the German side – made highly effective use of artillery fire to crush attacks. The added weight of this division's firepower would make any attempt by Ninth Army to reach safety in the west far more difficult to carry out.

During the evening of 25 April, Weidling reported to Krebs and Hitler in the Reich Chancellery bunker. He attended the evening briefing, noting that Krebs deliberately exaggerated the strength of Twelfth Army and what could be achieved. Amongst those present was Hanna Reitsch, the photogenic female test pilot who had set a series of world records prior to the war and tested an early helicopter as well as participating in the development of the Stuka dive-bomber, the Dornier Do.17 bomber, and the rocket-powered Messerschmitt Me-163. Flying a small Fieseler Storch plane, she had landed on an improvised airstrip created in central Berlin near the Tiergarten accompanied by Generalfeldmarschall Robert Ritter von Greim, a senior Luftwaffe officer who had commanded large-scale formations on the Eastern Front. As they flew in to land, their plane came under fire and Greim was wounded in the foot, but Reitsch was able to land safely and she and Greim were taken by a waiting half-track to the Reich Chancellery. Hitler now informed Greim that he was to replace Göring as head of the Luftwaffe. In improved spirits, the Führer talked confidently about the forces commanded by Steiner, Busse, and Wenck and their impending relief of

Berlin. For Weidling, who would have been able to guess the state of Busse's forces from the fighting that he had experienced on the Seelow Heights, the entire conference must have seemed utterly surreal.

Towards the end of the meeting, Reitsch offered to fly Hitler to safety, but once more he refused. This battle, he assured everyone, would be the decisive engagement of the war, and he couldn't ask the soldiers of the Reich to make such sacrifices if he wasn't prepared to stay with them in the capital. He also ordered a reorganisation of higher commands. Until now, *OKH* had been responsible for the Eastern Front while *OKW* controlled all other theatres, but the shrinking Reich and the use of Wenck's forces – technically under *OKW* – for an attack towards the Eastern Front made such arrangements redundant. Henceforth, *OKW* would be responsible for all operations. Krebs, who was to remain in the bunker with Hitler, would serve as a conduit for Hitler's instructions to *OKW*.[34] He reassured Weidling, telling him that the situation was about to improve greatly and that a decisive victory was at hand. After four hours of enduring the fantasies of Hitler and his inner circle, Weidling returned to his headquarters. Meanwhile, Krebs continued to pass on Hitler's instructions to other commands, more to placate the Führer than out of any expectation that there was any possibility of them being carried out.

Trapped to the southeast of Berlin, Busse attempted to prepare his units for a breakout. Heinrici had requested again that the Luftwaffe fly supplies to the surrounded army, but although several planes were dispatched, once more none reached their destination. The remnants of Ninth Army were now concentrated in a relatively small area – what remained of XI SS-Panzer Corps, V SS Mountain Corps, the Frankfurt garrison, V Corps, and smaller formations. The numbers were further swollen by crowds of rear area personnel – medical teams, female flak and signals personnel, labourers, and thousands of prisoners of war and even forced labourers and concentration camp inmates. Finally, there were tens of thousands of civilians who intended to take whatever chance might come their way to escape from the imminent vengeance of the Red Army. It is difficult to know how many people had gathered in the forests to the east of Halbe; the total may have been as high as 200,000. It was impossible to hide such a concentration of people from the Soviet forces and there were constant air attacks and artillery strikes. Having cleared many of the lakes and waterways that blocked their earlier advances, the surrounding Soviet units were now closing in, steadily compressing the pocket and killing and wounding hundreds with their fire.

Busse had received orders from Keitel to direct his breakout towards Berlin, but – perhaps for the only time in his career – he had no intention of following orders that were utterly unworkable. Instead, he planned to use two battlegroups in an attack towards Baruth, immediately to the west. If Ninth Army could concentrate in that area, it would be possible to launch a further attack that would reach the lines of Twelfth Army. The first battlegroup was made up of SS troops – parts of *SS-Frundsberg* that had been sent to the Cottbus area and had then joined Ninth Army, and yet another improvised unit, 35th *SS-und-Polizei-Grenadier* Division, raised in early 1945 using the personnel of a police training school. The commander of the battlegroup was Standartenführer Rüdiger Pipkorn, who had commanded this new division. Pipkorn had risen to the rank of Oberst in the army before being transferred to the SS; his new rank was regarded as temporary and unlike other SS officers, he was not given a formal SS membership number. He had served as chief of staff to II SS-Panzer Corps during the Battle of Normandy, winning the German Cross in Gold, and was widely respected both by his army and SS contemporaries.

The second battlegroup was made up of the remains of several armoured units and was commanded by Oberst Hans von Luck, a close friend of Pipkorn. Luck started the war with 2nd Light Division, remaining with it when it became 7th Panzer Division until the Battle of Moscow in late 1941. He was then sent to North Africa at the request of Rommel, who had been his division commander in the Battle of France in 1940; after serving with distinction in the desert battles, he fought in Normandy with 21st Panzer Division, and like Pipkorn was regarded as a highly capable panzer commander. He was now ordered to attack that evening with the objective of reaching Luckenwalde; he later recalled that the orders explicitly said that German civilians in the area were not to be made aware of the breakout, as it was feared that the presence of large crowds of refugees would hinder and slow the operation, but word had spread already:

> By 1900 a few more tanks had arrived at my command post, mainly the fast little *Hetzers*. Naturally, our preparations could not remain hidden. At nightfall hundreds of civilians gathered in the village with primitive carts and emergency bundles of belongings. I took no steps to send the pitiable women and children back. I could not and would not do so, though I had the gravest misgivings that they might become involved in fighting.[35]

Luck and his column set off at 2000, accompanied by hundreds of civilians. Pipkorn's group was moving parallel to Luck, a little to the south. The first objective, Baruth, was reached at midnight; here, for the first time, the Germans came under fire. To their alarm, they realised that the village was strongly held by Soviet armour, including heavyweight IS-2s. Fuel and supplies were tightly stretched – Luck had calculated that he had barely enough to reach the Elbe without any detours – but the Soviet defences were too strong to overcome. Luck decided to try bypassing Baruth to the north, with the intention of then clearing it with his panzergrenadiers from the west. Pipkorn's attack, reinforced by the last surviving tanks of *SS-Frundsberg*, also ran into difficulties when it encountered the Soviet 329th Rifle Division. The leading elements were dispersed by energetic flank attacks and only a few elements reached the first objective at Staakow. From here, they were able to continue west to Dornswalde before diverting north to link up with Luck's forces.

At the same time, Wenck's forces attempted to move closer to Busse. The *Ulrich von Hutten* division lost contact with *Theodor Körner* as Soviet units attempted to drive them back. Generalleutnant Gerhard Engel, commander of *Ulrich von Hutten*, later wrote about the fighting:

> The two regiments and their accompanying artillery and assault guns found themselves in battle east and southeast of Wittenberg against three Russian rifle divisions that had just completed their preparations for an attack. Here, as rarely occurred during the war, a proper encounter battle between two spearheads heading in opposite directions unfolded. Both knew little about the other. And as was often the case in the war, here too, with all modesty, I can say about the achievements of our troops that they had the greater energy and the stronger will. With less artillery, which could only take up position once the battle began, supported only by a few stationary anti-aircraft batteries that had previously protected bridges over the Elbe, the two regiments threw back the three Soviet rifle divisions deployed against them a distance of 10km over half a day, liberated isolated German units, and established a bridgehead 15km deep and 30km wide as far as Wittenberg.
>
> This bridgehead was crucial for all other measures taken by the army in its hasty regrouping towards Berlin and thus the basis for the potential rescue of hundreds of thousands of civilians and soldiers.[36]

Engel's success in establishing a substantial position triggered furious Soviet counterattacks, but even though the entire Twelfth Army possessed only a modest number of tanks and assault guns, these were all deployed with *Ulrich von Hutten* and *Theodor Körner* and their firepower permitted the Red Army's assaults to be beaten off. The next phase of Wenck's plan required Engel to move the main strength of his division a little to the north, to Belzig; during the evening, he was able to disengage from the Soviet units around Wittenberg and reach the new positions. But in addition to organising his forces, Wenck had to deal with a constant stream of instructions from *OKW*. Keitel ordered him to pull more troops out of his positions that faced the US Army and prepare them for an attack towards the east, and he was to notify *OKW* immediately with the details of these units. Shortly after, a further order arrived, directing Twelfth Army to attack from Wittenberg and Niemegk towards Jüterbog, where it was to make contact with the leading elements of Ninth Army. Then, the combined forces of the two armies were to turn north towards Berlin.

Trying to push east from Wittenberg would be difficult, given the strong Soviet units that had been identified – these were the formations of V Guards Mechanised Corps, easily strong enough to deal with all of Twelfth Army's modest forces – and it was highly unlikely that the weakened Ninth Army would be able to contribute anything to any attack towards Berlin. In keeping with the best traditions of the German general staff, Wenck and Reichhelm considered their options separately and then compared notes. They found that they had come to identical conclusions and had identified two possible options. The first was to attack towards Potsdam and then link up with forces breaking out of Berlin. Concentrating resources for this operation would be relatively simple and it was anticipated that the Soviet units in the path of the attack were not strong. If such an attack succeeded, contact with Busse's Ninth Army might then be established near Treuenbrietzen. The second option was to shift the centre of operations far to the north and approach Berlin from the northwest. This would take longer to prepare, but Wenck was aware of the presence of *Armeegruppe Steiner* in that general area and considered that combining his forces with those of Steiner might create a favourable situation. For the moment, both officers agreed that the first option should be pursued, as it required less preparation time.

Some distance from Berlin, there was a further noteworthy incident on 25 April. The leading units of Zhadov's Fifth Guards Army had reached the Elbe near the town of Torgau on the evening of 23 April and found the area clear of any opposing forces. During the morning of 25 April, soldiers from 58th Guards Rifle Division had a momentous encounter, as Zhadov later wrote:

> At 1330 near Stehla [to the southeast of Torgau], soldiers of 7 Company, 173rd Guards Rifle Regiment, 58th Guards Rifle Division, led by the company commander, Senior Lieutenant Grigory Stepanovich Goloborodko … noticed a group of soldiers approaching from the west. Our men were habitually wary but their instincts told them that these men were not the same as those they had fought throughout the war. Nevertheless, forming battle formation, Goloborodko's unit moved towards the strangers. As they soon discovered, it was a reconnaissance group of 69th Infantry Division of the US First Army. This group was commanded by Lieutenant [Albert] Kotzebue, a former student from Texas …

About an hour later, near Torgau, soldiers of ... the same 58th Guards Rifle Division noticed a man in military uniform was signalling them from the bell tower of the town church. Lieutenant Aleksandr Semenovich Selvashko tried to speak to him in German, but nothing came of it. Our soldiers fired several shots into the air and suddenly heard familiar words: 'Moscow! America!' It became clear to our Red Army soldiers that the man in the bell tower was an American. He was from the same 69th Infantry Division. Then an officer approached ... and asked our officer to accompany him to his battalion headquarters, some 15km from where the meeting took place.[37]

The US troops in the area were aware that they were about to encounter Soviet units and the need for caution had been stressed – the risk of a 'friendly fire' incident was considerable, and had to be avoided at all costs. The US officer in Torgau, Second Lieutenant William D. Robertson, later described the encounter:

Our division ... had come up to the banks of the Mulde River [about 17 miles to the southwest of Torgau] ... on about 21 April and we stopped and stayed on the west bank for a couple of days. And then the *Burgermeister* of Wurzen wanted the division to cross the river and occupy the town. So we did that and at that point, the Red Army and our army were coming closer together. We did not know where they were – all we knew was that they were somewhere out ahead of us. And they also, we understood later, did not know where we were ... So there was the anticipation of meeting the Red Army and we had instructions that they were going to paint a white stripe around their tanks and ... [they would use] flare signals. I guess there was some concern in higher levels that there might be an unfortunate encounter, that we might mistake each other for enemies ... I'm not sure that was really going to be a possibility because I think that there was so much anticipation in both armies ... that everyone was going to be cautious ...

At that time there were hordes, hundreds and hundreds of refugees of all descriptions – released prisoners, escaped POWs, German refugees and what I guess were called slave labourers who were coming into the American lines. I was an intelligence officer for our battalion ... it was my job to make plans for accommodating these refugees ... I can remember a group that came in of Allied prisoners that included men of almost all nations in the world. There were Sikhs with their turbans, black troops from Africa, French, Polish, all races ... One day I went out to count roughly how many hundreds were coming into our camp ... and I took a jeep with three men and went up and down several roads outside our town counting refugees, counting surrendering German troops too, and on one road we decided we'd go up aways and we kept on going until we got to Torgau ...

We were not fired on until we got to Torgau, then there was some scattered fire. We went across the town. After liberating some Allied prisoners in a prison camp in Torgau [we found] two Americans, one was an ensign from the navy, called Peck, and a sergeant. They had been in the OSS and they joined our patrol. There were now six of us … we made a makeshift flag and climbed a tower in a castle on the bank of the Elbe just by a blown-up bridge and we waved the flag. The Russians fired several times …, finally we encountered a Russian POW from the same prison camp who spoke German and instructed him to tell his Russian colleagues on the other side of the Elbe River that we were Americans and not Germans. So he shouted across and then the firing ceased … I crawled across the girders of this bridge …

We met the Russians and I have no recollections of any of their names now … We saluted each other, exchanged cap badges and wristwatches and mementos, we slapped each other on the back and shook hands. They produced some schnapps, and we toasted each other and all our leaders.[38]

The link-up between Soviet and US troops divided what remained of the Reich into two, bringing the end to the war closer.

Chapter 10

DISINTEGRATION: 26–28 APRIL

26 April

Stettin, close to the Baltic coast, had a long history of having a mixed population of Poles and Germans. Prior to Hitler's accession of power, the Polish population had gradually declined and numbered no more than about 2,000 by 1933; this small number dwindled still further after the Nazis enacted a number of discriminatory policies against Poles. A Polish-language school in Stettin was closed down, and many prominent Poles, including teachers from the school, were imprisoned and even killed.[1] After the war commenced, Stettin became a hub of a network of labour camps, many of them for Polish forced labourers; these workers helped manufacture armaments for the Reich. Despite the years of repression, there was still a small Polish community in the city and after the war accounts were published of the anti-Nazi resistance work of the Poles in and around Stettin. Given that the city became the Polish city of Szczecin, there was a clear political benefit in amplifying such stories, and more recently the accuracy of many of these accounts has been disputed.[2]

Almost inevitably, Stettin was one of the cities declared by Hitler to be 'fortresses', requiring their defence to the last bullet. By the end of 25 April 1945, it was clear to Manteuffel that Stettin would have to be abandoned. He had withdrawn much of the garrison to fight elsewhere, and the remaining defenders were now too weak to hold the defences. Moreover, Generalleutnant Alfred Jacobi, the fortress commander, reported that the morale of the men was close to collapse. During the night of 25 April, after beating off repeated Soviet incursions during the afternoon and evening, what remained of the garrison slipped away to the west almost unmolested. In his memoirs, Rokossovsky wrote about how his men took the city by storm, but whilst fighting had been intense on 25 April, the withdrawal of Jacobi's men was relatively uneventful. They left behind a city in which two thirds of the buildings had been destroyed. Last-minute demolitions in the port added to the damage.

Rokossovsky moved his headquarters into Stettin almost immediately, while the focus of fighting shifted to the west. He wrote about the intensity of the battles and the heavy losses that were inflicted on the retreating Germans, describing desperate counterattacks, but most of the units of Third Panzer Army were simply trying to pull back before they were overwhelmed. Morale in many units had plummeted. Manteuffel did what he could, shuffling units from one sector to another, but the disintegration of his Third Panzer Army was clear for all to see. For the moment, German artillery units continued to batter the advancing Soviet units, but it was inevitable that the line would break up at some point and Manteuffel asked Heinrici for mobile forces that might be able to intercept a Soviet breakthrough. In turn, Heinrici contacted Krebs. Continuing to demand an attack towards Berlin by *Armeegruppe Steiner* was pointless, he said, and Steiner's units would be far more effective if deployed in the north. Krebs was sympathetic, but Hitler refused, reiterating his orders for all available units to attack towards Berlin. Concluding that this made any further defence of Third Panzer Army's current positions impossible, Heinrici gave Manteuffel permission to pull back towards the west.

Following an early morning thunderstorm, the skies over Berlin were cloudless on 26 April, allowing Soviet aircraft to operate freely. Below them, the battle for the city continued. To the west of Berlin, Second Guards Tank Army – now largely reunited with its subordinate formations – pushed further into Spandau, capturing much of Siemensstadt during the day. Helmut Altner and his remaining comrades were in the area, marching back and forth in response to contradictory orders. They watched a young SS officer turning back any soldiers moving away from the front line, threatening them with his pistol; they were told that he had previously commanded a punishment battalion, driving his men to attacks that resulted in huge losses, and wouldn't hesitate to shoot anyone who refused to obey him. After losing several men in battles with Soviet tanks and accompanying infantry on 25 April, Altner and the other survivors were in the Siemens factory and were ordered to move to the western part of Spandau. It seemed that there were sounds of fighting all around and there was little by way of a formal front line – the units of both sides were entangled in the streets. After a couple of close encounters, Altner's group found themselves in an apartment block:

> The Leutnant suddenly enters the apartment saying that several companies are supposed to be on their way to reinforce us and we will soon be relieved, but I

do not believe it any more. We have been lied to too often. As always, we will have to make our own way out, and this bitter fighting will not end until death sets us free.

Once he has left the room, I go out into the back yard … some children are playing in a box of yellow sand in a corner of the yard and several of the tenants are standing around snatching a quick breath of fresh air after hours in the stuffy cellar. They are conjecturing about how the Russians will behave. The women are frightened, and they are all worried about the horrors the next few hours will inevitably bring. But it will be a new experience, and the end of what they have been going through. Better an uncertain future than the deadly present.[3]

A few moments later, shelling began and the civilians fled back to the shelter. Altner and his comrades exchanged fire with Soviet soldiers in the block facing them and a tank appeared. When the firing died down, the young soldiers realised that their major, who had seemed to be sitting quietly behind them, was dead. More Soviet tanks appeared, their gunfire reducing the German-occupied buildings to rubble, and the small group pulled back to a nearby police school. When they finally caught their breath, Altner and the others were forced to hand over their paybooks to an officer of the SS. One of the SS soldiers with him then quipped that the Red Army would shoot anyone captured without a paybook; the soldiers interpreted this as a cynical attempt to force them to fight to the death.

Shortly after, a column of men marched up:

The leader of this outfit, a political officer with an armband worked in gold, lets them fall out. A couple of the youngsters lie down near us. A small lad looks at our cigarettes with eyes full of longing and we call him over. He comes across slowly and sits down beside us. We ask him his age. 'Thirteen,' he replies.[4]

The boy told them that he and others had been rounded up by an officer of the SS and had been involved in fighting for several days, during which most had been killed. When their 15-year-old platoon commander had refused an order to move them to a new location – he wanted to send the survivors home – he had been hanged by two SS men.[5] They were part of a replacement draft organised for one of the last divisions to be raised by the SS, 32nd *SS-Freiwilligen-Division 30. Januar*, named after the day that Hitler became Reich chancellor in 1933. Nearly all of the 'soldiers' in this replacement battalion were teenagers, and most would be dead before the end of the war. There was no real justification for terming the unit *Freiwilligen* ('Volunteer'), and the original intention had been to create a new panzergrenadier division, but this proved impossible given the limitations on supplies of vehicles, fuel, etc. The bulk of the division was fighting with the encircled units of Ninth Army; there was never any possibility of this replacement battalion reaching its parent unit.

The attack into Spandau was made by the Soviet Forty-Seventh Army, which was trying to make up for its failed attack the previous day. This time, the attack was far more methodical with powerful artillery strikes at any suspected German positions preceding the infantry advance. When the riflemen moved forward, they carefully outflanked the remaining German positions. By the end of the day, the Germans were still clinging to the Havel crossings in the northern part of Spandau, but most of the rest of the district was in the hands of the Red Army. Here too, the big guns of the flak towers intervened; fired from five miles to the southeast, the 128mm shells from the Tiergarten Flak Tower struck into the rear area of Forty-Seventh Army, disrupting movements repeatedly.

Chuikov continued to batter his way into Neukölln. Although few if any of the senior commanders mentioned the rivalry between the commanders of the two Soviet Fronts, it seems to have been common knowledge amongst their subordinates. The commander of one of Chuikov's rifle corps encountered the journalist Vasily Grossman close to the front line and told him jokingly:

> Now we should be scared not of the enemy, but of our neighbours. I've ordered that the burnt-out tanks should be used to block our neighbours from getting to the Reichstag. There's nothing more depressing in Berlin than learning about the successes of your neighbours.[6]

This was the second day of air attacks ordered by Zhukov during which Rybalko's tank units suffered casualties, and Chuikov added to the chaos by ordering his artillery to bombard areas that he must have known by this stage were occupied by Third Guards Tank Army. To the north, the other Soviet armies attacking into Berlin's eastern sectors were meeting tough resistance and repeated counterattacks. The huge losses suffered by the rifle companies in their advance to Berlin left the Soviet units barely able to cope; with their infantry support thus reduced, the tank formations suffered heavy losses in close-quarter encounters with German defenders.

In his headquarters in Bendlerstrasse, just to the south of the Tiergarten, Weidling and his staff could see multiple threats developing. The advance by Soviet forces into southeast Berlin – by Eighth Guards Army – was steadily approaching the central part of the city. The line along the southern edge, following the canals of the city, was too thin to stand up to significant attacks, and to the west, it was essential to hold positions along the Havel in the hope that

Wenck's Twelfth Army would arrive in the next few days. The forces available to Weidling were too weak to deal with all of these for more than the immediate future, and he made his dispositions. What remained of *SS-Nordland*, backed by the small contingent from *SS-Charlemagne*, was to counterattack in the southeast in Neukölln; and 18th Panzergrenadier Division was to try to restore contact with 20th Panzergrenadier Division in the west. However, given the hopelessness of the situation, Weidling drew up plans for a breakout towards the area that he expected Wenck would be approaching.

That evening, after a difficult drive through the city streets – at one point, the car carrying Weidling and Refior, chief of staff of the Berlin defence forces, slipped into a shell crater and a low-hanging telegraph wire nearly decapitated Refior – Weidling briefly discussed the situation with Krebs before presenting his proposals to Hitler. He stressed the growing shortage of ammunition and the steadily accumulating casualties and then outlined his planned breakout. He intended to conduct the operation on 28 April with the most combat-worthy elements of LVI Panzer Corps, concentrated around about 40 operational tanks, leading the way. This group would be followed by what he described as the *Führergruppe* consisting of Hitler and other senior figures, escorted by *Kampfgruppe Mohnke*; the rearguard would consist of the survivors of the *Müncheberg* panzer division reinforced by other remnants.[7] Immediately, Goebbels objected angrily, but Hitler appeared to consider the plans with some care. He then replied that even if the breakout succeeded in penetrating the Soviet encirclement, it would merely represent escape from one encirclement into another. Rather than face the inevitable end in some isolated farmhouse or in the open air, Hitler told Weidling, he preferred to remain in the Reich Chancellery. He therefore refused permission for a breakout, with no regard for the fact that this decision forced the entire garrison to share his personal fate in the ruins of Berlin.

For Weidling, this was a great disappointment. He had not wanted to get his corps involved in the battle for Berlin, and now felt that his last hope of saving some of his men had disappeared. After he returned to the old army buildings on Bendlerstrasse where the July Plot had unravelled just a few months before, he was told that Goebbels wished to speak to him on the telephone. Weidling had placed Generalmajor Werner Mummert, commander of *Müncheberg*, in command of Berlin's Sectors A and B. But he now learned that Erich Bärenfänger, a young Wehrmacht officer who had enjoyed a spectacular rise through the ranks – aged just 30, he was a Generalmajor – had been transferred to the SS with the rank of Brigadeführer and was to replace Mummert. A devoted Nazi, Bärenfänger was a close friend of Goebbels and had used his influence to secure this post. For Weidling, struggling to prevent the complete collapse of his units in what was clearly the closing phase of the war against the Soviet Union, such machinations seemed utterly bizarre. Almost immediately, Bärenfänger started to take advantage of his new authority. Towards the end of the day, as units of *Müncheberg* fell back towards Alexanderplatz, Bärenfänger personally stopped them and issued *Panzerfausts* to their officers, ordering them to join the tank-hunter groups defending the city.

Krukenberg, who had inherited command of *SS-Nordland*, also visited the Reich Chancellery bunker, and complained about the dispersed state of his division. He was particularly unhappy that he was under the command of Siefert, a Wehrmacht officer – like several SS officers during the war, he resented being answerable to someone who was not in the SS. Fegelein and Mohnke were sympathetic, and the latter ordered Krukenberg to move his headquarters to a *U-Bahn* station in the city centre; his division was to take up defensive positions defending the government quarter to the east and southeast. Any relief that Krukenberg might have felt at receiving these instructions soon disappeared when he reached what he had expected to be a prepared location for his new headquarters:

> I thought that some sort of a defence had been set up for the centre of Berlin. I found absolutely nothing. In the *U-Bahn* station for example, where my command post was to be, and which I thought had already been set up, I found that there were no lights, no telephone, there was a single wagon standing in the station, and that was all. I now had to install all the necessary items that a command post needed. I didn't have the faintest idea what was going on because nobody had even supplied me with maps and I never did get correct maps showing the situation as it developed.[8]

None of the SS officers involved in this decision bothered to inform Weidling. He lost control of the division and learned about the decision only indirectly, adding to his already strong distrust of the SS.

In Neukölln, the counterattack launched by Weidling ran into units of Eighth Guards Army advancing in the opposite direction. A group of panzergrenadiers from *SS-Charlemagne* rapidly lost much of its strength in close-quarter combat but managed to battle through to Herzbergplatz, to the east of the Tempelhof airfield, but the counterattack soon found itself in an isolated salient with Soviet units on three sides with just a handful of Hitler Youth as reinforcements. Increasingly, men from different units were fighting alongside each other in improvised battlegroups. Many of the survivors of *SS-Nordland* found themselves

Disintegration: 26–28 April

to the northeast of Tempelhof; adding a number of survivors of *Müncheberg* and small groups of *Volkssturm* and Hitler Youth to their numbers, they took up defensive positions and waited for the next Soviet assault.

The fighting for Tempelhof saw heavy losses on both sides. Vladimir Ivanovich Abyzov, a soldier in 39th Guards Rifle Division, described the fighting and how he and his comrades grabbed abandoned German weapons and put them to use:

> Artillery roared and thundered. Mortars cracked angrily. Submachine-gunners fired continuously to the right and left and from somewhere above.
>
> All the city was ablaze. Thick, foul smoke lapped over the rooftops and lay heavily over the scarred landscape. It seeped into houses and basements through every possible gap. The air became unbreathable. But despite this, we ran, dropped to the ground between the roadblocks, then rose and ran further through gardens, along or across the streets, slinging hand grenades into the empty eye sockets of the windows.
>
> Our regiment had been involved in street fighting for more than five days now, a different kind of warfare from what we had been taught. There was no clear front line, nor was there a proper rear area, or even a battle plan that had been carefully thought through. Your front line was where you were – here on the first floor, with the ground floor your rear area. But in five or ten minutes it could all change and become utter confusion. The Germans somehow appeared on the ground floor and the second floor was engulfed by fire. Where was the front or rear area, as described in the infantry field manual?
>
> In the beginning of the street fighting, we tried to use camouflage, dropping to the ground and sometimes trying to dig foxholes with our entrenching tools. But later we had no time to dig in. Push on! Push on! Once though, we did wish for our entrenching tools. It was when we were fighting for Tempelhof. We were on one side of the runway and German tanks were dug into the other side. The Nazi tanks were firing armour-piercing rounds. They would strike in front of or behind us with hollow sounds, like fat quails falling on cut grass in the autumn. We used knives and our hands to dig in. Why had we thrown away our shovels?
>
> We burst into a five-floor building, throwing hand grenades through the doorway beforehand. We then swept the rooms. We took the first three floors. Half the building was in our hands, the other half still held by the Germans. We were separated by a very thick wall. Junior Lieutenant Sorokin called out to Medvedev: 'Breach the wall with your *Panzerfaust*!' Standing in a doorway, Medvedev aimed the weapon at the wall. There was a flash of flame and a blast, then a lot of dust and smoke. We could see nothing. We fumbled our way to the wall, expecting to find a big hole. But there was no hole, just a small crater.[9]

Tanks from First Guards Tank Army were meant to be operating in support of Chuikov's riflemen, but the chaos described by Abyzov was almost universal and often the tanks found themselves lacking infantry support, while the riflemen struggled to advance without armour. A column of T-34s attempted to push north between Neukölln and Tempelhof without infantry support but suffered heavy losses when attacked with *Panzerfausts*, and those that managed to drive past the German defenders ran into a King Tiger, suffering further losses. In another ambush, several unaccompanied Soviet tanks were destroyed in Hermannplatz, close to the northeast corner of Tempelhof, by two assault guns from *SS-Nordland*. But not all of the disorganisation was due to the chaotic circumstances of street warfare. Katukov made matters worse than they might have been:

> We had been advancing in the same zone as Chuikov's army, and according to Zhukov's orders he [Chuikov] was in charge. But the situation in the city was different and I asked the Front commander to give the tank army an independent zone of attack in Berlin. Zhukov agreed to my proposal. However, he ordered that 64th Separate Tank Brigade and the heavy assault gun regiment should be allocated to Eighth Guards Army as armoured support. I had to part with these units.[10]

It seems remarkable that Katukov effectively requested a zone in which he could operate without infantry support, and that Zhukov agreed. To an extent, this may have been due to inexperience of urban warfare; Katukov may have been motivated by a desire to compete for the prize of penetrating into the city centre first; and Zhukov was determined that his armies were going to the heart of Berlin before Konev's troops. It is impossible to know how many Soviet soldiers paid in blood for this determination to race ahead as fast as possible, but these tactics contributed greatly to the manner in which the front line became disordered, with isolated German pockets resurfacing behind advancing Soviet troops and adding to the general confusion.

A further heavy artillery bombardment by Chuikov's gunners in the early evening broke the back of the German resistance in Neukölln and the fighting continued into the night. Late in the evening, Soviet tanks reached Kurfürstendamm, one of the main thoroughfares of Berlin, close to the Kaiser Wilhelm Memorial Church. A young Soviet officer was in a tank that approached the church from the southeast:

> We didn't meet serious resistance until the intersection of Kurfürstenstrasse and Keithstrasse. Here, a large group of Hitlerites had gathered and opened fire with

all sorts of weapons, forcing the assault group to dismount and fight for every room and building until we broke into Keithstrasse. The street was reached with minimal losses but it wasn't possible to cross it. To make matters worse, the far side of the street had been reduced to rubble by bombing.

The Germans had prepared proper defences in this area. I can still remember the gates and doors, all barricaded from the inside. I remember a building on the corner to the left, from which anti-aircraft guns and machine-guns fired on the street. Snipers were everywhere. Our command issued orders: we were to take this intersection at all costs and take Kurfürstenstrasse as far as the zoo, so that we could later push on down Keithstrasse to the Landwehr Canal and the Tiergarten. After careful reconnaissance, we estimated that the enemy's strength was concentrated in the first 100–150m with fewer Germans further away. So after bypassing this group, we exploited our success quickly. Then Captain Kabanov, the tank battalion commander, took a bold step.

The majority of the group mounted up again on the tanks. The first group was armed with assault rifles. Several tanks moved forward first, a small distance ahead, and then raced at full speed through the streets and junctions held by the enemy. They were told to throw hand grenades at the enemy as they passed.

Covered by the thundering fire from our vehicles and constant rifle fire, the tanks raced ahead at top speed. Walls crumbled and glass shattered, bricks and plaster flew everywhere and dust and smoke filled the street. This dismayed the Germans so much that some of them ran away, throwing away their weapons, while others were too scared to raise their hands.

But some Germans continued to fire *Panzerfaust* rounds. The constant firing of the assault group kept them at bay and the *Panzerfaust* rounds fell short. A German machine-gun opened up but was quickly silenced. After driving through a dangerous road junction, the assault group surrounded a handful of Germans. Some were cut down, others surrendered, and the road to the Landwehr Canal was cleared.[11]

This rapid drive down Keithstrasse amounted to an advance of barely 200m, but it gives a good picture of the nature of the battle. The Soviet troops were now forced to deal with the flak tower complex located in the southwest corner of the Tiergarten. Some of the anti-aircraft personnel in the tower were sent into the neighbouring streets to engage Soviet armour with *Panzerfausts*, and some of these teams suffered injuries due to their inexperience with the anti-tank weapons, getting caught in the back-blast when they were fired. Red Army snipers began to drive gunners on the flak towers to take cover, but for the moment the Soviet forces remained mainly south of the Landwehr Canal. In places, the fighting was underground in the numerous *U-Bahn* and *S-Bahn* tunnels, where thousands of terrified civilians had taken shelter. Soldiers from *Müncheberg* took shelter in the tunnels near the Anhalter station, but suddenly they and the civilians experienced a new threat: the tunnels began to fill with water. Some accounts written after the war suggested that this was deliberately done by the SS, but given the number of military units that had their headquarters in the tunnels, this seems unlikely. The entire area was under heavy shellfire, and damage caused by the exploding artillery rounds is a more likely cause of the flooding. Desperately, the soldiers and civilians tried to climb to safety. Many were killed in the panic and crush.

Chuikov's thrust had – deliberately – crossed the boundary designated by *Stavka* between 1st Belarusian Front and 1st Ukrainian Front. Rybalko's tank army had intended to drive into this area, and if Konev had acted with the same level of disregard as Zhukov, his artillery would have inflicted heavy losses on Eighth Guards Army. Instead, Third Guards Tank Army angled away towards the northwest, avoiding a direct confrontation with Chuikov's troops. This was as much due to luck as it was to judgement; neither Front had a clear idea of the precise location of the formations of the other. On Chuikov's northern flank, the two shock armies continued their slow grind into the centre of Berlin. The fighting was now centred on the *Museumsinsel* ('Museum Island') in the Spree; backed by *Volkssturm* and Hitler Youth, a battlegroup from *SS-Nordland* put up fierce resistance, driving back elements of XI Tank Corps and their accompanying infantry. Loudspeaker appeals to the Germans to lay down their weapons and avoid unnecessary bloodshed went unanswered.

Nearly every part of Berlin was now experiencing artillery barrages, adding to the chaos and terror caused by Soviet air attacks. The anonymous female diarist was queuing for food when an air attack on Berlinerstrasse, in the northern part of the city, drove everyone to cover. Every attempt to venture out to search for food risked sudden death, but there were unexpected finds. When foraging in a nearby building, the diarist and several other civilians came across a horde of items – canned food, bread, alcohol, even a side of beef. They took what they could, sometimes clashing with others bent on similar looting, and returned to their shelter. Towards the end of the day, their building took a direct hit from an artillery shell, reducing much of it to rubble, but those hiding in the basement were safe for the moment:

> I want to go to sleep right away. I'm looking forward to it. The day's been packed to the brim. The net result: I'm healthy, bold and bright; for the moment my fear is mostly gone. My brain is full of vivid images of greed and rage. Stiff back, tired feet, broken thumbnail, a cut lip that's still smarting. So the saying's true after all: 'What doesn't kill you makes you stronger.'

One more thing. An image from the street: a man pushing a wheelbarrow with a dead woman on top, stiff as a board. Loose grey strands of hair fluttering, a blue kitchen apron. Her withered legs in grey stockings sticking out the end of the wheelbarrow. Hardly anyone gave her a second glance. Just like when they used to ignore the rubbish being hauled away.[12]

To the southeast of Berlin, the German Ninth Army continued its attempts to escape to the west. Hans von Luck had been told by Busse that his armoured group would be followed closely by infantry, but to Luck's dismay none appeared. Aware that his tanks had barely enough fuel and ammunition for the drive to the Elbe and Wenck's Twelfth Army, Luck signalled Busse that he wanted to press on to the north of Baruth before dawn. Busse ordered him to hold his positions until other elements of Ninth Army arrived. Pipkorn had joined Luck and the two men discussed the situation. Deciding that any delay would only give the Red Army time to strengthen their positions, they agreed to attack immediately. Pipkorn's tanks would try to pin down the Soviet troops in the eastern part of Baruth while Luck moved around their northern flank.

Almost immediately, the plan began to unravel. Pipkorn was killed when his tanks moved forward and, gathering all the remaining vehicles, Luck set off on his outflanking attempt. The German column was accompanied by crowds of civilians, and as they moved through dense woodland, they came under heavy artillery fire. Shells sprayed shrapnel and wooden splinters in all directions, slaughtering dozens of civilians and soldiers who were accompanying the armoured vehicles. Before long, the column found itself engaged by Soviet riflemen and anti-tank guns, followed by a strong Soviet attack from the south. Ammunition rapidly began to run short and Luck gathered his men for one last attempt. The last of the fuel was siphoned from all vehicles into the remaining tanks, which were ordered to try to break through to the west in small groups. The doctor attached to Luck's battlegroup volunteered to remain with the wounded; Luck himself decided to head back into the encirclement with his adjutant and a few others to report to Busse:

> I could see in each of them how hard the moment was for them, but also that my decision was understood. I had no wish to be regarded as a coward or a deserter; that much I owed myself. While the unit commanders said goodbye to each other, we grasped our machine-pistols and set off on foot along the route back into the pocket.
>
> As I heard many years later, a few small groups did in fact succeed in reaching the Elbe and falling into American hands. The bulk of my officers and men ended

up in captivity. As for the women and children, I have never been able to discover anything about their fate.[13]

Busse would later attempt to blame Luck for the failure of this first breakout, claiming that he should have waited until more troops arrived. But Luck knew that any delay cost him precious fuel; it is certainly arguable that responsibility for the failure lay with Busse for not ensuring that sufficient troops were gathered for Luck's attempt. In many respects, Busse was floundering as an army commander. He had served in the Reichswehr – the small army permitted by the Treaty of Versailles – between the wars, and for many years he had marked time while other more capable officers rose through the ranks. His later promotion was largely due to the rapid expansion of the Wehrmacht by Hitler. Unable to contemplate deliberate disobedience, and rarely showing much independence of thought, he refused to make any preparations for a breakout until he received explicit permission from Hitler, and this delay cost Ninth Army heavily.

Late on 26 April, fighting flared up again along the western side of Ninth Army's encirclement. There is little to suggest that this was instigated by any orders from Busse; rather, it was the result of elements of the three remaining corps in Ninth Army reaching the area and attempting to push west. They ran into the guns of 1st Guards Breakthrough Artillery Division and suffered heavy losses, often engaging the Soviet gunners at close range. After rallying, the Germans tried again, and were once more driven off. All the time, Soviet bombers and ground-attack aircraft were overhead, often bombing the dense woodland at random and killing dozens of German soldiers and civilians.

In the west, Wenck now attacked north towards Potsdam, hindered as much by hordes of refugees on every road as by Soviet resistance. Led by a modest reconnaissance detachment, *Ulrich von Hutten* moved north, with its eastern flank protected by two divisions – *Scharnhorst*, created from the remnants of two infantry divisions in March 1945, and *Theodor Körner*. Almost immediately, the advance ran into the Soviet VI Guards Mechanised Corps. Despite Hitler's proclamation being distributed freely in leaflets, thus depriving Wenck of any chance of achieving surprise, it seems that the Soviet troops were not expecting this attack. The corps commander, Major General Vasily Ignatyevich Koretsky, had taken up the post at short notice before the advance on Berlin began after the death of his predecessor near Oppeln, and his units fell back in disarray; several supply vehicles and a tank repair workshop were captured by the advancing Germans.

Konev had spent the preceding days with his earlier confidence and satisfaction slowly being eroded by concern at the attacks on his forces from the east and west. He responded rapidly, dispatching several rifle divisions to block any attempt by Ninth Army to escape. As 26 April progressed, he set up three defensive lines extending to a depth of up to 12 miles; if Busse's troops were to break out, they would have to fight almost all the way to Wenck's lines. Konev also wanted to send reinforcements to deal with Wenck's attack; in particular, he was frustrated that he was unable to divert X Guards Tank Corps to the south, but this formation was heavily committed in fighting around the western side of Berlin, attempting to defeat German troops defending the southern approaches to Wannsee and Potsdam. Here, any Soviet advance was hampered by the Havel and several large lakes, channelling the attackers into predictable channels. The defenders were under the command of Reymann, who had been dismissed as *Kampfkommandant* of Berlin just a few days before. With a rag-tag force of several thousand men, he put up fierce resistance, hoping that Wenck would be able to reach him before his men ran out of ammunition.

27 April

With Heinrici unable to give him the mobile forces he needed to restore his positions, Manteuffel effectively gave up any attempt to hold a strong defensive line against the advancing forces of Rokossovsky's 2nd Belarusian Front. A group of Soviet tanks burst through the German lines at Prenzlau and rapidly advanced west. As had been anticipated on the German side for several days, units now disintegrated completely, including 3rd Marine Division, which had been involved in fighting ever since the Soviet forces began their assault. The orders from Berlin continued to bear no relation to the reality on the ground. At midday, Krebs informed Heinrici that having failed to attack towards Berlin, Steiner was to be relieved of this task, which would now be conducted by Generalleutnant Rudolf Holste, commander of XVI Panzer Corps. He was to have two divisions – 25th Panzergrenadier Division and 7th Panzer Division – placed at his disposal. Heinrici had no intention of allowing these soldiers to be thrown into a pointless attack and ensured that they remained in the north.

What remained of 7th Panzer Division, which Manteuffel had commanded earlier in the war, was mainly some distance behind the front line. After fighting in Lithuania in late 1944, the division had been in almost constant action after Rokossovsky's forces burst into East Prussia in early 1945 and had retreated west across the Vistula before being driven into a small coastal pocket to the north of Danzig. From here, its soldiers – without any of their tanks and vehicles – were evacuated by sea first to the naval base at Hela, and then to northern Germany.

Officially, their units were to be re-equipped and restored to full strength, but the reality was that the soldiers were relieved to be taken west, thus reducing the risk of becoming prisoners in the Soviet Union. Some 82 tanks had been provided for the reconstitution of the division, but there was almost no fuel or ammunition for them and many had already been lost through immobility. Now, with the Red Army driving west towards the Danish border, Soviet captivity seemed a real threat once more, but both Manteuffel and Oberst Hans Christern, the division commander, intended to get as many of their men to the west as possible, where they could surrender to the British and Americans. Johann Huber had joined the division as a potential officer during the autumn of 1944 and had served as a tank crewman in the battles that followed; he kept a diary of his experiences. He and many other soldiers of the division were currently gathered into an improvised infantry formation and were billeted in a farm:

> In the morning, when we go outside, we can faintly hear the front to the east. It's rumbling; the Russians are coming. The Wehrmacht report, that we listen to every day, says nothing about it. Defensive fighting, everywhere defensive fighting, on the western front and of course against the Red Army, which is attacking Berlin. The dull sounds are from the front, about 40km away. The women are anxious. They tremble visibly, and the children cling to their mother, following her everywhere. The farmer's wife asks us what will happen now. We advise her: leave, flee! Our opinion is based on experience: what the Russians take, they never give back.
>
> I look at the women in silence, aware of what will happen to them if the front rolls over them. We know these situations only too well – rape, beatings, shootings, and plenty more. We have a horror of the atrocities perpetrated by the Russians on every sector of the front.
>
> We tell the people to hurry, to pack and flee, and they decide to do so an hour later. Finally!
>
> The grumble from the front, which has grown much louder, helps them make their decision. As there is nothing to do until midday, we help them to prepare the two carts for which they have horses. We advise them on what to take with them and what they should leave here. The farmer's wife stands hopelessly in front of her good porcelain, which is apparently very valuable. Plates, cups, dishes – and the table silver, which is antique. We bury it all beneath the threshing floor. 'Just in case we can come back!' Fritz and I look at each other – come back? We know that will never happen. The Russians will take away everything, nobody will see their property again.
>
> The big hole we dig in the threshing floor to bury valuables poses problems. We can't just stamp the earth down, as that will break something. So we have to

smooth the surface carefully, as best we can, pressing it down with our shoes, so that it looks like the rest of the floor and not like newly dug earth. The Russians find these things so quickly – they have a nose for such matters. Anyhow, we have helped the woman, and she's pleased that at least her good things have been hidden.

In the afternoon, a messenger summons us. The front is growing ever louder, and we are clearly waiting for orders to go into action. We are to assemble in the village square immediately. Our family continues to pack, and we go to Überend without our weapons to find out what the orders are.

Once we're assembled, our company commander, who has been living in the pastor's house next to the church, arrives. One of the Feldwebels calls us to attention. Oberleutnant P speaks to us in clipped phrases, saying that we are now facing hard times and that it might be good for us to have a field service. He has therefore spoken to the village pastor and the service is ready. So we march into the church, silently, everyone thinking that what P has arranged at this moment is probably the right thing to do. We sit silently and thoughtfully in the half-dark church and wait for the evangelical pastor, who is holding a service just for us. Nobody else is there. I have very mixed feelings and, when I look at my comrades, I see that they feel the same – everyone stares at his shoes, their faces down.

After the service is finished, Oberleutnant P passes the word. Quietly and calmly, he explains to us that the war is going to end. Like a flash, his words go through me, words that until now nobody was allowed to speak without being court-martialled. But P continues. He tells us that we should understand that the war can no longer be won. 'The war can only be ended with a compromise. Comrades, many of us no longer have a homeland – our homeland is now the regiment, our colours. Let us remain true to our colours, even if we no longer have a homeland.'

What he says is very cruel – we have until now fought through the months and years to keep the enemy from the homeland, from Germany! But actually it is also good, if things are coming to an end, and this dreadful war will finally be over. For me it is still all so unclear: how long will it last? What did he mean? Perhaps two months? I can't figure it out, and Fritz, who is standing next to me outside the church, also wonders how long the war can still go on.

Today no orders arrive, but we will have to assemble early in the morning. We can go back to our quarters for the rest of today. We go to our farmhouse. The whole family is waiting for us; they want to leave. It's high time. It's a parting with heartfelt words, sad for the women, sad for us, with everyone facing an unknown fate. We tell them, though, that we have been told that the war can no longer be won. We can say these things, now.

All day, the noise from the front has grown louder. Are the Russians getting closer? After our civilians have left, we conclude that we will have to go into action in the morning. After our advice, they set off very late, not far ahead of the Russians, whose tanks are fast enough to overhaul them.

It's another lovely spring evening, we feel, so we sit outside and chat. The front grumbles loudly to the east, but nobody mentions it.

Suddenly, there is an enormous thunderclap. We get up. Directly to the east, far, far away, a huge cloud of smoke rises into the air. The distance to the smoke is at least 25 kilometres, it must be in Neubrandenburg. It is an ammunition dump that has exploded. Slowly, the smoke column rises higher, it must already be 3km high, and it broadens, its underside lit up by dark red reflected flames. It must have been a tremendous explosion, and we wouldn't have wanted to be anywhere near it.

Everyone looks at the horrifying smoke, which is now 5–6km high – we check it every ten minutes, as it broadens and flattens. The Russians are therefore already there, it can't be more than 25km. So it's going to kick off again tomorrow, we can count on that.[14]

Keitel, who had left Berlin to join the leadership of the northern part of what remained of the Reich, visited Third Panzer Army that day – or according to some accounts, the following day – and was dismayed to find that Manteuffel was pulling back towards the west. Angrily, he summoned Manteuffel and Heinrici to an impromptu roadside meeting near the town of Fürstenberg. Fearing that their commander would be arrested and perhaps even executed, Manteuffel's staff took the precaution of taking their personal weapons with them. Keitel began by attacking Heinrici, accusing him of deliberately not following explicit orders to hold his positions at all costs. The army group commander replied calmly and quietly that Third Panzer Army was nowhere near strong enough to follow such instructions and added that he had repeatedly informed *OKH* (and therefore Hitler) that without substantial reinforcements, he would have to order a retreat. Keitel waved him away, shouting that there were no reserves; he then turned to Manteuffel and demanded that he order his army to return to its positions, where it was to hold fast. Heinrici interrupted, telling Keitel that while he was army group commander, no such order would be issued. Keitel now lost his temper completely. He accused the two generals of refusing to obey orders and of being cowards, saboteurs, and traitors. If Heinrici had shown greater resolve, he raged, and had executed anyone who would not stand firm, Third Panzer Army would have been able to hold its positions. 'If you want to take these men and have them shot,' replied Heinrici, indicating a column of men who had stopped in the town to rest, 'why don't you do it yourself?' Keitel started to speak, but then silently climbed back into his vehicle and drove away.[15]

That evening, Manteuffel spoke to Generalleutnant Ivo-Thilo von Trotha, Heinrici's chief of staff. He described the 'complete disintegration' of several of his divisions – *SS-Langemarck*, *SS-Wallonien*, and the marine divisions – and that order was rapidly breaking down:

> Now the battle is for the self-preservation of the army, moving everyone to the west. The columns of refugees contain the most valuable human cargo. They should have stayed at home. We don't have time anymore, the political leadership must act ... 100,000 human beings are fleeing.[16]

The end of the war seemed imminent, but casualties were still climbing on all sides. It is estimated that the two Soviet Fronts battering their way into Berlin were losing an average of nearly 13,000 men every day; after adding the casualties suffered in the battles immediately around the city, the total climbed to about 16,000 per day, and at least 100 tanks or assault guns lost.[17] These were the heaviest daily losses suffered by the Red Army in a sustained period of any phase of the war since the mass encirclements of 1941. Despite these losses, Zhukov kept up the pressure on his subordinates. Berlin had to be captured as quickly as possible, regardless of the cost.

The fighting of the previous days had left many of the Soviet units badly entangled and Berzarin had to pause major attacks by his Fifth Shock Army while he regrouped. The neighbouring Third Shock Army was also pausing attacks, not least because it faced the formidable Friedrichshain Flak Tower. During the afternoon of 27 April, Berzarin was able to resume his advance, edging closer to Alexanderplatz and the *Polizeipräsidium*, headquarters of Berlin's police. To the south, Eighth Guards Army – which had suffered heavier losses than any other Soviet army – continued to batter its way forward.

With the front lines difficult to define amidst the rubble and devastation, small groups of soldiers often found themselves isolated. One soldier from *SS-Charlemagne* managed to escape back to German lines, walking boldly down the street and assuring the Soviet soldiers that he was a slave labourer. Many SS personnel were carefully removing any badges that identified them as not being ordinary army soldiers, and with ammunition running short, the units trying to stop Chuikov from driving into the central parts of Berlin were slowly forced back. Red Army howitzers deployed in Viktoriapark, the highest ground in Berlin, rained shells down on the central area and the German defences along the Landwehr Canal were now threatened. Morale began to collapse with battle-hardened veterans deciding that further resistance was pointless; many were caught by the flying courts-martial that patrolled behind the front line and summarily executed. Mummert, commander of *Müncheberg*, objected strongly to the manner in which these enforcers of rigid loyalty were acting and issued orders that anyone attempting to implement summary executions in the area controlled by his division was to be shot.[18] The division's remaining tanks were now in the Tiergarten and as fuel ran out, some were turned into stationary anti-tank guns until they were knocked out by Soviet fire.

Like the French SS soldier who bluffed his way through the front line, men of the Red Army also attempted to take advantage of the confusion. A group of men from Eighth Guards Army used two captured German tanks – old Pz.38s, probably deployed by the Germans in desperation from a training depot before being captured by the Red Army – at the head of a column of T-34s. The group of tanks motored past the first German defenders, but were soon identified as Soviet tanks and destroyed at close range by assault guns from *SS-Nordland*.[19]

By the evening of 27 April, Chuikov's troops were on the very edge of the central district, but exhaustion forced a brief pause and the army commander told his subordinates to pause operations for half a day while ammunition and other supplies were brought forward. On the other side of the front line, the remnants of *SS-Nordland* were gathered in and around the air ministry building on Wilhelmstrasse. Some of the combat engineers that Ziegler had sent west to secure bridges for a possible breakout had returned to the city centre, and there was general despondency. Henseler, the junior officer in the engineer battalion who had earlier been on the Teltow Canal, was shocked to find Sturmbannführer Hermann Voss, the battalion commander, drunkenly sitting in the cellar with a female Luftwaffe secretary sitting on his knee. He greeted Henseler cheerfully, telling him that they probably had less than 24 hours of freedom left and should make the most of it. As they discussed what they should do, most of the officers decided that they would take their own lives rather than surrender to the Red Army, and Henseler wandered through the building in a daze, encountering drunkenness and couples indulging in sexual encounters without any regard for who might be watching. In the early evening, the mood changed. A Luftwaffe officer ran through the building, claiming to have received a signal stating that the 'Wenck Army' would arrive in Berlin in the next 24 hours. Hastily, the officers stumbled off to their posts for one last act of defence.[20]

Inevitably, the disregard of Zhukov and Chuikov for the designated boundary with Konev's 1st Ukrainian Front led to further incidents of 'friendly fire'. As Rybalko's depleted tank formations made their own attacks into southern Berlin, they reached the *S-Bahn* on Kolonnenstrasse to the west of Tempelhof and during

Disintegration: 26–28 April

the evening ran into a rifle regiment from Eighth Guards Army. Neither Soviet unit was aware of the presence of the other and a furious exchange of fire resulted, with losses on both sides. As news of the clash was passed up the chain of command, Rybalko and Konev both decided that they would respond to the bloody-mindedness of 1st Belarusian Front in a similar manner, though with the justification that the *Stavka*-designated boundary was in their favour. Rybalko's IX Mechanised Corps was ordered to continue its thrust towards the city centre. The result was that during the night of 27–28 April, at least one regiment of Chuikov's Eighth Guards Army found itself cut off from its parent body by the troops of Third Guards Tank Army.

In the west of the city, the remnants of Helmut Altner's company had suffered further casualties during the night of 26–27 April. Shortly before dawn on 27 April, the exhausted young soldiers were amongst the last to pull out of Spandau, and as they moved through the rubble-strewn streets, they often heard voices speaking in Russian around them, but they made their way slowly and carefully towards the Havel bridges from where they were to cross to the east bank. They encountered other German groups, but suddenly they were brought to a halt by machine-gun fire ahead of them. A flamethrower tank moved forward and cleared the way, only to discover that the fire had been coming from a German unit; the Germans, too, were suffering from friendly fire incidents due to the chaotic conditions. When they caught their breath in a ruined factory, they listened to the latest proclamation from Goebbels on a radio set. Then one of the soldiers tuned it to a different station and they heard a voice announce that they were listening to Radio Free Germany, being broadcast by the Western Allies. The voice described the overall situation, listing the towns around Berlin that had fallen to the Red Army, and a senior NCO silently marked them on a large-scale map while the others listened. Later, they contemplated the day's events:

> We sit here staring at the light, asleep with our eyes open. The day goes past like a film strip. The ruins of Spandau and the dead. Spandau has been abandoned by German troops, and our dead lie in the buildings of the town, in the Napola, in the Police School, at the Nordhafen, and in the woods. In Siemensstadt and elsewhere the companies are being burnt to cinders in no time at all. A straggler told us that 85 per cent of his company was lost at the Nordhafen, either dead or captured, and that is the scale of the casualties in virtually all the critical points in the fighting. Women, children, old men, *Volkssturm* and other civilians have suffered casualties that no one knows about, and which no one cares about.
>
> The Leutnant comes back into the room and stands near the candle. They he says suddenly, 'It will soon be over. No one can go on taking it much longer.'[21]

Later that day, Altner was on the east bank of the Havel near a bridge, and watched how two elderly Germans on the far bank reacted to the imminent end of the war:

> They stop right opposite me under the bridge. To their right a few steps lead down to the water, ending in a small platform for mooring boats. They look across at me, but seem not to notice me. We stand opposite each other, two civilians and a soldier, and the river separating us into two different worlds. Then they move. The man opens a gate in the frill that is scarcely visible. Between the water and the grill there is now only a short step ... They stand on the water's edge, on the stone wall that drops abruptly to the river. They hold hands and kiss. I am still standing there with no idea what all this means. Then suddenly they jump, their faces quite calm, quite without fear, as if they were no longer of this earth ...
>
> I slowly recall what a soldier told us yesterday about the bridge by the Nordhafen that was going to be blown up. When this became known, people went and stood on it, women with babies in their arms, mothers holding crying children by the hand, old men and youngsters of both sexes, even soldiers, and they would not let themselves be driven away, by threats or by force. They stood there quietly, not listening, just looking at the water and staying silent until the bridge was blown as the first tank appeared on the bank. A dark cloud rose slowly and flames shot upwards, and the people fell into the river in a cloud of fire and lightning. Yesterday I didn't want to believe it, but today I do.[22]

Altner then moved to a nearby building. After being slightly wounded when a volley of *Katyusha* rockets struck, he and the remnants of his company ventured out again. Finally, accompanied by just one other soldier, Altner encountered a woman and her two children who told the soldiers that the entire area was under Soviet control, but there were SS patrols that executed any stragglers they found. The woman gave Altner and his comrade civilian clothes, and they cautiously made their way east to the barracks where they had been stationed prior to the battle.

It seems that numerous bodies – SS, military police, and others – took it upon themselves to round up stragglers. In some cases, they ordered them back to the front line; in other cases, they simply executed them. Dieter Borkowski, a teenager who had been assigned to an anti-aircraft unit in Berlin, was attempting to reach safety when he came upon a typical scene:

> The bombardment was so devastating that the only way forward was to sprint from house to house. When I finally approached the Königstor [immediately to

the west of the *Volkspark Friedrichshain*], I spotted something strange from a distance. Five men were standing by the trenches in front of St Bartholomew's Church, as stiff and still as if they were on drill, while bullets struck all around. Barely 100m away, I called out excitedly from a hallway where I was waiting for a brief break in the firing: 'Take cover! Get into the trenches quickly!' No answer, nobody moved. As I approached, I jumped in shock: the five men were dead. Only from a distance did it look as if they were standing by the air raid trenches. In reality, they were hanging from trees behind them. One had a sign on his chest: 'We were too cowardly to protect Berlin from the Bolsheviks. We raised the white flag and thereby betrayed Germany and the Führer. That is why we had to die without honour!'[23]

The front line running through northern Berlin had reached the street where the anonymous diarist lived. Early in the morning, the first Soviet soldiers appeared in the street:

A Russian anti-aircraft battery was turning the corner, four barrels, four iron giraffes with menacing necks tall as towers. Two men were stomping up the street: broad backs, leather jackets, high leather boots. Jeeps pulling up to the kerb. Howitzers rattling ahead in the early light. The pavement alive with the din. The smell of petrol drifted into the kitchen through the broken windows …

We kept creeping up to the window and peeking out at the street, where an endless supply train was passing by. Stout mares with foals running between their legs. A cow drearily mooing to be milked. Before we knew it they had set up a field kitchen in the garage across the street. And for the first time we could make out faces, features, individuals – sturdy, broad foreheads, close-cropped hair, well fed, carefree. Not a civilian in sight. The Russians have the street entirely to themselves, but under every building people are whispering, quaking.[24]

The first soldier entered the cellar where she and her fellow residents were hiding shortly after, but departed when they told him they had no alcohol. More soldiers appeared, and a surreal atmosphere developed with Red Army personnel hesitantly talking to German civilians asking where they could get water for their horses or where they might find other items, while the thunder of artillery and gunfire continued nearby. Before long, the encounters developed a different nuance, with some of the soldiers clearly looking for young women. Towards evening, the first attempts at rape occurred; the diarist noted that the soldiers seemed to prefer plumper, buxom women. When three soldiers gathered around the wife of a baker, the diarist rushed into the street and found a Soviet officer who reluctantly followed her back to the basement:

> The officer joins the conversation, not with a tone of command but as among equals. Several times I hear the expression *ukaz Stalina* – Stalin's decree. Apparently Stalin has declared that 'this kind of thing' is not to happen. But it happens anyway, the officer gives me to understand, shrugging his shoulders. One of the two men being reprimanded voices his objection, his face twisted in anger: 'What do you mean? What did the Germans do to our women?' He is screaming. 'They took my sister and – ' and so on …
>
> Once again the officer speaks, calming the man down, slowly moving towards the door, and finally managing to get both men outside.[25]

The sense of relief lasted just minutes. When the diarist cautiously ventured out of the basement to check that the soldiers had gone, two of them grabbed her. To her horror, she heard the basement door slam shut behind her and she was raped; at one point, a woman in Red Army uniform appeared and watched, laughing. After the rape, she and a group of others went in search of the local Soviet commander to ask for protection. He dismissed them with the words, 'Come on, I'm sure they didn't really hurt you. Our men are all healthy.'[26] The group returned to the ruined apartment block, and the diarist was raped a third time that evening.

Other German civilians emerged from their shelters to face the new occupiers, many of them certain that they would simply be killed. Hermann Kasack and his wife had been hiding in the cellar of their house:

> As we stepped out of the front door, we saw a machine-gun set up in the entrance between the narrow front gardens opposite, with the muzzle pointed at the wide side of the empty street. The crew crouched on the steps. When we asked where we should go, they told us, 'On the lawn.' The interpreter stayed behind the machine-gun. I understood. We slowly crossed the road. On the sandy path in front of the lawn, my wife hugged me once more and I kissed her. 'It's over,' I said. 'Yes,' she replied. We were very calm. Someone asked, 'Are we going to be shot now?' 'Yes,' I said. I saw that half a dozen graves had been dug on the lawn. How quickly these things happen. We lined up next to each other in the middle of the lawn, facing our house. So that's how it is, I thought. Time stood still. After a while, the interpreter told us to go to the other side of the street. We turned and nobody said a word. From the moment we stepped onto the lawn to be shot, I felt I was one of the dead. The fact that death had not arrived didn't change the validity of the feeling.[27]

Meanwhile, Hitler continued to hope that Steiner would finally commence a powerful attack from the north. Fegelein had been dispatched to Steiner's headquarters on 26 April to reiterate the orders for the 'army group' to commence its offensive, but Steiner rejected Fegelein's demands. He had been told that he would get two further divisions from Third Panzer Army, he argued, and neither had appeared. Fegelein flew back to Berlin in a small plane and returned to the bunker beneath the Reich Chancellery. Here, amidst growing signs of complete dissolution – the air conditioning system struggled to cope, rubbish littered the corridors and common areas, and people drank alcohol and indulged in sexual encounters with little restraint – Fegelein met briefly with Obergruppenführer Hans Jüttner, head of the *Ersatzheer* ('Replacement Army'), telling him that he had no intention of dying in Berlin or joining the ranks of those who had proclaimed their intentions to commit suicide. He then left the bunker and went to his apartment nearby, from where – according to some sources – he telephoned Eva Braun, Hitler's mistress and the sister of his wife Gretl. It was common gossip that his relationship with Eva Braun was somewhat closer than would be normal between a man and his sister-in-law, and he now beseeched her to leave the bunker while there was still time.[28]

Hitler had already started to suspect that despite his constant assurances of complete loyalty, Fegelein was less than fully committed to the Führer and he soon became aware that he had disappeared. He promptly ordered Obersturmbannführer Peter Högl, deputy commander of the *Reichssicherheitsdienst*, a unit of the SS responsible for organising close protection of Hitler and other senior figures, to find Fegelein, and Högl took a group of soldiers to Fegelein's apartment. Here, they found him heavily intoxicated and dressed in civilian clothes and accompanied by an equally intoxicated red-haired young woman. There were several bags full of large quantities of money and jewellery, including items that belonged to Eva Braun. Högl also found a briefcase that contained documents relating to attempts by Himmler, the only person to whom Fegelein ever showed any significant loyalty, to negotiate with the Western Allies.[29]

The chronology of what followed Fegelein's enforced return to the bunker is imprecise. Eva Braun, whose sister was heavily pregnant, apparently pleaded with Hitler to show mercy and Hitler toyed with the idea that, stripped of his rank, Fegelein should be sent to serve in Mohnke's battlegroup defending central Berlin as a private soldier, but Bormann and others expressed concerns that this would simply result in Fegelein attempting to desert again. Fegelein drunkenly demanded to see Hitler, refusing to answer questions from Mohnke and insisting that he was answerable only to Himmler; Hitler refused to see him and ordered a court-martial to be held.

Mohnke presided over the court-martial, with Burgdorf, Krebs, and Gruppenführer Johann Rattenhuber (the commander of Hitler's personal SS bodyguard) assisting. Fegelein was still drunk and wept constantly; at one stage he lost control of his bladder. Mohnke concluded that although Fegelein's desertion was not in doubt, he was – under the terms of German military and civil law – in no state to stand trial at that moment, and handed him over to Rattenhuber.[30] According to some accounts, it was only at this stage that the documents relating to Himmler's negotiations were discovered when Fegelein's quarters were searched.[31] Either late on 27 April or the following day, Fegelein was taken out of the bunker and executed by a single shot to the back of the head.[32] It was a suitably ignominious end for a man who had behaved consistently with a cynical eye for self-promotion and hadn't hesitated to denigrate others or to take advantage of whatever opportunities might come his way, regardless of the consequences for others. His wife Gretl gave birth to a daughter a week later; she was named Eva in honour of her aunt. Gretl changed her name after the war and remarried in 1954, but the family continued to experience tragedy – after her boyfriend was killed in a car crash in 1975, Fegelein's daughter Eva killed herself by swallowing poison.

To the southwest of Berlin, Wenck's Twelfth Army could do little more. Its modest strength had been used to good effect, but Konev had rapidly strengthened his lines and driving east towards Ninth Army was clearly beyond its strength. After further discussions with his chief of staff, Wenck ordered a regrouping towards the north, where he still hoped for a drive towards Potsdam where he hoped to link up with the isolated troops gathered under Reymann's command. In order to free up men for this task, and also to avoid the deaths and destruction that would be the consequences of urban fighting, he ordered Wittenberg to be evacuated late on 27 April. Significantly, he issued these orders without informing *OKW* and sent them to the various units at the last possible moment – he wanted to avoid any recurrence of the fiasco of the last few days, when Berlin Radio had triumphantly broadcast his planned attacks to the entire world.

For the moment, Konev was content that he had sufficient forces in place to deal with any further attempt by Wenck to attack towards the east. This left him with three other issues demanding his attention. The battle for Berlin was continuing, and he must have been both exasperated and confused by the clashes with Zhukov's troops. To the south, the German counterattack against his southern flank had badly disrupted Second Polish Army, and he dispatched Petrov (his chief of staff) and Major General Vladimir Ivanovich Kostylev (his chief of operations) to take control of the situation. When they arrived at the headquarters of the Polish troops, they immediately dismissed the army commander, Lieutenant

General Karol Swierczewski. Kostylev now took command and recalled units that Swierczewski had dispatched in an advance on Dresden; he also requested reinforcements, and Konev diverted units from Fifth Army to the area.

But the main focus of Konev's attention was the German Ninth Army, which was now facing pressure from three of Zhukov's armies in the north and three of Konev's armies in the south and west. Throughout the hours of darkness before dawn on 27 April, groups of soldiers from Ninth Army made largely uncoordinated attempts to escape to the west. One such group managed to slip through the first two cordons of Soviet troops that had been deployed in their path and reached Neuhof, to the north of Baruth; another group edged past Baruth and reached the village of Paplitz, a mile to the west. In anticipation of such developments, Konev had ordered two units – 395th Guards Rifle Division from Thirteenth Army and 68th Guards Tank Brigade from Fourth Guards Tank Army – to be held in reserve, and these launched energetic counterattacks. Most of the German soldiers were killed or taken prisoner.

One of the units that was still relatively intact within the encirclement was 21st Panzer Division, and some of its officers now urged Generalleutnant Werner Marcks, the division commander, to take unilateral action and to break out to the west while the division still had sufficient strength to make the attempt. But Marcks, who had shown no inclination to prevent flying courts-martial from executing men of the division who were legitimately away from the front line and had showed unwavering loyalty to Hitler, refused to commit himself. Soviet formations continued to compress the encirclement from north, east, and south, and Busse struggled to keep in contact with all of his formations. An officer in *SS-30. Januar*, most of which was in the encirclement, described the growing chaos:

> [The encirclement of Ninth Army] had become split into several small pockets at Müllrose, Prieros, and elsewhere. The Prieros pocket was about 21km across. In it were about 10,000–14,000 German soldiers of all arms of service and also about 20,000 German civilians with their herds of cattle, individual animals, and personal possessions; families, women with children, some on foot, some with horse-drawn carts and handcarts. Everything was under constant artillery and mortar fire and air attack from the Russians, which couldn't fail to hit something each time. Conditions in the pocket were horrific. Soldiers, civilians, children, women, and vehicles trudged around in a circle, trying to avoid the fire like a giant, thousand-legged worm biting itself in the tail. Officers, soldiers, civilians with their families, whole groups of German people were shooting themselves. I looked across at this spectacle shattered, stunned, and helpless.[33]

28 APRIL

In the north, the front line broke up completely. Manteuffel's Third Panzer Army had hoped to be able to hold the *Wotanstellung* ('Wotan Line') for at least long enough for stragglers to catch up, but this would only have been possible if Hitler had permitted an orderly withdrawal to this shorter line before the Soviet offensive began, and the best that could be done now was to continue the retreat to the west, with the few remaining coherent units mounting local counterattacks to drive off Soviet spearheads. The improvised infantry battalion created with some of the tank crews of 7th Panzer Division was told to assemble, but Huber and his comrades were shocked to discover that overnight, the Oberleutnant in command of their company had disappeared. Two officers from division headquarters then appeared and one of them addressed the men, telling them that he intended to lead them for what remained of the war and would try to get them out alive. The company – in reality, just 20 men – left the village where they had assembled that afternoon, and soon found themselves struggling along roads choked with men streaming west from the front line, but they found themselves marching towards the approaching Red Army: they were to form part of the rearguard of Third Panzer Army.[34]

Amongst the men attempting to escape to the west were several groups of SS from the numerous divisions that Himmler had raised from the occupied territories. With the end of the war so close, they knew that they were unlikely to be taken prisoner by the Red Army, or to survive captivity if they weren't shot out of hand. By the early afternoon of 28 April, the town of Neubrandenburg was in Soviet hands and ablaze as Red Army soldiers set off on a spree of drunken looting and destruction, and soldiers from *SS-Wallonien* and other non-German divisions simply abandoned their posts and headed west. Neither Heinrici nor Manteuffel had any serious intention of making some sort of heroic last stand against the Red Army, but they both regarded it as essential for the retreat to the west to be conducted in as coordinated a manner as possible. Military police units were dispatched to set up catch lines in the rear in order to turn back soldiers from both regular army units and the SS who were withdrawing without permission.

In the Soviet-held parts of east Berlin, Berzarin – the commander of Fifth Shock Army – had been appointed governor of the city by Zhukov. He promptly issued a proclamation, declaring that the Nazi Party was hereby dissolved and that all German employees of the Party and government had to register with the Soviet authorities immediately. Public services were to resume work immediately and all weapons, radios, cameras, vehicles, and gasoline were to be handed over to the Red Army. Given the ongoing fighting just a very short distance away, the proclamation must have seemed bizarre to the civilians cowering in cellars, but few became aware of it immediately. Meanwhile, the battle continued with the same intensity as before. Attempts to approach Alexanderplatz from the north were frustrated by fire from the Friedrichshain Flak Tower to the north, and small German tank destroyer teams ventured out of the tower, attacking and destroying Soviet tanks that still lacked sufficient infantry protection. The *Polizeipräsidium* near Alexanderplatz saw particularly heavy fighting; it took over a day for the Soviet forces to overcome the German defenders, using artillery firing over open sights to smash each German firing point in turn. Most of the defenders were killed in the battle.

A little to the south, some of the tank crews were improvising their own solutions to the struggle against German troops armed with *Panzerfausts*. Sheets of metal or wire mesh were hastily attached as a form of 'spaced armour', so that incoming rounds would explode on striking this outer shell. The HEAT warheads of the *Panzerfausts* had to be in physical contact with the armour of the target when they exploded if they were to be effective, and this proved to be a useful solution. German tank-hunting teams adapted just as quickly. A first *Panzerfaust* was fired to blast off the outer shell, and a second was then aimed at the exposed turret or hull.

To the south of the central district, Soviet troops overcame tough resistance around Spittelmarkt, but a combination of disorientation in the intense fighting, compounded by difficulties in identifying particular locations in a heavily bombed city that was now being further devastated by constant artillery fire, prevented the Red Army from coordinating its efforts to maximum effect. The German lines immediately to the west of Spittelmarkt were almost non-existent, and a concentrated effort here might have reached the Reich Chancellery within a day. When he became aware of the threat, Siefert ordered a group of sailors, flown into Berlin in the preceding days, to take up defensive positions, but the 'naval infantry' – little more than naval personnel who had little or no training in land warfare – were driven to cover by Soviet artillery fire.

The Soviet troops to the west of Spittelmarkt were from IX Rifle Corps, part of Berzarin's Fifth Shock Army, and after a pause to regroup, they pushed north through the weak German lines. A desperate German counterattack took the Soviet units by surprise and forced a hasty withdrawal to Moritzplatz, but after further regrouping the Germans were scattered, with some finding themselves in the streets to the south of Spittelmarkt and therefore behind the Soviet units that had taken the area early in the day. Other elements of IX Rifle Corps pushed forward on the northern side of the Landwehr Canal, coming up against another group of non-German SS, this time Latvian soldiers. Counterattacks by what was officially a battlegroup of *SS-Nordland*, but in reality consisted of whatever soldiers could be gathered together, added to the overall confusion. Small pockets of German soldiers remained at large behind the advancing Soviet troops, with snipers taking a toll on both sides.

Chuikov's Eighth Guards Army was immediately to the west, preparing to clear the Germans from the Landwehr Canal. If he was aware of IX Rifle Corps to his immediate right, he made no allowances for this; nor did he take any account of the likely location of Rybalko's Third Guards Tank Army, operating in the same area as his troops, despite the repeated incidents of friendly fire between his and Rybalko's men. On a broad front, Eighth Guards Army attacked, taking advantage of *S-Bahn* and *U-Bahn* tunnels that passed under the canal; only small groups of men could move north through the tunnels, but Chuikov counted on them to create confusion when the main body of his army attacked. Pontoon bridges had been established before dawn in areas where Eighth Guards Army had already secured footholds on the north bank, and heavy fighting erupted with daylight.

The defenders were the now-usual mix of *Volkssturm* and Hitler Youth, with substantial groups of men from *SS-Charlemagne* and *SS-Nordland* providing the main resistance. Groups of soldiers became isolated from each other, and many German soldiers perished as they attempted to fall back to the north. One battlegroup managed to concentrate at the Kochstrasse *U-Bahn* station and attempted to counterattack towards the south, but was broken up by mortar fire after advancing no more than 50 metres. The survivors took up positions in a building overlooking Friedrichstrasse.

A little to the west, Chuikov's troops attempted to take the Anhalter railway station. This was also the objective of Rybalko's Third Guards Tank Army, with elements of 61st Rifle Division and Lieutenant General Ivan Prokofiyevich Sukhov's IX Mechanised Corps tasked with seizing the station – it should be remembered that according to the directives issued by *Stavka*, the station was effectively the boundary between 1st Ukrainian Front and 1st Belarusian Front, but was explicitly within the zone of the former. Chuikov therefore had no business attacking here. The attack by Sukhov was preceded by heavy artillery fire, and many of the shells struck areas already occupied by 82nd Guards Rifle Division, the most western unit of Chuikov's Eighth Guards Army. This unit immediately reported back to Chuikov's headquarters that they were under heavy fire from previously unidentified German artillery, but worse was to follow. The soldiers of 61st Rifle Division now moved forward, passing through the lines of 82nd Guards Rifle Division and then advancing towards the Anhalter station. There were fierce clashes between not only the German defenders and the advancing Soviet units, but between the units of the two Soviet Fronts. The scale of casualties suffered is not clear, but was clearly substantial.[35]

Finally, a senior commander intervened to stop the fratricidal battles. Konev later wrote:

> Taking into account the advance of Chuikov's troops to the west and trying to prevent our units from mixing with units of 1st Belarusian Front in the conditions that existed in urban warfare, I ordered Rybalko, after reaching the Landwehr Canal, to turn the most advanced units to the west and then to continue the offensive in the new zone of operations of 1st Ukrainian Front, which had just been established.
>
> The telephone conversation I had with Rybalko about this was unpleasant. He said that he didn't understand why the corps, already aimed at the city centre, was to turn west on my orders, changing the direction of its attack.
>
> I understood the commander's feelings perfectly, but I could only answer that the offensive of 1st Belarusian Front was proceeding successfully and the centre of Berlin, along the established dividing line, was now in the zone of operations of 1st Belarusian Front. Knowing Rybalko, I should add that his discontent was not due to eagerness to take a few more streets and squares for personal glory. He had already achieved great glory. But being on the battlefield, in the thick of it, and seeing a direct opportunity to contribute to the most rapid clearance of Berlin, he now had to overcome his feelings and carry out his orders. I am not inclined to condemn him for these personal views, which were perfectly understood by me.
>
> As for my own opinions, I believe it was necessary to establish a precise dividing line between the two Fronts during this period. It was essential to exclude any possibility of confusion, losses from friendly fire, and other unpleasantness that might arise from the mixing of troops, especially in urban fighting.[36]

The last paragraph fails to mention that such a 'precise dividing line' already existed – Zhukov had simply ignored it, and had ordered Chuikov to proceed as if it did not exist. Neither Zhukov nor Chuikov make any mention of the clash between the two Fronts on 28 April. Having favoured first one of his commanders, then the other, Stalin had conclusively decided to give the prize of capturing Berlin to Zhukov, perhaps calculating that the chastening losses incurred in storming the Seelow Heights would take the shine off Zhukov's glory. Konev was offered a consolation prize: after completing operations in the western parts of Berlin, he was to turn his armies south to capture Prague.

Having managed to slip past Soviet and SS patrols, Altner and his comrade Blaczek had slept in their barracks in Ruhleben, but awoke early on 28 April when fighting erupted nearby. As it grew light, the disparate group of soldiers realised that they were surrounded. Voices called to them to give up the fight and many slipped away, despite threats from their officers and NCOs. A counterattack reinforced by large numbers of Hitler Youth threw back the Soviet soldiers, probably because at this stage of the battle, fewer Red Army men were prepared to risk their lives in pointless combat, but as the German attack continued, machine-guns slaughtered dozens of the youngsters, many of whom were armed with obsolete rifles for which they had barely any ammunition. That afternoon, Altner and others were ordered to make another counterattack, this time towards Charlottenburg to the southeast. The small group was ordered to advance along a *U-Bahn* tunnel and resurfaced on the Kaiserdamm. They returned to the tunnel and ran into Soviet troops near the Berlin Opera House, shots and deafening explosions echoing from both ahead and behind:

> The firing doesn't stop. Our combat team spreads out even further apart and partly holds back. The roof to the road has been torn open beyond the Zoo station and the tunnel has fallen in, so we have to make our way carefully over a maze of torn concrete and twisted rails, collapsed beams and electricity cables, constantly followed and driven on by enemy fire, which seems to be coming from all directions. After negotiating each destroyed and demolished section, we vanish underground again. I have no idea how late it is, having lost all sense of time, and am surprised to be still alive. Our ranks have become thinner, but the Hitler Youth are fighting like devils, being driven on ceaselessly by their SS leaders.[37]

Covered in dust and with their numbers greatly reduced, Altner and his comrades finally reached the *U-Bahn* station on Kurfürstendamm close to the ruins of the Kaiser Wilhelm Church. Over the preceding two weeks, they had travelled back and forth. First, they went to the Seelow Heights; then, they retreated back to Berlin and returned to their barracks; from here, they were briefly sent west into Potsdam before returning once more to their barracks; and now, they were close to the centre of Berlin.

Much of Ninth Army was now gathered immediately to the east of Halbe, together with tens of thousands of refugees. During 28 April, there was heavy fighting as Kleinheisterkamp led most of the combat-worthy elements of Busse's troops in increasingly desperate, but ultimately futile, attacks. The Red Army's artillery, reinforced by the artillery breakthrough division and backed by unopposed air attacks, slaughtered hundreds of German soldiers as they struggled to break through to the west. A German civilian who had served in the First World War recalled the ferocity of the Soviet artillery fire:

> I had experience of the bombardments in Champagne during the First World War, and took part in the Battle of the Somme and the bitter assaults at Verdun, but what occurred in the Halbe encirclement during these days eclipsed all that I had seen before. From dawn to dusk, one bomber squadron after another delivered its deadly cargo with clockwork precision over the forests around Halbe, Teupitz, and Märkisch Buchholz, dropping bombs on the heavily congested country lanes. Rockets hissed in without pause, and guns hammered at the improvised positions dug by the German soldiers.[38]

Kleinheisterkamp, who appears to have conducted the attack without any authorisation from Busse, had clearly reached the limit of his patience with his superior. The headquarters of Ninth Army was now in the forest to the north of Märkisch Buchholz and Busse summoned all the available officers during the afternoon of 28 April. There was universal agreement that resources should be concentrated for a concerted attempt to break out towards where it was hoped Wenck's Twelfth Army was waiting. The only viable route was through Halbe, and the failed attacks of the morning demonstrated the strength of the Soviet units in the area. What remained of the *Kurmark* panzergrenadier division and the 14 surviving Tiger tanks of *SS-Schwere-Panzer-Abteilung 502* would lead the way, but coordinating the tangled masses in the encirclement was almost impossible. Radio contact with outside agencies was sporadic at best, and shortages of detailed maps further increased the difficulties.

That evening, Ninth Army's artillery fired one last barrage at Halbe; after all the available ammunition had been fired, the gunners then disabled their guns and joined the columns of infantry heading west. Kleinheisterkamp had been put in charge of the first wave and had organised the remaining tanks into two groups. The southern group was delayed in its start, giving the Red Army units in Halbe time to recover from the artillery bombardment, and the battle for the town rapidly became chaotic in the growing darkness. To add to the confusion, there were groups of *Seydlitz-Truppen* operating in the area; some directed German columns in the wrong direction, others took part in the battles. The limited command and control on the German side broke down almost immediately as Soviet aircraft began to intervene, bombing the area to the east of Halbe at random – they could hardly miss, given the crowds of soldiers and civilians compressed into the area.

At some point during that chaotic night, the Soviet units in and around Halbe were forced back by the waves of German soldiers and civilians pressing forward from the forests to the east. Meanwhile, many miles to the west, Wenck's divisions continued their attack north towards Potsdam. The *Scharnhorst* and

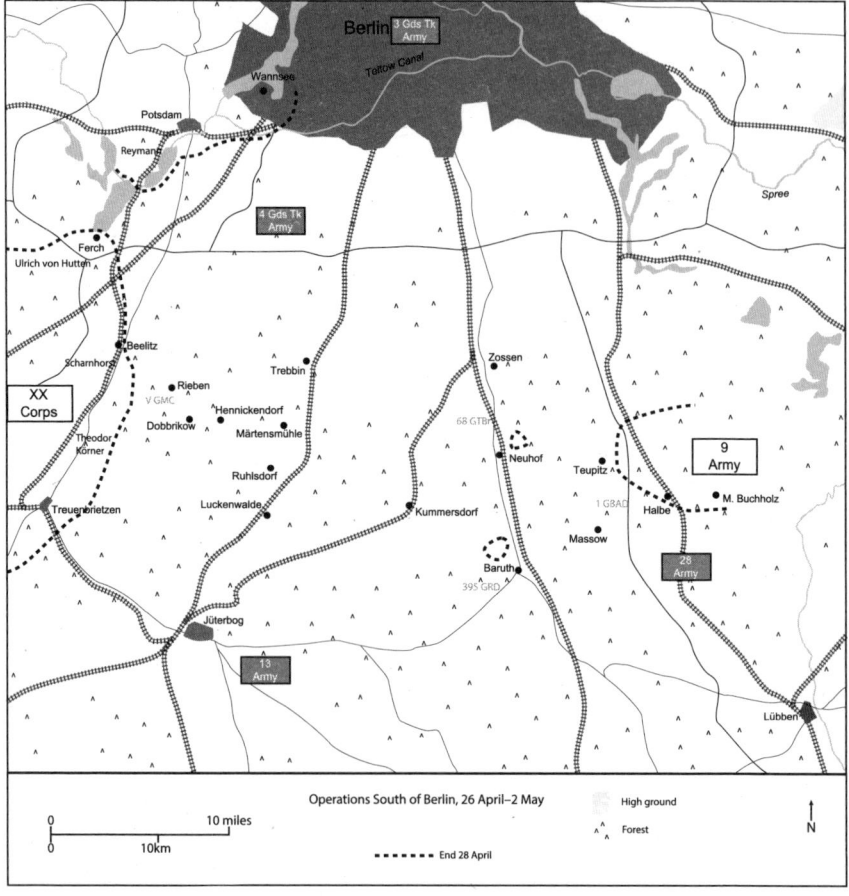

Operations South of Berlin, 26 April–2 May

Ulrich von Hutten infantry divisions reached a point about three miles north of Beelitz; an urgent signal was sent to Busse, advising him of the line that had been reached and adding that there was little prospect of advancing further to the east.

In Berlin, the documents that had been found by the SS – in either Fegelein's apartment or his office in the Reich Chancellery bunker – unequivocally showed that Himmler was attempting to negotiate a ceasefire in the west. During the afternoon of 28 April, Hitler learned that Stockholm Radio had confirmed this. Immediately, the Führer contacted Dönitz, the commander of all German forces in the north. Dönitz then spoke to Himmler, who denied the rumours, but a Reuters communiqué that evening reported further information about the attempted negotiations. Furiously, Hitler went to Greim, who had replaced Göring as commander of the Luftwaffe. After ordering him to mount immediate air attacks on the Soviet tanks that were nearby in Potsdamerplatz – where such planes were to be found was dismissed as an irrelevance – Hitler told Greim that he was to leave immediately to place Himmler under arrest. Greim and Hanna Reitsch were taken in a half-track to the Brandenburg Gate, where a small single-engined trainer aircraft was waiting. Reitsch took off, flying low over astonished Soviet soldiers. Fearing that they were witnessing Hitler's departure, they belatedly opened fire, but the plane was gone.

Back in the bunker, Hitler announced that he was to marry Eva Braun that evening. Walter Wagner, a local Party official who was empowered to conduct wedding ceremonies, was brought to the bunker. The ceremony was reduced to the bare minimum – which included declarations from the bride and groom that they were of unblemished Aryan stock and free from any hereditary diseases – and was witnessed by Goebbels and Bormann. After a brief, awkward celebration with glasses of champagne, Hitler retired to a separate room with his secretary Traudl Junge and dictated his personal testament. Dönitz was to become Reich president, Goebbels would be chancellor. Bormann became head of the Nazi Party. Karl Hanke, the *Gauleiter* of Breslau, still trapped in the besieged city in Silesia, was declared the new head of the SS following Himmler's dismissal.[39]

Other changes were announced that evening. Keitel, still smarting from the ill-tempered exchange with Manteuffel and Heinrici, sent a signal to Army Group Vistula. Heinrici was dismissed from his post. In an added touch of spite, Bormann signalled Dönitz, ordering him to have Heinrici brought before a court-martial for his failure to stop the Soviet advance on Berlin. Even if those in the bunker continued to behave as if the Reich still had enough of a future to make such measures meaningful, Dönitz had fewer illusions, at least on that count. He took no action against Heinrici. The new commander of Army Group Vistula was to be General Kurt Student, who had distinguished himself commanding German paratrooper formations earlier in the war. It would take several days for him to reach his headquarters; in the meantime, General Kurt von Tippelskirch – commander of the non-existent Twenty-First Army, which in theory had control of Steiner's forces and other units – stepped in as an interim commander. In reality, he had little to do. There was no longer any coherent structure to Army Group Vistula.

Chapter 11

THE BITTEREST OF ENDS: BERLIN, 29 APRIL–2 MAY

It had been increasingly obvious to all but a small group of diehards that the end of the war was coming, but by first light on 29 April, it was clear to everyone in Berlin that this end was imminent. Weidling informed Hitler that ammunition was rapidly running out and that his men would be unable to continue fighting beyond 30 April. Hitler enquired about the possibility of supplies being brought in by air; Weidling replied that the Luftwaffe had dropped about six tons of food and no more than 20 *Panzerfausts* the preceding night, and lacked the resources to conduct further air drops. Grudgingly, Hitler gave permission for the garrison to conduct a breakout to the west, where it was to continue resistance. Anticipating this, several officers had already commenced planning for such an operation. Late on 28 April, a young Leutnant from *Müncheberg* was told by Major Helmut Thoma, the division's operations officer, to go to the Zoo Flak Tower and to 'find out discreetly' if the Luftwaffe flak units there were prepared to join the panzer division in a breakout. Thoma added that under no circumstances was the Leutnant to speak to anyone from the SS.[1] The officers in the flak tower proved to be of a similar mind. They assured that they would cooperate, and would avoid sending any information by telephone. But once Hitler had given permission for a breakout, planning could continue without any further subterfuge.

The fighting in the eastern part of Berlin continued with the same intensity as before as Fifth Shock Army tried to batter its way to Alexanderplatz. A young Soviet artillery officer from 89th Guards Rifle Division was ordered to provide fire support, but by this stage his battery was reduced to just one gun:

> I ordered Senior Sergeant Kuzmov and his crew to carry out the mission. Even before the howitzer was rolled forward, I set up reliable covering fire using my

own resources. The troops from the other crews who no longer had guns moved into covered positions close to the howitzer. Every group was tasked with suppressing specific fire points that threatened our gun.

At my signal, they opened fire with machine-guns and assault rifles. Under cover of this fire, Senior Sergeant Kuzmov's crew dragged out the gun and started firing at the enemy. For about 90 minutes, Kuzmov's howitzer fired without interruption. The barrel and the working parts were so hot that they burned our hands. The gunners sweated profusely. The ammunition carriers could barely keep up.

Right on time, we heard the noise of engines approaching. The gunners increased the rate of fire to their maximum. Other guns could be heard somewhere to the right. Our tanks emerged from behind the ruins. They quickly crossed the street and managed to get to the square, firing on the move. But they had covered less than half the distance [to the *U-Bahn* station] when heavy fire struck them from the wrecked buildings and the station, with the Germans firing from new positions. A minute later, the square was engulfed in clouds of smoke. The tanks were forced back, one of them towing a burning vehicle that had taken a direct hit from a shell. The artillerymen then started firing with greater fury at the enemy's firing points that had been revealed.[2]

It took most of the day for the Soviet troops to overcome resistance around the *Polizeipräsidium*, particularly in the nearby *Rotes Rathaus* ('Red City Hall'), where the defenders clung on stubbornly. Using captured *Panzerfausts*, the soldiers of the Soviet 266th Rifle Division had to blast their way through the building, fighting for almost every room. The smoke and dust, the concussive blast of constant explosions, the thunder of gunfire in enclosed spaces, the uncertainty of whether the shadow briefly glimpsed was friend or foe – the terror of such warfare is almost beyond comprehension. It was not until late that night that the Germans were driven out of the *Rotes Rathaus*. A little to the south, Soviet troops reached the Spree near the Jannowitzbrücke *U-Bahn* station.

Further west, Zhukov once again issued orders explicitly subordinating First Guards Tank Army to Chuikov's Eighth Guards Army. The two armies had been fighting alongside each other from the first assaults on the Seelow Heights, but several attacks in Berlin by unsupported tanks resulted in heavy losses, and Zhukov issued this new order in an attempt to improve coordination between the two armies. Before they could continue their attacks towards the north, the Soviet troops had to deal with an energetic German counterattack. Several small battlegroups from what remained of *SS-Nordland* struck at first light, catching the Red Army by surprise, and moved forward two city blocks before being brought to a halt. The leading units of Berzarin's Fifth Shock Army then struck the Germans in their eastern flank; they also opened fire on riflemen of Eighth Guards Army in the maze of ruins. But despite his badly depleted ranks, Chuikov was determined that his army would be the first to reach the Reich Chancellery and the ruins of the Reichstag. Before dawn on 29 April, 27th Guards Rifle Division was pulled back across the river and replaced by 79th Guards Rifle Division – neither was remotely close to full strength, but Major General Viktor Sergeyevich Glebov, commander of 27th Guards Rifle Division, knew his men desperately needed time out of the front line to rest and reorganise.

Tanks were brought over the Landwehr Canal in large numbers, and from dawn on 29 April there was intense fighting in the streets to the north of the canal. In many places, the Germans were still in position on the canal itself, and Eighth Guards Army was involved in bitter battles as it attempted to secure a bridge that led to the Tiergarten. Chuikov described how the bridge was taken:

> The most intense battle took place around the humpbacked bridge. Under constant machine-gun fire, the sappers managed to remove the mines and two powerful explosive charges that were suspended under the trusses. The first attempt to rush the bridge was unsuccessful. A tank is a very obvious target and as soon as one moved into the square before the bridge, it drew a barrage of fire. A Tiger, dug in up to its turret, fired from somewhere in the depths of the Tiergarten.
>
> By evening, the disabled tank before the bridge had been pulled out of the danger zone and the tank crews called in artillery fire to provide a smoke screen. Under cover of the smoke, several machine-gunners from an assault detachment of 220th Guards Rifle Regiment managed to slip across the bridge and captured the corner house on the opposite side of the canal. But as soon as our tanks appeared, the enemy's firing points became active again. One tank, which had rushed up to the bridge, was knocked out by a *Panzerfaust* fired by a Nazi who had miraculously survived in his position on the third floor of the corner house, despite the rest of the house being captured by our machine-gunners.
>
> It seemed that this would be the end of the tankers' attempts to break through to the Tiergarten with their formidable machines. But again, the soldiers' ingenuity saved the day. They put smoke grenades and petrol on a tank and as it approached the bridge, they set them ablaze. The Nazis seemed confused: the burning tank was moving forward, still firing. Those few seconds of confusion were enough for the tank to slip across the bridge and disappear into the courtyard of the corner house. From here, cooperating with the machine-gunners, the tank crew began to clear the block, which we could then use as a springboard for further attacks.[3]

Close by, the Soviet units that had stormed the Anhalter station the previous day attempted to push on to the north, running into the survivors of the battalion from *SS-Charlemagne*. The French SS drove back the first probes with a mixture of gunfire and *Panzerfausts*; the Red Army responded with heavy artillery fire, but when they moved forward once more, they were brought to a halt again by defensive fire. The frustrated attackers were reinforced by a tank regiment, and its commander ordered his crews to charge down the broad Saarlandstrasse (now Stresemannstrasse) in line abreast. The attack started with eight tanks lined up side by side, but this rapidly shrank to just two as the vehicles struggled to pick their way through the rubble, and the French SS knocked them out at close range with their *Panzerfausts*.[4]

But even if *SS-Charlemagne* was able to hold off the Soviet troops for the moment, it was being outflanked. On their northern flank were the last of the Latvian SS, who had just received reinforcements. Many of these were the survivors of the combat engineer battalion of *SS-Nordland*; others were from the battalion of Spanish volunteers. Bitter attacks and counterattacks continued all day with little change in positions; during the evening, much of the fighting centred on the ominous buildings on Prinz-Albrecht-Strasse, where the Gestapo had its headquarters throughout the war.

Further to the west, the front lines remained completely entangled. If Weidling's breakout was to have any chance of success, it was vital that the bridges over the Havel were in German hands and a battalion from 18th Panzergrenadier Division was ordered to push down Heerstrasse to secure the crossings over the Stössensee and the Havel. Other units of 18th Panzergrenadier Division were gathering in the Grunewald area, immediately south of these crossings, and they detained a man in civilian clothing who appeared to be trying to escape from Berlin. He told the soldiers that he had top secret documents, and the officers reported to the division's command post close to the Zoo Flak Tower that these appeared to be Hitler's will and testament, naming Dönitz as his successor. Böttscher, the division's operations officer, telephoned the bunker beneath the Reich Chancellery and spoke to Bormann. He told him what had happened:

> Bormann: What the hell do you think you are doing? This is unacceptable! The man was ordered to take those documents out of Berlin. You are not permitted to arrest any of my people or to read such secret documents. You must forget what you have read immediately, or there will be severe consequences. Are you aware that you have stopped this man from carrying out the Führer's direct orders?
>
> Böttscher: I had no idea about any of this. Nobody told me he was going to try to pass through my lines. The commander has simply done his duty. We have

The Bitterest of Ends: Berlin, 29 April–2 May

firm orders to detain all deserters. If I had known, I would have offered the man protection while he crossed through my lines.

Bormann: I have sent two other men with the same orders and the same papers. Take care that they at least get through.

At that moment, a second man was detained with the same documents. The conversation continued:

Böttscher: We have captured a second man and he has been brought to my office. What am I meant to do with these two?

Bormann (now screaming): Send them back to the *Führerbunker*![5]

After their terrifying journey towards central Berlin along the *U-Bahn* tunnels, Altner and his comrades were stunned to be told that they were to return to Ruhleben in the west. Wearily, they retraced their footsteps before dawn, dodging bursts of gunfire that came from soldiers fighting on both sides. When they reached the *U-Bahn* station outside the Opera House, they were warned that Soviet troops had blocked the way further west, and they divided into two groups. One would continue along the tunnel, while the other – including Altner – would follow the main highway; the two groups would try to meet at Adolf-Hitler-Platz (now Theodor-Heuss-Platz). If there had been Soviet troops blocking their route, they had clearly moved on, and the two German groups reached their destination without incident and then continued northwest to their old barracks where they were able to get some sleep. Later, Altner was assigned to a group that was sent to a nearby foreign labourers' camp. At first, he wondered why he and the others were issued with plentiful weapons and ammunition:

> We have to search the huts. Apparently arms and equipment of foreign origin are hidden here.
>
> Each one of us is assigned a room. When I go into mine, some women cower in a corner and look at me fearfully. One of them speaks a little German and keeps repeating that there are no hidden weapons ... The girl who speaks German suddenly says that now a few more will be shot, just like yesterday. The other women start crying ... In order to stop the crying, I ask the interpreter about the men. 'Shot,' is all she says. 'Only those in the kitchen are left. The others were shot.'[6]

Altner and the others were told that the men in the camp had been executed the previous day because an illegal radio set had been found in the camp. In the nearby cookhouse was a group of SS soldiers, who boasted about how they had killed the prisoners. Dismayed and demoralised, Altner and the others returned to their barracks. They had been told that several Soviet soldiers had been taken prisoner while they were making their hazardous journey along the *U-Bahn* tunnels and after being questioned had been shot; quietly, some wondered what chance they would have if they were captured by the Red Army.

To the north of the city centre, the advancing Soviet troops had reached the Moltkebrücke over the Spree, immediately to the north of the Tiergarten. Troops from Third Shock Army's 171st Rifle Division managed to secure the damaged bridge but faced fierce battles to take the buildings on the south bank of the Spree. Other riflemen crossed the river a little to the east and reached the Brandenburg Gate, where they raised the Soviet flag. The Germans promptly tore it down, but by the end of the day the Soviet troops had pushed south from the Moltkebrücke to the Kroll Opera House on the edge of the Tiergarten.

Behind the front line, the anonymous diarist in northern Berlin endured further rapes. Like other women, she tried to find a single Soviet soldier – ideally an officer – who, in return for sexual favours, would protect her from other soldiers. To her surprise, she discovered that the presence of officers often resulted in no change in the behaviour of Soviet soldiers – 'apparently the strict Prussian order of ranks we're so used to doesn't apply here'.[7] Eventually, a young Ukrainian junior lieutenant named Anatol offered her a degree of safety, but at the price of having sex whenever he wished. Even women who had lived in terror during the Nazi years were unsafe. Ellen Goetz, a Jewish woman, had escaped from one of Berlin's prisons after an air raid and was repeatedly raped. Other German women attempted to explain to the soldiers that she was Jewish; the response of the soldiers was to shrug and reply, '*Frau ist Frau.*'[8]

In his bunker, Hitler learned of the death of Benito Mussolini, the former Italian dictator. Trying to escape to Switzerland, Mussolini had been captured by Communist partisans on 27 April and was taken to the small village of Giulino di Mezzegra, where he and his mistress Clara Petacci were shot on 28 April. Knowing that a similar fate or worse awaited him if he were captured, Hitler's determination to end his life rather than surrender was further reinforced. Late that evening, he sent a signal to Jodl. He demanded to know the location of Wenck's Twelfth Army and when it would attack; similarly, he asked where and when Ninth Army would break through and join the relief attempt. Finally, he wanted to know the location of the former *Armeegruppe Steiner*, now commanded by Holste. The replies to all these questions arrived shortly after midnight. None of the three forces were advancing towards Berlin. Wenck had been forced onto the defensive, as had Holste, and Ninth Army was completely isolated.

Communications with the outside world were now erratic at best. Radio contact had been via a set connected to an antenna that was held aloft by a

The Bitterest of Ends: Berlin, 29 April–2 May

balloon, but this had been shot down; the telephone lines from the bunker were also increasingly disrupted. Many in the bunker were aware that there was no possibility of negotiating an end to the violence until Hitler took his own life. In the meantime, the chances of anyone else emerging alive diminished almost by the hour. Late on 29 April, Krebs' aide Loringhoven decided that if he was going to escape, time was running out:

> I decided to go to see Krebs and tell him bluntly that I had no intention of getting myself killed in the bunker. I had reached the limit I had set myself. My job had been to collect as much intelligence as possible and transfer it to the maps. The interruption of the last link with *OKW* meant that I could no longer do my work. My military duty was over and all I had to do was look after my own welfare ... [It was] a hard decision and potentially fraught with consequences. I risked being taken for a deserter, which would mean immediate execution.[9]

Krebs was reluctant to give Loringhoven – and Hauptmann Gerhardt Boldt, Loringhoven's assistant – permission to leave and raised the matter with Burgdorf. Perhaps to Loringhoven's surprise, Burgdorf was more favourable, adding that his own aide-de-camp, Oberstleutnant Rudolf Weiss, should accompany the two men. He also asked that the three men should personally see Hitler before they left, and a strange interview followed. Despite the imminent collapse of everything, the Führer seemed calm and enquired about the route they intended to take. Given his familiarity with maps and the military situation, Loringhoven had been asked about possible escape routes by several people over the preceding days and he outlined two possible options. With his characteristic obsession with often-trivial details, Hitler became more animated and recommended the route that included making use of the Havel River through Spandau, adding that it would be best to find a boat with an electric motor as this was less likely to be heard by Soviet troops. Rather than indulge in a pointless discussion, Loringhoven assured Hitler that he would take heed of his advice. The three men were issued with written orders to leave Berlin and make their way to Wenck's headquarters and escaped into the darkness. The nearest Red Army soldiers were just 800 metres from the bunker.

On 30 April, the battle for the ruined city continued. From the west, Third Guards Tank Army and Twenty-Eighth Army, from Konev's 1st Ukrainian Front, edged closer to the central part of Berlin, a little to the south of the highway that Altner and his comrades had used a short time before. German resistance was strong, and it seems that some of the attacks were at best half-hearted. To the rear of this attack, there was bitter fighting as other elements of Rybalko's tank army tried to clear the Wilmersdorf district; by the end of the day, most of the German defences had been crushed.

Throughout the war, and particularly in connection with the attempt to assassinate Hitler in July 1944, many – perhaps most – German officers had refused to break the personal oath of loyalty they had taken to Hitler. Even now, in the midst of the catastrophe that had befallen Germany, the oath remained an obstacle for many. The elements of 18th Panzergrenadier Division that had gathered in and around the Zoo Flak Tower were meant to be preparing for a breakout, but several junior officers informed Böttscher, the operations officer, that they refused to take part in such an operation as they felt their oath required them to stay in Berlin while the Führer was still alive. Böttscher raised the matter with Rauch, the division commander, using the telephone link to the Reich Chancellery bunker, and Rauch replied that he would discuss it with Weidling. That evening, he telephoned Böttscher and told him that the matter had been raised with Hitler, who had relieved all soldiers of any obligation to stick to their oath. It is by no means clear whether any such discussions took place. Rauch or Weidling may have decided that given the manner in which events were unfolding, the oath was meaningless and nobody would have any opportunity to confirm what was being said.[10]

Chuikov's Eighth Guards Army continued to smash its way through the German defenders along the southern approaches to the Tiergarten. Zhukov contacted Chuikov repeatedly, asking anxiously whether Berlin would fall in time for the traditional Soviet May Day celebrations; Chuikov replied that resistance was weakening, but completion of the conquest of Berlin within the next day was unlikely. There was similar pressure on other armies. The Soviet troops that had spilled so much blood crossing the Spree at the Moltkebrücke the previous day were urged to drive on to capture the ruins of the Reichstag and began to move forward before dawn, even though in the darkness, dust, and smoke, nobody knew precisely where their objective was. As it grew light, Soviet soldiers attempted to attack across Königsplatz (now Platz der Republik) but were smashed by concentrated fire, including shells fired by the guns of the Zoo Flak Tower. Much of LXXIX Rifle Corps, part of Third Shock Army, now gathered its diminished strength at the southern end of the Moltkebrücke for a more organised attack. The first objective was to suppress the defenders in the ruins of the Kroll Opera House to the southwest, so that attacks towards the southeast and the Reichstag could proceed without flanking fire. The opera house came under heavy artillery bombardment before an attack was launched in the early afternoon by 207th Rifle Division, supported by tanks. Once again, heavy defensive fire brought the assault to a premature halt.

The Bitterest of Ends: Berlin, 29 April–2 May

German reinforcements – no more than a handful of men, a single King Tiger, and three assault guns – joined the battle. More Soviet tanks were ordered across the Moltkebrücke; many of them were promptly knocked out. A third attack towards both the Reichstag and the opera house in the early evening was also repulsed, but a message reached the headquarters of 1st Belarusian Front claiming that the Reichstag was in Soviet hands. This prompted a proclamation that was sent to all units of Zhukov's Front:

> Forces of Colonel General Kuznetsov's Third Shock Army, continuing the attack, overcame enemy resistance and seized the main building of the Reichstag and today, 30 April 1945, at 1425, raised our Soviet flag above it …
>
> The time is approaching for the final victory over the enemy. Our Soviet flag already flies above the main building of the Reichstag in the heart of Berlin.[11]

For the Red Army soldiers fighting and dying a little to the north of the Reichstag, this must have seemed an utterly bizarre message. Major General Semen Nikoforovich Perevertkin, commander of LXXIX Rifle Corps, demanded confirmation that a Soviet flag was flying above the ruins of the Reichstag. When Captain Stepan Andreyevich Neustroyev, one of his battalion commanders, replied that he could see no flags and doubted that any Soviet troops had reached the ruins, he was ordered to ensure that a flag was raised at least somewhere in the buildings that composed the Reichstag before the end of the day.

Gathering their strength, the Soviet troops attacked again at dusk, reinforced by a heavy tank regiment; many of its IS-2 tanks had been knocked out as they crossed the Moltkebrücke, with some being blown off the bridge entirely by the heavy guns of the Zoo Flak Tower. Although the Red Army placed great importance on capturing the Reichstag, the building had been in ruins since the fire of 1933 and the Germans do not appear to have regarded it as a vital location. Nonetheless, it had a substantial garrison. Neustroyev's troops finally entered the buildings shortly before midnight and a small group of riflemen occupied parts of the ruins. In an attempt to comply with Perevertkin's orders, regimental banners were hung from the windows.

Having left the bunker beneath the Reich Chancellery during the night, Loringhoven and the two men accompanying him went first to the Zoo *U-Bahn* station, where they were able to get a ride on an armoured car that took them west towards Pichelsdorf. They spent much of the day trying to find a boat, dodging Soviet patrols; finally, in a small canoe they paddled southwest to the *Pfaueninsel* ('Peacock Island'), where they sheltered amongst the reeds. Behind them, the final stages of the drama in the bunker were coming to their inevitable conclusion. Probably shortly before his conversation with Loringhoven and the other two officers, Hitler had ordered Feldwebel Fritz Tornow, who cared for his dog Blondi, to administer poison to the animal. Ostensibly, this was because Hitler couldn't bear the thought of the animal falling into Soviet hands; at a more practical level, it was an opportunity to test the efficacy of the cyanide capsules that were being distributed in the bunker. A few minutes after the Alsatian stopped breathing, Tornow shot Blondi's four puppies.

Shortly before receiving Jodl's reply to his questions about the whereabouts and movements of Ninth and Twelfth Armies and Holste's units, Hitler met several senior figures in his conference room at about 0200: Goebbels and his wife Magda; Burgdorf and Krebs, Mohnke, Rattenhuber, and Walther Hewel (a senior Nazi diplomat); his secretaries; and several of the high-ranking SS officers who had gathered in the bunker. He shook hands with each in turn. According to one source, he spoke a few words with each person, but the noise of the bunker's diesel generators drowned out his voice, reduced now just to a mumbling whisper.[12] Finally, he addressed them collectively, reiterating his intention to take his own life and freeing them all of any obligations under their oaths of loyalty – it is possible that Krebs then made Weidling aware of this, hence the outcome of the enquiries from 18th Panzergrenadier Division. Those who wanted to leave should do so without delay. He then retired to his personal rooms.

Shortly before dawn on 30 April, Hitler summoned Mohnke to ask him how long the soldiers defending the Reich Chancellery could hold out. Mohnke replied that the fighting would probably be over within a few hours. At midday, several figures met for the daily conference. Weidling reported that he was losing contact with many of his units and that coherent defence of the central part of Berlin was now impossible. At first, Hitler insisted that no units were permitted to surrender, but at the end of the discussion he issued a final order:

> In the event of the defenders of the capital city of the Reich facing a lack of munitions and supplies, I give my consent for a breakout. They must break out in small groups, and must look for units that are still fighting and join them. If they cannot find any, the small groups are to continue fighting in the forests.[13]

Several SS soldiers ventured out of the bunker and, under artillery fire, filled canisters with gasoline from abandoned vehicles. After a light meal, Hitler met Goebbels once more; in a last-minute change of heart, the propaganda minister urged the Führer to leave, but even if Hitler had been minded to follow this advice, it was far too late. He pointed out to Goebbels that there was nowhere to go, and he had no intention of being killed in the streets of Berlin – or worse still, being wounded and then being captured. There was one last round of farewells, after which Hitler said once again that he had been betrayed by the army, the SS, and the German people. Haunted by the reports of the mutilation of the corpses of Mussolini and his mistress, he stressed that his body was to be destroyed, and then he and his wife Eva retired to their rooms. Characteristically, his last words to his inner circle were that the epitaph on his tombstone should read *Das Opfer seiner Generäle* ('The victim of his generals').

On the floor above, discipline had collapsed completely and those in the main canteen indulged in heavy drinking, dancing, and uninhibited sex. The end of Hitler's rule descended to utter farce: a messenger was sent upstairs to urge the revellers to be silent as the Führer was about to end his life, but it had little effect. Some of those who were waiting outside Hitler's rooms heard a single shot. When they entered the rooms, they found that Hitler had shot himself. Next to him was Eva, who had taken a cyanide capsule. The two corpses were carried to the bunker garden, which was now under gunfire, and it took several attempts before the bodies could be placed a short distance from the entrance to the bunker. They were doused with the gasoline that had been gathered earlier and were set ablaze.

Weidling had returned to his headquarters, and issued orders for a breakout attempt to be made that evening. He then returned briefly to the bunker, where Krebs informed him of Hitler's death and swore him to secrecy. He also said that Siefert had been ordered to contact the commanders of the Soviet forces attacking central Berlin; he was to make them aware of Hitler's death and then commence negotiations for a final surrender. Goebbels joined the discussion, stressing that it was vital that Weidling cancel any plans for a breakout – even at this late stage, he still dreamed of negotiating a settlement that would leave the Nazi government in power, and wished to use the possibility of continued resistance in Berlin as a bargaining chip. But despite attempts to avoid others becoming aware of Hitler's death, the news began to spread rapidly. The soldiers in the Friedrichshain Flak Tower left their positions during the evening, slipping away towards the west. They left behind several hundred wounded men with medical personnel, and the formidable fortress was surrendered the following day.

Shortly before midnight on 30 April, Chuikov received an urgent radio message from Lieutenant General Vasily Asanavovich Glazunov, commander of IV Guard Rifle Corps. A German Oberstleutnant had appeared carrying a white flag and a set of documents that he said had to be passed to higher commands immediately. The German officer was Siefert, and he had informed Glazunov that his seniors wished to meet their Soviet counterparts. Chuikov immediately agreed to meet the German delegation. He was unable to hide his excitement at this development, and Vsevolod Vitalyevich Vishnevsky, a writer who was accompanying the troops of Eighth Guards Army, realised that something momentous was happening. He begged Chuikov for permission to accompany him. After informing the headquarters of 1st Belarusian Front, Chuikov left for his forward command post, where he awaited the German envoy:

> An agonising wait began. Only my adjutant and I were in the room. An hour and a half passed. It was deep night, but I didn't feel like sleeping at all. Memories flashed through my head. The war had been going on for four years already. The Volga was before my eyes, now distant and yet so close; burning oil had spilled over it, the raging flames were devouring everything – barges, boats. Here were leaflets from Goebbels' propaganda … Here I saw the night assault on Zaporozhye, and Nikopol, Odessa, Lublin, and Łódź. And finally Berlin. After defending the sacred line of the Volga, my Soviet soldiers were now standing on the Spree. They had temporarily put down their weapons and awaited the envoys from the Wehrmacht leaders, the very same ones who were recently certain of the imminent end of the Soviet state. Envoys from the leaders of the Third Reich – did these leaders now think that we had such short memories that we had already forgotten the millions killed, the tens of millions of widows and orphans, the gallows and the gas chambers, Majdanek and the other death camps?[14]

The group was then joined by Matvei Isaakovich Blanter, a composer, who was wearing civilian clothes; he had been sent to Berlin by Stalin to compose a symphony about the fall of Berlin and wanted to be present. Chuikov decided that it was inappropriate for a man dressed as a civilian to be in the meeting and ordered him to hide in a large cupboard and to remain silent. At about 0300, Krebs crossed the front line with Dufving, Weidling's chief of staff, and an interpreter – the latter wasn't strictly necessary, as Krebs spoke excellent Russian. Krebs was taken to Chuikov's command post where he said he wished to speak directly to Zhukov. Chuikov replied that he was empowered to listen to whatever Krebs had to say. Krebs informed him that he was the first non-German to be told that Hitler had taken his own life, and paused to see what effect his words would have. With commendable *chutzpah*, Chuikov – for whom this was momentous news – hid his surprise and replied blandly, 'We know that.' The discomfited Krebs then handed over three documents. The first was a note from Goebbels confirming Hitler's death and adding that he, Bormann, and Dönitz had inherited Hitler's various posts. The second was an authorisation for Krebs to conduct negotiations. The third was a copy of Hitler's will and testament, listing the various personalities who had been given control of the Reich.

Chuikov asked for clarity: was Krebs talking about surrender? Krebs responded that there were other ways of ending the fighting than complete surrender, and that formal negotiations with Dönitz should decide matters. There followed a staccato series of questions and answers – Chuikov reported what was happening by telephone to Zhukov, who then made him wait while he telephoned Stalin in Moscow. Eventually, Chuikov informed the chief of the German general staff that he was only prepared to discuss unconditional surrender. Krebs asked for a local ceasefire while he discussed matters with other senior figures and again Chuikov repeated his insistence for unconditional surrender:

> 'You must understand, *Herr General*,' I said, 'that we know what you want from us. You intend to warn us that you will continue the struggle, or rather, the senseless resistance will increase the number of pointless victims. Let me ask you directly: what is the meaning of your struggle?'
>
> Krebs looked at me silently for a few seconds, seemingly lost for words, and then blurted out, 'We will fight to the last.'
>
> I couldn't resist an ironic smile. 'General, what do you have left, with what forces do you want to fight?' Then, after a short pause, I added, 'We await your complete capitulation.'
>
> 'No!' exclaimed Krebs. He added with a sigh, 'In the event of complete capitulation, we will not exist legally as a government.'[15]

The meeting of Krebs, who had served in various posts on the Eastern Front during the war before becoming chief of the general staff, and Chuikov, the wiry-haired veteran who had defended Stalingrad with such tenacity and had then fought almost every step of the way from there to Berlin, was already taking on an air of unreality. It descended into comical surrealism when Blanter, who had been in his cupboard for several hours, suddenly fell out with a loud clatter. He had lost consciousness; two guards simply dragged him from the room while Krebs watched, nonplussed. Without a word of explanation, the negotiations continued. As a battery of *Katyusha* launchers hurled another salvo of rockets into central Berlin, Chuikov pointed out that the Swedish government was reporting on negotiations with Himmler – in other words, there did not seem to be any single authority left in Germany. By now, it was growing light and Chuikov and Vishnevsky – the latter diligently scribbling down every exchange – had been joined by General Vasily Danilovich Sokolovsky, deputy commander of 1st Belarusian Front. As Krebs appeared to be unable to accept unconditional surrender, Sokolovsky suggested that he should send Dufving, accompanied by a Soviet officer, back to Goebbels to report on the discussions. Despite coming under fire from nervous German soldiers, Dufving was able to return to the bunker. A local ceasefire was arranged so that a telephone cable could be run along Prinz-Albrecht-Strasse from the German front line to the Soviet side and Dufving then reported back. Goebbels had summoned Krebs back to the bunker with the Soviet demands in writing.[16]

Throughout the morning, the Soviet forces had been bringing forward ammunition and had regrouped for further assaults. On the other side of the front line, there were few supplies to distribute and few troops to reorganise. Krukenberg, commander of *SS-Nordland*, learned about the negotiations from Mohnke, who made him personally responsible for preventing the Red Army from taking advantage of the negotiations to infiltrate forward. The wording of Mohnke's instructions left Krukenberg in no doubt that such 'infiltration' included any forward movement of Soviet troops as a direct result of the negotiations. This appears to have been a deliberate attempt by Mohnke – who was a member of the SS – to prevent Krebs from agreeing any surrender unilaterally.

Despite the local ceasefire, the battle continued elsewhere. The leading troops of Berzarin's Fifth Shock Army had cleared the Kaiser Wilhelm-Brücke (now Karl-Liebknecht-Brücke) to the Museum Island and the Schlossbrücke across the western channel of the Spree. They now advanced west along Unter den Linden, storming the State Opera House and State Library, and continued towards the Brandenburg Gate. When they reached the iconic landmark, they linked up with riflemen from Chuikov's Eighth Guards Army, advancing from the south. A little to the west, despite the claims that the Soviet flag was flying over the ruins of the Reichstag at the end of 30 April, fighting raged on throughout 1 May. German resistance finally came to an end amidst the rubble that evening, with the last German defenders slipping away to the *S-Bahn* station a little to the northeast. The famous photograph of Red Army soldiers unfurling the Soviet flag above the Reichstag was actually staged the following day. In the meantime, fighting within the buildings continued. At first, the Soviet troops were unaware of the existence of an extensive system of basements, and in any case they were short of ammunition and other supplies. Neustroyev ordered his men to try to clear the basement anyway; the first attack cost over 50 dead or wounded. By now, German artillery was shelling the area, and in the second half of 1 May German troops counterattacked into the buildings before finally withdrawing as darkness fell.

Although Soviet artillery was still firing, many German soldiers noted that the intensity of combat had significantly slackened. One soldier later recalled that at least in his sector, things were far quieter:

> There was artillery fire on 1 May but no close-quarter combat. You'll know that everyone talks about the fighting around the Reich Chancellery and the

surrounding area – there was, but mainly it was artillery and sniper fire. I at least was able to walk along the streets. It seems to me that the Russians weren't too eager to fight – they too wanted to survive.[17]

In many locations, some officers started to send *Volkssturm* and Hitler Youth back to their families. But others took a different view. Aribert Schulz, aged 16, had been part of a draft raised during the winter and intended as replacements for 12th *SS-Hitlerjugend* Panzer Division, but had found himself in Berlin with a mixture of other youths, *Volkssturm*, and a few SS. As the battles for central Berlin began, Schulz and the others were advised to remove their SS insignia; Schulz scratched off the SS runes on his helmet, acutely aware that the shape of the scratches left little doubt that the insignia had been there. Shortly after, they captured a Red Army soldier who was emerging from a wrecked tank. The man was interrogated and then turned out on the street, but after he had walked a few paces towards his own lines, an older soldier in the unit shot him dead.

On 1 May, the small group received unexpected reinforcements when 76 sailors appeared. At first, Schulz and his comrades were excited at the thought that these men, wearing naval uniforms, were the vanguard of the long-awaited 'Wenck Army' – the previous evening, they had heard a radio broadcast claiming that Twelfth Army was very close and that a ceasefire had been agreed with the Western Powers – but they were soon told that they were merely soldiers transferred from elsewhere.

A newssheet entitled *Panzerbär* ('Armoured Bear', a reference to both the panzer arm and the bear emblem of Berlin) had been circulating for several weeks and a final edition appeared that day, informing Schulz and the others that Hitler was dead. Although there was consternation about what might lie ahead, there was apparently little genuine sorrow. Thiemer, the unit commander, gathered them together and made them swear allegiance to Dönitz, the new head of state. Shortly after, a loudspeaker truck approached and a German – a member of the Soviet-run *Komitee Freies Deutschland* – gave his name, rank, and serial number, and then called on them to lay down their weapons and avoid senseless deaths. Ammunition was running short, with each person having no more than 20 rounds, but Thiemer was determined to fight to the last bullet. Reinforced by two tanks and a vehicle-mounted quadruple 20mm anti-aircraft gun, the group – now numbering between 200 and 300 – attempted to retake Spittelmarkt. The fighting lasted from mid-afternoon until after dusk, with heavy losses on both sides – Thiemer was killed, together with about half his command. The remnants were ordered to pull back towards the Reich Chancellery, where they were meant to join others preparing to break out to the west.[18]

To the west, Soviet troops were steadily working their way into the Tiergarten. Although a few diehards from 18th Panzergrenadier Division reiterated their intention to stay and die in Berlin, the rest of the division's survivors, together with the flak crews of the Zoo Tower, prepared to make their bid to escape. Three columns were organised, with the intention of attempting to reach the Havel that night.

Meanwhile, in the bunker beneath the Reich Chancellery, Goebbels and Krebs discussed the results of the meeting with Chuikov. Goebbels was a veteran of the Nazi Party's struggles against the Communists in the Weimar years, and for him it was unthinkable that he should negotiate a surrender with people that he regarded as implacable enemies. He made a final, long-winded entry in his diary, but this section did not survive the war. When Hanna Reitsch had left the bunker, Magda had given her a letter for Harald Quandt, her son by a previous marriage:

> By now, we have been in the *Führerbunker* for six days already – Papa, your six little siblings and I, for the sake of giving our National Socialist lives the only possible honourable end ... You shall know that I stayed here against Papa's wishes, and that even on last Sunday [29 April] the Führer wanted to help me to get out. You know your mother – we have the same blood, for me there was no wavering. Our glorious dream is ruined and with it everything beautiful and marvellous that I have known in my life. The world that comes after the Führer and National Socialism isn't worth living in any longer and therefore I took the children with me, for they are too good for the life that would follow, and a merciful God will understand me when I give them deliverance ... Harald, my dear son, I want to give you what I learned in life: be loyal! Loyal to yourself, loyal to the people and loyal to your country ... Be proud of us and try to keep us dear in your memory.[19]

There is an unintended irony in these closing remarks. Magda had at least one affair during her first marriage, and at least two more – with Kurt Ludecke and Karl Hanke, both senior Nazis – in the 1930s when she was married to Goebbels, who was himself notorious for several affairs. Whilst both believed themselves to be unshakably loyal to the Führer, their loyalty didn't extend to their personal lives.

The six children, born between 1932 and 1940, were first put to sleep, by being given either an oral sleeping draught or a morphine injection. Their mouths were then held open while hydrogen cyanide was administered. The oldest, Helga, was later found to have bruises on her upper arms, suggesting that she had been held down forcibly while the poison was poured into her mouth. The couple had a last moment with Bormann and a few others, reminiscing about the 'good old days'. They then left the bunker and shot themselves just outside the entrance. Hauptsturmführer Günther Schwägermann, his adjutant, had been ordered by Goebbels to ensure that the couple was dead; Schwägermann ordered a guard to fire a couple of times into each body, and the corpses were then doused with petrol and set alight.

Even if Goebbels was not prepared to contemplate surrender to the hated Bolsheviks, others could see no point in further senseless deaths. Hans Fritsche, a senior figure in Goebbels' propaganda ministry, was aghast that Krebs and Goebbels were unwilling to accept Chuikov's terms and decided to try to bring the fighting to an end. His office in Wilhelmstrasse was a short distance from the bunker and he quickly went there to write a personal letter to Zhukov, offering the surrender of the city, but he had been followed by Burgdorf. Heavily intoxicated, Burgdorf burst into his room and threatened to shoot Fritsche, adding that as a civilian he had no authority to negotiate a surrender. A radio technician intervened, knocking Burgdorf's arm upwards as he attempted to shoot Fritsche; Burgdorf was then overpowered and taken back to the bunker. Shaken but unharmed, Fritsche wrote a note that was to be taken across the front line.[20]

It was now mid-evening, and like Fritsche Weidling decided that he would take matters into his own hands. After a brief discussion with Krebs, he headed for his own headquarters, intending to send a signal to the Red Army calling for a ceasefire. Mohnke gathered the commanders of the units still arrayed around the Reich Chancellery. He quickly brought them up to date, adding that Weidling intended to order his units to break off combat with the Red Army shortly after midnight; any that were able to move were to try to break out of Berlin. He then organised people into about ten groups, each of roughly 20, which were to leave the bunker at short intervals and head for the nearby *U-Bahn* station on Wilhelmplatz, from where they would follow the tunnels north in the hope of reaching the Stettiner station, in the northern part of Berlin. This was in marked contrast to the attempt by Weidling to concentrate forces around the Zoo Flak Tower prior to an attempt to break out to the west.

Shortly after midnight, Weidling sent a radio transmission to the Soviet forces:

> This is the German LVI Panzer Corps. This is the German LVI Panzer Corps. We ask that you cease your fire. At 0250 Berlin time, we will dispatch truce delegates to the Potsdamerbrücke. They will be carrying a white flag in front of a red light. Please reply. We are waiting.[21]

The reply was almost immediate, telling Weidling that his message was being passed up the chain of command. Chuikov then ordered a ceasefire around the Potsdamerbrücke, running over the Landwehr Canal to the south of the Tiergarten. Whilst his ultimate intention was to bring the fighting in Berlin to an end, Weidling's more immediate concern was with his breakout attempt; he hoped that by negotiating an immediate ceasefire, he might buy precious time for the soldiers and civilians who were hoping to escape to the west.

The first Germans to cross the Potsdamerbrücke were Dufving and two other staff officers. The commander of 47th Guards Rifle Division, Major General Vasily Minayevich Shugayev, was temporarily away from his command post and in his absence the division was led by his deputy, Colonel Semchenko. Chuikov had already sent him a message that he was to avoid negotiating with the Germans personally, and was to limit his conversation to asking how long it would take for the Germans to lay down their weapons. Dufving informed him that at least three or four hours would be needed, due to communications difficulties and potential problems ensuring that the SS units in the capital acquiesced to Weidling's orders. Semchenko reported this to Chuikov, who told him to send Dufving back to the German lines; he was to inform Weidling that only the unconditional surrender of all forces in Berlin would be accepted.

While he waited for Weidling to respond, Chuikov had a visit shortly before dawn on 2 May from another German delegation, this time from Fritsche:

> There were three delegates, all in civilian clothing, accompanied by a soldier in a helmet with a white flag. I ordered the soldier to leave. One of the others was an advisor from the propaganda ministry named Heinersdorf. I asked, 'What do you want and how can I help you?'
>
> Heinersdorf handed me a letter in a pink folder. I read it; Vishnevsky, Pozharsky, Vainrub, and Tkakencho studied it over my shoulders:
>
> 'As you have been informed by General Krebs, former Reich Chancellor Hitler is no more. Dr Goebbels is no longer alive. As one of the surviving officials, I ask you to take Berlin under your protection. You will be aware of my name: [Signed] Dr Hans Fritsche, Director of the Propaganda Ministry.'
>
> I read this, amazed by the course of events in the last few days and even hours. After Hitler, Goebbels had been appointed, and after Goebbels – who would be next? Whoever it was, this was effectively the end of the war.[22]

The delegation informed Chuikov that they accepted the requirement for unconditional surrender. They added that Fritsche was a well-known personality

The Bitterest of Ends: Berlin, 29 April–2 May

and it was likely that German forces would obey orders issued by him; Fritsche was prepared to make a radio broadcast to this effect.

The civilian delegation was still with Chuikov when Weidling arrived at the command post of 47th Guards Rifle Division. Semchenko asked him if his proposed surrender of LVI Panzer Corps had the approval of Goebbels; Weidling replied that he had decided to act without the knowledge of any remaining government figures.

Chuikov now ordered a more general ceasefire and ordered that Weidling be brought to his command post. In the meantime, he spoke to Zhukov by telephone and then told Heinersdorf to return to Fritsche, who was to issue a written order and speak on the radio telling all German troops to surrender. As the civilians left, they met Weidling at the door. The exhausted commander of LVI Panzer Corps glared at them and said, 'This should have been done earlier!'[23]

Immediately, Chuikov questioned Weidling. He asked him for the whereabouts of Krebs; Weidling replied that he had seen the chief of the general staff the previous day and believed he would commit suicide. He added that Krebs, Goebbels, and Bormann had rejected Chuikov's terms the previous evening, but Krebs had later changed his mind. Chuikov asked if Weidling's command extended to all German forces in Berlin. The answer was unsurprisingly evasive, given the confusing overlapping of commands in the capital.

Chuikov then told Weidling to issue an order for immediate surrender. Weidling declined, saying that communications difficulties might make such an order impossible to implement quickly, and that with so many soldiers still unaware of Hitler's death, the previous prohibitions on surrender would still be seen by many as being in force. According to some sources, Weidling added that he was no longer in a position to issue orders as he had personally surrendered, and there was a pause when the German general – who had commanded his corps in increasingly difficult conditions with almost no sleep since the fighting in the urban area commenced – had to take a break. Finally, with Dufving's help, he drafted an order that was to be disseminated as widely as possible, and would be read out via loudspeakers:

Berlin, 2 May 1945.

On 30 April 1945, the Führer committed suicide, and thus abandoned all of us who had sworn loyalty to him.

In accordance with the Führer's orders, you believed that you had to continue to fight for Berlin, even in the face of shortages of weapons and ammunition and in an overall situation that made the battle senseless.

> Every hour that you continue to fight prolongs the terrible suffering of the civilian population of Berlin and of our wounded. Anyone who is still killed in combat in Berlin makes his sacrifice in vain.
>
> In agreement with the high command of the Soviet forces, I order you to cease fighting immediately.
>
> Weidling, General of Artillery and Commandant of the Berlin Defensive District.[24]

The original draft included the word 'former' before Weidling's status as commander of the Berlin garrison, but Chuikov and Sokolovsky told him that he should remove it. A few hours later, Chuikov – who, like Weidling, was functioning on very little sleep – met Fritsche. By now, they had both learned that Dönitz, from his headquarters in the north, had broadcast a message stating that he accepted Hitler's decision to nominate him as president and that he would continue the struggle.

It was the end of Weidling's contribution to the battle. He became a prisoner of war and wrote detailed accounts of the battle for Berlin for his captors. In 1952, he was charged with war crimes committed in the Soviet Union in zones under his control, particularly the deliberate infection of prisoners with typhus, and was sentenced to 25 years' imprisonment. By this time, he was 61 and in poor health. Soviet records state that he died of heart failure in November 1955 in a prison in the city of Vladimir, but this may not be accurate. When Adenauer, the first chancellor of West Germany, successfully negotiated the release of all remaining prisoners in Soviet hands, many were already dead, but the dates of their deaths had not been recorded accurately or often at all. The Soviet authorities therefore improvised, adding dates of death that happened to be between the date of Adenauer's visit and the final release of prisoners.

Weidling was a competent if unspectacular military commander, and in some respects was fortunate not to rise above corps command – at this level, he was well within his capabilities, and he was not exposed to the likely negative effect on his reputation of taking command of a field army in the years of defeat. There is no doubt that he was aware of the crimes committed in his jurisdiction in the Soviet Union, and that is a major blemish on his record. Although he wished to avoid the civilian casualties that would result from fighting in Berlin, he nonetheless obeyed orders from above, even when he must have known that these orders were both wrong and would make no difference to the final outcome of the war. But in this respect, he was no better or worse than most of his contemporary German officers. The instinct to obey instructions remained strong to the end.

The Bitterest of Ends: Berlin, 29 April–2 May

After Goebbels' rejection of Chuikov's terms the previous day, there had been a further spell of heavy shelling of the centre of Berlin, but now the guns were falling silent and after so many days of battle, many of the survivors on both sides found the lack of noise and smoke unsettling. Cautiously at first, Soviet soldiers moved forward, disarming the Germans they found and marching them away. There were still occasional exchanges of fire, but most men from both the Wehrmacht and the Red Army, not to mention the tens of thousands of civilians in the city, were grateful that the Soviet assaults had come to an end. The bunker beneath the Reich Chancellery, which had been badly overcrowded for many days, was now eerily empty. Many had left in a desperate last-minute attempt to escape capture by the Red Army, but others had followed the example of Hitler and Goebbels. Krebs and Burgdorf shared a bottle of fine Cognac and then took their own lives before dawn on 2 May – most accounts state that they shot themselves, but a few suggest that Burgdorf, at least, took poison.[25] It is possible that they feared the personal consequences of becoming prisoners – they had held posts that could have resulted in prosecutions for war crimes. But both had served as junior officers in the First World War and had endured the humiliation of national defeat and it is likely that, like many others, they simply couldn't face the prospect of living through the aftermath of another surrender.

Others in the bunker also chose to end their lives. Brigadeführer Alwin-Broder Albrecht, a former naval officer who spent much of the war as an adjutant to Hitler, was seen amongst the defenders of the central District Z, firing a machine-gun at attacking Soviet riflemen, but is believed to have killed himself.[26] Obersturmbannführer Franz Schädle, commander of Hitler's last bodyguard detail, had been wounded by shrapnel on 28 April and was only able to move around with crutches; knowing that it would be impossible to escape in such a condition, he shot himself. And across Berlin – indeed, in many parts of Germany – there was a wave of suicides, with more than 7,000 Berliners taking their lives. In numerous cases, parents killed their small children before committing suicide themselves. Motivations varied. In many cases, there was justifiable fear of what would happen when the Red Army arrived. Goebbels' propaganda ministry had ensured that all Germans were aware of the atrocities committed by Soviet troops as they entered East Prussia. There was also an awareness that this was not purely because they were 'barbarous Asiatic hordes', as Goebbels described the Red Army. Knowledge – or at least suspicion – of German atrocities abroad was widespread. But the level of indoctrination of the German population is perhaps the most difficult factor to comprehend when viewed from the present. During their years in power, the Nazis strictly controlled all media, and despite the suffering that many attributed to the Nazi regime, there was widespread acceptance of Hitler's declarations that the only alternative to victory was death.[27]

Zhukov gave an account of the final advance to the ruins of the Reich Chancellery in his memoirs:

> The fighting on the approaches and inside this building was particularly fierce. The senior political officer of IX Rifle Corps, Major Anna Vladimirovna Nikulina, was part of the assault group of 1050th Rifle Regiment. Together with the soldiers Davidov and Shapovalov, she made her way through a hole in the roof and, pulling a red cloth from under her jacket, tied it to a metal pole with a piece of telegraph wire. The Red Banner now flew over the Reich Chancellery.[28]

It is possible that Nikulina did indeed raise a red flag over the ruined buildings, but there was actually very little fighting in and around the Reich Chancellery. The first Soviet soldiers to reach it were from 301st Rifle Division, part of Fifth Shock Army's IX Rifle Corps. Led by Colonel Ivan Isayevich Klimenko (spelled 'Klimenke' in some accounts), the riflemen cautiously entered the ruins. Klimenko was under orders to find senior Nazis, dead or alive – Berzarin, commander of Fifth Shock Army, had promised a medal to any soldier who found Hitler's body – and the Soviet soldiers picked their way past the corpses of several German officers who had clearly taken their own lives and lay in congealed puddles of blood. Klimenko later described the tunnels as having a strong stench of death.[29] According to some accounts, Klimenko was accompanied by a special detachment from *SMERSH* – the counter-intelligence arm of the security services – but others suggest that this unit arrived at the bunker immediately after the troops from Fifth Shock Army seized the area; it is likely that the unit had been monitoring radio traffic. A detachment of sappers had been commandeered by the *SMERSH* team to check for booby traps and as soon as they had completed their checks, they were ordered to leave.

Somewhat to his surprise, Klimenko and the *SMERSH* unit found few people alive aside from two doctors and two nurses, aided by several volunteer helpers, who were treating dozens of wounded. A man who introduced himself as a stoker led the Soviet soldiers to Hitler's quarters, where they found a portrait of Frederick the Great and two of Hitler's greatcoats, but little else. Klimenko's solders then found a few more civilians, including Wilhelm Lange, the chef of the Chancellery kitchens, and Karl Schneider, a car mechanic; the latter told Klimenko about the orders to deliver several cans of petrol, which he assumed had been used to incinerate the Führer's corpse. The partly burned corpses of Magda and Joseph Goebbels were found outside the bunker entrance, identifiable by Goebbels' leg brace and a gold Nazi Party badge and gold cigarette case engraved with Hitler's signature, but the main prize – Hitler's body – was impossible to find.[30] The charred remains had been dispersed by shellfire and wind. Inside the bunker, the German medical staff tending the wounded later recalled that the *SMERSH* team was punctiliously correct in their behaviour, but that as they left, their officer told the German women that they should lock their doors that night.[31]

The bodies of the Goebbels family were formally identified by Vizeadmiral Hans-Erich Voss, a naval liaison officer who had been in the bunker to the very end. The Soviet authorities removed the bodies and buried them, but they were repeatedly re-interred before being buried in a special *SMERSH* facility in Magdeburg in early 1946. In 1970, they were dug up once more on the orders of Yuri Andropov, head of the *KGB*; he had ordered their complete destruction. The remains were incinerated and the ashes scattered in one of the tributaries of the Elbe.[32]

Weidling had done all he could to gain time for a breakout. Others, too, had adopted a similar strategy. In the Zoo Flak Tower, there were thousands of civilians and over a thousand wounded soldiers, crowded together in terrible conditions. On 30 April, aware that storming the formidable structure would be hugely costly, the commander of the Soviet 79th Guards Rifle Division had sent several German prisoners across the front line with an ultimatum scribbled on a sheet of paper, urging the garrison to surrender. During the morning of 1 May, one of the soldiers returned with a note signed by an Oberst named Haller, who claimed to be the garrison commander: the defenders would surrender at midnight that night. In the meantime, the heavy guns on the roof fell silent. Haller wasn't the commander of the flak tower; the delay was to give the troops planning to break out to the west sufficient time to complete their preparations.

There was, therefore, still one last phase of the battle left: the attempt by the remnants of the garrison to escape. And outside Berlin, the ordeal of Ninth Army and the thousands of German civilians accompanying it was also coming to a head.

CHAPTER 12

THE ROADS TO THE WEST: 29 APRIL–8 MAY

While the final battles were raging in Berlin, the steady retreat of the units of Manteuffel's Third Panzer Army towards the west continued. The improvised infantry company from 7th Panzer Division, made up of tank crews who no longer had vehicles, was tasked with forming a rearguard, and early on 30 April Johann Huber and his comrades reached the village of Gross Flotow, 11 miles west of Neubrandenburg. They found the village was deserted; all civilians had fled west already. As they ascended a low slope to the west of the village, they saw Soviet armoured vehicles were already approaching Gross Flotow. After a brief exchange of fire, the Germans pulled back and the following morning they passed through the small village of Alt Gaarz. Here, they found a group of youths in the uniforms of the *Reichsarbeitsdienst* ('Reich Labour Administration' or *RAD*) preparing to defend their homes:

> It's the first German unit that we have seen, albeit not Wehrmacht, that has organised troops. We slow down. They are really young chaps, the oldest perhaps 17 or even younger, real kids' faces, each of them carrying a rifle. We ask them what they're trying to do here. They reply: their unit has been deployed as *Volkssturm* and they have been working in this role since the beginning of the year. Their military and combat training is precisely nil. A unit commander of the *RAD* comes up to us and asks some questions. We tell him that he and his young lads should take off, Ivan is right behind us. From his face, as he stares at us, it's clear that he has no idea what this means. If these young soldiers are still in their positions with their rifles – it's all they have – and they open fire, there will be a bloodbath. None of them will get out alive – the Russians behind us are combat-hardened troops, who

have learned about warfare over many years and know what they're doing when they open fire. The commander explains to us that he has had difficulty with the march, as all of them are footsore and can't march any further.[1]

Leaving the *RAD* detachment behind them, Huber and the others continued their retreat. Later that morning, they encountered another group of people:

> They must be prisoners, as they all have grey-white striped jackets and trousers, prisoners' clothing. One of them comes over to us and asks us if we have anything to eat. They look emaciated and are in bad shape. Most are Poles, and they all have shaved heads, even the women, as we can see now. One of them speaks to us – in German. What does he want? We ask him what they are doing here, and he asks us if we've heard of the concentration camps, and whether we have anything to eat. We all stare dumbly. He explains that they were in the Litzmannstadt [Łódź] concentration camp and they were evacuated as the Russians advanced. Here, as the war appears to be coming to an end, they were released, without supplies. It's been very bad for them, and some of them have simply given up. And again, he asks whether we have anything to eat. All of us have no more than a quarter of a commissary loaf, but we all break off a chunk. He says, 'At least I can give something to my comrades.' He tells me that he was an actor in Berlin and as a result of political statements he made, he was sent to the concentration camp three years ago …
>
> We look at him without comprehension. He asks us, 'Don't you know these things? Those with the yellow triangles on their arms, they are Jews, and we, with red triangles, are political prisoners; the blue ones are criminals, serious criminals, who have something to eat.' The man is so emaciated that his cheekbones stand out, and the prison uniform is too big. I ask him what they plan to do here. He replies: 'We are not going another metre, and we're waiting until the Russians come – they will have something for us to eat. We can't go any further.'
>
> Troubled, we turn away, marching on, but not before all of us have shaken his hand and wished him good fortune. We tell him that the Russians are right behind us, good news for him, it seems. As we turn away, we stare at a couple of young Polish girls, who look bizarre with their shaved heads.[2]

Most concentration camp prisoners were treated well by the Red Army, but there were also exceptions. In some cases, female prisoners were raped despite their emaciated condition.

The Soviet pursuit of Third Panzer Army was perhaps not as energetic as Rokossovsky might have wanted, but nonetheless pressed hard on the heels of Huber and others. Later on 1 May, the Germans came across a large quantity of industrial alcohol and debated whether they should burn it. Concluding that the Soviet soldiers were certain to drink it, they left the containers intact in the hope that intoxicated soldiers would pursue them with less energy. But the collapse of Third Panzer Army raised the possibility of Soviet troops reaching objectives further west than had originally been planned. Whilst the partitioning of Germany had been largely agreed in the Yalta Conference in February 1945, Stalin now saw the possibility that a rapid advance might permit Rokossovsky to reach Denmark before the Western Allies. Even if such an advance would involve seizing parts of northern Germany that would ultimately have to be handed back to the Western Allies, the occupation of the Danish peninsula, guarding the entrance to the Baltic Sea, would be of huge importance. Accordingly, he ordered Rokossovsky to make haste.

The northwest part of Germany would become the British occupation zone, and by the end of April the British forces closing in on Hamburg and other Baltic ports were aware of the rapid advance of the Red Army. Accordingly, the British VIII Corps was ordered to advance swiftly to ensure that Lübeck and the southern coast of Lübeck Bay, immediately to the east of the town, were occupied by British forces first, thus blocking any Soviet advance into Denmark. Lieutenant General Evelyn Barker, the corps commander, had 11th Armoured Division and 6th Airborne Division as his main units; he dispatched the former towards Lübeck and the latter towards Wismar.

One of the brigades of 6th Airborne Division included a Canadian battalion, and elements of this unit – riding on the decks of 11 light M2 tanks – approached Wismar during the morning of 1 May. It was a diminutive force, and as it ventured into the town, its commander discovered that the bridges over the Mühlenbach River that ran through Wismar were still intact. As he considered whether he should attempt to seize them or await reinforcements, a German officer approached and offered to lead the British across the bridges. Cautiously, the small group followed him. As they approached an airfield on the edge of Wismar, the Canadians came under fire, but the gunfire suddenly stopped and a German officer ran forward, his hands raised; he apologised, saying he and his men had mistaken the Canadians for Soviet troops.

The rest of 6th Airborne Division began to arrive later on 1 May, having covered about 60 miles in about eight hours. That evening, at about 2100, the leading elements of the Soviet III Guards Tank Corps arrived, a pair of motorcycles with sidecars and two armoured cars. Seeing British and Canadian troops ahead of them, they slowed and approached cautiously, guns at the ready, but then relaxed and there was much handshaking and sharing of alcohol. But as quickly as it had begun, the bonhomie came to an abrupt end following a radio message.

The small Soviet patrol pulled back and began to assemble a road block on the edge of Wismar.[3] The town was to be part of the Soviet zone of occupation and the Canadian and British soldiers were ordered to withdraw a few days later, but not before an ominous incident, as described below.

Not far from Wismar, Huber and his comrades continued to fend off pursuing Soviet units. Late on 2 May they joined a small group of SS soldiers and the following day they reached Bankzow, to the south of Schwerin. Here, they encountered American troops who disarmed them:

> The truck lurches, engages gear and drives on, and we realise: we are now prisoners of war. We stare at each other as this realisation dawns; the war is now over for us. Someone says, 'At least nobody can shoot us now, whatever happens! We have survived this war, which is soon going to be over anyway.' Fritz Renner, who is sitting next to me, chats with me. 'So, we have apparently lost this war, and there hasn't ever been a war like this in the history of the world. We have lost a total war.'
>
> But oddly enough, life goes on. Nobody is executed, nobody is shot. The total destruction of all life, that had been predicted so often, doesn't happen. It's true, we're alive![4]

The senior officers of Third Panzer Army were also being taken prisoner. Manteuffel and his staff surrendered to the British in Hagenow on 3 May. Manteuffel was released in late 1946 and became a politician in West Germany, but in 1959 he was charged with ordering the execution of a deserter in 1944. The soldier's court-martial had sentenced him to imprisonment, but Manteuffel changed this to a death sentence. He was given an 18-month sentence, and died in 1978. Heinrici, who had been dismissed as commander of Army Group Vistula, joined Dönitz's headquarters in Plön, close to the Danish border, and was taken prisoner by the British in late May. He was released in 1948 and helped the US Army Center of Military History create an operational history of German campaigns. He died in 1971 and received full military honours at his funeral. He was fortunate not to be handed over to the Soviet authorities; numerous war crimes had been committed in areas controlled by his troops, particularly in 1941 and 1942, and other officers in similar circumstances were charged and executed by the Soviet Union after the war.

Not far away, Fritz Altner and the survivors of 20th Panzergrenadier Division also surrendered to US troops, near Ludwigslust:

> In front of us was a Luftwaffe convoy that had already sent an envoy to the Americans. Then a vehicle arrived with large white flags on it and an American

officer inside. He took the pistols from our officers and waved us on. At 1830 we drove across the American lines into captivity. We gave up our weapons on the way. Most of us lost our watches too. Some of the Americans were drunk, apparently from looted schnapps. Liberated Poles were firing pistols and taking farmers' cows from their stalls. It was mildly comforting to see that the people still waved to us.[5]

Steiner, who had fallen from favour following his refusal to attack towards Berlin, accompanied the former *Armeegruppe Steiner*, now renamed *Armeegruppe Holste*, as it slowly withdrew to the west. To his surprise, he found himself the effective commander of the force; his replacement, Rudolf Holste, disappeared on 1 May and then resurfaced in Wenck's headquarters shortly after, having abandoned his men. Like Heinrici and Manteuffel, Steiner became a prisoner of war of the Western Allies. He was originally listed as one of those who would be prosecuted at Nuremberg, but when the tribunals were reduced in scale he was released in 1948. After the war, he became a founder member of *HIAG*, lobbying on behalf of former SS soldiers and portraying the Waffen-SS as nothing more than ordinary soldiers who were not involved in war crimes. Whilst his attempts to whitewash the Waffen-SS were misleading at best and deliberately dishonest at worst, his devotion to his subordinates was unquestionable. He deliberately avoided allowing his men to be sacrificed in a futile assault towards Berlin in April 1945, and it was perhaps fitting that he was still with them when they finally surrendered. He died in 1966.

Throughout the final struggles in Berlin, the armies of Wenck and Busse continued their battles to the south of the capital. An attack by the *Scharnhorst* division took the Red Army by surprise, allowing the Germans to retake Beelitz, where there was a complex of hospitals and sanatoriums. Wenck later wrote:

We had bypassed the Russians near the Beelitz sanatoria with our attack. As we pulled back to the hospitals, wounded men and nurses stared in astonishment from the windows. They couldn't believe that German soldiers were standing before them again. They had probably heard the sounds of fighting, but didn't know what they meant. When they now saw that it really was a German unit, their eyes filled with tears. They thought: we can still get out of this. Now we still have hope of rescue. During their three days of occupation, the Russians had behaved generally correctly. They had just removed rank badges and epaulettes from the doctors. They then left, leaving just some guards. I went to the medical superintendent and assured him that the army would do all it could to move the wounded as quickly as possible. All who could walk should immediately set off towards the west.[6]

A little to the north of Beelitz, Reymann, the former commandant of Berlin, had gathered his troops – numbering nearly 20,000 men – in readiness for the arrival of Wenck's columns. He was informed by Twelfth Army that it had come as close as it could by seizing Ferch, and he was ordered to break out. Early on 29 April, his men made tentative contact with the leading elements of *Ulrich von Hutten*, and Wenck ordered him to complete the link-up by forcing a way through the Soviet forces that continued to engage both *Ulrich von Hutten* and *Gruppe Reymann*. As had already been the case, these plans were made more difficult by the radio broadcasts emanating from Berlin and elsewhere. The latest *OKW* announcement early on 29 April informed the world that 'The divisions deployed from the west are throwing back the enemy in bitter fighting on a broad front and have reached Ferch.' When they heard the broadcast, Wenck and his staff officers looked at each other with a mixture of dismay and amazement, astonished that their movements were being made public in this manner.

There was a small bit of good news for Wenck: Köhler, commander of XX Corps, which had overseen the advance by *Ulrich von Hutten*, reported that he had made radio contact with Ninth Army. A message was passed to Busse, advising him that the previous plan to link up near Jüterborg was unlikely to succeed – anticipating such an attempt, the Red Army had now massed far more forces in the area than the Germans had available to them. A better option was between Jüterborg and Beelitz, where reconnaissance suggested that the Soviet forces were relatively weak. Twelfth Army would attempt to hold its current positions, but to do so for more than a day or two would be beyond their ability. Just before dusk on 29 April, Wenck advised *OKW* that despite linking up with Reymann's troops near Potsdam, an advance towards Berlin was impossible.

The soldiers of Ninth Army needed little urging to try to head west. It would be incorrect to see the fighting that followed as a battle coordinated by Busse's headquarters; by now, he had, at best, only intermittent contact with his corps and division commanders. The desperate fighting around Halbe finally led to the Soviet defenders being forced back by sheer weight of numbers, and throughout 29 April German soldiers and civilians poured through the town. Kleinheisterkamp, commander of XI SS-Panzer Corps, had been captured the previous day and committed suicide either on 29 April or a day or two after; the remnants of his units hurried past the corpses of those killed in the battle for Halbe. They were followed by Wäger's V Corps, reduced to three battlegroups that collectively had less combat strength than a full-strength infantry division. As the day progressed, Konev's troops began to recover; in particular, the breakthrough artillery division that he had sent to the area put Halbe under increasingly heavy artillery fire. In the congested roads, the death toll amongst soldiers and civilians was terrible. When V SS-Mountain Corps – effectively, no more than a weak battlegroup from *SS-30. Januar* – reached Halbe, a Soviet counterattack once more blocked the road and bitter fighting erupted once more. Losses climbed rapidly on both sides, but although the German rearguard was now separated from the other elements that had passed through Halbe, the renewed fighting drew the attention of Konev and other senior commanders to the battle. For a brief time at least, those who had already broken through had an opportunity to continue their escape.

By this time, the leading elements of the breakout – with the last Tiger tanks of *SS-Schwere-Panzer-Abteilung 502* – had reached the highway running between Cottbus and Berlin. They crossed the road and took shelter in woodland to the east, where a forestry lodge had been designated as an assembly area. Amongst those following these Tigers was Rudi Lindner, an officer-cadet in 712th Infantry Division, part of XI SS-Panzer Corps, and he described what happened when he reached the highway, riding on an assault gun:

> Suddenly in front of us was the nose of an armoured vehicle. 'Take cover! One man forward to reconnoitre!'
>
> After ten minutes came the report that it was an assault gun. Its crew, who had their dead commander aboard, were about to cross the *Autobahn* under cover of the morning haze, but didn't know if the woods opposite were occupied by the enemy or not, and were also afraid that there might be flanking anti-tank gun fire along the *Autobahn*, so they were happy to see us and for us to find out for them. A brief order: 'Under simultaneous covering fire, over the *Autobahn* in bounds.' We were soon on the other side. All we found on the other side were foxholes and dead bodies. We welcomed the chance to drive our assault gun several kilometres in the westerly direction ordered for the breakout to the assembly point at the forest warden's lodge at Massow. We found ourselves on a woodland track on which soldiers were moving along in groups of all sizes.
>
> We soon arrived at Ninth Army's assembly point, reported in, and received 16 men's worth of rations and ammunition to divide among the remaining five of us, sufficient to eat ourselves full once more, for we didn't know when we would get any more. Here, the extent of the tragedy at Halbe quickly became apparent. Many comrades were missing from our unit, the majority of our company of grenadiers having been killed or wounded; there was no accurate account.[7]

After a brief pause, the soldiers who had gathered began to move west once more. Lindner noted that there was little command and control. There were few senior officers anywhere, and the soldiers were no longer in coherent battalions or regiments – merely agglomerations of survivors trying to escape. Riding in a half-track, Busse joined the leading elements during the afternoon and informed the Tiger tank crews that there was still a considerable distance to travel; some later recalled that he mentioned a distance of 36 miles, but the closest elements of Twelfth Army were a little more than half that distance away. None of the remaining armoured vehicles had sufficient fuel for a 36-mile journey; Busse told the crews that they would have to seize whatever fuel they could in order to remain mobile.

The renewed fighting in Halbe meant that the columns of soldiers and civilians arriving from the east slowed to a trickle, and, concluding that few if any would be following, the assembled troops headed west. Energetic junior officers, NCOs, and even ordinary soldiers took it upon themselves to try to organise combat-worthy elements consisting of the few armoured vehicles accompanied by infantrymen who were still able to fight. These led the way, followed by a few vehicles carrying wounded; the civilians and stragglers, now much reduced in numbers, trailed behind as best they could. Shortly before dusk, the leading elements reached the line from which Luck and Pipkorn had conducted their ill-fated breakout attempt three days earlier. A small group of Tigers was dispatched to shield the northern flank of the continued march, but the plan misfired after an unknown German Oberst appeared and ordered the tanks to a new location, threatening their commander with court-martial if he refused. It is likely that this was another of the so-called *Seydlitz-Truppen* deployed by the Red Army.[8]

After crossing the Baruth–Zossen road, the survivors gathered once more in dense forest. A few of the Tigers and a handful of Panther tanks from the *Kurmark* panzergrenadier division were still running, and these would be vital if the breakout was to succeed. As it grew dark, there were several more encounters with suspicious individuals in German uniform who insisted they knew safe ways out of the encirclement. Some were ignored, and others were shot – it rapidly became a byword amongst the survivors of Ninth Army that anyone in a clean, tidy uniform was likely to be a *Seydlitzmann*. There were occasional air attacks, adding to the confusion, but the advance continued towards Kummersdorf, leaving behind a trail of dead soldiers and abandoned vehicles, the last drops of fuel carefully siphoned from their tanks.

Soviet soldiers from III Guards Rifle Corps – from Luchinsky's Twenty-Eighth Army – attacked the breakout group, breaking it into two segments; those in the smaller segment were driven away to the south where they were ultimately forced to surrender. But the leading group of Ninth Army was made up of those most determined to escape and they continued west. By the end of 29 April, they had covered perhaps half the distance between Halbe and Beelitz, overcoming several Red Army blocking positions. Behind them, there was growing chaos. Most of the armoured reconnaissance battalion of 21st Panzer Division succeeded in fighting its way past the Soviet troops that had retaken Halbe, but when the Germans reached the Cottbus–Zossen highway, they found that the Red Army had once more set up strong positions and they were rapidly overwhelmed. In the nearby forest, the soldiers could hear the screams of German women who were being raped repeatedly.[9] Erika Menze, a 17-year-old civilian, was trying to escape with the soldiers, and she later described her experiences:

> I don't know now how I got across the railway lines at Halbe station. What I saw was horrible. The tanks rolled down Lindenstrasse covered all over with wounded soldiers. One fell off and the next tank rolled right over him, squashing him flat, so that the next tank rolled through a pool of blood. There was nothing left of this soldier. It happened in seconds ...
>
> The pavement near the Drassdo Bakery was covered in corpses, all German soldiers. Many more dead were lying alongside the houses, stacked up at an angle, leaving no cobblestone or piece of pavement uncovered. I had to pass over these dead soldiers, their heads yellow, grey, crushed flat ... a horrific scene ...
>
> Heavy weapons were roaring and Stalin-organs were mentioned. Heavy and light machine-guns were rattling and tracer bullets whistled over us. 'Don't move! They're firing at anything that moves,' a woman near me cried out. This lasted from early afternoon until dusk. The barrage must have lasted six hours. The woman next to me was wounded twice, her brother-in-law too. They comforted each other as best as they could.
>
> After hours of bombardment, it became quieter. During the bombardment we had seen many shot-up ruins collapse. Night began to fall. A Russian took a large glass of what looked like sugar or semolina from a handcart standing not far from us. I thought, so he comes and helps himself and we have to stay still. But he only looked very shyly towards us. He needed it as much as we did. As we looked back there was no horizon to be seen. Everything was covered in smoke. We all tried to stand up, then noticed how cold we had become.
>
> German soldiers came and hurried us on. The Russians had been driven off and we should get away quickly towards the *Autobahn*.[10]

Most of the German rearguard was broken up and destroyed piecemeal, but small groups managed to slip through to the west in the confused fighting that raged across a wide area. The German losses in and around Halbe were so great that many commanders in the Red Army units believed that they had actually overwhelmed all of Ninth Army, unaware that a substantial part had broken out towards the west. But those units were in poor shape, and that evening, Busse sent a signal to Wenck:

> The physical state and morale of the officers and men, as well as the levels of ammunition and supplies, permit neither a new attack nor prolonged resistance. The misery of the civilians who have fled out of the pocket is particularly bad. Only the measures taken by all the generals have enabled the troops to stay together. The fighting capacity of Ninth Army is clearly at an end.[11]

The comment about the contribution of senior commanders is both misleading and self-serving. Most memoirs of survivors suggest that it was the determination of men far lower down the chain of command that had held things together thus far.

On 30 April, the struggle continued. The leading elements, still accompanied by five surviving Tigers, reached Kummersdorf. For some, it was familiar territory: there was a training area close to the village, where many of them had spent their early military careers. There were repeated clashes with both Red Army troops and *Seydlitz-Truppen*. The survivors gathered once more in woodland between Kummersdorf and Trebbin and sent a reconnaissance group forward; it soon returned, reporting that there was a strong Soviet cordon along the road running south from Trebbin to Luckenwalde. Wäger, commander of V Corps, was with the group and he now took command of the leading elements, ordering all remaining fuel to be given to the last tanks. The group would wait until dusk for as many stragglers as possible to reach them; then, they would make a final attempt to head west. They were just 11 miles from Beelitz, where they hoped Wenck's troops were waiting for them.

Erika Menze reached the forest warden's lodge near Baruth, accompanied by a crowd of other civilians and dispirited soldiers. They were all exhausted by their ordeal:

> The soldiers had long lost their will to carry on fighting. They also knew that this war had become nonsensical in the government's final desperation.
>
> Then came some officers, one here, another further off: 'Where is your weapon?' 'Lost in battle!' Then the soldiers had to take the officers' carbines and were ordered up front. One of them didn't want to follow orders and was sworn at and threatened with a pistol.
>
> It must have been midday when we came to Luckenwalde. We had to keep moving, though we seemed to be going around in a circle. Shot-up trees, broken-down vehicles, lost or discarded equipment, pieces of clothing and other items

were all lying around. Again we saw dead German soldiers. A young girl wearing a steel helmet sat leaning against a tree. One soldier said that she was asleep, but she was dead.[12]

Accompanied by two *Volkssturm*, she reached Ruhlsdorf, immediately north of Luckenwalde, where some women from the village gave them shelter; they also produced civilian clothes so that the *Volkssturm* could abandon their uniforms. A couple of days later, the local mayor told them that it would be best if they simply returned to their homes.

The main breakout attempt was unfolding a little further north. Spurred on by the hope that escape was close, the German soldiers rushed across the Trebbin–Luckenwalde road with the last tanks in the lead. They regrouped in Märtensmühle, where Standartenführer Hans Kempin – the commander of *SS-30. Januar* – told them that another group had already succeeded in reaching the lines of Twelfth Army. Fuel was now in critically short supply; until this moment, the last remnants of *SS-Nederland* had managed to bring about 50 badly wounded men with them, but they now had to be left behind. Elsewhere, Soviet units overwhelmed isolated bands that were plodding through the forests, and by the end of the day Konev's 1st Ukrainian Front claimed that it had taken another 20,000 men prisoner.

Perhaps realising a little belatedly that a large portion of Ninth Army had managed to slip through Halbe and was heading west, Konev dispatched further units to block the German escape. In particular, Lelyushenko's Fourth Guards Tank Army was ordered to turn its two mechanised corps south, one to drive back Wenck's Twelfth Army and the other to intercept the breakout group. At the same time, Luchinsky urged his division commanders to show more energy in breaking up and destroying the German forces, but with only limited results. Many of the soldiers of Twenty-Eighth Army had not been resupplied for several days; they were surrounded by opportunities to gather loot and to search for women; and everyone knew that the end of the war was imminent. After spending months or years doubting that they would survive to see such a day, it was inevitable that many soldiers now decided that they would avoid taking further unnecessary risks in battles that would make no difference to the final outcome.

In the early hours of 1 May, Busse and a few other senior officers discussed the best options for continuing to the west, but as had been the case since the breakout began, they found that they had little or no control over events. Shortly after midnight, the last tanks fired up their engines and started moving west before any orders had been given and the exhausted soldiers and the few civilians who were still with them simply followed. They covered nearly half the distance to Beelitz before dawn. As it grew light, the tank crews saw that there were Soviet tanks, anti-tank guns, and *Katyusha* launchers in the meadow in front of Dobbrikow and they prepared to attack, but as they began to move, thousands of soldiers and civilians emerged from the forest on either side and surged west. Major Otto-Christer von Albedyll, commander of the armoured reconnaissance battalion of the *Kurmark* division, was killed in the fighting, and many of the remaining armoured vehicles finally ran out of fuel. But the Soviet units withdrew and by mid-morning Busse was in Hennickendorf. Here, he came under fire but moved on rapidly.

As the morning progressed, Soviet resistance became far stronger. Scharführer Ernst Streng, in one of the last King Tigers, described the attempt to push on:

> Our tanks rolled along the Hennickendorf–Dobbrikow road. Halfway along we came under artillery fire from woodland to the right. Anti-tank guns? We couldn't tell for certain. Suddenly, a heavy blow struck our Tiger and the track guards clattered to the road. Our gun blazed away at the woodland at a range of about 350–400m. There were some bright explosions, and branches and foliage whirled into the air.
>
> Like lightning, there was a second direct hit on the hull of our tank. A shell struck the right side with enormous force and was deflected upwards. There was then another terrifying impact. We clenched our fists and gritted our teeth. 'Hit on the right side of the turret! Driver, hard left! Quick, go, go!' I screamed on the intercom. Our tank reared up and rolled left into a field sloping down to a small lake. After a few hundred metres, we turned to the right. Meanwhile, the other tanks had silenced the Russian anti-tank guns and the gathered thousands continued their trek.
>
> We ran out of fuel but somehow we got hold of some more and drove on. As we climbed back aboard, our tank was hit from half-left across the lake by a Russian tank that we had not spotted. I was wounded in the left arm and left thigh. They laid me down inside the tank and Läbe took over. The Wenck Army was only a few kilometres away, but the Russian cordon here at Wittbrietzen–Rieben–Zauchwitz seemed impenetrable.[13]

The village of Rieben was captured by the Germans in heavy fighting, despite repeated Soviet air attacks on both the troops in the forefront of the battle and those attempting to follow them. As they drove northwest towards Beelitz, Streng and his crew encountered more Soviet guns. Even as they engaged and destroyed an anti-tank gun and a tank, another Soviet tank that they had not spotted fired on them and set their Tiger ablaze, forcing them to abandon it. A few seconds later, another Tiger was also destroyed and it became clear that the Soviet lines here were too strong to be forced. But other groups turned to the southwest and found that there were few enemy soldiers in their path. As they crossed the Beelitz–Treuenbrietzen road, they saw yet another line of trenches before them, but to their joy they realised that they were occupied by German soldiers. They had managed to reach the lines of Twelfth Army.

Over the rest of the day, groups of varying sizes reached Wenck's lines. The best estimates suggest that about 25,000 soldiers from Ninth Army, accompanied by 5,000 civilians, escaped the encirclement. Inevitably, the Soviet accounts give smaller numbers. When the German forces encircled in the Battle of Cherkassy in early 1944 succeeded in breaking out to safety, Konev – who had assured Stalin that the Germans would be completely destroyed – made claims that of those who escaped, most were then killed in energetic Soviet attacks. Now, he described much the same thing, writing that although about 30,000 reached the general area to the southeast of Beelitz, only about 4,000 succeeded in reaching safety and the rest were killed.[14] Wenck went forward to meet Busse, stressing that the ordeal of the escapees was not over: Twelfth Army was now under heavy pressure from the north as Lelyushenko's tanks and riflemen began to drive back the units that had linked up with Reymann. A full-scale withdrawal to the Elbe was ordered, commencing during the evening of 1 May.

The two mechanised corps directed against the German Twelfth Army by Lelyushenko were putting considerable pressure on the German lines, and although Wenck had originally intended to send all escaping units of Ninth Army to reinforce his positions, it was clear to everyone that the exhausted survivors who had managed to escape via Halbe would be unable to contribute much by way of fighting strength. As a result, priority was given to these men to cross the Elbe. Using improvised trains, the few remaining trucks for which there was fuel, and often resorting simply to marching on foot, the remnants of Busse's army reached the river. Fortunately, a large bridging column was amongst the various units that had congregated, as much by luck as planning, in Twelfth Army's area, and it was already at work repairing a partly demolished bridge at Tangermünde.

The following morning, the pressure on the eastern face of Wenck's positions intensified. The northern flank of Twelfth Army, made up of LXI Corps, was isolated and driven away to the northwest. In order to prevent the Red Army from rolling up the German positions from the north, XXXIX Panzer Corps, defending along the Havel, was ordered to pull back its northern flank to the Elbe, while XX Corps was to pull back to the Tangermünde crossing and to free up units that could be sent to shore up the northern flank of Twelfth Army. Whilst the survivors of Ninth Army were at the end of their strength, the men of Twelfth Army were in little better shape, having fought hard against numerically superior Soviet forces in order to link up with their comrades near Potsdam and then to hold their positions until Busse's troops reached them. Now, under constant pressure, they had to conduct a difficult withdrawal. Despite having few units that had spent much time fighting alongside each other, the soldiers of the improvised formations in Wenck's command performed admirably. By early morning on 3 May, it seemed as if the line was stabilising once more, with pressure on the German lines easing. There were probably several reasons for this. Firstly, many of Konev's units were being ordered to pull out of the front line in preparation for being sent south to capture Prague. Secondly, the general reluctance of men to risk their lives so close to the end of the war probably played a part.

Even as the soldiers and civilians headed for the Elbe, Wenck commenced negotiations with the US forces beyond the river. He had already submitted a request for his units to surrender to the US Army, and on 4 May he dispatched Generalleutnant Maximilian von Edelsheim, commander of XLVIII Panzer Corps, to Stendal for detailed discussions. Major General James Moore, the chief of staff of the US Ninth Army, wrote an account of the meeting:

> General von Edelsheim informed me that the forces which he represented were the Twelfth German Army and the remnants of the Ninth German Army which had been fighting on the Eastern Front. He stated that the strength of the force was approximately 25,000 unarmed soldiers, 40,000 men in battle formations and 6,000 wounded. He also stated that there were approximately 100,000 civilians in the area which he wished to evacuate to the west bank of the Elbe. He stated that they had a considerable amount of transport and about a week's supply of food in army stores, plus that which was carried on the individual soldier. He also stated that they had adequate field hospitals and medical personnel to care for their wounded ...
>
> General von Edelsheim was told that the Russians were our allies and fighting the Germans with us – that we had all the German prisoners that we wanted and more too. He was told, however, that if Germans appeared on the west bank of the Elbe River with their hands up, or under a white flag, under custom of war they would be accepted as prisoners and they would not be fired on while they were crossing the river. It was made clear, however, that we accepted no responsibility for any action on the part of the Russian forces opposing him and, if they cut him off from the river or fired on his troops while they were crossing, that he would have to meet that problem as best he could ...
>
> General von Edelsheim was told that there would be no movement of civilians from [the] east to [the] west bank of the Elbe River.[15]

The Western Allies were increasingly concerned about the difficulties that they faced in feeding the German civilian population. The disruption caused by the last year of the war and the wholesale mobilisation of men into the *Volkssturm* meant that the harvest in 1945 would be a fraction of what was required. In such circumstances, they were unwilling to accept more civilians from the east. At various levels, they were aware of the rapes and other acts of violence occurring in the areas occupied by the Red Army, but at least to an extent this was offset by a growing awareness of the scale of crimes committed by Nazi Germany. In many cases, attitudes towards the German population hardened in the spring of 1945 after the liberation of concentration camps as American and British soldiers saw first-hand how the regime had treated those it regarded as enemies. As a further restriction, Moore advised Edelsheim that motorised vehicles would not be permitted to cross the repaired bridge at Tangermünde – only foot traffic was to cross. Edelsheim had no choice but to accept the terms that he was offered.

Soldiers began to cross the Elbe in large numbers. Throughout 5 May, there was fighting from time to time along the eastern perimeter; ammunition began to run out, but the German defences remained intact for the moment. The following morning, heavier Soviet artillery began to fire on the enclave and some shells landed on the west bank. The US Ninth Army was promptly ordered to pull back a short distance and, equally promptly, the Germans used the opportunity to start ferrying civilians across the Elbe. By the second half of 7 May, only the German rearguard remained east of the river. The last armoured vehicles were rendered unusable and their crews walked across the Tangermünderbrücke. It seems that many were turned back by the US troops who awaited them on the west bank. Like the Waffen-SS, Wehrmacht soldiers of the panzer arm wore black uniforms with death's-head badges, derived from the old hussar regiments of the Prussian Army, and it is possible that the tank and assault gun crewmen were mistakenly identified as SS and sent back to surrender to the Red Army.[16] At dusk on 7 May, Wenck crossed the Elbe in a small boat accompanied by Riechhelm, his chief of staff, two other staff officers, and a handful of soldiers. Soviet riflemen reached the bank before he had crossed and opened fire, wounding three of the occupants of the boat, one fatally. Despite the restrictions of the agreement between Moore and Edelsheim, several thousand civilians had succeeded in crossing and thus avoided the tribulations of being in the Soviet zone of occupation, but several thousand more were not so fortunate.

It was the end of the struggle for Twelfth Army, which despite having been created in haste around several improvised divisions, had performed creditably in difficult circumstances. Like the men who had managed to reach safety either breaking out of Potsdam with Reymann or after the gruelling breakout from the Halbe encirclement, these soldiers were now in US custody. They still faced considerable hardships. Many would be held for several months in open compounds, often with rations that were barely adequate – there were widespread food shortages everywhere across Europe, and former German soldiers were given a relatively low priority. Many would later complain that they were mistreated, with watches, medals, and other items being seized by their captors. The justification for such treatment was that after the complete surrender of Nazi Germany, the US Army reclassified prisoners of war as 'disarmed enemy forces', a category that did not require the level of care stipulated by the Geneva Convention. There were many deaths during captivity, with some of the more extreme claims suggesting that as many as a million Germans – both soldiers and civilians – died due to starvation; this is almost certainly a considerable over-estimate, with most estimates suggesting a total significantly lower, many suggesting a figure of 1 per cent or less of those held.[17]

But even as Wenck's and Busse's soldiers were completing their relatively orderly exit from the war, others were still trying to get out of Berlin. Early on 1 May, Kurt Eberhard, a 50-year-old Berliner who had been conscripted into the *Volkssturm*, was in an air raid shelter at the Anhalter station, having been given a written order from his commander to return to his home, when SS military police appeared, demanding that those who could fight should return to the front line. One of them shouted at the people in the shelter:

'The *Kampfkommandant* hereby orders the shelter to be vacated ... It will be blown at 0600. March along the north–south subway tunnel at once. Gather at the Stettiner station ... take only small pieces of baggage. Leave behind anything cumbersome – baggage, bicycles, and baby carriages! You can get more when Berlin is free again! Move out! Long live the Führer!'

For a moment there was silence and in this silence there came from somewhere a burst of scornful laughter ... the SS commander turned suddenly, shrugged, and squeezed his way through the crowd and disappeared.

The crowd began to move north in fits and starts. They moved from station to station as the dull grey light of dawn filtered through the street grating above. When they reached the station at Unter den Linden, someone far to the back of the column shouted, 'Blasting!' Soon there was wild shouting from the rear and people pressed hard against each other as a cold blast of air swept through. The mass of people in the tunnel began to push forward as a stream of water poured over their feet.[18]

The Roads to the West: 29 April–8 May

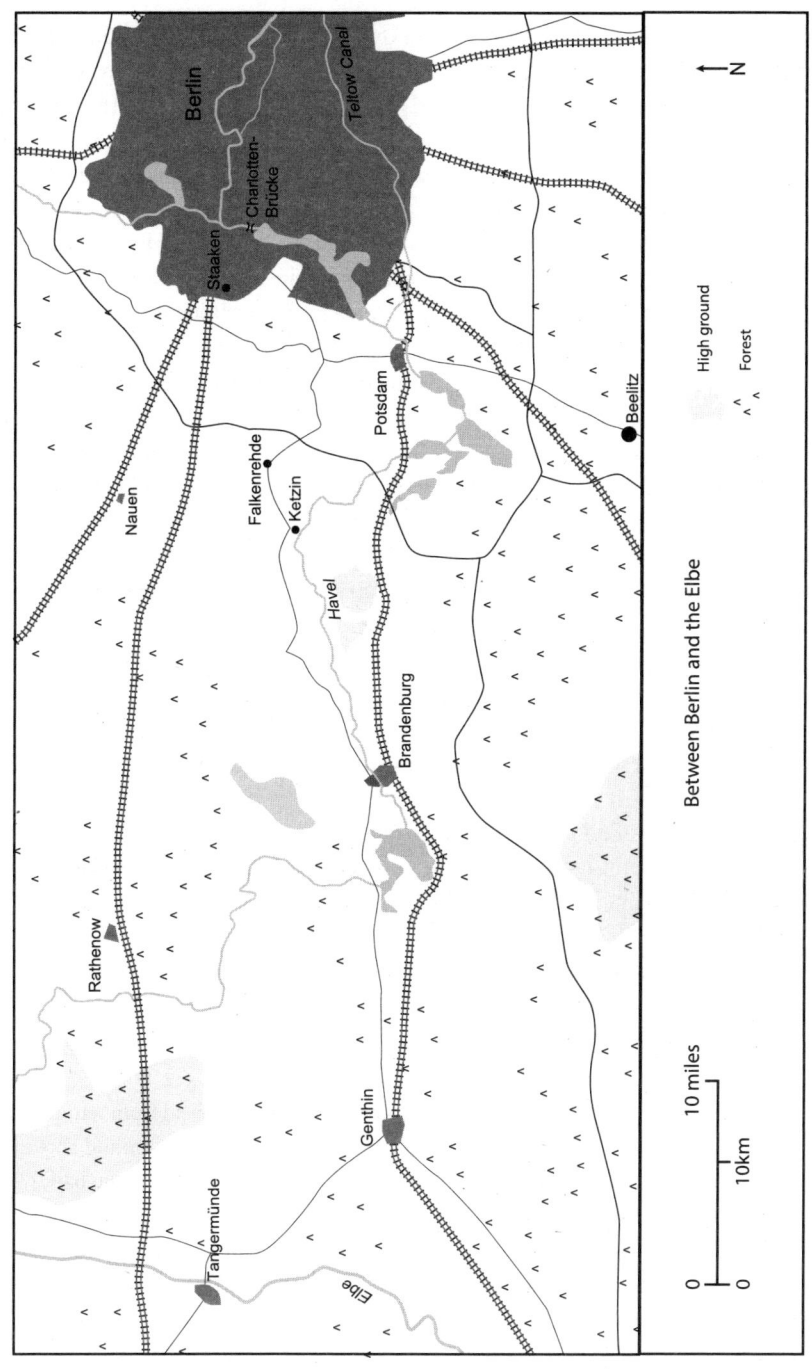

Between Berlin and the Elbe

Many of the civilians hiding in cellars and *U-Bahn* stations remembered a loud explosion at this moment that made the ground shake. As has already been described, the *S-Bahn* tunnel under the Landwehr Canal had been blown, and water poured through the underground network and hundreds of people frantically waded through the darkness to escape, an unknown number drowning in the darkness. The SS had prepared demolition charges in the tunnels and it is possible that they detonated these to hinder the advance of Soviet troops into the central district; if this is the case, they failed to take into account how long it would take civilians to move to safety. An alternative explanation is that the ongoing shelling in the area detonated the charges that resulted in flooding.

Elsewhere, a large group had gathered near the Zoo Flak Tower and Generalleutnant Otto Sydow, commander of *Flak-Division Berlin*, took command. The group set off for Charlottenburg late on 1 May, led by the surviving tanks of 18th Panzergrenadier Division and the *Müncheberg* panzer division. Their first objective was the Charlottenbrücke, a little to the north of where Helmut Altner and his comrades had gathered in their barracks; just like Altner's unit, many of the soldiers and civilians moved from the Tiergarten area to the approaches of the bridge via the *U-Bahn* tunnels.

The first vehicle to attempt a crossing was a half-track, and it tried to race across the open area quickly. Immediately, Soviet gunners opened fire. During the morning of 2 May, Altner and his comrades were gathered together and ordered to head west. They joined the columns attempting to cross the Havel. First, they headed for the railway bridge to the south of the Charlottenbrücke, only to find that it had already been destroyed. As they came under fire from Soviet soldiers, the crowds of soldiers and civilians surged back and forth in search of cover:

> All hell has broken loose. Machine-gun salvoes hit the walls, grenades explode and walls collapse, then we are through and fall exhausted into a quieter pace.
>
> There are ruins left and right. The flood of people has eased off, pressed tight under cover ... Only the odd soldier, woman, civilian, or child is getting through alongside the buildings, and others are sitting down in the rubble resting ... The buildings look as if they have been sawn off, mostly at the first storey and their cellars have collapsed and, amid their broken brickwork, people are struggling through to us, through the ruins and the streets with only one aim, one hope: to get to the west to the Wenck Army, away from Berlin's rubble waste, this vast cemetery. Everyone runs, racing through the fire. The dance of death has begun and the big reaper is mowing his broad swathes through the rows of women, children and soldiers.[19]

Altner soon reached the Charlottenbrücke:

> Occasionally a few people jump up out of the shelter of the steps and run across the bridge. The mass of people growing behind us in the dead angles begins to spill over. Beside me among the soldiers are women with babies in their arms, old women, children, and young teenagers of both sexes. I look carefully over the top step. Shots are racing across the bridge and the horror hits me, for the bridge is swimming in blood ...
>
> The road surface is slippery with blood and there are bodies lying around and hanging over the bridge railings. Vehicles and tanks race across, grinding the bones with a crack ...
>
> Now shells are hitting the bridge. I jump up again. I can see figures ahead of me running and stumbling as if through a fog ... Everyone is for himself and has no time to think of others. Then I reach the end of the bridge and crouch down behind the barricade, gasping for air. Shots wing over my head and hit the bodies. The number of figures on the bridge is increasing. Women with babies in their arms and holding children by the hand, Hitler Youth, girls, civilians, old men and women, fall to the ground, dragging down others with them, riddled with bullets and streaming with blood. Death plays his dance, mowing his bloody path. Tanks roll over the bridge, over people, squashing them to pulp, churning them up with their tracks and a wide street of death and blood, of bits of corpses and torn bodies spans the river murmuring beneath the bridge.[20]

Amongst those who died on the bridge was Ernst Himmler, brother of the former head of the SS. Despite the high loss of life, the sheer weight of people crossing forced the Soviet units out of their positions.

On the west bank, Sydow attempted to organise the survivors for a further move to the west. Slowly, constantly under fire both from Soviet soldiers and aircraft, Altner and the others made their way to Staaken in the western part of Spandau, about 2.5 miles from the bridge. From time to time, SS officers attempted to issue orders, but most of the men ignored them. By mid-afternoon, Altner's company – originally 150 men strong – was reduced to just eight survivors. Sydow gathered together the few remaining vehicles and as the column set off once more, heavy firing commenced, and everyone attempted to climb onto the vehicles:

> The trucks are stormed by the troops. Although according to the orders only the wounded should climb aboard, nobody cares about that any more, for no one is prepared to give up the place he has fought for ... Everyone is pressed tight

together on the trucks with women, children, soldiers, and civilians piled up on top of one another in the back. I sit on the left front wing of a truck, having no proper hold, my fingers having to press into the slits on the bonnet. A young girl is sitting on the right front wing holding on tight, and people are clinging like burrs to the cab, the running boards, and the sides of the truck. Then the truck moves off, the engine roaring into life and we shoot along the street, a strong slipstream hitting me in the face, making my eyes water. I clutch on tightly, bracing my feet against the thin front bumper …

There is a scream, and the right hand wing is empty. Two slender hands clutch the metal of the bonnet and slip away. Trees and houses fly towards us. We take the bends with the truck skidding, driving over dead and wounded, threatening to tip over as we take the curves at top speed, taking off and slamming down hard again.[21]

The column came to a halt a short time later and almost immediately was hit by artillery fire, blowing apart vehicles and their occupants. Wounded in a foot by shrapnel, Altner stumbled away and reached a military training area, where he had been told soldiers of Wenck's Twelfth Army would be waiting. Instead, he found the area had become a rendezvous for the small bands filtering out of Spandau. Once more, the soldiers and civilians set off, reaching the village of Falkenrehde during the late afternoon. They were now 13 miles from the Havel crossing, and remarkably were still accompanied by a small number of tanks. During the evening, they crossed the Havel once more at Ketzin on an improvised bridge. From here, they headed west towards Brandenburg, coming under fire as it grew dark. Everyone was dismayed when local people told them that they had no idea of the whereabouts of Wenck's Twelfth Army. The column disintegrated into smaller groups, each left to find its own way to safety, but at dawn on 3 May the main group, of which Altner was a part, still numbered about 500 men, led by a major from an administrative post who clearly had no experience of field command.

Shortly after dawn, Altner's group sheltered in a small patch of woodland; the lucky few who still had food took the opportunity to eat, many sharing their meagre supplies with their comrades, while they waited for the morning mist to clear. A young officer from the Waffen-SS had joined them, and the men were now reorganised into makeshift platoons, even though they had few weapons or ammunition. As the rising sun burned off the mist, the soldiers – still accompanied by a few civilians – were horrified to see that there were Red Army tanks and soldiers on a nearby road. They hastily moved deeper into the woodland before finding a route west. Later that morning, they stumbled across tanks once more, but this time they were surprised to find that they were the vehicles that had accompanied them the previous day, laden with wounded. As they continued west, small groups continued to break off in the hope of finding their own ways to safety, and Altner estimated that the group who remained with the tanks now numbered no more than a hundred. Local civilians gave them small amounts of food as they passed and warned that Soviet troops were everywhere. They were now about eight miles northeast of Brandenburg, and the group dispersed almost completely. Led by an officer of the *Volkssturm*, Altner and seven others continued across country. Exhausted and struggling with his wounded foot, Altner was horrified when the group heard shouts behind them:

> We turn around and see that they are Russians. We start to run across the field to the wood that means salvation to us. Suddenly shots ring out and plough into the field …We keep going, unable to grasp that it is all over now, that the dance of death of the last few days has all been futile – the pain, the hunger, the misery. Our lungs are panting. Then we stop and look back. I throw my pistol far away into the field and soon they are standing in front of us. The flight has ended, the hunt is over …
>
> [They were marched back to the nearby road.] We all have the same question inside us: what now? Will we be killed as we were told? Or do we have a short time before execution? Suddenly one of the Russians stops and waits for me, as I'm the last. This is the end. I slowly go up to him. Then he takes my arm. I am afraid that he will take me aside somewhere and put an end to me, but then I notice that he is supporting me, walking in step with me and guiding me. He gives me a cigarette and lights one for himself. 'War over! All go home!' he says to me. I am astonished. The immense tension of the last few days gives way inside me, and I am suddenly unable to hold back the tears, tears of relief that the enemy is human after all, and that I could ever have believed otherwise.[22]

Altner was taken by truck to Brandenburg where his wound was treated, and he was soon allowed to return to his home in Berlin. Others were less fortunate; many were taken to prison camps to the east and put to work. Some remained prisoners until 1955 when Konrad Adenauer, the West German chancellor, made his historic visit to Moscow and negotiated their release. A few soldiers managed to reach the Elbe and cross to the west bank – when he was captured, Altner was about 30 miles from the river – but most of those who had survived the crossing of the Charlottenbrücke were killed or rounded up and captured. Sydow, who had led the attempt, was captured a day or two after Altner. He was one of those who was held until 1955. He died in 1970.

Böttcher, the operations officer of 18th Panzergrenadier Division, waited in the Zoo Flak Tower on 1 May in vain for Rauch, his division commander, to join the breakout attempt, and then decided to try to escape before it was too late. At the deadly bridge, he realised that most of the devastating enemy fire was coming from a house on the far bank and he directed the crew of a quad anti-aircraft gun to fire on it. In the lull that followed, he succeeded in crossing, but was unable to follow the main group towards Staaken, diverting instead towards Potsdam. Accompanied by about 20 others, Böttcher hid in woodland, their numbers slowly diminishing; one of the officers had an infected arm wound and they managed to get civilian clothing for him and sent him to a nearby parsonage where wounded men were being tended. On 9 May, they were startled when a civilian approached their hideout, calling out Böttcher's name. He told them that he had been sent by the wounded officer with a sack of civilian clothing. He also informed Böttcher that Germany had surrendered unconditionally the day before.

Accompanied by his adjutant, Bottcher went to the makeshift hospital where their wounded comrade was being treated, but a Soviet officer suddenly appeared and accused them of being soldiers. The adjutant had lost an arm earlier in the war, and angrily remonstrated with the Red Army soldiers that he was an invalid. The Soviet officer stared in astonishment as the adjutant removed his prosthetic arm and showed the gathered Soviet soldiers how it functioned, while Böttcher pretended to be a medical orderly looking after the wounded. After the officer and his men departed – promising to return later and warning them not to leave – the parson and his daughter provided Böttcher and his adjutant with improvised documentation that described them as workers of a local industrial company. The two soldiers then walked to Jüterborg, where Böttcher's aunt lived, before continuing towards their homes in Silesia. When he reached his home town, Böttcher learned that his wife had fled to Czechoslovakia; he remained in the town for about a year before an opportunity arose for him to head west and escape from the Soviet occupation zone. Some time later, he was reunited with his wife.[23]

Another breakout attempt took place immediately to the north of the Reich Chancellery involving some of the surviving defenders of the central district and the groups who had left the *Führerbunker*. Unlike the groups that made the bloody crossing of the Charlottenbrücke, they planned to link up with the former *Armeegruppe Steiner*, unaware that Steiner had already retreated to the west. Mohnke led a group to the Spree where they found a metal footbridge. They crossed during the night of 1–2 May, while a second group attempted to storm the Weidendammerbrücke, about 300 metres to the east. The assault was led by the last Tiger tank of *SS-Nordland* and an assault gun. Followed closely by hundreds on foot – a mixture of Wehrmacht and SS soldiers, and many civilians – the Tiger roared across the bridge, smashing its way through Soviet barricades, but intense fire on the north bank brought it to a halt. As on the Charlottenbrücke, there was terrible loss of life as gunfire swept the crossing, and the Red Army soon restored its hold on the north bank, but not before small groups of Germans managed to slip past.

Unfortunately for the Germans, the Soviet units in the area had been alerted by another breakout attempt. The Humbolthain Flak Tower in the northern part of Berlin had held out throughout the fighting and from here, a group of soldiers – a mixture of Wehrmacht troops and Luftwaffe paratroopers – slipped through the Red Army's lines and headed north. As alarming reports reached him of German groups attempting to escape from central Berlin, Zhukov issued immediate orders for strong measures to be taken; he was aware that despite having captured the German capital, his personal standing with Stalin was not what it had been and would fall still further if any senior Nazi figures managed to get out of the city. As a result, the Red Army units in this area were fully prepared when the German groups that had managed to cross the Weidendammerbrücke reached the next line of resistance.

Unterscharführer Georg Diers was the commander of the last Tiger tank that had succeeded in crossing the bridge and he managed to get moving again. He found himself in a small group led personally by Erich Bärenfänger, one of the commanders who had overlapping responsibilities in the central district:

> General Bärenfänger was attempting to bring some order into the chaos and he requested us to drive to the other side of the street through a subway underpass and to take point. After a short drive we ran onto German mines. General Bärenfänger came back immediately and I reported to him that we were immobilised for the moment, but would be ready for action again in one hour. General Bärenfänger said to me then: 'My boy, see to it that you blow up your tank and, most importantly, that you get your boys home safely. We have lost the war.'[24]

Diers set off a destruction charge in his Tiger and he and his crew slipped away into the ruins. The rest of this group was rapidly dispersed by Soviet patrols. Bärenfänger managed to reach a bunker underneath a nearby brewery where his wife and brother-in-law had taken shelter; the three of them killed themselves on 2 May.

One of the groups that had managed to follow Diers' Tiger across the bridge consisted of Artur Axmann, the head of the Hitler Youth who had sent teenagers to their deaths on the Seelow Heights, and others from the Reich Chancellery. These included Bormann, Johannes Baur (Hitler's personal pilot), Ludwig Stumpfegger (one of the senior medical personnel in the bunker), Werner Naumann (who had been nominated as head of the propaganda ministry when Goebbels became Reich chancellor after Hitler's death) and Obersturmbannführer Erich Kempka, who had often served as Hitler's personal chauffeur. They were caught in the blast of a shell or rocket that struck the lone Tiger tank and Axmann was wounded, but he, Bormann, Baur, and Stumpfegger were able to escape into the ruins of Berlin.

Behind them, a second attempt to force the Weidendammerbrücke, led by a half-track and a quadruple 20mm flak mount, was also brought to a halt by heavy defensive fire from the north bank. Two more futile attempts followed, each leaving the bridge littered with more corpses. Meanwhile, Axmann and the others in his group decided to split up. After dodging a Soviet patrol, Axmann turned back and attempted to follow the others; he came across two bodies, which he identified as Bormann and Stumpfegger.[25] Naumann, who had managed to escape into the darkness, later claimed that Bormann had been working with Soviet agents and escaped alive, ending his days in Moscow, but the remains of the corpses described by Axmann were located in 1972 and in 1998, DNA testing confirmed their identities.[26]

Continuing to dodge Soviet patrols, Axmann – despite being wounded – was able to escape into the countryside. Here, he attempted to adopt an alias of Erich Siewert, and became involved in a Nazi underground movement. This proved to be a mistake – the group was being monitored by US intelligence officers and he was arrested at the end of 1945. After several months in US captivity, during which he was extensively interrogated, Axmann had to appear before a Denazification court. This court had the option of coming to one of four conclusions. It could exonerate defendants entirely; it could find them guilty of being 'fellow travellers' of the Nazi Party, i.e. having been members but not advancing the aims of the Party; it could declare them as being 'major offenders', active members who had worked to further the Party's aims; or it could refer defendants for further prosecutions for war crimes. In Axmann's case, despite his major role in the Hitler Youth, Axmann was not referred for further investigation or prosecution and was given a three-year prison sentence for being a major offender. In 1958, he was prosecuted once more and on this occasion was fined heavily for indoctrinating young Germans with National Socialist beliefs, but once again he was found not guilty of war crimes. He died in 1996.

Yet another group that attempted to fight its way out of central Berlin consisted of a largely SS contingent that coalesced around Krukenberg. This included Ziegler, the former commander of *SS-Nordland*, and Krukenberg was able to lead them safely across the Spree. They continued north nearly two miles before they ran into strong Soviet resistance near the Gesundbrunnen *U-Bahn* station; here, Ziegler was mortally wounded by the explosion of a shell. Several others were killed, and Krukenberg led the survivors back south and they dispersed. Dressed in civilian clothes, Krukenberg managed to reach a suburb in southwest Berlin, but surrendered to the Red Army a week later. He was charged with war crimes and given a long prison sentence in the Soviet Union, but like thousands of others he was released in 1955 and returned to Germany, where he died in 1980.

Mohnke's group was unable to find a route through the Soviet troops in its path and rapidly split up. Three of Hitler's secretaries – Gertraud ('Traudl') Junge, Gerda Christian, and Else Krüger – were in the group. Junge was eventually able to reach the Elbe near Wittenberge but was unable to cross to the west bank and returned to Berlin. She was arrested by Soviet troops in June 1945 and extensively interrogated, but was then released without charge.[27] The Denazification court declared her to be a 'fellow traveller', and she died in 2002.

Mohnke and most of his group ended up in the cellars of a brewery on Prinzenallee. Here, they surrendered to the Red Army a day later; some of the group shot themselves before they could be captured. Together with several of his fellow officers, Mohnke was invited to a banquet arranged by Chuikov's chief of staff, Colonel Vitaly Andreyevich Belyavsky; as the meal drew to an end, the German officers were led into an adjoining room where they were kept under guard before being handed over to the *NKVD*.[28] Mohnke was taken to Moscow where he was held in solitary confinement for several years before being sent first to the Lubyanka Prison, and then to an officers' prison camp. He was released in 1955. Although he was accused of involvement in the killing of British and Canadian prisoners in Normandy in 1944, no charges were brought against him and he died in 2001.

After the main breakout group left the Zoo Flak Tower, the garrison surrendered to the Red Army the following day; several junior officers from 18th Panzergrenadier Division who had refused to join the breakout attempt killed themselves. About 350 men went into captivity. In northwest Berlin, another German stronghold that remained defiant until the very end was on an island in the Havel, in Spandau. On 1 May, Perkhorovich, the commander of the Soviet Forty-Seventh Army, ordered Major Vasily Grishin, who had been in charge of broadcasting demands for the Germans to surrender by loudspeaker, to negotiate with the fortress garrison. The German position was suspected to be held by SS troops and Grishin turned down a request by Konrad Wolf, a German Communist who would be a prominent film maker in East Germany after the war, to accompany him. Instead, he took Vladimir Samoilovich Gall, a close friend of Wolf who was working with Grishin's propaganda department, as his translator.

When the two Soviet officers approached the German positions carrying a white flag, a rope ladder was lowered to them. Inside the fortress they met the garrison commander, Oberst Gerhard Jung, and a group of other officers. One of them told the Soviet pair that Hitler had issued clear orders that anyone attempting to surrender was to be shot. Gall explained that most of Berlin was under the control of the Red Army – at this stage, he was unaware that Hitler was dead – and that contact had been made with US troops on the Elbe. Germany was rapidly collapsing, and there was no point in prolonging the fighting. He promised good treatment if the garrison surrendered, but added that this would not necessarily apply if the Red Army was forced to storm the German defences:

> We are all soldiers and we all know that a great deal of blood would be shed. And if many of our soldiers die in the process, I cannot answer for the consequences. Also, if you refuse to surrender, you will be responsible for the deaths of all your civilians here. Germany has lost so much blood that each life must surely be important for its future.[29]

Gall was Jewish, and it was clear that many of the Germans had recognised this. Faced by their stony stares, Grishin told Gall to advise the Germans that they had until 1500 to lay down their arms. As they climbed back down the rope ladder, Grishin and Gall feared that the Germans might cut the ladder, but they returned safely to their lines. At precisely 1500, two figures appeared on the balcony and climbed down the rope ladder. They were taken to Grishin and Gall and informed them that they required the terms of surrender in writing. A suitable document was hastily drawn up and after being encouraged to drink copious amounts of Cognac, the two German officers returned to the fortress. The main gates were then opened and the garrison emerged. As he met the officers with whom he had negotiated a few hours earlier, Grishin was shocked to discover that at least one of them spoke excellent Russian, having lived in St Petersburg for many years. At one point during the negotiations, he had been on the verge of telling Gall to promise whatever the Germans wanted to hear, with no intention of sticking to his promises. Amongst those who emerged from the fortress were several hundred civilians who had sheltered there. Whilst fear of surrender to the Soviet forces was one of the reasons that had driven them to seek shelter, they were in little doubt that such a surrender was better than enduring a Soviet assault on the fortress.

The two officers who had negotiated with Gall and Grishin – Jung, and his deputy Edgar Koch – were actually senior scientists involved in research on nerve agents. A Soviet officer recognised that their shoulder boards bore the symbol of technical officers and told his superiors that the men should be interviewed further, but a detachment of *NKVD* arrived and took them away. Together with others captured at Spandau, Jung and Koch were held in captivity for nearly a decade and there were repeated attempts by the Soviet authorities to get them to help develop Soviet chemical weapons. Led by Jung, the Germans refused to cooperate and were ultimately released in 1954.

In Berlin, the ruins of the Reichstag – which had been left in its devastated state after the fire of 1933 – became a magnet for Soviet soldiers. Yakov Fadeyev, who had been shocked to be appointed commander of an assault platoon just before the offensive began, was concussed in the fighting for the building and emerged to find soldiers celebrating:

> There was a lot of shooting, but not in combat, purely in victory. Our guys were dancing on the steps and there were journalists and photographers. Nearly all of my entire platoon died during the storming of the Reichstag; only three were pulled out from under the rubble – me, Vanya Bashmakov, the radio operator, and Zhora Kuznetsov, the linesman. The three of us were photographed in vanquished Berlin. This is my only photograph from the front line, and I have kept it as my most precious relic. On the seventh column from the entrance, I and others wrote on the walls. I wrote: 'I, Fadeyev, reached Berlin'.[30]

Weary columns of German prisoners were gathered and began to march out of Berlin. Some Soviet soldiers gathered to jeer at them, but most were either busy celebrating, or simply glad that the fighting was over. All around them, the civilian population waited in trepidation for what lay ahead.

CHAPTER 13

CONCLUSION: AN UNEASY SILENCE

Throughout the last weeks of the war in Europe, almost all operational attention had been on the battlefields of Germany, particularly around Berlin. But further to the east, two groups of German soldiers fought on in isolation. The largest was in northeast Latvia, where Army Group Courland – the remnants of Sixteenth and Eighteenth Armies – continued to hold out. To their south, around the Vistula estuary, the so-called *Armee Oberkommando Ostpreussen* ('Army High Command East Prussia') clung to its small coastal enclave.

Ever since the two armies that had once marched to the gates of Leningrad had been cut off in Courland in late 1944, there had been repeated suggestions that they should be evacuated by sea. They contained large numbers of battle-hardened soldiers who might have helped Germany defend itself more effectively, but Hitler refused to countenance any wholesale withdrawal. Instead, divisions were pulled out individually from time to time, arriving in a trickle that did little to alleviate the problems faced by the German forces attempting to hold back the Soviet advance on Berlin. The Führer insisted that the rest should remain in the east where they were to hold a 'bridgehead' from which future offensive operations might one day be launched, and gave numerous other reasons for retaining a toehold in the eastern Baltic – for example, if the tide of war was to be turned by the new, more effective U-boats that were about to enter service, it was essential for the U-boat training areas in the Baltic Sea to be protected.

The troops of *AOK Ostpreussen* were the survivors of the armies that had been ground down in East Prussia and around Danzig, but their role was different from that of the men trapped in Courland. From late January until the very end of the war, the German Navy mounted a huge evacuation operation codenamed

Hannibal. Mass evacuation of the eastern territories was anathema to Hitler and senior Nazis and regarded as synonymous with defeatism, but hundreds of thousands of desperate refugees had gathered in the ports of the eastern Baltic. As commander of the navy, Dönitz ordered Konteradmiral Conrad Engelhardt, head of the navy's sea transport department, to organise *Hannibal* as an evacuation of U-boat training personnel from their bases in the east. The real reason for *Hannibal* was hidden further down the operational orders: in addition to bringing the U-boat trainees and their instructors to the west, Engelhardt's ships were also to evacuate wounded soldiers, military personnel who were not needed in front-line roles, and any civilians who could be accommodated.

As the operation unfolded, this last category became the largest. By the end of the war, over two million people, military and civilian, had been brought west, though this figure is inflated slightly by some evacuees being put ashore at ports in Pomerania and then being evacuated a second time. During the evacuation, three of the five worst losses of life at sea took place after attacks on the ships carrying people to safety. The liner *Wilhelm Gustloff* and the freighter *Goya* were sunk by Soviet submarines on 30 January and 16 April respectively; and the liner *Cap Arkona* was sunk by RAF Typhoons on 3 May. But despite these losses, the operation was a huge success, with fewer than 1 per cent of passengers losing their lives.[1] It was the responsibility of *AOK Ostpreussen* to hold back the Red Army for as long as possible so that the evacuation could be completed.

By late April, Engelhardt's motley fleet of small warships, coastal freighters, and a few former ocean-going liners, was struggling to continue operations. Shortages of fuel, mechanical breakdowns, and damage from air attacks had all taken their toll. Nonetheless, almost all civilians in the remaining German-held ports had been brought west, and the race was now on to see if the remnants of Army Group Courland and *AOK Ostpreussen* could also be evacuated. To buy as much time as possible, Dönitz – now head of the German government – tried to shore up the defences facing the enemies of the Reich. He had no illusions about achieving a wildly improbable victory; what mattered now was to evacuate as many soldiers from the east as possible.

This strategy soon unravelled. Third Panzer Army's surviving formations were rapidly pulling back towards the west, fighting no more than a rearguard action, and when the British 7th Armoured Division approached Hamburg, Generalmajor Alwin Wolz, the city *Kampfkommandant*, decided that his forces – the usual mixture of survivors of regular formations, rear area units, *Volkssturm*, Hitler Youth, naval and Luftwaffe personnel, and a few small groups of diehard SS – were incapable of defending such a large city. He sent a delegation across the front line to negotiate with the British, with a Hauptmann who had studied at

Conclusion: An Uneasy Silence

Oxford University before the war as interpreter. Wearing his scarf with the colours of Christ Church College, the Hauptmann explained the mission of his small group, and they were taken to the headquarters of 7th Armoured Division. Here, the leader of the German delegation – with the rank of Oberst – asked if he could speak confidentially to his British counterpart. The two men walked a short distance from the others, and the Oberst asked if it was likely that the officers of the garrison would be sent to Siberia. If that was the case, he continued, should they commit suicide instead? The British officer was dumbfounded. 'That's entirely up to you,' he replied.[2]

On 3 May, Wolz surrendered Hamburg without a fight. Even as news of this arrived in Dönitz's headquarters, there was a further blow. Tippelskirch's makeshift Twenty-First Army was meant to be holding back the British and US troops pressing into northern Germany, but Dönitz now learned that Tippelskirch was taking advantage of the rapid advance of the Western Allies to open talks about a ceasefire. As he evacuated his headquarters in Plön and set off for Flensburg, Dönitz ordered negotiations to begin with the Western Allies on a larger scale. His preferred solution remained that of so many Germans – a ceasefire in the west, but continuation of the war in the east, ideally with the aid of the Western Allies. Admiral Hans-Georg von Friedeburg and General Eberhard Kinzel, accompanied by the politician Lutz Graf Schwerin von Krosigk, were sent to meet the British in north Germany.

Meanwhile, Tippelskirch met General James Gavin, commander of the US 82nd Airborne Division, on 3 May. Aware of Dönitz's intentions, he asked for a ceasefire in the west while he continued to fight in the east. Gavin refused. Tippelskirch suggested a compromise, drawing up a document for Gavin to forward to higher commands:

> Twenty-First Army is continuing the withdrawal action from the enemy and is preventing Russian breakthroughs. Personnel who encounter the Anglo-American forces in the course of this withdrawal are to stop fighting and to surrender to them, laying down their weapons.[3]

The document deliberately made no mention of ceasing hostilities against Soviet forces. Gavin made a few minor modifications, and then agreed. Over the days that followed, 82nd Airborne Division – numbering barely 10,000 men – accepted the surrender of tens of thousands of German soldiers with barely a shot fired.

Meanwhile, Friedeburg and his delegation travelled through the front lines to the headquarters of Field Marshal Montgomery. The German admiral told the

British commander that he wished to negotiate the surrender of all forces in this last corner of the Reich to the Western Allies, but Montgomery rejected this, replying that as they were fighting against the Red Army, they should surrender to the Soviet forces. In an attempt to persuade the Germans of the hopelessness of their situation, Montgomery showed them the current positions of forces on the Western Front; Friedeburg, who seems to have been completely unaware of just how bad things were, broke down in tears, and an embarrassed Montgomery suggested a short break. When the talks resumed, he made three points. Firstly, he demanded the unconditional surrender of all German forces in the Netherlands, Schleswig-Holstein, and Denmark, and in exchange offered a cessation of British air attacks on German targets to the east. Secondly, he was prepared to discuss further details of the occupation of these regions after the surrender had been completed. Thirdly, if the Germans didn't agree, he would prosecute the war to the bitter end.

This was actually far more than Montgomery was authorised to offer. Eisenhower was insisting on complete unconditional surrender, but Montgomery saw this as an opportunity to bring fighting in northwest Europe to a swift end. The losses suffered by all Allied armies in Normandy in 1944 had been heavy, and Britain was now hard stretched to find sufficient men to replace its casualties, with conscription being extended to previously exempt groups. There remained the grim prospect of at least another year of fighting against Japan, and a rapid end to hostilities in Europe was of great importance. The longstanding rivalry between Montgomery and Eisenhower played a part too – Montgomery had an opportunity to secure the surrender of a huge number of Germans. The following day – 4 May – the German delegation returned and signed a surrender document. A ceasefire would come into effect the following morning. The German delegation then flew to Rheims, to hold discussions with Eisenhower. Throughout the day, Engelhardt's diminished fleet continued its evacuation of the east, and at one stage British aircraft appeared overhead. The Germans watched nervously, but no bombs fell. Montgomery had honoured the agreement he had reached with Friedeburg.

It was inevitable that Montgomery would make the most of the German surrender. His war diary entry is both self-serving and dishonest:

> When I review the campaign as a whole, I am amazed at the mistakes that we made. The Supreme Commander [Eisenhower] had no firm ideas as to how to conduct the war and was 'blown about by the wind' all over the place ... The staff at SHAEF ['Supreme Headquarters Allied Expeditionary Force'] were out of their depth all the time.[4]

Conclusion: An Uneasy Silence

For the moment, it seemed as if Dönitz had at least partially achieved his aim, but the delegation in Rheims faced a far more intransigent set of discussions. Jodl had joined the German team, and he informed Eisenhower that it would take at least 48 hours for all German forces to be informed that a surrender was being implemented. Whilst communications problems were undoubtedly an issue, the true reason was of course to win an opportunity to allow *Hannibal* to continue. Eisenhower flatly rejected all suggestions of continued German military activity in the east, and the Americans added that all German forces would have to surrender to whichever Allied forces they faced. Late on 6 May, Jodl was given just 30 minutes to agree to complete surrender or face continuation of the war with no further discussions. His American counterparts pointed out wryly that the agreed time for cessation of hostilities – midnight on 8–9 May – would still permit sufficient time to deal with any communications delays. Jodl sent a signal to Dönitz:

> I see no alternative other than chaos or signing. I request immediate confirmation by radio whether I have permission to sign the surrender document. It will come into effect immediately. Hostilities will cease on 9 May, 0000 hours.[5]

Dönitz had been informed by Engelhardt that complete evacuation of *AOK Ostpreussen* and Courland would take at least three full days, and even that would require more fuel and shipping than was currently available, but he had to bow to reality. He gave permission to Jodl to sign the surrender. In a final desperate effort, the last ships raced east on 8 May so that they could load aboard as many men as possible for one more run. Every ship involved took on dangerously large numbers of men, often with the decks of the few remaining warships so crowded that it would have been impossible for their guns to be used if they came under attack. In the two days before *Hannibal* came to a close, roughly half of the 120,000-strong *AOK Ostpreussen* was successfully evacuated. An armada of 175 vessels, ranging from small freighters to motorboats, took 23,000 men from Courland, leaving nearly 200,000 to surrender to the Red Army. Luftwaffe engineers stripped armour from the last fighter aircraft in Courland to make space for them to carry a single passenger each, and the pilots flew to the west, taking with them ground crew who had been selected on the basis of being fathers of young children or the last surviving sons of families.

In Berlin, Soviet troops roamed through the ruins in search of the last pockets of resistance. There were occasional exchanges of fire with those who were determined to fight to the death, but many of the Red Army personnel were more interested in searching for things other than diehard German soldiers.

Civilians were searched repeatedly for valuables and women of all ages were subject to repeated rapes. After the war, official Soviet accounts denied that such rapes took place, and few veterans were willing to speak about the subject. Officially, rape was punishable by immediate execution, but this was rarely the case. Red Army soldiers had been encouraged to approach this last phase of the war in a spirit of vengeance, perhaps in an attempt to overcome war-weariness, and as the mass mobilisation of German males for last-ditch military service left Berlin and other cities with predominantly female occupants, they bore the brunt of the desire for revenge. Added to this was the consequence of long service in the Red Army with little or no opportunity for contact with women – the Wehrmacht had organised brothels for its personnel, often forcing local women to work in them, but there was no such arrangement for Soviet soldiers. With the constant threat of death now gone, the soldiers celebrated by venting their pent-up emotions on any women who were at hand. It wasn't until July 1945 that serious steps were taken to bring the rapes to an end.

As already described, the desire to rape and loot was driven by many factors. Quite often, the items taken were of no use whatever to either the individual soldiers or to the Soviet state: typewriters were loaded into railcars by the hundred, even though they would be useless in the Soviet Union with its Cyrillic alphabet; electrical items were shipped home to towns and villages with no electrical supply; and even porcelain toilets were sent east, despite there being no plumbing to which they could be attached. Soldiers were given monthly weight allowances, based on rank, that they could use to ship loot home. Senior officers frequently took whatever they wanted.

After the first wave of looting and rape had passed, the systematic dismantling of German industrial plant began. The leaders of the Allied Powers had agreed that Berlin would be partitioned among the victorious Allies – originally, this was to create Soviet, British, and US zones, but the Anglo-Americans gave up parts of their zones so that a French zone of occupation could be created – and Berzarin, the governor of the city, was under orders from Stalin to ensure that everything of possible use in the Soviet Union was to be shipped out before parts of the city were handed over. Factory machinery, sewing machines, even ventilation equipment – everything was loaded onto trains and sent back to the Soviet Union. Most of it proved impossible to use, sometimes because German prisoners, who had been forced to dismantle it, had deliberately removed key items. Such activity added to the general devastation of Berlin.[6]

The Soviet soldiers weren't the only ones picking through the ruins of Berlin in search of items of value. One of the civilian survivors of the fighting travelled around the city a couple of weeks after the surrender:

Conclusion: An Uneasy Silence

The final six days of fighting have destroyed more of Berlin than ten heavy air raids. Only occasionally does one spot an intact building ...

People with weary faces poke around in the ruins, here and there recovering some battered 'trophy' or charred beam ...

We arrive at the Tiergarten. Or rather, what's left of it. Aghast, I look at the torn-up trees. Smashed, blasted, mutilated beyond recognition ... On Charlottenburger Chausee the smell of decaying bodies. On closer inspection we see it is only the skeletons of horses. People living in the neighbourhood have cut the meat off the dead animals' bones piece by piece ...

We turn into Wilhelmstrasse. Ruins and dust. Dust and ruins. Wherever a cellar has remained intact, trophy hunters are at work, struggling up and down the stairs like maggots on cheese ... Before the entrance [to the Reich Chancellery] a Russian soldier is on guard. His gun across his knees, he leans comfortably back in a green silk-covered armchair. In the middle of the so-called Court of Honour, an image of perfect peace. The sight makes us smile. Certainly this is not the sort of guard the Nazis had imagined for their Führer and Chancellor.[7]

It wasn't until July that the Western Allies began to arrive in Berlin to take over their respective occupation zones. Until then, the Soviet occupiers took every opportunity to seize whatever they could. All public clocks in the city were put on Moscow time, and construction of a memorial commenced, using marble from the Reich Chancellery – it was to stand in the Tiergarten area, deliberately selected because it would be in the western part of Berlin and would act as a reminder to the Western Allies that the Red Army had reached Berlin first. The towering figure of a Soviet soldier would become known to Berliners as the *Denkmal für den Unbekannten Vergewaltiger* ('Memorial to the Unknown Rapist').

For the Soviet soldiers who had occupied Berlin, it was a time of revelry. Now that Germany had surrendered, the sense of relief at surviving such a bloody war must have been overwhelming. Inevitably, the constant drunkenness and over-exuberant celebration of victory resulted in injuries and fatalities, but the survivors felt that they had earned the right to take such risks. The price that the Red Army paid for its great victory was immense. Estimates of the casualties suffered by both sides between the commencement of the attacks along the Oder–Neisse line and the end of the fighting in Berlin vary. The Red Army claimed that it killed over 396,000 German soldiers and captured a further 390,000.[8] German assessments are a little different, giving a total of about 100,000 killed, 220,000 wounded, and 480,000 taken prisoner.[9] In addition, about 125,000 civilians were killed in the fighting.[10] Soviet casualties between

16 April and 2 May for 1st and 2nd Belarusian Fronts and 1st Ukrainian Front are put at about 352,000 dead, wounded, or missing. In addition, the Polish formations in the assault suffered a further 8,900 casualties.[11] Losses of tanks and assault guns were also substantial, with nearly 2,000 destroyed. The number knocked out during the fighting was far higher – many were recovered from the various battlefields and eventually repaired. Many regiments and battalions lost over three quarters of their strength in the fighting. The fears of US commanders of heavy casualties had they attempted to take Berlin were probably correct.

However, it is worth considering: how realistic were these US concerns? When the Western Allies surged across the Rhine, they advanced rapidly to encircle the German Army Group B in the Ruhr area, and killed or captured about 327,000 German soldiers for the loss of just 10,000 killed, wounded and missing.[12] Although some German troops facing the Western Allies – particularly the SS – fought with the level of fanatical determination demanded by Hitler, most simply laid down their arms. It was common knowledge in German military circles that the Western Allies treated prisoners of war fairly well, despite attempts by Goebbels' propaganda machine to suggest widespread mistreatment. If US and British troops had attacked Berlin, how hard would the Germans have fought to stop them? Wenck's Twelfth Army had already put up a strong fight for Magdeburg, blocking the headlong advance of the US Army, but the sheer weight of resources available to the Western Allies would surely have permitted them to bypass any units that did choose to stand and fight. It is certainly arguable that the bitter determination shown by German forces in trying to hold back the Red Army – first in the Soviet advance over the Oder and Neisse, then in Berlin – was driven by determination to prevent Soviet forces, which were expected to behave with brutality towards the civilian population, from reaching the capital. If that is the case, it is equally arguable that resistance to an advance by the Western Allies would have been far less determined. But a battle for the urban area of Berlin – the capital of Germany – would perhaps have hardened the resolve of the city's defenders. The US assessment that an advance *might* cost 100,000 casualties is certainly correct, and the decision to avoid such losses was therefore valid.

By April 1945, the only realistic hope for the Germans was that fissures would open in the alliance arrayed against Nazi Germany. At the very least, the Western Allies might be persuaded to accept a ceasefire while the Wehrmacht continued to hold off the Red Army in the east, allowing a relatively peaceful occupation of Berlin by western armies; at best, the British and Americans might be persuaded that the threat of Soviet domination of Europe was sufficiently great to justify the complete disintegration of the anti-German alliance, with the armies of the Western Allies fighting alongside the Germans against the Soviet Union. Such hopes were in vain, but nor were they entirely without foundation. Churchill in particular was convinced of the need to prevent further Soviet expansion into Europe and actively considered the possibility of British forces fighting alongside German units against the Red Army. On 9 May, he sent a telegram to Eisenhower expressing concern that the Germans might destroy their remaining aircraft as they surrendered:

> I hope that this policy will not be adopted in regard to weapons and other forms of equipment. We may have great need of these some day and even now they might be of use ... I think we ought to keep everything worth keeping.[13]

Montgomery agreed entirely with this. He travelled to the front line in Wismar on the same day to meet Rokossovsky to calm nerves after an incident that had taken place a few days before. Although rapes committed by the soldiers of the Western Allies were far less frequent than those committed by Red Army soldiers, they nonetheless took place. It should also be noted that there were consensual sexual encounters in all occupation zones, often motivated by the need for German women to secure the protection of individual occupying soldiers or to barter sex for food and other items. Many of the paratroopers in Wismar had been roaming through the town in search of both alcohol and women on 5 May, and late that day, a group of drunken Soviet soldiers appeared on the steps of the hospital in Wismar, shouting to a British sentry, '*Wir wollen Frauen!*' ('We want women!') When the sentry refused to allow them entry into the hospital, tensions rose rapidly. Some of the Canadian paratroopers appeared, many of them armed, and in the confusion of drunken shouting, shots were fired – it isn't clear which side started the violence. The Soviet soldiers rapidly departed, leaving six or seven dead.[14] When he met Rokossovsky, Montgomery agreed with the Soviet commander that it would be best to draw a veil over the incident. On his return to his headquarters, Montgomery issued orders that German weapons were not to be destroyed, but were to be retained and stored close to prisoner of war compounds in case they might be needed at a later date. Clearly, the intention was that if hostilities with the Red Army erupted, the Germans could be rearmed rapidly.

Another famous commander also shared Churchill's views. A few days later, General George Patton, who had led the US Third Army in its advance across Europe, spoke to a few close friends in Paris:

> Day after day, some poor bloody Czech or Austrian or Hungarian, even German officers, come into my headquarters ... With tears in their eyes they say, 'In the

name of God, General, come with your army the rest of the way into our country. Give us a chance to live before it's too late – before the Russians make us slaves forever.' That's what they tell me, and every damned one of them has offered to fight under my flag and bring their men with them. Hell, a German general offered his entire air force, the Third [this was presumably Generalleutnant Alexander Holle, commander of *Luftflotte 3*], to fight the Russians if necessary! I'll tell you this: the Third Army alone, with very little other help and with damned few casualties, could lick what's left of the Russians in six weeks. You mark my words. Don't ever forget them. Some day we'll have to fight them and it will take six years and cost us six million lives.[15]

Such a statement – that Third Army alone could crush the Red Army with little help – was of course wildly optimistic at best, but thought was given to such an operation. Churchill ordered his Joint Planning Staff to consider how an attack on the Soviet forces in Europe might unfold. After considering the forces available and the likely strength of the Red Army, the planners reported on 22 May that 'without the help of US forces, Britain alone would find it beyond our power to win a quick but limited success and we would be committed to a protracted war against heavy odds'.[16] A further iteration of the plan was then drawn up with a proposed implementation date of 1 July 1945; this called for 47 British and US divisions to attack in central Germany, backed by ten rebuilt German divisions. Any chance of success, the planners wrote, relied almost entirely on surprise. If rapid success was not realised, the numerical advantage enjoyed by the Red Army would result in a prolonged war with uncertain outcome. The plan was quietly dropped and remained classified until 1998.[17]

After almost every major operation, the Red Army instigated high-level reviews of how its forces had performed and drew up lists of recommendations for future improvements. This practice played a large part in the steady improvement of the Red Army through the war, but it was not without flaws. For much of the war, the same problems were repeatedly identified. Artillery preparation might have been heavy, but was often too inaccurate to destroy German defences. Infantry, armour, artillery, and aircraft rarely cooperated as efficiently as expected, and crucially fell far short of the performance of German forces. If and when a major advance began, supplies and reinforcements often failed to keep up with the advancing forces. Armoured formations lost as many vehicles to mechanical breakdowns or terrain difficulties as through enemy action, but engineering support was inadequate to return vehicles to action quickly – again, the integrated tank recovery and repair teams that were a feature of panzer divisions from their very inception gave them a significant advantage

Conclusion: An Uneasy Silence

over their Soviet opponents. And senior commanders often lost control of their units, allowing them to be squandered in costly attacks that achieved little.

Implementing changes to remedy these problems, however, proved difficult. For artillery preparation to be more effective, better reconnaissance was essential, and Soviet forces suffered from a lack of dedicated aerial reconnaissance aircraft. Identifying German defences from ground observation was difficult, and unlikely to locate all bunkers and firing positions; attempts to provoke the Germans into opening fire by carrying out reconnaissance in force was costly and generally ineffective. Most reviews recommended major improvements in training to ensure better all-arms coordination, but several factors worked against this. The Soviet system of training – adopted from the Imperial Russian Army, and still largely in use in the modern Russian Army – relied on field units completing much of the training required to turn recruits into effective fighting men. In units that had suffered heavy losses, there were often few opportunities for such training and few men to conduct it; instead, the recruits had to learn as they fought. This inevitably resulted in higher casualties, thus exacerbating the problem. The lavish provision of trucks and other transport by the USA, Britain, and Canada did a great deal to improve Red Army mobility as the war progressed, greatly alleviating the difficulties of resupply that featured repeatedly in the early parts of the war, but German destruction of bridges and railway installations as they retreated also increased in intensity. One area where there was steady and sustained improvement, though, was increased provision of engineering support for armoured formations. By the end of the war, tank units could expect large numbers of repaired vehicles to be returned to service during an operation, allowing them to sustain advances for longer than had been the case in earlier years.

The quality of senior commanders and their ability to control their units did improve, but they faced many problems. Compared to German units or those of the Western Allies, Soviet formations had far fewer radios, making communication difficult. The requirement to obey orders or risk punishment – ingrained through the use of terror during the 1930s – made many junior and middle-ranking officers almost completely resistant to showing any initiative, and as a result they often persevered in costly assaults on positions that had already proved to be too strong rather than attempting to bypass them. Ultimately, at every level the Red Army was something of a blunt instrument – a cudgel rather than a finely crafted sword. As the war progressed, the cudgel improved and was wielded rather more effectively, but it remained an instrument of brute force. The consequence was heavy casualties in every operation that was undertaken, and the callous indifference of men like Zhukov to the losses their armies suffered meant that little was done at a high level to modify tactics to reduce casualties. The rivalry between Zhukov and Konev also contributed to avoidable casualties: Zhukov urged his armies forward regardless of the cost, even when this led to friendly fire incidents. Zhukov and others wrote after the war that they had tried to minimise losses, but there is nothing in their operational orders that suggests this was the case.

In earlier phases of the war, there had been a general view that, at every level, German formations could deal with Soviet units one step above them in size – thus, German divisions were seen as the equivalent of a Soviet corps, German corps as the equivalent of a Soviet army, German armies as the equivalent of a Soviet Front. By 1944, this was no longer true, though German divisions were individually able to outfight a Soviet division, German corps could outfight a single Soviet corps, and so on. But the maps of the battles around Berlin often show that individual German divisions were attempting to hold back Soviet armies – in other words, they were forced to defend against formations two stages above them in size. This is a reflection of the numerical superiority of the Red Army in this closing phase of the war in Europe, but despite this, the Soviet forces suffered shocking casualties. This surely undermines the claims by senior Soviet commanders that they took strenuous steps to reduce losses.

The Soviet advance from the Vistula to the Oder–Neisse line in early 1945, which established the start line for the final drive to Berlin, was in many respects a major success, with the Germans losing far more men than the Soviet and Polish forces. But nonetheless, there were developments that were good indicators of the difficulties that lay ahead for any attack towards Berlin; on this occasion, there was no general staff review with recommendations for improvements. To a large extent, this was because the Berlin Operation was mounted shortly after the end of the advance to the lower Oder, leaving little or no time for detailed analysis. There was also a strong awareness that the end of the war was close, and despite the difficulties encountered in the advance across Poland, Pomerania, and Silesia, the Germans were surely at the end of their resources. As a result, key developments were missed, with serious consequences.

One such development was the effectiveness of German anti-tank weaponry. In a report presented to Hitler on 8 March, Generaloberst Erhard Raus, commander of Third Panzer Army at the time, described the recent fighting in Pomerania. His army – temporarily renamed Eleventh SS-Panzer Army – had launched a counteroffensive intended to cut off and destroy Soviet units that had reached the lower Elbe, but had been driven back towards the northwest. Nonetheless, the fighting in Pomerania had not been without success:

> As a peculiarity of the Pomeranian battle, I can report that of the 580 enemy tanks which have been knocked out up to this time, 380, or two thirds, were

destroyed by the *Panzerfaust* – that is, by the courage of the individual soldier. Never before has an army achieved so much success with the *Panzerfaust*.[18]

There were many reasons for this, but the very nature of the *Panzerfaust* changed the way in which tanks could be engaged. The weapon had a relatively short range and most variants in use in 1945 could only hit targets up to 60–100 metres away, but in combat in an increasingly built-up environment, this was of less importance than might have been the case on the open terrain of the Soviet Union. The shaped charge of the *Panzerfaust* could blast through the armour of any tank it struck, and German soldiers in upper floors of buildings had the advantage of being able to fire onto the thinner decks of enemy tanks. It was also a very easy weapon to use – Goebbels boasted that even a child could use it with accuracy. It is noteworthy that despite having to engage German forces in the dense hedgerows and woodland of Normandy, British tank losses attributed to *Panzerfausts* amounted to only 6 per cent of all tank losses, partly due to a high level of all-arms cooperation. But nonetheless, losses from *Panzerfausts* rose rapidly as British forces approached German territory, partly reflecting the growing shortages of other anti-tank resources for German units and their increasing reliance on *Panzerfausts*.[19]

Whilst Raus' claim that 380 tanks were 'destroyed' (as opposed to disabled) by *Panzerfausts* may be an overestimate, the efficacy of this weapon was unquestionable, but during their preparations for the Berlin Operation, Soviet formations made no organised changes in their tactics to try to counter it. Some tank companies fitted additional armour panels to the exterior of their tanks, held a small distance from the main hull with brackets; this early form of 'spaced armour' was fairly effective, but the practice wasn't adopted wholesale. Increasingly as the assault proceeded, infantry units were ordered to accompany the tanks into battle so that they could flush out German defenders, but the poor training that had been identified in earlier campaigns continued to be a problem. After the end of the battle for Berlin, XI Tank Corps analysed its performance and confirmed that, apart from its own specialist motorised infantry units, cooperation with infantry from Fifth Shock Army remained difficult:

> During the course of the fighting in Berlin it was obvious that in a single street it was impossible to deploy more than a single company of tanks. Infantry had to be deployed in echelons. Infantry that went into action in close support with the tank corps had to be able to exploit the successes of the tanks and had to guard the tanks against tank destroyer teams. During the fighting in Berlin, the tank brigades were attached to each of the motor rifle battalions of the corps' motor

rifle brigades. This was required as the infantry of Fifth Shock Army often failed to protect the tanks adequately. The riflemen usually moved into cellars and buildings. As a result, tanks in the streets were left without protection. As they moved forward, the infantry didn't accompany them and forced to wait for infantry support, the tanks suffered heavy losses.[20]

Analysis of the losses suffered by individual tank units highlights the efficacy of *Panzerfausts* in the hands of even inexperienced soldiers, but also shows how much better the Red Army had become at recovering and repairing tanks. One heavy tank brigade reported that it had 39 IS-2 tanks totally destroyed, of which 11 were attributed to *Panzerfausts*. A further 28 were damaged, but were repaired. In a brigade with an establishment of about 65 tanks, this large number of 'recycled' tanks was vital for the unit to remain in action. Another heavy tank brigade reported that it suffered 30 total losses, 18 of which were due to *Panzerfausts*, and had 41 tanks disabled but later repaired – given that this exceeds the establishment strength, several tanks were damaged and repaired more than once. But even if tanks could be repaired, the crews were harder to replace. Each of these brigades lost between 340 and 390 men killed or wounded; when its explosive charge burned through the hull of a tank, the *Panzerfaust* blasted the interior with hot shrapnel that ricocheted around inside the crew compartment.

Even as the smoke and dust lingered over Berlin, myths were arising about the battle. Stalin had already decided that the official story of the war would stress that the defeat of Nazi Germany was accomplished by the combined strength and will of the Soviet people, led by the infallible Communist Party – and as the head of the Communist Party, he was also infallible in how he conducted the war. Anything that detracted from this version of events was either downplayed or simply ignored. Zhukov was anxious to be seen as the conqueror of Berlin, and for many years attempted to diminish the importance of the contribution of Konev's 1st Ukrainian Front to the Soviet success; on occasion, he even implied that, as had been the case in earlier operations, he had overall control of more than just his own 1st Belarusian Front and coordinated all Soviet forces advancing on Berlin. But there could be little question that the assault on the Seelow Heights had been a costly and poorly conducted operation. The use of searchlights on the first day of the attack, resulting in more inconvenience for Soviet troops than German defenders, and the deployment of massed armour in unsuitable terrain, leading to avoidable tank losses, were clear mistakes. This raises an important question: were there any alternatives?

The terrain in front of 1st Belarusian Front was highly favourable for defensive fighting. The ridge of the Seelow Heights was a formidable obstacle, and the land

Conclusion: An Uneasy Silence

to the north and west of the ridge, with dense woodland, made rapid advances almost impossible. If Zhukov had instead shifted the main point of effort to his northern flank, he might have avoided the worst of the difficult terrain, but would still have had to contend with dense woodland. Such a shift might also have exposed his advancing units to a German counterthrust from the south. In some respects, the benefits of such alternatives are clearer with hindsight than might have been the case at the time, but Zhukov's planning was without doubt over-optimistic. His failure to take proper note of terrain difficulties, which he blandly acknowledged in his memoirs, was not a new feature. During his oversight of operations around the Rzhev salient to the west of Moscow in 1942, he repeatedly ordered massive assaults on the German positions through terrain that was even more unsuitable for an attack. In the case of the Berlin Operation, this was compounded by confidence that the losses inflicted on the Germans during the advance from the Vistula to the Oder ensured that there was little strength left in the Wehrmacht.

After the end of the fighting, Zhukov became the first commander of all Soviet troops in the Soviet occupation zone, encompassing what would become the German Democratic Republic or 'East Germany'. Perhaps belatedly, he issued decrees to restore order, imposing and enforcing severe punishments for rape and looting; recognising the growing threat of starvation, he also made urgent requests for large quantities of food to be delivered to his zone. But his prominence in the army resulted in him being accused of 'egoism' and of promoting a personality cult. Such accusations were frequently instigated by Stalin, who was happy to recognise the perils of personality cults involving anyone but himself. In 1946, Zhukov was stripped of his role as commander-in-chief of the Soviet Army and sent to command the Odessa Military District, regarded as a major demotion. From here, he was sent to take command of the Urals Military District in 1948, a further deliberate humiliation. There were growing attempts to bring about his downfall, with Lavrentiy Beria, head of the *NKVD*, arresting and mistreating some of Zhukov's close associates in attempts to extract incriminating confessions and denunciations, and a search of his apartments resulted in a significant number of valuable items looted from Germany being seized. He was forced to issue an apology, and remained sidelined until the death of Stalin in 1953, when he became deputy defence minister. He took part in the arrest and trial of Beria and was appointed defence minister, but his close relationship with the new leader of the Soviet Union, Nikita Khrushchev, proved to be short-lived. Perhaps fearful of Zhukov's influence increasing once more, Khrushchev had him sidelined again. He returned to favour after Khrushchev's fall from power in 1964, but by then his health was failing. He was permitted to publish his memoirs, and died in 1974.

Konev, Zhukov's great rival, replaced Zhukov as commander-in-chief of the Soviet Army in 1946, but in 1950 he too was sidelined; he was sent to take command of the Carpathian Military District. Like Zhukov, he returned to prominence after Stalin's death and was part of the group that toppled Beria. He became the first commander-in-chief of the armed forces of the new Warsaw Pact and in this role played a major part in the suppression of the Hungarian Revolution in 1956. He retired from army service in 1960 but was recalled a year later and sent to Berlin, taking command of Soviet forces in East Germany. Here, he was instrumental in the decision to build the Berlin Wall. He died in 1973.

Rokossovsky, who had been bitterly disappointed to be removed from command of 1st Belarusian Front prior to the Vistula–Oder Offensive, became commander of Soviet forces in Poland. He was related to Polish aristocracy on his father's side and in 1949 Stalin had him appointed Minister of National Defence in Warsaw. Almost all senior military positions in Poland were under the control of men like Rokossovsky who could claim Polish nationality but were devoutly loyal to the Soviet regime, and this often resulted in resentment and friction; there is a long history of distrust and hostility between Poles and Russians, and at one stage Rokossovsky complained angrily that the Poles treated him like a Russian, while the Russians treated him like a Pole.[21] In his attempts to ensure rigid adherence and loyalty to Soviet doctrine, Rokossovsky was frequently heavy-handed and brutal, putting about 200,000 Poles who were regarded as politically unreliable – often because they had family members living in the west – into labour battalions, and he showed no hesitation in using soldiers and tanks to suppress protests against food shortages in Poznań in 1956. Indeed, he wanted to use even greater force to ensure that Poland remained strictly loyal to Moscow, but was overruled by Khrushchev. The Polish government took advantage of this to request his removal from office as defence minister. He moved back to the Soviet Union and held various posts until he retired in 1962. He died in 1968.

The German defenders of Berlin fought bitterly, often to the last round, before they were overwhelmed or forced to surrender. The determination to fight when defeat must have been clearly obvious was due to many factors. From the perspective of the 21st century, it is often difficult to understand the level of indoctrination of the populations of Germany and the Soviet Union. All media had been under strict control in Germany since 1933 (even longer in the Soviet Union), and many of the young defenders of Berlin had few memories of a time before Hitler came to power. It was an era in which the superiority of the white man was almost taken for granted, not only in Germany but in much of the western world too; in the case of Germany, this was further nuanced by a belief that amongst the European nations Germany was inherently superior and had a

Conclusion: An Uneasy Silence

right to a predominant status. This contributed to a belief that, despite all setbacks, the superior German people would ultimately triumph over their foes. An additional feature of such thinking was the use made by the Nazis of the theories of Social Darwinism – just as individual animals competed for survival and success, they saw nations competing in the same way. This belief in 'survival of the fittest' meant that if Germany failed to prevail, it would be doomed to destruction. Such a 'zero-sum' attitude ensured that, faced with what they saw as the end of Germany and its people, many chose to fight on regardless of the odds stacked against them. Such tendencies were reinforced by the obsession of senior Nazis with setting heroic examples that would inspire future generations, even though when the critical moment came, many of those senior Party figures attempted to slip away rather than seeking a glorious death in battle.

The conduct of the Red Army in territories that it had already occupied also contributed to the determination of German soldiers to fight on. Soviet units reached German territory in East Prussia in the autumn of 1944, briefly advancing to the village of Nemmersdorf before being driven back, and when German units retook the area they found the corpses of civilians littering the village and surrounding area. Many – probably most – of the women had been repeatedly raped before they were killed, and Goebbels was quick to take advantage of this, amplifying and exaggerating the scale of the crimes. Lurid tales of atrocities circulated in Germany, with the ominous threat that further Soviet advances would expose more German people to such bestial behaviour, and when the Red Army surged forward in early 1945, similar episodes occurred across much of Poland and the eastern provinces of Germany. The constant portrayal by Goebbels of the Red Army as an undisciplined horde from the east, led by 'Jewish Bolsheviks', may have been an exaggeration, but was based on a foundation of real crimes. Inevitably, this hardened the resolve of German soldiers at every level to hold out as long as possible in the hope that somehow the civilian population of Germany could be spared such mistreatment. Many hoped that the Western Powers would reach Berlin first; others hoped that even at this late stage, Hitler would accept reality and would negotiate a surrender that would at least alleviate the mistreatment of civilians. A few clung to the belief that wondrous new weapons would appear at the last moment and would turn the tide in Germany's favour. All such hopes were in vain.

The determination to defend German civilians from the wrath of the Red Army was also influenced by an awareness that the Soviet Union was bent on revenge. Although many German veterans at all levels later denied personal knowledge of atrocities committed in the occupied territories in the east, the reality is that such German crimes were so widespread that almost every military unit was involved, either providing logistic support or directly participating in the crimes. Reports of massacres of civilians spread not only through the army, but also through the civilian population of Germany when men returned home on leave. In cities like Berlin, many civilians might have persuaded themselves that their Jewish neighbours had been resettled in lands to the east, but most suspected – or knew – that the truth was far worse. Again, this hardened the resolve of many to fight to the bitter end.

It seems almost inconceivable from a modern perspective to comprehend that many Germans at this stage of the war still believed that there was a chance of victory, but this is unquestionably the case. Civilians chatted about rumours of miraculous weapons that would destroy Germany's enemies; others spoke about a brilliant master plan in which the advance of the Allies onto Germany was part of a scheme to trap them in a devastating final battle from which Germany would emerge triumphant. Some – particularly amongst the ranks of the Nazi Party – saw Hitler's escape from the July Plot as the intervention of Providence: he had been spared so that he could save Germany. Just how widespread such views were is hard to estimate. Many accounts describe how those who suggested such things in the closing weeks of the war were met with jeers and contempt, but even at that stage, there was widespread awareness that everyone was being watched and any 'defeatist' tendencies would result in swift, arbitrary, and severe punishment. Unsurprisingly, many civilians and soldiers therefore kept their doubts to themselves.

Writing after the war, Konev gave perhaps one of the best assessments of the defenders of Berlin:

> Goebbels, at the head of all civilian authorities [as *Gauleiter* of Berlin] was responsible for the preparation of the civilian population for defence of the city. Weidling, when he was given the post of commander of the defences of Berlin, was given a categorical order by Hitler to defend the capital to the last man ...
>
> When defending the city, the Germans made widespread use of underground structures, which were very numerous in the city. Bomb shelters, subway tunnels, sewers, drainage ditches – all types of underground passages were used both for moving troops and for bringing ammunition to the front lines. By using these underground routes, the city's defenders created an extraordinarily high level of difficulty for us. Our troops would capture an area of resistance and it would appear that at this point everything was done, but the Germans would use the underground tunnels to move into our rear with reconnaissance groups, individual saboteurs, and snipers. Groups of men with automatic weapons, snipers, mortars, and *Panzerfausts*, moving through the tunnels, fired on vehicles, tanks, and gun crews that were moving through streets that had already been

Conclusion: An Uneasy Silence

captured, and cut our lines of communications, creating difficult conditions behind our front line ...

The *Volkssturm* battalions, predominantly made up of elderly people and teenagers, were particularly heavily armed with *Panzerfausts*. It was just the weapon for people who were not trained in warfare, giving them a psychological confidence that, despite having become soldiers just a day or two earlier, they could really achieve something today. As a rule, these *Faustniks* fought to the very end, showing at this late stage greater determination than many German soldiers who had seen action but were worn out by many years of defeats and fatigue.

As in earlier battles, the soldiers surrendered only when there was no other way out for them. The same applied to their officers. But they had little fighting spirit left. All that remained was the grim, hopeless resolve to fight until they received orders for capitulation.

In the ranks of the *Volkssturm* during the decisive battles for Berlin, there was a feeling of almost hysterical self-sacrifice. These last defenders of the Third Reich, including small boys, saw in themselves the personification of the last hope for a miracle which, in spite of everything, they still believed would occur at the very last moment.[22]

The first occasion that Hitler and his close associates demanded increased 'fanaticism' from German soldiers was during the crisis outside Moscow in the winter of 1941–42, and as the war progressed such demands grew ever more strident. Whilst the determination to fight is an important characteristic in any army, there is a limit to how much it can compensate for shortages of manpower, equipment, and ammunition, but Hitler's inevitable response to the steady tide of setbacks suffered by Germany was to demand ever greater self-sacrifice and 'fanatical resistance'. When such exhortations failed to achieve the desired outcome, he would blame the army for failing to show sufficient determination, and there may be some truth in Konev's assertion that regular German soldiers involved in the last battles of the European war were weary and less willing to fight than in earlier years. But faced with the fall of Berlin, they fought with determination in a vain attempt to prevent the Red Army from wreaking its vengeance on the population of the capital. The intentions of Heinrici, Busse, Weidling, and others to avoid fighting in the urban area came to naught. The policies of Nazi Germany, which few in Germany had questioned during the years of victory, yielded their inevitable bitter harvest. Just as ordinary Soviet civilians bore the brunt of Hitler's genocidal plans in the Soviet Union, it was ordinary civilians in Berlin and the surrounding area who paid in full when the Red Army exacted its terrible revenge.

As Ursula von Kardorff walked through the centre of Berlin late on 3 February, after the devastating daylight air raid, she surveyed the wreckage and the dazed, battered survivors who tried to salvage a few belongings from the rubble. 'Why does no one stand on the street and shout "Enough! Enough!" Why is no one going crazy? Why is there no revolution?'[23] But it was too late for any such measures, and far worse destruction was imminent. Gradually, after the fighting, work began on clearing the rubble, the corpses, and the wrecked vehicles that littered Berlin in May. With so few German men left in the capital, much of the burden fell on the women, many of whom became known as the *Trümmerfrauen* ('rubble women'), stacking usable bricks and other items. Amidst the ruins and the traumatic memories of the recent past, Berliners began to think about a future as the days grew warmer. One diarist wrote that 'the breath of spring has chased away the stench of smoke, decay and corruption. It soothes the brows of the unburied dead, be they soldiers, men, women, or children.'[24] Today, the signs of the terrible battles can still be seen, from the huge buried mounds of the Friedrichshain and Humboldthain Flak Towers to the bullet scars on the railway arches in central Berlin. Much has changed, but the irreverent, independent, distinctive spirit of modern Berliners would be familiar to former residents. They take pride from the memory of ordinary Berliners tearing down the wall that divided the city during the Cold War, but remember the dark days of the past, and the part that their city played in it.

NOTES

INTRODUCTION: THE ROAD TO BERLIN

1. A. Hitler, *Mein Kampf* (Houghton Mifflin, Boston MA, 1939), pp.950–51
2. Quoted in U. Saft, *Krieg im Osten* (Militärbuch Verlag, Walsrode, 2002), p.9
3. Quoted in S. Sebag Montefiore, *Stalin: The Court of the Red Tsar* (Phoenix, London, 2004), p.318
4. P. Hausser, *Soldaten wie Andere Auch* (Munin, Osnabrück, 1982)
5. W. Breuer, *Top Secret Tales of World War II* (John Wiley, London, 2000), pp.218–20

CHAPTER 1: THE CITY ON THE SPREE

1. T. Ludewig, *Berlin: Geschichte einer Deutschen Metropole* (Bertelsmann, Munich, 1986), p.278
2. J. Huret, *Berlin um Neunzehnhundert* (Tasbach, Berlin, 2014), p.14
3. Quoted in D. Large, *Berlin* (Basic Books, New York, 2007), pp.17–18
4. H. Vizetelly, *Berlin Under the New Empire* (Greenwood, New York, 1968, 2 volumes), Vol. I, p.63
5. G. Brandes, E. Christensen and H.-D. Loock, *Berlin als deutsche Reichshauptstadt. Erinnerungen aus den Jahren 1877–1883* (Colloquium, Berlin, 1989), p.11
6. Letter to *Chicago Daily Tribune* 3 April 1892
7. O. Pflanze, *Bismarck and the Development of Germany* (Princeton University Press, Princeton NJ, 2021, 3 volumes), Vol. II, p.392
8. *Metropolitan Magazine* (Walker, Harvey & Macfadden, New York, 1913) No.38, p.63
9. *Illustrated London News* (London) 27 October 1906
10. R. Stremmel, *Modell und Moloch: Berlin in der Wahrnehmung Deutscher Politiker vom Ende des 19. Jahrhunderts bis zum Zweiten Weltkrieg* (Bouvier, Bonn, 1992), p.55
11. Ibid., p.235
12. H. Kessler, *Berlin in Lights: The Diaries of Count Harry Kessler, 1918–1937* (Grove, New York, 2000), p.60
13. P. Broué, *The German Revolution, 1917–1923* (Haymarket, Chicago, 2007), pp.276–77

14 M. Bauer, *Konnten wir den Krieg Vermeiden, Gewinnen, Abbrechen?* (Scherl, Berlin, 1919), p.58
15 P. Kilduff, *Iron Man: Rudolf Berthold, Germany's Indomitable Fighter Ace of World War I* (Grub Street, London, 2012), pp.133–34
16 Quoted in H. Ostwald, *Sittengeschichte der Inflation, ein Kulturdokument aus den Jahren des Marksturzes* (Neuhaus & Henius, Berlin, 1931), p.100
17 R. Manvell, and H. Fraenkel, *Doctor Goebbels: His Life and Death* (Skyhorse, New York, 2010), pp.75–77
18 For a detailed account of the Horst Wessel affair, see D. Siemens, *The Making of a Nazi Hero: The Murder and Myth of Horst Wessel* (Tauris, London, 2013)
19 Quoted in A. Kaes, M. Jay and E. Dimendberg (eds), *Weimar Republic Sourcebook* (University of California Press, Oakland CA, 1995), p.426
20 Quoted in D. Clay Large, *Berlin: A Modern History* (Allen Lane, London, 2001), p.289
21 P. Gay, *My German Question: Growing Up in Nazi Berlin* (Yale University Press, New Haven CT, 1998), pp.133–35
22 Quoted in A. Read and D. Fisher, *Berlin Rising: Biography of a City* (W. W. Norton, New York, 1994), p.217
23 G. Kennan, *Memoirs 1925–1950* (Little, Brown & Co, Boston, 1967, 2 volumes), Vol. I, pp.401–03
24 A. Hillgruber and H. Picker, *Hitlers Tischgespräche im Führerhauptquartier 1941–1942* (Deutscher Taschenbuch-Verlag, Munich, 1968), p.182
25 Quoted in H. Weihsmann, *Bauen Unterm Hakenkreuz. Architektur des Untergangs* (Promedia, Vienna, 1998), p.278
26 A. Speer, *Inside the Third Reich* (Weidenfeld & Nicolson, London, 1995), pp.121–22
27 Ibid., pp.124–26

Chapter 2: 'Call Me Meier'

1 N. Moss, *Nineteen Weeks: America, Britain and the Fateful Summer of 1940* (Houghton Mifflin Harcourt, Boston MA, 2004), p.295
2 N. Fleming, *August 1939: The Last Days of Peace* (Davies, London, 1979), p.171
3 W. Shirer, *Berlin Diary 1934–1941: The Rise of the Third Reich* (Promotional Reprint Co, London, 1997), p.238
4 A. Grayling, *Among the Dead Cities* (Bloomsbury, London, 2006), p.47
5 N. Longmate, *The Bombers: The RAF Offensive Against Germany 1939–1945* (Hutchinson, London, 1983), p.121
6 Ibid., p.126
7 M. Hastings, *Bomber Command* (Pan, London, 1999), p.154
8 A. Harris, *Bomber Offensive* (Pen & Sword, Barnsley, 2022), p.52
9 R. Rürup, *Berlin 1945: Eine Dokumentation* (Willmuth Arenhövel, Berlin, 2003), p.11

10 M. Vassiltchikov, *The Berlin Diaries 1940–1945* (Pimlico, London, 1999), pp.51–52
11 Ibid., p.37
12 M. Connelly, *Reaching for the Stars: A History of Bomber Command* (I. B. Tauris, London, 2014), p.115
13 Speer, *Inside the Third Reich*, pp.393–95
14 Vassiltchikov, *The Berlin Diaries*, pp.107–09
15 T. Findahl, *Letzter Akt – Berlin, 1939–1945* (Hammerich & Lesser, Hamburg, 1946), pp.187–88
16 O. Lubrich (ed.), *Travels in the Reich, 1933–1945: Foreign Authors Report From Germany* (University of Chicago Press, 2010), p.281
17 Rürup, *Berlin 1945*, p.11
18 D. Miller, *Eighth Air Force: The American Bomber Crews in Britain* (Aurum, London, 2007), pp.41–56
19 Quoted in Rürup, *Berlin 1945*, p.16
20 U. von Kardorff, *Berliner Aufzeichnungen aus die Jahren 1942–1945* (Deutsche Taschenbuch Verlag, Munich, 1964), pp.202–03
21 Rürup, *Berlin 1945*, p.21
22 C. Webster and N. Frankland, *The Strategic Air Offensive Against Germany 1939–1945* (HMSO, London 1961, 3 volumes), Vol. III, p.100
23 Rürup, *Berlin 1945*, p.13
24 Vassiltchikov, *The Berlin Diaries*, p.89
25 Air Force Historical Research Agency, Maxwell AFB, AL, Message CS-93-JD Doolittle to Spaatz 30 January 1945, reel B5046 frame 1808
26 Air Force Historical Research Agency, Maxwell AFB, AL, Report, Eighth Air Force Operations Analysis Section, subject: Analysis of Attack on Berlin 3 February 1945, dated 24 February 1945, reel A5680 frames 445–447
27 R. Davis, *Bombing the European Axis Powers: A Historical Digest of the Combined Bomber Offensive 1939–1945* (Air University Press, Maxwell AFB AL, 2006), p.500
28 See, for example, E. Smit, E. Staikos, D. Thormann, and H. Lieser, *3. Februar 1945: Die Zerstörung Kreuzbergs aus der Luft* (Kunstamt, Berlin, 1995), p.12
29 Library of Congress, Washington DC, Spaatz Papers, Letter Spaatz to Arnold, 5 February 1945
30 Air Force Historical Research Agency, Maxwell AFB, AL, Memo for General Anderson, subject: Operation CLARION, Col Thetus Odom, asst deputy commander operations, USSTAF, 9 January 1945, reel A5687 frame 779
31 Air Force Historical Research Agency, Maxwell AFB, AL, UAX 64613, Spaatz to Doolittle, Eaker, Twining, Vandenburg, Saville, 21 February 1945, reel B5047 frame 722
32 Webster and Frankland, *The Strategic Air Offensive Against Germany*, Vol. III, p.112
33 Quoted in Rürup, *Berlin 1945*, p.20
34 Davis, *Bombing the European Axis Powers*, pp.541, 549

35 K. Bahm, *Berlin 1945: The Final Reckoning* (Amber, London, 2014), p.47
36 Rürup, *Berlin 1945*, p.13
37 Y. Tanaka and M. Young (eds), *Bombing Civilians: A Twentieth-Century History* (New Press, New York, 2009), p.84
38 J. Dower, *War Without Mercy: Race and Power in the Pacific War* (Faber & Faber, London, 1986), p.41
39 F. Pike, *Hirohito's War: The Pacific War, 1941–1945* (Bloomsbury, London, 2016), p.1054
40 W. Ralph, 'Improvised Destruction: Arnold, LeMay, and the Firebombing of Japan' in *War in History* (Sage, London, 2006), Vol. 13 No.4, pp.519–21

Chapter 3: Preparing for the Last Stand: The German Defences

1 F. Bokov, *Vesna Pobedy* (Mysl, Moscow, 1985), p.74
2 Hausser, *Soldaten wie Andere Auch*, p.134
3 H. Eismann and F. Steinhardt, *Unter Himmlers Kommando 1945 – der Kampf von Heeresgruppe Weichsel an der Ostfront: Die Persönlichen Erinnerungen von Oberst Hans-Georg Eismann, Ia von Heeresgruppe Weichsel* (Melchior, Wolfenbüttel, 2010), pp.55–56
4 M. Hastings, *Das Reich: The March of the 2nd SS Panzer Division Through France, June 1944* (BCA, London, 1981), p.36
5 Eismann and Steinhardt, *Unter Himmlers Kommando*, p.65
6 Ibid., pp.61–63
7 A. Babadzhanian, *Dorogy Pobedy* (Molodaya Gvardiya, Moscow, 1975), p.238
8 V. Chuikov, 'Na Berlin' in *Novaya i Noveyshaya Istoriya* (Rossiyskaya Akademiya Nauk I Institut Vseobshchey Istorii RAN, Moscow, 1965) No.2, p.7
9 V. Chuikov, 'Vislo-Oderskaya Operatsiya' in *Oktyabr* (Soyuz Pisateley RSFSR, Moscow, 1964) No.4, pp.128–29
10 H. Guderian, *Erinnerungen eines Soldaten* (Kurt Vowinkel Verlag, Neckargemünd, 1960), p.383
11 *Bundesarchiv-Militärarchiv*, Freiburg, N265/153, Bl.6f
12 Eismann and Steinhardt, *Unter Himmlers Kommando*, p.81
13 Quoted in C. Ryan, *The Last Battle* (Simon & Schuster, New York, 1966), p.74
14 Guderian, *Erinnerungen*, pp.388–90
15 H. Altner, and T. Le Tissier, *Berlin: Dance of Death* (Spellmount, Staplehurst, 2002), p.4
16 Ibid., p.15
17 T. Le Tissier, *With Our Backs to Berlin* (Sutton, Stroud, 2001), p.95
18 Ryan, *The Last Battle*, pp.239–41
19 Quoted in T. Le Tissier, *Marshal Zhukov at the Oder* (History Press, Cheltenham, 2008), p.183

20 *Cornelius Ryan Collection* (Ohio University, Athens OH), Box 68 Folder 3, Heinrici interview, pp.12–14
21 Altner and Le Tissier, *Berlin: Dance of Death*, pp.56–59

Chapter 4: The Red Army: Plans For Vengeance

1. A. Beck (ed.), *Bis Stalingrad … 1941–1943* (H. Abt, Ulm, 1983), p.197
2. K. Rokossovsky, *A Soldier's Duty* (Lancer International, New Delhi, 1985), p.267
3. P. Grigorenko, *V Podpole Mozno Vstretit Tolko Krys* (Zvenja, Moscow, 1997), p.82
4. G. Zhukov, *Vospomimaniya I Ramyshleniya* (Olma, Moscow, 2002, 2 volumes), Vol. II, pp.43–44
5. For a full account of the fighting for the Rzhev salient, see P. Buttar, *Meat Grinder* (Osprey, Oxford, 2022)
6. P. Batov, *Von der Wolga zur Oder* (Deutscher Militärverlag, Berlin, 1965), pp.311–13
7. T. Le Tissier, *Slaughter at Halbe: The Destruction of Hitler's Ninth Army* (History Press, Cheltenham, 2021), p.14
8. See for example V. Dyatlov and V. Milbach, 'Sovetskaya Artilleriya v Konflikte na Khalkin-Gole' in *Voyenno-Istoricheskiy Zhurnal* (Ministerstva Oborony SSSR, 2013) No.1, pp.34–38
9. Interview with A. Pokrovsky in *Oktyabr* (Moscow, 1990) No.5, pp.38–39
10. *Voyenno-Istoricheskiy Zhurnal* (Ministerstva Oborony SSSR, 1965) No.4, pp.25–26
11. I. Konev, *Sorok Pyatyy* (Voyenizdat, Moscow, 1970), pp.139–40
12. V. Karpov, *Izbrannye Proizvedeniya* (Khudozhestvennaya Literatura, Moscow, 1990, 3 volumes), Vol. III, pp.704–05
13. S. Shtemenko, *The Soviet General Staff at War 1941–1945* (Progress, Moscow, 1970), p.320
14. M. Katukov, *Na Ostriye Glavnogo Udara* (Voyenizdat, Moscow, 1974), pp.390–91
15. V. Chuikov, *Ot Stalingrada do Berlina* (Sovetskaya Rossiya, Moscow, 1985), p.607
16. Babadzhanian, *Dorogy Pobedy*, p.267
17. Interview with Y. Fadeyev, available at https://iremember.ru/memoirs/pekhotintsi/fadeev-yakov-ivanovich/
18. Interview with A. Vesterman, available at https://iremember.ru/memoirs/tankisti/versterman-arkadiy-grigorevich/
19. G. Krivosheyev, *Soviet Casualties and Combat Losses in the Twentieth Century* (Greenhill, London, 1997), pp.85–97
20. N. Antipenko, *Na Glavnom Napravlenii* (Nauka, Moscow, 1967), p.249
21. Ibid., pp.251–52
22. Interview with A. Gordeyev, available at https://iremember.ru/memoirs/letchiki-istrebiteli/gordeev-anatoliy-nikolaevich/
23. S. Rudenko, 'Nad Visloy, Oderom Berlinom' in V. Vosnesensky and D. Rubezhnyi (eds), *9 Maya 1945 Goda. Vospominaniya* (Nauka, Moscow, 1970), pp.599–600

24 M. Badigin, *Boy Trepuget Podviga* (Voyenizdat, Moscow, 1980), pp.105–06
25 I. Galitsky, *Dorogu Otkrivaly Sapery* (Voyenizdat, Moscow, 1983), pp.268–69

Chapter 5: The Storm Bursts: 16 April

1   V. Kazakov, *Artilleriya, Ogon!* (DOSAAF, Moscow, 1975), p.223
2   Le Tissier, *With our Backs to Berlin*, pp.100–01
3   Altner and Le Tissier, *Berlin: Dance of Death*, pp.61–62
4   Interview with A. Ivanov, available at https://iremember.ru/memoirs/samokhodchiki/ivanov-aleksey-petrovich/
5   V. Chuikov, *Konets Tretyego Reykha* (Sovetskaya Rossiya, Moscow, 1973), p.148
6   Interview with V. Myasnikov, available at https://iremember.ru/memoirs/drugie-voyska/myasnikov-vladimir-vladimirovich/
7   Interview with D. Osinovsky, available at https://iremember.ru/memoirs/artilleristi/osinovsky-dmitriy-filippovich/
8   Chuikov, *Ot Stalingrada do Berlina*, p.609
9   Ivanov interview
10 Le Tissier, *With our Backs to Berlin*, p.101
11 A. Hamilton, *The Oder Front 1945: Documents, Reports, Personal Accounts, and Maps* (Helion, Solihull, 2014), pp.324–25
12 Vesterman interview
13 Interview with U. Polyakov, available at https://iremember.ru/memoirs/samokhodchiki/polyakov-uriy-nikolaevich/
14 Ivanov interview
15 Katukov, *Na Ostriye Glavnogo Udara*, p.396
16 A. Getman, *Tanki Idut na Berlin* (Voenizd-vo Ministerstva Oborony SSSR, Moscow, 1982), p.194
17 Quoted in Le Tissier, *Marshal Zhukov at the Oder*, pp.249–51
18 Le Tissier, *With our Backs to Berlin*, p.106; P. Gostoni, *Bitva za Berlin v Vospominaniyach Ocevidcev 1944–1945* (Centrpoligraf, Moscow, 2013), pp.157–59
19 Bokov, *Vesna Pobedy*, pp.146–47
20 Quoted in Le Tissier, *Marshal Zhukov at the Oder*, pp.257–58
21 Bokov, *Vesna Pobedy*, p.152
22 Chuikov, *Konets Tretyego Reykha*, pp.189–90
23 N. Pukhov, *Gody Ispyitanyy* (Voyenizdat, Moscow, 1959), pp.80–81
24 Konev, *Sorok Pyatyy*, pp.148–49
25 A. Zhadov, *Chetire Goda Voyny* (Voyenizdat, Moscow, 1978), pp.250–51
26 V. Zaitsev, *Gvardeyskaya Tankovaya* (Sred-Ural, Sverdlovsk, 1989), p.154
27 Interview with I. Maslov, available at https://iremember.ru/memoirs/tankisti/maslov-ivan-vladimirovich/
28 Zhukov, *Vospomimaniya I Ramyshleniya*, Vol. II, p.257

29 Ibid.
30 Babadzhanian, *Dorogy Pobedy*, p.269

CHAPTER 6: BREAKTHROUGH: 17–18 APRIL

1   Ryan, *The Last Battle*, pp.290–300
2   D. Lelyushenko, *Moskva-Stalingrad-Berlin-Praga. Zapiski Comandarma Sayt* (Nauka, Moscow 1987), p.264
3   Karpov, *Izbrannye Proizvedeniya*, Vol. II, p.710
4   *Tsentralnyi Archiv Ministerstva Oboronyi Rossyiskoi Federalyy* (henceforth cited as TsAMO RF), Moscow, f.315, op.4440, d.538, L.60
5   D. Shein, *Tanki Vedet Rybalko. Boyevoy Put 3-y Gvardeskoy Tankovoy Armii* (Eksmo, Moscow, 2007), p.293
6   J. Greenacre and D. Giles, *The Battle for Berlin: A Battlefield Reader* (self-published, 2019), pp.99–100
7   Ivanov interview
8   A. Hamilton, *The Oder Front*, Vol. II, p.352
9   Ibid., Vol. I, p.134
10 Quoted in Le Tissier, *Marshal Zhukov at the Oder*, p.283
11 Ibid., pp.287–88
12 Quoted in Le Tissier, *With our Backs to Berlin*, pp.103–04
13 Zaitsev, *Gvardeyskaya Tankovaya*, pp.156–57
14 Shein, *Tanki Vedet Rybalko*, p.294
15 Konev, *Sorok Pyatyy*, p.158
16 Chuikov, *Ot Stalingrada do Berlina*, p.614
17 Babadzhanian, *Dorogy Pobedy*, pp.268–69
18 Quoted in Le Tissier, *Marshal Zhukov at the Oder*, p.299
19 Altner and Le Tissier, *Berlin: Dance of Death*, p.69
20 Quoted in Hamilton, *The Oder Front 1945*, Vol. I, p.132
21 R. Teuber, *Die Bundeswehr 1955–1995* (Militair-Verlag K D Patzwall, Norderstedt, 1996), p.46
22 T. Busse, 'Die Letzte Schlacht der 9. Armee' in *Wehrwissenschaftliche Rundschau* (Mittler, Darmstadt, 1954), p.164
23 Ryan, *The Last Battle*, pp.290–91
24 Chuikov, *Ot Stalingrada do Berlina*, p.617
25 G. Khetagurov, *Ispolnenye Dolga* (Voyenizdat, Moscow, 1977), p.171
26 Altner and Le Tissier, *Berlin: Dance of Death*, p.71
27 Ibid., pp.71–72
28 Babadzhanian, *Dorogy Pobedy*, p.272
29 Quoted in Le Tissier, *With our Backs to Berlin*, pp.107–08
30 Interview with S. Tsvang, available at https://iremember.ru/memoirs/razvedchiki/tsvang-semen-ruvimovich/
31 Quoted in Le Tissier, *With our Backs to Berlin*, p.116

32 *Cornelius Ryan Collection*, Box 66, Folder 2, Lohmann interview, p.1
33 Quoted in W. Tiecke, *Tragedy of the Faithful: A History of III (Germanisches) SS-Panzer-Korps* (Fedorowicz, Winnipeg, 2001), p.276
34 Lelyushenko, *Moskva-Stalingrad-Berlin-Praga*, pp.267–68
35 Shein, *Tanki Vedet Rybalko*, p.95
36 H. Spaeter, *History of the Panzerkorps Grossdeutschland* (Fedorowicz, Winnipeg, 2000, 3 volumes) Vol. III, pp.398–400, 420
37 Quoted in J. Fest, *Inside Hitler's Bunker: The Last Days of the Third Reich* (Pan, London, 2012), p.31

Chapter 7: To the Gates of Berlin: 19–20 April

1 *Cornelius Ryan Collection*, Box 67, Folder 12, Reymann interview, pp.10–12
2 W. Willemer, *The German Defense of Berlin* (US Army Historical Division, Karlsruhe, 1953), pp.50–51
3 B. Freytag von Loringhoven, *In the Bunker with Hitler* (Weidenfeld & Nicolson, London, 2007), p.111
4 D. Stahel, *Operation Barbarossa and Germany's Defeat in the East* (Cambridge University Press, 2007), p.277
5 C. Barnett (ed.), *Hitler's Generals* (Grove Weidenfeld, New York, 1989), p.152
6 Loringhoven, *In the Bunker with Hitler*, p.112
7 J. Fest, *Die Unbeantwortbaren Fragen: Notizen über Gespräche mit Albert Speer Zwischen Ende 1966 und 1981* (Rowohlt, Hamburg, 2006), p.143
8 H. Peiper, *Fegelein's Horsemen and Genocidal Warfare: The SS Cavalry Brigade in the Soviet Union* (Palgrave Macmillan, Basingstoke, 2015), pp.86–120
9 Loringhoven, *In the Bunker with Hitler*, p.106
10 Eismann and Steinhardt, *Unter Himmlers Kommando,* p.60
11 Loringhoven, *In the Bunker with Hitler*, p.80
12 Gostoni, *Bitva za Berlin*, pp.173–74
13 National Archives and Records Administration, College Park MD (henceforth cited as NARA) RG242 T-311/169/7221931
14 Quoted in Le Tissier, *Marshal Zhukov at the Oder*, p.331
15 Le Tissier, *With our Backs to Berlin*, p.117
16 *TsAMO RF*, Moscow, f.315, op.4452, d.566
17 Ivanov interview
18 Khetagurov, *Ispolnenye Dolga*, pp.172–73
19 Getman, *Tanki Idut na Berlin*, pp.260–62
20 Katukov, *Na Ostriye Glavnogo Udara*, pp.400–01
21 Altner and Le Tissier, *Berlin: Dance of Death*, p.74
22 Quoted in Le Tissier, *Marshal Zhukov at the Oder*, p.342
23 W. Tiecke, *Das Ende Zwischen Oder und Elbe: Der Kampf um Berlin 1945* (Motor Buch Verlag, Stuttgart, 1981), pp.152–53
24 Tiecke, *Tragedy of the Faithful*, pp.284–85

25 Interview with V. Golovach, available at https://iremember.ru/memoirs/tankisti/golovach-v-vladimir-nikitovich/
26 NARA MS TS-9, *Der Kampf um die Oder im Abschnitt der Heeresgruppe Weichsel, Februar bis April 1945*
27 Konev, *Sorok Pyatyy*, pp.159–60
28 NARA RG242 T-311/169/7221952
29 V. Zolotarev (ed.), *Russkiy Archiv: Velikaya Otecestvennaya* (Terra, Moscow, 1994–96, 23 volumes) Vol. XV, pp.141, 168, 180
30 Fest, *Inside Hitler's Bunker*, p.44
31 Osinovsky interview
32 Anonymous, *A Woman in Berlin* (Virago, London, 2011), pp.17–21
33 Rokossovsky, *A Soldier's Duty*, p.327
34 Spaeter, *History of the Panzerkorps Grossdeutschland*, Vol. III, pp.420–21
35 TsAMO RF, Moscow, f.236, op.2712, d.359
36 NARA RG242 T-311/170/7222035
37 Ibid.
38 Ryan, *The Last Battle*, pp.338–39
39 Fest, *Inside Hitler's Bunker*, p.47

CHAPTER 8: *DER KRIEG IST VERLOREN*: 21–22 APRIL

1 Quoted in Hamilton, *The Oder Front 1945*, Vol. I, p.146
2 Batov, *Von der Wolga zur Oder*, p.405
3 Zhukov, *Vospomimaniya I Ramyshleniya*, Vol. II, p.258
4 Le Tissier, *Marshal Zhukov at the Oder*, p.356
5 Babadzhanian, *Dorogy Pobedy*, p.273
6 Katukov, *Na Ostriye Glavnogo Udara*, p.402
7 Altner and Le Tissier, *Berlin: Dance of Death*, pp.89–91
8 Quoted in Tiecke, *Tragedy of the Faithful*, p.291
9 E. Gerasimov (ed.), *Shturm Berlina: Vospominaniya, Pisma, Dnevniki Uchastnikov boev za Berlin* (Voyenizdat, Moscow, 1948), p.202
10 A. Beevor, *Berlin: The Downfall 1945* (Viking, London, 2002), p.266
11 Ibid., pp.266–67
12 Lelyushenko, *Moskva-Stalingrad-Berlin-Praga*, p.268
13 Konev, *Sorok Pyatyy*, p.162
14 Spaeter, *History of the Panzerkorps Grossdeutschland*, Vol. III, pp.421–22
15 Beevor, *Berlin: The Downfall 1945*, p.261
16 R. Lakowski and K. Stich, *Der Kessel von Halbe 1945. Das Letzte Drama* (Mittler, Hamburg, 2013), p.42
17 Loringhoven, *In the Bunker with Hitler*, p.58
18 E. Kuby, *Die Russen in Berlin 1945* (Moewig, Rastatt, 1988), p.108
19 Anonymous, *A Woman in Berlin*, p.28

20 K. Skorobogatkin, *50 Let Vooruzhuzhennykh Sil SSSR* (Voyenizdat, Moscow, 1968), p.501
21 A. Hamilton, *Bloody Streets: The Soviet Assault on Berlin* (Helion, Warwick, 2020), p.165
22 Ibid., p.163
23 F. Vorobyev and I. Parotkin, *Poslednii Shturm: Berlinskaia Operatsiia 1945g* (Voyenizdat, Moscow, 1975), pp.251–52
24 Chuikov, *Ot Stalingrada do Berlina*, pp.620–21
25 Quoted in Spaeter, *History of the Panzerkorps Grossdeutschland*, Vol. III, pp.423–24
26 G. Williamson, *German Commanders of World War II* (Osprey, Oxford, 2006, 2 volumes), Vol. II, pp.15–16
27 H. Coppi, K. Inachin, K. Langer, G. Diederich, I. Garbe, F. Bersch, A. Wagner, A. von Borries, M. Niemann, D. Graf von Schwerin, D. Krüger, and A. Leo, *Widerstand Gegen das NS-Regime in den Regionen Mecklenburg und Vorpommern* (Friedrich-Ebert Stiftung, Schwerin, 2007), p.120
28 Loringhoven, *In the Bunker with Hitler*, p.83
29 Fest, *Inside Hitler's Bunker*, p.65
30 W. Gorlitz (ed.), *The Memoirs of Field Marshal Wilhelm Keitel* (First Cooper Square Press, New York, 2000), pp.201–02
31 Ibid., pp.203–04
32 *Bundesarchiv-Militärarchiv*, Freiburg, MS G1/976, p.28
33 D. Bradley, *Walther Wenck, General der Panzertruppe* (Biblio, Osnabrück, 1981), p.352
34 G. Gellermann, *Die Armee Wenck: Hitlers Letzte Hoffnung. Aufstellung, Einsatz und Ende der 12. Deutschen Armee im Frühjahr 1945* (Bernard & Graefe, Bonn, 2007), p.48
35 Fest, *Insider Hitler's Bunker*, pp.68–69

Chapter 9: Into the City: 23–25 April

1 M. Gwiazdowska, 'Konzepte des Wiederaufbaus der Stettiner Baudenkmäler nach, und Möglichkeiten ihrer Durchführung' in *Biuletyn Polskiej Misji Historycznej* (Uniwersytet Mikołaja-Kopernika, Torún, 2012)
2 Chuikov, *Ot Stalingrada do Berlina*, pp.621–22
3 Babadzhanian, *Dorogy Pobedy*, p.276
4 Myasnikov interview
5 Interview with Z. Krasilchikov, available at https://iremember.ru/memoirs/razdeivchiki/krasilchikov-zakhar-evseevich/
6 T. Hillblad and E. Wallin, *Ragnarök: Historien om SS-Divisionen Nordlands Pansarspaningsavdelnings Kamp och Undergång I Pommern, Brandenburg och Berlin* (Self-published, 1996), pp.79–80
7 *Cornelius Ryan Collection*, Box 68 Folder 18, Haas interview, p.5

8   Anonymous, *A Woman in Berlin*, p.39
9   Tiecke, *Das Ende Zwischen Oder und Elbe*, p.201
10 Konev, *Sorok Pyatyy*, p.165
11 Lelyushenko, *Moskva-Stalingrad-Berlin-Praga*, p.272
12 S. Komornicki, *Polnische Soldaten Stürmten Berlin* (Verlag des Ministeriums für Nationale Verteidigung, Warsaw, 1967), pp.128–34
13 This account of Weidling's visit to Berlin is based on Hamilton, *Bloody Streets*, pp.178–79, which is derived from post-war interviews with Weidling, Knapp, and Dufving. See also Beevor, *Berlin: The Downfall 1945*, pp.286–87
14 Speer, *Inside the Third Reich*, p.640
15 Ibid., pp.643–44
16 Altner and Le Tissier, *Berlin: Dance of Death*, p.99
17 Ibid., pp.100–01
18 Hamilton, *Bloody Streets*, pp.200–01
19 Le Tissier, *With our Backs to Berlin*, pp.119–20
20 Hamilton, *Bloody Streets*, p.194
21 Translated from reproduced leaflet in Hamilton, *Bloody Streets*, p.190
22 Anonymous, *A Woman in Berlin*, p.43
23 Gellermann, *Die Armee Wenck*, pp.78–79
24 Quoted in T. Le Tissier, *Death Was Our Companion: The Final Days of the Third Reich* (Sutton Publishing, Stroud, 2003), pp.187–88
25 R. Forbes, *For l'Europe: The French Volunteers of the Waffen-SS* (Helion, Solihull, 2006), pp.283–84
26 Batov, *Von der Wolga zur Oder*, pp.415–16
27 Hamilton, *Bloody Streets*, p.209
28 Ibid., p.220
29 R. Michaelis, *Die 11. SS-Freiwilligen-Panzergrenadier-Division Nordland* (Dörffler, Eggolsheim, 2009), p.110
30 Chuikov, *Ot Stalingrada do Berlina*, p.632
31 Konev, *Sorok Pyatyy*, pp.171–72
32 Shein, *Tanki Vedet Rybalko*, p.300
33 Zhukov, *Vospomimaniya I Ramyshleniya*, Vol. II, p.259
34 G. Förster and R. Lakowski, *1945 – Das Jahr der Endgültigen Niederlage der Faschistischen Wehrmacht* (Militärverlag der Deutschen Demokratischen Republik, Berlin, 1985), p.337
35 H. von Luck, *Panzer Commander: The Memoirs of Colonel Hans von Luck* (Cassel, London, 2002), pp.261–62
36 Quoted in Bradley, *Walther Wenck*, pp.354–55
37 Zhadov, *Chetire Goda Voyny*, pp.249–50
38 Interview with W. Robertson, recorded 31 August 1989, available at https://archive.org/details/WilliamDRobertson

Chapter 10: Disintegration: 26–28 April

1. T. Białecki, *Historia Szczecina: Zarys Dziejów Miasta ad Czasów Najdawniejszych do 1980. r* (Zakład Narodowy im. Ossilińskich, Wrocław, 1992), pp.20–55
2. See for example J. Musekamp, *Zwischen Stettin und Szczecin: Metamorphosen Einer Stadt von 1945 bis 2005* (Harrassowitz, Wiesbaden, 2010), pp.201–02
3. Altner and Le Tissier, *Berlin: Dance of Death*, p.140
4. Ibid.
5. Ibid., pp.147–48
6. *Gosudarstvennyy Arkhiv Literatury I Iskusstva*, Moscow, 1710/3/51, p.241
7. Hamilton, *Bloody Streets*, p.261
8. Quoted in ibid, p.278
9. V. Abyzov, *Poslednyy Shturm* (Novosti, Moscow, 1985), pp.49–50
10. Katukov, *Na Ostriye Glavnogo Udara*, p.405
11. Gerasimov, *Shturm Berlina*, pp.121–22
12. Anonymous, *A Woman In Berlin*, p.63
13. Luck, *Panzer Commander*, p.264
14. J. Huber, *So War Es Wirklich: Das Letzte Kriegsjahr an der Ostfront: Ein Panzermann Berichtet. Mein 20. Lebensjahr* (Vowinckel, Berg am See, 1994), pp.360–61
15. E. Ziemke, *The Battle for Berlin: End of the Third Reich* (Macdonald, London, 1969), p.122
16. *Bundesarchiv-Militärarchiv*, Freiburg, RH 19-XV MA 5, *Kriegstagebuch Heeresgruppe Weichsel 27/04/1945*
17. Krivosheyev, *Soviet Casualties*, p.158
18. T. Le Tissier, *Race for the Reichstag* (Pen & Sword, Barnsley, 2022), p.136
19. H. Heiber and D. Glantz (eds), *Hitler and his Generals: Military Conferences 1942–1945. The First Complete Stenographic Record of the Military Situation Conferences, from Stalingrad to Berlin* (Enigma, New York, 2004), p.731
20. Hamilton, *Bloody Streets*, p.297
21. Altner and Le Tissier, *Berlin: Dance of Death*, pp.160–61
22. Ibid., pp.169–70
23. Quoted in Rürup, *Berlin 1945*, p.32
24. Anonymous, *A Woman in Berlin*, pp.66–67
25. Ibid., p.72
26. Ibid., p.74
27. Rürup, *Berlin 1945*, p.56
28. I. Kershaw, *Hitler: A Biography* (Norton, New York 2008), p.942; Fest, *Inside Hitler's Bunker*, p.98
29. Kershaw, *Hitler*, p.942; A. Joachimsthaler, *The Last Days of Hitler: The Legends, The Evidence, The Truth* (Brockhampton, London, 1999), pp.277–78
30. J. O'Donnell, *The Bunker: The History of the Reich Chancellery Group* (Houghton Mifflin, Boston MA, 1978), pp.182–83
31. Fest, *Inside Hitler's Bunker*, p.100

32 H. Eberle and M. Uhl, *Das Buch Hitler: Geheimdossier des NKWD für Josef Stalin, Zusammengestelt Aufgrund der Verhörprotokolle des Persönlichen Adjutanten Hitlers, Otto Günsche, und des Kammerdieners Heinz Linge, Moskau 1948–1949* (Lübbe, Bergisch Gladbach, 2005), p.436
33 Quoted in Lakowski and Stich, *Der Kessel von Halbe 1945*, pp.104–05
34 Huber, *So War Es Wirklich*, pp.363–64
35 See for example Vorobyev and Parotkin, *Poslednii Shturm*, p.374
36 Konev, *Sorok Pyatyy*, pp.174–75
37 Altner and Le Tissier, *Berlin: Dance of Death*, p.200
38 Quoted in Lakowski and Stich, *Der Kessel von Halbe 1945*, p.108
39 H. Trevor-Roper, *The Last Days of Hitler* (Pan, London, 1955), pp.156–57

CHAPTER 11: THE BITTEREST OF ENDS: BERLIN, 29 APRIL–2 MAY

1 Hamilton, *Bloody Streets*, pp.338–39
2 Gerasimov, *Shturm Berlina*, pp.292–93
3 Chuikov, *Ot Stalingrada do Berlina*, pp.653–54
4 W. Fey, *Armored Battles of the Waffen-SS 1943–1945* (Fedorowicz, Winnipeg, 1990), pp.315–16
5 *Cornelius Ryan Collection*, Box 68 Folder 4, Böttscher interview, pp.2–5
6 Altner and Le Tissier, *Berlin: Dance of Death*, pp.216–17
7 Anonymous, *A Woman in Berlin*, p.90
8 Beevor, *Berlin: The Downfall 1945*, pp.345–46
9 Loringhoven, *In the Bunker with Hitler*, pp.173–74
10 *Cornelius Ryan Collection*, Box 68 Folder 4, Böttscher interview, p.6–7
11 Tsentralnyi Arkhiv Ministerstva Oboronyi Rossyiskoi Federalyy, Moscow, *Zhurnal boyevykh deystviy 1-go Belorusskogo fronta za aprel' i pervuyu dekadu maya 1945 g*, p.367
12 Fest, *Inside Hitler's Bunker*, p.108
13 Ibid, p.110
14 Chuikov, *Ot Stalingrada do Berlina*, pp.659–60
15 Ibid., p.667
16 This account is based upon Chuikov's memoirs, and *Cornelius Ryan Collection*, Box 69 Folder 1, N. Gladky, *Kapytulyatsiya Berlinskogo Garnizona*
17 *Cornelius Ryan Collection*, Box 67 Folder 10, Lampe interview
18 *Cornelius Ryan Collection*, Box 70 Folder 14, Schulz interview
19 P. Longerich, *Goebbels: A Biography* (Random House, New York, 2015), pp.684–86
20 Fest, *Inside Hitler's Bunker*, pp.137–39
21 Quoted in Fest, *Inside Hitler's Bunker*, pp.139–140
22 Chuikov, *Ot Stalingrada do Berlina*, p.692

23 Ibid., p.694
24 Weidling's surrender order is available at https://www.liberationroute.com/pictures/735/german-capital-surrender-2_1280_1280_fit_90.jpg
25 R. Misch, *Der Letzte Zeuge* (Pendo Verlag, Munich, 2008), pp.231–32
26 Joachimsthaler, *Last Days of Hitler*, p.289
27 For a detailed discussion, see C. Goeschel, *Suicide in Nazi Germany* (Oxford University Press, 2009)
28 Zhukov, *Vospomimaniya I Ramyshleniya*, Vol. II, p.264
29 *Der Spiegel* (Hamburg, 1965) No.19, 5 May, pp.94–99
30 R. Ainsztein, 'How Hitler Died: The Soviet Version' in *International Affairs* (Oxford University Press, 1967), Vol. 43 No.2, pp.307–18
31 Beevor, *Berlin: The Downfall 1945*, pp.389–91
32 V. Vinogradov, *Hitler's Death: Russia's Last Great Secret from the Files of the KGB* (Chaucer, London, 2005), pp.333–36

Chapter 12: The Roads to the West: 29 April–8 May

1 Huber, *So War Es Wirklich*, p.367
2 Ibid., p.369
3 C. Whiting, *Finale at Flensburg* (Leo Cooper, London, 1973), p.100
4 Huber, *So War Es Wirklich*, p.372
5 Le Tissier, *With our Backs to Berlin*, pp.121–22
6 Quoted in Bradley, *Walther Wenck*, p.363
7 Quoted in Le Tissier, *Death Was Our Companion*, p.198
8 Le Tissier, *Slaughter at Halbe*, p.176
9 Le Tissier, *Death Was Our Companion*, p.203
10 Le Tissier, *Slaughter at Halbe*, pp.185–87
11 Busse, 'Die Letzte Schlacht der 9. Armee', p.168
12 Le Tissier, *Slaughter at Halbe*, p.190
13 Tieke, *Das Ende Zwischen Oder und Elbe*, p.339
14 Le Tissier, *Slaughter at Halbe*, p.227
15 Gellermann, *Die Armee Wenck*, pp.186–88
16 Bradley, *Walther Wenck*, p.76
17 For a controversial assessment of German deaths due to starvation, see J. Bacque, *Other Losses* (Stoddart, New York/Ontario, 1989); see also N. Ferguson, 'Prisoner Taking and Prisoner Killing in the Age of Total War: Towards a Political Economy of Military Defeat' in *War in History* (2004) Vol. 11 No.2, pp.148–92
18 Hamilton, *Bloody Streets*, p.405
19 Altner and Le Tissier, *Berlin: Dance of Death*, p.252
20 Ibid., pp.252–53
21 Ibid., pp.257–58

22 Ibid., pp.285–86
23 Hamilton, *Bloody Streets*, pp.424–28
24 Fey, *Armored Battles*, p.317
25 Trevor-Roper, *Last Days of Hitler*, p.193
26 J. von Lang, *The Secretary. Martin Bormann: The Man who Manipulated Hitler* (Random House, New York, 1979), pp.410–36
27 T. Junge and M. Müller, *Bis zur Letzten Stunde: Hitlers Sekretärin Erzählt ihr Leben* (List Taschenbuch, Berlin, 2003), pp.213–42
28 O'Donnell, *The Bunker*, pp.331–32
29 Quoted in Beevor, *Berlin: The Downfall 1945*, p.374
30 Fadeyev interview

Chapter 13: Conclusion: An Uneasy Silence

1 See P. Buttar, *Battleground Prussia: The Assault on Germany's Eastern Front 1944–1945* (Osprey, Oxford, 2010), pp.218–35; H. Schön, *Ostsee 45: Menschen, Schiffe, Schicksale* (Motorbuch Verlag, Stuttgart, 1998)
2 Whiting, *Finale at Flensburg*, pp.101–02
3 Ike Skelton Combined Arms Research Library Digital Library, Ft Leavenworth KS: 82nd Airborne Division After Action Report N11709, p.48
4 Quoted in P. Caddick-Adams, *Monty and Rommel: Parallel Lives* (Arrow, London, 2012), p.450
5 Quoted in Schön, *Ostsee 45*, p.606
6 For an excellent account of Berlin immediately after the end of the war, see G. Milton, *Checkmate in Berlin* (John Murray, London, 2021)
7 R. Andreas-Friedrich, *Battleground Berlin: Diaries 1945–1948* (Paragon, New York, 1990), pp.23–26
8 Zolotarev, *Russkiy Archiv*, Vol. XV, p.95
9 R. Müller, *Das Deutsche Reich und der Zweite Weltkrieg* (Deutsche Verlags-Anstalt, Stuttgart, 2008, 13 volumes), Vol. X, p.673; D. Glantz, *The Soviet-German War 1941–1945: Myths and Realities. A Survey Essay* (Strom Thurmond Institute of Government and Public Affairs, Clemson SC, 2001), p.95
10 P. Antill, *Berlin 1945: End of the Thousand Year Reich* (Osprey, Oxford, 2005), p.85
11 Krivosheyev, *Soviet Casualties*, p.220
12 C. Macdonald, *Victory in Europe, 1945: The Last Offensive of World War II. US Army in World War II European Theater of Operations* (US Government Printing Office, Washington DC, 1973), p.372; S. Zaloga and P. Dennis, *Remagen 1945: Endgame Against the Third Reich* (Osprey, Oxford, 2006), p.87
13 Quoted in Hansard (House of Commons, London, 1954), Vol. 535, *Debate on the Address*, 1 December 1954
14 Whiting, *Finale at Flensburg*, pp.104–05
15 This speech is quoted in Whiting, *Finale at Flensburg*, p.158, and elsewhere, but a definitive source has proved impossible to find.

16 National Archives, Kew, *Operation Unthinkable: British War Cabinet Joint Planning Staff 22 May*, CAB 120/691
17 For a more detailed account, see S. Hines, *Operation Unthinkable. Its Significance in the Development of the Cold War* (GRIN, Munich, 2016); J. Walker, *Operation Unthinkable: The Third World War* (History Press, Cheltenham, 2013)
18 P. Tsouras, *Panzers on the Eastern Front: General Erhard Raus and his Panzer Divisions in Russia, 1941–1945* (Frontline, Barnsley, 1996), p.220
19 T. Place, *Military Training in the British Army, 1940–1944: From Dunkirk to D-Day* (Frank Cass, London, 2000), p.160
20 S. Platonov, *Geschichte des Zweiten Weltkrieges, 1939–1945: Militärhistorischer Abriss* (Deutscher Militärverlag, Berlin, 1961), pp.29–30
21 W. Białkowski, *Rokossowski – na ile Polak?* (Alfa, Warsaw, 1994), p.326
22 Konev, *Sorok Pyatyy*, pp.181–82
23 Kardorff, *Berliner Aufzeichnungen*, p.231
24 Quoted in R. Moorhouse, *Berlin at War: Life and Death in Hitler's Capital, 1939–1945* (Vintage, London, 2011), p.388

BIBLIOGRAPHY

Air Force Historical Research Agency, Maxwell AFB AL
Bundesarchiv-Militärarchiv, Freiburg
Cornelius Ryan Collection, Ohio University, Athens OH
Gosudarstvennyy Arkhiv Literatury I Iskusstva, Moscow
Ike Skelton Combined Arms Research Library Digital Library, Ft Leavenworth KS
Library of Congress, Washington DC
National Archives, Kew, London
National Archives and Records Administration, College Park MD
Tsentralnyi Archiv Ministerstva Oboronyi Rossyiskoi Federalyy, Moscow

Chicago Daily Tribune
Der Spiegel (Hamburg)
Hansard (House of Commons, London)
Illustrated London News (London)
International Affairs (Oxford University Press)
Metropolitan Magazine (Walker, Harvey & Macfadden, New York)
Novaya i Noveyshaya Istoriya (Rossiyskaya Akademiya Nauk I Institut Vseobshchey Istorii RAN, Moscow)
Oktyabr (Soyuz Pisateley RSFSR, Moscow)
Voyenno-Istoricheskiy Zhurnal (Ministerstva Oborony SSSR)
War in History (Sage, London)
Wehrwissenschaftliche Rundschau (Mittler, Darmstadt)

www.iremember.ru

Abyzov, V., *Poslednyy Shturm* (Novosti, Moscow, 1985)
Altner, H. and Le Tissier, T., *Berlin: Dance of Death* (Spellmount, Staplehurst, 2002)
Andreas-Friedrich, R., *Battleground Berlin: Diaries 1945–1948* (Paragon, New York, 1990)
Anonymous, *A Woman in Berlin* (Virago, London, 2011)
Antill, P., *Berlin 1945: End of the Thousand Year Reich* (Osprey, Oxford, 2005)

Antipenko, N., *Na Glavnom Napravlenii* (Nauka, Moscow, 1967)
Babadzhanian, A., *Dorogy Pobedy* (Molodaya Gvardiya, Moscow, 1975)
Bacque, J., *Other Losses* (Stoddart, New York/Ontario, 1989)
Badigin, M., *Boy Trepuget Podviga* (Voyenizdat, Moscow, 1980)
Bahm, K., *Berlin 1945: The Final Reckoning* (Amber, London, 2014)
Barnett, C. (ed.), *Hitler's Generals* (Grove Weidenfeld, New York, 1989)
Batov, P., *Von der Wolga zur Oder* (Deutscher Militärverlag, Berlin, 1965)
Bauer, M., *Konnten wir den Krieg Vermeiden, Gewinnen, Abbrechen?* (Scherl, Berlin, 1919)
Beck, A. (ed.), *Bis Stalingrad … 1941–1943* (H. Abt, Ulm, 1983)
Beevor, A., *Berlin: The Downfall 1945* (Viking, London, 2002)
Białecki, T., *Historia Szczecina: Zarys Dziejów Miasta ad Czasów Najdawniejszych do 1980. r* (Zakład Narodowy im. Ossilińskich, Wrocław, 1992)
Białkowski, W., *Rokossowski – na ile Polak?* (Alfa, Warsaw, 1994)
Biuletyn Polskiej Misji Historycznej (Uniwersytet Mikołaja-Kopernika, Torún, 2012)
Bokov, F., *Vesna Pobedy* (Mysl, Moscow, 1985)
Bradley, D., *Walther Wenck, General der Panzertruppe* (Biblio, Osnabrück, 1981)
Brandes, G., Christensen, E. and Loock, H-D., *Berlin als Deutsche Reichshauptstadt. Erinnerungen aus den Jahren 1877–1883* (Colloquium, Berlin, 1989)
Breuer, W., *Top Secret Tales of World War II* (John Wiley, London, 2000)
Broué, P., *The German Revolution, 1917–1923* (Haymarket, Chicago, 2007)
Buttar, P., *Battleground Prussia: The Assault on Germany's Eastern Front 1944–1945* (Osprey, Oxford, 2010)
Buttar, P., *Meat Grinder* (Osprey, Oxford, 2022)
Caddick-Adams, P., *Monty and Rommel: Parallel Lives* (Arrow, London, 2012)
Chuikov, V., *Konets Tretyego Reykha* (Sovetskaya Rossiya, Moscow, 1973)
Chuikov, V., *Ot Stalingrada do Berlina* (Sovetskaya Rossiya, Moscow, 1985)
Connelly, M., *Reaching for the Stars: A History of Bomber Command* (I. B. Tauris, London, 2014)
Coppi, H., Inachin, K., Langer, K., Diederich, G., Garbe, I., Bersch, F., Wagner, A., Borries, A. von, Niemann, M., Schwerin, D. Graf von, Krüger, D. and Leo, A., *Widerstand Gegen das NS-Regime in den Regionen Mecklenburg und Vorpommern* (Friedrich-Ebert Stiftung, Schwerin, 2007)
Davis, R., *Bombing the European Axis Powers: A Historical Digest of the Combined Bomber Offensive 1939–1945* (Air University Press, Maxwell AFB AL, 2006)
Dower, J., *War Without Mercy: Race and Power in the Pacific War* (Faber & Faber, London, 1986)
Eberle, H. and Uhl, M., *Das Buch Hitler: Geheimdossier des NKWD für Josef Stalin, Zusammengestellt Aufgrund der Verhörprotokolle des Persönlichen Adjutanten Hitlers, Otto Günsche, und des Kammerdieners Heinz Linge, Moskau 1948–1949* (Lübbe, Bergisch Gladbach, 2005)

Eismann, H. and Steinhardt, F., *Unter Himmlers Kommando 1945 – der Kampf von Heeresgruppe Weichsel an der Ostfront: Die Persönlichen Erinnerungen von Oberst Hans-Georg Eismann, Ia von Heeresgruppe Weichsel* (Melchior, Wolfenbüttel, 2010)

Fest, J., *Die Unbeantwortbaren Fragen: Notizen über Gespräche mit Albert Speer Zwischen Ende 1966 und 1981* (Rowohlt, Hamburg, 2006)

Fest, J., *Inside Hitler's Bunker: The Last Days of the Third Reich* (Pan, London, 2012)

Fey, W., *Armored Battles of the Waffen-SS 1943–1945* (Fedorowicz, Winnipeg, 1990)

Findahl, T., *Letzter Akt – Berlin, 1939–1945* (Hammerich & Lesser, Hamburg, 1946)

Fleming, N., *August 1939: The Last Days of Peace* (Davies, London, 1979)

Forbes, R., *For l'Europe: The French Volunteers of the Waffen-SS* (Helion, Solihull, 2006)

Förster, G. and Lakowski, R., *1945 – Das Jahr der Endgültigen Niederlage der Faschistischen Wehrmacht* (Militärverlag der Deutschen Demokratischen Republik, Berlin, 1985)

Galitsky, I., *Dorogu Otkrivaly Sapery* (Voyenizdat, Moscow, 1983)

Gay, P., *My German Question: Growing Up in Nazi Berlin* (Yale University Press, New Haven CT, 1998)

Gellermann, G., *Die Armee Wenck: Hitlers Letzte Hoffnung. Aufstellung, Einsatz und Ende der 12. Deutschen Armee im Frühjahr 1945* (Bernard & Graefe, Bonn, 2007)

Gerasimov, E. (ed.), *Shturm Berlina: Vospominaniya, Pisma, Dnevniki Uchastnikov boev za Berlin* (Voyenizdat, Moscow, 1948)

Getman, A., *Tanki Idut na Berlin* (Voyenizd-vo Ministerstva Oborony SSSR, Moscow, 1982)

Glantz, D., *The Soviet-German War 1941–1945: Myths and Realities. A Survey Essay* (Strom Thurmond Institute of Government and Public Affairs, Clemson SC, 2001)

Goeschel, C., *Suicide in Nazi Germany* (Oxford University Press, 2009)

Gorlitz, W. (ed.), *The Memoirs of Field Marshal Wilhelm Keitel* (First Cooper Square Press, New York, 2000)

Gostoni, P., *Bitva za Berlin v Vospominaniyach Ocevidcev 1944–1945* (Centrpoligraf, Moscow, 2013)

Grayling, A., *Among the Dead Cities* (Bloomsbury, London, 2006)

Greenacre, J., Giles, D., *The Battle for Berlin: A Battlefield Reader* (self-published, 2019)

Grigorenko, P., *V Podpole Mozno Vstretit Tolko Krys* (Zvenja, Moscow, 1997)

Guderian, H., *Erinnerungen eines Soldaten* (Kurt Vowinkel Verlag, Neckargemünd, 1960)

Hamilton, A., *The Oder Front 1945: Documents, Reports, Personal Accounts, and Maps* (Helion, Solihull, 2014, 2 volumes)

Hamilton, A., *Bloody Streets: The Soviet Assault on Berlin* (Helion, Warwick, 2020)

Harris, A., *Bomber Offensive* (Pen & Sword, Barnsley, 2022)

Hastings, M., *Das Reich: The March of the 2nd SS Panzer Division Through France, June 1944* (BCA, London, 1981)

Hastings, M., *Bomber Command* (Pan, London, 1999)

Hausser, P., *Soldaten wie Andere Auch* (Munin, Osnabrück, 1982)

Heiber, H. and Glantz, D. (eds), *Hitler and his Generals: Military Conferences 1942–1945. The First Complete Stenographic Record of the Military Situation Conferences, from Stalingrad to Berlin* (Enigma, New York, 2004)

Hillblad, T. and Wallin, E., *Ragnarök: Historien om SS-Divisionen Nordlands Pansarspaningsavdelnings Kamp och Undergång I Pommern, Brandenburg och Berlin* (Self-published, 1996)

Hillgruber, A. and Picker, H., *Hitlers Tischgespräche im Führerhauptquartier 1941–1942* (Deutscher Taschenbuch-Verlag, Munich, 1968)

Hines, S., *Operation Unthinkable. Its Significance in the Development of the Cold War* (GRIN, Munich, 2016)

Hitler, A., *Mein Kampf* (Houghton Mifflin, Boston MA, 1939)

Huber, J., *So War Es Wirklich: Das Letzte Kriegsjahr an der Ostfront: Ein Panzermann Berichtet. Mein 20. Lebensjahr* (Vowinckel, Berg am See, 1994)

Huret, J., *Berlin um Neunzehnhundert* (Tasbach, Berlin, 2014)

Joachimsthaler, A., *The Last Days of Hitler: The Legends, The Evidence, The Truth* (Brockhampton, London, 1999)

Junge, T. and Müller, M., *Bis zur Letzten Stunde: Hitlers Sekretärin Erzählt ihr Leben* (List Taschenbuch, Berlin, 2003)

Kaes, A., Jay, M. and Dimendberg, E. (eds), *Weimar Republic Sourcebook* (University of California Press, Oakland CA, 1995)

Kardorff, U. von, *Berliner Aufzeichnungen aus die Jahren 1942–1945* (Deutsche Taschenbuch Verlag, Munich, 1964)

Karpov, V., *Izbrannye Proizvedeniya* (Khudozhestvennaya Literatura, Moscow, 1990, 3 volumes)

Katukov, M., *Na Ostriye Glavnogo Udara* (Voyenizdat, Moscow, 1974)

Kazakov, V., *Artilleriya, Ogon!* (DOSAAF, Moscow, 1975)

Kennan, G., *Memoirs 1925–1950* (Little, Brown & Co, Boston, 1967, 2 volumes)

Kershaw, I., *Hitler: A Biography* (Norton, New York, 2008)

Kessler, H., *Berlin in Lights: The Diaries of Count Harry Kessler, 1918–1937* (Grove, New York, 2000)

Khetagurov, G., *Ispolnenye Dolga* (Voyenizdat, Moscow, 1977)

Kilduff, P., *Iron Man: Rudolf Berthold, Germany's Indomitable Fighter Ace of World War I* (Grub Street, London, 2012)

Komornicki, S., *Polnische Soldaten Stürmten Berlin* (Verlag des Ministeriums für Nationale Verteidigung, Warsaw, 1967)

Konev, I., *Sorok Pyatyy* (Voyenizdat, Moscow, 1970)

Krivosheyev, G., *Soviet Casualties and Combat Losses in the Twentieth Century* (Greenhill, London, 1997)

Kuby, E., *Die Russen in Berlin 1945* (Moewig, Rastatt, 1988)

Lakowski, R. and Stich, K., *Der Kessel von Halbe 1945. Das Letzte Drama* (Mittler, Hamburg, 2013)

Lang, J. von, *The Secretary. Martin Bormann: The Man who Manipulated Hitler* (Random House, New York, 1979)

Large, D., *Berlin* (Basic Books, New York, 2007)

Lelyushenko, D., *Moskva-Stalingrad-Berlin-Praga. Zapiski Comandarma Sayt* (Nauka, Moscow 1987)

Le Tissier, T., *With Our Backs to Berlin* (Sutton, Stroud, 2001)

Le Tissier, T., *Death Was Our Companion: The Final Days of the Third Reich* (Sutton, Stroud, 2003)

Le Tissier, T., *Marshal Zhukov at the Oder* (History Press, Cheltenham, 2021)

Le Tissier, T., *Slaughter at Halbe: The Destruction of Hitler's Ninth Army* (History Press, Cheltenham, 2021)

Le Tissier, T., *Race for the Reichstag* (Pen & Sword, Barnsley, 2022)

Longerich, P., *Goebbels: A Biography* (Random House, New York, 2015)

Longmate, N., *The Bombers: The RAF Offensive Against Germany 1939–1945* (Hutchinson, London, 1983)

Loringhoven, B. Freytag von, *In the Bunker with Hitler* (Weidenfeld & Nicolson, London, 2007)

Lubrich, O. (ed.), *Travels in the Reich, 1933–1945: Foreign Authors Report From Germany* (University of Chicago Press, 2010)

Luck, H. von, *Panzer Commander: The Memoirs of Colonel Hans von Luck* (Cassel, London, 2002)

Ludewig, T., *Berlin: Geschichte einer Deutschen Metropole* (Bertelsmann, Munich, 1986)

Macdonald, C., *Victory in Europe, 1945: The Last Offensive of World War II. US Army in World War II European Theater of Operations* (US Government Printing Office, Washington DC, 1973)

Manvell, R., and Fraenkel, H., *Doctor Goebbels: His Life and Death* (Skyhorse, New York, 2010)

Michaelis, R., *Die 11. SS-Freiwilligen-Panzergrenadier-Division Nordland* (Dörffler, Eggolsheim, 2009)

Miller, D., *Eighth Air Force: The American Bomber Crews in Britain* (Aurum, London, 2007)

Milton, G., *Checkmate in Berlin* (John Murray, London, 2021)

Misch, R., *Der Letzte Zeuge* (Pendo Verlag, Munich, 2008)

Moorhouse, R., *Berlin at War: Life and Death in Hitler's Capital, 1939–1945* (Vintage, London, 2011)

Moss, N., *Nineteen Weeks: America, Britain and the Fateful Summer of 1940* (Houghton Mifflin Harcourt, Boston MA, 2004)

Müller, R., *Das Deutsche Reich und der Zweite Weltkrieg* (Deutsche Verlags-Anstalt, Stuttgart, 2008, 13 volumes)

Musekamp, J., *Zwischen Stettin und Szczecin: Metamorphosen Einer Stadt von 1945 bis 2005* (Harrassowitz, Wiesbaden, 2010)

O'Donnell, J., *The Bunker: The History of the Reich Chancellery Group* (Houghton Mifflin, Boston MA, 1978)

Ostwald, H., *Sittengeschichte der Inflation, ein Kulturdokument aus den Jahren des Marksturzes* (Neuhaus & Henius, Berlin, 1931)

Peiper, H., *Fegelein's Horsemen and Genocidal Warfare: The SS Cavalry Brigade in the Soviet Union* (Palgrave Macmillan, Basingstoke, 2015)

Pflanze, O., *Bismarck and the Development of Germany* (Princeton University Press, Princeton NJ, 2021, 3 volumes)

Pike, F., *Hirohito's War: The Pacific War, 1941–1945* (Bloomsbury, London, 2016)

Place, T., *Military Training in the British Army, 1940–1944: From Dunkirk to D-Day* (Frank Cass, London, 2000)

Platonov, S., *Geschichte des Zweiten Weltkrieges, 1939–1945: Militärhistorischer Abriss* (Deutscher Militärverlag, Berlin, 1961)

Pukhov, N., *Gody Ispyitanyy* (Voyenizdat, Moscow, 1959)

Read, A. and Fisher, D., *Berlin Rising: Biography of a City* (W. W. Norton, New York, 1994)

Rokossovsky, K., *A Soldier's Duty* (Lancer International, New Delhi, 1985)

Rürup, R., *Berlin 1945: Eine Dokumentation* (Willmuth Arenhövel, Berlin, 2003)

Ryan, C., *The Last Battle* (Simon & Schuster, New York, 1966)

Saft, U., *Krieg im Osten* (Militärbuch Verlag, Walsrode, 2002)

Schön, H., *Ostsee 45: Menschen, Schiffe, Schicksale* (Motorbuch Verlag, Stuttgart, 1998)

Sebag Montefiore, S., *Stalin: The Court of the Red Tsar* (Phoenix, London, 2004)

Shein, D., *Tanki Vedet Rybalko. Boyevoy Put 3-y Gvardeskoy Tankovoy Armii* (Eksmo, Moscow, 2007)

Shirer, W., *Berlin Diary 1934–1941: The Rise of the Third Reich* (Promotional Reprint Co, London, 1997)

Shtemenko, S., *The Soviet General Staff at War 1941–1945* (Progress, Moscow, 1970)

Siemens, D., *The Making of a Nazi Hero: The Murder and Myth of Horst Wessel* (Tauris, London, 2013)

Skorobogatkin, K., *50 Let Vooruzhuzhennykh Sil SSSR* (Voyenizdat, Moscow, 1968)

Smit, E., Staikos, E., Thormann, D. and Lieser, H., *3. Februar 1945: Die Zerstörung Kreuzbergs aus der Luft* (Kunstamt, Berlin, 1995)

Spaeter, H., *History of the Panzerkorps Grossdeutschland* (Fedorowicz, Winnipeg, 2000, 3 volumes)

Speer, A., *Inside the Third Reich* (Weidenfeld & Nicolson, London, 1995)

Stahel, D., *Operation Barbarossa and Germany's Defeat in the East* (Cambridge University Press, 2007)

Stremmel, R., *Modell und Moloch: Berlin in der Wahrnehmung Deutscher Politiker vom Ende des 19. Jahrhunderts bis zum Zweiten Weltkrieg* (Bouvier, Bonn, 1992)

Tanaka, Y. and Young, M. (eds), *Bombing Civilians: A Twentieth-Century History* (New Press, New York, 2009)

Teuber, R., *Die Bundeswehr 1955–1995* (Militair-Verlag K. D. Patzwall, Norderstedt, 1996)

Tiecke, W., *Das Ende Zwischen Oder und Elbe: Der Kampf um Berlin 1945* (Motorbuch Verlag, Stuttgart, 1981)

Tiecke, W., *Tragedy of the Faithful: A History of III (Germanisches) SS-Panzer-Korps* (Fedorowicz, Winnipeg, 2001)

Trevor-Roper, H., *The Last Days of Hitler* (Pan, London, 1955)

Tsouras, P., *Panzers on the Eastern Front: General Erhard Raus and his Panzer Divisions in Russia, 1941–1945* (Frontline, Barnsley, 1996)

Vassiltchikov, M., *The Berlin Diaries 1940–1945* (Pimlico, London, 1999)

Vinogradov, V., *Hitler's Death: Russia's Last Great Secret from the Files of the KGB* (Chaucer, London, 2005)

Vizetelly, H., *Berlin Under the New Empire* (Greenwood, New York, 1968, 2 volumes)

Vorobyev, F. and Parotkin, I., *Poslednii Shturm: Berlinskaia Operatsiia 1945g* (Voyenizdat, Moscow, 1975)

Vosnesensky, V. and Rubezhnyi, D. (eds), *9 Maya 1945 Goda. Vospominaniya* (Nauka, Moscow, 1970)

Walker, J., *Operation Unthinkable: The Third World War* (History Press, Cheltenham, 2013)

Webster, C. and Frankland, N., *The Strategic Air Offensive Against Germany 1939–1945* (HMSO, London, 1961, 3 volumes)

Weihsmann, H., *Bauen Unterm Hakenkreuz. Architektur des Untergangs* (Promedia, Vienna, 1998)

Whiting, C., *Finale at Flensburg* (Leo Cooper, London, 1973)

Willemer, W., *The German Defense of Berlin* (US Army Historical Division, Karlsruhe, 1953)

Williamson, G., *German Commanders of World War II* (Osprey, Oxford, 2006, 2 volumes)

Zaitsev, V., *Gvardeyskaya Tankovaya* (Sred-Ural, Sverdlovsk, 1989)

Zaloga, S. and Dennis, P., *Remagen 1945: Endgame Against the Third Reich* (Osprey, Oxford, 2006)

Zhadov, A., *Chetire Goda Voyny* (Voyenizdat, Moscow, 1978)

Zhukov, G., *Vospomimaniya I Ramyshleniya* (Olma, Moscow, 2002, 2 volumes)

Ziemke, E., *The Battle for Berlin: End of the Third Reich* (Macdonald, London, 1969)

Zolotarev, V. (ed.), *Russkiy Archiv: Velikaya Otecestvennaya* (Terra, Moscow 1994–96, 23 volumes)

INDEX

References to maps are in bold.

Abyzov, Vladimir Ivanovich 313, 314
Adenauer, Karl 360, 385
aircraft 59, 67, 70, 82, 99, 139–140, 148, 168, 170, 192, 247, 292, 297, 299, 337
    Boeing B-17 (US) 67, 74
    de Havilland Mosquito (UK) 60, 76, 228
    North American P-51 Mustang (US) 67, 70
Allied bombing raids 57, 58–59, 60, 63–66, 73–74, 75–79, 100, 225, 228, 234, 259, 269, 294
Allied strategy 22–23, 57, 67–68, 70–72, 73, 75–76, 102, 194–195, 264, 290, 379
    and fears of post-war Soviet expansion 401–402
    and the partitioning of Germany and occupation zones 22, 23, 24, 102, 129, 194, 264, 367, 368, 386, 398, 399, 407
    and unconditional surrender 353, 358, 396
Altner, Fritz 284, 368–369
Altner, Soldat Helmut 107–108, 114, 150, 192, 197, 222, 230, 243–244, 281–282, 308–309, 325–326, 335–336, 345–346, 382–384, 385
ammunition consumption 142, 147, 179
ammunition supplies 70, 73–74, 100, 111, 161, 179, 193, 194, 198, 207, 246, 292, 311, 317, 320, 322, 323, 336, 337, 341, 355, 379
anti-aircraft fire 58, 66–67, 69, 71, 73–74, 78
    and flak towers 66–67, 69
Antipenko, Lt Gen Nikolai Aleksandrovich 138, 142, 149, 153
antisemitism in Germany 29, 85, 96 *see also* Jewish community, the
Arbeitsgemeinschaft Deutscher Musikkritiker, the 48
Ardennes offensive, the 71, 81, 95
army discipline 120–121, 122–123
Arnold, Gen Henry 75, 79

astrological predictions 114–115
Autobahn network, the 55, 229, 246, 289–290, 371
Averdieck, Feldwebel Fritz 199–200, 215
Axmann, Artur 215, 387–388

Babadzhanian, Col Aranesp Khachaturovich 92, 93, 133, 158, 175, 191, 192, 197, 198, 218, 220, 230, 242, 271
Babelsberg garrison 247, 248
Bärenfänger, Generalmajor Erich 311–312, 387
Batov, Col Gen Pavel Ivanovich 123–124, 235, 239, 240, 252, 292–293
Battle of Baranovichi (July 1944), the 123–124
Battle of Cherkassy (1944), the 125, 377
Battle of Khalkin Gol (1939), the 120, 125
Battle of Kursk (1943), the 123, 130, 131
battle of Letschin (April 1945), the 162, 163–164
Battle of Moscow (1941–42), the 107, 118, 121, 125, 131, 160, 166, 301
Battle of Stalingrad (1942–43), the 92, 117, 118, 120, 131, 132
Bauer, Oberst Max 38–39
Belov, Col Gen Pavel Alekseyevich 160–161, 171
Berchtesgaden, Bavaria (Hitler's mountain headquarters) 18, 238, 263
Beria, Lavrentiy 407, 408
Berlin 25–30, 32, **115**, 206, **229, 258, 288, 381,** 412
    and 1848 protests 26, 27
    after the surrender and ceasefire 361, 398–399
    and attitudes to the Nazis and the war 51–52, 61, 73
    and bombing raids 58, 63–66, 68–70, 73–74, 76, 77–79, 107–108, 259, 412
    as capital 27, 28, 52
    and culture and entertainment 43, 45, 47, 48, 177
    and expansion of 42
    and the First World War 34–36

and German Communists 281, 294
and industry 33–34, 43
and infrastructural developments 28, 32
and the Jewish community 28–29, 43, 48, 49–50
and political unrest after 36–38, 40–41
and post-war architectural plans 52–55
and preparation for defeat 177
and social classes 29, 38
and underground tunnels and *U-bahn* network 66, 69, 271, 316, 334, 336, 345, 346, 357, 362, 380, 382, 410
and vice and crime 43 *see also* German strategy
Berlin Philharmonic Orchestra, the 177–178
Berlin Wall, the 408, 412
Berzarin, Gen Nikolai Erastovich 164, 165, 230, 285, 323, 332, 343, 354, 362, 398
Biehler, Oberst Ernst 189, 221
Bismarck, Otto von 27, 31–32, 52
Blanter, Matvei Isaakovich 352, 353
Blondi (Hitler's dog) 280, 350
Bogdanov, Col Gen Semen Ilyich 131, 133, 166, 191, 228, 276
Bokov, Lt Gen Fedor Yefimovich 164, 165
Bolshevik revolution (1917), the 36, 38
bomb loads and effectiveness 59–60
Borkowski, Dieter 326–327
Bormann, Martin 89, 205–206, 212–213, 214, 263–264, 281, 329, 339, 344–345, 352, 357, 359, 388
Böttcher, Oberst Friedrich 275, 344–345, 348, 386
Bradley, Gen Omar 22, 23
Braun, Eva 212, 280, 329, 339, 351
Braun, Gretl 212, 329, 330
bridgeheads 168–170, 178, 183, 194–195, 198, 202, 204, 230, 241, 252, 253, 254, 274, 302
  at Oder River 81–82, 92, 98, 99, 110, 116
  and pontoon bridges 138, 139, 144, 168, 235, 334
  Sandomierz bridgehead 107, 125, 148, 179
British Army, the
  6th Airborne Division 367
  7th Armoured Division 394–395
  21st Army Group 22, 102
  VIII Corps 367
British Joint Intelligence Committee, the 71
British strategy 59–60, 63
Burgdorf, General Wilhelm 210, 211, 213, 214, 250, 278, 330, 347, 350, 357, 361
Burgfrieden, the 34

Burmeister, Generalleutnant Arnold 200, 279
Busse, General Theodor 97–98, 99, 100, 101, 105–106, 111, 116, 179–180, 182, 193, 194, 200, 205, 207–208, 224, 226, 227–228, 237, 244, 245, 251, 253, 254, 261, 264, 267–268, 275, 278, 279, 287, 299, 300–301, 317, 318, 331, 337, 338, 369, 370, 372, 374, 375, 376, 377, 411

Carinhall (Göring's residence) 109, 110, 231
Catholic Bavaria and German unification 27
Charlottenbrücke crossing, the 382–385, 386
Cherwell, Lord Frederick 59, 60
Chuikov, Col Gen Vasily Ivanovich 92, 93, 132, 152, 153, 154, 157, 158, 164, 165, 166–167, 181, 190–191, 195–196, 198, 200, 201, 217, 218, 219, 220, 221, 228–229, 242, 248, 257, 261, 271, 274, 282, 295–296, 310, 314, 323, 324, 334, 335, 342, 343, 348, 351–353, 354, 356, 357, 358, 359, 360, 361
Churchill, Winston 22, 59, 71, 76–77, 129, 401, 402
civilian clothing as a means of escape 261, 274, 326, 329, 344, 375, 386, 389
civilians *see* Berlin; refugees
command structures and decision-making 83–84, 131, 137
Communist Party (Germany), the 46
Communist Party (Soviet Union), the 23, 143, 144, 406
concentration camps, the 21, 51, 77, 98, 101, 230, 231, 247, 366, 379
Cottbus bombings (February 1945) 225
currency instability 42

deaths 22, 40, 47, 103, 108, 123, 125, 133, 136–137, 139, 151, 164, 184, 203, 218, 222, 227, 228, 257, 259, 260, 274, 296, 298, 309, 311, 316, 323, 325, 333, 335, 336, 355, 370, 371, 373, 377, 380, 387, 396, 399–400, 403, 404
  of civilians 20, 41, 58, 59, 60, 67, 70, 75–76, 79, 88, 101, 225, 252, 281–282, 300, 316, 317, 326, 329, 331, 361, 371, 382–383, 385, 409–410, 411
  and mass suicides 329, 361, 387, 389
  of POWs 278
  of senior Nazis and Wehrmacht officers 356–357, 361, 370 *see also* executions

'Dehousing Paper,' the 59–60
demarcation boundaries 170, 173, 296, 297, 298–299, 316, 324–325, 334, 335
   Lübben demarcation line 127–129, 261
Denazification courts 388, 389
Der Angriff (newspaper) 44
Dolchstoss legend, the 96, 97
Dönitz, Admiral Karl 112, 278, 338, 339, 344, 352, 353, 355, 360, 368, 394, 395, 397
Dremov, Maj Gen Ivan Fedorovich 220, 229
Dresden bombing raid (February 1944), the 75, 76, 77, 79
Dufving, Oberst Theodor von 275, 279, 352, 353, 358, 359

Ebert, Friedrich 38, 39–40
Edelsheim, Generalleutnant Maximilian von 378, 379
Ehrhardt, Korvettenkapitän Hermann 39, 41
Eisenhower, Gen Dwight 23, 396, 397, 401
Eismann, Oberst Hans-Georg 87, 88, 90, 91, 94, 97, 99, 182, 212, 226–227, 237, 244
Engelhardt, Konteradmiral Conrad 394, 396, 397
executions 22, 31, 40, 41, 74, 97, 165, 193, 211, 230, 243, 244, 255, 322, 324, 331, 345, 368, 398
   of POWs 345
   of stragglers and deserters 108, 326–327, 347, 368 *see also* deaths

Fadeyev, Yakov Ivanovich 134–135, 391
Fedyuninsky, Col Gen Ivan Ivanovich 253, 277
Fegelein, Gruppenführer Hermann 211–212, 213, 267, 278, 291, 312, 329–330
First World War, the 34, 35, 51, 85, 96, 97, 100, 125, 133, 147, 337
flak towers, Berlin 66–67, 69, 315
   Friedrichshain 284, **286,** 323, 333, 351, 412
   Humboldthain 294, 387, 412
   Tiergarten 310, 315
   Zoo 341, 344, 348, 349, 356, 357, 363, 382, 386, 389
food shortages 35, 51, 60, 62, 108, 316, 379, 380, 408
forestry warfare 168, 170–171
Franco-Prussian War (1870–71), the 28, 30
Frankfurt-an-der-Oder garrison 189, 221, 276–277
Freikorps, the 36, 37, 38, 39, 41, 105
   Iron Division 40
   Marinebrigade Ehrhardt 39

Friedeburg, Admiral Hans-Georg von 395–396
Friedrich II, King 26, 115
Friedrich III, Elector 25–26
Friedrich Wilhelm IV, King 26
'friendly fire' 198, 199, 218, 247, 304, 324–325, 334, 335
Fritsche, Dr Hans 357, 358–359, 360
fuel supplies 139, 180, 182, 200, 201, 207, 240, 244, 290, 292, 317, 320, 324, 372, 374, 375, 376
Fürstenwalde satellite work camp 230

Gall, Vladimir Samoilovich 390, 391
German atomic weapons programme, the 77
German chiefs of staff commander selection and training 87–88
German economy and inflation, the 41–42, 47
German strategy and tactics 51, 57, 83–85, 87, 91, 98–99, 102–110, 139–140, 148, 161–162, 164–165, 171, 179–180, 182, 189, 200–202, 205, 235–238, 239–240, 253–254, 289, 400–401, 410
   and breakdown in communications 251–252, 254–255, 260, 263, 279, 295, 346–347
   and breakout and escape attempts 300–301, 311, 317–318, 337, 341, 344, 347, 349–350, 351, 358, 363, 372–373, 375, 380, 386–389
   and defence of Berlin 17, 18, 66–67, 73–74, 114, **115,** 167, 208–210, 215–216, 244–245, 246, 249, 256, 265–268, 269, 270–271, 273–274, 275, 276, 277, 278–279–280, 282, 284, 285–291, 294–295, 299–300, 310–312, 315, 316–318, 319, 323–324, 330, 333, 335–336, 337–338, 339, 341, 342–343, 348–349, 354–355, 369, 408, 410–411
   and delaying tactics 92, 138, 194, 225, 227, 382, 403
   and intent to flee west to escape Soviet occupation 208, 224, 266, 285, 320, 331, 332, 370–374, 375–377
   and managing surrender 202, 227–228, 264, 267, 272, 338, 351, 352–354, 356, 357–360, 378, 379, 390, 394–397, 409, 411
   and multiple defensive lines 110–113, 114, 116–117, 166, 188, 205, 220, 226

Index

at Müncheberg 182, 197, 199–200, 218, 219, 220, 224, 226
and Operation *Barbarossa* 18–20, 118, 121
and reinforcements 112, 115–116, 192–193, 205, 209, 222, 225, 241, 285, 344
and retreats and withdrawals 81, 102, 110, 151, 192, 194, 223, 224, 225, 226, 227, 236, 237–238, 242, 244, 250, 251, 277, 293, 307–308, 322, 332, 365, 366, 368, 369, 378, 393–395, 397
at Seelow Heights 153–156, 157, 194
and *Sonnenwende* counter-attack 91, 93, 201
German unification 26, 27
foreign policy after the Franco-Prussian War 30–31
German Wehrmacht, the 17, 19, 38, 39, 83, 97, 101, 102, 121, 351, 361, 398
Armies
Eighteenth 393
Eleventh 91, 105
Fifteenth 102
Fifth Panzer 95
First Panzer 96
Fourth Panzer 106–107, 179, 180, 188, 192, 194, 205, 217, 237, 249, 251
Ninth 84, 90, 94, 98, 99, 100, 105, 106, 112, 180, 192, 193, 194, 197, 205, 207, 209, 214, 215, 226, 227, 237, 238, 242, 244–245, 248, 250, 251, 253, 254, 256, 261, 264, 265, 267, 275, 276, 277, 278, 279, 280, 287, 292, 299, 300, 301, 303, 310, 317, 318, 319, 330, 331, 336, 337, 346, 363, 369, 370, 371, 372–373, 374, 375–377, 378
Second 84, 85, 90, 94, 95
Sixteenth 393
Sixth 85, 120
Sixth SS-Panzer 71
Third Panzer 91, 94, 95, 98, 102–103, 111, 112, 193, 194, 201, 207, 227, 234, 235, 237, 240, 241, 245, 251, 253, 269, 292, 293, 302, 308, 322, 329, 332, 365, 366, 367, 368, 394, 404–405
Twelfth 264–265, 267, 277, 279, 289, 299, 311, 330, 337, 346, 355, 369, 370, 372, 375, 377–378, 379–380, 384, 400
Twenty-First 339, 395

Army Groups
Armee Oberkommando Ostpreussen 393, 394, 397
Armeegruppe Reymann 276, 370
B 85, 400
Centre 106–107, 110, 112, 114, 119, 120, 188, 238, 244, 263, 277
Courland 393, 394, 397
Don 85
F 84
North 94
South 105, 109, 263
Vistula 84, 86, 87, 88, 89–90, 94–95, 96, 97, 98, 110, 115, 193, 211, 212, 214, 225, 226, 237, 244–245, 264, 271, 280, 285, 292, 339
Corps
CI Corps 106, 162, 215, 227, 228, 237, 242, 251, 253, 292
Korps Oder 104
LVI Panzer 106, 107, 182, 201, 215, 217, 218, 227–228, 237, 244, 245, 251–252, 253, 254, 275, 278, 279, 280, 294, 311, 357, 359
LXI 377
Panzerkorps Grossdeutschland 107, 169
V 107, 251, 300, 370, 374
XLVI Panzer 104
XLVIII Panzer 378
XVI Panzer 319
XX 265, 289, 370, 377
XXXII 104
XXXIX Panzer 99, 100, 377
Divisions
1st Flak 274
1st Marine 104, 269
3rd Marine 104, 237, 244, 245, 254, 319
5th Jäger 106, 116, 183, 200, 222–223, 237, 244, 245, 254
7th Panzer 207, 269, 270, 293, 301, 319–320, 332, 365
9th Fallschirmjäger 106, 109, 151, 163, 164, 184, 185, 186, 193, 200–201, 223
11th Infantry 208
18th Panzergrenadier 105, 182, 186, 215, 275, 311, 344, 348, 350, 356, 382, 386, 389
20th Panzergrenadier 106, 108, 149–150, 154–155, 185, 199–200, 215–216, 252, 255, 283, 284, 311, 368–369
21st Panzer 188, 290–291, 331, 373

439

25th Panzergrenadier 98, 99, 106, 161,
162, 182, 183, 193, 200, 222–223,
237, 245, 254, 269–270, 279, 319
72nd Infantry 107
169th Infantry 106
218th Infantry 51–52
250th Infantry *(División Azul)* 285
251st Infantry 276
275th Infantry 107, 225, 259
281st Infantry (Security) 104,
239–240, 253
286th Infantry 106
297th Infantry 117
303rd *Infanterie-Division Döberitz* 106,
181, 192
337th Volksgrenadier 94
342nd Infantry 107, 169, 205, 225, 259
344th Infantry 116, 226
344th Volksgrenadier 249
391st Security 106
402nd 104
541st Volksgrenadier 161
545th Volksgrenadier 169, 205
547th Volksgrenadier 104, 105
549th Volksgrenadier 104, 227, 241
606th Infantry 106, 116, 161, 183
610th Security 104
712th Infantry Division 106, 371–372
Brandenburg panzergrenadier 188, 205
Division Rägener 106
Divisionsgruppe Müller 104
Divisionsgruppe Voigt 104
Ferdinand von Schill infantry 289
Flak-Division Berlin 382
Führer-Begleit panzergrenadier 178, 180,
186, 205, 225, 236, 249, 259–260
Infanterie-Division Berlin 116, 162–163,
184, 223, 255, 275
Infanterie-Division Klossek 104
Panzer-Division Müncheberg 98, 106, 157,
164, 165, 181, 182, 285, 311, 312,
313, 316, 324, 341, 382
Panzergrenadier-Division Kurmark 106,
337, 372, 376
Scharnhorst infantry 289, 318,
337–338, 369
Theodor Körner infantry 289, 290,
302, 318
Ulrich von Hutten infantry 289, 290, 302,
318, 337–338, 370
Ersatzheer (Replacement Army) 86, 329

Flak-Regiment 21 104
Friedrich Ludwig Jahn infantry 276
Gruppe Wellmann 235
Kampfgruppe 1001 Nachts 161–162
and officers' oath to Hitler 348
Panzer-Ausbildungsverband Böhmen 178
Regiments
18th Panzergrenadier 200
35th Panzergrenadier 200
119th Panzergrenadier 162
652nd 164
Volkssturm battalions 90, 91, 104, 108, 109,
113, 185, 204, 209, 213, 214, 218,
221, 223, 226, 227, 235, 241, 243,
249, 250, 254, 257, 259, 261,
270–271, 274, 276, 278, 281, 282,
284–285, 313, 316, 325, 334, 355,
365, 375, 379, 380, 385, 394, 411
see also SS, the
Goebbels, Joseph 20, 21, 43–44, 45, 47, 48, 49,
51, 60, 62, 63, 68, 69, 73, 89, 108,
114–115, 178, 207–209, 210, 213,
214, 227, 231, 238, 249, 250, 264,
270–271, 273, 311, 325, 339, 350,
351, 352, 353–354, 356, 358, 359,
361, 363, 388, 400, 405, 409, 410
Goebbels, Magda 350, 356, 363
Gordeyev, Anatoly Nikolayevich 140, 141
Gordov, Col Gen Vasily Nikolayevich 144,
248, 276
Göring, Hermann 46, 51, 57, 60, 61, 72,
109–110, 112, 115, 210, 211, 212,
231, 238, 245, 263, 280–281, 299, 338
Gräser, General Fritz-Hubert 106–107, 180, 188,
205, 249
Grebennik, Maj Gen Kuzma Yevdokimovich 124,
240, 293
Greim, Generalfeldmarschall Robert Ritter von
299, 338–339
Grishin, Maj Vasily 389, 391
Grynszpan, Herschel 49, 51
'Guards' status in the Red Army 135
Guderian, Generaloberst Heinz 84, 89, 95–96,
99–102, 210, 213, 214, 264
Gusakovsky, Col Iosif Irakliyevich 158–159

Hamburg 63, 394–395
Gomorrah bombing raid (July 1943) 67–68
Hanke, Karl 339, 356
Hardenbergstellung, the 110–111, 112
Harmel, Brigadeführer Heinz 249, 260–261

Harris, Air Marshal Arthur 58, 60, 63, 66, 76, 77
Hausser, Oberstgruppenführer Paul 20, 86
Havel island fortress, Berlin 389–390
Heinrici, Generaloberst Gotthard 96–99, 102,
    109–110, 111, 112–113, 114, 116,
    143, 148, 151, 153, 156, 163, 179,
    182, 189, 192–193, 200, 202, 207,
    214, 215, 217, 218, 224–225, 227,
    237–238, 240, 241, 244, 245,
    250–251, 253, 267, 268, 269, 270,
    277, 279–280, 285, 300, 308, 319,
    322–323, 332, 339, 368, 369, 411
Henseler, Untersturmführer Hans 255, 282, 324
Herriot, Eduart 247–248
Herrmann, Oberstleutnant Harry 193, 201
Hess, Rudolf 60–61
*HIAG (Hilfsgemeinschaft auf Gegenseitigkeit der
    Angehörigen der Ehemaligen Waffen-SS),*
    the 20, 369
Himmler, Heinrich 51, 62, 85–87, 88–90, 91,
    94, 95–96, 97, 98, 112, 115, 202,
    211–212, 264, 267, 329, 332, 338,
    339, 353
Hindenburg, Gen Paul von 39, 46
Hitler, Adolf 17, 18, 22, 24, 34, 35, 40, 43, 46,
    48, 49, 51, 91, 94, 99, 102, 116, 208,
    209, 210, 215, 228, 231, 233, 234, 236,
    245, 250, 268, 278, 279, 281, 299, 318,
    322, 329, 346, 404, 409
  and architectural plans for Berlin 52–53, 54,
    57, 69
  and daily conferences 212, 213–214,
    261–263, 267
  and decision to remain in Berlin 238,
    262–265, 280, 300, 311, 350–351
  and farewells and death 346, 347, 350–351,
    352, 355, 358, 359, 361, 362
  and fortress cities 189, 244, 307
  and Himmler 95, 96, 338–339
  and the July 1944 assassination plot 22, 84,
    88, 178, 236, 410
  and last will and testament 339, 344–345
  Mein Kampf (book) 18, 20
  and micro-management of strategy 81,
    83–84, 113
  and military orders and directives 103,
    111–112, 155, 162, 171, 194, 202,
    205, 222, 225, 237, 238, 239, 244,
    250, 251, 256, 275, 280, 281,
    287–289, 308, 311, 332, 341, 390,
    393, 410, 411
  and mistrust and treatment of senior generals
    84, 85, 88–89, 99–101, 210–211, 214,
    265–266
  and officers' oath of loyalty to 348, 350
  and purges of the SA and Nazi Party 41, 45,
    47, 105
Hitler Youth, the 182, 215, 223, 224, 271,
    273–274, 276, 281, 285, 312,
    313, 316, 334, 336, 355, 383,
    387–388, 394
Holste, Generalleutnant Rudolf 319, 346,
    350, 369
Huber, Johann 320–322, 332, 365–366, 368

ice floes 138–139
indoctrination and racial superiority 408–409
industrialisation in Germany 33–34
insignia, medals, patches and badges 155,
    363, 379
  and removal of conceal identity 323, 355
intelligence 19, 71, 77, 91, 94, 113, 132, 178,
    179, 194, 220, 388
Ivanov, Aleksei Petrovich 151, 218

jazz and American culture in Nazi Berlin 48
Jewish community, the 28–29, 30
  in the medical and legal professions 48
  and Nazi policy on 62–63
  and persecution of 43, 46–47, 48, 49–51,
    193, 239
Jodl, Generaloberst Alfred 89, 210, 213, 214,
    251, 262, 263, 264, 265, 266, 267,
    278, 279, 280, 293, 346, 350, 397
July 1944 Plot, the 22, 74, 84, 88, 98, 101, 178,
    214, 410
Jung, Oberst Gerhard 390, 391
Junge, Gertraud 'Traudl' 339, 389

Kapp, Wolfgang 39, 40–41
Kardorff, Ursula von 69, 412
Käther, Oberst Ernst 250, 279
Katukov, Col Gen Mikhail Yefimovich 131–132,
    158, 166, 191, 198, 220–221, 229,
    230, 243, 314
Kazakov, Col Gen Vladimir Ivanovich 148–149,
    151, 152, 174, 175
Keitel, Generalfeldmarschall Wilhelm 100, 101,
    210–211, 262–263, 264–265, 266,
    267, 278, 279, 280, 300, 302–303,
    322, 323, 339
Khetagurov, Maj Gen Georgy Ivanovich 219, 220

Khrushchev, Nikita 407
kill claims 223
Kinzel, Generalleutnant Eberhard 94–95, 395
Kleinheisterkamp, Obergruppenführer Matthias 106, 192, 217, 336, 337, 370
Klimenko, Col Ivan Isayevich 362
Köhler, General Karl-Erik 265, 289, 370
Konev, Marshal Ivan Stepanovich 23, 24, 107, 125–126, 133, 144, 148, 150, 167–168, 179, 188–189, 204, 241, 248–249, 275–276, 277, 282, 290, 296, 299, 316, 318–319, 330, 331, 347, 370, 371, 375, 377, 403, 406, 408
   and command style 126
   and demarcation lines 128–129, 261, 298, 324–325
   and memoirs 127–128, 129, 188, 297–298, 335, 410–411
   and speed of advance 170, 171, 173, 174, 178, 186, 189–190, **204,** 205, 217, 226, 236, 244, 246, 261
Königsberg and East Prussia 26–27, 248
Krebs, General Hans 100, 102, 112, 210, 213, 214, 235–236, 237–238, 246–247, 250, 256, 261, 267, 278–279, 280, 291–292, 299, 300, 308, 311, 319, 330, 347, 350, 351, 352–353, 354, 356, 357, 359, 361
Kriegsmarine, the 99, 112, 393–394
Kristallnacht 49–51
Krukenberg, Brigadeführer Gustav 291–292, 294–295, 312, 354, 388–389
Küstrin 92, 98–99, 100, 103, 106, 109, 139, 185
Kuznetsov, Col Gen Vasily Ivanovich 184, 223, 230, 349

Lammerding, Gruppenführer Heinz 88, 94, 95, 97
Landwehr Canal, the 36, 209, 295, 296, 315, 323, 333–334, 335, 343, 358, 382
leaflet drops 72, 192, 271, 287, 289, 318, 352
Lelyushenko, Gen Dmitry Danilovich 131, 144, 170, 173, 178, 179, 202–203, 226, 236, 261, 276, 284, 290, 293, 375
Liebknecht, Karl 35, 36–37, 38
logistics and supplies 17, 19, 83, 92, 93, 121, 138–139, 142, 167, 189, 229 *see also* ammunition supplies; fuel supplies
Loringhoven, Major Bernd Freytag von 210, 211, 212, 213, 262, 347, 349, 350
Luchinsky, Lt Gen Aleksandr Aleksandrovich 248, 375

Luck, Oberst Hans von 301, 317–318, 372
Ludendorff, Gen Erich 38, 39
Luftwaffe, the 57, 60, 70, 72, 99, 111, 112, 113, 139, 140, 142, 179–180, 210, 247, 252, 292, 299, 338, 341, 397, 402
   as ground units 154–155, 161, 163–164, 184, 193, 245
   Kampfgeschwader 200 99
Lüttwitz, Gen Walther von 39, 40, 41
Luxembourg, Rosa 35, 36–37, 38

Magdeburg 264, 400
maintenance and repairs 137, 402, 406
Majdanek concentration camp 21
Manstein, Generalfeldmarschall Erich von 85, 105
Manteuffel, General Hasso von 95, 98, 103, 104, 105, 207, 227, 241, 252, 253, 269, 293, 307, 308, 319, 322, 323, 332, 339, 365, 368, 369
Märkische Schweiz, the 195
matèriel losses 21, 58, 66, 67, 70, 99, 131, 155, 159, 182, 224, 226, 228, 314, 400, 405
memoirs 20, 89, 92, 107, 119–120, 121–122, 124, 126, 129, 133, 136, 140–141, 142, 148–149, 167–168, 174–175, 188, 195, 211, 217, 261, 298, 307–308, 362, 374, 407 *see also* war diaries
Menze, Erika 373, 374–375
Mietskasernen (rental barracks) 28, 30, 54
military awards 159, 198, 362, 368
military production 21, 35, 67, 75, 111
military strengths and complements 17, 104–107, 121, 126–127, 132, 162, 179, 201, 213, 215–216, 221, 239, 255, 257, 266, 269–270, 289, 295, 370, 378, 404
minefields 143
Mohnke, Brigadeführer Wilhelm 278, 312, 329–330, 350, 354, 357, 386, 389
Montgomery, Field Marshal Bernard 22, 102, 395–396, 401
Moore, Maj Gen James 378, 379
morale 71, 144, 169, 222
   of civilians 72–73, 75
Mummert, Generalmajor Werner 311, 324
Müncheberg 218–219, 221, 224, 226, 230
Mussolini, Benito 346
Myasnikov, Vladimir Vladimirovich 152, 271–272

INDEX

Nazi Party, the 43, 44, 45, 46, 47, 85, 96, 209, 250, 252, 266, 332, 339, 356, 388, 409, 410, 411
and flight from Berlin 249–250
Gauleiters 49 *see also* Hitler, Adolf
Neisse river, the 167–168
Nemmersdorf, East Prussia 21, 409
Neu Trebbin, Germany 184, 193, 200, 223
Neustroyev, Capt Stepan Andreyevich 349, 354
NKVD, the 118, 230, 389, 391, 407

Oderbruch, the 110, 111, 116, 130, 132, 156, 157, 163, 175
OKH (Oberkommando des Heeres), the 77, 78, 84, 94, 100, 112, 179, 193, 194, 210, 213, 225, 235–236, 237, 246–247, 264, 269, 280, 300, 322
OKW (Oberkommando der Wehrmacht), the 89, 210, 213, 278, 292, 300, 302–303, 330, 347, 370
Operations
  Allied
    Clarion (February 1945) 75–76
    Gomorrah (July 1943) 67–68
    Market Garden (September 1944) 22–23
    Pointblank (June 1943 – April 1944) 70
    Thunderclap 70–71, 73–74
  German
    Barbarossa (June – Dec 1941) 18–19, 94, 97
    Eclipse 22
    Hannibal (Jan – May 1945) 393–394, 396, 397
  Soviet
    Bagration (June – August 1944) 119, 120, 123, 125, 127, 140
    Uranus (November 1942) 85
Oradour-sur-Glane massacre, the 88
Osinovsky, Dmitry Filippovich 153, 232–233

Panzerbär (newssheet) 355
Papen, Franz von 46, 47
Patton, Gen George 401–402
Perkhorovich, Maj Gen Frantz Iosifovich 161, 389
Petrov, Gen Ivan Yefimovich 128, 178, 179, 330
Pipkorn, Standartenführer Rüdiger 301, 302, 317, 372
political unrest and violence 36–38, 40–41, 44, 45, 46, 47
Portal, Air Chief Marshal Charles 58, 60, 71, 76–77

POWs 19, 20, 59, 70, 76, 117, 135, 137, 165, 178, 222, 224, 230, 231, 233, 247, 259, 278, 300, 304, 305, 331, 345–346, 360, 363, 368, 375, 378, 391, 398, 400, 401
and post-war German prisoners 360, 369, 385, 389, 391
and US reclassification of 380
press and censorship, the 47–48
propaganda 44–45, 62, 74–75, 79, 81, 101, 361–362, 400
Prussia and unified Germany 27
public attitudes to war 51–52
Pukhov, Col Gen Nikolai Pavlovich 167–168, 169, 226, 277, 290

RAD (Reichsarbeitsdienst), the 276, 365–366
Radio Free Germany 325
RAF, the 57, 58, 60, 66, 71, 75, 79, 234
  Bomber Command 58, 63, 71
rail gauges 121, 139
railway infrastructure 75, 76
Rath, Ernst vom 49, 51
Rattenhuber, Gruppenführer Johann 330, 350
Rauch, Generalleutnant Josef 186, 348, 386
Raus, Generaloberst Erhard 95, 404–405
Ravensbrück concentration camp 231
reconnaissance 19, 82, 109, 111, 113, 116, 135, 140, 142–143, 148, 156, 157, 163, 165, 167, 189–190, 203, 204, 235, 246, 254, 257, 370, 374, 403
Red Army, the 17, 19, 20, 21, 57, 71, 81–83, 85, 91, 94, 98, 102, 105, 106, 110, 111, 113, 115, 116, 117, 121, 133–137, 157, 177, 208, 228, 268, 320, 361, 366, 369, 372, 383, 385, 389, 390, 396, 397, 399, 401, 402, 409
  8th Independent Penal Battalion 182
  Armies
    Eighth Guards 92, 93, 99, 126, 130, 132, 152, 154, 157, 158, 165–167, 173, 175, 181, 190, 195, 217, 218–220, 228–229, 230, 242, 248, 255, 257–259, 261, 270, 274, 282, 295–296, 297, 310, 312, 316, 323, 324, 325, 334, 342, 343, 348, 352, 354
    Fifth Guards 126, 130, 169, 170, 186–188, 190, 202–203, 225, 226, 236, 249, 277, 303
    Fifth Shock 81, 82, 93, 126, 130, 163, 164, 165, 184, 185, 195, 217, 228,

230, 242, 271, 284, 285, 294, 316,
323, 332, 333, 341, 343, 354, 362,
405–406
Fifty-Second 127, 130, 277
First Guards Tank 126, 131, 133, 158,
159, 173, 193, 217, 220, 229, 230,
242, 255, 257, 297, 314, 342
First Polish 126, 130, 160, 161, 183, 200,
227, 230
First Tank 93
Forty-Ninth 126, 235, 240
Forty-Seventh 126, 130, 161, 162, 183,
200, 228, 230, 231, 293, 310, 389
Fourth 118
Fourth Guards Tank 127, 131, 170, 174,
178, 202, 203, 247, 276, 293, 331, 375
Second Guards Tank 126, 131, 133, 165,
185, 191, 193, 201, 215, 217, 220,
223, 224, 228, 242, 276, 308
Second Polish 127, 130, 254, 277, 330
Second Shock 126, 130, 235, 253, 269
Second Tank 93
Seventieth 126, 235, 240
Sixty-Fifth 123, 126, 235, 239, 240, 241,
252, 292, 293
Sixty-First 126, 130, 160, 182
Sixty-Ninth 119, 126, 130, 242
Third 126, 130, 242
Third Guards 126, 130, 135, 144–145,
169, 189, 225, 248, 276, 277, 347
Third Guards Tank 127, 130–131, 134,
171, 174, 178, 179, 202, 203, 204,
236, 248, 261, 274, 275, 276, 277,
282, 299, 310, 316, 325, 334
Third Shock 126, 130, 162, 163,
183–184, 200, 223, 228, 230, 231,
242, 256, 284, 285, 294, 316, 323,
346, 348, 349
Thirteenth 126, 130, 167, 169, 205, 226,
277, 290, 331
Thirty-Third 126, 130, 242, 277
Twenty-Eighth 127, 248, 275, 277, 347,
372, 375
Brigades
1st Mechanised Infantry 292
10th Guards Mechanised 290
17th Tank 292
35th Guards Mechanised 293
44th Guards Tank 158, 159, 230
45th Guards Tank 218
54th Guards Tank 188
61st Guards Tank 170–171, 186
64th Separate Tank 314
65th Guards Tank 247, 293
68th Guards Tank 331
Corps
I Guards Cavalry 160
I Guards Tank 235, 292
I Mechanised 228
III Guards Rifle 372
IV Guards Rifle 157, 181, 242, 257, 351
IX Guards Tank 276
IX Mechanised 325, 334
IX Rifle 185, 274, 333–334, 362
IX Tank 228
LXXIX Rifle 231, 256, **258,** 348, 349
LXXXIX 161
V Cavalry 118
V Guards Mechanised 203, 290, 303
VI Guards Mechanised 202–203, 276, 318
VI Guards Tank 226
VII Guards Cavalry 256
VII Rifle 284
VIII Guards Mechanised 158,
220–221, 229
X Guards Tank 170, 178, 203, 319
X Tank 203
XI Guards Mechanised 226
XI Guards Tank 92, 133, 158, 159,
218, 220
XI Tank 158, 181, 316, 405–406
XII Guards Rifle 223, 294
XII Guards Tank 228
XLVI Rifle 235
XXI Rifle 225
XXIX Guards Rifle 82, 181, 197, 219,
220, 270
XXVI Guards Rifle 164, 284, 285
XXVII Rifle 226
XXVIII Guards Rifle 181, 270
XXXII Guards Rifle 170
XXXII Rifle 284, 285
XXXIV Guards Rifle 170
Divisions
1st Guards Breakthrough Artillery
299, 318
15th Rifle 124
27th Guards Rifle 343
37th Guards Rifle 240, 293
39th Guards Rifle 313
44th Guards Rifle 293
47th Guards Rifle 157, 358, 359

58th Guards Rifle 169, 303, 304
61st Rifle 334
69th Rifle 293
79th Guards Rifle 343, 363
82nd Guards Rifle 196, 219, 334
88th Guards Rifle 270
89th Guards Rifle 341–342
108th Rifle 293
144th Rifle 271
171st Rifle 346
193rd Rifle 253
207th Rifle 348
266th Rifle 184, 342
301st Rifle 362
328th Rifle 293
329th Rifle 302
395th Guards Rifle 331
413th Rifle 293
and engineering support 402, 403
Fronts 167, 173, 174
   1st Baltic 120
   1st Belarusian 23, 91, 92, 114, 118–119, 124, 125, 126, 127, 128–129, 138, 140, 142, 147, **160**, 173, 174, 175, **180**, 188–189, 190, 191–192, **196**, 203, 209, **216**, 220, 248, 274, 276, 293, 297, 316, 325, 334, 335, 349, 352, 353, 406–407
   1st Ukrainian 23, 107, 114, 119, 124, 125, 126–127, 128–129, 130, 131, 138, 144, 147, 148, 150, 167–168, 171, **172, 187,** 189–190, 193, **204**, 207, 220, 225, 226, 228, 244, 248, 259, 261, 274, 276, 297, 316, 324, 334, 335, 347, 375, 406
   2nd Belarusian 23, 91, 93, 114, 119, 126, 130, 139, 193, 227, 234, **234**, 239, 241, 252, 291
   2nd Ukrainian 125–126
   3rd Belarusian 120
and NCOs 134
Regiments
   50th Guards Heavy Tank 287
   220th Guards Rifle 343
Refior, Oberst Hans von 208, 209, 249, 311
refugees 71, 75, 87, 150, 177, 260, 301, 304, 318, 320, 323, 331, 336, 379, 394
   and cover from Soviet forces 66, 252, 285, 289, 309, 328, 333, 380, 382, 390
   and evacuations 68, 79, 209, 231, 249, 320–322, 379, 393–394

and food supplies 379
Reich Chancellery, the 74, 100, 263, 265, 267, 275, 278, 291, 296, 299, 311, 312, 329, 333, 338, 343, 348, 349, 355, 356, 361, 362–363, 386, 388, 399
Reichhelm, Oberst Günther 289, 303
Reichstag, the 35, 53, 133, 296, 310, 343, 348, 349, 354, 391
   burning of 46
Reichswehr, the 85, 105, 318
Reitsch, Hanna 299, 300, 339, 356
relocation of German factories, the 68
Remer, Generalmajor Otto-Ernst 178, 236, 249, 260, 261
replacement drafts 107, 108, 113, 132, 134–137, 193, 205, 239, 309–310, 355 *see also Ersatzheer* (Replacement Army), the
Reymann, Generalleutnant Helmuth 208–210, 214, 249, 250, 270, 276, 278, 279, 319, 330, 370
Ribbentrop, Joachim von 18, 280
right-wing coup attempt (March 1919) 40–41
Röhm, Ernst 47, 85
Rokossovsky, Marshal Konstantin Konstantinovich 93–94, 117, 118–119, 129–130, 173, 174, 193, 234, 235, 239, 252–253, 269, 291, 307–308, 319, 366, 367, 401, 408
Roosevelt, F. D. R. 22, 114, 115, 129
Rote Fahne (newspaper) 37, 47
Rudenko, Col Gen Sergei Ignatyevich 140–142
Ruhr industrial region, the 33, 57, 58, 102, 265, 400
Rybalko, Gen Pavel Semenovich 130–131, 134, 144, 171, 173, 179, 188, 204, 226, 236, 248, 261, 274, 275, 282, 283, 297, 298, 310, 316, 324, 325, 334, 335, 347
Rzhev salient, the 125, 221, 407

SA (Sturmabteilungen), the 44, 45, 46, 47, 48, 49–50, 51, 85, 105, 281–282
Sachsenhausen concentration camp 51, 77, 230
Schleicher, Gen Kurt von 46, 47
Scholze, Generalmajor Georg 255, 283
Schöneck, Soldat Friedhelm 162–163, 184, 200, 223
Schörner, Generalfeldmarschall Ferdinand 106–107, 110, 112, 114, 171, 188, 244, 260, 277, 299
Schwerbelastungskörper, Berlin, the 54–55

SD *(Sichersheitsdienst)*, the 60, 68, 72
searchlights 151, 163
Seeckt, Gen Hans von 39, 41
Seelow Heights, the 110, 116, 130, 132, 149,
    153, 154–161, **160**, 163, 167, 171,
    173, 174, 175, 178, 180, 181, 182,
    185, 186, 190, 191, 194, 195, 196,
    205, 217, 218, 220, 221, 226, 228,
    255, 294, 335, 342, 388, 406–407
    Reichstrasse I 155, 157, 159, 182, 191, 196,
        219, 228, 242
Semchenko, Col 358, 359
Seydlitz-Truppen, the 184, 197, 252, 255, 295,
    337, 372, 374
Shalin, Lt Gen Mikhail Alekseyevich 158, 220
Siefert, Oberst Ernst 295, 312, 333, 351
Siegessäule ('Victory Column'), the 30
Sixt, Generalleutnant Friedrich 106, 242
SMERSH 124, 362, 363
Sokolovsky, Gen Vasily Danilovich 353, 360
soldiers' attitudes and war weariness 143–144
Soviet Air Force, the 139–140, 185, 297
    Sixteenth Air Army 140
Soviet purges, the 117–118
Soviet strategy and tactics 21, 23–24, 91–94,
    112, 114, 118–120, 122–124,
    125–127, 138–140, 152–153, 160,
    163–170, 173–175, 182–185, 186,
    189–192, 195–196, 197–198, 200,
    217–220, 230–231, 234–236, 239,
    240–241, 248, 372, 373–374
    and air and ground coordination 140–142
    and artillery 147–150, 153, 163, 165, 168,
        180–181, 195, 292, 296, 310,
        336–337, 370, 402, 403
    and bridgeheads 110, 116, 144–145, 198,
        230, 252, 253, 254
    and engagement with escaping German units
        375, 376–377, 378, 379
    and fighter escorts 140
    and the German surrender 352–354,
        357–360, 363
    and plan to occupy Denmark 367–368
    and plan to seize Berlin 17, 127–130,
        131–133, 138, 178–179, 202–205,
        217, 220–221, 226, 228–229,
        241–243, 245–246, 252–253,
        256–259, **258**, 261, 270, 271–274,
        275, 276–277, 282, **283**, 283–285,
        287, 290, 292–294, 295–298, 300,
        308, 309, 310, 312–316, 318–319,
    323, 324–325, 327, 330–331,
    332–335, 337, **338,** 341–344, 346,
    347–349, 354, 387, 391, 397–398,
    404, 405, 406, 407
    and post-war recommendations for
        improvement 402–403
    and reconnaissance in force 116, 142–143,
        155, 203, 204, 403
    and the removal of German industrial plant
        398
    and searchlights 151–152, 163, 406
    and tanks 157–158, 170–171, 184, 188–189,
        405–406
    and the Vistula-Oder Operation 17, 21, 71,
        81, 93, 107, 132, 133, 140, 166, 319,
        404, 407, 408
Spaatz, Gen Carl 73, 75, 76, 77
Spandau barracks, Berlin 107–108
spare parts 19, 137
Spartacists, the 35, 36, 38, 39, 41, 42
SPD (Social Democratic Party), the 28, 31, 34,
    35, 37, 42, 46, 50
Speer, Albert 21, 63–64, 68, 75, 177, 211, 280
    and architectural plans for Berlin 52–55
SS, the 20, 41, 46, 60, 62, 85–86, 101, 102, 104,
    112, 167, 210, 211, 230, 267, 277,
    281, 285, 308, 309, 316, 323, 326,
    332, 336, 338, 339, 341, 345, 350,
    351, 358, 368, 369, 382, 383,
    388–389, 394, 400
    Allgemeine-SS 108
    Battalions
        SS-Schwere-Panzer-Abteilung 502 337, 371
        SS-Schwere-Panzer-Abteilung 503 223
        Waffen-SS 86, 108, 369, 379, 384
    Corps
        II SS-Panzer 301
        III SS-Panzer *(Armeegruppe Steiner)* 104,
            105, 201–202, 214–215, 224, 228,
            245, 254, 255, 256, 261–262, 269,
            278, 292, 293, 303, 308, 346, 369, 386
        V SS-Mountain 90, 106, 227, 251, 300,
            371
        X SS 90
        XI SS-Panzer 106, 179, 192, 201, 217,
            218, 227, 300, 370, 371
        XVI SS 90
    Divisions
        1st *SS-Panzer Division LSSAH
            (Leibstandarte-SS-Adolf-Hitler)* 278
        2nd *SS-Panzer Division Das Reich* 88

Index

4th *SS-Polizei* Panzergrenadier 214–215, 227, 245
10th *SS-Panzer-Division Frundsberg* 225–226, 249, 260–261, 301, 302
11th *SS-Panzergrenadier Nordland* 104–105, 182, 200, 201, 202, 214, 223, 224, 225, 245, 253–254, 255, 259, 273–274, 282, 291, 292, 294, 311, 312–313, 314, 316, 324, 334, 342–343, 344, 354, 387, 389
12th *SS-Panzer Division Hitlerjugend* 355
15th *SS-Waffen-Grenadier* 227, 285
23rd *SS-Panzergrenadier Nederland* 104, 105, 182, 193, 200, 202, 214, 218, 224, 225, 245, 375
27th *SS-Grenadier-Division Langemarck* 105, 162, 253, 323
28th *SS-Grenadier-Division Wallonien* 105, 241, 323, 332
32nd *SS-Freiwilligen-Grenadier Division 30. Januar* 309–310, 331, 371, 375
33rd *SS-Grenadier Division Charlemagne* 105, 291, 295, 311, 312, 323, 334, 344
35th *SS-und-Polizei-Grenadier* 301
SS-Panzergrenadier-Division Grossdeutschland 106, 178
Einsatzgruppen 20, 239
Eleventh SS-Panzer Army 93, 105
and foreign recruits 291, 294, 332, 334
and military police 380
Regiments
11th SS-Panzer 200–201
24th *SS-Panzergrenadier-Regiment Danmark* 259, 274, 287
Reichssicherheitsdienst 329 *see also* German Wehrmacht, the
Stalin, Josef 18–19, 22, 24, 120, 131, 192, 328, 352, 353, 367, 377, 406
and military control 23, 119
and the purges 83, 117–118, 120
and Zhukov and Konev 23, 92, 120, 121–123, 124, 126, 127–129, 173–174, 188–189, 217, 335, 387, 407, 408
Stavka, the 93, 119, 123, 128, 173, 174, 179, 203, 248, 297, 298, 299, 316, 325, 334
Steiermark (train), the 87, 88, 98
Steiner, Obergruppenführer Felix 105, 201–202, 214, 215, 224, 245, 251, 259, 262, 264, 267, 278, 293, 299, 319, 329, 339, 369, 386

Stettin, Germany 104, 200, 240, 241, 253, 254, 269, 292, 307–308
strikes and industrial unrest 34, 35–36, 39–40, 45–46
Sydow, Generalleutnant Otto 382, 383, 385

Tams, Leutnant Karl-Hermann 108, 149–150, 185–186, 198–199
tank identification 188
tanks 136, 137, 154, 324, 343, 373, 383, 404–405
Hetzer tank destroyer (Germany) 183, 301
IS-2 (USSR) 154, 155, 157, 216, 287, 301, 349, 406
Panther (Germany) 157, 159, 216, 224, 285, 372
T-34 (USSR) 155, 181, 185, 186, 198, 223, 224, 230, 314, 324
T-35 (USSR) 154
Tiger (Germany) 157, 159, 188, 199, 223, 337, 343, 371, 372, 374, 377, 387
King Tiger (Tiger II) 314, 349, 376
Telegin, Lt Gen Konstantin Fedorovich 191, 192
Teltow Canal, Berlin, the 275–276, 277, 282, 283, 299
terrain factors 109, 110, 111, 131–132, 166–167, 174, 180, 184–185, 195, 221, 405, 406–407
Thirty Years War, the 25
Timoshenko, Semen Konstantinovich 117, 118, 119, 122
Tippelskirch, General Kurt von 339, 395
trade unions in Germany 34, 42
training 87, 105, 107, 112, 114, 133–134, 136, 137, 166, 213, 403, 405
Treaty of Versailles (1919), the 38, 85, 318
Trümmerfrauen ('rubble women'), the 412
typhus 106, 134

U-boats 393
Unter den Linden, Berlin 30
urban warfare 242, 271, 272–273, 294, 296, 297, 298, 314
US Army, the 285, 289, 291, 303, 368–369, 378, 380, 390
Armies
First 303
Ninth 378, 379
Third 102, 401, 402
Divisions 22
69th Infantry 303, 304
82nd Airborne 395

447

Historical Division 20, 101
US/Soviet encounter, Torgau 303, 304–305
USAAF (US Army Air Force), the 67, 74, 75, 78, 79, 225, 290
  Eighth Air Force 73, 76
  Twentieth Air Force 79

Vasilevsky, Marshal Aleksandr Mikhailovich 119–120, 123, 128
Vassiltchikov, Marie Illarionovna (Missie) 61–62, 63, 64–65, 72–73
Vesterman, Arkady Grigoryevich 135–136, 155
Vishnevsky, Vsevolod Vitalyevich 351–352, 353
Voigt, Wilhelm 32–33
Voigtsberger, Generalmajor Heinrich 163, 255, 275
Volksmarinedivision, the 36

Wäger, General Kurt 107, 370, 374
Wall Street Crash and world depression, the 44, 47
Wannsee Conference (January 1942), the 74
war crimes and atrocities 20–21, 88, 101, 193, 232–234, 278, 360, 361, 368, 409–410
  and raping and looting 231–232, 320, 327–328, 332, 346, 366, 373, 375, 379, 398, 401, 407, 409
war diaries 61–62, 68, 69, 107–108, 193, 320–322, 356, 396, 412
  of anonymous female journalist 233–234, 252, 274, 289, 316–317, 327, 328, 346
  see also memoirs
war reparations 38, 41
Warsaw Uprising, the 101, 294
weaponry 66, 132, 256, 275, 284, 294
  88mm AA gun (Germany) 154–155, 164, 259–260
  DShK machine gun 272–273
  Katyusha rocket (USSR) 149, 151, 197, 199, 222, 326, 353, 376
  Panzerfaust (Germany) 114, 186, 197, 215, 216, 224, 226, 240, 242, 246, 257, 261, 271, 273, 275, 281, 284, 294, 296, 312, 313, 315, 333, 341, 342, 343, 344, 404–405, 406, 410, 411
  SU-76 assault gun (USSR) 181, 235
  V-1 and V-2 flying bombs (Germany) 70, 162, 231
weather conditions 73, 77
Weichs, Generalfeldmarschall Maximilian von 84–85

Weidling, General Helmuth 106, 215, 237, 244–245, 251, 253, 254, 275, 278, 279, 282, 294, 295, 299, 300, 310, 311, 312, 341, 344, 348, 410, 411
Weiss, Generaloberst Walter 94, 95
Wenck, General Walther 100, 102, 263, 264–265, 266–268, 277, 278, 287, 289, 290, 299, 302, 303, 318, 319, 330, 337, 346, 369, 370, 374, 375, 377, 378, 379, 384, 400
Werwolf resistance, the 230
Wessel, Horst 44–45
  Horst Wessel Lied (song) 45
Westerman, Gerhart von 177–178
Wilhelm I, Kaiser 27, 31
Wilhelm II, Kaiser 31–32, 33, 34, 36
Wismar and Soviet zone of occupation 367–368
Wolz, Generalmajor Alwin 394, 395
workforce shortages 19
Wotanstellung, the 111, 332

Yalta Conference (February 1945), the 22, 24, 77, 367

Zaitsev, Col Vasily Ivanovich 170–171, 186
Zhadov, Col Gen Aleksei Semenovich 169–170, 186, 202–203, 236, 249, 277, 303
Zhukov, Marshal Georgy Konstantinovich 91, 92, 93, 117, 119, 120–125, 127, 130, 131, 140, 142, 144, 150, 151, 152, 157–158, 173–174, 188, 190, 192, 195, 201, 218, 221, 229, 241, 245, 256, 261, 282, 284, 323, 332, 342, 348, 352, 353, 357, 387, 407, 408
  and discipline 120–121, 122–123, 125
  and disregard for boundary lines 310, 314, 316, 324, 335
  and memoirs 121–122, 123–124, 129, 174–175, 261, 298, 362, 404
  and reputation 92, 93, 119, 120, 123, 124–125, 126, 136, 403–404, 407
  and rivalry with Konev 23–24, 126, 133, 173–174, 178, 190, 217, 228, 241, 242, 248, 287, 296–297, 298–299, 314, 335, 403–404, 406
Ziegler, Brigadeführer Joachim 254–255, 292, 295, 324, 389
Zobel, Hauptmann Horst 158, 159